AS SHE AGED, EVERYONE HAD SOMETHING TO SAY ABOUT LUCILLE BALL

HERE'S HOW, AFTER HER DIVORCE FROM DESI AND HER EMERGENCE AS A SHOW-BIZ MOGUL, LUCILLE WAS "REVIEWED" BY SOME OF HER CONTEMPORARIES, AND HOW, IN THE LATTER DECADES OF HER LIFE, SHE REVIEWED HERSELF.

"Lucille Ball slept in a bedroom that adjoined that of her second husband, Gary Morton. When she needed to be 'serviced,' she went clang-clang on that bell."
—Vivian Vance

"Joan Crawford and Bette Davis are bigger bitches than I am."
—Lucille Ball

"When I became head of my own studio, I was mailed a lot of frontal nudes from young actors willing to lie on my casting couch."
—Lucille Ball

"I'll always love Lucy. But loving Lucille Ball is another thin'."
—Desi Arnaz

"If William Holden came knocking on my door, I would have kicked out either Desi or Gary Morton."
—Lucille Ball

"There was a lot of laughter. But there was despair. Oh, such despair."
—Lucille Ball

"I never told anyone this before, but Judy Garland once propositioned me."
—Lucille Ball to Vivian Vance

"That damn dyke, Judy Holliday stole the lead in Born Yesterday from me. I should have walked home with Oscar and slept beside him that night."
—Lucille Ball

"Sammy Davis Jr. told me I didn't know what real sex was like until I did it with a black man."
—Lucille Ball.

"Bea Arthur, Ann Sothern, Eve Arden, eat your hearts out. Not one of you came anywhere near topping me."
—Lucille Ball

"My most frequent co-star, Bob Hope, was revered in some quarters. In private, he was a womanizing rake. No Las Vegas chorus gal was safe from him. Once, he tried to attack me, but I told him to call Marilyn Maxwell instead."
—Lucille Ball

Lucille Ball with her second husband, **Gary Morton**.

"I switched from a Cuban to a Jew, and this time I got it right. What it lacked in passion, it made up for in loyalty."

This is the concluding volume of a two-part biography of television's most famous *comedienne* and business mogul.

Volume One, released in May, 2021, is available now, through Amazon.com and other booksellers worldwide.

Runner-up to the First Prize Winner in 2021's category of General Nonfiction from **The New York Book Festival**, it's

LUCILLE BALL & DESI ARNAZ
THEY WEREN'T LUCY AND RICKY RICARDO
978-1-936003-71-6

THE SAD & TRAGIC ENDING
OF LUCILLE BALL

VOLUME TWO (1961-1989)
OF A TWO-PART BIOGRAPHY

DARWIN PORTER AND DANFORTH PRINCE

THE SAD & TRAGIC ENDING OF LUCILLE BALL

VOLUME TWO (1961-1989)
OF A TWO-PART BIOGRAPHY

by Darwin Porter and Danforth Prince

Unless otherwise stated, all texts are copyright
© 2021 Blood Moon Productions, Ltd.
with all rights reserved.

www.BloodMoonProductions.com

ISBN 978-936003-80-8

Covers and Book Design by Danforth Prince
Front cover photo of Lucille Ball courtesy Alan Light

Distributed Worldwide through Ingram,
Amazon.com, and internet vendors everywhere.

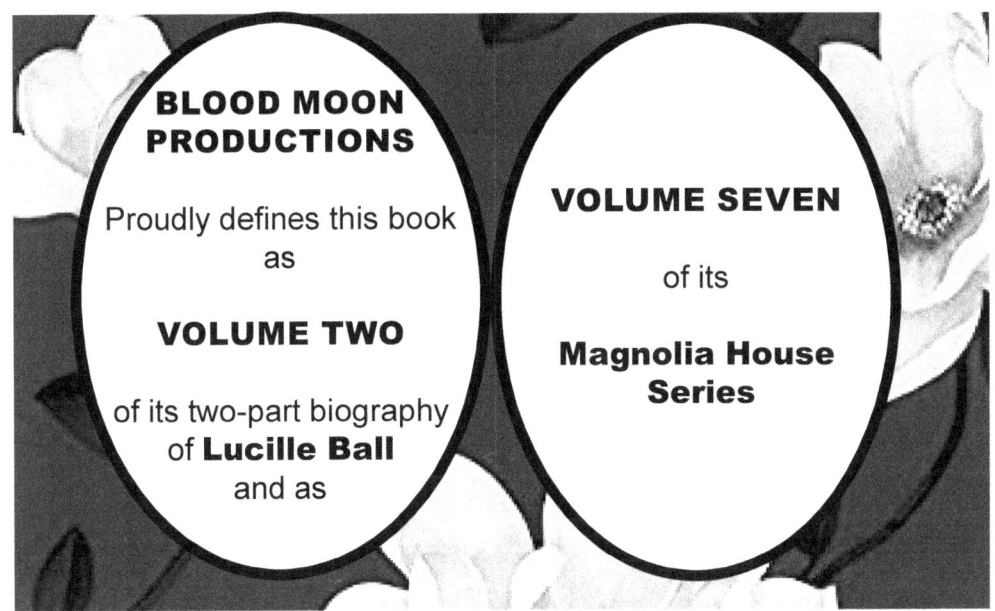

CONTENTS

CHAPTER ONE
    Lucille Launches Act Two of a Turbulent Life   page 1

CHAPTER TWO
    Lucille's Back-As a Solo   page 25

CHAPTER THREE
    As Co-Owner of Desilu, Lucille Emerges as
    the Most Powerful Woman in Hollywood   page 55

CHAPTER FOUR
    The Lucy Show   page 87

CHAPTER FIVE
    Lucille Sells Desilu to Gulf + Western   page 121

CHAPTER SIX
    Television & The March of Time   page 143

CHAPTER SEVEN
    Here's Lucy   page 175

CHAPTER EIGHT
  Celebrity Feuds   page 205

CHAPTER NINE
  Lucille Confronts the Generation Gap: Sex, Drugs,
  Rock & Roll, and Her "Babe Magnet" Son   page 231

CHAPTER TEN
  As Hollywood's Aging Stars Fade & Begin to Die,
  Like Troupers, the Few Who Remain Attempt to
  Boost Ratings for *Here's Lucy*.   page 269

CHAPTER ELEVEN
  Defying the Odds, Lucille Emerges as the
  Last Survivor of Vintage, Golden-Age Television
  Lucy Plays *Mame* as a Flaming Drag Queen   page 303

CHAPTER TWELVE
  After the Lingering, Long-Awaited Death of
  Here's Lucy, Lucille Forges Ahead with a Frenzied
  Campaign to Re-Invent Herself   page 327

CHAPTER THIRTEEN
  Lucille's Career Declines. As It Falters, Her
  Children Struggle for Industry Recognition   page 357

CHAPTER FOURTEEN
  Aging Gracefully? Lucille Becomes a Key Figure
  In Televised Odes to Vintage Hollywood.   page 393

CHAPTER FIFTEEN
  Like Many Mothers of the 1970s and Early '80s,
  Lucille Struggles with Her Son's Drug Addiction.   page 433

CHAPTER SIXTEEN
  Lucille Gets Nostalgic and Patriotic *(Again & Again*
  & Again) with Bob Hope. Bravely, They Morph into
  Predictable, "Past Their Expiration Date" Television
  Fixtures & Icons of "The American Century"   page 475

CHAPTER SEVENTEEN
  Lucille's Last Hurrah   page 507

EPILOGUE   page 542

AUTHORS' BIOS   page 547

WHAT IS BLOOD MOON PRODUCTIONS?

"Blood Moon, in case you don't know, is a small publishing house on Staten Island that cranks out Hollywood gossip books, about two or three a year, usually of five-, six-, or 700-page length, chocked with stories and pictures about people who used to consume the imaginations of the American public, back when we actually had a public imagination. That is, when people were really interested in each other, rather than in Apple 'devices.' In other words, back when we had vices, not devices."

—*The Huffington Post*

Previous Works by Darwin Porter
Produced In Collaboration with Blood Moon

Biographies from Blood Moon's Magnolia House Series

Lucille Ball & Desi Arnaz: They Weren't Lucy & Ricky Ricardo
(Volume One—1911-1960) of a Two-Part Biography

Marilyn: Don't Even Dream About Tomorrow
(a 2021 revised version of the best-selling
Marilyn at Rainbow's End: Sex, Lies, Murder, &
the Great Cover-Up (2012)

The Seductive Sapphic Exploits of Mercedes de Acosta
Hollywood's Greatest Lover

Jacqueline Kennedy Onassis, Her Tumultuous Life & Her Love Affairs

Judy Garland & Liza Minnelli, Too Many Damn Rainbows

Historic Magnolia House: Celebrity & The Ironies of Fame

Glamour, Glitz, & Gossip at Historic Magnolia House

***

Biographies from Blood Moon
Not Associated with Its Magnolia House Series

Burt Reynolds, Put the Pedal to the Metal

Kirk Douglas, More Is Never Enough

Playboy's Hugh Hefner, Empire of Skin

Carrie Fisher & Debbie Reynolds,
Princess Leia & Unsinkable Tammy in Hell

Rock Hudson Erotic Fire

Lana Turner, Hearts & Diamonds Take All

Donald Trump, The Man Who Would Be King

James Dean, Tomorrow Never Comes

Bill and Hillary, So This Is That Thing Called Love

Peter O'Toole, Hellraiser, Sexual Outlaw, Irish Rebel

Love Triangle, Ronald Reagan, Jane Wyman, & Nancy Davis

Pink Triangle, The Feuds and Private Lives of Tennessee Williams, Gore Vidal, Truman Capote, and Famous Members of their Entourages.

Those Glamorous Gabors, Bombshells from Budapest

Inside Linda Lovelace's Deep Throat, Degradation, Porno Chic, and the Rise of Feminism

Elizabeth Taylor, There is Nothing Like a Dame

J. Edgar Hoover and Clyde Tolson Investigating the Sexual Secrets of America's Most Famous Men and Women

Frank Sinatra, The Boudoir Singer. All the Gossip Unfit to Print

The Kennedys, All the Gossip Unfit to Print

The Secret Life of Humphrey Bogart (2003), and *Humphrey Bogart, The Making of a Legend* (2010)

Howard Hughes, Hell's Angel

Steve McQueen, King of Cool, Tales of a Lurid Life

Paul Newman, The Man Behind the Baby Blues

Merv Griffin, A Life in the Closet

Brando Unzipped

Katharine the Great, Hepburn, Secrets of a Lifetime Revealed

Jacko, His Rise and Fall, The Social and Sexual History of Michael Jackson

Damn You, Scarlett O'Hara,
The Private Lives of Vivien Leigh and Laurence Olivier

Film Criticism
Blood Moon's 2005 Guide to the Glitter Awards
Blood Moon's 2006 Guide to Film
Blood Moon's 2007 Guide to Film, and
50 Years of Queer Cinema, 500 of the Best GLBTQ Films Ever Made

Non-Fiction
Hollywood Babylon, It's Back! and *Hollywood Babylon Strikes Again!*

Novels

Blood Moon,
Hollywood's Silent Closet,
Rhinestone Country,
Razzle Dazzle
Midnight in Savannah

Other Publications by Darwin Porter Not Directly Associated with Blood Moon

Novels

The Delinquent Heart
The Taste of Steak Tartare
Butterflies in Heat
Marika (a roman à clef based on the life of Marlene Dietrich)
Venus (a roman à clef based on the life of Anaïs Nin)
Sister Rose

Travel Guides
Many Editions and Many Variations of *The Frommer Guides,*
The American Express Guides, and/or *TWA Guides,* et alia to:

Andalusia, Andorra, Anguilla, Aruba, Atlanta, Austria, the Azores, The Bahamas, Barbados, the Bavarian Alps, Berlin, Bermuda, Bonaire and

Curaçao, Boston, the British Virgin Islands, Budapest, Bulgaria, California, the Canary Islands, the Caribbean and its "Ports of Call," the Cayman Islands, Ceuta, the Channel Islands (UK), Charleston (SC), Corsica, Costa del Sol (Spain), Denmark, Dominica, the Dominican Republic, Edinburgh, England, Estonia, Europe, "Europe by Rail," the Faroe Islands, Finland, Florence, France, Frankfurt, the French Riviera, Geneva, Georgia (USA), Germany, Gibraltar, Glasgow, Granada (Spain), Great Britain, Greenland, Grenada (West Indies), Haiti, Hungary, Iceland, Ireland, Isle of Man, Italy, Jamaica, Key West & the Florida Keys, Las Vegas, Liechtenstein, Lisbon, London, Los Angeles, Madrid, Maine, Malta, Martinique & Guadeloupe, Massachusetts, Melilla, Morocco, Munich, New England, New Orleans, North Carolina, Norway, Paris, Poland, Portugal, Provence, Puerto Rico, Romania, Rome, Salzburg, San Diego, San Francisco, San Marino, Sardinia, Savannah, Scandinavia, Scotland, Seville, the Shetland Islands, Sicily, St. Martin & Sint Maarten, St. Vincent & the Grenadines, South Carolina, Spain, St. Kitts & Nevis, Sweden, Switzerland, the Turks & Caicos, the U.S.A., the U.S. Virgin Islands, Venice, Vienna and the Danube, Wales, and Zurich.

BIOGRAPHIES

From Diaghilev to Balanchine, The Saga of Ballerina Tamara Geva

Greta Keller, Germany's Other Lili Marlene

Sophie Tucker, The Last of the Red Hot Mamas

Anne Bancroft, Where Have You Gone, Mrs. Robinson?
(co-authored with Stanley Mills Haggart)

Veronica Lake, The Peek-a-Boo Girl

Running Wild in Babylon, Confessions of a Hollywood Press Agent

HISTORIES

Thurlow Weed, Whig Kingpin

Chester A. Arthur, Gilded Age Coxcomb in the White House

Discover Old America, What's Left of It

This Book Is Dedicated to:

VIVIAN VANCE
For her commentaries on, and begrudging loyalty, to Lucille Ball

and to

GARY MORTON
For the indignities he suffered as the
husband and business manager of a relentlessly famous Hollywood diva

and to

THE FRIENDS AND FRENEMIES OF LUCILLE BALL
Many of whom had a LOT to say about the tumultuous last decades of her life

Biographies
from Blood Moon Productions

More Biographies
from Blood Moon Productions

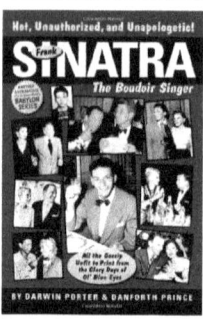

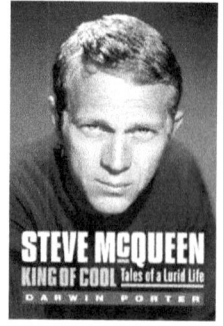

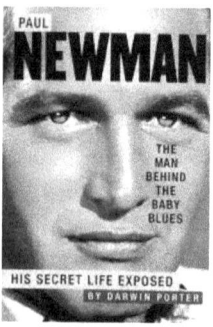

Coming Next from Blood Moon Productions

A pithy overview of the most famous and most dysfunctional father/daughter act in show-biz history:

JANE & HENRY FONDA

(For more information, check out the final pages of this book.)

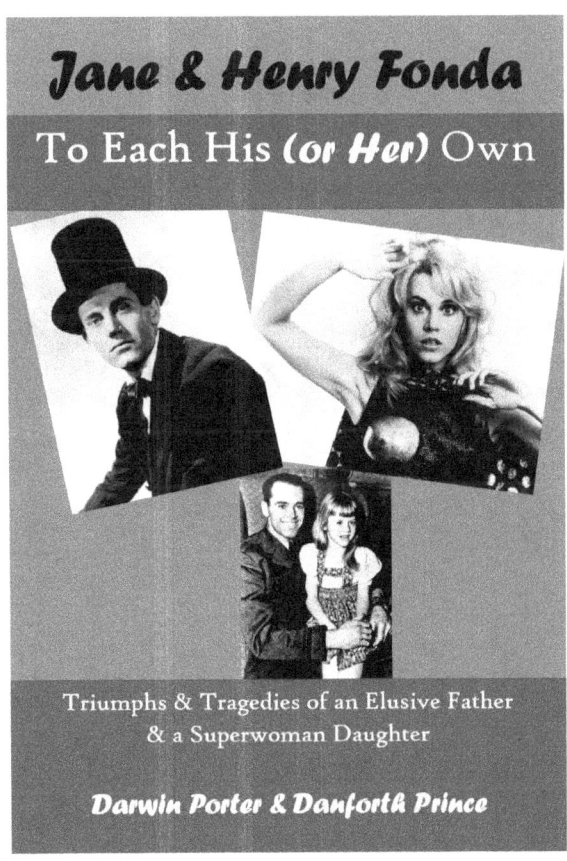

CHAPTER ONE

LUCILLE LAUNCHES
ACT TWO
OF A TURBULENT LIFE

In Beverly Hills at her home, Lucille Ball woke up early on the morning of March 3, 1960 to dress for her appearance in the Santa Monica Superior Court later that day. At long last, she was divorcing Desi Arnaz, "that philandering bastard," as she'd come to call him.

She'd married him on November 30, 1940 in Greenwich, Connecticut, when she was twenty-nine, and he was only twenty-three.

She called their affair "cradle snatching on my part." In Manhattan, she had been sleeping with him every night during his gig with his Cuban band at The Roxy.

The wedding had been haphazard and badly planned. On the morning of the day it happened, she didn't even know when she'd awakened in bed with him that this would be her wedding day.

He told her to get dressed because, "We goin' upta Greenwich to get married."

"This is the first I've heard of it," she said in shocked surprised.

"I tole you las' night between rumbas," he answered.

Right from the beginning of their marriage, he had developed a pattern of seducing young women, preferably blonde or redheaded, although he didn't reject a glamourous brunette.

When he had turned fifteen in his native Santiago, Cuba, his father had taken him to a brothel. Since then, he had seduced beautiful girls by the dozens. "The world was, and is, my oyster," he claimed. "What I want, I need only to ask for."

"Desi loved sex," said actor Cesar Romero, who was in love with him. "He couldn't get enough."

After his marriage, he told an Army

Actress Wins Divorce

Lucy Suing for a Divorce, Charges Desi with Cruelty

To millions of their fans, headlines like the one displayed above from a March, 1960, newspaper in Detroit were virtually unthinkable....Until it happened.

buddy, "Your wife is your wife. Fooling around in no way affects your love for her. Your marriage is sacred, and a few peccadilloes mean nothing."

Johnny García, a member of his Cuban band, claimed, "Desi didn't know the difference between sex and love. To put it bluntly, love was a good fuck. He could get that anywhere…and did. I should know. I was often with him and two gals in the same bed."

"He was a total lech," Garcia said. "Any female from thirteen to thirty, he'd bed, or so he told me. But there was an immediate problem with Lucille: Just months after his marriage, she would turn thirty in August. So right from the beginning, she had reached the far frontier of his age limit for seduction."

Lucille tolerated this womanizing until 1944, when she told her mother, DeDe, "I don't think Desi ever intends to settle down and become a good, steady, faithful husband—not as long as there are Army nurses, Hollywood starlets, pickups along the highway, and *putas* (his word for prostitutes) in the bordellos of Tinseltown. And as long as Betty Grable, Lana Turner, and Ginger Rogers—even that ice-skating Norwegian whore, Sonja Henie—keep inviting him into their bedrooms."

When she starred with Red Skelton in *Du Barry Was a Lady* (1943), she said to him, "Desi just can't keep it zipped up. He has a cheating heart. My marriage isn't working."

In 1944, when Desi was still in the U.S. Army, Lucille moved ahead and filed for divorce. On October 15, 1944, she was due in court to testify against him. But he came over to see her the night before. As she later admitted, "He delivered the sexual performance of his life."

The following morning, she woke up before him and beside him. After that night of shared passion and bliss, he had assumed that she'd abandon plans to divorce him.

But she told him she'd bought a chic new outfit, and the reporters and photographers expected her to make an appearance. "It's a great publicity break," she assured him.

The hearing that day in court was brief, and she did not charge him with adultery, but cited his carelessness with money and his frequent and abusive temper fits. When it was over, she was granted an interlocutory decree. Back at her home, she spent the rest of the day in bed with him. He was aware that according to California law, if a couple co-habited during a one-year waiting period, the divorce decree became invalid.

Every year that their marriage survived after that, she threatened to divorce him if he didn't give up his constant phi-

To TV audiences' horror, it suddenly became clear that adorable photos like the blissful domestic scene above were neither blissful nor particularly domestic

landering. But he never gave up his pursuit of women.

Now, sixteen years later, in March of 1960, Lucille knew that this divorce would be for real.

***

Dressed in a form-fitting black-and-white tweed suit, she held her head high as she emerged from a chauffeur-driven limousine hired for the occasion. She was mobbed by reporters and photographers, and she stopped and posed for pictures before entering the courthouse.

In front of Judge Orlando H. Rhodes, she gave a tearful testimony, charging "extreme mental cruelty which constantly causes me anguish. Mr. Arnaz has a violent temper, a Dr. Jekyll and Mr. Hyde personality."

Desi had not shown up to contest their divorce. She was granted custody of their two children, Lucie and Desi Jr., but he would be allowed to visit whenever he wished. He was ordered to pay $450 monthly in child support for each of his kids. Reporters thought paying less than a thousand dollars a month for both of them was very lenient.

Together, they held joint ownership of Desilu Productions, a large and rambling compound of studios previously known as RKO. For a time, RKO had been owned by the billionaire aviator and movie producer, Howard Hughes.

Desilu had originated in 1950, with Desi as President, Lucille as Vice President. From it, millions in revenue had been generated during the 1950s by the hit TV series, *I Love Lucy*. Its success had allowed them to buy RKO Studios and its offices, all of it valuable, "gold-plated" real estate.

Although Desilu later went public on the Stock Exchange, Desi and Lucille still owned fifty percent of its

In the middle photo, snapped in 1958, **Lucille** and **Desi** leave their offices at Desilu, where they were a big success. But in the lower photo, the tension between them was obvious.

"Lucy is becoming an old lady," Desi told Cesar Romero, "and I like 'em young."

stock. As part of their divorce settlement, the shares were divided equally between them, each receiving a twenty-five percent share of the company's stock.

To the court, Lucille's attorney, Mickey Rudin, presented a 68-page document dividing up their assets. She would retain ownership of their lavish home on Roxbury Drive in Beverly Hills and also their property in Rancho Mirage.

Desi was awarded their villa in Del Mar near the racetrack there and retained ownership of his ranch in Corona.

After leaving the courthouse, from her home on Roxbury Drive, Lucille phoned Vivian Vance, her longtime friend and co-star on *I Love Lucy*, where she'd played Ethel Mertz. Months before, Vance had finalized a divorce from her third husband, Actor Phil Ober.

"The last five years with Desi have been living hell," Lucille told Vance. "After this, there will be no more reconciliations. The last two or three times he tried to have sex with me, he couldn't even get it up. But apparently, it's rock hard for all the whores he seduces."

Although he didn't show up in court, Desi, that same afternoon, released his own statement to the press:

"After long consideration, we have not been able to work out our problems and have decided to separate. Our divorce is completely amicable, and there will be no contests. Lucy will pursue her career in television in another series without me, and I will continue in my duties as President of Desilu."

Vivian Vance's marriage (to **Phil Ober**, depicted here with his wife) was disentigrating, too.

An often out-of-work actor, Ober seemed to resent his wife's success. He warned her, "Cool it with all that hugging and kissing with Lucy. You come off like a couple of dykes in heat."

When news of their divorce was announced on radio and TV, many of their fans were shocked. Thousands of letters poured in from their devoted followers, who claimed that they were "devastated."

To millions of Americans, Lucille Ball and Desi Arnaz, so they believed, were just playing themselves on all those episodes of *I Love Lucy* which—because of their nine-year run (October 15, 1951, to April 1, 1960) seemed by now to be woven into the fabric of American life.

According to Lucille, "Our public thought we were actually Lucy and Ricky Ricardo. The Ricardo family had nothing in common with the Arnaz family."

In 1971, she looked back on that March day in court, defining it as "the worst time of my life. Since our divorce, neither Desi nor I have ever been the same, either mentally or physically."

***

Lucille's first appearance on television in

the new decade of the Sixties was not the final episode of *I Love Lucy*, but on the star-studded *Hedda Hopper's Hollywood*, a special NBC telecast that aired on January 10, 1960.

As Lucille was interviewed by Hopper, they stood together outside the Desilu Workshop, where young actors were trained. She talked briefly about her plans for the Playhouse (which actually would soon be shut down) and even referred to her husband without mentioning her plan to divorce him in two months. She then tells Hopper goodbye before heading off in her golf cart to her next duty as Desilu's vice president.

Having flexed her muscles as a leading gossip columnist, Hopper had assembled a bevy of other major-league stars to also appear with her on the telecast. They included Debbie Reynolds, Anthony Perkins, Gary Cooper, and Bob Hope. Brushing off the stardust of yesterday, and as a nostalgic tribute to them, she also included stars from the Silent era. They included the long-ago screen vamp, Gloria Swanson, and the two stars of the silent, 1925 version of *Ben-Hur*, Ramon Novarro and Francis X. Bushman.

HEDDA HOPPER

More Pictures For Lucy, Desi

Although the syndicated (much feared) columnist **Hedda Hopper** was sometimes spectacularly vicious with other Hollywood players, she usually puffed, fussed over, praised, and promoted anything associated with Lucille.

When *Variety* ran a review of Hopper's telecast, Lucille was "seriously pissed off" (her words) at how they phrased it: "Lucille Ball looked puffy and overweight, and she wore tons of makeup to cover up a lot of 'sins.'"

As recalled in Volume One of this biography, March 2, 1960 (Desi's 43rd birthday and also the date of the telecast that had preceded Lucille and Desi's divorce), had been a historic day in television. He and Lucille co-starred in "Lucy Meets the Mustache," with comedian Ernie Kovacs and his singer-*comedienne* wife, Edie Adams.

After filming 179 episodes of *I Love Lucy* with Fred and Ethel Mertz (Vivian Vance and William Frawley), plus thirteen one-hour specials, the Ricardos were turned out to pasture after almost a decade of frenzied telecasting.

After the broadcast of the final episode, the Ricardos and the Mertzes were sentenced to television heaven in the form of decades of reruns that would be broadcast around the world.

Based on the advance publicity it generated, CBS thought the episode with the Kovacs would be among the most-watched of the entire series. It therefore came as a shock that the telecast became the lowest-rated of the *I Love Lucy* series.

More bad news was on the way, as Westinghouse announced it would cancel the *Desilu Playhouse* at season's end, too. "We didn't sell enough light bulbs sponsoring it," one of its executives at its headquarters in Pittsburgh said.

The 1960s had arrived, and Lucille had been haunting Hollywood sound stages since 1933. She wasn't alone, and change was in the air: At this point in their careers, two of Hollywood's greatest stars, Bette Davis and Joan Crawford, were reduced to starring in a horror film (*What Ever Happened to Baby Jane?;* 1962), and the fabled blonde goddess, Marilyn Monroe, was soon to die.

In contrast, Elizabeth Taylor, Audrey Hepburn, Shirley MacLaine, Natalie Wood, and Elvis Presley (despite all those bad movies) still had star power, and new faces were on the horizon.

As Hollywood insiders already knew, the animosity between **Joan Crawford** (right) and **Bette Davis** dated from the 1930s. It was on grotesque display in the horror film, *What Ever Happened to Baby Jane* (1962).

After Lucille went to see it, she vowed, "I'm not going to let that happen to me. Nobody's going to reduce me to a monster on screen."

***

Lucille's agent finally came up with a movie for her. Her former co-star and longtime friend, Bob Hope, arranged a co-starring role for her in his latest film, *The Facts of Life*. Critics later reviewed it as "a sexless farce about adultery."

When Lucille first read its script, she was surprised, as it was an unusual vehicle for Hope. "What is this?" she asked. "The Road to Infidelity?"

[*That was a snide reference, of course, to all those "Road" movies Hope had made with Bing Crosby and Dorothy Lamour:* Road to Singapore *(1940) and* Road to Morocco *(1942) among many others.*]

The movie was shot at Desilu Studios, but Desi deliberately stayed away from the set, not wanting to distract Lucille from her work. From time to time, she spoke to reporters. They kept asking the same questions over and over:

"How does it feel to be a free woman again?"

"What are your plans to remarry, and are you going steady with any man right now?"

"What's it like to be the richest woman in Hollywood?"

Lucille and Bob Hope were not the original stars considered as the leads for *The Facts of Life*. At first, the script was presented to Olivia de Havilland, with William Holden or James Stewart suggested as her male counterpart. [*Some critics asserted that the film might have been inspired by David Lean's* Brief Encounter *(1945), starring Celia Johnson and Trevor Howard.* Brief Encounter *was remade in 1974 as a TV film with Richard Burton and Sophia Loren. In both versions, a man and woman meet by chance at a railway station and embark on a spontaneous but temporary romance.*]

The Hope/Ball film was a joint effort of Norman Panama and Melvin Frank. Panama was both the co-director and co-producer. He had written its screenplay based on a story by Frank, who was also co-director. Before working with Lucille and Hope, Panama and Frank had turned out such movie fare as *Mr. Blandings Builds His Dream House* (1948) with Cary Grant.

They had first worked with Hope on *My Favorite Blonde* in 1942 and again on *Road to Utopia* (1946), co-starring Bing Crosby. One of their biggest hits was again with Crosby, *White Christmas* (1954).

Johnny Mercer wrote the music for the opening titles of *The Facts of Life*, the song sung by Steve Lawrence and his wife, Eydie Gorme.

In a minor role was Phil Ober, the former husband of Vivian Vance.

The movie would win Oscar nominations, including one for Edith Head for costume design. Lucille herself would be nominated for a Golden Globe for "Best Actress in a Comedy."

Screen and TV writer, Larry Gelbart, said, "Hope fooled around a lot with anyone who was young and mobile and guest-starred on his show, but Lucille was not one of them. She would give him a friendly kiss—and that was that."

Privately to friends, Lucille confided, "Some gossips have linked me sexually with Hope. Believe me, it never happened. I don't find him sexy at all. He's spent a lifetime cheating on his wife, Dolores, but not with this kid. I heard two of the biggest names he's seduced were Dorothy Lamour, his Road picture co-star, and Paulette Goddard after Chaplin dumped her."

The plot of *The Facts of Life* has Lucille cast as Kitty Weaver, a bored Pasadena housewife with a dull husband named Jack (Don DeFore). In the role of Larry Gilbert, Hope is equally bored

The vintage *Brief Encounter* (1945) starring **Trevor Howard and Celia Johnson** was based on a passionate extramarital affair that played out in the months before World War II. It became the inspiration for the blandly vanilla **Bob Hope and Lucille Ball** farce, *The Facts of Life* (1960).

In it, Lucy and "Ski Nose"—correctly interpreting it as a G-rated, "family friendly' picture, never make it to bed.

Sixteen years later, however, in a 1976 made-for-television updated version of *Brief Encounter*, **Sophia Loren and Richard Burton** ignited the main character's adulterous passion once again.

with his wife, Mary (Ruth Hussey).

Usually, the couples go on vacation together, but for some reason, Hussey and DeFore can't make it one summer. Hope and Lucille decide to go anyway, and somewhere along the way—although they make an unlikely pair—love blossoms. Since this is a family-friendly picture, expect by the final reel that they will have second thoughts and return to their dull spouses.

Hussey had long been a screen favorite and had been Oscar nominated for Best Supporting Actress in *The Philadelphia Story* (1940), in which, as a photographer, she is in love with James Stewart. Their co-stars were Cary Grant and Katharine Hepburn.

The following year, exhibitors voted Hussey the third most popular star in Hollywood, which came as a surprise to everyone, including her. Over the years, her leading men included Robert Young, Robert Taylor, Van Heflin, Ray Milland, and Alan Ladd in F. Scott Fitzgerald's *The Great Gatsby* (1949).

DeFore was known mainly for his TV sitcom roles in such series as *Ozzie and Harriet* (1952-57) and *Hazel* (1961-65) starring Shirley Booth. Two of DeFore's most notable feature films were *A Guy Named Joe* (1943) and *Thirty Seconds Over Tokyo* the following year.

In *The Facts of Life,* Phil Ober and Marianne Stewart were cast as the Masons, another married couple.

From the beginning of the shoot, everyone, especially Lucille, seemed accident-prone. Hope quipped, "The movie should have been shot at Cedars of Lebanon Hospital."

One afternoon, on location for *The Facts of Life,* Lucille suffered a serious injury on camera as she tried to climb into a boat floating on the studio lake. Falling nine feet, she slashed her right leg and seriously bumped her forehead. By the time an ambulance rushed her into the Cedars of Lebanon Hospital for a two-day stay, her head injury had swollen to the size of a goose egg.

After her release, she retired with her children to the Arnaz villa at Del Mar.

After her return to the set, she walked with a limp and needed heavy makeup to conceal the black and blue bruises on her forehead.

When Desi heard of the accident, he was furious, placing an angry call to Hope. "I played straight man to Lucy for nine years, and never set her up for an accident. Why can't you guys follow my example? You should never have let her do such a stupid stunt." Then he slammed down the phone.

During the shoot, Hope and some members of the crew also suffered accidents.

Desi had rushed to Lucille's bedside and visited her every day during her recovery. That led to speculation that they'd get together again until her cousin, Cleo Morgan, told the press, "There is no hope for a reconciliation."

Lucille herself claimed, "Desi and I will never be together as man and wife, only as business associates."

After shooting was wrapped for the Hope picture, Lucille entered the hospital again, this time with a case of viral pneumonia. When news of that made the press, she was bombarded with get well cards. Many were sent by friends who hoped that she and Desi would reunite. An oft-repeated phrase was, "You two made the perfect couple."

The New York Times reviewed *The Facts of Life* as "a refreshingly flip yet moral picture." The critic cited it as one of the finest comedies of the year."

Variety judged it "a lively, witty romp."

Time magazine defined it as the finest movie since the release of *The Apartment,* that Billy Wilder picture that had starred Jack Lemmon and Shirley MacLaine.

The Facts of Life opened in November of 1960, earning $3.3 million at the box office. It became the last good movie Hope would ever make, and certainly the best of several in which he co-starred with Lucille.

In 1973, Melvin Frank would direct *A Touch of Class* starring George Segal and Glenda Jackson, which brought her a Best Actress Oscar. Like *The Facts of Life,* it dealt with a middle-aged couple trying to have an adulterous love affair during the course of a disaster-soaked trip to a destination where they would not be recognized. Although the plot and theme of each of the two were very similar it was never presented or defined as an outright remake.

During the filming of *The Facts of Life,* Lucille received an estimated 10,000 letters, many with marriage proposals, the writers ranging in age from sixteen to seventy-five. All of them wanted to marry her, and she was very flattered. Some sent frontal nudes, often with erections.

She told Vance and others, "I reached the bottom of my despair during the making of that Bob Hope picture. I detest failure in any form, and a failed marriage, followed by divorce, is one of the worst horrors a woman ever has to face. I figured I'm at rock bottom so anything from now on is up.

"I'm still getting scripts, really awful ones, mostly variations ripped off from episodes of *I Love Lucy.* I turn every one of these rip-offs down. Enough with this Lucy Ricardo shit! I've decided to do something I've wanted to do all my life. I want to star in a Broadway musical."

***

"I didn't have Ann Miller's tap-dancing feet or Judy Garland's powerful, memorable voice," Lucille recalled. "So what did I do? I headed for Broadway to do a musical called *Wildcat* where I played a hoydenish, gun-shooting Annie Oakley wildcatter, a blue jean-clad woman in boots who bamboozles roustabouts into letting her take control of their Oklahoma oil fields."

The play was set in 1912.

"My part was written for a 27-year-old, and I was pushing fifty. But since Desilu was putting up more than $400,000—later a lot more—to produce it, I got the lead. Money talks, darling."

In Manhattan, Lucille, with her attorney, signed a run-of-the-play contract, thinking that *Wildcat* might last a year, maybe a lot more, thanks to Lucille's star power and her millions of fans.

That same day, she signed a one-year, $50,000 lease on a luxurious apartment in the Imperial Hotel at 150 East 69th Street. The venue had been recommended to her by Joan Crawford, one of its charter residents. Consisting of two once-separate apartments with views of both the Hudson and East Rivers, it would provide ample room for Lucille, DeDe, and her two children, Lucie and Desi, Jr.

To please Desi, she enrolled her children in a local Catholic school. To her regret, they found winter in Manhattan gray and gloomy, preferring sunny California, where their friends were.

One of her neighbors turned out to be John Charles Daly, the host of the hit TV show, *What's My Line?* He invited Lucille to become a celebrity mystery guest on his show. Its theme revolved around four blindfolded panelists who each tried to figure out who she was. Of course, she'd have to disguise her voice. The moment she uttered a sentence with her natural (i.e., non-disguised) voice, the panelists would guess her identity.

The script for *Wildcat* had been written by N. Richard Nash. Born in Philadelphia, he had started life as a boxer for ten dollars a match. Before breaking into the theater, he had written two books on philosophy, including *The Athenian Spirit*.

Wildcat, which had hoped to propel Lucille into stardom as a Broadway star, disappointed virtually everyone.

The show had serious problems almost from the start, with a blizzard forcing the rescheduling of opening night, negative reviews, and a very unwell Lucille, who collapsed onstage after an already prolonged absence.

The production closed June 3, 1961, after 171 performances.

His first play on Broadway, *Parting at Imsdorf*, had opened in 1940, but he didn't achieve major success until he created *The Rainmaker*, a Broadway play that starred Geraldine Page. In 1956, it was adapted into a film starring Katharine Hepburn and Burt Lancaster.

Originally, Mary Martin had considered starring in *Wildcat*, but apparently, she didn't have confidence in the two composers (Jimmy Van Heusen and Sammy Cahn), who had signed to create the music. Although they'd been successful in movie musicals, they'd never (yet) had a success record on Broadway.

Lucille had no fears about them, considering them extremely talented. In spite of the age difference between her and her character, she believed that she could pull off the role of the brazenly outgoing Wildcat (aka "Wildy") Jackson.

Eventually, Michael Kidd, the director, decided not to hire Van Heusen and Cahn, opting to engage two other young composers, Cy Coleman and Carolyn Leigh, instead. Leigh had written the lyrics for the hit Broadway production of *Peter Pan* (1954), which had starred Mary Martin.

For other productions, Coleman and Leigh had jointly written such songs as "Witchcraft," "Firefly," and "The Best Is Yet to Come." For *Wildcat*, they would emerge with one hit, "Hey, Look Me Over," sung by Lucille and later recorded by other singers.

Kidd, the director, was also a dancer and choreographer who was known in theatrical circles for weaving dance movements into the plots of whatever he was directing at the time. This was in contrast to many musicals where the star would spontaneously burst into song without any motivation in the script.

Kidd was also noted for "athletic" dancing, as best seen in the rousing musical, *Seven Brides for Seven Brothers* (1954).

Kidd was the first choreographer to win Five Tony Awards. Before *Wildcat*, he had worked on such Broadway musicals as *Guys and Dolls, Can-Can,* and *Finian's Rainbow*.

Two views of **Lucy in** *Wildcat*: Upper photo shows **Valerie Harper** onstage on Broadway, and (lower photo), **Lucille with Paula Stewart** in a replica of the play as presented on *The Ed Sullivan Show* in 1961.

Long after the stage version of *Wildcat* folded, he would go on to choreograph a famous cinematic flop, the musical movie, *Hello, Dolly* (1969) starring Barbra Streisand.

[*Shortly after its release, it won three Oscars—Best Art Direction, Best Score of a Musical, and Best Sound—and nominated for Best Picture of the Year. Initially, it generated mostly favorable reviews. After that, however, it was critically re-assessed. Although the film version of* Hello, Dolly! *had cost nearly as much to produce as* Cleopatra (1963) *starring Elizabeth Taylor and Richard Burton, it made far less at the box office, thus earning it a reputation as one of Hollywood's "foremost turkeys."*

A critic for Slant Magazine *claimed, "More infamous for bringing Fox financially to its knees than for being the last major musical directed by Gene Kelly,* Hello, Dolly! Is one big-assed bull in a china shop.": *The consensus was that Streisand was miscast."*]

Broadway had to include a love interest for Lucille and the wildcatter she'd portray, so Nash created "Joe Dynamite," a swaggering foreman for the drilling crew, a young hunk in tight blue jeans.

Kirk Douglas had the necessary bravado, and he would have been "age appropriate" for Lucille, but he priced himself out of the running. Then Gordon MacRae, who had made all those musicals for Warner Brothers, actively campaigned for the role but was rejected.

Lucille recommended Stephen Boyd, a son of Ireland, who had thrilled her in the 1959 blockbuster rendition of *Ben-Hur* in which he had starred opposite Charlton Heston. Cleft-chinned and rugged, Boyd had a macho charm that seemed tailor made for Joe Dynamite. Then, to everyone's regret, it became known that he'd already signed to make a feature film called *The Big Gamble.*

Then they considered Gene Barry, whom they thought might be ideal, based on his 1953 performance as a saloon keeper in the Yukon with a roving eye for another redhead, Rhonda Fleming, billed at the time as "The Queen of Technicolor." But to Lucille's regret, he was committed to his hit TV series, *Bat Masterson* (1959-1961), and had to reject their offer.

As her leading man, Lucille finally settled on Keith Andes, whom she remembered from *Clash by Night* (1952), in which he played opposite Marilyn Monroe. During its filming, Marilyn was servicing both Andes and its female star, Barbara Stanwyck.

"He looked great in the early Fifties," Lucille said to Nash, the scriptwriter. "Bring him to New York. I want to see what he looks like today."

Since she was the play's "virtual producer," the conduit to Desilu's money, Lucille got her wish. Andes flew to New York, and Lucille liked what she saw. After meeting with him, she told Nash, "He's a bit older, but still great looking. I don't want him to look as young as he did when he played opposite Marilyn."

During rehearsals, rumors spread along the gossipy Broadway grapevine that Lucille was having an affair with her leading man, Keith Andes.

At first, she denied it, but years later, she admitted to having had a brief fling with him. "It wasn't all that much," she recalled. "Maybe four or five times, perhaps more."

Andes admitted to the affair but not at the time. "She was so very lonely, and I did my best. She wasn't that turned on by me. I really wanted the role since my career was going nowhere. So I performed stud duty, but it was strictly physical between the two of us, no real emotional involvement. Then Gary Morton came along. He was more her type."

When Lucille dated Andes, he was in the process of divorcing his first wife, Jean Alice Cotton, whom

Marilyn Monroe and **Keith Andes** in *Clash by Night.* Off screen, his sexual competitor for MM's affections was the star of the picture, Barbara Stanwyck.

In *Wildcat* on Broadway years later, playing "Joe Dynamite," Andes was Lucille Ball's leading man.

he had married in 1946 after his stint in the U.S. Army during World War II. A former nurse, she and Andes had produced two sons.

In the wake of that divorce, during a lull in the production of *Wildcat*, he met and married Sheila Hackett, a dancer in the chorus. Months later, it was Hackett who replaced Lucille during the second act after she collapsed on stage during one of her evening performances.

Actress Paula Stewart played Lucille's younger sister in *Wildcat*. She never really became a super star, although she was talented and beautiful in a low-key kind of way. The daughter of a doctor and an actress, she in time joined the Broadway production of *Seventeen* in 1951. Her career on stage, in film, and TV consisted mainly of bit parts and supporting roles.

Stewart married two famous performers.

The first was in 1953 when she wed Burt Bacharach during her gig at the Versailles Club, where he was her accompanist and scored arrangements for her night club act.

[Located at 151 E. 50th Street, The Versailles was billed as "New York's distinguished continental rendezvous."] Divorced in 1958, Stewart would go on to marry comedian Jack Carter in 1961. During the run of *Wildcat*, she was already dating Carter.

In addition to playing opposite Lucille on stage, Stewart would become a key figure in setting her up with another husband.

By far the best dancer in the original Broadway show was Swen Swenson. Born in Iowa in 1930, he was twenty years old when he wowed Broadway with his skill as a dancer. Lucille was amazed at his movements.

He would go on to really dazzle Broadway when he performed in the

Looking exhausted, **Lucille** is depicted here with her co-star, **Paula Stewart**, the colleague who eventually introduced her to Gary Morton, around the time of the staging of the Broadway production of *Wildcat*.

Stewart defined her as "my savior".

America loved Lucy, and **Lucille** still loved (and endorsed) cigarettes, as shown in this ad for the "Big Clean Taste of Top Tobacco...**Chesterfields**."

A pack of them is prominently displayed beneath her photo on this announcement of the "out-of-town" opening (at the opulent, since-demolished, Ehrlanger Theater in Philadelphia) of *Wildcat*.

1962 musical *Little Me,* in which he performed a dance number so spectacular that he often received a standing ovation for it. Openly gay, he also won a Tony nomination. He would later star in *No, No Nanette, I Remember Mama,* and the 1981 revival of *Can-Can.*

In 1993, Swenson died of an AIDS-related illness.

***

Even before opening on Broadway in *Wildcat,* as a result of injuring her leg on the set of *The Facts of Life,* Lucille faced a health emergency. She thought that her injured leg had healed, but in New York it became infected. Surgery was required at the Polyclinic Hospital on West 50th Street in Manhattan. A surgeon had to open the festering wound and scrape way the infection.

For days in the hospital, with her leg in a cast, she invited members of the cast to come to her hospital room and rehearse lines with her.

She recalled *Wildcat* as her most strenuous theatrical performance, surpassing any of the antics she'd executed on *I Love Lucy.* During its Broadway run, she suffered several severe bruises, a sprained ankle (three times), and a pulled tendon in her left leg caused by a "too athletic" dance number.

The first time an audience got to see *Wildcat* was on Thanksgiving Day, 1960, at a tryout in Philadelphia. Her voice was hoarse, she was not in good health, she was saturated with painkillers, and still aching from the injuries she'd sustained during the filming of *The Facts of Life.*

One critic wrote: "She began muffing her lines, even forgetting the words of some lyrics, which were not that good to begin with. On two occasions, she stopped cold and turned to the audience, asking for their indulgence. That request was met with thunderous applause before she resumed her role."

At some point, she became Lucy Ricardo, as noted by the Philadelphia press. One critic claimed that "Adding Lucy Ricardo to the Wildcatter role was like adding maraschino cherries to a tuna fish salad."

At the show's preview in

WILL BROADWAY LOVE LUCY?

"As a young wannabe actress in the early 1930s, I dreamed of becoming a star on Broadway," **Lucille** said.

"In *Wildcat*, I got my chance, but, as it turned out, I postponed my Broadway debut for too long, Physically, I was not up to the demanding role of a dancing and singing version of a wildcatter in the oil fields."

Philadelphia on October 2, 1960, an enthusiastic critic for *Variety* was in the audience, later predicting it will be "a surefire hit when it will open on the Great White Way. Miss Ball sings acceptably, dances with spirit, shines as a *comedienne*, and even does a couple of dramatic scenes with ease and polish."

Yet as if to signal the upcoming doom of *Wildcat*, it opened on December 16, 1960 as a blizzard swept over New York City, one of the most paralyzing in years. "The poison pen critics of the New York press—all snobs about Hollywood stars starring on Broadway—had it in for me," Lucille claimed.

It opened with pizzazz: She received a standing ovation when she walked out onto the stage, wearing blue denim. Then she burst into song, "Hey, Look Me Over."

A lone figure wanders an almost deserted avenue of Manhattan during one of the city's worst blizzards: **December of 1960.**

On their way from Philadelphia, three trucks carrying props, sets, and costumes faced a miles-long shutdown on the New Jersey turnpike. It threw the opening of *Wildcat* into chaos.

As the crowd roared its approval, Desi Arnaz rose from the front row with a bouquet of flowers.

After the opening, he staged an elaborate party at the chic Twenty-One, inviting key members of the cast and production staff. As the honored guest, Lucille attended but didn't stay long, telling him, "I am tired, exhausted beyond belief."

En route back to her apartment with two male attendants, she asked to stop at a newsstand with the intention of retrieving the morning papers and their reviews of *Wildcat*.

Then the barbs were released: *The New York Times* wrote that, "Miss Lucille Ball is up there on stage, all right, doing all the spectacular and animated and energetic and deliriously accomplished things she can do, but what happened? It is simply the unsmiling libretto of N. Richard Nash, who created *The Rainmaker*, that makes her seem to be performing by proxy."

Walter Kerr of *The Herald Tribune* panned it: "The general temperature is mild for a big Broadway fandango, and the rueful silences are many. It's the time, it's the place, but where is the star?"

The *Journal-American* offered no solace to Lucille: "This mishmash could have been conceived on any TV-Western assembly line."

Critic Howard Tauman later wrote, "*Wildcat* went prospecting for Broadway oil, but drilled a dry hole. Everyone wanted to love Lucy, and she worked hard singing and dancing with zest and reading her lines with expert timing. *Wildcat* did seem to test her full capacities as a performer. But the musical has as much spirit and excitement as a tame old tabby."

En route back to Los Angeles, Desi voiced his opinion to his current girlfriend, Sheilah Dare, and out-of-work blonde showgirl he'd met in Manhattan. "Fans are coming to see Lucy Ricardo as they remembered her. What they get is an aging showgirl past her expiration date."

Nash gave his own review: "Lucille was in her fifties, and her age sure did show. She was almost there, but not quite., She has aged prematurely."

"It was not believable that a woman of her years would be doing shenanigans more appropriate to a late teenager," said director Kidd.

Despite the negative reviews, *Wildcat* was a hit with Lucille's fans, some of whom came from distant cities such as Chicago or St. Louis. The Alvin Theater had 11,200 seats, and most of them were filled every night.

During its six-month run on Broadway, and every night of the show, a hundred, sometimes two hundred fans gathered nightly at the theater to see her exit. Of course, she couldn't even begin to sign all those autograph books, so in almost every instance, she was rushed to a waiting limousine as soon as possible. All she could do was wave and blow kisses.

Any longtime success of *Wildcat* on Broadway was doomed by Lucille's deteriorating physical condition. Throughout the run of the play, she suffered from nervous exhaustion, and was constantly getting colds. At one point, she came down with a serious viral infection, and on occasion, she suffered from torn muscles that never seemed to heal because of her intricate stage movements and dance steps.

Around Valentine's Day, her doctor recommended she shut down the play and take a vacation in some sunny clime. Palm Beach was recommended, but she chose Jamaica.

She flew to Montego Bay with Lucie and Desi Jr. "Bad choice," she said later. "It was so humid I passed out twice. Not only that, but there was some sort of revolution going on."

When she returned to the Broadway stage, her vacation didn't seem to have done her any good. By then, Desilu's investment in the doomed production had risen to $750,000. Desi—enraged, frustrated, and back in Hollywood—was "going out of my mind" with fear that disaster was near and that their company would be stuck with a "lemon" and suffer a major loss.

In her weakened condition, Lucille feared that she did not have the strength to deliver two performances on Saturday, April 22. At one point, she fainted on stage.

Performing with her at the time was Edith King, a young actress who broke her fall. In doing so, Edith herself suf-

After the "died-with-a-whimper'" closing of Lucille's Broadway version of **Wildcat**, Hollywood producers considered **Debbie Reynolds** as her replacement for a film adaptation, but the project died before it got started.

In the photo above, Reynolds sings and dances up a storm a few years later, in 1964, as a "country girl who got rich quick" in *The Unsinkable Molly Brown*.

fered a fracture of her right wrist. Both women had to be assisted off the stage by the stagehands.

Kidd emerged from the wings and came out onto the stage to announce that the show would continue in fifteen minutes. Against house rules, Lucille's understudy, Betty Jane Watson, had gone home early. Furious and in a red-alert emergency mode, Kidd yanked Sheilah Hackett, a choreographer and dancer from the chorus, to finish Lucille's musical number. Although Hackett did so admirably, the audience wanted (and demanded) Lucy. When Hackett first came on, there were boos from the audience, and in the aftermath of her performance, many fans demanded their money back from the box office.

After her fainting spell, Lucille was out of the show for a week, as her understudy, Watson, took over the role. But fans were coming to see Lucille more than they wanted to see *Wildcat*. There was a loud outcry for refunds from the box office. Some nights, the seats in the audience were only one-fourth full.

Lucille never really escaped the pain of her many broken bones and injuries. In reference to her opening night on Broadway, she later asserted, "I felt as if I'd been stabbed with a red-hot butcher knife. One night, I fell into the footlights. During the short run of the play, I dropped twenty-five pounds."

Before Lucille bowed out, Kidd wanted to keep *Wildcat* going. It was a common occurrence on Broadway to replace "a star with a star" when the originator of a role wanted to leave. He negotiated with Ginger Rogers, Mitzi Gaynor, and Gwen Verdon, but none of them wanted "to follow Lucille Ball."

Inevitably, when the production closed on May 24, 1961 after a six-month run, the box office was forced to return $165,000 of advance ticket sales. Unwilling to immediately face family

One of the "dictators" of fashion during Lucille's heyday on Broadway was the spectacularly bitchy "**Mr. Blackwell,**" seen above in this ad from 1962 promoting him as a Czar of Impeccable Taste.

Every year, female celebrities lived in dread, waiting for the release of his "Worst-Dressed List."

In 1961, **Lucille Ball** (upper left photo) topped Blackwell's list as a "Worst Dressed."

Runners-up that year were **Kim Novak** (upper right). **Anne Baxter** (lower left) and **Brigitte Bardot** (lower right).

17

and friends, Lucille immediately left for Europe, flying to London and continuing on to Rome. Eventually, she rented a villa on the Isle of Capri to be alone and to recover from her ordeal.

When she flew back to New York, she learned that a dubious honor had been bestowed on her. The flamboyant "Mr. Blackwell" designated her as "the worst-dressed actress in the world." Runners-up included, in first place, the French sex kitten Brigitte Bardot, followed by Kim Novak and Anne Baxter.

Months later, Seven Arts flirted with the idea of bringing *Wildcat* to the screen, starring Ann-Margret. Later, Debbie Reynolds was viewed as the ideal choice for the lead, opposite any number of actors, notably Rory Calhoun. But it was never filmed.

***

Years later, Keith Andes reflected on having co-starred on Broadway with Lucille Ball in *Wildcat*:

"She was recovering from her divorce from Desi Arnaz, and I was also having marital troubles. Frankly, I think she was shopping around for her next husband. I knew right from the start I would not be her choice, although she was physically attracted to me."

"As a stage actress, she lacked discipline," he said. "Forgive the expression, but she shot her wad in the first act, leaving nothing left for the second act. Also, she wasn't really a singer or dancer. Let's face it: On the stage, you've got to get t right the first time, unlike the movies where you can do retakes. She screwed up time and time again, but we had to keep it rolling. I knew she was a real professional, but I think something was wrong with her mentally and also physically."

Years after that, this time in June of 2004, Andes reflected once again on his work with Lucille in *Wildcat*.

"If she'd been in better shape, I think *Wildcat* could have gone on for years, considering her worldwide popularity. Any visiting couple from out of town wanted to see 'Lucy' on the stage. In private, she insisted on being called Lucille. Fans gathered at the stage door at night to see her retreat. My God, she was the most famous woman on the planet."

"In contrast, I was always met by a small coterie of fans who held out an 8" x 10" glossy for me to sign. Onstage, at least, I was often shirtless. My fan base, such as it was, consisted of a lot of gay men and some older women who'd been teenagers in the 1950s."

A few months later, another reporter asked Andes rather bluntly if he'd made it with either Marilyn Monroe or Lucy…or both of them.

"No, I never made it with Lucy, but I did become intimate with Lucille. (Never refer to her as Lucy.) I'm not for bragging, but she had high praise for my body and my equipment. But there was something missing in our relationship. Passion. I went through the motions on the set of *Clash by Night* with Monroe. She just performed mechanically. Frankly, I came to feel that at the time, she was enjoying lesbian sex with our star, Barbara

Stanwick, more than she did with me."

***

In the late 1950s, Arlene Dahl, the stunning red-haired beauty of MGM films, bonded with Lucille. At the time, she was married to Fernando Lamas, who had become a good friend of Desi, even though they often competed for which of them would become the premier Latin lover of the silver screen. (Lamas won.)

But they'd usually put jealousy aside and often went out together on night-crawling "poontang hunts," where, together, they'd uncover one girl after another willing to accept their invitations to get better acquainted.

Before Lamas, Dahl had been married (1951-52) to the screen Tarzan, Lex Barker. Their marriage began foundering shortly after their wedding as Barker was lured away and into the arms of Lana Turner. At the time, he was hailed as "The Sexiest Body Beautiful on the Planet." On television, years later, Dahl spoke of the "big package" behind that loincloth on the screen.

In reference to the time and attention she devoted to her grooming, Lamas confessed to Desi, "Being married to Arlene is fine at night in bed. But during the day, it's like being married to Elizabeth Arden."

At first, it was not men but astrology that drew Lucille and Dahl together. To cope with their errant husbands, they turned to the stars through Carl Righter, hailed at the time as America's leading astrologer. Twice a week, they attended his lectures. He later met privately with them, hoping to understand their husbands better. *[Desi was a Pisces, Lamas a Capricorn.]*

"We were each redheads married to Latin lovers with roving eyes," Lucille said. "But why?" everyone asked, "would Fernando cheat on Arlene when she was hailed in some quarters as the most beautiful woman in the world, rivaling Hedy Lamarr in the 1940s and Ava Gardner in the 1950s."

Left to right: **Arlene Dahl** with husband no. 1 (1951-1952, **Lex Barker**, aka "Tarzan"); with husband #2 (1954-1960; **Fernando Lamas**); and with husband #3 (1960-1964, **Christian Holmes**).

In 1960, during rehearsals for *Wildcat*, when Dahl was living in New York and divorcing Lamas, Lucille bonded with her again. Dahl sometimes set up double dates for herself and Lucille, most often with "stage door Johnnies." The cast and crew of *Wildcat* jokingly referred to Dahl as "Lucy's pimp."

Lucille rarely interpreted any of these blind dates as suitable, realistically romantic choices. Some of them were theatrical agents hoping to sign her up as a client. On one occasion, she was paired with a notorious Mafia Don who evoked her "gun moll" days when she dated the mob-linked actor George Raft in the 1930s.

Although Lucille never found a suitable candidate for marriage through any of her blind dates, Dahl did. In 1960, she met Christian R. Holmes, a Texas oil millionaire, and married him. That union lasted until 1964.

In the 1970s, Dahl worked for Sears & Roebuck as their director of beauty products, earning $750,000 annually.

Like Lucille, **Arlene Dahl** had deeply entrenched sense of what was commercially viable. Here, she appears as a Valentine's Day pinup in the mid 1950s, during her MGM years.

***

During the heady weeks before *Wildcat* opened on Broadway, Danny Welkes, a theatrical agent, was having dinner with Lucille at Danny's Hideaway, a dimly lit Midtown Manhattan bistro that attracted the cast and crews of Broadway productions.

At the next table, Mickey Hayes, a hawker of cut-rate men's clothing, was finishing his meal with Gary Morton, a stand-up comedian who at the time was appearing at Radio City Music Hall.

Hayes knew Welkes and stopped to greet him after paying his check. Beside him was Morton, who was introduced to Lucille. As he leaned over to shake her hand, his gray tie dipped into her coffee.

She took a salt shaker and sprinkled some of it on his tie. "That way it won't stain."

Soon, after the clothing salesman and Morton were out the door, Lucille turned to Welkes. "That guy is what I call ugly handsome, if that makes sense. He looks rough and tough, but strangely alluring. A real man's man who might also spare some time for a lady. Get me his address. I'm going to call Saks in the morning and order three elephant gray ties delivered to him."

She followed through on that promise, and the ties were delivered to a cheap hotel on the Upper West Side.

Although unknown to Lucille, Morton was well-known in certain circles. She set out to learn what she could about him. She'd never seen his stand-up comedy routine, although he'd been "second banana" to a number of opening acts, including Frank Sinatra, Dean Martin, Sammy Davis Jr., Milton Berle, and Lena Horne.

The son of a truck driver from the Bronx, Morton was born Morton Goldaper in 1924, which made him thirteen years younger than Lucille. Even though still quite young, he covered his head with a *toupée*.

As a stand-up comic, Morton got his start working in the "Borscht Belt," the nickname of a string of Jewish resorts in the Catskills, a three-hours' drive north of New York City.

Morton had started out playing the trumpet—"I was no Harry James"— but soon found he had a talent for stand-up comedy.

He'd had a very brief and unsuccessful marriage to actress Susan Morrow, whom he'd wed on December 17, 1953. They separated a few months later, but didn't have their marriage annulled, in Los Angeles, until 1957.

Amazingly, Morton was unfamiliar with Lucille's career, having seen her only in "two or three of her movies." Because he worked at night, he'd never watched any episode of *I Love Lucy* on television. When he wasn't working, he was not known for chasing after women, like Desi. Instead, he was an avid golfer and had "this thing" for vintage cars.

She was shocked that he'd never seen an episode of *I Love Lucy*. "Here I was, the third most famous woman in history, and millions had seen my series," she said.

A souvenir (and relic) of yesterday, when cigarettes were legal indoors: an ashtray from **Danny's Hideaway**, the Manhattan eatery where Lucille met Gary.

Here is a rare press photo of then-working-comedian **Gary Morton** during his Borscht Belt *schtick* in 1959.

It's one of the few stand-alone photos of Gary Morton. Most of the others in public circulation show him in some kind of interaction with his spectacularly famous wife, Lucille.

"Who do you consider the two most famous women?" Dahl once asked him.

"Mary, the mother of Jesus, and Eve, Adam's trick in the Garden of Eden," Morton adroitly answered.

Lucille and Morton began going out on double dates with Paula Stewart, the actress who played her kid sister in *Wildcat,* and her fiancé, Jack Carter, the Brooklyn-born comedian who was sometimes referred to as "the Poor Man's Milton Berle."

Their first double date was at the Silver Moon Pizza Parlor, ten blocks from Lucille's apartment at the Imperial Hotel. It soon became their hangout for late-night suppers after everyone got off from work.

On their first date, she "tested" Morton to see if she could boss him around. Over pizza, she tossed him a package of Chesterfield cigarettes, ordering him to "light one for me." He picked up the package and tossed it back at her. "Light it yourself."

She burst out laughing. "My kind of man!" Then she kissed him gently on the lips. "I can see you're not the type of man who can be pussy-whipped."

After dinner that night, Morton took Lucille back to the Imperial in a cab, but she didn't invite him upstairs.

He told her he had to get up early the next day. His gig at the Radio City Music Hall had ended, and he had to leave for a booking "in some remote town in Ohio." He promised he'd call her every day he was away, and he kept that commitment.

When he returned from Ohio, he began to date her steadily. On his fourth night back, she invited him for a sleepover. After two weeks of steady dating, he popped the question: "Will you be my gal?"

"I'll think about it," she promised.

Morton later told Carter, "I was struck by Lucille's carriage. When she enters a room, everybody takes notice."

In the months ahead, Paula Stewart and Lucille became so closely involved, respectively, with Jack Carter and Gary Morton that they were almost like men with their wives. Soon, they'd each marry their respective suitors.

Stewart would wed Carter in 1961. After that, they performed as a team in theaters and clubs around the country, including at The Versailles Club in New York where Desi had frequently appeared.

They also were booked into a gig at the Waldorf Astoria, where Desi had gotten his start with Xavier Cugat's band. Before her gig with Lucille in *Wildcat*, Stewart had been featured in the revue *From A to Z*, starring Hermione Gingold.

Lucille told Stewart, "After Desi, I vowed never to marry again: I'd had many lovers...I mean, a whole troop of them, but nothing compared to all the *putas* he seduced. I'm bitter after my failed marriage to him. He had too much power in my relationship. I don't want a Nellie for a husband. I DO want a powerful man, but one I can control. I know I seem to be contradicting myself and not making sense. I have all these mixed feelings about what I want. I prefer a man who will stand up to me, but one I can cut down to size. What I like most about Gary is that he is the very antithesis of Desi Arnaz."

During one of Lucille's conversations with Arlene Dahl, the two gossipy women talked about marriage. Dahl was on the verge of marrying her Texas oil millionaire and perhaps leaving the screen. "I haven't liked many of my roles. I've played a nymphomaniac, a kleptomaniac, and even a dipsomaniac. Now I may be some *grande* lady hanging out with other wives married to very rich men."

Dahl was eager to know what Morton was like. "Where do I begin?" Lucille said. "First, the really important thing. Yes, both Desi and Gary are great in bed. But there's a difference of an inch, perhaps an inch and a half of skin, between them."

The very hip Dahl knew at once that Lucille was saying that Morton, as a Jew, was circumcised whereas Desi was not.

She also confided to Dahl that in many ways, Morton reminded her of actor Broderick Crawford, with whom she'd had an affair in the late 1930s when there was talk of a possible marriage.

"Broderick was burly and brutish, but with a commanding presence," she said. "Gary is more polished, but still evokes the image of my long-ago beau. Let's face it: Desi will always be the love of my life. But you can't have a husband who's intent on plugging every starlet in Hollywood. I hear that our First Lady, Jacqueline Kennedy, can put up with her husband's philandering, but I'm tired of it. I'll never love Gary in the same way I did Desi. But so what? At least Gary will be the man around the house, unlike Desi, who visited on occasion."

After one of Lucille's performances in *Wildcat*, Hollywood's matron of gossip, Louella Parsons, came backstage one night. As a journalist, she pointedly asked if she planned to marry Gary Morton.

She was not ready to formally announce any plans. And when she did, she planned to give Hedda Hopper the scoop.

"Hell no!" Lucille shot back at Parsons. "I've had it with marriage. It's taken me a long time to realize something. I loved Desi, but Desi didn't love me. It took me a lot of time to face the truth."

She told her close friend and future co-star, Carole Cook, "Here I am, world famous, filthy rich, loaded and lonely, nearing the half-century mark. Along comes Gary. There will be problems, of course. After all these years in Hollywood, I've become tough. In honor of my last name, I now swing a big pair of balls. Weak men would find it heard to live with a woman as powerful as I am. But somehow I think Gary can."

In time, Lucille became a close friend of the ardent movie fan, Robert Osborne, who would become famous for hosting *Turner Classics* on TV. One night, she spoke to him of the decision that led her to marry Morton.

"She told me how he could make her laugh but also comfort her when she was depressed. It's always been hard for really big-time stars like Judy Garland, Bette Davis, or Joan Crawford, to find suitable mates. Morton seemed to be the answer to Lucille's lonely nights., Of course, he would not be a replacement for Desi, but something new and completely different. I suspect that Lucille at heart is a one-man woman and will never really get over Desi. She confided that there was only one man in Hollywood that she'd run off with, leaving Desi behind, and that was William Holden."

One night, Morton asked Lucille a question that had been nagging him. "For men, it is important to know when contemplating marriage to a woman who has been married before: Am I bigger than Desi?"

"Comparisons are odious," she said, dismissing the question.

Lucille's divorce from Desi came through on May 12, 1961. That summer, she moved ahead with plans to marry Morton that fall.

Author Charles Higham described him like this: "Morton had the qualities necessary to become a successful husband to a major star. He was unselfish, unshakeable, sturdy, deferent when that was needed, and good at countering insecurities, fragility, and self-doubt. He could shrug off Lucy's temper; he was not, like Desi, volatile, nervous, and passionate."

Before any wedding took place, there were certain agreements that had to be understood. Lucille told him she did not want a "part-time husband" like she'd had with Desi. She warned him to give up his career as a stand-up comic working night clubs and resorts. *[It was agreed, however, that he could fulfill any contracts he'd already signed.]*

After she left *Wildcat*, she accompanied him to some final engagements, but she let him know that she was eager to return with him to Hollywood, where she wanted him to get involved in aspects of her television production.

Two days before their actual wedding, she insisted that he sign a pre-nuptial agreement. He agreed, telling her, "I'm no god damn gold digger. There has been a lot of gossip in the press that I'm marrying you for your millions. Maybe this agreement will put an end to that speculation."

On November 19, 1961, Lucille married for the second time, only eleven days before what would have been her twenty-first wedding anniversary to Desi. She invited him to the wedding, but he did not respond.

The wedding took place at the Marble Collegiate Church on lower Fifth Avenue in Manhattan. She asked her friend and mentor, Norman Vincent Peale, to preside. Paula Stewart was her matron of honor, and Stewart's new husband, Jack Carter, was Morton's best man.

Lucille invited her mother, DeDe, and her brother, Fred Ball. Likewise, both Desi Jr. and Lucie attended. Morton's relatives took the subway from the Bronx.

For the occasion, Morton purchased a new *toupée*. Although voted worst-dressed woman of the year, Lucille "dropped a few thousand" on a designer outfit of "windowpane silk and a matching tulle headdress," in a bluish-green color.

As the happy couple left the church, more than a thousand fans were waiting outside to throw rice.

In front of the church, before she stepped inside her "getaway limousine," a reporter from the *Daily News* called out to her.

"Lucy, is this time forever?"

"Hell no!" she snapped. "I plan to remarry every twenty years."

And off they went, but not for a honeymoon. Perhaps that would come later. Right now, each of them had (separate) gigs to complete. His involved a final round-up of night clubs and resorts, and hers was a made-for-TV movie with a "beau from yesterday," Henry Fonda.

When Arlene Dahl called the next day to congratulate her, Lucille said, "I read that F. Scott Fitzgerald once said that there are no second acts in American lives. He was wrong. Yesterday, the curtain went up on my second act."

CHAPTER TWO

LUCILLE'S BACK —AS A SOLO!

Lucille, With Viv but Without Ricky Ricardo, Orchestrates a TV Comeback

The famous Broadway producer, Leland Hayward, purchased the screen rights to a script by Walter Lord called *The Good Years,* a made-for-TV film that covered the era from the turn of the century to the coming of World War I in 1914.

Hayward offered the role to Mary Martin, but she was too busy performing in the Broadway stage version of *The Sound of Music*. He then offered it to Lucille, who accepted it. After signing a contract, she learned that her co-star would be Henry Fonda, her boyfriend of yesteryear.

Three days later, he was already in makeup and fully dressed in clothing appropriate to the World War I and the Jazz Age.

Lucille went to his dressing room to greet him, hugging and kissing him. "The last time I spent the night with you, you were wearing that black rhinestone jockstrap Joan Crawford gave you. Still got it?"

"Some memories are best forgotten," he said. "Why didn't you and I get married? Do you remember?"

"I didn't marry you because your wives commit suicide," she said.

"You're still the naughty girl you always were. Good to know that some things

Theatrical impresario **Leland Hayward** with the fifth, and probably the most fascinating, of his five wives, the British-born socialite and ultimate powerhouse fundraiser of the U.S. Democratic Party, **Pamela Digby Churchill Harriman.**

25

in life don't change. I wish your new husband all the luck in the world. He'll need it."

"Let's cut out the shit, Hank, and see what this god damn script is all about."

Her role was that of the legendary prohibitionist Carry Nation, who in one scene wields an axe in a barroom. As her supporting players, director Franklin J. Schaffer had hired Mort Sahl and Margaret Hamilton. Hamilton, of course, had immortalized herself in movie history by starring opposite Judy Garland as "The Wicked Witch of the West," in *The Wizard of Oz* (1939).

The press announced the casting of Lucille in *The Good Years* as "her television comeback."

Fonda was both the star and narrator. One might wonder why it was called *The Good Years* since it depicts, almost in documentary style, the San Francisco Earthquake, the human carnage brought on by a yellow fever pandemic, the financial panic of 1907, the desperation of newly arrived immigrants on Ellis Island, the launch of the income tax, and the emergence of Lenin, Einstein, and Freud.

On her first day on the set, Lucille also met Hayward, reminding him that he had rejected her when she'd tried out for a role in the stage version of *Stage Door*, though she would win a part (alongside the then-more-heavily featured stars Katharine Hepburn and Ginger Rogers) in the 1937 movie version.

Configured as a kaleidoscopic variety show, one skit within *The Good Years* called for Fonda and Lucille, as vaudeville performers, to sing a duet entitled "Tell Me Pretty Maiden."

In another skit, set in a courtroom, Lucille is cast as a woman arrested for disorderly conduct for singing "The Turkey Trot" and also "Everybody's Doin' It."

The Good Years was telecast by CBS on January 12, 1962. Lucille watched it with Fonda. At the end, she turned to him and said, "I hated it."

"So did I," he shot back.

Jack Gould in *The New York Times* wrote, "Leland Hayward's production wavers so awkwardly between documented history and theatrical simulation that it loses all touch with the buoyancy and innocence of those years. As straight history, however, the film has spirit and

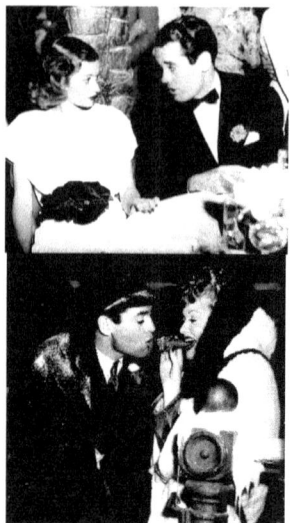

Fonda and Ball shared a long, complicated, and highly nuanced past:

Upper photo shows **Lucille Ball** with **Henry Fonda** on a date during their early "breakthrough years" in Hollywood.

The middle and lower photos are associated with their co-starring roles as dysfunctional country-boy-meets-tough-as-nails-girl in *The Big Street*, an "inverted romance" released in 1942.

captures some of the vivacity and spirit of the time. The numbers in which Ball appears with Fonda are on the stilted side, as if *The Good Years* is terribly afraid to enjoy itself. The sketches are heavy handed, and Mort Sahl's comments on the era are never winning or penetrating."

***

After the filming of *The Good Years*, Lucille joined Gary Morton on the road as he fulfilled the last of his appearances as a stand-up comic. Before leaving New York for the road tour, she spoke to columnist Earl Wilson. She denied that she and Morton were going to work together as a comedy team, as she'd done with Desi: "My fans wouldn't stand for it," she claimed.

Morton's first appearance was in Palm Springs at the Chi Chi Club. On one night, from her perch in the audience, she was seen sitting between Dean Martin and Frank Sinatra.

On another booking, she flew with him to Miami Beach for Morton's warm-up act for singer Johnny Ray, who opened his show with a rendition of "Cry."

Then it was off to New York where he drove her to the Catskills. There, at Grossinger's, he was the opening act for singer Tony Bennett.

Hesitant at first to interfere, she mustered her courage and gave him some advice about how to sell a joke. He didn't seem offended. The first night he followed her suggestion, he got bigger laughs. "Hell, why not listen to you? I'm married to the Queen of Comedy."

Morton's last gig was at Lake Tahoe, and Lucille went there with him, too. She had arrived with seven movie scripts, and in the suite they shared, the one she read first was by the gay novelist and playwright, James Kirkwood Jr. It was based

Based on a best-selling book by Walter Lord first published in 1960 about the years leading up to World War I, *The Good Years* was a confusing hodge-podge of sketches and musical numbers about the time period 1900 through 1920.

Lucille, one of the most sophisticated women in Hollywood, played the humorless anti-liquor crusader, Carry Nation, the perhaps psychotic Prohibition crusader with a hatchet and a penchant for breaking up bars.

The upper photo shows **Lucille** with **Henry Fonda**, dressed in turn-of-the-20th-century pro-Prohitiion garb.

The lower photo shows a frumpy-looking **Lucille**, between takes, dressed as Carry Nation, facetiously quaffing beer.

on the novel he'd written in 1960, *There Must Be a Pony*.

Kirkwood was the biological son of two well-known silent screen stars, James Kirkwood Sr., and Lila Lee. His mother had been Valentino's leading lady in the silent picture, *Blood and Sand* (1922), in which he was cast as bullfighter Juan Gallardo.

There Must Be a Pony was the story of Rita, a fading actress trying for a comeback after her release from a mental hospital. She's also trying to re-establish her relationship with her gay son, Josh, while involving herself with a handsome but somewhat mysterious new suitor.

[Regrettably, soon after her departure from Lake Tahoe, complications arose for Lucille back in California, and she abandoned plans for the film.

Like so many scripts in Hollywood, *There Must Be a Pony* was shelved until 1986 when Elizabeth Taylor discovered it and brought it to the screen with co-star Robert Wagner. Chad Lowe, the brother of actor Rob Lowe, was cast as Taylor's son, Josh. Its final screenplay was written by Matthew Crowley, far better known for his gay play, *The Boys in the Band*, which premiered Off-Broadway in 1968.

The *New York Times* reviewed, unflatteringly, this made-for-television film. "Talk about grinding it out. It brings new meaning to the words 'chopped liver.'"

In spite of some critical blasts, the movie version of There Must Be a Pony later developed a following by young men forever drawn to any Elizabeth Taylor movie and who might have identified with the character of Josh.]

Lucille Ball was the first actress to recognize the dramatic possibilities in James Kirkwood's script for *There Must Be a Pony*.

Kirkwood, a long-time friend of this book's co-author, Darwin Porter, was later instrumental in the development of the script for the spectacularly profitable Broadway play, *A Chorus Line*.

What fascinated both Lucille and Elizabeth was *There Must Be a Pony's* female lead, a hysterical, fast-fading movie diva desperate for a comeback.

As Lucille envisioned it, the project was abandoned, but years later, **Elizabeth Taylor**, through a different producer, won the pithy role, appearing opposite her long-time friend, **Robert Wagner.**

There were rumors of an affair.

***

Lucille was sometimes the first choice for the female leads in feature films that eventually went to other actresses. Jerry Wald met with her about starring in *Mr. Hobbs Takes a Vacation*, which was distributed by 20th Century Fox in 1962. She was anxious to co-star in it with James Stewart, one of her most admired of all Hollywood actors.

But many months after reading the script, she agreed with Bosley Crowther who stated in *The New York Times*, "The general thesis of *Mr. Hobbs Takes a Vacation* is that the family unit is perhaps the most anomalous and irritating social arrangement ever devised by so-called civilized man."

Although Wald was quite ill at the time he met Lucille, he continued to work. Regrettably, soon after discussing the project with her, he suffered a heart attack and died at the age of fifty.

The director who replaced him, Henry Koster, preferred the red-haired Irish actress, Maureen O'Hara as Stewart's on-screen wife. O'Hara had been Lucille's co-star in that long-ago film, *Dance, Girl, Dance* (1940).

Over the years, Lucille had maintained at least a surface friendship with Frank Sinatra. He'd once punched Desi in the nose for his depiction of Italian Americans in *The Untouchables,* but they had later made up.

She not only admired Sinatra as a singer, but as a screen actor, too.

She admitted to being flattered that he had wanted her to play one of the key roles in his latest film, *The Manchurian Candidate* (1962), a neo-*noir* psychological political thriller.

[Its plot centers on a Korean War veteran, Raymond Shaw (Laurence Harvey), who was brainwashed by Chinese communists after his Army platoon was captured. He becomes an unwitting assassin in a conspiracy to subvert and overthrow the U.S. Government. In other words, it becomes clear, early in the film, that he has emerged as "a sleeper agent." Sinatra, cast as Major Bennett Marco, later emerges as a hero who prevents the assassination.]

Sinatra had always appreciated Lucille's skills as a dramatic actress, a quality he had seen at its best-developed in two of her films from the late 1940s. He recommended her for the role of Mrs. Eleanor Iselin, who is recklessly promoting the candidacy of her husband, Senator John Yerkes Iselin (played by James Gregory). Scheming, ruthless, amoral, and cunning, she's also the mother of Shaw, the brainwashed veteran.

When Lucille read the first version of the script by George Axelrod, based on a novel by Richard Condon, she was shocked to read that Mrs. Iselin is leveraging her son's brainwashing to have sex with him.

Years after filming it, its female lead, **Angela Lansbury**, praised *The Manchurian Candidate* as "The most imporfant movie I was ever in."

With more than a bit of envy, Lucille heard about Lansbury's assessment, since she had been one of the leading contenders for Lansbury's role.

In her words, she lost out on the role because of her "*I'm a funny lady, I'm Lucy Ricardo*" image.

29

Lucille wanted to depict that incestuous mother on the screen. "People will forget I was ever Lucy Ricardo." To her chagrin, the taboo topic of incest would be downplayed within the script. Instead, Eleanor would kiss Shaw on the lips to "merely imply" her incestuous attraction to him.

[Regrettably, director John Frankenheimer rejected Sinatra's casting suggestion and assigned the role to Angela Lansbury instead. He had worked with her on the movie All Fall Down *(1962), in which she starred with Warren Beatty in a role that also evoked an incestuous relationship.*

Lucille's hunch about the power of the role was affirmed when Lansbury was nominated for an Oscar as Best Supporting Actress. [She lost to Patty Duke for her performance as Helen Keller in The Miracle Worker.*]*

***

Back in Hollywood, Lucille ran into Bob Hope at one of the first parties she attended with Morton. From another part of the room, Hope approached her: "I hear you've ended up with a second-banana comic, that Gary Morton guy. Don't tell me you're settling for less."

"Bobby, boy, just so long as the banana is big enough, I'm satisfied."

"Hey, kid, let's make another picture together."

"I'm game," she said.

"Did you get to see Henry Fonda, another one of your bananas, in *Critic's Choice* on Broadway?"

"I did, and I loved it."

"Good. I'm considering doing the movie version of it with you playing my wife. You should probably know, before you accept, that I'm screwing Marilyn Maxwell when Arnaz isn't humping her, and I've promised her a supporting role."

"Bring on the whoring bitch," Lucille said.

"I've also talked with Rip Torn about taking the secondary male lead, and he's interested. Rip and I enjoyed a steambath together. Talk about big bananas."

"Thanks for the heads up," she said. "Good to know that in case Gary can't get it up one night. So far, that is not his problem."

***

In the autumn of 1962, during the interim between the last telecast (in April of 1960) of the *Lucille Ball-Desi Arnaz Show* and the first airing of her new series, *The Lucy Show*, she often appeared on television as a guest on someone else's telecast. She

Natural, brilliant, and relaxed, the genius-level comedienne, **Carol Burnett**, steals his show from talk show host, **Garry Moore**, just before the entrance, on camera, of another scene-stealer, Lucille Ball.

wasn't new to this kind of "scattershot" booking: Early in 1960, she'd made random appearances to plug her "project of the moment," the Broadway musical, *Wildcat*.

In September of 1960, she was seen on the CBS network in an episode of *The Garry Moore Show*. Her co-star was Carol Burnett. Although the two *comediennes* might have been bitter rivals, they actually bonded into a close friendship. Also on the show were singer Eydie Gorme and comedian Alan King.

A feature of the program, "Somebody Goofed," showed embarrassing outtakes while filming. Lucille was depicted "goofing" and spoiling a take on her latest movie, *The Facts of Life* with Bob Hope. During the screening, she bursts into laughter at herself.

During the run of *Wildcat*, when she had occupied a luxury apartment at the Imperial Hotel in Manhattan, the South Africa-born journalist and game show host, John Charles Daly, had been her neighbor. She accepted his invitation to appear on the show he moderated, *What's My Line?* Four blind-folded guests had to guess who she was. Of course, she had to disguise her voice, which was already rather hoarse that night.

One of the panelists she confronted was columnist Dorothy Kilgallen, whose husband, Richard Kollmar, had sexually pursued Desi during the late 1930s.

The program was aired on the first day of January 1961.

About two weeks later, she did little more than lend her presence to *Eleanor Roosevelt's Diamond Jubilee*, a program that celebrated the former First Lady's 76th birthday, proceeds going to her Cancer Research Foundation. Appearing with Lucille were such guests as Carol Channing, Mary Martin, Paul Newman, and even Senator John F. Kennedy and Vice President Richard M. Nixon. Bob

LUCY! HITS THE GAME! SHOWS!

Game show host **John Daly** (right) with regular *What's My Line* panelists Arlene Francis (left), publisher **Bennett Cerf**, and entertainment columnist **Dorothy Kilgallen**.

On January 1, 1961, during the heat of her involvement in *Wildcat*, **Lucille Ball** appeared as a mystery guest on one of early television's most popular game shows, *What's My Line?*

She used a hoarse, low, and deliberatly camouflaged voice to answer questions posed by blindfolded panelists.

One of them, Faye Emerson, the daughter-in-law of Eleanor Roosevelt, correctly guessed Lucy's identity by saying "Are you a red-headed Wildcat?"

In the bubbly chitchat that followed, Lucille said she had lost twelve pounds during rehearsals for that musical.

The moderator then reminded everyone that she and Bob Hope had a new film coming out, *The Facts of Life*, and suggested to millions of TV viewers that it might be up for an award.

Hope was the host of the telecast.

Again to promote *Wildcat*, Lucille was also a guest on an episode of *I've Got a Secret*, hosted by Garry Moore. On the panel, she joined Johnny Carson, Betsy Palmer, and Bess Myerson.

Hope asked her to appear as his guest on the *Bob Hope Buick Sports Show*, broadcast on NBC on February 15. She was surprised to find herself collaborating with the divorced Jane Wyman and Ronald Reagan, who were also Hope's guests. On the air, Jane Russell and Jayne Mansfield indulged in a "Battle of the Bosoms," and Dean Martin and Esther Williams also showed up, as did Ginger Rogers, Lucille's friend and Desi's former lover from the late 1930s.

The *Bob Hope Buick Sports Awards Special* was broadcast from California on February 15, 1961. Two-time world heavyweight boxing champion **Floyd Patterson** could not attend the ceremony on the West Coast, so he was filmed accepting an award from **Lucille** in Manhattan.

At the time, to wild audience approval despite its many flaws, she was appearing on Broadway in *Wildcat*.

The show was a comedy awards telecast honoring the best and worst athletes. Lucille did a stint with boxing champ Floyd Patterson.

Four nights later, she was on *The Ed Sullivan Show,* mainly to promote *Wildcat*. She joined her Broadway co-star, Paula Stewart, in a rendition of the song, "Hey. Look Me Over."

Regrettably, what was slated to have been yet another TV special was canceled when Lucille became ill and opted to drop out. Tentatively entitled *Lucy Goes to Broadway,* it would have been a star-studded event with Hedda Hopper, Bob Hope, Ethel Merman, and director Michael Kidd.

The telecast would have been the only reunion of the Arnazes with the Mertzes, and it would also have been the first time Lucie and Desi Jr. would have starred on TV with their divorced parents.

***

Installed once again in her home on Roxbury Drive in Beverly Hills, Lucille faced a dilemma. Would Lucie and Desi, Jr.—both of whom were extremely fond of their own father— take to their new stepfather, or would they resent the intrusion?

Even before her marriage, both Lucie and Desi Jr., had insisted that she sit through many screenings of *The Parent Trap*. That was a 1961 movie in which Hayley Mills (who played both members of a set of identical twins) tries to get her estranged parents back together again.

[It would be remade in 1998 starring Lindsay Lohan in her film debut. In it,

she also played twins.]

Lucille sat through all the many screenings her children foisted upon her but had to make it clear: "For Desi and me, there will be no reconciliation...ever!"

On their first communal meeting, Morton was kind, friendly, and understanding with both the boy and the girl. In contrast, they were each rather open about their resentment of him. As he told Lucille later that night, "It will take time. Of course, they resent me. It's typical of children meeting a new stepfather."

Within her house on Roxbury Drive, Lucille began renovating and redecorating, perhaps eliminating traces of Desi. The biggest change involved the installation of a rock-rimmed pool with a waterfall.

Within the kitchen of their (shared) new home, Morton made a pronouncement: "No more Arnaz tortillas for breakfast. I'll replace them with Morton's Jewish bagels with cream cheese."

"Gary came from such a different world, the Bronx, from my children, who had a privileged upbringing in Beverly Hills. He tried to be a caring, loving stepfather, but the odds were not in his favor. I didn't expect my kids to love him like they would Desi. I'd settle for resenting him less."

The Parent Trap (1961) starred **Hayley Mills** and was produced by Walt Disney. Cutesy and family-friendly, it described a family whose children tried to bring their divorced parents together again.

Lucille brusquely informed her own kids that the tactics it promoted would NOT bring about a reconciliation with herself and their father (her ex-husband) Desi.

Actually there wasn't that much of a family life, anyway. Lucie and Desi Jr. were growing up and away from Lucille and Gary's new *ménage* much of the time. Lucille enrolled her son in St. John's Military Academy, and her daughter attended Immaculate Heart for Girls.

Her son's stay at the military academy was short. According to Lucille, "It was hell for the kid. He told me that he had been held in detention for eight hours. The other cadets bullied him. He was miserable the whole time, and he couldn't sleep, and when he did sleep, he was plagued by nightmares. When I heard all that, I took him out of school at once."

In part because of her new husband, Lucille's social life changed, and she began to receive more frequent invitations to Hollywood parties. *[During the final years of her marriage to Desi, the couple had been more or less blacklisted because of his heavy drinking which often escalated into violent outbursts at parties.]*

Lucille was very clear about wanting to introduce Morton to Desi, since she wanted her new husband to be hired on the production side of the television industry. Desi was an expert on that. Perhaps she hoped that they might gracefully collaborate on the business side of Desilu.

"The two men circled each other at first, like two fighting roosters in the ring, sizing up the competition," she claimed. "But at least on the surface, they seemed friendly enough, and I felt that in spite of their different backgrounds, they could get along. Someone characterized the two of them as '*olé meets oy vay.*'"

Indeed, although there was at least surface politeness, behind their backs, Desi, for reasons of his own, called Morton "Barry North," and the comic referred to Desi as "My ex-husband-in-law."

To his dismay, Morton soon learned that under adverse working conditions, Lucille could frighteningly morph into either "Dr. Jekyll or Mrs. Hyde."

Sometimes, when he approached her on the set, she would rush to hug and kiss him. But when she was having a bad hair day, she would sometimes loudly confront him with, for example, "What in hell are you doing? Why don't you go and try to nail something down in case a typhoon hits this afternoon?"

When he was asked about his life with Lucille, Morton often responded with humor. One afternoon, Hedda Hopper visited their home. Over coffee, he told her, "I didn't marry Lucille for her cooking. Last night, she cooked a steak for me. It tasted like hockey pucks."

In contrast to the marital infidelities of girl-crazy Desi, Lucille had no real problems on that front from Morton. There is no evidence that he ever committed adultery during their time together. His passion outside the home was directed at acquiring vintage cars, which he could never afford before.

She decided to ensure that he accumulated the vintage cars his heart desired. She told a reporter, "He can have a love affair with old cars, but if he strays, I'll cut him up into steaks."

She financed his automobile collection, beginning with a Rolls-Royce previously owned by Hedda Hopper. That was followed by a Mercedes 300-SS once driven by David Niven, plus two Karman Ghias, a Mark II Lincoln, an antique Stutz Bearcat, and even a Model-T once owned by film pioneer D.W. Griffith.

One afternoon, as Lucille and Morton rested beside their swimming pool, the maid announced a visitor at

"Just a normal, *(YEAH, RIGHT!)* everyday American family."

Here is a press release photo, courtesy of TWA, snapped at Idlewild Airport on November 18, 1961, a day before Lucille's November 19 wedding to Gary Morton.

the door, producer Joe Vogel. Lucille had changed her unlisted phone number, and instead of approaching her through agents, he decided to make a direct pitch to her during an unannounced, unscheduled visit.

"Send him in," she said to her maid.

Vogel talked with Morton and her for about an hour, pitching a movie he wanted to produce. He wanted to co-star her with James Cagney, whose talent she admired.

"It's called *Here Lies Ruthie Adams,* emphasis on "lies." Cagney will play a psychiatrist who's married to you, a chronic liar."

She told him that although she was intrigued with the script, she would not be available. Only the week before, she had signed to make another movie with Bob Hope.

***

Having seen the play, *Critic's Choice,* starring Henry Fonda, on Broadway, Lucille felt the film version should rightfully feature her former co-star, too. But he had another, more enticing offer.

As she told Morton, "This is not a Bob Hope movie. Since Fonda turned it down, it would be better cast with James Stewart...even Fred MacMurray." *[She concealed her casting choice from Hope, who had already cast his longtime girlfriend, Marilyn Maxwell, as the third lead. As she told Morton before heading for Warner Brothers, "Perhaps Maxwell and I can compare notes about how good—or bad—Desi is in bed."]*

As **Lucille** and **Bob Hope** aged, many deals were suggested that derived from adaptations of earlier projects. One of them was *Critic's Choice*, a coyly flirtatious movie based on a Broadway play with the same name that had starred Henry Fonda.

Some of them called for a new "screen team" that included the now "romantically available" Lucille in the aftermath of her very famous divorce from Desi Arnaz.

One windy day in March, she arrived at the gate of Warner Brothers to make her fourth and last feature film with Bob Hope. Its script had been adapted from a play by Ira Levin. *[Although Levin had already crafted novels which had morphed into big movie hits,* Rosemary's Baby *(1968) and* The Stepford Wives *(1975), Lucille suspected that* Critic's Choice—*eventually released in 1963— would not be in that league.]*

Hope was cast as a brutal drama critic, Parker Ballantine, perhaps based on the real life of the Broadway writer and drama critic Walter Kerr. Ballantine is married to Angie, a promising playwright.

On Lucille's first day on the set, Director Don Weiss came out to greet her. Within the hour, she'd been introduced to Marilyn Maxwell, who extended her hand. Lucille ignored it. Maxwell had been cast as Hope's ex-wife, Ivy London.

After locking her arm with that of Rip Torn, cast as Dion Kapakos, a director, Lucille said to him, "Let's have some coffee, stud, and you can tell me all the dirt on Geraldine Page, your new wifey-poo."

Two views of Lucille's "I'll hate you to the grave" contender for the affections of Desi Sr., **Marilyn Maxwell**.

In the left photo, Maxwell appears as a mid-war MGM pinup fantasy from 1943, and (right photo) in *Champion* (1949) as the beguiling mistress of boxing champ **Kirk Douglas** in an Oscar-winning classic about the degeneracy of a prizefighter.

Other supporting players in *Critic's Choice*, each a minor name in the early 1960s, included Jessie Royce Landis, Jim Backus, Marie Windsor, and Jerome Cowan.

Trouble in the Ballantine marriage arises when Angie writes a Broadway play. Should her husband review it? If he praises it, he'll be accused of being prejudiced in its favor. If he pans it, it might catalyze a divorce.

Hope's biographer, Richard Zoglin, wrote, "In a ludicrous slapstick climax, he shows up sloshed for his wife's Broadway opening. In one of his rare drunk scenes, he gets shunted to the balcony because the play has already started, and he winds up dangling his heels over the orchestra seats—and still manages to get back to the office in time to write a devastating review of his wife's play for the morning paper."

During filming, many famous people wanted to visit the set, including Peter Lawford, who was married at the time to Patricia Kennedy, sister of President John F. Kennedy. The producers of the film gave the president's sister a bit part.

After its release, a reviewer for *The New York Times* claimed, "Unfortunately, the director, Don Weis, has tried to upholster the shaky plot with slapstick and broad burlesque. Both Hope and Ball, old hands at this sort of thing, go through their paces with benign good humor, but their subtler comic talents remain untapped."

Variety was more promising: "The vehicle provides Miss Ball with little opportunity to act up in her accustomed manner, but her warm, sincere portrayal of his rather shallow-sighted, unappealing wife is quite an achievement."

The *New York Daily News* critic found that "The film contains little material for laughter. Most of the picture's running time is taken up with the couple's quarrels. These are not conducive to laughter."

The movie flopped at the box office, generating $1.2 million. *Critic's Choice* would be Lucille's last appearance in a feature film until 1967, and even then, she would be only a guest star.

***

At the 15th annual ceremony for the Emmy Awards, broadcast on May 22, 1962, the show was hosted by comedian Bob Newhardt in Los Angeles. Johnny Carson in New York, and David Brinkley in Washington, D.C.

Lucille was so cleverly made up and beautifully gowned that rumors spread that she'd had a major facelift.

In her appearance, she presented the Comedy Writing Emmy to Carl Reiner for *The Dick Van Dyke Show*. [Spanning five seasons (1961-66) it was filmed at Desilu Studios.]

But despite Lucille's gracious delivery, it was Edie Adams who stole the show that night when she spoofed Marilyn Monroe singing "S'Wonderful."

On June 24, on *The Ed Sullivan Show*, Lucille joined an array of stars to salute Sullivan for his 14th year on television. She had finished *Critic's Choice* with Bob Hope, and she looked glamourous, wearing a chic wig from that movie and a velvet top with a fur collar. As the camera pulled back, she is exposed sitting on an elephant, which then dutifully hauls her offstage.

That summer, *The Lucy-Desi Comedy Hour* was presented on CBS in thirteen re-runs that the pair had made for either Ford or Westinghouse. Lucille recorded voice-overs, using many of them as a chance to hype her upcoming TV series, *The Lucy Show*, set for telecast that autumn.

***

Desi was still president of Desilu, and talk was in the air that Lucille might return to television in a projected new series—one that would not include him. He was too busy handling the business affairs of Desilu, but admitting to associates, "I'm bored with this job."

He rejected all proposals, as did Lucille herself, that a new comedy team of her with Gary Morton be hyped to CBS. "I get letters every day, a

Patricia Kennedy Lawford was sometimes reviewed as the most sophisticated and beautiful of President JFK's sisters, as she appeared on her wedding day in 1954.

Years later, perhaps as a vehicle to better promote the film, she was persuaded by her then-husband, Peter Lawford, to appear in a very brief (and uncredited) scene in *Critic's Choice*

barrage of them, and all of them want me to kiss Lucy and make up with her," Desi claimed.

In the early 1960s, Desilu was drawing most of its income from the funds generated by returns on the crime drama, *The Untouchables, (1959-63) and from rentals of its* studio facilities.

When *The Untouchables* came under fire for depicting too much violence, Desi had ordered that the TV series become tamer. However, when ratings fell off, he demanded more violence be reinstated in the scripts. He told the press, "Those gangsters at the St. Valentine's Day Massacre in Chicago weren't throwing violets at each other."

He also responded to the charge that there was too much sex on TV. "There is not too much sex on the tube. There is no sex on TV."

"Desi was hanging in there, but he was also falling apart," said Vivian Vance, who ran into him one afternoon at the studio. "He was no longer Ricky Ricardo."

They both hugged and kissed and recalled happier times when they had starred as Ricky and Ethel. Tears came to both of their eyes., She noted that time was catching up with her former co-star and boss. His hair was almost the color of the old gray mare (her words). His eyesight was failing him, and to read a document or letter, he had to wear thick, horn-rimmed glasses. The burden of time had descended on his stooped shoulders.

He still wore expensive business suits, but his belt wrapped around an expanding waistline.

After Vance shared her observations with Lucille, she said, "Time was also moving in on her in her fifties. But she could cover it up more with makeup, and she moved about with a far greater vitality than Desi, even though she was much older than him."

The annual meeting of Desilu's stockholders was held in August of 1962 with Desi presiding. *[For his managerial role within the company, he drew an annual salary* of $156,000 .]

Dressed in lime-green slacks and a sunflower yellow blouse, Lucille sat beside him, still drawing her yearly salary of $25,000 as vice president. Of course, most of their money came from their control of the stock, corporate profits, and dividends.

A reporter for the *Los Angeles Times* covered the meeting, later writing that, "It was Hollywood's uncut, unrehearsed version of *How to Succeed in*

Lucille had already proven her "Kissability Quotient," as witnessed by the U.S. Postal Service (top photo) that commemorated Desi Arnaz's attraction to the character she played in *I Love Lucy.*

But after their divorce, the names of other contenders for her affection began popping up frequently.

Offscreen, although it was widely understood that Hubby #2, Gary Morton, ruled as her "main squeeze," others, including **Bob Hope** (lower photo) maneuvered their way into the public consciousness as a screen partner for a woman now being watched regularly in re-runs.

Business by Really Trying," parroting the title of the recent (1961) hit Broadway musical.

Desi predicted a bright future for Desilu and spoke at length about the success of renting out the old RKO Studios. He commented on all the TV series and feature films Desilu was filming on its grounds at the time. He also suggested that Desilu might launch a new TV series featuring Lucille.

That spring and summer of 1962 was a busy time for cameras, crew, and casts. Desilu produced *The Kraft Mystery Theater* for NBC.

[*The Kraft Mystery Theater ran for sixteen weeks as a temporary replacement for* The Perry Como Show, *which was on vacation during its run.*

Como, an Italian singer and rival of Frank Sinatra, would return in the fall, informally clad in a cardigan sweater and sitting on a stool. Whereas he'd been a fixture on TV since 1948, The Perry Como Show *itself had made its debut in September of 1955.*]

Ben Casey, also filmed at Desilu but produced by Bing Crosby Productions, was a medical drama starring the matinee idol Vince Edwards in the title role, that of an intense, idealistic neurosurgeon at the County General Hospital.

Lucille once visited Edwards' dressing room, and was somewhat surprised to see that he had posted an 8" x 10" frontal nude of himself on his dressing room mirror.

"That was taken in the locker room at Ohio State when I was on its swim team. We won the United States National Championship."

"I can see why," she said. "I hear you have a twin brother. Care to give me his phone number? I also hear you share something in common with Desi, a compulsive gambler."

"You've nailed me," he admitted.

Also shot at Desilu was *The Joey Bishop Show*, created by Danny Thomas, as a spin-off from his own hit TV series. It had premiered in September of 1961 but would be canceled by NBC in January of 1964 because of low ratings.

Perry Como was "the man who invented casual" thanks to his penchant for cardigans and smooth ballad-style mood music.

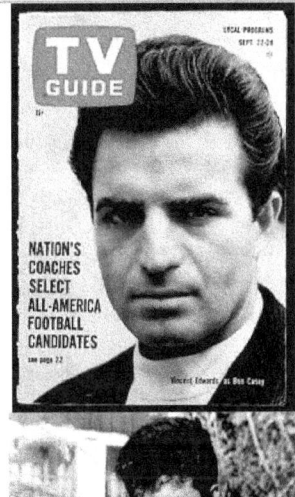

Two views of **Vince Edwards**, well known to TV audiences as *Dr. Ben Casey.*

That "medical drama' series was filmed at Desilu Studios under the supervision, even after their divorce, of Lucille, Desi, and Bing Crosby

CBS picked it up and telecast it for its fourth and final season. Actress Abby Dalton was brought in as Bishop's wife and to add some sex appeal to the series.

Having begun in October of 1960, *The Andy Griffith Show* was another hit TV show emerging at the time from Desilu. Actor Andy Griffith was cast as Andy Taylor, the cornpone sheriff in the small (fictional) town of Mayberry, North Carolina, a site that was loosely based on Griffith's hometown of Mount Airy, NC. Drawing huge audiences nationwide, it would run for 249 episodes over a span of eight seasons.

Ron Howard (who morphed, as an adult, into a major-league producer and director in his own right) was cast as Griffith's young son, and Don Knotts played the goofball Barney Fife, his deputy sheriff.

When *The Andy Griffith Show* went off the air in 1968, it joined two other shows, *I Love Lucy* and *Seinfeld*, both of which had ended their seasons when they were still among the Top Ten Nielsen-rated TV shows.

Yet another TV series shot at Desilu was *The Dick Van Dyke Show*, which first was telecast in October of 1961. Created by Carl Reiner, it starred Van Dyke with Mary Tyler Moore as his wife.

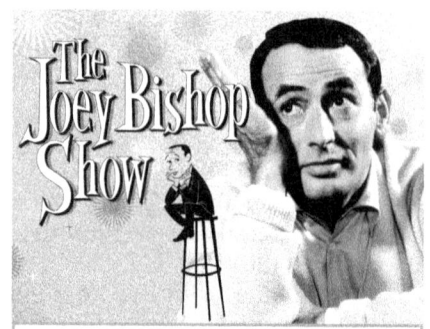

Bronx-born **Joey Bishop** was not a womanizer, nor was he a drunk or a gambler. Yet Frank Sinatra invited him to join his notorious Rat Pack.

"The guy's always good for a laugh, fun to be with. He never fails me on that score."

Also emerging from Desilu under the supervision of Lucille and Desi was the affectionately cornpone (and spectacularly successful) *The Andy Griffith Show*.

In addition to the "recluse in real life" Aunt Bea, it featured, left to right, **Don Knotts** as Deputy Sheriff Barney Fife; **Ron Howard** (center) as Opie; and **Andy Griffith** as the Sheriff of Mayberry, Andy Taylor.

Lucille once lunched with Moore, who told her she almost skipped the audition. "I walked into this vast waiting room where there were sixty other actresses competing. I didn't think I had a chance, but I stuck it out."

Moore also said that in a way, she modeled her character on First Lady Jacqueline Kennedy.

During its run, *The Dick Van Dyke Show* would walk off with fifteen Emmy Awards.

Lucille always tried to watch another hit TV series, *My Three Sons*. Filmed at Desilu, it starred one of her favorite actors, Fred MacMurry, whose career spanned a half century and a hundred films ranging from the *film noir*, *Double Indemnity* (1944), with Barbara Stanwyck, to *The Egg and I* (1947) with Claudette Colbert.

He was married to the blonde-haired actress, June Haver.

MacMurray's peak year was 1943 when his annual salary was $420,000, making him the highest-paid person in the nation.

Lucille later paid a tribute to MacMurray: "This guy could hold his own against the biggest names in Tinseltown, even Sidney Greenstreet. He seemed to specialize in legends like Humphrey Bogart, Marlene Dietrich, Katharine Hepburn, Henry Fonda, Carole Lombard, and Joan Crawford.

Lucille had another interest in watching *My Three Sons.* Originally, it featured William Frawley as the maternal grandfather and housekeeper to the three sons. Because of illness, Frawley had to drop out and was replaced with William Demarest, his long-time rival.

Launched in 1960, *My Three Sons* had a long run, remaining highly visible for 380 episodes (196 of them in color) until eventually going off the air in 1972.

Since 1957, the TV series, *Lassie,* had been shot at Desilu. It was inspired by the seven feature films MGM released in the 1940s, whose star was a spectacularly well-trained female Collie dog. For a long time, *Lassie,* as a TV series, was the fifth most-watched TV program in America and held on for an amazing seventeen seasons.

Desilu also provided film sets for the casts and crews of feature films. A case in point was *The Caretakers* (1963), starring Robert Stack, Desilu's money-maker from *The Untouchables,* plus Polly Bergen and Joan Crawford.

Set in a mental hospital, *The Caretakers* evoked *The Snake Pit* (1948), one of Olivia de

"**Dick Van Dyke** could clown, could dance, could sing...perhaps he belonged to the old era of vaudeville," Lucille said. His *The Dick Van Dyke* show became classic TV, winning him three Emmy Awards.

In 1960, *My Three Sons,* starring **Fred MacMurray,** became a hit as a TV sitcom.

"Back in my day of making feature films," Lucille said, "I campaigned several times to make Fred my leading man, but failed. I had the hots for him, even though that is not a very ladylike expression."

"Desi and I rented **Lassie** rental space at Desilu," Lucille said. "Elizabeth Taylor once told me that Lassie was a female, and I thought he was a male. But what does Liz known about male anatomy?"

Havilland's greatest roles.

Lucille never liked Crawford, but out of respect for her past performances, she called on her two or three times during her shoots on Desilu's sound stages.

"From gay actor Rock Hudson to Clark Gable, from Barbara Stanwyck to John F. Kennedy, Joan Crawford dropped her panties a lot," Lucille claimed.

She witnessed a scene at Desilu where Crawford played the head nurse, Lucretia Terry, an aging, hardened medical professional. *Variety* later wrote that, "Miss Crawford doesn't so much play her handful of nurse scenes, but dresses looking as if she were *en route* to a Pepsi board meeting."

[At the time, Crawford was married to Alfred Steele, Pepsi's CEO.]

One of the most ambitious films shot in part at Desilu was George Stevens' *The Greatest Story Ever Told* (1965). It was the retelling of the Biblical narrative of Jesus of Nazareth, from his Nativity to his Ascension.

Max von Sydow played Jesus; Dorothy McGuire portrayed the Virgin Mary; Charlton Heston was John the Baptist; and Claude Rains (in his final movie role) was Herod.

"I always despised **Joan Crawford**, but I let her film *The Caretakers* at Desilu," Lucille said.

"Her co-star was that divine Robert Stack, star of *The Untouchables*. Crawford played an aging, hardened bitch of a head nurse. Talk about type casting."

Location shots were in Nevada, Arizona, and Utah. California's Death Valley was the setting for Jesus's 40-day sojourn in the wilderness.

At Desilu, on acreage that had previously belonged to RKO, nearly fifty sets were constructed to depict ancient Jerusalem at the time of Christ. Most of them were systematically demolished soon after the picture was wrapped.

Although Desi was sometimes configured as the onscreen host of TV series which had been nurtured to fruition by other producers, he consistently failed, time and again, to launch his own series.

Two of what might have evolved into his biggest successes (or failures) would have starred Carol Channing in a comedy series, and Spencer Tracy in a legal drama.

After seeing Channing on Broadway with her big hit, *Hello, Dolly!*, Desi had thought she would go over big on TV. He was disappointed. The comedy pilot she shot was brusquely rejected by potential sponsors.

Likewise, Desi had long admired the screen roles of Tracy, and ordered a legal drama, *Without Consent,* be developed in which the vintage actor would play a defense attorney. But attempts to develop a suitable script failed, and Desi was told that no company could (or would) insure Tracy because of his perceived unreliability and his heavy boozing.

***

As president of Desilu, Desi faced mounting financial problems. "After all the bills were paid, there was not that much left over in our purse. We needed a hit, and our pilots or projected scripts were facing rejection. I tried, for example, to get *The Victor Moore Show* a sponsor for the 1962-63 season but failed."

In March of 1962, he learned that *The Ann Sothern Show*, shot at Desilu, was going off the air.

Another sitcom, *Angel*, featuring Marshall Thompson and also part of the Desilu repertoire, was also biting the dust, as was Pat O'Brien's *Harrigan and Son*. It had ended its run in 1961 and was not renewed.

That same year, the same fate also was in store for Joanne Dru's *Guestward Ho!*. Dru's great successes in a roster of film classics, including *Red River* (1948), *She Wore a Yellow Ribbon* (1949) and *All the King's Men* (also 1949), did not carry over into television.

High drama unfolded at Desilu when scenes from T*he Greatest Story Ever Told* were shot on their lot. It was a grueling, 18-month ordeal for actor **Max von Sydow**, who'd been cast as Jesus in the blockbuster "swords and sandals" overview of Christ's birth and resurrection.

In his own words, Von Sydow noticed that "some of my close friends began treating me with reverence. Playing the role of Christ was like being in a prison. It was the hardest part I've ever had to play in my life. I couldn't smoke or drink in public. The most difficult part was that I had to keep up the image around the clock."

December Bride had been a money maker for Desilu. Its plot centered on the adventures of Lily Ruskin, a spry widow played by Spring Byington whose character has moved in with her daughter and son-in-law.

In time it became the second most-successful TV program from Desilu, outranked only by *The Untouchables*. It ran for five seasons (1954-1959). At least some of its high ratings derived from its scheduling right after the highly popular *I Love Lucy*.

Lily Ruskin's next door neighbor was Pete Porter (Henry Morgan), an insurance agent married to his unseen wife, Gladys.

A spinoff was plotted by Desilu entitled *Peter and Gladys*, starring Morgan. His wife was played by Cara Williams, who won an Emmy for the series and was hailed as "The New Lucille Ball." The Nielsen ratings, however, were poor, and *Pete and Gladys* ran only from 1960 to 1962.

***

To rescue the upcoming 1962-63 season, Desi needed a hit to make up for the many failures. He told Lucille that she was still Desilu's "Most salable property."

"That makes me sound like a whore on the market," she said.

"We need you, and Bill Paley at CBS has already indicated he will greenlight a series with you. There was talk of calling it *They Love Lucy* because you'll be the mother of two kids. But the latest title is simply *The Lucy Show*."

[It was agreed that for the first eight episodes of The Lucy Show, Desi would also be the executive producer.]

Desi was far too busy to continue to star in a weekly series. He had to oversee 3,000 employees, run three studios, and deal with the daily production problems—"and the disasters"—occurring on thirty-five sound stages. "It was the blood-hungry Frankenstein monster at my throat every hour of the day and often throughout much of the night," he claimed.

The news that Desi would not be Lucille's co-star in any future series was greeted with disappointment from thousands upon thousands of Lucy/Desi fans. Critic Edith Efron expressed the disappointment best by saying, "It would be like sitting through a new version of *Gone With the Wind* where Scarlett O'Hara appears without Rhett Butler."

As Desi went to work casting it and lining up the writers, Lucille gloomily predicted, "We will always be second rate to *I Love Lucy*. Let's face it: We'll never top that."

"I know that," he said. "The reason being that I was the star of the series but will not be of the second."

"Your ego gets out of bound at times," she claimed.

Life magazine, in its January 1962 issue, placed a photo of Lucille on its cover and broke the news: "LUCY IS BACK!"

For the inaugural episodes, Desi rehired his familiar writing team, including Madelyn Pugh (now going by her married name of Martin), plus "The Three Bobs"—Carroll, Weiskopf, and Schiller.

For their source material, the screenwriters were inspired by the Irene Kampden novel, *Life Without George* (1960). Its plot swirled around two female *divorcées* living with their children in a shared home in Connecticut.

CBS objected to Lucille being cast as a divorced woman, preferring to have her configured as a widow instead. The dictatorial James Aubrey,

Despite Desi's constant tinkering with ideas for new-fangled TV series, Lucille still remained Desilu's biggest moneymaker.

Therefore, it was unanimously agreed that **Lucille** with **Vivian Vance** (and without Desi) would recreate the shenaningans they'd made famous with *I Love Lucy*—this time in a recycling of her time-tested, widely adored character.

"More of the same," cynical insiders made clear.

who had become president of the CBS television network in 1959, claimed, "If Ball plays a *divorcée*, that means she will have divorced Ricky Ricardo. That simply won't go over. Make her a widow."

In her new role, Lucille would be Lucy Carmichael, the mother of a teenage girl and an eight-year-old son. The second woman, a *divorcée*, would be a character named Vivian Bagley, a role intended for Vivian Vance. The two stars, each without a husband, would be "man-hunting, middle-aged mothers."

When Desilu contacted Vance about it, she was living with her fourth husband in Connecticut. She told Desi, "I'm not interested. I even want to forget that I played Ethel Mertz on TV."

When Desi met with his staff and Lucille, Ann Sothern was suggested for the part. "I think Sothern is getting beyond her expiration date," Desi said. "How about Gale Storm?"

[*A Texas beauty, born in 1922, Storm was more than a decade younger than Lucille. She had launched her film career in 1940 and later became a big star at Monogram on Poverty Row.*

Storm's real fame did not come until 1952 when she starred in the TV series, My Little Margie, *with former silent film star, Charles Farrell, playing her father. The series had begun as a summer replacement for* I Love Lucy. *In 1956, Storm starred in* The Gale Storm Show on TV, *this time featuring another star who became famous in the silent era, ZaSu Pitts.*

Then, in a surprise move, Lucille adamantly opposed the casting of Storm. "I want Vivian, and I'm flying East to convince her to take the co-star role."]

AMERICA LOVES HER AND SHE'S GOOD FOR SALES!

As America dangled over the precipe of the Cold War, TV viewers couldn't get enough of their favorite redhead, viewing her return to an all-new (admittedly derivative) TV series. with fanfare

Here, a trio of highly emotive Lucys peer out from the cover of a January, 1962 edition of *Life*, which celebrated the premier of *The Lucy Show* with a *tsunami* of advance publicity.

Ironically, the same edition also contained a brief feature about the Eisenhower's trip, with their grandchildren, to Disneyland, and an optimistic editorial forecast about then-president John F. Kennedy's "next three years" in office.

Vance had divorced actor Phil Ober in 1959 and had married literary agent John Dodds in January of 1961. He was six years her junior, and they lived together in a home in Stamford, Connecticut.

It took a lot of persuading, but Lucille finally wangled Vance's collaboration as her co-star, and with the stipulation that her "stage name" would be changed to "Vivian." She also demanded that she would not look like "that frumpy Ethel Mertz" and that she'd be fashionably, even glamourously, attired. She also insisted on equal billing and a doubling of her salary.

During the first season, Vance was invited to live in the guest cottage behind Lucille's house on Roxbury Drive in Beverly Hills.

At the time, a lot of rumors were spread along the Hollywood grapevine. Vance's husband was said to be bisexual. *[The same charge had been leveled against her previous spouse, actor Phil Ober.]*

Not only that, but rumors were spread that Lucille and Vance were engaged in a lesbian relationship. Behind their backs, the crew of the new *The Lucy Show* referred to the series as "The Dyke Show Without Dick."

As the series remained unfocused and in development, Lucille had many long talks with her new director, Brooklyn-born Jack Donohue, three years her senior. He was multi-talented, not just a director but an actor, producer, choreographer, screenwriter, and composer.

In the 1920s, he'd danced in the *Ziegfeld Follies* before migrating to Hollywood in the 1930s. Once there, he taught child star Shirley Temple how to do the "Hula" in *Curly Top* (1935). The year before, he'd taught her how to dance in *Bright Eyes*.

Donohue made his TV debut in the 1950s, working on *The Frank Sinatra Show*.

He would remain with *The Lucy Show* until 1968, helming her through ninety-six episodes. He later said, "She was not the type to take direction, a real do-it-yourself dame."

In 1928, he'd married the celebrated Broadway star, Marilyn Miller. On stage, she usually played rags-to-riches Cinderella damsels. Her life was short, as she'd died in 1936. Her time on earth was marred with disappointments, tragedy, and frequent illness. She'd had an ill-fated marriage to Jack Pickford, the brother of Mary Pickford.

One night, Donohue discussed with Lucille a screenplay he was writing about Miller near the

When Vivian Vance protested long and loudly about getting involved in another series based on the *Lucy* theme, Lucille and Desi, then in charge of Desilu, approached **Gale Storm**, depicted above as "My LIttle Margie" and a time-tested daytime comedy star.

No dice...Lucille, remarkably consistent as a powerhouse and frenemy, rejected Storm as a possible replacement

Ann Sothern, too, was briefly considered as a replacement for Vance, with scads of fans who thought she'd be terrific. Surprisingly, she, too, was rejected as a possible co-star for **Lucille.** Was Lucy afraid of the competition?

The photo above derives from a 1959 episode of Sothern's own show (*The Ann Sothern Show*). Lucy has come to town and caused mayhem to Sothern's love life, with a style that audiences predicted in advance and seemed to love anyway.

end of her days. He "detested" how his former wife had been depicted in biopics, the most visible of which had been *Look For the Silver Lining* (1946) starring June Haver and Gordon MacCrae, who had been cast as her first husband, Frank Carter, an acrobatic dancer.

[Judy Garland had portrayed Miller in Till the Clouds Roll By, *MGM's 1946 biopic of Jerome Kern. A biographer had described Miller as "Ziegfeld's most dazzling star and the premier musical comedy star of the Jazz Age."]*

Lucille flirted with the idea of taking on the role, but decided she was too old and that she didn't have the voice that Miller had.

Among the cast of *The Lucy Show,* Vance was a familiar face but, surprise, she looked younger than Lucille. Secretly, she'd slipped away to Manhattan and had had a facelift.

Desi and William Frawley were not in the cast, so Vance and Lucille had to work with a new set of actors, some of whom were hired late during the film sequences of the show.

Candy Moore was cast as Lucille's teenaged daughter, Chris, with James Garrett playing her eight-year-old son, Jerry. Ralph Hart won the role of Vance's ten-year-old son, Sherman.

Additional characters were added, including Charles Lane, cast as the banker, Mr. Barnsdahl, for whom (according to the plot) Lucy worked. Her next-door neighbor, Harry Connors, was played by Dick Martin.

Instead of her real daughter, Lucie Arnaz, Lucy's teenaged TV daughter, Candy Moore, was an actress from New Jersey born in 1947. She'd begun her career with appearances on the TV series *Leave It to Beaver.* Before working with Lucille, she had starred in two episodes of *Rawhide* (1961-62) and had appeared as a hiker in a telecast of *My Three Sons.*

In the first episode, *Lucy Waits Up for Chris,* televised on October 1, 1962, Moore played Lucy's fourteen-year-old daughter. Lucy waits up for her when she comes home long after her curfew.

"Lucy was wonderful to me," Moore said, "and so was the cast. The stinker was our director, Donohue. I don't think he dug kids. My character of Chris was rather plastic, and I struggled to make the girl real."

Here's **Marilyn Miller**, a Broadway star with whose memory and talent Lucille did NOT want to compete, as she appeared on the June 23, 1922 edition of *Movie Weekly.*

In the photo above, **Judy Garland** sings up a storm in a style perhaps inspired by Marilyn Miller—something Lucille opted to avoid—in *Till the Clouds Roll By.*

Jimmy Garrett, as Jerry Carmichael, Lucy's young son, was born in 1954 in Los Angeles. He had first faced a camera when he was only nine months old, in a TV commercial for Bell Telephone. He was in the show at its premier and would remain there until he was written out of the script when Lucy relocates from New England to California.

Re-calibrating **Lucille and Vivian** for a new reprise series (*The Lucy Show*) without any husbands in sight.
The original cast of *The Lucy Show* (left to right): **Jimmy Garrett** (as Jerry Carmichael), **Candy Moore** (Chris Carmichael), **Lucille Ball** (Lucy Carmichael), **Vivian Vance** (Vivian Bagley), and **Ralph Hart** (as Sherman Bagley).

The young actor later told the press that Lucille "was lovely to me, but I really dug Dick Martin. What a guy! I was only seven, and he let me have my first taste of beer from his Budweiser can. Not only that, but I got to take two puffs from his cigar."

Vance told Garrett, "You're getting all those Fred Mertz lines in our present scripts. The difference is that you say them better than that old poop."

Born in 1952, Ralph Hart was a blonde and good-looking kid, and he beat out dozens of competitors before being cast as Sherman Bagley, the ten-year-old son of Vance. "Vivian never had a child and didn't know how to relate to me. Even though she'd been cast as my mother, I found her cold and distant."

"With Donohue, it was a different story," Hart claimed. "He was a former choreographer. During breaks, he taught me how to dance—you know, the soft-shoe routines."

After he left the show and went on to become a hydro-geologist, Hart never wanted to have anything else to do with later observances, always refusing to attend the annual "Lucy Fest" in her hometown of Jamestown, New York.

Charles Lane was born in San Francisco in 1905, two years before an earthquake destroyed the city. In the new series, he would be cast as Mr. Barnsdahl, Lucy's cantankerous banker boss.

He and Lucille had had a long friendship. Before teaming with her, he had played supporting roles in several Hollywood classics during a career that spanned 72 years. His most memorable films included *Mr. Smith Goes to Washington* (1939) and *It's a Wonderful Life* (1946), both of them starring James Stewart.

In 1931, he'd married Ruth Covell Lane, and was still married to her when she died in 2002. *Variety* wrote, "And gossips say Hollywood marriages don't last."

Lucille and Desi had first used him on the *I Love Lucy* series. His specialty was playing scowling, beady-eyed, short-tempered, no-nonsense professionals, a perfect comic foil for the scatter-brained Lucy Ricardo.

On *The Lucy Show,* he was eventually let go when he could no longer remember his lines. There was another reason, too: Her original choice had been Gale Gordon. When he was free from other contractual obligations, she fired Lane and replaced him with Gordon.

Actually, "that veteran geezer," Lane, continued to work until the age of 101, appearing as a narrator in 2006, a year before his death. During the course of his career, he appeared in more than 250 feature films and dozens upon dozens of TV shows.

The comedian, Dick Martin, was soon introduced to the series, making his debut on October 8, 1962, in *Lucy Digs Up a Date.* He played Harry Connors, her next-door neighbor.

"I guess they didn't want Lucy to be sexless," Martin said. "I was working with Dan Rowan in a gig in Sparks, Nevada (not Las Vegas!) when I got this call from Desi. He had me flown to Hollywood in this twin-engine Cessna. I did the warm-ups that Desi used to do in front of a live audience. After I left the show, Lucille ordered Gary Morton to do them."

Desi was asked by a reporter what he thought of Morton's comic warm-up before Lucille came on with the show. He answered, "Do you mean that cucumber who took over my house, my wife, and my two kids? I sat through one of his routines before Lucy came on. He did not get one chuckle from me, although once I accidentally farted."

A native of Battle Creek, Michigan, Martin would go on to sensational fame on his own TV show, the hit sketch comedy series, *Rowan &*

Charles Lane was Lucy's cantankerous, short-lived boss in *The Lucy Show* before he was fired (for forgetting his lines) and replaced by Gale Gordon.

The fussy and perpetually crabby **Gale Gordon** appears here with **Lucille Ball** in "Lucy Flies to London" on *The Lucy Show.*

Early in the series, Lucille (and the character she played) grew adept at soothing, coddling, and placating this well-known character actor.

One critic reviewed him as "always indulgent, always forgiving, always susceptible to being "handled" by his irrepressible and frequently annoying employee."

Martin's Laugh-In, telecast from 1968 to 1973. He had first teamed with Rowan in 1952, playing the night club circuit.

Their TV show was an immediate hit, becoming number one only two months after its debut. It was fast-paced, with a stream-of-consciousness style of gags, *double entendre*, topical satire, and catchphrases.

Its cast of unknowns soon became famous, too—Goldie Hawn, Lily Tomlin, Arte Johnson, and "the purse beater," Ruth Buzzi.

Martin told Lucille, "When I'm not working, I devote my life to women, lots and lots of women…and parties. What else is there in life?"

After Martin left the show, she encountered him one night in a club. He had married Dolly Read, formerly one of Hugh Hefner's "Playboy Playmates," in 1971. She had been the lead star in the raunchy *Beyond the Valley of the Dolls* (1970).

Both Desi and Lucille knew actress Joanne Dru when she had starred on Desilu's *Guestward Ho!* in the early 1960s.

For an appearance on *The Lucy Show* that aired on January 7, 1963, they met and befriended her younger brother, actor Peter Marshall, who came into the world in West Virginia in 1926.

Dan Rowan (left) with his partner, **Dick Martin,** became TV legends with their hit show, *Rowan & Martin's Laugh-In.*

Martin was familiar with Desi and Lucille, having worked with them before. He recalled seeing Desi in his straw hat smoking a huge Havana cigar.

"He was brilliant going through an entire script and remembering every line from memory. Then, one day, I guessed shit hit the fan. After a few episodes of *The Lucy Show*, he just up and disappeared."

Their father had committed suicide when Peter was ten, and the family moved to New York, where his mother worked as a costume designer.

With Lucy, he appeared as brother-in-law, Hughie, in the episode *Lucy's Sister Pays a Visit.*

Marshall loathed his time on the show. First, Donohue tried to direct him, then Lucille took over. Even Vivian told him how to act.

"Desilu offered me $750 a week to become a regular, but I wasn't prepared to take all that crap from three loonies."

In 1966, Marshall became a household name when he hosted *The Hollywood Squares* for a thirteen-week gig. That booking stretched out for fifteen years and more than 5,000 episodes, finally coming to an end in 1981.

Donald Briggs of Chicago was the same age as Lucille. At first, when he was brought in for some episodes, he assumed that he would portray her boyfriend. As it turned out, during the first season, he was assigned the role of Eddie Collins, boyfriend of the Vance character. The following year, he made only one appearance before his character was dropped.

However, in 1970, when Lucille was starring in a new series, *Here's Lucy,* he was called back for an episode entitled *Lucy the Crusader.*

***

Mike Dunn, chief of programming at CBS, said, "All of us were acting like we were at the Gates of Hell when *The Lucy Show* had its premiere on October 1, 1962. We felt that Lucy without Desi, as Ricky Ricardo, would bomb. But she held her own."

From CBS headquarters, James Aubrey Jr. announced, "We are certain that millions of Lucy fans will welcome her back to television with great affection."

From its first telecast, *The Lucy Show* was a hit, ranking as the fifth most-watched TV program, according to the Nielsen ratings. At the time, the biggest hit on television was *The Beverly Hillbillies*. *Candid Camera* also ranked near the top, as did *Bonanza* and *The Red Skelton Show*. *Saints and Sinners* at NBC was going strong, too, as was *The Rifleman* at ABC.

Newton Minow, head of the FCC (Federal Communications Commission), sat through the top shows of that season, series that included *Petticoat Junction* and *My Favorite Martian*. He admitted, "I absolutely deplored *The Beverly Hillbillies*. Just how low can public taste go? Television has become a vast wasteland."

William Paley, the CEO at CBS, said, "TV today has degenerated into broads, bosoms, and fun."

For the most part, the first season of *The Lucy Show* was well received by critics.

The New York Times wrote: "Lucille Ball is back in her first weekly series since *I Love Lucy,* and she is as remarkable a gal as ever. Put her in the wildest half-hour of improbability, the sort of far-fetched doings that regularly trip up many TV notables, and she makes it all seem not only quite likely, but diverting fun in the bargain.,"

Another reviewer claimed, "Ever since Lucy retired, TV *comediennes* have been competing for the crown of Lucille Ball. Last night, that contest was decided. Miss Ball herself is back."

Since many Americans did not have a color television set at the time, episodes, performed in front of live audiences, were formatted in black and white.

Without Ricky Ricardo, the series took on more of a family comedy plot. Lucy Carmichael worked as a secretary at the First National Bank in Danfield, Connecticut. Her best friend and companion was the *divorcée* portrayed by Vance.

She was delighted to be using her real first name in the series, since hundreds of people she met still called her Ethel. "I didn't like Bagley as a

Feared, loathed, and despised, having carved out a bloody niche for himself as the man who helped bring down Judy Garland as a TV entertainer, CBS honcho **James Aubrey** loudly applauded the return to network TV of Lucille Ball.

He became influential in her resurrection, without Desi, as a prototypical but reincarnated LUCY.

last name, however. I disliked the word 'bag.' At least as a *divorcée*, my loyal fans could well understand why I divorced Fred Mertz."

In one of the weaker episodes, telecast on March 25, 1963, Elliot Reid was brought in. In a silly plotline, Lucy is invited to the Kennedy White House to present him with a miniature, "accurate to scale" version of the White House crafted by the local cub scout troupe. But the replica is destroyed during the train ride, leading to emergency measures to reconstruct it from sugar cubes.

At the time of his appearance with Lucille, Reid was an accomplished impersonator, famous for his mimicry of John F. Kennedy. In fact, unlike the TV script, he had actually been invited to the White House to perform in person in front of JFK.

The actor had immortalized himself, more or less, when he starred as Jane Russell's love interest in *Gentlemen Prefer Blondes* (1953) with Marilyn Monroe.

Reid had first worked on an *I Love Lucy* episode in 1953. She liked him and asked for him to come back on *The Lucy Show* in 1965 in the episode entitled *Lucy the Stockholder*.

In the sixth season of her later series, *Here's Lucy*, Reid, in 1974, had a reunion with the star in the episode, *Lucy the Sheriff*. That same year, he joined her as one of the guests on the televised show, *Milton Berle's Life of the Party*.

A television critic ranked the top ten episodes from the six-year (1962-1968) run of *The Lucy Show*. Three episodes, each from 1962, made the list:

Ranking in the number three spot was *Lucy and Her Electric Mattress*, which aired for the first time on December 17. Slapstick reigned supreme in this sketch, where viewers got to see Lucy walk on stilts.

"Lucy loved to rehearse," Dick Martin claimed, "especially on those damn stilts. She was the exact opposite of that laidback Dean Martin—more like Carol Burnett."

Ranking fifth among the Top Ten was *Viv Sues Lucy*, aired on December 3. In this episode, Vivian falls and injures her ankle on an abandoned toy. Lucy hasn't renewed her liability insurance and is afraid of being hauled into court.

This episode marked the last appearance of Charles Lane as Mr. Barnsdahl. Writer Bob Schiller said, "We brought in Gale Gordon, who had finished his stint on *Dennis the Menace*."

Lucy Is a Kangaroo for the Day was televised on November 12, and it made the sixth position on the top ten list. From the bank, Lucy leaves to deliver contracts to clients, but ruins her suit along the way. The only costume she can find is a kangaroo outfit, which she wears to make her house calls.

Gary Morton insisted that Lucille hire his cousin, Sid Gould, if only in a small walk-on. Most of the fellow cast members found him to be a "jerk," but he became a regular on the show, popping up in various bit parts for the next fifteen years.

In Episode No. 22, *Lucy and Viv Learn Judo*, Dick Martin co-starred with them for the telecast that aired for the first time on February 23, 1963.

After a rash of burglaries in their neighborhood, the girls take up judo in case a bandit breaks in on them.

"Lucy and Viv were the female Laurel and Hardy," Martin said. "After this episode, I was written out of the series. I think they should have kept me in as a romantic interest to show Lucy's femininity."

Writer Bob Schiller agreed: "Keeping Lucy dateless was a mistake, but my objections were overruled."

Episode No. 23, telecast on March 4, 1963, introduced Lucie Arnaz, cast as Lucy's twelve-year-old daughter. This show was called *Lucy Is a Soda Jerk, A.K.A. Lucy Is a Drum Majorette*.

Her daughter wants to be a drum majorette, but Lucy claims that she can't afford the forty-dollar costume that she needs. To earn the money, Lucie takes a job as a soda jerk.

On the day of the parade, the drugstore owner won't release Lucie, so Lucy and Vivian fill in as soda jerks—with disastrous results.

Both Candy Moore and Jimmy Garrett, co-stars, found Lucie very talented and predicted a big future for her in show business.

In episodes like the one partially replicated above (*Viv Sues Lucy*), audiences and studio executives alike all seemed to agree:

"She **(Lucille)** still has what it takes to make audiences laugh—even without Desi."

Lucie would return for the April 8, 1963 broadcast of *Lucy Is a Chaperone*. She and her classmates want to spend a weekend at the beach, and Lucy and Vivian insist on accompanying them as chaperones. The two older women decide to act like teenagers themselves.

***

Vance noticed how different the atmosphere on *The Lucy Show* was from back in the 1950s when they filmed comic episodes of *I Love Lucy*.

"There was tension in the air," she said, "at times unbearable. I dreaded going to work in the morning. Every time Desi, often drunk, wandered onto the set, he seemed to enrage Lucille. Once, she had great faith in his judgment. Now, she challenged almost anything that came out of his mouth. She had become more demanding herself, a real perfectionist, dictating everything from our performances to the set decorations, even wardrobe."

"She also questioned how Desi ran the company, as his drinking became even heavier. She complained so much to her brother, Fred Ball, who worked for Desilu, that one day, without Lucy's knowledge, he went to the head office to confront the boss man."

Ball must have felt protected by his sister, because he challenged Desi that day. As was later reported, he charged him "for being real sloppy in running production." He cited his heavy drinking and a series of questionable judgments he'd made that had cost Desilu a lot of money."

"Lucille and I want you to pull yourself together and shape up for God's sake," Ball said.

"Who in hell do you think are, you little creep?" Desi asked. "Someone who has sponged off Lucy for all your rotten life. Who wants to know who's running this company? You're looking at him., You want me to make better decisions? I'll begin with you. You're fired! If you're not off our grounds within the hour, I'll have security guards toss you out the gates on your dingleberry-coated ass."

The firing of Fred Ball was just one of the bad decisions Desi made that day. His judgment seemed so wrong that many on his staff secretly went to Lucille to direct them as to what they should do.

Day by day, it was becoming more obvious that Desi's days at Desilu were numbered. He frankly admitted, "I can't wait to get out of this hell hole."

Few other stars maintained links as strong and loyal to their parents as Lucille and Desi did with their respective mothers. Perhaps it was a result of their having, as families, survived the deprivations of poverty and in the case of the Arnaz family after their exits from Cuba, spectacular falls from economic grace.

Snapped in 1952, the photo above shows **Lucille** with her mother, **Desirée**, and **Desi** with his mother, **Dolores**, each of them clad in the best and most distinguished, age-appropriate finery that money in that era could buy.

It was more than just show-pretend: Many of her contemporaries cited Lucille, especially, as ferociously loyal to her mother, regardless of her sharp tongue and trenchant criticisms.

CHAPTER THREE

AS CO-OWNER OF DESILU,

LUCILLE EMERGES AS THE MOST POWERFUL WOMAN IN HOLLYWOOD

In the summer of 1962, Desi told Lucille that he was ready to bolt from Desilu. Because she was aware of his long-standing discontent, she was not as shocked as she might have been. It did not take her long to meet with her lawyers and exercise an option in her contract that ensured that she'd be the first person who bid on the acquisition of his stock.

Since he was in ill health and needed a long period of recuperation, she found him easy to negotiate with. He desperately wanted to leave his post as the studio's president and willingly accepted her offer of $2.5 million for the sale of his shares.

After signing the takeover contract, he turned to Lucille and said, "I wish you luck, kid. It's a hell of a job, guaranteed to age you five years for every one year on the job."

She didn't want to hear that.

Film history had been made: Lucille—now the company's president—owned fifty-two percent of Desilu's stock. As such, she was the first woman in Hollywood to serve as the head of a major studio; and the most powerful woman in Hollywood.

The closest that a woman had ever come to holding such power in the entertainment industry had occurred back in the heyday of "America's Sweetheart," Mary Pickford, who in 1919 had established United Artists with Douglas Fairbanks Sr., D.W. Griffith, and Charlie Chaplin.

Variety reported that Lucille's purchase of Desi's stocks was a "fire price sale," noting that Westinghouse, two years earlier, had offered $20

Lucille and **Mary Pickford** (depicted above as "America's Sweetheart" during the silent film era) had a lot in common:

Each was cited as having the most recognizable face on the planet during their respective heydays. And behind Pickford's curly haired heroics, and behind Lucille's zany antics lurked shrewd, and hardworking businesswomen.

million to buy Desilu.

After the sale was announced, reporters and photographers clamored for her attention outside her office door. As her administrative headquarters, she chose not to occupy Desi's former office, and for many months to come, refused to let any other person use it either.

Eventually, she emerged to speak to the press, telling them, "Desi has wanted to sell out and retire for many years. Perhaps he'll have a comeback in the future that I don't know about. At this point, I think he doesn't know either. I honestly believe that he loved founding Desilu more than he did running it."

"He's a great showman and a great business executive," she continued. "I am very proud of the empire he created and that I'm now running. It's unfortunate that in the past two or three years, Desi let things slide a bit. There are people like him, those who build and then destroy. But all of that is in the past. I'm in charge now, and I'm giving it hell. We're coming back bigger and better than ever."

Three weeks later, Desi talked to reporters at the Del Mar racetrack. Denying that Lucille forced him to sell so that she could transfer the management of Desilu to Gary Morton, he said, "My selling out had nothing to do with Barry Norton—that's my nickname for Morton. I started the company in 1950, a different time and a different ball game. But after many a year, even the best ballplayer in the game can have an umpire call three strikes and you're out. I was that umpire who called myself out. It was time for me to go."

"In the fight for love and glory in Hollywood," he continued, "both executives and performers can find the going too god damn tough. They turn to pills like Judy Garland, or to liquor like Alan Ladd. You find yourself on the Tinseltown merry-go-round, not a place you'd want to ride forever."

As the newly designated director of Desilu, Lucille knew at once that she didn't have enough business savvy for the job. No longer could she place a call to Desi for advice, He had already made it clear that for a while at least, he planned to go into hiding.

She then turned to Oscar Katz, an executive at CBS whom she had long admired. She'd first been exposed to his good business sense when she'd worked with him on her radio show, *My Favorite Husband*.

A deal was struck during some phone calls to New York, and he arrived soon after at Desilu as her fulltime business advisor.

Even before the takeover, Jerry Thorpe had been vice president in charge of pro-

Lucille is seen at a meeting of Desilu stockholders with her new business "whiz," **Oscar Katz**, who reigned as executive vice president in charge of production at Desilu from 1964 to 1966.

He told stockholders that he had purchased 22 television pilot scripts, which he hoped to turn into hit shows.

gramming. In the aftermath of her ascension, he said, "As the weeks went by, Lucy got tougher and tougher. I think she'd begun to imitate such studio moguls as Darryl F. Zanuck over at Fox, Louis B. Mayer at MGM, and Harry Cohn, that tiger at Columbia."

"The major difference among Lucy and those moguls was that she did not demand that beautiful Hollywood starlets have sex with her."

Since Lucille lived in gossipy Hollywood, she generated unconfirmed reports that every now and then, a good-looking, studly member of her staff, perhaps a grip or a construction worker, might have caught her lustful eye.

One of her first decisions involved re-hiring her brother, Fred Ball, who had previously been fired by Desi. For some strange reason, she "re-invented" his job description, unexpectedly designating him as responsible for Desilu's real estate holdings in Arizona.

Reports surfaced in the press that she was about to name Gary Morton as Vice President of Desilu, but that did not happen. It wasn't until four years later (1966) that she put him in charge of TV programming.

Later in life, Desi told a reporter, "I have loved Lucy ever since I met her in 1940, even though at the time, she was dressed as a prostitute on a film she was shooting. Loving Lucy is one thin', loving Lucille Ball is another thin'."

Fred Ball is shown here with his sister, **Lucille**, about midway through her *I Love Lucy* series of the 1950s.

Her brother's first wife was also named Lucille, creating two Lucille Balls within the same family. The first of them (i.e., the television star) said, "One of us has to go, and it ain't gonna be me, sweet cheeks."

Indeed, perhaps having "caved in" to pressure, Fred's wife began identifying herself as "Zo," and remained married to Fred until his death at the age of 91 in 2007. His ashes were buried in Jamestown's Lake View Cemetery, near those of his famous sister and their parents and grandparents. Zo herself died six years later at the age of 93.

***

During her first months as president, Lucille failed in several attempts to launch TV pilots for potential sitcoms. She had high hopes for the development of series tailor-made for both Ethel Merman and for the super-talented Donald O'Connor (for a series tentatively entitled *The Hoofer*), but her enthusiasm wasn't shared with others.

She had long admired the talent of Glynis Johns, who was not only an actress but a dancer, pianist, and singer.

"Glynis had this uniquely appealing husky voice," Lucille said, "and she was bright-eyed, with a sparkling and upbeat personality."

Johns is remembered today for creating the Broadway role of Desirée Armfeldt in *A Little Night Music,* for which she won a Tony Award, in part for her introduction of the song "Send in the Clowns.". *[Inaugurated on Broadway in 1973 and adapted into a film with Elizabeth Taylor in 1977, it featured music and lyrics by Stephen Sondheim and a book by Hugh Wheeler.]* Johns also starred in Walt Disney's *Mary Poppins* (1964), in which she was cast as Winifred Banks singing "Sister Suffragette."

Lucille ordered that a television pilot be developed for her (it was entitled *Glynis*) by Jeff Oppenheimer, one of the creators of the Lucy Ricardo character. As *Glynis'* co-star, Lucille brought back Keith Andes, her former co-star and off-stage lover from Broadway's *Wildcat.*

According to the vision of Oppenheimer and Lucille, *Glynis* would be a modern-day version of William Powell and Myrna Loy in their *The Thin Man* series from the 1930s. Johns would play a mystery writer, and Andes, her celluloid husband, would be a criminal defense attorney.

Glynis (the TV series) had a short life span. First telecast in September of 1963, it never received much of an audience. A few months later, shortly before Christmas, Lucille shut it down.

[As of this writing in 2021, Glynis Johns, born in South Africa in 1923 to British parents, is still alive. Her roots were in South Wales. After the death of Olivia de Havilland, who immortalized herself as Melanie in Gone With the Wind *(1939), Johns became the oldest living movie star of the Golden Age of Hollywood. Her third and last husband, Elliott Arnold, died in 1980, and she never remarried.]*

Lucille's creative ego suffered an even bigger blow when she was notified that *The Untouchables* was going off the air. [It had been the nation's most controversial crime drama, a hit for

In 1963, one of the many TV series that Desilu, under the direction of Lucille, tried to launch was *Glynis*, starring what some reviewers considered the madcap British incarnation of Lucille herself, **Glynis Johns**, depicted in both photos, above.

To spice up the plots and premises of *Glynis*, Lucille hired **Keith Andes**, depicted as he appeared in *Blackbeard the Pirate (1952)*, as her soulmate and partner in crime solving.

Even with Andes, the series, as nurtured by Desilu, was yanked from TV sets after only three months. Insiders interpreted it as just another monument in the graveyard of TV series that never survived.

years. Desi had even been threatened with assassination for his depiction of the Italian American crime figures it included. But the world had moved on.]

Finally, Lucille was presented with a television script she liked, although she was startled by its title: *The Greatest Show on Earth*. [In 1952, Cecil B. De Mille had walked away with a Best Picture Oscar for directing a feature film (also a circus drama) with the same name. At the time, to her everlasting regret, Lucille — who had been cast in the film as "the elephant girl," had to drop out because of pregnancy. The role was eventually assigned to Gloria Grahame.]

The lead character in the TV series under consideration was Johnny Slate, a rough and tough circus master who gets involved in the private lives of his performers. The first actor Lucille considered for the role was Rory Calhoun, but that didn't work out.

Briskly, Lucille moved on to consider a number of other actors, but none of them seemed quite right until Jack Palance was suggested. Right away, she thought he might be ideal.

Palance had made a name for himself as an actor as the sinister star of *Sudden Fear* (1952), in which he played the murderous husband of Joan Crawford; and *Shane* (1953), in which he was cast as a creepy gunslinger menacing Alan Ladd.

On meeting Palance in person, she reportedly found him craggy, with looks suitable for the character he was eventually cast as — the series' hard-driving circus manager. In some ways, he evoked her long ago lover, Broderick Crawford.

Even though he'd been known for playing hard-bitten cowboys from the American West, he had actually been born into a family of recent immigrants from the Ukraine (his birth name was Volodymir Ivanovich Palahniuk) in the anthracite coal-mining community of Lattimer Mines,

Lucille liked tough guys, perhaps as an evocation of her early days in Jamestown as a gun moll to Johnny DaVita

Here are two views of an actor whose career she nourished: **Jack Palance**.

Noted for his ability to play a convincing villain, he excelled at football, boxing, and dangerous military missions before becoming an actor.

In the upper photo, he menaces **Joan Crawford** in *Sudden Fear* (1952) and in the lower frame, he smiles threateningly at someone he's about to bully in *Shane* (1953).

Pennsylvania.

A former boxer, this celluloid tough guy, standing six feet, three inches, had his special appeal to those who wanted "a man's man" and not one of the pretty boys of the 1950s like Tab Hunter.

During the run of the series, Lucille spent a lot of time in Palance's dressing room, leading to gossip that they were having an affair. That was neither confirmed nor denied.

Once, a reporter from *Variety* dared ask her what she found attractive about Palance:

Unexpectedly, she replied, "We were drawn to each other by our love of Swiss chard, which is our favorite vegetable," she said. "Jack is a vegetarian. We have to have our helping of chard every day. That alone would make me want to marry him. Gary Morton is not that much into the vegetable, and Desi didn't like it at all."

"Incidentally," she continued, "and in case you didn't know, Jack was Marlon Brando's understudy in the stage version of Tennessee Williams' *A Streetcar Named Desire.*"

Right from the time the Palance series went on the air, it faced stiff competition, notably from the long-running *Jack Benny Show* (which as a TV series ran from 1950-1965) and from *Petticoat Junction* (1963-1970), a spin-off from that mega-hit, *The Beverly Hillbillies.*

The Greatest Show on Earth aired on December 10, 1963. In it, in an episode entitled *Lady in Limbo,* Lucille assigned herself the role of Kate Reynolds, a horse trainer who becomes the temporary mother of an animal trainer's orphaned son.

Her episode and the series itself were generally savaged by critics, despite the fact that she cast a dozen actors who were well-known because of their previous film performances.

The roster included such stars as Don Ameche, Joan Blondell, Joe E. Brown, Red Skelton, Spring Byington, Dennis Hopper, Fabian, Yvonne De Carlo, Bruce Dern, Tony Franciosa, Ricardo Montalban, Edmond O'Brien, Cliff Robertson, Tuesday Weld, and Betty Hutton. *[Hutton, incidentally, had also appeared in the original 1952 feature version of* The Greatest Show on Earth.*]*

Lucille cast veteran actor Stuart Erwin as the circus business manager, Otto King. He'd starred in films since 1928, waiting more than two decades before making his debut on television. In *The Stu Erwin Show,* his co-star was his wife, June Collyer.

The Greatest Show on Earth was first telecast on September 17, 1963. Lucille did what she could to publicize it and to attract a large audience but was forced to take it off the air on April 24, 1964. During the course of its brief life, she hired and fired eight screenwriters and four directors.

***

After his departure from Desilu, and after he had disappeared for several months, *Variety* asked in a headline—WHATEVER HAPPENED TO DESI ARNAZ?

As it turned out, he was living on a 45-acre horsebreeding farm in Corona, California, about 49 miles southeast of Los Angeles. His horse stable at the time numbered fifty animals, the prize being that racing champ, "Nashville." Highly valued as a stud horse, Desi had paid $300,000 for him, and rented him out at six thousand dollars for every live foal he sired.

Desi's other two prize horses included Amerigo's "Fancy," a beautiful animal with a chestnut coat and all-white legs. Yet another prize in his stable was "Soldier Girl," who held several records.

Initially, all he had to say about his retirement was, "Now I was able to buy a truckload of shit if that's what I wanted. I wouldn't have to worry about Lucy objecting. And there'll be no more catering to my commercial sponsors."

In his autobiography, which was not published until 1976, he spent little time documenting his philandering during the course of his marriage to Lucille. Referencing their last years, he said, "At our home, I no longer slept in the master bedroom, but in the cottage behind our house. That went on for more than a year, and I fulfilled my sexual needs outside."

Then, in a candid admission that he knew his wife had indulged in extramarital affairs, too, he went on to claim, "And so did she."

He told friends such as Dean Martin, "Lucy would never have strayed if I'd been with her at night. But I was gone, sometimes for months at a time. I can't blame her, really. There was a lot of temptation at Hollywood parties and elsewhere—even some of her leading men."

"Playing around is what married men do in Hollywood," Martin said. "That's one of the rewards of being a star. Just ask Sinatra."

After their professional breakup, thanks to Lucille's purchase of his Desilu stock, Desi built a vacation retreat opening onto the Pacific at Las Cruces in Baja California, Mexico. Perhaps inspired by Liberace's piano-shaped pool, Desi ordered a construction contractor to install a large swimming pool in the shape of a guitar.

At the age of forty-five, he looked much older, but still indulged in what he called "tomcatting."

"That's my favorite word," he once said. "With millions in the bank, and di-

Desi Sr. mugs for the camera after his marriage ceremony with **Edith (Edie) McSkimming, a.k.a. Mrs. Clement Hirsch**. At one point, her estranged husband, a wealthy horse-breeder, had the couple followed by two detectives as part of a plan to charge her with adultery in court proceedings associated with their upcoming divorce.

Desi promised her that she didn't need Hirsch's money, since he could take care of her financially.

That was not entirely true. Living off capital, and overinvesting in real estate and horses, he was going through his millions fast, telling her, "I'm not going to live so long that I will outlive my money."

vorced, I think I was pursued by every gold-digging starlet in Hollywood. I took advantage. Even with all this available stuff, I still visited bordellos. I really didn't have to find a *puta* with so many starlets available, but I went anyway. What the hell!"

Even with this steady supply of partners, a new love interest entered his life, someone he'd known for some time. Her name was Edith McSkimming, and he'd flirted with her when she was a cigarette girl at a Del Mar night club. He hadn't seen her for years, and one day, as he was walking, he discovered that she was his neighbor in Del Mar. Their friendship resumed.

She had married the super-wealthy Clement L. Hirsch, the founder of the Oak Tree Racing Association and the most famous thoroughbred racehorse owner in California. Desi made an effort to get to know him.

He was amused to learn that many of Hirsch's millions derived from dog food. In 1936, he'd founded the Dog Town Packing Company, a business venture which later morphed into Kal Kan Foods.

Desi began an affair with Mrs. Hirsch (aka Ms. Edie McSkimming)—her husband had taken up with other mistresses—and he soon learned that she planned to divorce Hirsch that very year.

Desi nicknamed her "Edie," and later said, "She was a redhead like Lucille, but she had the face of Doris Day. Like me, she was a horse-racing fan, and we began to attend all the races at Del Mar together. We were known as 'horseholics.'"

One day, he ran into Clement Hirsch, who greeted him warmly. "I'm glad you're taking that aging filly off my hands. Right now, I'm skipping along with three little wildcats. Wasn't that the name of a play Lucy did on Broadway? It's all I can do to keep up. After all, I was born in 1914."

"I'll give you a tip if you're planning to marry my wife," Hirsch said. "Throughout our marriage, I screwed around. She tolerates a husband who is a womanizer."

Frank Sinatra provided a massive wedding cake for **Desi and Edie**.

Jokingly, Sinatra told his best pal, Dean Martin: "I had the baker fill it with hormones, because, according to some of the same *putas* I shared with Desi, his Cuban salami was not always reliable."

He was happy to get that report from her soon-to-be ex-husband. He told friends, "Lucy was jealous, always on my case for my fucking around. I've learned that Edie is just the opposite of that. She'll give me my freedom if we get married. That was the same deal my old papa had with my *madre,* Lolita, in Santiago."

"In my way, I love her, but it's a different love than what I have for Lucy. When Edie came back into my life, I was at low tide. Everything seemed hopeless, and my drinking had gone haywire. That's an English word, right? Her giving me her love brought hope back into my life."

During the course of his engagement to Edie, every month, Desi gave her $5,000 for "operating costs" and another $5,000 for betting on the horses.

In Juárez, Mexico, when she was 45 years old, Edie divorced Hirsch. She had been a friend of Desi for years, and Lucille had met her several times at Del Mar.

Desi said, "My ex-wife and my wife-to-be got along. I mean, they weren't crazy about each other, but they didn't start a hen fight."

Hirsch was delighted with the divorce. "She could have gone for my millions. But she settled only for child support for our five-year-old boy."

On March 2, 1963 (Desi's forty-sixth birthday), at the Sands Hotel in Las Vegas, he married for the second time. Judge David Zenoff officiated at the ceremony, and Frank Sinatra supplied the wedding cake.

Even though she'd been invited, Lucille did not attend. Instead, she sent a floral arrangement in the shape of a "good luck" horseshoe, telling friends, "Poor Edie will need all the luck she can get in this marriage."

Jimmy Durante and Van Johnson were witnesses. Edie chose Durante's wife, Marge, as her matron of honor, and Desi selected Dr. Marc Rabwin, his long-time friend, as his best man.

The press described Edie as "a Lucille Ball lookalike with reddish-gold hair."

Back in Beverly Hills, Lucille said, "I feel sorry for Edie. I heard she had to drag Desi from the Vegas gambling tables for their honeymoon at Indian Wells Country Club outside

Edie with Desi and their wedding guest, an aging *"schnozzola,"* comedian **Jimmy Durante**, at the Sands Hotel in Las Vegas in March of 1963. The occasion was also Desi's 46th birthday.

He told Edie, "I don't know what we'll find in this new venture we're about to embark on. The only thing I can promise you is that it won't be dull."

Insofar as their careers were concerned, **Gale Gordon** (left in photo), had a lot in common with **Lucille.** He had trudged his way through a radio career, fine-tuned his comedic craft in dozens of previously not particularly successful entertainment venues, and eventually emerged as a consummate master of stage business and the vaudeville-inspired "slow burn and double-take."

Here, he's seen with **Bea Benaderet** in 1950 in the then-popular radio comedy, *Granby's Green Acres.*

Like Lucille, he was a tough-minded survivor in the politics of show-biz, a male version of the Vivian Vance that Lucille considered as essential to her ability to "sell" a joke and a comedy *schtick*.

Palm Springs."

***

Lucille was hesitant about being nailed down for a second season (1963-64) of *The Lucy Show,* despite demands from CBS and General Foods. James Aubrey, the network president, phoned her almost every day. The CBS chairman, William Paley, even flew to Los Angeles for an urgent meeting.

Paley met her new husband, Gary Morton. Used to dealing with Desi, he found Morton a quiet, rather subdued man. He concluded, "Morton is the kind of guy to light Lucy's cigarettes."

One low-level assistant detested Morton, in part because he had an anti-Semitic streak in him. "I think Ball hires the Jew to wipe her royal ass, a position in times of yore held by a fag to Louis XIV."

"When I get into a fight with the kids at home, or with some of my employees, Gary steps in as the peace-maker," Lucille said. "Unlike Desi, he's a real homemaker, and is a true father to my children. Desi gave us plenty of homes to live in but was rarely around to indulge in daily family life. Gary is easy-going, a real family man. The gal was right when she said, 'It's so good to have a man around the house.'"

Finally, on the first days of spring, 1963, Lucille announced that she would star in the second season of *The Lucy Show*. She designated Jack Donohue as director/producer and named Elliott Lewis as "top dog" (i.e., executive producer), a title previously held by Desi.

The major cast change for the series involved introducing Gale Gordon as a replacement for Charles Lane as Lucy Carmichael's curmudgeonly boss at the bank where she worked. Gordon was immediately reassigned the name of Theodore J. Mooney.

"I was terribly disappointed that she chose Gordon over me," Lane lamented. "But that's show business."

"With Gordon, we'll improve or at least maintain our ratings," she said. "Gale is the funniest man on the planet."

Screenwriter Madelyn Pugh Martin claimed, "*The Lucy Show* began its long, slow decline. Because of Lucille's star power, it would remain on the

Like Lucille, **Mary Jane Croft** was already a polished radio-comedy pro by the time she was hired as an on-again, off-again sidekick for Lucy in *The Lucy Show.*

The man who made that possible was her husband, **Elliott Lewis**, also a consummate pro as it related to every aspect of radio and later, television production. Lucille frequently turned to him for advice in the immediate absence of Desi from her life.

air long beyond its expiration date. She was not the same anymore. She ceased to take time to memorize her lines. Instead, from that point, she relied on cue cards."

A New Yorker, Elliott Lewis became the major business source in Lucille's life. She began to turn to him as she had to Desi in the early days of their TV programming.

Lewis had been a star ("Mr. Radio") during the golden age of a medium he'd been working in since he'd been 18, way back in 1936. In the late 1940s, he'd even worked on Lucille's own radio show, *My Favorite Husband.]*

Having evolved into a television artist, Lewis could work either behind the scenes or in front of the camera as an actor.

His best-known role on radio came after he'd served as a master sergeant during World War II. Back in civilian life, he played the hard-living, trouble making, left-handed guitar player, Frankie Remley in NBC's *The Phil Harris-Alice Faye Show*. In all, during the course of his career, he was involved in 1,200 radio productions.

During his time at Desilu, Lewis cast his wife, Mary Jane Croft, as Lucy's sidekick in several episodes of *The Lucy Show*. He lasted only until the second season, stepping down in 1964 to join Bing Crosby Productions.

***

Money was definitely a consideration in Lucille's decision to launch the second season (1963-64) of *The Lucy Show*. On paper, at least, it looked promising at first. In 1963, Desilu had grossed $21 million. But after the bills were paid, the company found itself $650,000 in the red. One pilot after another had failed to find a network to air it and a commercial sponsor to pay for it.

At the time, newspapers were filled with scandalous stories of an adulterous affair Richard Burton and Elizabeth Taylor were having in Rome during the filming of Hollywood's latest version (1963) of *Cleopatra*. As such, although it was later interpreted as a bad decision, the episode that Lucille and her staff selected as the first of their new season seemed like a good idea at the time.

Episode No. 31, *Lucy Plays Cleopatra,* was aired

Although cashing in on Elizabeth Taylor's "Cleopatra Craze" of 1963 seemed like a good idea at the time, the skit she acted out with Vivian Vance seemed rather silly, more like an envious jab at Taylor and Burton's over-budget movie than an amusing skit and satire.

In the photos above, **Lucille** (left) and **Taylor** each do their best to evoke, with differing degrees of self-satire, the Queen of the Nile.

on September 30, 1963. In it, Lucille did not attempt to satirize (or even overtly refer to) Burton and Taylor. Nevertheless, it was decided that a script would be crafted in which she could deliver her own interpretation of the Egyptian queen in a zany spoof (i.e., an amateur production) staged by Hans Conried. Both Lucy and Vance wanted to play Cleopatra as a vamp, but Lucy won, with Vance (deliberately) miscast as Marc Antony.

[Conried had been one of Lucille's favorite actors since their days of working together on her radio show, My Favorite Husband, *in the late 1940s. He told her he was delighted to be appearing with her in a comedy. "I'm still trying to get over the stigma of my playing a Nazi in all those World War II dramas."]*

Also included in the cast were Mary Jane Croft. When Vance eventually bolted from the series, Croft was designated as Lucy's new sidekick.

[Croft had first met Lucille when she'd had a small part on My Favorite Husband. *She'd also appeared in the final season (1956-1957) of* I Love Lucy.

Croft's husband, Elliott Lewis, was the executive producer of The Lucy Show, *and Croft had also worked with two of Lucille's competitors—Joan Davis and Eve Arden—on their respective TV shows.*

Two views of **Hans Conried**. In the left photo, he portrays the effete but evil Captain Hook in *Peter Pan*.

One of the best character actors in the business, and a favorite of Lucille, Conried was tall, slender, and nuanced. One critic put it like this: "He put his aquiline nose, disdainful look, and aristocratic voice to good use in the creation of sundry snobs and eccentrics."

Naturally and incorrigibly funny: Character actor **Mary Wickes** had been Lucille's original choice for the character of Ethel Mertz. Wickes rejected the offer, fearing that working so closely with Lucille would damage their close friendship. "I had great respect for Lucille," Wickes said. "But she scared some people sometimes. She could be abrupt."

The scene on the left is a still photo from Season One of *I Love Lucy*. Telecast as "The Ballet" in 1952, it features Wickes as Madame Le Mond, a dance instructor, who quickly realizes that **Lucille** will never become another Margot Fonteyn.

Also in the Egyptian episode was Mary Wickes, Lucille's longtime friend and one of her favorite actresses. *[She, too, had appeared on episodes of I Love Lucy. Right before joining in the second season of The Lucy Show, she had co-starred with Robert Preston in the feature film, The Music Man (1962).*

During her adolescence in St. Louis, Wickes had planned to become a lawyer, but ended up in supporting film roles, usually cast as a secretary, nurse, nun, or housekeeper. She was known for making sarcastic remarks to the lead characters in whatever secondary role she played.

A tall, gangling woman, she'd appeared opposite Bette Davis in Now, Voyager (1942), playing a wisecracking nurse.]

As the Cleopatra episode aired across the country, critics sharpened their knives. The *Hollywood Reporter* wrote: "The telecast was a tired retread of all the lampoons of amateur theatricals there ever was. The debut of the new season of *The Lucy Show* revolves around a gag as trite as this is just coasting on the *I Love Lucy* reputation."

The Cleopatra episode was followed by an even worse one, *Kiddies Parties, Inc.*, which aired on October 7. Its plot has Lucy and Vance deciding to go into business hosting parties. Of course, they will screw everything up, and Lucy will end up floating away on a helium balloon.

Lyle Talbot, upon whom she'd had a crush in the 1930s, was her guest star.

"Trouble was, you never asked me out on a date," she said. "You were called studly handsome, and you're still looking good."

"I wish you'd signaled your desire a little more strongly," he said.

"I saw some of your pictures as you emoted with Bette Davis, Bogie, even Mae West," she said.

"I did more than emote with Mae," he claimed.

"My friend Carole Lombard told me you were a champ in the

Then-matinee idol **Lyle Talbot** with **Loretta Young** in *She Had to Say Yes* (1933).

According to Talbot, as he remembered it years later, "I was good-looking, a real stud, and no leading lady ever turned me down. My most fabled asset, however, could not be revealed on screen."

As he moved into middle age, **Lyle Talbot** lost most of the sex appeal which had defined him in the 1930s.

Nonetheless, he and **Mary Jane Croft**, as Joe and Clara Randolph, seemed ideal as neighbors and friends of Ozzie and Harriet Nelson in their long-running sitcom.

Eventually, from 1955 until its demise in 1966, the Randolphs became regulars as "the perfect neighbors" on *Ozzie and Harriet.*

boudoir," she said. "Joan Blondell agreed."

[*Despite the dozens of film roles he'd played, Talbot became best known for the decade he spent as a regular on the long-running (1952-66) ABC sitcom,* The Adventures of Ozzie and Harriet. *Although during the course of his career he appeared in some 150 movies, and despite his rugged sex appeal, major stardom forever eluded him.*

To his chagrin, Talbot ended up working for the worst filmmaker in town, Ed Wood. Campy, technically awful, eccentric, and according to many critics, relentlessly embarrassing, Wood's films weren't well known until 1980, when he was awarded a posthumous Golden Turkey Award for Worst Director of All Time. Talbot was assigned a highly visible role in Plan 9 from Outer Space. *One film survey defined it as "the worst film ever made in the history of Hollywood."*

Talbot followed that with another dubious role in another of Ed Wood's (horrible) films, Glen or Glenda. *"I usually try to seduce my leading lady, but in that crap I didn't know if I was getting Glen or Glenda. Talk about transformation of the genitals!"*]

In *The Lucy Show's* episode No. 33, *Lucy and Viv Play Softball* (aired on October 14, 1963), Lucille and Vance appeared with actor William Schallert. In it, they've volunteered for a post-season charity baseball game. Within minutes, the team manager, Mr. Cresant (Schallert), surmises that Lucy is a rotten player, but through some quirks, she saves the day for the team.

[*A native of Los Angeles, Schallert holds the record of appearing in films or on TV either as a regular or as a guest more times than any other actor in TV history. His best known role was as Martin Lane on* The Patty Duke Show. *He also had an occasional role in a feature film, most notably when he co-starred with Doris Day and Rock Hudson in* Pillow Talk *(1959).*

From 1979 to 1981, he was president of the Screen Actors Guild, following in the footsteps of Ronald Reagan.]

Never a leading man, **William Schallert** was defined by The New York Times as "a high-caliber embodiment of the working actor."

He appears in the lower photo as the TV father of **Patty Duke** in her namesake series, The Patty Duke Show around the time she was having an affair with Desi Arnaz Jr.

***

In Episode No. 34, *Lucy Gets Locked in a Bank Vault* (October 21, 1963), she is united once again with Gale Gordon, her longtime favorite co-star. "We dated back to 1947 when he joined me on radio," she said. In the role of Theodore J. Mooney, he is a bank manager and the tight-fisted trustee of her trust fund.

Through some tricky plot twist, she ends up getting trapped in a bank vault overnight and has to be rescued through some slapstick attempts to free her.

Not only that, but she gives Mooney's son—a role played by child actor Barry Livingston, who was ten years old at the time—the worst haircut of his life.

Livingston later said, "I heard that Lucy was a real pro, a master of comedy, but she screwed up our scene together in front of a live audience."

The actor/comedian Dick Martin tuned in to the telecast and later commented, "I wasn't as crazy about Gale Gordon as most people were. They should have kept me in the series to add some romantic interest for Lucy Carmichael. As it now plays, she comes off sexless. Lucy Ricardo on *I Love Lucy* was one smart cookie. The Carmichael dame comes off silly, dumb, and tacky."

The problem Martin cited was not solved in Episode No. 36, *Lucy Goes Duck Hunting* (November 7) for which she hired Keith Andes as her co-star. He'd played Joe Dynamite opposite her in the Broadway production of *Wildcat* (1960). No mention was made of their dressing room affair back then.

She convinces him she is the world's best duck hunter, but, of course, she is not, as later disastrous results reveal. However, she does know how to make the world's best duck call.

Her antics continued in yet another episode (No. 39), a farce entitled *Lucy Puts Out a Fire at the Bank*. Her favorite co-stars, Mary Wickes and Mary Jane Croft, joined her.

Alan Hale Jr with **Bob Denver**, irrepressible co-stars of *Gilligan's Island*, appear in the upper photo.

Many critics said that their co-stars (**Jim Bacchus** and **Natalie Schafer**, playing socialites as depicted in lower photo) were much funnier than Hale and Denver.

When Natalie Schafer died in 1991, she left the millions she'd accumulated from real estate investments to her beloved poodle, making him the richest dog in history.

The plot involves a conflict with the Volunteer Fire Department and with the Danfield city authorities. Lucy might not know how to put out a fire, but she sure knows how to start one.

Her co-star was the rugged Alan Hale Jr., the son of a far more famous actor, Alan Hale Sr. Junior's career would span four decades, during which he became best known for his long-lived performance as The Skipper in TV's oft-rerun sitcom, *Gilligan's Island* (1964-1967). Hale Jr. began his acting career in 1941 and would not end until he'd been cast in some 200 movies and TV shows.

He'd starred with such actors as Kirk Douglas, Ray Milland, and James Cagney. One day after leaving the studio, having completed a project with Lucille, a reporter asked him, "What was it like?"

"I'd rather not talk about it," he said.

Perhaps that comment did not get back to Lucille, since she later re-hired him for her new series, *Here's Lucy*.

For the final telecast of 1963, Lucille hired the talented Wally Cox in *Lucy Conducts the Symphony* (December 30). Cast as Vance's cousin, he is a symphony percussionist with so much anxiety about his upcoming performance that she has to hypnotize him so that he'll relax. Later, she can't bring him out of his trance.

She, therefore, fills in for him, and naturally, manages to disrupt the concert. Her director, Jack Donohue, played the angry conductor of the orchestra.

Cox made himself famous by starring in the hit TV series, *Mister Peppers* (1952-55). In his private life, he was the best friend and long-time lover of Marlon Brando, who openly admitted he was bisexual. Brando once told a reporter, "If Wally were a woman, I would have married him."

Cox died at the age of 48 in 1973. After his body was cremated, Brando took the ashes home with him and kept them in his bedroom. After that, he admitted to having talks with Cox every night.

Wally Cox (left) with **Marlon Brando**. When Lucille first met Cox, she asked him, "As a lover, how is Brando in bed?"

"Naturally funny" **Kathleen Freeman**, is seen here as a comic foil to **Jerry Lewis** in *The Ladies' Man* (1961).

According to Freeman, "Lucille Ball was a great comedian because she was fearless. I appreciated all the work she gave me over the years, but I never forgave her for not casting me as Ethel Mertz."

***

To launch the 1964 season of *The Lucy Show,* she starred in an episode named *Lucy Plays Florence Nightingale.* It aired on January 6.

Mr., Mooney (Gordon) has broken his leg, and Lucy visits him in the hospital.

Knowing Lucy, it is not just a sympathy visit: There's another reason: She wants to trick the man who controls her trust fund to endorse a check, since he's cut off her allowance for the month. She wants to purchase an expensive gown for her daughter Chris (Candy Moore) to wear to a dance.

Naturally, Lucy manages to turn the hospital into a madhouse.

The episode brought Lucille together with the very talented Kathleen Freeman, a native of Chicago, who sometimes played nurses as she would do in this sequence. She was also skilled when cast as secretaries, busybodies, schoolteachers, acerbic maids, and battleaxes.,

She was also known for appearing in Jerry Lewis comedies of the 1950s.

To the set every day she brought her longtime lover, Helen Ramsey. "They were a very devoted and loving couple," Lucille said. "I had come to realize that lesbian relationships can be just as devoted or romantic as straight ones, sometimes even more so."

Freeman would return to appear with Lucille again in future shows.

***

For *Lucy Goes to an Art Class* (January 13, 1964), she hired two talented actors as her co-stars, Robert Alda and John Carradine.

In this episode, Lucy and Vance meet a good-looking bachelor in an art

If you like the father, ya gotta like the son, too... Above left, is **Alan Alda**, the very famous son of **Robert Alda**, as shown in an episode of *M*A*S*H*.

John Carradine (right) appears with **Charles Laughton** in *Captain Kidd* (1945) and (lower photo) as Preacher Casey in *The Grapes of Wrath* (1940).

Carradine was only half-joking when he suggested to Lucille that they could co-star in an episode called *The Bride of Dracula,* a facetious reference to a horror movie he had starred in, *House of Dracula* (1945).

"As my bride, I'm sure you could be frightening enough to top Elsa Lanchester in *Bride of Frankenstein."*

store. Hoping to get a date with him, they enroll in his art class.

Vance beats her to him, and Lucy plots to sabotage their first date.

This marked Alda's first appearance on one of the Lucy shows, and in the future, he would be called back, on occasion, to do other telecasts with her.

She had first seen Alda on Broadway when he originated the role of Sky Masterson in *Guys and Dolls* in 1950 for which he won a Tony. The movie version starred Marlon Brando as Sky. Alda was the father of actors Alan and Antony Alda.

Also cast in *Lucy Goes to Art Class* was John Carradine, a fabled character actor. He started out in Cecil B. De Mille's stock company, later joining the John Ford troupe. He popped onto the screen in horror movies, in Westerns, and was also adept in Shakespearean plays.

He was familiar with creating characters who were eccentric, insane, or diabolical. He told Lucille, "I lost out on getting cast as Dracula. Perhaps you'll co-star me in *The Bride of Dracula*."

Michael J. Pollard with **Faye Dunaway** in *Bonnie and Clyde (1967).*

Although perhaps she wasn't being serious, Lucille told reporters that in 1968, she voted for Pollard during his run for President of the United States against Richard Nixon and Hubert Humphrey.

He claimed that he'd been cast into movies before he got billing, and later boasted of having been in 450 films, although some historians have challenged that.

Lucille had first worked with him in that taut drama and "disaster movie," *Five Came Back* (1939).

A week later, *Chris Goes Steady* was aired, this time with the very short Michael J. Pollard as her guest star. Her TV daughter Chris (Candy Moore) is going steady with Mr. Mooney's son Ted (Pollard). Lucy schemes to break up the couple, but her plot backfires.

Pollard was a rather odd choice for the role. He was a few years from his greatest role in *Bonnie and Clyde* (1967), a classic film he made with Warren Beatty and Faye Dunaway after Jane Fonda turned down the role. Pollard, who was born in 1939 in Passaic, New Jersey, would win critical acclaim along with an Oscar nod for his portrayal of C.W. Moss.

At the age of twenty, he was seen on television in Alfred Hitchcock Presents. He went on to star in the Broadway production of *Bye Bye Birdie*. Because he was so short, he could often play youthful roles even into his late twenties.

Film critic Roger Ebert wrote: "There is something about Pollard that is absolutely original and seems to strike audiences as irresistibly funny and deserving of affection. It's easy to become addicted to him."

A week later, Lucille made another unusual casting choice in *Lucy Takes Up Golf* (telecast January 27, 1964). She introduced her husband, Gary Morton to TV audiences, hoping that fans would not protest or compare him unfavorably to Desi.

Morton was an avid golfer, and he was joined on the show by two top golf professionals, each a sports star at the time, Jimmy Demaret and F.G. ("Bo") Wininger).

In the plot, Lucy is a horrible golfer but—knowing her—she manages to triumph in the end, winning the tournament.

Some of the cast and crew liked Morton's performance so much they urged her to make her husband part of the ongoing series. She rejected the idea.

Issued for the first time in September, 1994, this U.S. postage stamp both recognized **Ethel Merman** as an entertainer, and thanked her for her work promoting, with music, the merits of the recently inaugurated ZIP code system.

***

The highlight of the 1963-64 season was the episode entitled, *Lucy teaches Ethel Merman to Sing (A.K.A. Lucy Meets the Merm).* It aired February 3, 1964.

She and Merman had been friends since the early 1930s when Lucille was a Goldwyn Girl.

Vivian Vance had known Merman since the days on Broadway when she'd been her understudy in *Anything Goes* (1934).

Both Merman and Lucille lamented the failure of not getting her pilot, *Maggie Brown,* picked up by either a network or a sponsor. "You were terrific in it," Lucille assured her.

It took Bob Schiller's writing skill

Many viewers began laughing the moment they heard the link of the very loud and very undiplomatic **Ethel Merman** with the "tender sensitivities" of adolescent youths, i.e., **The Boy Scouts**.

But that was the the theme developed by Lucille, Merman, and their production staffs. The episode remains memorable to this day.

to create a plot wherein Lucille, no real singer, teaches "The Belter" how to do it.

The episode ended up as No. 2 on the Top Ten episodes of *The Lucy Show.*

It was so successful that Lucille asked Merman, "on bended nylon," (her words) to follow it up with yet another episode, this one entitled *Ethel Merman and the Cub Scouts Show.* There was only a week between telecasts, but the second show was shot a month later. Merman had to take four weeks off for her Las Vegas debut.

When she came back to shoot another *Lucy Show,* both she and Lucille had greatly altered their appearance, especially their hair. Vance had been in the sun for a month. In the first episode, she had been vanilla white, but in the second, her skin had darkened to the color of an overripe apricot.

The highlight of the second show was Merman singing "Everything's Coming Up Roses" from her Broadway hit *Gypsy*.

"Working with Lucille was great," Merman said. "We'd been pals for years. But right after that last TV show, I made the mistake of my life. I married Ernest Borgnine, no great beauty. Our marriage was the shortest in Hollywood history. It lasted less than an hour."

***

Episode No., 51, *Lucy Takes a Job at the Bank,* reunited her with her regulars, Mary Jane Croft and Carole Cook. She also rehired her lesbian friend, Kathleen Freeman, since she'd gone over so well with the audience.

In the new plot, a very reluctant Mr. Mooney, president of the bank, agrees to hire Lucy, much to his regret. Somehow, she manages to instigate a run on the bank.

A week later, on March 2, Episode No. 52, *Viv Moves Out,* depicts Lucy having an argument with Vance and her young son. They pack up and leave.

To fill in the gap, and because she needs the money, Lucy agrees to share her home with Roberta Schaeffer, an entertainer, and her young son, also a performer. Their constant and loud rehearsing nearly drives Lucy crazy.

The actual stars of the episode were Roberta Sherwood and her son, Jerry, both of them seasoned in show-biz. Unusual for a singer, Sherwood became known as a torch singer at the age of 43. *Billboard* cited her as the 19th most popular "album artist" in America, and *Life* called her "flashy and richly sentimental, unsubtle in her crashing cymbal and as unpretentious as a $49.50 dress."

His television exposure was also beneficial for her real son, Jerry Lanning, who had a strong baritone voice.

On a trivia note, Lucille had ordered a pilot starring Gale Gordon and Sherwood, who—according to its script, have produced a singer—played by Jerry—as their son. But no sponsor went for it.

Based on a play by Sherwood Schwartz, **Mr. and Mrs.** was weirdly evocatve of the recently deceased marriage of Lucille with Desi Arnaz, or so it was gossiped about at the time.

Lucille was hoping to morph it into a prototype for a new sitcom that would replace *The Lucy Show.*

Sherwood had heard rumors going around that Lucy and Desi, back in 1940, had never been legally married.

***

At first, Lucille was reluctant to co-star with

Bob Hope in the hour-long *Lucille Ball Comedy Hour* entitled *Mr. and Mrs.* telecast for the first time on April 18, 1964. The script by Richard Powell was obviously a thinly veiled parody of her own failed marriage to Desi Arnaz.

It had originated as a play in a suburb of Chicago. Although its author, Sherwood Schwartz, had nurtured hopes of taking it to Broadway, the farthest he got was to produce and stage it as a summer "dinner theater" tour with actors who included Marilyn Maxwell, Jackie Coogan, and Steve Dunne.

Eventually, it attracted the attention of producers at CBS-TV, who paid Lucille $30,000 to appear in its reconfiguration into an hour of television comedy that included a rather complicated play-within-a-play. Jeff Oppenheimer, who always claimed credit for originating the character of Lucy and Ricky Ricardo, was hired as its executive producer, and one of Lucille's long-time collaborators, Jack Donohue, was called upon to direct.

As the scatter-brained director of a Hollywood studio, Lucy tries to locate Bob Hope, thinking he might attract a large audience in whatever vehicle he was placed, and that his reflected glory might reinforce her position as the female head of production at a major studio. Gale Gordon plays a nasty banker-investor who is trying to force her out of her position.

Hope is finally located in the Philippines, and Lucille, from afar, manages to lure him back to Los Angeles for their joint appearance as television's favorite sweethearts, a happily married couple. *[To keep up appearances, they also must pretend to be married off-screen, even though they frequently bicker and argue. That aspect of the plot was torn directly from the pages of Desi's actual marriage to Lucille.]*

The most famous costume designer in Hollywood, Edith Head, was hired to design Lucille's wardrobe. "I had never looked so gorgeous," Lucille said about herself. "Even though I was in my fifties, I looked twenty-nine."

She was always willing to work with Hope. He had first hired her in the immediate aftermath of World War II for his popular radio show. They had remained friends and sometimes co-starred in feature films.

The special represented one of Lucille's first television appearances in color. "My fans could get a better look at me. Before that, they had to settle for me in black and white."

***

The final episode of the season, No. 58, *Lucy Enters a Baking Contest*, had her cast with Mary Jane Croft and Carole Cook with a return appearance of Kathleen Freeman.

Lucy and Viv enter a pie-baking contest, which ends up in a pie fight to equal any Mack Sennett silent comedy.

However, a dispute with her writers led to their mass exit.

When Lucille had read the first draft of the baking contest episode, she flew into a very temperamental mood. "I hate this damn piece of shit," she shouted at the writers. Then she tossed the script onto the floor, spat on it, and stormed out toward her dressing room.

Her longtime writers, Madelyn Pugh and Bob Carroll Jr., decided they had had it, even though Lucille did not plan to fire them.

Collectively, they packed up their possessions and left the studio. In a show of support, "The Two Bobs," Schaffer and Weiskopf, also resigned.

Once freed of their Desilu contracts, the writers could be more candid in expressing their impressions of Lucille.

Hailing from Indiana, Madelyn Pugh and her family eventually moved to Los Angeles, where she found work as a radio writer, first for NBC, then for CBS. There, she met Bob Carroll Jr., and they began dating, later talking of marriage. But in the end, they decided to be friends instead. Their writing partnership lasted for fifty years, and, as a team, they wrote scripts for more than 400 television shows and 500 radio episodes. Their link with Lucille dated back to her radio show, *My Favorite Husband* in the late 1940s.

Pugh and Carroll also created a Broadway vaudeville act for Lucille and Desi, which became the basis for the pilot episode of *I Love Lucy*.

They teamed with Jess Oppenheimer, and later, with Bob Weiskopf and Bob Schiller in the fifth season of the show, eventually tackling thirty episodes. Their efforts brought them three Emmy nods.

Madelyn Pugh and **Bob Carroll** Jr. were the head writers of *I Love Lucy*. They later revealed a behind-the-scenes look in a memoir entitled *Laughing With Lucy*. "It wasn't always laughter," Carroll said.

They later complained about not getting residuals for reruns of the shows they'd written.

Lucille had a different spin: "Bob and Madelyn got a little too rich and eventually quit. The big thing in this business is residuals, and they became millionaires very quickly."

In 2005, Pugh and Carroll published a book entitled *Laughing With Lucy*.

After walking off *The Lucy Show*, they would later make up with her and return to work on some of her other episodes.

Shortly before he died in 2007, Carroll complained that he and Pugh did not receive any compensation for the reruns of *I Love Lucy*. He told a reporter, "Do you think I would be sitting here now if I had gotten a royalty? Hell, no! I would have flown you down to a beach in Cuba for this interview."

"The Two Bobs," Weiskopf and Schiller, had organized themselves as a writing team in 1950 when television was a new medium. Their first job was to write gag lines for comedian Fred Allen. In time, they would write dozens of scripts, not only for Lucille but for Eve Arden's *Our Miss Brooks* and another hit, *All in the Family.*

In the 1950s, Schiller, a native of San Francisco, worked with Weiskopf on such popular shows as *Make Room for Daddy, The Bob Cummings Show, The Lucy-Desi Comedy Hour,* and *The Ann Sothern Show.*

"After bolting from Lucille's clutches, Bob and I took a big-paying job with a variety show," Schiller said. "Lucille had become a real pain in the ass, god damn bossy. She wasn't that good at selecting scripts. Actually, Desi had been brilliant, but after he'd gone to greener pastures, we missed him terribly. Whereas whenever Desi told us what was wrong with a script, we could fix it. But whenever Lucille attacked one of our scripts, we hated her."

Weiskopf suggested, "Bob and I should have fled when Desi did. He knew when the time had come to leave the party. We sure missed him."

"Ball was surrounded by 'yes' men who had no balls," Pugh said. "No one would stand up to her, even though all of us knew she was wrong. Whenever she called some flunkie to bring her a double scotch, we knew we were in for it."

"Desi believed in paying guest stars a lot of money," Pugh said. "I wish he'd been more generous with his writing staff. Lucille was the least generous of all."

"Fortunately, we didn't have to work with Bill Frawley," Weisskopf said. "He was a real bigot."

Schiller summed up their experiences most graphically: "There was a great deal of similarity in writing some of those *I Love Lucy* episodes with sexual intercourse. You were never certain you were going to get it up."

After the departure of Lucille's writing team, her Nielsen rating dropped to eighth position. When her show had premiered, she was in a third-place tie with *Bonanza.*

Let's Tell It to Lucy, Lucille's 1964 radio talk show, "was pretty vanilla," she claimed. "I wanted to ask provocative questions, but wasn't allowed. When Doris Day came on, I itched to grill her about her affairs with Jack Carson, Tyrone Power, and Ronald Reagan, who wanted to marry her before he made Nancy pregnant."

"I also wanted to ask her about her affairs with black men like basketball player Elgin Baylor of the L.A. Lakers and the lead singer of *Sly and the Family Stone.*

***

As if Lucille weren't busy enough as a performer and as president of Desilu, in 1964, she signed to host a daily radio talk show for CBS entitled *Let's Tell It to Lucy.* Gary Morton was the producer, lining up interviews with famous guests who included Danny Kaye, Dean Martin (whom Morton suspected of having once had an affair with his wife), Jack Benny, ("a fag, if I ever saw one"), Barbra Streisand, Doris Day, Carol Burnett, Bob Hope, Mary Tyler Moore, Andy Griffith, Frank Sinatra, Eva Gabor, and Dick Van Dyck.

Once, Lucille interviewed her son, Desi Jr., and she also "grilled" Vivian Vance and Gale Gordon.

Red Skelton and Agnes Moorehead agreed to come on the show, as did Hedda Hopper. The columnist told Lucille, "I'm the one who usually asks the questions."

Critics attacked them, one of them defining **Dino, Desi, & Billy**, a "boy band" that flourished between 1964 and 1969, as "innocuously bland in the extreme."

Left to right, **Dino Martin** (son of Dean Martin); **Desi Arnaz Jr.**; and **Billy Hinsche**.

Their biggest hit was "I'm a Fool," released in 1965.

Let's Tell It to Lucy was broadcast for only one season, ending in 1965.

The reason Lucille invited Desi Jr. onto her radio show was to publicize the debut of his hot new rock group. Her son was only twelve when he organized a trio known as "Dino, Desi, & Billy." The other members of the threesome included Dino, the thirteen-year-old son of Dean Martin; and aspirant musician Billy Hinsche. Aged fourteen, he was the oldest member of the trio.

After Sinatra first heard them perform, he used his influence to get them an album deal at Reprise Records. The mega hit on their album was "I'm a Fool."

Soon, the trio was making guest appearances on *The Ed Sullivan Show,* and, of course, Dean Martin invited his son and the other two onto his TV show. The trio also went over big at The Hollywood Palace. In very little time, the trio formed their own music publishing company just to deal with songs they had written themselves.

Although the boys were drawing $4,000 for each gig, but when they first started out, "We didn't even make enough for transportation to and from," Desi said.

Lucille let them perform before her live audience as a warm-up before she taped her show. When it came time for payment, she told them her budget wouldn't allow for it.

She also arranged for them to make appearances at the homes of friends at their A-list parties. The millionaire movie hosts were moderately more generous, giving the trio a five-dollar bill, which was to be mutually shared.

Although Lucille had serious fears about Desi Jr.'s entrance into show business, his father was immensely pleased. "I struggled for years to make it as a musician, but Desi Jr. has not only shot to fame, but become a sex symbol, although I could do without that long hair. After every show, girls chase after them. They even get love letters from teenaged boys."

***

After *The Untouchables* faded into TV history, Lucille, as president of Desilu, continued her struggle to launch TV pilots that she believed had potential to morph into hit series. Time after time, she failed to find a producer or sponsor.

Her own producer and director, Jack Donohue, even tried to greenlight *Letters of a Hoofer to His Ma*, but it bombed.

Joan Blondell and Herschel Bernardi plotted *Hooray for Hollywood*, a spoof of the silent screen era, but it, too, failed. Jack Carter's comedy series drew no interest. Singer Gogi Grant's series went the way of her hit song, "Gone With the Summer Wind."

At the August 1964 stockholders' meeting, Lucille spoke triumphantly of almost two dozen pilots in development at Desilu. She predicted that half of them would become big hits—"At least that's what I think."

She cited one of them, *The Green Horns*, as "the most ambitious TV Western ever attempted."

She also revealed that her staff was at work on series that would star such singers as Jane Powell, who was virtually out of work now that the MGM era of musicals had wound down. Another series, at least according to Lucille, might be built around singer Julie London.

"We've been searching for a replacement for *The Untouchables,* and I think we'll hit pay dirt with another taut police drama called *Assignment 100*," she said.

Jess Oppenheimer even returned to his former studio and was welcomed by Lucille, who was forever grateful to him for his success during the creation and early months of Lucy Ricardo. However, this time around, he did not succeed in launching a song-and-dance series, tentatively entitled *Papa G.I.*, for Dan Dailey.

From this "pile of proposed debris," in the words of one stockholder, "only one future series would emerge—-and that was the sci-fi *Star Trek.*"

Candy Moore was Lucy's daughter on *The Lucy Show.*

Many viewers, especially those caught up in the counterculture of the mid-60s penchant for **SEX & DRUGS & ROCK & ROLL**, thought it was annoying and just too, too wholesome.

***

None of the episodes of the third season

(1964-1965) of *The Lucy Show* made the Top Ten list of the series. In retrospect, many, but certainly not all, of her fans considered them a bit lackluster.

Scriptwriter Bob Schiller, who had left the series, put a lot of the blame on the writer who replaced him, Milt Josefsberg. "He was a gag writer, not a comedy plot line scribe," he said.

A New Yorker, Josefsberg had gotten his start writing for Bob Hope's radio program. From there, he later signed on as a writer for *The Jack Benny Program,* also on radio, a position he held for twelve years. He then joined the writing staff of Benny's TV show.

He would not only write for *The Lucy Show,* but for her later series, *Here's Lucy,* too. He also penned scripts for *The Odd Couple* and for *All in the Family.*

Lucy and the Plumber: If your pipes are clogged, who better for **Lucille** to call than **Jack Benny**?

Although in the past they'd had a feud or two, both were professionals and overlooked their former arguments.

According to Benny, "Lucille just had to learn that I was a far more skilled comedian than she was. Bob Hope was also on that show. Without cue cards and joke writers, he would have amounted to nothing."

The new season led off with *Lucy and the Good Skate,* telecast on September 21, 1964. It was a poor choice for a premier. In the plot, Lucy wants to spend more time with her TV daughter Chris (Candy Moore). They both decide to go roller skating, with predictable results and lots of pratfalls.

Moore was later quoted as saying, "It was at this point that our series began to fall apart. Many of the scripts didn't work and were often silly instead of comical, with a few exceptions, but stars were not used, and Lucy appeared with actors the general public had never heard of. The reason they were hired was that they came cheap. She was a real tightwad when it came to money."

Moore was young and rather innocent, and she admitted that she was shocked at Lucille's "foul mouth and dirty jokes. I turned beet red. Not only that, but she was always lecturing me to pick up my tempo."

The first telecast starred Charles Drake. On the big screen, he had starred in supporting roles with such star names as Humphrey Bogart and James Stewart. In 1955, he'd switched to television, starring on such shows as *Robert Montgomery Presents.*

Fearing a drop in her Nielsen ratings, Lucille called on "the big guns," Bob Hope and Jack Benny, and included them as guest stars in the episode airing on September 28, *Lucy and the Plumber.*

The plumber, as it turned out, was a dead ringer for, of all people, Jack Benny.

This was the first show of the season that did not feature Vance, who wanted to spend more time in Connecticut with her fourth husband, John Dodds.

"Jack Benny was his usual comic self," said Jimmy Garrett, cast as Lucy's son. "But Hope skipped the rehearsals, showed up right before shooting, just in time for makeup, and then fled from the studio the moment his scene was over."

In her next episode, *Lucy and Winter Sports* (October 5), her co-star was Keith Andes. As mentioned, he'd been her co-star and off-stage lover during the Broadway production of *Wildcat* in 1960. "As I get older, you get younger. You really keep that body of yours in great shape. No wonder Marilyn Monroe went ape shit over you."

In *Lucy the Camp Cook* (October 28), she and Vance take over the kitchen at a boys' camp, and all but destroy that kitchen.

Harvey Korman played a camp counselor. Lucille had long admired his comedic skills, and she would work with him again.

At the time he co-starred with her, he was appearing on CBS's *The Danny Kaye Show*. Of course, his greater fame would come from his prolonged gig on *The Carol Burnett Show*, which made its TV debut in 1967.

Korman suggested she do a show with his boss, Danny Kaye, and she phoned him and the comedian agreed to be her co-star on the final telecast of the year, December 18. *Lucy Meets Danny Kaye* was one of the better episodes of a dull season. Bob Schiller and Bob Weiskopf were called back to create its script.

Perhaps resenting them for resigning as her writers, she made working with her extremely difficult. Although she ridiculed their script, she starred in it anyway.

Director Jack Donohue often became the victim of Lucille's rage.

Depending on what time of day it was, Lucy could be a holy terror. She

Two views from "**Lucy Meets Danny Kaye**."

Candy Moore, who appeared frequently on screen with Lucille, claimed "Other than Ethel Merman, I never saw Lucille defer to anyone more than she did to Danny Kaye. I think she was a little in awe of him."

"Like hell she was," Kaye claimed when he heard that assessment. "She was always telling me how to pull off a skit, even with a cream pie dumped on my head. I was doing comedy back when she was trying to be a B chorus girl."

once yelled at a New York actor because he was mumbling. "Who in hell do you think you are?" she asked. "Marlon Brando? You're fired! Get your ass out of here!"

She was used to treating underlings like that. But Donohue claimed, "I didn't expect her to treat Danny Kaye like that actor."

She objected to Kaye's last scene with particular venom. "You think that's funny? I do not. I'll act it out for you and show you how it should be done. The way you're doing it, you won't get one laugh."

In anger, he retaliated, snapping at her, "Who in hell do you think you are?"

She shot back, "You're full of shit, that's who I am."

Although they parted in anger, they would later make up.

***

Vance told Lucille she was tired of commuting to Los Angeles from her home in Connecticut, and Lucille had no alternative but to grant her a vacation.

Lucille is depicted above with the veteran, time-tested comedienne **Ann Sothern**, who interacted with her, comedically, to great effect.

Many Lucy fans still wonder why Lucille didn't grab Sothern as a full-time replacement for the increasingly demanding Vivian Vance.

Was Lucille threatened that she might be upstaged?

As Vance's replacement, she chose Ann Sothern, her friend, frenemy, and rival on TV. In *Lucy and the Countess* (aired February 1, 1965), Sothern played the broke and widowed Countess Framboise, who comes to live with Lucy while Vance is away. The highlight of the episode is when they attend a wine-tasting party and each become intoxicated. They'd done similar drunken scenes before on TV.

Sothern stayed around to co-star with Lucy in *My Fair Lucy*. Telecast on February 8, 1965, it was a spoof of the 1957 hit Broadway musical (and later, 1964 film) *My Fair Lady*. Lucy played a scrubwoman, Liza Lumpwhomper, who evolves into a glamourous lady.

The least successful of the Ball/Sothern pairings was *Lucy and the Countess Lose Weight* (February 15). Actually, Sothern was beginning to indulge her life-long tendency to gain weight, so she was perfectly cast. Somehow, however, the episode didn't come off.

Sothern was still available for one final show, *Lucy and the Old Mansion* (March 1).

Although Vance returned for an appearance in this episode, she told Lucille that she didn't want to continue as her co-star under her present terms.

"The situation was tense," Sothern said. "Vance and Lucy snapped at each other several times."

Vance had met with her lawyers. She had a lot of demands, mostly a vast increase in salary. She demanded co-billing and wanted to be given more to do in her "sidekick" role. She also asked to direct and produce episodes. Vance confided that one of the reasons she wanted to stay in the East was because she learned that her husband, John Dodds, was having sex with men whenever she was away in California.

Lucille believed at the time that she could not afford Vance's demands and rejected them.

When Sothern learned of Vance's imminent departure, she pressured Lucille to allow her to take over the role. After thinking it over, Lucille turned her down.

Joan Blondell learned that Vance's slot might be available, and although she promoted herself, she, too, was rejected.

"Blondell is a fine actress, and I've worked in the past with her and would again in our future. But there is just no chemistry between us," Lucille said.

In another episode, *Lucy and Arthur Godfrey* (March 8), Lucy and Vance, according to the plot, travel to Virginia to meet "The Old Redhead."

In the 1950s, Godfrey had been one of the biggest stars on television. By mid-60s, however, he had greatly curtailed his schedule.

Both Vance and Lucille had heard terrible stories about him in which he'd been accused of everything from sexual harassment to anti-Semitism. But Lucille liked him and found him easy to work with.

The last show of the season was a sad event. *Lucy and the Disc Jockey* was telecast on April 12, 1965. It was noteworthy for its farewell appearances by some of the regulars on the show, including Vance herself.

Author Audrey Kuperberg wrote, "The truth of the Vance-Ball relationship was not one of dominance and subservice. Nor was it one of bosom-buddy equality. The true nature of their friendship lies somewhere in between. Lucy could be a stern taskmaster, for sure, but her fondness and respect for Vance was genuine."

The scriptwriter, Bob Weisskopf, claimed, "Lucy was a bitch to get along with, and she and Vance often had arguments over scripts. But behind the surface, they were true friends."

After their most recent disagreement faded a bit, Vance would return to Los Angeles at least three more times for appearances on *The Lucy Show*.

It was with great regret that Candy Moore (who had played Lucille's daughter, Chris) learned that she'd been written out of future episodes for the coming season. The premise of the show had been reconfigured.

"I had no warning," Moore recalled. "It hit me like a bolt of lightning. I was depressed for weeks."

Ralph Hart, who had played Vance's son, was also disheartened. "Lucy, Viv, and the gang had been like a family to me. It was like my own family was kicking me out of our happy home. I was devastated."

"I love Lucy dearly," said Mary Wickes, her frequent guest star. "But sometimes she could be a bit harsh, even with me. Of the cast and crew, Vance was the one who could stand up to her now that Desi had fled from the scene. I couldn't believe it, but one hot afternoon, I heard Vance tell Lucy, 'You are full of shit.'"

"You can't be sure, but one reason I think Lucy closed her heart was because she never got over the loss of Desi," Wickes claimed. "She seemed to shut down the compassionate side of herself, as if she never wanted to be hurt like that again. In her way, she seemed to love Gary Morton, I guess, but somehow it wasn't the same. Not at all."

After threatening to drop *The Lucy Show* at the end of the 1964-65 season, Lucille finally acquiesced to the demands of CBS. On March 6, she signed a contract for its fourth (1965-66) season. Her production budget would be $90,000 per episode, the highest fee ever paid at the time to produce one half-hour segment.

It was later revealed that it had been Lucille's idea to can Moore. Originally, CBS opposed the move because the young actress was popular with teenagers. As such, she had frequently been featured in magazines geared for the youth market.

"We needed a youthful look to the show," said James Aubrey at CBS. "Teens won't tune in to see some old bags."

When CBS ordered Lucille to retain Moore, she protested that she would "retire" unless Moore was fired.

Only Jimmy Garrett was retained, but he would appear in only two more episodes before he, too, was phased out of the series.

Perhaps the "massacre" of some of the cast members had been motivated by corporate greed: Otto Katz, one of Desilu's vice presidents, said, "If you go into a network with the same series but with a radically different format, the contracts allow for a greater re-negotiation."

"By dropping all of us," Moore explained, "Desilu was able to get a lot more money out of CBS for the continuation of *The Lucy Show*."

***

Celebrity Seer John Cohan was known in the entertainment industry as "The Celebrity Psychic to the Stars." His predictions for the year ahead have appeared annually for many years in Cindy Adams' column in *The New York Post*.

Over the years, many in show-biz have turned to him for insights during their crises and for guidance for their futures. Cohan played an influential role in the lives of Elizabeth Taylor, Inger Stevens, Nicole Brown Simpson, and Sandra Dee, whom he defines as having been "The Love of My Life."

As stated by Danforth Prince, "John is deeply spiritual, he has valuable insights into the agonies of 'the celebrity experience,' and he's an empathetic guiding force for anyone barging a path through the insecurities and doubts of a career in show-biz."

Celebrity Seer John Cohan

In a memoir, Cohan once wrote, "My gift is something that has been with me since I was born. During my adolescence, I spent time and energy ignoring or suppressing my psychic ability, because I didn't know what it was that possessed me. Finally, I grasped hold of it and embraced my talent."

In Beverly Hills, one of Cohan's clients was Mrs. Jack Haley Sr., the former Florence McFadden (1902-1996) of Wilkes-Barre, Pennsylvania.,

In 1921, she'd married "The Tin Man" (Jack Haley Sr.) from *The Wizard of Oz* (1939) starring Judy Garland.

After Haley's death in 1979, and with money he'd left her, she opened a chic beauty salon. Several highly visible film stars (including Lana Turner and Susan Hayward) were among her clients.

The couple produced a son, Jack Haley Jr., in 1933. He became a successful film producer and married Liza Minnelli as part of a troubled union that lasted from 1974 to 1979.

Cohan had once befriended Judy Garland, perhaps the most deeply disturbed client he ever advised. Many of his insights and revelations have been published in *Catch a Falling Star*, an overview of his life as a psychic to show-biz celebrities.

He frequently warned his friends and clients to expect disappointment in marriage and love and the importance of not becoming bitter and disillusioned.

Advice from the Celebrity Seer? "I've been disappointed but never pessimistic. True love is the one infallible shield against all the ugly and harmful things in the world. Once you find it, hold onto it and cherish it carefully, forever."

It was through Florence Haley that Cohan met her neighbor, Lucille Ball. After he made the mistake of calling her "Lucy," she told him, "It's either Lucille or Miss Ball. Don't call me 'Lucy.'"

"Even though she'd divorced him, Desi remained her "one and only" even after her marriage to Gary Morton," Cohan said.

"There came a time I could no longer tolerate Desi's philandering," Lucille said. "Perhaps the end came one afternoon when I wasn't feeling well. I left the studio at two o'clock and drove myself home. When I entered the house, it was quiet, but suddenly, I heard noises coming from a bedroom upstairs, and I went to investigate. I opened the door to catch Desi in bed with two hookers, both of them sleazy-looking. I kicked him out of our home, where I was trying to raise two kids. After that, he moved into the guest house in back."

"Since we were parents, I did meet with him on occasion, and for a while, we both had to make business decisions for Desilu."

"There was occasional talk of getting together again, but it came to nothing," Lucille said. "I knew in my heart that he wouldn't give up his womanizing until he could no longer get a rise out of what he nicknamed his 'Cuban salami.'"

"His glory days were over," she continued. "In his office at Desilu, he'd started drinking at 10AM. That was the martini hour, an hour that continued for most of the rest of the day."

She became rather candid about her marriage to Gary Morton, admitting, "It is one of convenience. He is at my beck and call, and he's a good man. But after three months of marriage, I moved him into an adjoining bedroom because I wanted to be alone. My secret reason was that I didn't want him to see what I looked like in the morning without my makeup. Cameramen had to film me in soft focus. For so-called close-ups, I demanded to be shot from the waist up, no more full-face closeups."

Even though Lucille eventually designated Morton as Vice President of Desilu, Cohan also learned that she would still, on occasion, treat him like an errand boy. However, if a photographer or a member of the press was present, she would hug and kiss her husband.

Even after Desi sold his Desilu stock to Lucille, he would sometimes show up at the studio to watch their kids, Desi Jr. and Lucie perform in an episode.

One afternoon, when Lucille was behaving autocratically, perhaps in a style inspired by Erich Von Stroheim, Desi made a private remark to Desilu director Maury Thompson. "Lucy has become as tough as a ten-minute hard-boiled egg."

***

With some reluctance and after a dragged-out delay, Lucille signed for the fourth (1965-1966) season of *The Lucy Show*. In this new plot, she had moved from Danfield, Connecticut to Hollywood.

Her trust fund has been transferred to the Westland Bank, where *'lo and behold*, in the oddest coincidence, the tight-fisted Mr. Mooney (Gale Gordon) is once again in charge of her account.

Although as part of its filming, she'd be reunited with some familiar faces, a whole new cast of characters, including Joan Crawford, would enter her life.

She'd also become entangled in the lives of two male performers whose personalities she later defined as "twisted."

The Lucy Show, in which **Lucille and Vance** still showed flashes of comedic skill, perhaps genius, albeit, one thinks, with increasing difficulty. Here's a scene from *Lucy and Viv Put in a Shower*

CHAPTER FOUR

THE LUCY SHOW (1962-68)

How Was Lucille's Performance as a Hollywood Mogul and Studio Honcho?

Answer: "Hit and Miss"
(aka, Sometimes Successful, Sometimes Not)

As the fame of Lucille Ball spread around the world, more and more people began commenting on her physical appearance, her style and stamina, on her fashion sense and grooming, and her ability as an executive.

Author Ron Alexander asserted that Lucille "has the talent of a clown and the steel trap mind of a tycoon."

As her age advanced and as the years moved on, she relied more and more on makeup artist Hal King, who employed surgical tape and elastic foundations to simulate the effects of a face-lift.

Earl Blackwell Jr., notorious for his bitchy evaluations of star wardrobes, continued to include Lucille on his lists of the worst-dressed women in Hollywood. He announced to the press, "In spite of her great comedy flair, offstage, Lucille is a clown caricaturing an actress who borrowed her wardrobe from the studio costume department. She is a Halloween trick without the treat. Lucy, dear, shoulder pads went out with the Black Bottom."

[Editor's note: Popular during the Jazz Age, and danced solo or by couples, the Black Bottom originated among African Americans in the rural South before becoming a national craze in the 1920s.]

After Vivian Vance left *The Lucy Show,* Lucille hesitated to sign for its Second (1963-64) Season. Desi and William Frawley had long ago departed, leaving Lucille alone on the stage. Fearing that she might not be able to carry the show by herself, she urgently needed a replacement for Vance. During her search for one, she developed a lot of oddball casting ideas, including using her children and even her mother DeDe.

Director Maury Thompson was with Lucille and her mother when the offer was presented to DeDe. "Fuck that!" the older woman said. "I have no desire to perform in this piece of shit. Count me out, kiddo!"

Thompson later said, "at last I know where Lucille got her foul mouth."

Around this time, Lucille also contemplated a return to the big screen. She wanted to be cast in the title role of the screen adaptation of the long-running Broadway play, *Hello, Dolly!*, which had been such a hit for Carol Channing.

Fox had already purchased the screen rights. Although Channing herself desperately wanted to reprise her iconic role, other candidates being considered by Fox for the role of Dolly Levi included Doris Day, Shirley MacLaine, Julie Andrews, and Elizabeth Taylor. All of them lost to Barbra Streisand, who really was too young for the part of the matchmaker.

Is it Lucille? NO! It's **STREISAND**, acting and singing up a storm in the movie role (Dolly Levi in *Hello, Dolly!)* for which Lucille was considered, and for which Carol Channing would have killed for.

***

Around the same time, Lucille also began maneuvering for yet another highly publicized feature film role that eventually eluded her.

Like every other actress in Hollywood, Lucille read one of the first copies printed of Jacqueline Susann's sensational and controversial novel, *Valley of the Dolls*.

In 1966, film rights for this bestseller were purchased by Fox for adaptation into a movie.

Lucille was fascinated to read Susann's descriptions of her novel's fading diva, Helen Lawson. [*It was widely suggested that Susann drew upon the personal histories of Judy Garland and Ethel Merman, and on a few of her own personality traits, too, during her creation of the very flamboyant and very unstable Helen Lawson.*]

Lucille lost out on the movie adaptation of *Hello, Dolly!*. However, she gave her own impersonation of Dolly Levi in *Lucy and the Undercover Agent*, an episode of *The Lucy Show* that was telecast in November of 1966. She even sang a few bars from this hit Broadway musical.

A miffed Carol Channing told the press, "Good try, Lucy, but you bombed, kid."

Everybody in show biz in those days either returned Lucille's calls or agreed to meet with her. Keenly aware that a portrayal of Helen Lawson might be a superb dramatic device for her, Lucille inaugurated a dialogue about it with Fox executives, who told her, "If you want the role, it's yours."

However, after discussing it with Gary Morton and considering her overloaded schedule, she withdrew.

She soon read in *Variety* that the role of the demented diva had been assigned to Judy Garland, who, as noted above, had been one of Susann's main inspirations for the character.

[*Ethel Merman was furious, knowing that much of her personality had been funneled into the Lawson role, too. She phoned Lucille, admitting the truth, "Jacqueline and I used to be lovers. She's just doing this to get back at me for dumping her. I'm glad you're not going to play Helen Lawson."*]

As fans of Judy Garland learned at the time, Garland, after being awarded the part, screwed it up in ways that made tabloid fodder for days. After frequent no-shows and after consistently arriving late and in many cases, emotionally sloppy and heavily drugged, she was fired.

Eventually, the role was assigned to Susan Hayward, who delivered—efficiently and on time—her usual brilliant performance. Critics later agreed that the role of the "coming unglued" Helen Lawson was far better suited to her than to either Lucille or Garland.

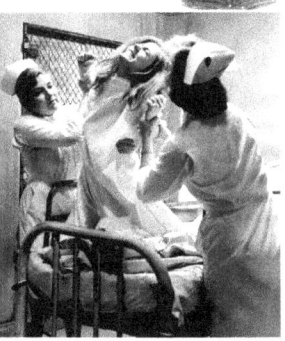

Jacqueline Susann (top photo) toured America to promote her controversial (some said "sleazy") bestseller, *Valley of the Dolls*.

In its film adaptation, the hysterically disturbed character played by **Patty Duke** (lower photo) is restrained by psychiatric nurses

***

In 1965, CBS began to film *The Lucy Show* in color. At last, fans could see Lucille's tango red hair. "I was afraid I'd run out of henna, thinking it might no longer be produced. I stored up enough to take me to the end of the century. Henna was shipped in from Cairo. As rumor had it, Cleopatra used the dye to entice studly Marc Antony into her bedchamber."

Still consumed with doubt about finding a workable replacement for Vance, Lucille made one final call to her long-standing co-star, who was at her home in Connecticut. She demanded (some say "extorted") $500,000 for another season,

In the ladies' toilet of a chic reception, **Patty Duke** (left) and **Susan Hayward** tangle in the most infamous scene in *Valley of the Dolls*. In an act of catty vengeance, Duke has stolen Hayward's wig and is about to flush it down the toilet.

"As an actress, Susan was very humiliated having to do that scene," Duke claimed.

a price Lucille found too steep. Originally, Vance had worked on *I Love Lucy* for $350 a week.

Although Lucille urgently needed a replacement, she had a hard time finding one who was suitable. Ann Sothern, who wanted the role, would make three more guest appearances as the Countess Framboise before Joan Blondell came on for two more appearances. Lucille, however, had already determined that there was no chemistry between them the way it had flowed with Vance.

Finally, Lucille decided her new best friend would be Mary Jane Croft, the frequently cheerful wife of the former Desilu producer, Elliott Lewis. Croft's history with Lucille dated back to her first appearance (in 1954) on *I Love Lucy,* when she'd been cast as the rich, haughty friend of Lucy Ricardo.

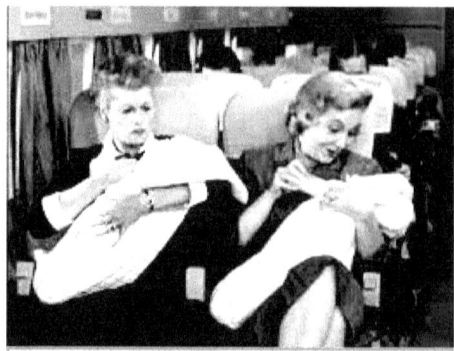

Lucille and **Mary Jane Croft** in "Return Home from Europe." It was telecast on May 14, 1956.

Croft holds a real baby in her arms, but Lucille is cuddling a huge slab of Italian cheese. She has exceeded her luggage allowance, and she heard that infants travel free.

Croft later said, "Lucy broke me up when she took a swig of baby formula."

In 1956, at the finale of *I Love Lucy's* fifth season, Croft returned, playing a bewildered traveler seated next to Lucy on an airplane in *Return Home from Europe.* It marked the last episode that Jess Oppenheimer, the virtual creator of the series, would produce before migrating to CBS's rival studio, NBC.

Croft also appeared in two episodes during the sixth and final season of *I Love Lucy.* In April of 1957, she appeared in *Country Club Dance* and later in *Lucille Raises Tulips,* in which she tangles with a runaway lawn mower.

In desperate need of a character to fill the gap in the void left by Vance's departure, Croft was brought back and re-configured, this time as Lucille's #1 "co-conspirator." It all happened in time for *The Lucy Show's* Fourth (1965-1966) Season. Croft did not, however, get the billing and publicity she wanted or deserved.

By 1966, Lucille was depicted as a single woman living in Hollywood. Characters representing her son and daughter had been written out of the series.

Feeling daring, and bored with the character she'd been reprising again and again, Lucille showed signs of wanting to change her image completely. In an interview with a newsman from the *Hollywood Reporter,* she said, "I want to star as a rich Carole Lombard-like fashion designer."

Of course, no one on her administrative team, or any potential sponsor, agreed to collaborate with such a radical change.

In lieu of the "regulars," she'd been appearing with, Lucille, for her next series of episodes, went after big name stars such as George Burns, John Wayne, Bing Crosby, and Bette Davis. Many would turn her down, but a few accepted her offer.

As the producer of *The Lucy Show*, Tommy Thompson got generally good reviews. Words like "stylish, elegant, adventurous, and meticulous" were used to describe him. Lucille found him bright, loyal, and steadfast. *[A native son of Los Angeles, Thompson was a close friend of the famous director and producer Robert Altman, having worked with him on such movies as* McCabe & Mrs. Miller *(1971), starring Warren Beatty and Julie Christie.]*

Lucille's newest director, Maury Thompson, would in time receive an Emmy for his work on *The Lucy Show*. He had worked his way up the Desilu ladder rung by rung, beginning as a camera coordinator.

He was apprehensive after reading the script, *Lucy at Marineland*, telecast on September 13, 1965. It launched the Fourth Season of *The Lucy Show*. Harvey Korman came back to co-star with her, and she demanded that Desi Jr. and Lucie also be in the cast.

It would require a location shoot at Marineland (aka Marineland of the Pacific, aka Hanna-Barbera's Marineland**)**, an oceanarium on the Palos Verdes Peninsula in southwestern Los Angeles County. Lucille found it uncomfortable, windy and chilly, and she was afraid of water in which she had to wear a wet suit. The 300-pound dolphins also alarmed her, but she was told that they like people, and one of them ended up towing (in a swimming pool) her rubber raft.

***

After Jerry Thorpe, Desilu's vice president in charge of programming, left, Lucille needed a strong business executive to oversee her empire. She turned to Oscar Katz, luring him away from CBS, where he had worked for twenty-six years.

With him at her side, she would, to an increasing degree, represent Desilu at stockholders' meetings.

Among his many decisions in the months to come, Katz would be partially responsible for the launch of the hit series, *Star Trek* and *Mission: Impossible*.

Variety asserted, "The job of Oscar Katz was to restore Desilu's rating as the supplier of network primetime merchandise, the studio's only such series now being the one starring the network's boss."

After Desi left, Lucille had refused to allow any executive to take over his office. *[Luxurious, and for Lucille, loaded with memories, it contained a working fireplace, a piano, a kitchen with a small dining room, a massage room, and an elegant bathroom.]*

On the night *Lucy at Marineland* was telecast, Lucille was seen making a guest star appearance on *The Steve Lawrence Show*. The campy and very gay Charles Nelson Reilly was another guest star.

A scene showing Lucille in the pool at Marineland with the dolphins was shown on *The Steve Lawrence Show*. When it was over, she and Lawrence performed a duet. "Hey, Look Me Over," from her Broadway production of *Wildcat*.

***

On September 19, on camera but from a position in the audience, she was introduced from the stage by the host of *The Ed Sullivan Show*. She had arrived for a performance by her son in his rock group, *Dino, Desi, & Billy*.

She had become increasingly worried about him, having found a stash of marijuana in his room. There were reports that even at his age of twelve, he was drinking, evoking an unflattering (to her, at least), image of his fa-

Working girls: The photo on the lower left shows the hat-wearing gossip mogul, **Hedda Hopper** with **Lucille Ball** at the dedication ceremony for the NY World's Fair. They're emulating the "palm prints in wet cement" rituals that were then in vogue in front of Hollywood's Grauman's Chinese Theater.

The photo on the lower right shows **Lucille** *oooooh-ing* and *ahhhhhh-ing* beside a scaled-down model of the World's Fair's **Unisphere**, a then-futuristic commemoration of the metallurigical skills of U.S. Steel.

ther.

She also suspected that he indulged in recreational "pill popping" like some of the characters in Jacqueline Susann's *Valley of the Dolls*.

She later made an enigmatic remark she never explained: "By the time Desi Jr. turned nine, he was thirty-six years old."

After her sighting at the taping of *The Ed Sullivan Show,* as she was exiting from the theater, a reporter asked her if she were going to use her son's trio on her own show. "I can't afford them. I pay only $400, but they want $4,000 for an appearance."

***

Despite the blazing heat of August 31, 1964, Lucille and Morton flew to Manhattan to celebrate "Lucy Day" at the World's Fair in Flushing Meadows, Queens.

"The whole town turned out to greet me," she recalled. "Only Elvis drew a bigger crowd.":

At the time, she was near one of the peaks of her popularity, her *Lucy Show* being telecast in forty-four countries.

The gossip columnist Hedda Hopper had remained supportive of Lucille since her early film career, and she flew East with her and Gary Morton to record the event.

When Lucille, that same summer, faced another stockholder's meeting, she dreaded it, since all of her projected TV pilots had bombed. It was reported to stockholders that the profit for Desilu for the past year was only $455,000.

From the audience, a stockholder, John Gilbert *[no relation to the silent screen star of the 1920s]* protested, objecting that her annual compensation of $500,000 (for her role as president of Desilu and for her role as its most visible TV entertainer) should be slashed to $75,000 annually.

A fistfight broke out between Gilbert and a security guard. Gilbert's glasses were broken when someone stepped on them. Finally, order was restored.

Following a report that the price of Desilu stock had plunged from a high of $29 a share to $7, Lucille rose to put a optimistic spin on the studio's future.

In front of the stockholders, she delivered high hopes for an upcoming pilot about a series entitled, *My Son, the Doctor.*

She was also optimistic about another projected series, *My Lucky Penny,* about two working wives trying to put their husbands through dental college. It had already been cast with Brenda Vaccaro, Joel Gray, and Richard Benjamin.

All of these pilots would bite the dust, as would *Frank Merriwell,* another series based on dime novels from 1900. She'd already cast that one with Beau Bridges and Tisha Sterling, the daughter of Ann Sothern.

When that series, like all the others, found no sponsor, Lucille called Sothern. "You break the bad news to your daughter. I can't do it."

Yet another projected series, *The Good Old Days,* also defined its backdrop as the beginning of the 20th Century. But it, too, found no sponsor.

Based to some degree on all these business failures, Lucille entered a period of depression.

There was a rescue on the way: It came from Outer Space and was entitled *Star Trek.*

***

To save Desilu, if for no other reason, as part of a deal totaling $12 million, Lucille agreed to sign on with CBS for the Fifth (1966-1967) Season of *The Lucy Show.* The deal guaranteed $90,000 for the production of each episode, and granted ownership to Desilu of all re-runs.

Then, in spite of all those failed pilots, CBS allocated $650,000 to film further projected pilots. If these films also failed, CBS planned to broadcast them as summer re-runs.

In the meantime, Lucille had to star in all those episodes remaining unfilmed and unfinished from the Fourth Season.

Lucy and the Golden Greek, telecast on September 20, 1965, is notable in that Mary Jane Croft replaced Vivian Vance as Lucy's next door neighbor, Mary Jane Lewis. *[The "Lewis" derived from Croft's status as the real-life wife of former* The Lucy Show *producer Elliott Lewis.]*

Lucy arranges a blind date for Mary Jane and when the candidate arrives to pick her up for dinner at a Greek Restaurant, he is very very shy and much shorter than she is. But when he hears musicians playing the *bouzouki* music of his native land, he undergoes a radical personality change and becomes a tiger hell-bent on pursuing and seducing her.

Jimmy Garrett, who played Lucille's son on *The Lucy Show,* evaluated how Lucy emoted with her newest co-star, Mary Jane Croft. He delivered a scathing verdict: "No one can replace Vivian Vance, and the show suffers from her disappearance."

A week later, America got to see Lucille emote in *Lucy in the Music World.* That brought her into the orbit of her guest star, the composer, actor, and author Mel Tormé, nicknamed "The Velvet Fog."

Decades previous to that, after his appearance with Frank Sinatra in the Big Band musical film *Higher and Higher* (1944), Tormé became a teen idol. As a solo singer for Decca, he sustained success with such hits as "Careless Hands." His recording of "Blue Moon" became his signature song.

Lucille had watched every telecast she could when Tormé appeared as a regular on CBS's *The Judy Garland Show* (1963-64). In the aftermath of many wrenching arguments and disputes, Garland fired him.

In episode 87 of *The Lucy Show,* Lucille is working for the president of a record company. Tormé, her neighbor, is an aspirant songwriter, and she schemes to get his career launched. They went over so well together that she would invite him back later on.

For the two episodes that followed, Joan Blondell, who had desperately wanted to permanently replace Vance, as mentioned, was hired. The first, release on October 18, was entitled *Lucy and the Stunt Man*. In it, Lucy tries to fix her up with studly Keith Andes, a man who had sustained a friendship with her since they'd co-starred together on Broadway in *Wildcat*.

It was said that Lucille interpreted Blondell as too aggressive in trying to extract commitments, but in spite of her criticisms, they managed to get through the episode together with friction but not all-out war.

In *The Lucy Show's* next episode, *Lucy and the Stunt Man* (telecast October 18), Blondell returned to the series. In this episode, Blondell has a boyfriend who is a stuntman. Lucy replaces the injured man and saves the day by performing (with disastrous but occasionally comic results) his dangerous stunts.

All did not end happily for the two female leads. At the end of Blondell's big scene, Lucy confronted her. "So you think you know how to do comedy?" she asked. "You didn't make one of your lines the least bit funny."

"That's because your writers only fed me straight lines to deliver to you," Blondell protested.

At this point, Lucille mockingly mimed the act of pulling the "flush" chain of an old-fashioned toilet and imitated the sound of flushing.

"Why are you doing that?" Blondell asked.

"Because you stink and I'm flushing it."

"Fuck you, Lucille Ball!" Blondell shouted at her before storming off the set, never to return.

Later, members of that day's (live) audience spoke to the press, relaying what had happened: "We were stunned," said a fan who had driven up from San Diego.

In the next episode, *Lucy and the Countess Have a Horse Guest* (October 25), she re-teamed with Ann Sothern. In this sequence, the Countess Framboise (who is broke) arrives on Lucy's doorstep with "tons" of luggage but no money. Her only asset is a pregnant racehorse. She's hoping that Lucy's boss, the fussy bank manager, Mr. Mooney (Gale Gordon), will finance the animal's care and training.

For sentimental reasons, Lucille brought back William Frawley, casting him as a horse trainer, even though she knew he was in a weakened condition. At the end of his brief cameo, she hugged and kissed him goodbye.

Frawley's last physical exam was conducted in the office of a "Dr. Gerson." He was brought there by his friend, John Stephens. After the checkup, Stephens conferred with the doctor.

"Frawley should have died a year ago," his physician said. "He's living

A rare photo of **William Frawley** and **Vivian Vance** taken from off the film set, where they actually appear to like one another.

Privately, she called him "the old goat," and he referred to her as "the fat old bag."

on borrowed time. Make that borrowed minutes."

In the months ahead, his health went into serious decline.

On March 5, after watching a film, Frawley and his nurse were walking slowly along Hollywood Boulevard. Suddenly, he experienced a seizure and collapsed onto the street. A doorman and another man helped carry him into the lobby of the Roosevelt Hotel. A doctor was summoned, but by the time he reached Frawley, he was dead. His fatal heart attack occurred just five days after his 79th birthday.

At his funeral, Fred MacMurray was one of the pallbearers. [*Frawley had co-starred with him on his hit TV series*, My Three Sons. *Illness had forced him out of the series.*] Joining MacMurray as a pallbearer was Desi.

Lucille was greatly saddened by the news. She told the press, "He was one of the great character actors of all time. Those of us who knew him and loved him will miss him."

Desi took out a full page in the *Hollywood Reporter,* complete with a photo of Frawley as Fred Mertz. His exit line was "BUENOS NOCHES AMIGO!"

Although not known to fans at the time, Vance and Frawley had loudly and vocally detested each other since they'd first met. But when asked to comment on his death by a reporter, Vance said, "There's a great big amusing light going out in this world tonight."

It was later revealed that at the time of his death, the value of Frawley's estate totaled $92,000.

***

The November 1965 lineup of *The Lucy Show* began unsuccessfully with the telecast of the badly titled *Lucy Helps Danny Thomas.*

Maury Thompson, its director, said that each of the episode's stars (Lucille and Danny Thomas) competed in directing it themselves. "Those two forces of nature were in constant conflict. I was caught between two powerful egos."

Lucille falls into the muscular arms of **Clint Walker**, cast as a construction worker. "Apparently, I was her kind of man. She liked 'em big and strong. I also had done a show with Jack Benny. He, too, liked 'em big and strong."

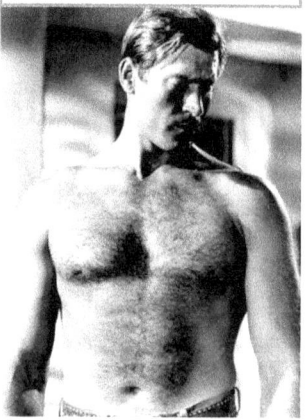

Actor **Clint Walker** was known for his spectacularly photogenic physique. He stood six feet, six inches, with a 45-inch chest and a 32-inch waist. But his proudest measurement, according to his gay agent, Henry Willson, was 10 1/2 inches.

Its unfunny plot was flat and not believable. Although Lucille herself was deep into middle age, it called for the character she played to audition for a role in a lineup of chorus girls, beating out younger, more beautiful dancers.

A week later, *Lucy Helps the Countess* reunited her with Ann Sothern for a reprise of an already-developed theme. In this one, Sothern, Lucy, and Mr. Mooney (Gale Gordon) find themselves locked up for the weekend in an ultra-modern apartment. Among their deprivations is a total lack of food.

The pace picked up by November 15 in *Lucy and the Sleeping Beauty*. Its star was Clint Walker cast as a very appealing construction worker. According to Thomas, she was in awe of this powerfully built former U.S. Merchant Marine.

Then his agent, Henry Willson, arrived to invite his client and Lucille out to lunch. Flamboyantly gay and very campy, he was the most notorious actor's agent in Hollywood. Known as "the man who created Rock Hudson," Willson also represented Nick Adams, Robert Wagner, Guy Madison, Tab Hunter, Troy Donahue, Mike Connors, Rory Calhoun, John Derek, and those screen beauties Lana Turner and Rhonda Fleming.

In the middle of lunch, after Walker headed for the men's room, he was trailed by three or four guys, who all seemed compelled to urinate at the same time.

Willson turned to Lucille and said, "I can fix you up. I have personal knowledge that Clint is big all over."

"I'll take a rain check," she responded.

***

The growing popularity of the James Bond movies, especially those starring 007 Sean Connery, led to a number of satires, spoofs, and spinoffs.

Screenwriter Bob O'Brien devised one of them, *Lucy the Undercover Agent*, telecast on November 22, 1965 with guest stars Ann Sothern and Jack Cassidy.

Lucy, with the Countess (Sothern), and with Mr. Mooney (Gordon) view a James Bond movie. Later, in a restaurant, they spot two men who look suspicious, and they determine that they must be spies. They set out to entrap them, leading, as always on an episode of *The Lucy Show*, to disastrous results.

Although Lucille had not been cast as Dolly Levi in the hit Broadway musical, *Hello, Dolly!*, in this episode, she gets to impersonate Carol Channing as she appeared

Looking devilish and handsome, **Jack Cassidy** was married to Shirley Jones. He became the father of two teenage idols, David Cassidy and Shaun Cassidy.

Bisexual, closeted, and suffering from a severe bipolar disorder, he led a scandalous secret life.

in that stage role.

During the filming of the episode, Lucille became intrigued by Jack Cassidy, an actor and singer who excelled in TV, feature films, and on the stage. He had already received multiple Tony Award nominations, as well as a Grammy for his performance in the 1963 Broadway musical *She Loves Me.* He had been married to actress Evelyn Ward, with whom he had a son, David, who became a teen idol.

At the time Lucille met him, Cassidy was wed to singer/actress Shirley Jones. They had three sons, including Shaun Cassidy, who also became a teen idol in the late 1970s.

Jack had the professional *persona* of a witty, urbane, confident egotist with a dramatic flair.

Lucille found him one of the most fascinating men she'd ever met. She denied rumors of any romantic involvement, claiming instead, "No one amuses me more than Jack. Whatever my cares and woes, he makes me forget them."

Even though married, he was carrying on numerous affairs, mostly with men, as he was well-known as a bisexual.

She continued to see him over a number of years, noting with alarm that his behavior was becoming more and more erratic.

He once described his long, perhaps sadistic sexual involvement with composer Cole Porter, who was disabled and confined to a wheelchair. According to Cassidy, "I strip down and sit in an armchair on one side of his living room, and he is on the other. My ritual is that I make him crawl all the way across his carpet to get to the goodies."

It was later determined that Jack suffered from alcoholism and a severe case of bipolar disorder. Neighbors reported that before watering his front lawn, he sometime stripped buck-naked. Shirley Jones later asserted that he had told her that he was convinced that he had been Jesus Christ in a previous life.

By 1976, he was living alone in a penthouse in West Hollywood. On the night of December 11, 1964 he was seen drinking with actress Nanette Fabray. Earlier in the evening, he'd phoned Lucille and asked her to join him at a night club, telling her he had "something really vital to talk over with her." Because she was hosting a dinner party at the time, she declined. However, she invited him to join her guests, and he declined.

In the pre-dawn hours, he fell asleep on his Naugahyde sofa, dropping a cigarette which ignited the couch. Flames spread quickly through his apartment. By the time the fire department arrived, all that was left was a burnt-out ruin and a smoking, charred corpse.

Lucille later regretted that she had not met with him that night. "I might have saved him," she said. "I'll go to my grave wondering what he had to tell me that was so vital."

***

Milton Berle had a reunion with Lucille when he agreed to star with her in a November 6, 1965 episode, *Lucy Saves Milton Berle.* Alongside Mary

Jane Croft and Gale Gordon as Mr. Mooney, her character agreed to volunteer in a soup kitchen. Berle arrives incognito, wanting to learn the ropes for his performance in a new movie. The trio thinks Berle is his impoverished brother, "Soup Kitchen Arthur."

On writer Mart Martin's list of Hollywood seductions, Lucille is at the top of the list of Berle's conquests. *[The array of stars he seduced during the course of his eventful career includes Theda Bara, the original screen vamp, and Wendy Barrie, Linda Darnell, Veronica Lake, Audrey Meadows, Ann Sheridan, and Marilyn Monroe.]*

Lucille had met Berle in the late 1930s and had begun an affair with him then. When he wasn't with her, Berle sometimes joined Desi to sample the wares at Polly Adler's notorious bordello in Manhattan. Wearing drag, he had appeared with Desi and her on an episode of *I Love Lucy*. He said, "My drag is too gay to be gay."

Betty Grable asserted, "They say the two best-hung men in Hollywood are Forrest Tucker and Milton Berle. What a shame. It's never the handsome ones. The bigger they are, the homelier."

"I might have married **Milton Berle** back in the late 1930s, but his overprotective mother thought I was white trash," Lucille claimed.

"The only thing bigger than Uncle Miltie's age was his legendary prick. Marilyn Monroe told me it was the biggest she'd ever seen."

Berle was known in television circles in the early 1950s as "Uncle Miltie" or "Mr. Television." He told Lucille that he had first appeared on TV in 1929, performing in a closed-circuit experimental broadcast.

"I'm known for telling some off-color jokes," Lucille said, "but Berle had me beat. His jokes were the filthiest I've ever heard."

Two nights after her telecast with Berle, she joined Danny Thomas to perform skits on *The Wonderful World of Burlesque*. *[She and Thomas had made up after they'd conflicted on an episode of* The Lucy Show. *She was appearing on his special as a "payback" for his agreeing to be a guest on her show. The cast also included Jerry Lewis, Shirley Jones (she and Lucille talked about Jack Cassidy), Jimmy Durante, and Sheldon Leonard.]*

Dressed as a stripper, Lucille appears to be singing a rendition of "Poor Butterfly." Actually, her voice was dubbed by Carole Cook.

Later, she joined Lewis and Thomas in a spoof of *White Cargo* (1942), that movie in which Hedy Lamarr, then voted as the most beautiful woman in the world, had starred as a seductive native girl with a penchant for being banished from missionary circles for her "amoral influence." In that film, Lamarr uttered her most iconic line, "I am Tandellayo."

***

The 97th episode of the *The Lucy Show*, entitled *Lucy the Choirmaster*, was telecast on October 13, 1966. Lucille's character invited students at her son's military academy to sing carols at the bank. The episode is notable in that it marks the final appearance of Jimmy Garrett, who had played her son in so many other episodes.

"I was heartbroken that I had been written out of the show," the boy said. "No more would I be Jerry Carmichael, son of Lucy. Standing outside the gate of Desilu, I looked back wondering where to go from here," Garrett said. "I feared I'd never get another gig in show business. Lucy could at least have told me goodbye and wished me luck."

The year of 1965 came to an end with *Lucy Discovers Wayne Newton* (December 27), in which she had allowed Gary Morton to co-star. It depicted how Lucy discovers a young singer and then tries to help him by arranging a distribution commitment from "Mr. Morton" (his real name is used), the president of a recording studio.

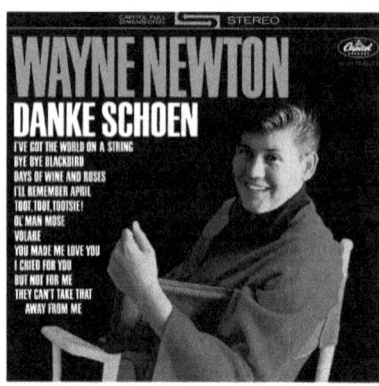

Lucille gave **Wayne Newton**'s musical career a big boost when she cast him on *The Lucy Show* in December of 1965. It became one of the best episodes of that season.

Newton is seen here on the cover of his most popular album, *Danke Schoen*.

Newton later claimed that this show was partially responsible for "sending me up the ladder to stardom."

A son of Virginia, Newton had a father who was half Powhatan (an alliance of Algonquian-speaking American Indians living in the Tidewater region of Virginia when English settlers landed at Jamestown in 1607), and a mother who was half Cherokee.

Two years before meeting Lucille, he had recorded his big hit, "Danke Schoen." Actually, Lucille preferred his other hit, "Red Roses for a Blue Lady."

In time, Newton would evolve into one of the best-known entertainers in Las Vegas, where he was nicknamed "The Midnight Idol," "Mr. Las Vegas," and "Mr. Entertainment."

In later years, he was plagued with more lawsuits and financial problems than any entertainer in Las Vegas history. In 1992, he filed for bankruptcy after running up $20 million in debt.

***

Lucille knew that if Desilu were to survive as a business entity, it would need more than her faltering TV series, *The Lucy Show,* to keep it solvent. Costs were drastically increasing year by year, and competition was keen.

She called in Oscar Katz, Desilu's Chief in charge of Production, and his associate, Herb Salow, and confronted them with a daunting challenge. She wanted them to develop scripts for pilots of gestating TV series that might morph into hits.

Within days, they turned to Gene Roddenberry, mostly known for his television series, *Have Gun, Will Travel.*

At the time, as a change from the Western theme he was known for, he was working on a sci-fi script entitled *Star Trek,* an adventure into Outer Space. It centered on the crew of the "one day in the distant future" *USS Enterprise.* On board, a brave group of men and women set out on a five-year mission into space, "to go where no man has ever gone before." The time and place would be the year 2260 and the outer fringe of the Milky Way Galaxy.

A son of El Paso, Roddenberry grew up in Los Angeles, where his father had been a police officer. In time, his son, Gene, also joined the force.

At night, he began to write scripts, hoping to sell them to TV producers. Some of his stories appeared on *Have Gun, Will Travel* starring Richard Boone.

By 1964, he was at work on *Star Trek,* which premiered in 1966 and ran for three seasons. Once *Star Trek* went into syndication, it grew in popularity, resulting in a stream of sequels, many of which continued to involve Roddenberry or his estate.

When he died in 1991 at the age of 70, he would be one of the first humans to have his ashes launched into orbit.

Many of her most avid fans never knew that Lucille was behind the launch of *Star Trek.* "If it were not for Lucy, there would be no *Star Trek* today," claimed its developer, Gene Roddenberry.

Lower photo: In their most iconic roles, **William Shatner** was cast as Captain Kirk, with **Leonard Nimoy**, the humorless by-product of a union between a Vulcan and an Earthling, cast as Doctor Spock.

During his first meeting with Lucille, he told her he interpreted *Star Trek* as "an intergalactic version of *Wagon Train,* leading the *Enterprise* crew into exotic locales in Outer Space, many of them on menacing planets."

Originally, the actor Jeffrey Hunter was tapped to play the lead role: Commander of the *Enterprise.* But when production was delayed, he bowed out to accept another film role. The producers then designated a Canadian actor, William Shatner, who was handsome, terse, masculine and ideal as a candidate for a matinee idol.

During its first season, there would be some adjustments in the cast. Actor Leonard Nimoy, with the help of a lot of makeup, would become famous as the unflappable Mr. Spock, a mixed-race Earthling/Vulcan who's challenged and baffled by anything approaching Earthling humor.

George Takei was cast at Lt. Sulu, and DeForest Kelly would play the ship's doctor, Leonard (Bones) McCoy.

Also joining the cast as the ship's communications officer was Nichelle Nichols as Nyote Uhura. The first African American woman to have a key role in a TV series, she made television history when she shared TVs first interracial kiss with Captain Kirk. *[In an early prototype, Uhura was cast as the ship's second in command, but NBC reconsidered, with the belief that that would be far too daring.*

Later, when she considered dropping out of the series, Martin Luther King Jr. phoned her and urged her to stay: "Your role on television means a lot to your brothers and sisters. They are so proud of you. You've become a role model for young black girls. You are an inspiration to future black actors and actresses that in the future we will play much larger roles in the industry. Our day will come."]

Lucille hired Bill Theis, telling him that he not only had to come up with uniforms for the crew aboard the *Enterprise*, but that he'd need to dress the aliens, too: Vulcans, Klingons, Romulans, Tallarites, Andorians, and Gideonites.

When *Star Trek* was first presented to CBS, Lucille's home studio, "the brass" there rejected it. She later learned why: CBS was fashioning its own outer space adventure series, *Lost in Space*, the saga of a family adrift in the galaxy.

NBC eventually agreed to pick up the series, which was regularly featured from 1966 to 1969 in cooperation with the Norway Corporation.

That entity had been established by Gene Roddenberry himself. *[Why he named it after Norway is not known.]*

Desilu needed a partnership because it was severely cash-poor and desperate to replicate some of its previous successes. The billing for the first episodes of *Star Trek* was phrased like this: "A Desilu Production in association with Norway Corporation."

When Desilu and Paramount merged midway through *Star Trek's* Second Season, the billing was changed to "A Paramount Production in Association with Norway Corporation," which is how it remained for the rest of the program's run. In the final accounting, it was resolved that Desilu would produce its Season One and the first half of its Season Two.

When NBC decided to move *Star Trek* to Friday night at 10PM, Roddenberry was furious, since that was considered a "suicide slot" for TV programming. Burned out from his struggles with both the network and the studio, Roddenberry resigned.

Ed Holly, the treasurer of Desilu, urged Lucille to drop the series because of its "excessive" production costs.

She was adamant about keeping the series running. Privately, Holly told Katz, "Lucille Ball was a lady who became a man."

She later heard that comment and told critic Rex Reed, "If I had wanted to be a man, I would have undergone a sex change long ago. I've been in awe of men all my life, inviting them into my board room and into my boudoir. I never wanted to get on the business side of Desilu, but when Desi and I broke up, I found myself in charge. It was one hell of a responsibility I didn't want, but I plan to carry it out to the best of my ability."

The premiere broadcast of *Star Trek* on September 8, 1966 drew mixed reviews and had a poor Nielsen rating. *Variety* predicted that it would be a failure, as "It's an incredible and dreary mess of confusion and complexities." Some critics praised *Star Trek* for its innovations. An early fan was Nelson Rockefeller, the governor of New York.

A survey revealed that its most devoted fans consisted of scientists, museum curators, doctors, psychiatrists, and university professors. Later, it developed a cult following among young people who were nicknamed "Trekkers" or "Trekkies."

After Lucille sold Desilu in 1967, Paramount took over the production of *Star Trek,* and then canceled it after three seasons and 79 episodes.

There was life after death, however. In the 1970s, the series became a hit in syndication and developed an even wider cult following.

In time, it would spawn a franchise consisting of eight TV series and thirteen feature films. Today, it's hailed as one of the most popular and influential TV shows in the history of the medium.

In the years that followed, Lucille's role in the launch of *Star Trek* was respectfully noted. One TV critic wrote, "Were it not for Lucille Ball, there would have been no *Star Trek.*"

***

Beset with business worries, Lucille spent many sleepless nights at her home in Beverly Hills while her husband, Gary Morton, slept peacefully in an adjoining bedroom. She needed rest but didn't want to become a pill-popping addict like Judy Garland frenziedly nearing the end of her career.

As she later revealed, "I had to confront my face every morning in the mirror, and that often was the worst ordeal of the day for me. I obviously was losing the battle of age, as all movie stars do. Let's face it: You can't be twenty-one forever."

"Plastic surgery was not an option for me. Doctors told me my skin was too sensitive for an operation. Otherwise, I would have turned myself over to the beauty butchers."

"I once had my eyes tucked. This is often a rather simple operation. But it took nearly nine months for me to recover, and for my skin to return to normal."

"Red patches of discolored skin remained around my eyes, and they drove my makeup artist, Hal King, crazy. 'Bring on the pancake makeup and lay it on heavy,' I told him."

All this heavy makeup did not go unnoticed by the critics. Harold Klein wrote, "Lucille Ball is desperately trying to look glamourous, which means it takes her at least two hours to make up her face every morning, or so it is rumored. She wears so much make-up she doesn't look real anymore. It's like she's pretending to be a movie star like Ava Gardner and Lana Turner in their heyday and not the Lucy Ricardo we knew yesterday."

There were rewards, or at least a nomination for an Emmy at the 1965 annual ceremony. She was hoping to be named Best Actress in a Comedy Series. However, Mary Tyler Moore won instead for her performance as Laura Petrie in *The Dick Van Dyke Show.*

The Lucy Show was still bringing in money, but she knew she could not coast much longer depending on revenue from that series alone.

Every day at Desilu would be devoted to finding or developing scripts for the shooting of pilots.

Eventually, she turned to another creative project, one being steered by Bruce Geller.

Geller's original title for it was *Briggs Squad,* but he later changed it to *Mission: Impossible.* He later told reporters that he had been inspired by the movie *Topkapi* (1964) about an exotic jewelry heist filmed in Istanbul. It had starred Melina Mercouri and Peter Ustinov.

Original 1966 cast from *Mission: Impossible*, left to right: **Greg Morris** as Barnard "Barney" Collier, **Barbara Bain** as Cinnamon Carter, **Steven Hill** as Dan Briggs, and **Martin Landau** as Rollin Hand.

Mission: Impossible evolved into a cloak-and-dagger espionage thriller TV series chronicling the exploits of secret government agents known as *The Impossible Mission Force (IMF).* As projected, each episode would open with a fast-paced montage played against a background of staccato-sounding theme music by Lala Schifrin.

The star of that series, a handsome, laser-focused rogue named Dan Briggs, would receive instructions for his next life-threatening assignment. Once the pre-recorded instructions were delivered, the audiotape would self-destruct.

The instructions always ended with this sinister disclaimer: "As always, should you or any of your IMF force be caught or killed, the Secretary will disavow any knowledge of your actions."

The small team of secret agents working for the United States would battle the villain of the day, often as part of a covert mission to destroy a despotic dictator or an evil crime lord.

In the beginning, Lucille met daily with the project's creator, Bruce Geller, a New York-born Yale graduate who had majored in psychology.

Instead of going into the field of mental health, he chose to write scripts for television. He met with great success after his early involvements with *Have Gun, Will Travel,* starring Richard Boone. His biggest break came when he was named co-producer of the hit TV series, *Rawhide* (1964-65), starring Eric Fleming and Clint Eastwood.

It was while working on *Rawhide* that Geller devised *Mission: Impossible*. He decided to take it to Desilu, where he met with Lucille, who seemed intrigued with the show's premise.

As it turned out, it was initially financed and filmed at Desilu, which scheduled its television premiere through CBS in September of 1966. First, a pilot had to be scripted and filmed, and a cast chosen before William Paley at CBS finally greenlighted it for an hour-long timeslot every Saturday from 9 to 10PM.

As Lucille was debating her approval of the pilot, she heard the voice of doom from her treasurer, Ed Holly, warning her about the costs. Even though CBS had approved an allotment of money to develop the series, it had become clear that she would have to come up with an extra $65,000 for each episode. "This series could drive Desilu into bankruptcy."

It was pointed out that even though indoor scenes could be shot at Desilu, each episode of Mission: Impossible would require a different physical location. The cast and crew would have to move frequently between them, making costs soar.

Ignoring his advice, she ordered, "Full speed ahead. Let the cameras roll."

Expenses at Desilu were soaring. As such, Lucille faced a hostile audience at its annual gathering of stockholders. One of them, Ralph Charles, publicly defined her as "The Evita Perón of Television."

[That was a reference to the inspirational but spectacularly corrupt Argentine dictator, Eva Perón (1919-1952), wife of that country's military leader, Juan Perón, who dipped heavily into her country's budget to finance Rolls Royces, mink coats, designer gowns, a major-league collection of diamonds and rubies, and frequent young gigolos for sex, even though she got Fernando Lamas and Tyrone Power for free.]

To launch Mission: Impossible as a TV series, both Geller and Lucille made a casting mistake by signing actor Steven Hill for the lead role of Dan Briggs. As a devout Orthodox Jew, he would not/could not work beginning every Friday night until the end of Sabbath on Saturday.

On the set, at least when he wasn't emoting before a camera, Hill organized prayer meetings with the Jewish faithful among the crew. There were many Jews working for Desilu, and Lucille chastised him for distracting workers from their jobs.

Both Geller and Lucille decided to fire him after the First Season was shot. After his dismissal, Hill left Hollywood for an Orthodox Jewish community in Rockland County, north of New York City. *[In 1990, he returned to Hollywood, starring as a district attorney on the TV series, Law & Order.]*

The pilot that launched Mission: Impossible was filmed at St. Mary's College, north of Brentwood Airport. Frank Sinatra lent his private plane to Lucille so she could fly there.

For the second season, she replaced Hill with actor Peter Graves, changing the character's name to Jim Phelps.

The brother of *Gunsmoke* star, James Anress, actor **Peter Graves** finally hit it big when he was cast as Jim Phelps, head of a spy team on the long-running TV series, *Mission: Impossible*.

Before that, in *Beginning of the End* (1957), he had to save the world from giant grasshoppers.

Graves would retain the role of the IMF leader for the remaining six seasons (1967-73) of the original series and return for its 1988-90, two-season revival. The Minnesota-born actor had taken the name of Graves so as not to be confused with his older brother, James Arness, star of the hit TV series, *Gunsmoke*.

After service in the United States Army Air Force during World War II, Graves arrived in Hollywood, where over a period of time he would be cast in some seventy feature films and TV roles.

Much later in his career, he refused to play Jim Phelps in the first feature film (released in 1996, entitled *Mission: Impossible*, and starring Tom Cruise) derived from the TV series because he didn't want to disappoint his many fans. The script called for Phelps' exposure as a traitor and villain. Jon Voight had no such problem about replacing him in the role.

Ohio-born Greg Morris, an African-American, starred throughout the course of the original TV series as Barney Collier, an electronics expert, and he would remain with the series throughout its initial run. In 1996, Morris attended the first installment of the full-length version starring Tom Cruise.

After sitting through half of it, he abruptly exited from the theater, telling a reporter, "Both this movie and Cruise are an abomination. Both are total disasters.:"

Morris died that same year, on August 27 at the age of 62.

Leonard Nimoy was better known as "Mr. Spock" on *Star Trek*. The Bostonian portrayed that character on TV and in the movies for nearly half a century, beginning with its pilot in 1964 and ending with his farewell performance in 2013.

After the original *Star Trek* series, he starred in *Mission: Impossible* for two seasons.

In 2015, an asteroid was named "4864 Nimoy" in his honor.

He told Lucille, "When I started out, everyone mocked the size of my big ears, claiming they were large enough to launch me into Outer Space. I reminded them that Clark Gable in his early days faced the same problem, and he, big ears and all, became the King of Hollywood."

Peter Lupus sauntered onto the set and introduced himself as one of

Years after joining the cast of *Mission: Impossible*, **Greg Morris** modestly claimed that part of the reason he got the job was because he was African-American.

"The word was getting out that it was necessary to cast a black in your TV dramas, perhaps to enhance and expand the viewing audience."

The winner of a "Mr. Hercules" contest, bodybuilder/model **Peter Lupus** also joined the cast of *Mission: Impossible*.

"Because of my willingness to pose for beefcake, I joined the league of actors like Steve Reeves, Sylvester Stallone, and Arnold what's-his-name."

the latest stars who had been cast. Not since Clint Walker had Lucille seen such a powerfully built man: all 6'4" of him. He'd won the body-building titles of "Mr. Indianapolis," "Mr. Indiana," "Mr. Hercules," and "Mr. International Healthy Physique."

He became one of the many bodybuilders to follow in the footsteps of Steve Reeves, "Mr. Body Beautiful" or "Mr. Muscles," who had starred in those "swords-and-sandals" epics of the 1960s.

Right before joining the *Mission: Impossible* cast, Lupus had starred in *Muscle Beach Party* (1964) in which he played "Mr. Galaxy."

In nearly all episodes of *Mission,* he was cast as the strong, silent type. As the series progressed, a decision was made to write him out of the shows. But when an outcry arose from fans, he was reinstated.

In its edition of April 1974, Lupus became one of the first well-known actors to pose full-frontal nude for *Playgirl* magazine, a favorite not just of playgirls, but a host of gay men, too.

In 1970, Lesley Ann Warren, a New Yorker, was brought into the series to portray the character of Dana Lambert. She had made her debut on Broadway in 1963, and two years later, received a lot of critical acclaim for starring in the title role in the TV musical *Cinderella.*

In 1983, she'd be Oscar nominated for Best Supporting Actress in her role of the two-faced floozie girlfriend of James Garner in *Victor, Victoria.* He seems more interested in what appears to be a male in drag., Never fear: It's really Julie Andrews impersonating a man.

After *Star Trek* was launched, Lucille devoted much of her time to *Mission: Impossible,* which got off to a slow start. It didn't really develop a fan base until the second season. *[Many fans didn't know that Desilu produced the First Season for CBS and the first half of Season Two.]*

Ultimately, it would run for seven seasons (1966-73) and be revived in 1988 for two more seasons. It became the sixth-longest-running TV series. *[Despite* Mission's *undeniable success,* Gunsmoke *eventually emerged as the champ in terms of longevity, hanging around for two decades (1955-1975).* **At the end of** Gunsmoke's **run in 1975, a columnist for the** Los Angeles Times **wrote: "Gunsmoke was the dramatization of the American epic legend of the west. Our own** Iliad **and** Odyssey, **created from standard elements of the dime novel and the pulp Western…It was ever the stuff of legend."]**

For Bruce Geller, *Mission: Impossible* won an Emmy for him as producer and another Emmy for Outstanding Writing Achievement. He could have lived for many decades in luxury from royalties pouring in, but on May 11, 1978, he died at the age of 47 in an airplane crash at Santa Barbara.

The *Mission: Impossible* theme morphed into the greatest career event in the life of Tom Cruise. In 1996, when many male movie stars his age were finding roles more scarce, he launched a series of feature films, casting himself as agent Ethan Hunt.

As of 2021, that series of films was still flourishing.

***

Star Trek and *Mission: Impossible* were only some of the distractions that occupied Lucille's time and energy. Under her direction, Desilu still rented out studio space for the filming of other productions such as *Batman* and *Lassie*.

"We were all part of one family. Different casts wandered around our lots. When Lassie spotted 'Vulcans' and 'Klingons,' and refugees from Outer Space in *Star Trek*, that dog went after them for the kill."

With fitful and sometimes unsuccessful results, knowing she had to increase revenue, Lucille struggled to finance pilots that might have launched other TV series. For a period, at least, she wanted scripts for a possible sitcom that would have starred comedian Shelley Berman.

As part of another experimental venture, she was particularly hopeful for a Western series starring Robert Lansing, hoping it might compete successfully with *Rawhide* or *Have Gun, Will Travel*.

Robert Lansing is celebrated on the cover of *TV Guide* for his involvement in *Twelve O'Clock High*, a series that Lucille wished Desilu had developed.

[*She had seen Lansing on television, performing in three seasons of NBC's Twelve O'Clock High beginning in 1964. In this military drama about American bomber pilots during World War II, he'd been cast as Brigadier General Frank Savage. "We didn't sell it," Lucille said, "but my faith in Lansing proved on target when he later appeared in a Western, cast as a bounty hunter on* Gunsmoke.*"]*

She also endorsed, without success, a sitcom about present-day Gypsies and an Irish schoolmarm that would have starred Gary Marshall and Jerry Belson.

Yet another negative outcome derived from the failure of Lucille's *April Savage*, a projected Western series by Gene Roddenberry of *Star Trek* fame. ABC had initially showed interest in broadcasting it.

Robert Lansing was set to star in its title role, playing a homesteader whose wife, daughter, and son were killed by a gang of renegades in 1871, one of whom was his own brother. But to Lucille's frustration and rage, about a week before she'd been scheduled to sign a contract, ABC abruptly canceled the series.

This string of frustrations and failures continued. Oscar Katz had nothing but bad news for her. Of the nearly two dozen Desilu-financed pilots, William Paley at CBS only okayed *Star Trek* and *Mission: Impossible*.

With all those failures, it appeared that Katz's days at Desilu were nearing an end. He was replaced by his assistant, Herbert Frank Solow, born into a Jewish family in New York.

In addition to being a TV producer, he also was a screenwriter and a former talent agent.

Katz later said, "I was brought in at a bad time. Desilu's revenue was down, and the big studios were starting to produce their own TV shows. Desilu faced severe competition. More and more independent and under-financed 'ma and pa' studios were going out of business."

Initially, Katz's judgment was sound when he helped launch *Star Trek* and *Mission: Impossible*, but he was gone before those TV series really started to "haul in the bucks" (Lucille's words).

By 1967, Lucille, thanks in part to a lot of help from Katz and others, did succeed with her own impossible mission: She had made Desilu profitable once again.

It was at this time that she began to think of selling it. But who would buy it?

***

Still a money-maker, *The Lucy Show* moved into January of 1966, eventually to conclude its Fourth Season. Alarmed by Nielsen polls that revealed that her ratings had slipped, she suggested to her director Maury Thompson and other key members of her staff, that "We should cast me with big name guest stars. That'll draw the viewers!"

> Lucille claimed that she liked **Art Linkletter** personally and worked smoothly with him. "The problem was, as a co-star, we just didn't click."

To lead off 1966, *Lucy the Rain Goddess* was aired on January 3.

The plot, which was set against a Native American backdrop, was poorly received. Some viewers defined it as "racially insensitive." A tribe believes that Lucy is a rain goddess, and as such, she is pressed into a tribal dance. Two Indian braves were played by Jamie Farr and Alan Reed Jr. *[Reed was the son of the voice of TV's Fred Flintstone. About six years later, Reed and Farr would each become better known for their roles in the TV smash hit, M*A*S*H (1972-1983).]*

Lucille's desire for a big-name guest came true on January 10, 1966 in an episode called *Lucy and Art Linkletter*. Born in Moose Jaw, Saskatchewan, a year after Lucille entered the world, Linkletter had eventually migrated to the United States.

Like Arthur Godfrey, he had evolved into one of the most famous personalities in radio and television. For twenty-five years on CBS radio and television, he was the creative force behind *House Party*. For another nineteen years, he was the host of *People Are Funny* which aired on NBC.

In 1942, he became a naturalized U.S. citizen.

In the plot, Lucille appears a guest on *The Art Linkletter Show*. There, she agrees to keep her mouth shut for twenty-four hours. To ensure that she lives up to her agreement, Helen Cosgrove (Doris Singleton) was cast as her chaperone.

On the set, Singleton and Lucille had a reunion. The New York actress is best remembered for her appearance as Lucy Ricardo's nemesis/frenemy, Carolyn Appleby, in the *I Love Lucy* series of the 1950s.

Her professional relationship actually dated back to 1948, when Singleton had starred in the radio series, *My Favorite Husband* with Lucille and Richard Denning. Singleton's final appearance on *I Love Lucy* was in an episode entitled *Lucy and Superman.* It featured daytime TV's superman, played by George Reeves, who died in June of 1959. *[Debates still rage as to whether the cause of death was murder or a suicide.]*

Singleton later revealed that she had previously been hired as a regular on Lucille's third season of *Here's Lucy.* In 1968, at the last minute, she'd been dumped, as Lucille cast her son and daughter, Desi Jr. and Lucie Arnaz instead. Singleton did, however, appear on *Here's Lucy's* premiere episode (i.e., Season One, Episode One), *Mod, Mod Lucy.*

Also on the Linkletter episode was another New Yorker, Jerome Cowan, a character actor born in 1897, a star of stage, film, and TV. *[Appearing in more than a hundred films, Cowan's classic was as the private eye partner of Sam Spade in* The Maltese Falcon *(1941) starring Humphrey Bogart. Cowan had also starred as Thomas Mara, the hapless district attorney, who had to prosecute Santa Claus in* Miracle on 34th Street *(1941), starring John Payne, Maureen O'Hara, and Edmund Gwenn as St. Nick.]*

Another big name, Mickey Rooney, came Lucille's way when he signed to star in *Lucy Meets Mickey Rooney* (January 24).

Although his once-illustrious career was in deep decline, the pint-sized star had been a Hollywood box-office champ in the late 1930s and early 1940s thanks in part to all those Andy Hardy movies. Lucille had long admired his comedic skills but had never worked with him before.

He arrived for rehearsals a day before the show was scheduled for taping and met with Lucille for lunch. She told him that she had met Tennessee Williams at a party and he'd told her, "Without a doubt, Mickey Rooney is the most talented actor in Hollywood."

"That's good to know," he said. "I didn't know I was that playwright's

In the late 1930s and early 1940s, **Mickey Rooney** and **Judy Garland** co-starred in several Andy Hardy movies, wholesome family fare.

Louis B. Mayer told the actor, "You're Andy Hardy. You're the United States, You're the Stars and Stripes. Behave yourself! You're a symbol!"

Rooney's first wife was sultry **Ava Gardner**, a Tarheel fresh from the hills of North Carolina.

The first time he took her to bed, she warned him: "If you knock me up, you little son of a bitch, I'll kill you."

type. It's usually the Rock Hudsons who proposition me."

Recalling his screen roles, Rooney told her, "In my heyday, I was age fourteen for thirty years in all those movies. At the time I had plenty of money in my jeans, any time I wanted to, I could get laid. A lot of starlets were after me, but I often preferred to go to that bordello across the street from MGM. There, I would join Clark Gable plus a lot of other male stars from Mayer's stable, and work my way through some of the most beautiful gals in Tinseltown."

She never knew what was going to pop out of Rooney's foul mouth. He confessed that he'd lost his virginity at age ten. "An older woman seduced me."

That was a reference to an eleven-year-old girl named "Ann," who was a year ahead of him when they attended Vine Street Elementary School in Hollywood.

"The most women I ever had at one time was a total of sixteen in a bordello in Tokyo," he confessed.

In spite of his small size, he also seduced a number of big name stars—Norma Shearer, Gene Tierney, stripper Tempest Storm, and Betty Grable.

He told Lucille that even though he'd been married many times (eventually, a total of eight), his first wife, Ava Gardner, was still the love of his life. "Her breasts had nipples like those wonderful golden raisins of California."

"I'm the only star in Hollywood whose marriage license reads, "To whom it may concern."

According to the script of their joint appearance on *The Lucy Show,* Rooney arrives at the bank where she works. He wants an appointment with Mr. Mooney, seeking a loan with the intention of opening an acting school. *[Critics pointed out that the mechanics of how one star after another arrived to see Mr. Mooney had become an overworked plot device.]*

The highlight of the episode featured Lucy with Rooney in a burlesque "Little Tramp" skit in the style of Charlie Chaplin, in front of a live audience.

She had clearly instructed Gary Morton to entertain the audience during her costume changes, while she made herself up. As part of an earlier skit, a vegetable cart had been hauled onto the set. While she was off the stage, as part of his *schtick,* Morton strolled over to it and chose the biggest cucumber he could find, one at least ten inches long.

He stuffed it into his jockey shorts and then reappeared before the audience "with a massive hard-on." He winked at Lucy's fans before telling them, "Now you know why The Redhead married me."

After the show, when she heard about his stunt, she called him into her dressing room and berated him for his "vulgarity. You've disgraced not only me but our family show."

He promised he'd never pull a stunt like that again.

Then he made her even madder by saying, "At least I got a bigger laugh than anything else in the show."

***

Her next show, *Lucy and the Soap Opera*, telecast on the last day of January, 1966, immediately became the one she most wanted to forget. Her co-star was the comedian Jan Murray, and she conflicted with him from the beginning.

He was nervous about appearing with her. But instead of trying to calm his nerves and let him gradually work into the role, she stormed off the set. "You give me nothing to work with," she shouted back at him.

In the show, she impersonated a Japanese gardener. One critic attacked her performance as "racist, guaranteed to offend every viewer in Tokyo. This is the single worst episode of any Lucy show I've ever seen."

She fared better in her next show, *Lucy goes to a Hollywood Premiere* (February 7). To attend the gala event, and, hopefully, get a chance to meet the stars, she purloins an usher's uniform and shows up on the night of the premiere.

The script was weak but enlivened by the guest appearances of such big name stars as Edward G. Robinson, Kirk Douglas, and Vince Edwards, with whom she had co-starred in the past. She still harbored a crush on the handsome actor ever since in his dressing room, he had shown her a frontal nude of himself.

Dean Martin hugging **Lucille Ball.**

A reporter once asked her if she'd ever gone to bed with the notorious womanizer.

"How in hell do I know?" she responded in anger. "I'm supposed to remember the names of all the men I've known?"

Later, Lucille made two TV appearances, each with Dean Martin. The first, on February 10, was on *The Dean Martin Show*, with other guests who included Kate Smith, Bill Cosby ("What a letch," she claimed), and Rowan and Martin.

[Dean Martin had long been one of Lucille's favorite entertainers, preferring this Rat Packer over his close buddy, Frank Sinatra. Martin always had the same greeting for her, "Hi ya, Redhead!" Dean had once joked with her over lunch, "In Hollywood, if a guy's wife looks like a new woman, she probably is."

Not all of Martin's conquests delivered reviews as good as Lucille's. June Allyson asserted that one night, she wanted to talk with him after they'd had sex, but Martin turned over in bed, and—with his back toward her—curtly told her, "Wanna talk? See a priest."

Lana Turner told Lucille, "Dean Martin is a bastard. At night, it's wine, roses, and champagne. But in the morning, it's a pat on the ass with the promise, 'See you around.'"]

"Dean had a subtle wit about him," Lucille claimed. "I much preferred his dry wit to the zany antics of his former partner, Jerry Lewis. Who did that crazy Jerry think he was? I always suspected he was trying to steal my act as a zany (male) version of Lucille Ball."

During one of their skits on the *Dean Martin Show*, Martin and Kate Smith delivered a duet of songs from the early days of 20th Century vaudeville. As a chorus girl in the background, Lucy had acted her way through a pantomime of their lyrics.

As "repayment" for agreeing to star on his show, Martin returned the favor by appearing in an episode of her show in *Lucy Meets Dean Martin* (February 14).

There's a zany aspect to its plot, as always. Lucy wants him to take her out on a date, but he's too busy. He tells her that he's going to fix her up instead with his stunt double, Eddie Feldman.

But at the last minute, Eddie is not free, so Martin goes instead. Without knowing it, Lucy dates the real Dean Martin, thinking the man she's with is merely a stand-in.

She later told its scriptwriter Bob O'Brien, "That was my favorite episode of all time."

That left him wondering why: "I didn't think it was any good."

Two weeks later, at a Hollywood party, Lucille chatted with Jerry Lewis, Martin's former partner.

"Back in the day when we were part of the same act, the most gorgeous dames went for him," Lewis claimed. "Actually, I've fucked more broads than he has, but most of them just wanted to burp me."

In *The Lucy Show's* next episode, she would co-star with the most notorious actor in Hollywood.

Hollywood, time and time again, spoofed Nazis and didn't always play them as monsters.

The most bumbling "idiot Nazi" ever seen on TV was **John Banner**, seen in the photo above with **Bob Crane**, the star of *Hogan's Heroes*, set in a German prisoner-of-war camp during World War II.

"**Bob Crane** was handsome and charming," **Lucille** said.

"I invited him for a weekend at my home when Gary Morton was in New York. Did I go to bed with him? Hell no! I don't think I would have survived his scenes of bondage, submission, leather belts, sado-masochism, and maybe even a touch of cannibalism."

***

In the wake of *The Dean Martin Show*, Lucille invited another well-known TV actor, Bob Crane, to co-star with her on a February 21 telecast, *Lucy and Bob Crane*.

In the now-familiar and deeply clichéd plotline, Bob Crane arrives at Mr. Mooney's bank as a new client. He is immediately attracted to Lucy, finding her very feminine. Unexpectedly, Mr. Mooney can later "blackmail" her into performing as "Iron Man" Carmichael, a stunt stand-in on Crane's new picture. So how, exactly, were the producers at Desilu (confusingly) portraying her? As an enduring symbol of female beauty or as an "Iron Man?"

At the time, Crane was the star of the hit TV series, *Hogan's Heroes* (1965-1971), set in a Nazi-operated prisoner-of-war camp during World War II.

Crane was not an obvious candidate as Lucille's amorous partner. He was eighteen years younger than her and looked even younger. She asked Maury Thompson, her director, "Do you think viewers will think he's my son?"

Although on screen they weren't convincing as romantic partners, off-screen was a different matter. He seemed attracted to her, and she accepted his invitation to lunch.

She found him fascinating and deliberately mysterious, as if he were concealing something. Before he shot to stardom, he had, like Desi Arnaz himself, been a drummer. Later, he morphed into a personality on radio and once had a late-night gig as a disc jockey.

In 1956, Lucille on occasion had listened to his morning show, which had featured high profile guests like Marilyn Monroe and Lana Turner. The show grew in popularity, until Crane got labeled as "The King of the Los Angeles Airways."

After that episode of *The Lucy Show* was wrapped, Crane learned from Gary Morton that he had to fly to New York that upcoming Friday night to meet with CBS. Because Lucille didn't want to make the flight, she delegated the rather routine business trip to Morton.

Knowing that Morton would be out of town, late the following Saturday morning, Crane phoned Lucille and asked if he could come over that afternoon. "There are things I want to talk over with you."

Since she had nothing else to do except read scripts, she invited him over at three o'clock.

When he arrived looking moody and depressed, she tried to cheer him up. She soon learned that he had just come from a bitter fight with his first wife, Anne Terzian.

As he told Lucille, he didn't want to go to a hotel where he might attract attention, and he wondered if he might move into her house for a few days. She offered her hospitality.

After dinner that night, he told her he'd brought along some tapes that he'd like to watch with her. Even though she suspected that they might be boring home movies, she agreed to it anyway. As she'd later tell her director, Maury Thompson, "They were home movies all right—porno ones!"

She soon learned he'd made a fetish of filming his adulterous escapades, often teaming on camera with his best friend, John Henry Carpenter, the regional manager of Sony Electronics.

"I witnessed the sexual mating habits of these two horndogs," Lucille said. "They'd filmed themselves with a changing array of girls. I think they indulged in every known sex act ever committed, including a lot of bondage scenes."

"Anything goes in his tapes, even golden showers," she claimed. "I hope Gary never finds out that I entertained this pervert for the weekend!"

Crane confessed to her that his favorite form of sex involved BDSM."

"I'm not exactly an innocent virgin, but what in hell is BDSM?"

He then launched into a detailed description. Basically, as he explained it, it involved sexually expressive strings of erotic role-playing, including consensual acts of bondage, discipline, dominance, submission, and sado-masochism.

As a for-the-most-part uninvolved *voyeur*, she was horrified.

He did not interpret her reaction accurately, assuming at first that she might be "erotically intrigued." He revealed his plans for an orgy scheduled for Sunday afternoon—"a sexual marathon," he called it—and he was hoping it could be staged in her home. "Your husband and children are away, and I assume you give Sunday off to the help? If you want to join in, I'll let you torture my cock and balls, and then I'll become a renegade on your breasts. After you join in, many sensual experiences will follow: Pinching, scratching, strategic applications of ice cubes, ropes, handcuffs, melted candle wax, erotic spanking, riding crops, leather straps, ropes, and chains."

She rose to her feet in horror: "Bob, I was going to invite you to use one of the bedrooms upstairs, but I think you'd be better off in my guest cottage. None of this is my scene."

In the aftermath of his father's death, years later, Bob Crane's son, Scotty Crane, revealed that Bob was a sex addict, and had started filming sex videos in 1956. In 2001, to raise some cash, Scotty reportedly launched a website featuring scenes from his dad's porn collection. At the time, he denied that Bob had once had a penile implant.

Lucille didn't see Crane after that, and never relayed any of the details of his visit to Morton after his return to L.A.

More than a decade later, she read about Crane in the papers and listened to what happened to him on TV news:

In June of 1978, he had moved into an apartment at Winfield Place in Scottsdale, Arizona. He was performing in a play, *Beginner's Luck*, at the Windmill Dinner Theatre. His co-star was Victoria Ann Berry.

She'd agreed to meet him for lunch on June 29 at one o'clock. When he hadn't appeared by 2:30PM, she went to his apartment to investigate. There, with the help of the apartment manager, she discovered his corpse. He had been bludgeoned to death with some unknown instrument, and an electrical cord had been forcefully tied around his neck. Blood had been discharged from his inner organs through his mouth.

An investigation was launched, but no one was arrested. On the day of his funeral (July 5) at the St. Paul Apostle Catholic Church in Westwood, many actors from *Hogan's Heroes* showed up, as did an unlikely pair, Carroll O'Connor and Patty Duke, the future girlfriend of Desi Arnaz Jr.

The murder trial wasn't held until 1994, sixteen years after his death, when Carpenter, Crane's former partner and his co-star in all those sex tapes, was charged. At the trial, Crane's son, Robert, testified that his dad had ended his relationship with Carpenter hours before his murder.

As it happened, not enough evidence was presented to convict Carpenter, and he was eventually acquitted of the charge.

Crane's death remains a mystery and the subject of much speculation even to this day. Lucille, without a lot of strong evidence, continued to suspect that Carpenter had killed Crane.

His life and eventual murder was depicted in the film, *Auto Focus* in 2002 with Greg Kinnear cast as Crane, with Carpenter played by Willem DaFoe. The film depicts the men descending into a life preoccupied with strip clubs, sex addictions, and BDSM.

> Hollywood insiders predicted that the aging comedienne, **Lucille Ball**, would be jealous of the fast-emerging, fast-rising **Carol Burnett**, who threatened her status as "The Queen of Television Comedy."
>
> But the two actresses had admiration for each other and developed a friendship, often co-starring together. According to Lucille, "Carol and I had one thing in common: Neither of us had any tits."

***

Carol Burnett could be seen as a rival, certainly a potential TV attraction to challenge Lucille's reign on the medium, but she chose to claim her as a friend. Even though her comic style was different from that of Burnett, Lucille admired her greatly.

Although Burnett's first TV series flopped after only one season, Lucille remained a faithful watcher of *The Entertainers,* a variety show that aired on CBS from September of 1964 to March of 1965 when it was pulled because of low ratings. Produced by Joe Hamilton, it featured three hosts, one of whom was his wife, Carol Burnett. The other two hosts were poker-faced Bob Newhart and Caterina Valente.

Before she could accept the gig, Burnett had to drop out of her Broadway musical, *Fade Out, Fade In.* The show's producers later sued her for breach of contract.

Burnett, along with the other hosts, received such guest stars as Phil Silvers, Chita Rivera, and Boris Karloff. Thelma Ritter and Dom DeLuise would also join the show's regular performers.

Lucille wanted to sign Burnett to a weekly sitcom produced by Desilu.

Burnett turned it down because she was pursuing a bigger deal. In 1967, she would premier *The Carol Burnett Show,* which would become one of the most-watched comedy series in television history, surviving on the airways for eleven years.

***

For Lucille's next episode of *The Lucy Show,* Jay North would be her co-star in *Lucy the Robot* (February 28, 1966). She had seen several of his telecasts as *Dennis the Menace,* many co-starring Gale Gordon, in 1962 and 1963.

The boy actor and Gordon shared a reunion, getting along much better than they had in that TV sitcom.

A victim of a troubled childhood, North had been deserted by his alcoholic father when the boy was four. The director of North's TV show changed his strawberry red hair to blonde. His parents on TV were Herbert Anderson and Gloria Henry.

Jay North as he appeared in 1962. He became a household name for his starring role in the TV sitcom, *Dennis the Menace*, driving his neighbor, played by Gale Gordon, crazy.

Like so many child stars, he never made it after his series went off the air. He fled to Florida and settled in the Panhandle, eventually fading into obscurity.

For his appearance every week, North was paid $350. His fee was eventually raised to $2,500 per episode.

In *Lucy the Robot,* North played Mr. Mooney's bratty nephew. He was such a menace that he had sent half a dozen babysitters fleeing. Lucy thinks she can solve the problem with a mechanized robot, an "artificial babysitter" invented by her friend.

The boy gave Lucille an idea for a new dramatic TV series: It addressed the issues associated with what becomes of a child actor, formerly (and briefly) adored by millions, who is dumped, never to find another acting gig.

Lucille was keenly aware that Mickey Rooney and Judy Garland were rare exceptions as teen-aged successes who would move on to adult roles. Shirley Temple tried to make the crossover but bombed. Many child stars ended up abandoned and forgotten.

Like so many Desilu pilots, this idea for a series was never developed.,

She never knew what happened to North. As it turned out, he ended up working for the Florida Department of Corrections.

In his last public statement, he told a reporter, "I plan to live in Lake Butler (North Florida, between Tallahassee and Jacksonville) with the people I love, and kind of vanish into the mists of time."

At the time that North co-starred with Lucille, he was also appearing with her former co-star, super-macho Clint Walker in a movie entitled *Maya* (1966).

It was a coming-of-age saga about a young man (North) who travels to the jungles of India to meet his father, played by Walker.

In her own projection room, Lucille arranged for a screening of *Maya*. North showed up with Walker, who renewed his acquaintance with her. She got him to agree to star in her next episode of *The Lucy Show*.

It was a busy year for the actor, who had recently starred in *The Night of the Grizzly* (1966), a western adventure film. Walker was cast as a lawman who inherits a ranch in Wyoming, where a treacherous grizzly on a murderous rampage appears as just one of many deadly threats.

Walker had also starred in *Cheyenne*, a Western television series broadcast on ABC from 1955 to 1962. The show was the first hour-long Western on TV, and the first hour-long dramatic series of any kind ever broadcast on TV.

Cast as Cheyenne Bodie, he had portrayed a physically large cowboy with a gentle spirit in search of frontier justice as he wanders across the West during the Civil War.

Before filming his episode with Lucille, Walker had dinner with Gary Morton and her. He wanted to star in another Western series, a search for gold in the West. But the story line he envisioned was vague, without a lot of details other than how it would be set in Arizona, Texas, and what he called, "Old Mexico."

He told Morton and Lucille that it would be in the genre of Zane Grey and Louis L'Amour. "I see it as having plenty of action, fascinating characters, and lots of romance,"

Since the project was so underdeveloped—other than having its hero in pursuit of *Yanqui Gold*, its eventual title—it didn't get off the ground.

Walker continued to pursue his dream, however, and in the autumn of 2003, *Yanqui Gold* appeared as a paperback Western novel that he co-authored with a more solidly established writer, Kirby Jones.

The episode of *Lucy and Clint Walker* (March 7) was critically well-received. One writer cited Walker as "the perfect on-screen mate for Lucille. She should make him her co-star. Once she is subdued by his macho charm, she'll forget all about Ricky Ricardo."

Cowboy **Clint Walker** as Cheyenne Bodie on the front cover of the August 15, 1956 edition of *LIFE* magazine.

Since he was short of cash, Lucille advised him to make a short porn film for a private collector in San Francisco.

In the 30-minute episode, Walker played a construction worker for whom she knits a red sweater, because it's his birthday. As it turns out, he detests the color red and angrily interprets the sweater as a freakish misfit.

At the time Lucille worked with him, Walker was going through a troubled period in his marriage to his first wife, Verna Garver. After their separation, she became the country's first female commercial pilot.

Walker seemed to be having money problems, and he turned to Lucille to talk over some offers he was receiving from other producers. Word of his physicality, especially his endowment, had spread, not only to a string of adoring females, but to a large gay base, too. Agent Henry Willson funneled the offers to Walker.

One was from a gay millionaire in San Francisco, who would pay him $25,000 to masturbate on film as supplement to his private collection of porn.

"How long does it take you to pop off?" Lucille asked.

"About five minutes, more or less," he confessed.

"Twenty-five grand for a five-minute gig," she said. "Sounds reasonable to me, particularly since it's for a private collector."

***

Near the conclusion of the Fourth Season of *The Lucy Show,* Lucille and Robert Stack co-starred in *Lucy the Gun Moll* (March 14, 1966). In Bob O'Brien's plot, the FBI calls on Lucy to impersonate a gun moll to spy on a gangster.

According to the script, she's a dead ringer for his floozie, Rusty Martin. The co-star of the episode was Bruce Gordon, who, along with Stack as Eliot Ness, had starred in the hit TV series, *The Untouchables.*

At the beginning of her reunion with Stack, she greeted him warmly, as she'd known him for years. "As one after another of our pilots bombed, your show has kept our bank account full," she told him.

"For years, Lucille told me how handsome and sexy I was, but she never asked me to take her to bed," Stack later claimed. "Maybe she was waiting for me to make the first move, but I didn't."

"Maybe I should have, because the next day, she began to be real bossy, trying to direct me. I told her, 'You're forgetting one thing: I know how to play this damn role. You see, I was on a hit TV series called *The Untouchables.* Perhaps you didn't watch it, but I think I know more about how to do the role than you do.'"

"Properly chastised, Lucille got off my back and we continued. Some critics claimed our on-camera mating made it the best episode of the season."

One day, when she was more relaxed, she told him, "I feel at home playing a gun moll. As a teenager, I hung out with the local hoodlum in Jamestown, New York. In my early days in Hollywood, I was the girlfriend of George Raft, that movie star gangster with ties to the mob."

In one scene in the episode, Lucy sings, "My Heart Belongs to Daddy," which Mary Martin had sung on Broadway.

Martin was out of the United States at the time and missed it. Later, she saw it as a re-run. "I don't know who Lucille was impersonating," she said. "But it sure in hell wasn't me."

***

As part of the (implausible) plotline of the final show of the season, *Lucy the Superwoman* (telecast on March 21, 1966), she has to lift a one-ton machine off the foot of Mr. Mooney, where it has fallen. Doctors quickly discover that she has a "stuck" adrenal gland and define it as the cause of the extreme strength which made such a Herculean feat possible.

"That episode bombed," she said, "but by then, I was worrying about how we'd survive getting through our Fifth (1966-1967) Season."

"Suddenly," she said, "I'm told to pick up the phone line. On the other end of the long-distance line was Charles Bluhdorn of Gulf + Western. Little did I know at that moment, but my life would be changed forever."

In the portrait above, **Billy Bob Thornton** portrays the ruthless, abrasive, and deeply feared corporate mogul, **Charles Bluhdorn** in a biopic about Robert Evans, who became head of Paramount.

Throughout the 1980s, Bluhdorn was the engineer of dozens of takeover deals, some of them spectacularly successful. Most of them were funneled through the multinational giant he orchestrated, Gulf+Western, the eventual owner of Paramount Pictures.

It acquired Desilu and, according to many Hollywood cynics, Lucille too.

Little did she know at the time of his inaugural phone call the degree to which he'd change her life, and the degree to which she'd begin to loathe him.

CHAPTER FIVE

Yours, Mine, and Ours

LUCILLE SELLS DESILU TO
GULF + WESTERN

AND CONCLUDES, AFTER SIX TRAUMATIC AND GRUELING SEASONS, THAT IT'S

TIME TO KILL *THE LUCY SHOW*

The man on the other end of the telephone, Charles Bluhdorn, the chief executive of Gulf + Western, was an American industrialist whose spectacular rise to power is shrouded in mystery.

Born in 1926 in Vienna to Jewish parents, he was considered a "hellion" in his youth, so out of control that his father sent him to a harsh boarding school to discipline him.

At sixteen, he was in New York attending City College, but he dropped out to take a $15-a-week job on the Cotton Exchange.

From such lowly beginnings, he established a company that would make him a tycoon, a titan of industry, before he was thirty. In 1956, he took over Michigan Bumper, a small auto parts dealer in Grand Rapids, that grew rapidly. From such a small beginning, he assembled the vast conglomerate, Gulf + Western.

"This sure in hell beats walking the streets selling typewriters door to door," he once told a board meeting.

During the heyday of what became known in the 1960s as "the conglomerate boom," thanks in part to easy regulations, low interest rates and highly leveraged buyouts, his auto parts company diversified into deliberately unrelated industries. It absorbed Paramount Pictures, Madison Square Garden, and Simon & Schuster into the same wildly diversified corporate entity.

It carried implications for the tourism and filmmaking industries, especially for the Caribbean, where he bought vast tracts of land in the Dominican Republic, developed them into golf courses and the then-cutting edge Casa de Campo resort with its (associated) replica of a medieval fortified village, Altos de Chavón. Bluhdorn, in collaboration (or at least cooperation) with the blood-soaked iron fist of the country's dictators at the time, the Trujillo family, eventually becoming known as "The Father of Dominican Tourism."

As Paramount expanded, it needed more land. Its vast studio lots adjoined the sprawling real estate holdings of Desilu. That's why he wanted Lucille on the phone. He wanted to make her an offer for Desilu's real estate and film properties.

In contrast to many of his relatively dour (some said "uninterested" in moviemaking and the quirks of its stars) colleagues at Gulf + Western, **Charles Bluhdorn** took a vivid and gregarious interest in the creative processes for which Paramount was known.

In the photo above, Bluhdorn occupies VIP "center stage" during the making of a film to which it was said he was emotionally attached, *The Godfather III*, but which ended up aborted, unprofitable, and unloved, despite his backing.

Its controversial, later "much fallen from grace" heavily bearded director, **Francis Ford Coppola,** is seen on the right.

Although Lucille knew a lot about Paramount Pictures, the burgeoning universe of Gulf + Western and the fast-growing reputation of Charles Bluhdorn as a mergers and acquisitions carnivore were almost unknown to her.

[*Whereas Paramount had barely survived the Depression of the 1930s, it had been saved by the Pre-Code and then-risqué movies of Mae West. Although it had flourished during World War II, its prosperity in the Postwar 1950s had diminished. Paramount, under Bluhdorn, had been plotting to expand its involvement into television, and it needed more studio space for its ability to compete in the "New Hollywood."*]

Lucille would always remember Bluhdorn's voice during that phone call in February of 1967. "I'll pay you $17 million in Gulf + Western stock for Desilu. My accountants figured out that even after you pay off your stockholders, you'll still end up with $10 million."

"My God!" she almost shouted in shock. "I'll really need to think this over. I'll need quite a bit of time."

"I understand," he answered. "You have exactly seventy-two hours: If I don't hear from you by then, the deal is off." Then he slammed down the phone.

She immediately called her lawyer and business manager, Mickey Rudin. When she presented him with the offer, he immediately recommended that she accept it. "Let's face it: The day of the independent producer like Desilu is coming to an end. We're at low tide here. Although there's a ton of money coming in, it's bringing in only a wheelbarrow of profit."

To escape the pressure, Lucille left immediately with Gary Morton in tow, and flew to Miami Beach, where they hid out in a hotel. Rudin tried to track her down, eventually fingering the hotel where she was staying, but she refused to take his calls, even though the clock was ticking on Gulf + Western's offer.

Her ostensible reason for flying to Miami involved a meeting with Jackie Gleason. "The Great One" was broadcasting his hit TV show from Miami Beach.

She wanted to pitch to him a new idea for a sitcom based on the life of Diamond Jim Brady and the fabled actress, Lillian Russell.

In desperation, Rudin flew from Los Angeles to Miami to confront Lucille directly. He sensed that she'd flown to Florida as an escape from the tension of having to confront the possibility of such a major change.

He painted a gloomy picture of what would happen if she didn't sell Desilu: "Our studio will have to finance at least two dozen pilots. If we're lucky, we'll get a sponsor for two of them, maybe three. We'll continue to be awash in red ink. Time is wasting, girl."

"I haven't even met this Austrian," she said. "Maybe he's a Nazi. A lot of Nazis are still alive and thriving in Austria, or so I've heard."

"Bluhdorn isn't a damn Nazi," Rudin said. "C'mon, Lucy, we have only hours left to accept his offer."

She waited until the final hour. After a lot of aggressive re-hashing of the deal, Lucille relented and let Rudin telephone Bluhdorn: "Lucy will ac-

This press and PR photo celebrates **Lucille** as the executive-in-charge ("the buck stops here") of Desilu after the departure of her ex-husband, Desi, from the lot.

Lucille found the position neurosis-inducing and stifling, with insatiable demands on her time and energy.

To whom did she turn? **Mickey Rudin**, a 52-year survivor of a law practice which had included Frank Sinatra and Marilyn Monroe among its clients.

cept the Gulf + Western deal," Rudin said. "I can't put her on the phone right now because she's sobbing."

"At least that proves she cares," Bluhdorn said. "We'll have our lawyers work to close the deal, which might take until sometime this summer."

In July, contracts were signed. Lucille told Rudin, "I'm no longer a tycoon. It's a man's world after all."

After the sale, she spoke to a reporter from *Variety*. "Making movies was a lark at first, but in time it was like tangling with a creature from a deep, dark lagoon, a real swamp monster."

"As for being president of Desilu, I had to run three studios and one time I was wanted on eighteen different phone lines, each person on the other end reporting a disaster. Try being mama to three-thousand members of cast and crew spread across three dozen sound stages. What's the fun of that?"

Bluhdorn announced his acquisition to the press. "We at Gulf + Western and Paramount are happy to welcome Miss Lucille Ball to our family. She is one of the great performing artists of all time.":

As part of the deal, Paramount made a generous offer to Lucille to star her in two feature films a year if suitable scripts could be found.,

She was still making payment to Desilu for her $3 million purchase of his stocks, and one of the benefits of her new deal would allow her to pay off any lingering debt to her divorced husband.

In February of 1967, **Lucille** announced she would sell Desilu to Gulf + Western, a decision which was formalized on July 27, 1967.

The act of selling Desilu to Gulf + Western brought it under the same parent company as its next-door neighbor, Paramount Pictures.

The event was commemorated with a dramatic ceremony in which Lucille cut a ribbon of film stock which had replaced a wall which had previously separated the two production studios.

She left the Desilu lot the very same day taking her own hugely popular *The Lucy Show* with her.

It was the only studio asset not included in the sale.

She still had not met Bluhdorn until one day, during a visit to Paramount next door, Bluhdorn decided to walk over and meet her at Desilu.

He had a lot of trouble getting through the gates of the studio he now owned.

It is not known what was said at that meeting. All she had to say was, "He travels fast, he talks fast, and he acts on impulse. I hope he stays alive. Who knows—if he goes, I might end up with some bastard to make my life miserable."

Many Hollywood insiders felt that Lucille sold at the wrong time, since she would not be able to benefit from the success of either *Star Trek* or *Mis-*

sion: Impossible. Not only that, but another hit TV series, Mannix, starring Mike Connors, was in pre-production.

During the final months of 1967, Bluhdorn became very disappointed at having acquired Desilu. "A lot of dough going out and precious little coming in."

Time, however, would eventually prove that in the long run, he made the right decision. By 1994, his purchase of Desilu for $17 million generated a profit of $1.2 billion.

***

Before selling Desilu, Lucille had concluded a deal with United Artists to distribute her latest feature film, Yours, Mine, and Ours, set for a 1968 release.

As director, she had chosen Melville Shavelson, who was also a screenwriter and producer. He'd gotten his start in the entertainment industry as a writer for Bob Hope's radio shows. Lucille had met and been impressed with him when he'd directed Hope and her in Sorrowful Jones (1949).

Ultimately, Yours, Mine, and Ours became her alltime favorite feature film. John Wayne had been her first choice as leading man, although Art Carney and Jackie Gleason were temporary candidates too. None of those three was available, but Henry Fonda was. So once again, and for the final time, she was reteamed with her former co-star and off-screen lover. She desperately wanted this movie to be a hit, since she felt she'd bombed in her last picture, Critic's Choice, with Bob Hope.

The plot of Yours, Mine, and Ours was based on a true-to-life story. In a nutshell, it described a widowed mother of eight who marries a Naval officer—father of ten—who was also widowed.The real Helen Beardsley wrote an autobiography entitled Who Gets the Drumstick?. It described her life as the story of a man and a wife coping with a schoolyard of their own kids.

Lucille insisted on personally casting each of the kiddie roles herself, and for a brief period, she considered casting Lucie and Desi Jr. among the horde of children who eventually appeared in the film. At the

Henry Fonda and **Lucille Ball** were together again when they co-starred in Yours, Mine, and Ours, with kids running all over their house.

As one reviewer put it: "Fonda and Ball don't have to be seen in bed to convince us they know what to do when they get there. These professionals can convey more about love in a look or gesture or a mumbled word than a lot of screen newcomers can with ten pages of dialogue or five minutes of hard-breathing amorous acrobatics."

last minute, however, she changed her mind.

As pre-production got underway, Fonda at the last minute wanted to accept another role instead. She turned to Fred MacMurray as a replacement, but then Fonda changed his mind and came aboard, although MacMurray might have been better-suited for the father, as he'd had such a hit with the TV sitcom *My Three Sons.*

Although her long-ago affair with Fonda was a distant memory, Lucille had long maintained a friendship with him. He'd once told her, "If you had married me, Desilu could have been named Fondalu."

Before the beginning of filming, she told *Variety*, "I'm getting tired of mini-skirted beauties ruling Hollywood. Our movie will mark a return to family values."

In his biography of Henry Fonda, Devin McKinney wrote: "*Yours, Mine, and Ours* is less honest than the youth-oriented exploitation movies it means to counteract. We wonder why Lucy, opposing the miniskirt oligarchy, goes through the film wearing thickly painted lips and false lashes that curl over her eyes like fried spiders. We ask how traditional morals are advanced by a screenplay sprinkled with, in Renata Adler's words, 'all sorts of sleazy, dirty lines, and cozy bedroom scenes and smiley, hesitant conversations about puberty.'"

Although Van Johnson, her longtime friend and former co-star, was no longer the box office attraction he'd been in the 1940s. she hired him as the third lead, Darrel Harrison, who convinces the pair that "you guys are made for each other."

Tom Bosley had a minor role as the family doctor.

Yours, Mine, and Ours became United Artists' number one hit of the year and one of the top-grossing comedies of its era.

Made for $1.2 million, it took in more than $25 million at the box office.

To Lucille's regret, in this era of comparatively high income tax, most of her take-home pay ($2 million dollars) went to the IRS.

Time magazine asserted that the movie "relies for its levity on two unassailable assets, Fonda and Ball. At 62, Fonda can still leave a line wry and dry. At 56, Ball commands a solid slapstick style." The *Philadelphia Inquirer* noted that the two stars "curb their instincts for the extravagance the story suggests."

Variety found the film's overall impact to be wholesome—in the best sense of the word. *[The word* wholesome *is rarely used these days without derogation.]*

As the new owner of Desilu, Paramount pocketed $2 million of the revenue from the box office bonanza the film generated, thereby retrieving a chunk of the money they had paid to purchase Desilu. "That money could have gone to me," Lucille lamented.

Her accountants did not anticipate that *Yours, Mine, and Ours* would be such a windfall, so they had not prepared a workable "tax shelter" for her in advance.

***

Following the Fifth Season of *The Lucy Show*, Lucille contracted with 20th Century Fox to appear in a brief cameo in *A Guide for the Married Man* (1967).

In an amusing sketch, and under the direction of Gene Kelly, she starred with Art Carney, as her on-screen husband. Their enduring dynamic involves his picking a fight with his wife every time he's tempted to stray into an outside-the-marriage affair.

In addition to Lucille and Carney, the bedroom farce starred Walter Matthau, Robert Morse, and Inger Stevens.

Kelly also arranged for an impressive list of stars to appear, like Lucille, in cameos. Foremost in prestige and box office potential was Jack Benny, followed by Terry-Thomas, Sid Caesar, Carl Reiner, Jayne Mansfield, Wally Cox, Joey Bishop, and Polly Bergen.

Lucille enjoyed working with Kelly again. Their friendship dated from when he'd been her leading man in *Du Barry Was a Lady* (1943).

According to the plot, Paul Mannings (Matthau) has a beautiful wife (Stevens), but flirts with intention of adultery. His best buddy, Ed (Morse) sets out to teach him the fine art of infidelity.

As always, Lucille made it a point to get to know the stars better, always with an eye to possibly casting them in a film of her own. She was toying with the idea of setting up her own movie production company once again.

Matthau is best remembered for playing opposite Jack Lemmon in *The Odd Couple* (1968) and in *Grumpy Old Men* (1993). He'd won an Oscar as Best Supporting Actor for his performance in the Billy Wilder movie, *The Fortune Cookie* (1966).

Matthau's partnership with Lemmon became one of the most enduring collaborations in Hollywood. These two life-long friends co-starred in ten feature films.

A New Englander, Morse was best known for his starring role in the 1961 Broadway production and later (1967) film adaptation of *How to Succeed in Business Without Really Trying*. Over the years, he would receive several nominations for a Tony or an Emmy.

A beauty from Stockholm, Inger Stevens, had become a household name because of her hit TV series, *The Farmer's Daughter* (1963-1966). In feature films, she'd "mated" with Henry Fonda, Richard Widmark, Dean Martin, Robert Mitchum, and Clint Eastwood.

Two co-stars of her boudoir included

> **Lucille** had a very busy schedule, and she ensured that her cameo appearance in *A Guide to the Married Man* took very little of her time. Art Carney played her adulterous husband,
>
> "Playing the wife of a womanizer was familiar turf for me," she said. "After all, I was once married to Desi Arnaz, who didn't know how to keep it zipped up.":

Bing Crosby, who promised to marry her, and Burt Reynolds.

Aspects of her private life remain mysterious even to this day. Was she really married to Ike Jones, an African American? Did her relationship with Reynolds turn abusive and violent, possibly leading to her death? Or was her death a suicide?

After directing *A Guide for the Married Man*, Gene Kelly became a director again when he helmed Barbra Streisand in the 1969 musical film *Hello, Dolly!"*

The New York Post called *A Guide for the Married Man* "elaborately sly, sexy, and stylish."

The New York Times claimed that "the most amusing episode was the one in which Art Carney teams with Lucille Ball." And *The New York Daily News* weighed in with: "And they said it couldn't be done — a Hollywood comedy all about sex that isn't cause for leering and sneering."

***

After selling his shares in Desilu to Lucille, Desi Arnaz had gone into semi-retirement, devoting most of his time to gambling in Vegas or betting on the horse races in Southern California.

At one point, he told friends, "I'm itching to get back into the television game." He set about launching his own production company, calling it Desi Arnaz Productions.

His first attempt to make his newly formed company profitable involved his endorsement of a pilot for what was envisioned as *The Carol Channing Show.* He wanted CBS to pick it up with a sponsorship from General Foods.

He had first seen Channing perform back in 1949 in the Broadway Musical, *Gentlemen Prefer Blondes.* He thought she should also have been chosen to star as Dolly Levy in *Hello, Dolly!*, which she had also performed so brilliantly on Broadway in 1964. However, the role went instead to Barbra

The tragic life of **Inger Stevens,** a beautiful, blue-eyed, Swedish-American blonde, is explored more fully in Blood Moon's biography of **Burt Reynolds**, the leading box office attraction of the 1970s.

Was Inger's death a murder or a suicide? The bio presents the details and allows the reader to decide.

Her co-star, Rod Steiger, once said, "You would have to be an idiot not to know this lady was not too happy with the false poetry of living. There was always a bit of terror in the corner of her eye."

Streisand.

In Hollywood, Desi invited Channing to lunch at the Brown Derby. He was surprised when she arrived with her own food in a plastic container. She asked the waiter to bring her only a glass of water, cutlery, and an empty plate.

When the (empty) plate arrived, she put her lunch on it: Fresh chopped zucchini, fresh raw carrots, and fresh raw celery. In contrast, Desi ordered several glasses of bourbon and a thick juicy steak served bloody and rare.

For dessert, he dined on lemon meringue pie as she nibbled at a small portion of pumpkin seeds.

During their meal, they discussed the series and the character she'd play, i.e., a caricature of herself. Future guest stars for Desi's new TV venues were talked about too.

Later, he tried valiantly to arrange for the production of a pilot that would get Channing launched as the centerpiece of a new series, but CBS rejected it, as did ABC and NBC. Each agreed that the series would be too similar to a recent one starring Jean Arthur that barely made it through one season, always with very low ratings.

Finally, Desi hit upon an idea and phoned and met with Bob Carroll Jr. and Madelyn Pugh (now Davis), the writers who had crafted some of the best of the *I Love Lucy* episodes. After some persuasion from Desi, they agreed to write the script for a new pilot.

It was to be a situation comedy, *The Mothers-in-Law.* Desi even hired one of his original *I Love Lucy* directors, Elliott Lewis, to helm the project.

Ever since her big TV hit, *Our Miss Brooks* (1952-1956), Eve Arden had been looking for another gig, and she agreed to star in this projected series.

At first, Ann Sothern was chosen as the co-starring mother-in-law. Later, however, executives decided that the Arden and Sothern were "too similar," and asked Desi to replace Sothern with another star.

He chose the macho-looking *comedienne* Kaye Ballard. She had broken into musical comedies in the 1940s, and he'd last seen her when she was a regular on *The Perry Como Show* in 1963.

Ballard recalled working with Desi. "I dreaded when he took over an episode to direct. He was critical of almost everything I did. He always said, 'Lucy would have done it this way' and then he transformed himself into Lucy Ricardo to show me how to do it. Finally, I lost my temper

Kaye Ballard (left) and **Eve Arden** appear together in this publicity photo for *The Mothers-in-Law.*

Ballard had her disputes with Desi, but basically, he charmed her. "He had the ability to make you love him. Especially women. I bought his house in Palm Springs. For years, I had women knocking on my door asking, 'Does Desi still live here?'"

and told him, "I am not Lucy, nor do I intend to be. I'm Kaye Ballard, and I'll do it my way.' He never pulled that Lucy shit on me again."

Desi himself appeared in four episodes of *Mothers-in-Law*. He was cast as a matador named Raphael Delgado y de Acha III. The wives had called his phone after dialing a wrong number, and he became somewhat of a family friend. On the show, he used his Ricky Ricardo accent and trademark mispronunciations of English-language words to full effect.

Desi must have envied the success of *The Lucy Show*. At the end of 1967, it was the highest Nielsen-rated show on TV. The *Mothers-in-Law* evolved into a minor hit, but not among the Top Twenty. Its sponsor, Proctor & Gamble, complained to Desi that many of the episodes were "old hat."

Don Jenkins at the *Hollywood Reporter* had known Desi for years. He was invited to the press party celebrating the launch of *The Mothers-in-Law*.

"I had not seen Desi since his semi-retirement and had heard he'd put on a lot of weight. But he was really slimmed down when I met him at the party. His hair was of the old gray mare color. He looked really gaunt. I made a mistake in asking him about his health."

"He told me he had had to wear a bag. That certainly must have interfered with his love life."

"I suggested to him that he should check into a clinic up in Santa Barbara for a long rest instead of trying to launch a TV series. That did it! Boy, did he lose his temper."

"Get the fuck out of here!" he yelled at Jenkins, causing the other press party members to become silent as they registered what was going on.

Jenkins retreated to the door while Desi was still "wildcat mad." Although he later apologized to Jenkins, the damage to their friendship had been done.

***

Before the name "Desilu" faded into the dust of Hollywood history, the studio produced the first half of a detective series that was eventually aired on CBS.

In 1967, Lucille had launched a pilot called *The Name Is Mannix,* which was shortened to *Mannix* before it was ever telecast on CBS.

At the time, Desilu was being dissolved, and *Mannix* soon came under the ownership of Paramount Television, a Gulf + Western subsidiary.

It would become one of the longest-running series of the 20th Century, lasting until 1975.

Mike Connors, who had starred in the pilot, remained the star until the very end.

The detective series was originally developed by Bruce Geller, the creator and executive producer of *Mission: Impossible.* In the first part of the season, Joe Mannix works for Interact, a large detective agency in Los Angeles. Computers are used to help solve crimes. Lucille considered the computers "too high tech" and ordered most references to them removed from future telecasts.

Mannix doesn't follow company rules and often disobeys the orders of his boss, Lew Wickersham, played by actor Joseph Campanella.

Connors always acknowledged Lucille for getting the series launched. He told a reporter from *Variety*, "The show itself started a whole new genre in detective stories. No more cynical *film noir* private eyes like the Sam Spade character inspired by Humphrey Bogart in *The Maltese Falcon*."

"Mannix is more of an all-around human being. He can be taken advantage of by a pretty face, and he can shed a tear on an emotional level. He is very close to his father and his family. In other words, in spite of his adventures, he is more normal than those hard-nosed detectives of those 1940s pictures."

Lucille liked working with Connors, a native son of California who had grown up in Fresno. "He was handsome, seductive, and ruggedly masculine. A lot of the gals on our crew went for him, and some of the boys made passes at him. But he seemed very much in love with his wife, Mary Lou Wiley, whom he'd fallen in love with when they were students at UCLA."

She had first seen him on the screen in 1952 in *Sudden Fear,* a thriller starring Joan Crawford and Jack Palance.

"I was told that to launch himself in the film industry, he had to lie on agent Henry Willson's notorious casting couch," Lucille said. "In that, he was following in the path of Rock Hudson, Tab Hunter, Rory Calhoun, Guy Madison, and so many others. Willson preyed on good-looking, wannabe actors—he was a real son of a bitch!"

Connors confided to Lucille, "It was Willson who gave me my stage name of Connors. He didn't go for my birth name, which is Krekor Ohanian Jr. I'm of Armenian descent, actually a cousin of Charles Aznavour, my favorite singer."

"Willson came up with the name 'Touch' Connors. I'd played football in college, where I got the nickname of Touch. I feared I'd be labeled with all the other first names in Willson's stable: Tab, Rock, Guy. Also, with a name like Touch, I feared a lot of people might see that as an invitation to feel—to touch—my basket. I kept the Connors part, but chose Mike as a first name."

What had convinced Lucille to cast him was not the Crawford movie,

Mike Connors as *Mannix*, a tough but charming detective on television.

"He had to lie on Henry Willson's casting couch back when he was known as 'Touch Connors,'" said Lucille. "But once he made it as a star, he would give none of us a break, and remained faithful to his devoted wife."

but a more recent one released in 1967. He had been leading man to Susan Hayward in *Where Love Has Gone*. It had co-starred Bette Davis.

When he came over to Desilu, Lucille lunched with him the first day, and he talked of having starred as a card shark in the 1966 remake of *Stagecoach* (1939), that film that had marked the debut of superstardom for John Wayne.

Lucille, at the beginning, paid so much attention to Connors that it aroused the jealousy of Gary Morton. "I was an ugly duckling compared to this good-looking stud, and she was gazing at him with goo-goo eyes. I never gave them a chance to be alone together after their first luncheon date."

According to Connors, "I tried to convince Morton that I was happily married to my wonderful wife Mary, but he didn't really believe me. He seemed to think I was a male whore because of the way I'd broken into show biz using Willson's influence."

From the beginning of filming with Desi, Connors took a beating pulling off the stunts required in the script. It began with the pilot. In that sequence, the actor dislocated his shoulder, running away from a *From Russia With Love*-type of pursuit from a helicopter. He also broke his left wrist punching a stuntman, who at the time was wearing a protective steel plate on his back.

It was during the filming of the first episodes of *Mannix* that Desilu was incorporated into Gulf + Western, which later integrated its operations into Paramount Pictures, which later morphed into Paramount Television. Connors would ride through to the very end of the long-running series.

***

Before Lucille could make any big career moves, she first had to complete the Fifth Season (1966-1967) of *The Lucy Show*, for which she had committed herself contractually.

Bob O'Brien had been promoted to executive producer, and Maury Thompson was still the director. Gale Gordon would still play Mr. Mooney, her boss at the bank, and Mary Jane Croft would be her sidekick in a role that used to be cast with Vivian Vance.

Late in the summer of 1966, Lucille was invited as a guest on *The Milton Berle Show*. After a decade off the air, "Uncle Miltie" was back as a regular on television.

In his off-color manner whenever the cameras weren't rolling, he approached to give Lucille "a big smooch" the moment she arrived at the studio.

"Tell me, honeybun, didn't I used to bang you long ago? As I remember, you weren't red down there."

"Cut the crap, Berle," she said. "You're still as vulgar as ever."

They forged an agreement: "You appear on my show, and I'll be a guest on yours."

One of his appearances had been on the Ninth Season of the *I Love Lucy* series. That episode, aired on September 25, 1959, had been entitled *Milton Berle Hangs Out at the Ricardos*.

Actually, it was with another famous comedian that Lucille opened the Fifth Season of *The Lucy Show*. George Burns joined her for its September 11 telecast. The now-familiar plot had the veteran comedian visiting the bank to talk to Mr. Mooney. There, he meets and is impressed with Lucy, inviting her to perform with him on his show. Lucille later said, "I did my best impression of Gracie Allen," his wife and former co-star who had died in 1964.

TV critic Bob Wolff said, "If fans haven't already noticed, Lucy Carmichael is getting dumber and dumber in every episode."

Burns gave Lucille some advice. "Don't give up. Defy age. Keep working until you're told the undertakers are at the door."

He followed his own advice and continued to perform until a few weeks before he died of cardiac arrest in 1966.

The September 11, 1966 telecast of *The Lucy Show* was called *Lucy the Bean Queen*, and her co-star was Ed Begley, a character actor who starred on the stage, on film, and on TV.

[Before working with Lucille, Begley had won a Best Supporting Actor Oscar for playing a corrupt political boss in the 1962 film adaptation of Tennessee Williams' Sweet Bird of Youth starring Paul Newman as a hustler and Geraldine Page as a fading movie queen. Lucille had seen Begley recently in The Unsinkable Molly Brown (1964) starring Debbie Reynolds. She told Begley, "If I had been a bit younger, I would have pursued that role for myself. I would have been fabulous as Molly Brown. I'm already, as the world knows, unsinkable."

"And that you are, little girl," Begley said. "That you are."]

In the *Bean Queen* episode, she and Mary Jane (Lewis) read an ad suggesting that if you don't like Bailey's Baked Beans, you can return them for double your money. Consequently, she and Mary Jane buy up every box of Bailey's Beans in town. Of course, their scheme doesn't turn out as planned.

***

On September 28, in an entertainment event not associated with *The Lucy Show*, Lucille appeared on TV as a guest star on the *Bob Hope Special* alongside a bevy of leading ladies from Hope's comedies, some of them dating back to World War II.

Backstage, she had a reunion with her still-beautiful friend, Arlene Dahl, before privately asking Hope, "Have all these lovely ladies slept with you?"

"Most of them," he said. "Except Joan Fontaine and Jane Russell. I never made it with Paul Lynde. And I didn't want Phyllis Diller."

"Well, I know Dorothy Lamour and Hedy Lamarr, not to mention Marilyn Maxwell, made it to your bed. And for all I know, you're still working on those sex goddesses, Joan Collins, Anita Ekberg, and probably Rhonda Fleming, too. As for Virginia Mayo, probably not—she's more into the Steve Cochran type."

In Bob Hope's telecast, Lucy is seen pedaling a tandem bike with Jerry Colonna, an actor known for his trademark, a walrus mustache. In one of the skits, each of the female stars begin competing for the role of Scarlett O'Hara in a remake of *Gone With the Wind.* Surprise of surprises, at the end of the skit, Phyllis Diller was cast as Scarlett.

***

Lucy in London, telecast on October 24, was one of the most-watched of the Lucy Shows that season. She took control herself, naming herself executive producer.

Filmed in London, it has a plot that, refreshingly, has moved away from Mr. Mooney's bank. Lucy Carmichael has won an all-expenses paid trip to England, but once she gets there, she's granted only one day for sightseeing.

When her plane landed in London, it was immediately obvious that she wouldn't confront the throngs of fans she had during the peak of her *I Love Lucy* heyday in the 1950s, even though she was still a highly popular entertainment figure among the British public.

Then at the height of his popularity, the actor and singer, Anthony Newley, would be her co-star. He had recorded one of her best-loved songs, "What Kind of Fool Am I?"

One of the skits in a *Bob Hope Special* telecast in the autumn of 1966 featured **Phyllis Diller,** pictured here in a basket, auditioning for the role of Scarlett O'Hara in *Gone With the Wind.*

Competing with her for the role are such beauties as Joan Collins, Rhonda Fleming, Anita Ekberg, Arlene Dahl, Hedy Lamarr, Joan Fontaine, and Jane Russell.

As part of the gag, as the audience laughed raucously, Hope rejects all of them—including his off-screen mistress, Marilyn Maxwell—and asserts that Diller will make the perfect Scarlett.

Actually, years before, it had been Lucille herself, in a real-life audition, who had tried to convince David O. Selznick that she could play Scarlett in the 1939 epic.

Newley had been one of the most innovative early rock stars on the British scene, and, much later, his biggest success involved his co-authorship of both the music and lyrics for the musical, *Stop the World, I Want To Get Off. [It opened as a hit in London's West End in 1961 before moving to Broadway a year later.]*

At the time, he was married to the British sex goddess, Joan Collins. Lucille first met Newley in his dressing room, where he ordered late morning tea.

Noticing a large framed picture of his seductive wife, Joan Collins, on his dressing room table, she jokingly asked, "If I had been a bit younger, would you have chosen me over Joan?"

"You know I would," he said, none too convincingly. He got up from his stool and went over to a chest of drawers nearby, from which he removed a record album and handed it to her as a gift. "It's devoted to my reciting poetry," he said, "As you can see, I'm displayed nude on its sleeve. Back then, I was a young model. Look at it! See what you missed out on for not marrying me?"

"Impressive," she said. "Anthony Newley in all his manly glory. I'm not surprised that fans bought it, and not just because of its poetry!"

In *Lucy in London,* Newley escorts Lucille on a whirlwind one-day tour of the British capital, hauling her through the city in a sidecar attached to his motorcycle. One of the scenes unfolds at midnight in the Chamber of Horrors in Madame Tussaud's Wax Museum.

A near disaster occurred when they shot a scene in a boat floating on the River Thames. As the cameras rolled, she stood up, lost her balance, and fell into the river, one of the most polluted in Europe. She was quickly rescued. "That sure wasn't in the script. But maybe we should leave it in for a laugh," Newley said.

"It was no laughing matter for me," she said. "I almost drowned."

***

Back in Los Angeles, Lucille learned that Desi Arnaz had been arrested three nights ago on his property at Del Mar, and that two teenaged boys from San Diego had charged him with assault with a deadly weapon, telling the press that he had tried to kill them. Desi was said to have fired at them with his .38 caliber revolver, a gift for him from the crew who worked on his TV series, *The Untouchables.*

Desi claimed that as he and his wife, Edie, along with Jimmy Durante, were building a bonfire at the waterside edge of his beachfronting property, the teenagers, from their cars, "were calling me every dirty name in the book," Desi told the judge. "I couldn't get rid of them. I did have the gun, but I fired it into the ground as a warning to them to leave us alone."

After he fired that warning shot, the boys drove away.

At the courthouse, Desi was charged, but after he posted bail, he was released.

When the case came to trial, the judge lent Desi a sympathetic ear and dismissed the case.

***

The next episode of *The Lucy Show*, telecast on October 31, teamed Lucille with Carol Burnett in *Lucy Gets a Roommate.* Lucille referred to Burnett and herself as "The Two Redheads."

It marked the first of many TV appearances in which Lucille would star with Burnett. In a way, they were rivals, each with scores of hard-core devotees. The debate raged as to which of the two was funnier.

In this episode, Lucy has advertised for a roommate to help with her expenses. At her door, Burnett shows up, a quiet, shy librarian. At least that is who she appears to be at first.

Don't believe it: She quickly breaks out of her shell, most notably during her hilarious performance in a burlesque in front of Lucy's (otherwise staid) party guests.

"Carol & Lucy" worked so well that Burnett was invited back for the next episode. *Lucy and Carol in Palm Springs.* Lucy fibs to her boss, Mr. Mooney, feigning illness so she can secretly join Burnett at the desert resort for a golf tournament. As might have been anticipated, Mr. Mooney also shows up, exposing Lucy's lie.

One of the episode's co-stars was Dan Rowan, star of the hit TV series *Rowan & Martin.* That was the first time he'd appeared without Dick Martin.

Martin had played Lucy's romantic partner in a few episodes of the First Season (1962-1963) of *The Lucy Show.*

During rehearsals, Lucy confided to Burnett, "Dick and I did more than rehearse in my dressing room. Our rehearsal heated up. You know how these things happen."

"No, I don't know," Burnett protested, "but I'd like to learn."

Also cast in the Palm Springs episode was Gary Morton, who kept a protective eye trained on Lucille, as if he was expecting another sexual advance on her from Rowan. That never happened.

***

On November 28, 1966, Lucille shared a reunion with John Wayne, who had appeared with her previously in an earlier episode. In this one, she pays a visit to the set, where he is shooting his latest movie. As might be expected in any episode of *The Lucy Show,* she throws the entire shooting schedule into chaos.

For the barroom brawl scene, Wayne took over from director Maury Thompson after telling him, "I've had more experience with these saloon brawls than you have."

Before a live audience, Wayne was supposed to be splattered with catsup,

It had been more than a decade since **Lucille** had co-starred with **John Wayne** on an episode of *I Love Lucy.*

"The Duke and I were never lovers," she told director Maury Thompson. "If I had a crush on that type of strong Western hero, it would have been Gary Cooper. Duke and I got along just fine, even though I never found him sexy...I mean, not at all."

"He did confide to me that of all the women he'd bedded, none was more thrilling than Marlene Dietrich."

but the scene didn't come off, and it had to be reshot later, after the fans had filed out.

When Lucille encountered Wayne again, he was not faring as well as he had in the past. Young Americans were protesting the Vietnam War, which The Duke (loudly and very visibly) supported. Many previous fans had turned against him, and most of young America—who had never really been ardent fans of his—boycotted his movies.

The sexual "conquests" he had made were fewer than those associated with many other male stars of his generation. Heading the list had been Clara Bow, a goddess of the silent screen. When he'd co-starred with Joan Crawford, she'd spread the word: "Get him out of the saddle, and you've got nothing."

He had also co-starred with Marlene Dietrich, in reference to whom he once told a reporter, "Best lay I ever had."

Other affairs were with Claire Trevor, his co-star in his breakthrough performance in *Stagecoach* (1939); Paulette Goddard with whom he'd made *Reap the Wild Wind* (1942). His most serious romance had transpired with the doomed Gail Russell, his co-star in *Angel and the Badman* (1947).

One afternoon, he confessed to Lucille that "Women scare the hell out of me. I've always been afraid of them."

He also told her that he'd received unwanted sexual advances from the British actor, Laurence Harvey, his co-star in *The Alamo* (1960).

"Tonight? Please, please, Duke, tonight," Harvey had pleaded. "Just once... I'll be the queen, if you'll be the king."

The Duke rejected the royal offer.

Years later, a much different offer would come in, this time from George Wallace, long-time Governor of Alabama. At the time, he was running for President on the ticket of the American Independence Party, and he wanted Wayne to run as his Vice President.

The Duke declined.

Lucille met her match when she re-teamed with the bombastic comedian **Phil Silvers**. Their episode together ended the 1966 season of *The Lucy Show*.

He was known as a "take over" star, and so was Lucille. Who would come out as the one in charge?

Silvers won. As the picture above reveals, he knew how to get Lucy "to shut her trap."

***

At the end of 1966, Lucille co-starred in an episode entitled, *Lucy and Phil Silvers* (December 12).

At the time, Silvers was widely hailed as "The King of Chutzpah" [*translated from the Yiddish as "extreme self-confidence or audacity"*] His greatest popularity had derived from his hit series, *The Phil Silvers Show* (1955-1959), a sitcom set in a U.S. Army post where he was cast as Sergeant Ernie Bilko.

Before working with Lucille, he had starred in two feature film hits, *It's a Mad, Mad, Mad World* (1963), and *A Funny Thing Happened on the Way to the Forum* (1966).

Brooklyn born to Jewish parents, Silvers had been a supporting player in Marilyn Monroe's last picture, the unfinished *Something's Got to Give* (1962). He told Lucille fascinating stories from Marilyn's last days on a film set.

Lucille had known Silvers for years, and they had appeared on TV shows together on several occasions. She knew that Silvers had something in common with Desi: Both were compulsive gamblers. He confessed to her that one night at the Cal-Neva Lodge near Lake Tahoe, he had gambled away every penny he had except for cab fare.

"Getting into a taxi, I told the cabbie, 'Don't expect a tip. I'm flat broke. I left my wad at Cal-Neva.'"

After wishing Silvers good luck, Lucille faced an uncertain future. "Like everybody else in Hollywood," she added.

Even before finishing the final episode of the Fifth Season of *The Lucy Show* in March of 1967, she had to decide if she wanted to commit to a Sixth Season (1967-1968).

***

Looming before Lucille were all the issues associated with the final episodes of the second-to-last season (1966-1967) of *The Lucy Show*. Each was eventually aired between January and March 1967.

The first of them, *Lucy's Substitute Secretary*, was telecast on January 2, 1967. From her character's home in Connecticut, she is planning a vacation at Lake Arrowhead in California. Mr. Mooney hires Ruta Lee (played by Audrey Fields) as her replacement. As it turns out, Audrey is a schemer who plots to take over Lucy's job as secretary, arranging things so that Mr. Mooney will tell Lucy she's fired the moment she returns.

Lucy learns of the deception. Instead of flying to California, she remains at home and undergoes various disguises in attempts to get Audrey dismissed.

Roy Roberts was cast as Mr. Cheever, Mooney's boss. Roberts went over so well in the role that Lucille requested that he become a regular in her next season of *The Lucy Show*.

A Canadian actress of Lithuanian descent, Lee was young, short, and pretty, with a deep voice. She had appeared in a number of films, notably in that classic musical, *Seven Brides for Seven Brothers* (1954), starring Jane Powell and Howard Keel.

Over the course of Lee's career, she would work with a wide range of stars: Sammy Davis Jr., Marlene Dietrich, Roy Rogers, Audrey Hepburn, Frank Sinatra, and Tyrone Power.

Months before she was cast with Lucille, she received a lot of newspaper publicity when she wrote and publicized an appeal to the Soviet leader

Nikita Khrushchev, asking him to free her grandmother, Ludvise Kamandulis, who had been locked away in a prisoner-of-war camp since 1945.

The most powerful man in the U.S.S.R. granted her request, and the grandmother came to live with Lee in Hollywood. In poor health, she died two years later.

In the following episode, Lucille re-teamed with Vivian Vance, of Ethel Mertz fame, to appear in the January 9 telecast of *Viv Visits Lucy*.

The two former friends and former co-stars "buried the hatchet" (Vance's words) and ended their feuds of yesterday, vowing "friendship to the end" (Lucille's words).

Whereas fans had grown used to Lucille's looks as she aged, they were rather shocked to see Vance's face after her absence. It revealed that time, indeed, had marched on. One critic defined her as "puff-faced."

In the script, the two women try to rescue Herbie, the son of their friends. He has succumbed to the hippie lifestyle. Long-haired, unwashed, and "sexually ambivalent" (although that is not the term used on the air), Herbie was portrayed by Les Brown Jr., the son of one of America's most famous bandleaders.

Vance stayed with Lucille at her home, where they talked privately about their respective marriages. Lucille revealed that her union with Gary Morton was "working out well enough. Things are fine. He performs like a husband ought to and Desi never did. All women don't have to be madly in love with their spouses."

Vance claimed, "I'm still married to John (Dodds). I've gotten used to his occasional weekend trips to Manhattan, allegedly on business. I know he's shacked up there with some young man in a hotel. But he always returns home to Mama."

***

For Lucille, it was payback time. Carol Burnett had co-starred with her, and now Lucille would appear with her in a TV special entitled *Carol + 2*. The third member of their trio would be Zero Mostel, with whom Lucille had starred in the 1943 musical film, *Du Barry Was a Lady*.

The highlight of the telecast occurred when Lucy and Carol appear in an office building as charwomen. In one musical number, "Chutzpah," they sing and dance about, wrecking the office.

Before the end of January, Lucille brought back her close friend and former co-star Mary Wickes in an episode entitled "Lucy the Baby Sitter" (January 16).

Lucy leaves her bank job for another position, this one as the babysitter for "The Marquis Chimps." Wickes later admitted, "I still adore Lucille, but I noted she has become even more bossy. I think her toughness is merely a façade to disguise her insecurity. She often insulted actors and ordered them around, but she knew what she was doing. As a director, she was usually right. After all, she had been in the business longer than any of us."

"Lucille had a good heart," Wickes said. "She wouldn't admit it, but she often provided a helping hand when a friend or former co-star fell on bad days, as so many of us do in show biz."

"During my time working with her, I almost got killed," Wickes said. "The guys brought in this big fat elephant for one of our scenes. This ghastly beast developed the hots for me and tried to rape me. Before he could mount me, his trainer had to beat him off with a club. I didn't get raped with old elephant dick, but I ended up with a broken arm."

***

Mel Tormé made a return visit to co-star with Lucille again. He'd last taped an episode, *Lucy in the Music World,* in September of 1965.

His two new back-to-back shows were aired on January 23 and 30 and were entitled *Main Street, U.S.A.* and *Lucy Puts Main Street on the Map.*

The plot, and not much of one at that, has Mr. Mooney sending Tormé and Lucy to Bancroft, a small American town where the locals need money to finance the construction of a modern freeway.

Carole Cook, a frequent co-star, was back on the set. A talented dancer, John Bubbles, was the first African American to be billed as a guest star on her series.

Director Maury Thompson wasn't particularly happy with either show. "Working on these two episodes was a fucking nightmare. Everyone was running around like crazy, especially Lucille. The only grace note was Tormé's music. I had five extra martinis when it was all over."

In addition to a reunion with Tormé, Lucille was scheduled for another reunion with yet another former co-star for a telecast on February 27: country singer Tennessee Ernie Ford. He had last appeared with her in episodes of *I Love Lucy* back in 1954 and 1955.

Carole Cook played Ernie's wife, Efie. The highlight of the episode was a barn dance staged to make Ernie feel at home. He praised Lucille for knowing how to pull off some hillbilly stunts.

Regrettably, during its filming, Lucille and her director, Maury Thompson, got into at least three major fights in full view of the cast and crew. Ernie recalled "a bit of name-calling. Lucille cursed like a drunken sailor, and Thompson used words best confined to a Marine barracks after dark."

As it happened, Thompson was overdue for a vacation. While he was away, the director of the coming season had to be selected. He sent word to Lucille through his agent, asserting that he would return to work only if his salary were doubled.

The producer, Tommy Thompson, transmitted his demand. She listened, not responding at first. Finally, she blasted out, "Tell the fucker to go to hell! He was never any good anyway. Hand me the damn phone."

She dialed her former director, Jack Donohue. "Jack! Good to hear your voice. Have you signed for anything for the next season?"

"Nope. Just sitting around playing with myself and waiting for the phone to ring."

"Well, the phone has rung. Zip up your pants and get your ass over here. Have I got a job for you!"

***

To round out the Fifth Season, *Lucy Meets Sheldon Leonard* was aired on March 6, 1967.

In the plot, Leonard approaches Mr. Mooney, asking him if he could shoot a scene for a TV series within his bank.

Lucille and another co-star, Mary Jane Croft, did not hear the dialogue clearly and think that Leonard and his gang are plotting to rob the bank. They set out to apprehend him.

A New Yorker, Leonard was also a producer and director and was well known to Lucille. In fact, he was one of her "tenants," having rented studio space to shoot TV series that included *The Andy Griffith Show* (1960-1968); *Gomer Pyle, U.S.M.C.* (1964-1969) with Jim Nabors; and *I Spy* (1965-1969) with Robert Culp and Bill Cosby.

***

Joey Bishop and Hugh Downs hosted the 19th Annual Emmy Awards, broadcast on June 4, 1967. Lucille attended but told friends, "I don't expect to walk off with an Emmy. I'm sure my series is considered old hat at this point."

As if to confirm that, Don Rickles in his Vegas nightclub act had elicited laughter from his audience by saying, "Lucille Ball has been around so long that she helped Alexander Graham Bell invent the telephone."

At the Emmy Awards, and to her astonishment, she was announced as the winner in the category of "Outstanding Actress in a Leading Role of a Comedy Series."

She beat out Marlo Thomas for her performance in *That Girl* and Agnes Moorehead for *Bewitched.*

Fighting back tears, she said, "The last time you gave me one of these, I thought it was for having a baby." *[She was referring to the episode where Lucy Ricardo gives birth. That series was aired the night Desi Arnaz Jr. was born (January 19, 1953). The Ricardos had a boy, and almost simultaneously, in real life, Lucille gave birth to a son.]*

The night was a kind of "last hurrah" for Desilu Productions. The soon-to-be-dissolved studio garnered fourteen Emmy nominations for the 1966-1967 Season. *Mission: Impossible* and *Star Trek* were nominated for "Most Outstanding Drama Series," with *Mission* winning. Its female lead, *Barbara Bain,* was honored, as was writer Bruce Geller.

Director Maury Thompson was nominated as Best Director for his helming of *The Lucy Show.*

"Lucille had recently fired me as director, but I thought she could at least have been gracious enough to seat me at the Lucy table with the others like Gale Gordon. But I ended up sitting at a nearby table with Sid Caesar and others. I lost and at one point, she walked right by me without even a nod or a promise of 'maybe next time.'"

After winning the Emmy that night, Lucille told reporters, "I'm going to sign for another season (1967-1968) of *The Lucy Show*. But it will be for the last time."

To launch the 1967 season of *The Lucy Show* in January of 1967, **Vivian Vance** and **Lucille** reteamed, marking Vance's first appearance on *The Lucy Show* since early 1965.

Bob O'Brian, the scriptwriter, claimed, "It was fun watching these two old TV warhorses plowing again, putting aside their past feuds."

Les Brown Jr., the son of the celebrated bandleader Les Brown, recalled working with these time-tested veterans now in their 50s. He was quoted as saying, "Makeup, it seems, can only hide so much. Time marches on, and it always wins."

CHAPTER SIX

TELEVISION & THE MARCH OF TIME

"It was the 60s, darling…"

TRYING TO BRIDGE THE GENERATION GAP
LUCILLE (BARELY) MANAGES TO REINVENT HERSELF
AS A SITCOM STAR WITH

HERE'S LUCY
A TIRED AND REPETITIVE SPIN ON AN OVERUSED THEME

DESI'S LAST HURRAH:
WHY THE STUDIOS REJECTED "THE CONGA KING"
AS A HAS-BEEN

Lucille had been hesitant to commit herself to the Sixth Season (1967-1968) of *The Lucy Show*. But since it was still riding high on the Nielsen ratings, CBS made her an offer she could not refuse.

She was presented with a $12 million package deal, $7.8 million of which would go to allowing Paramount to take over the re-runs of *The Lucy Show*, as well as remaining episodes yet to be filmed for the upcoming Sixth Season.

Desperate to maintain the status quo with *The Lucy Show*, she rehired Jack Donohue as its director; Bob O'Brien as executive producer; and Tommy Thompson as its producer.

She would repeat her role of Lucy Carmichael. Gale Gordon would return as her curmudgeonly boss, bank president, Mr. Mooney, and her sidekick, Mary Jane Croft, would retain control of her character of Mary Jane Lewis.

In contrast to the acquiescence of Lucille's other co-stars, Vivian Vance rejected an offer to appear in any capacity within this concluding season of *The Lucy Show*.

Originally, Charles Bluhdorn of Gulf + Western had assured Lucille that Desilu Productions could continue as a semi-autonomous subdivision within his conglomerate. But as time went by, it became increasingly obvious that that had been merely "a promise," and not a contractual commitment. *[Eventually, Bluhdorn successfully maneuvered for Desilu's integration (some said "dissolution") into the network of Paramount Television.]*

He also announced that episodes from the *I Love Lucy* series would no longer be available as part of the weekly lineup of CBS programming. Instead, they'd be negotiated as nostalgic gems and released to the highest bidder for general syndication worldwide.

Almost from the beginning of Desilu's takeover, Lucille had conflicts with the Gulf + Western management, particularly with John Reynolds, who had been put in charge of the conglomerate's television programming.

Right from their first meeting, he got off to a bad start by telling her, "I was never a fan of *I Love Lucy*. I thought it was uninspired farce. I'm more of a Carol Burnett fan. The Ricardos just didn't do it for me."

Marlene Dietrich, appearing above as she did in her last film, *Just a Gigolo* (1978), famously used some of the cosmetic techniques (some said "masochistic self-flagellations) later adopted by Lucille Ball to render herself alluring in front of the "cruel, cruel cameras."

It was an artful and artsy West German "black comedy" that Dietrich morphed into her "swan song. "Her presence added luster to a film that might otherwise have been overlooked. Many commentaries focused on how "well" she was "preserved."

Her co-star was David Bowie, playing a down-on-his luck German Army officer working in a brothel run by Kim Novak between the World Wars during the rise of the Nazi menace.

Ridiculed by critics and audiences and generally viewed as a commercial failure; the film's reception led Bowie to quip that it was "my 32 Elvis Presley movies rolled into one."

Even though Lucille felt deeply insulted, she kept quiet, knowing she'd be forced to work with this executive on many different levels.

She reflected sadly on the loss of the corporate name "Desilu," a moniker that she and Desi had chosen back in 1942 when they moved into their ranch home in Chatsworth in the San Fernando Valley.

Her relinquishing of the Desilu franchise evolved into its disintegration. Many of her most loyal and long-serving employees were fired, as new ones from Gulf + Western replaced them. "Those who remained got a demotion and a huge cut in salary," she said.

Lucille was dismayed when she read what Phil Carstairs, a minor Gulf + Western employee in New York, told *Advertising Age:* "Stars of yesterday like Jack Benny and Lucille Ball, who are still on the payroll, should have been retired long ago. What's best for them now is to take a long, long rest in a wheelchair in some nursing home."

"As time goes by," he was quoted as saying, "TV viewers more and more are tuning out *The Lucy Shows*, which rely on an old bag of zany gags from yesteryear. We need new blood, fresh new ideas, and more challenging scripts to reflect more of today's generation and their rapid changes going on in the world. Right now, what we get with Lucy is a superfluous vaudeville pie—and one overbaked one at that."

Mocking her declining popularity, *Rowan & Martin*, both of whom had appeared on her program, took special delight in sarcastically bidding her goodnight at the conclusion of one of their shows.

"They should name my last season, *Lucy at Twilight*," she said, ruefully.

Steeling herself in preparation for the upcoming filming, she frenziedly set about making herself look younger. Calling in her longtime makeup pro, Hal King, she ordered him, "Take off fifteen years...at least!"

Before he began his labors, she scheduled what evolved into a very painful appointment with her hairstylist, Irma Kusely, who removed chunks of Lucille's henna-dyed hair and tied strands of them up with bobby pins. To her scalp, Kusely then stretched a "skull fracture bandage," with the understanding that cosmetically, it would force a lift to her stagging face. *[Marlene Dietrich had submitted to this harsh cosmetic treatment before every concert appearance for years.]*

Then, over the bandage, Kuseley stretched an orange-colored wig. For Lucille, this was a painful process. Sometimes her scalp bled, but bravely, she carried on, saying, "No one said it would be easy to take fifteen years off my sagging puss."

After the hair stylist departed, King was called in. With bravado, Lucille instructed him to "Lay on the makeup and repaint the trademark 'Cupid lips' of what used to be known as 'Lucille Ball.'"

***

As the opening episode of the Sixth Season of *The Lucy Show*, Lucille called on her old friend (and former lover from the late 1930s) Milton Berle. Both of them were past their prime, but *[Lucille's words]* "still hanging in there."

Lucy Meets the Berles (September 11, 1967), written by Bob O'Brien, has her working for Berle as his temporary secretary. She was recommended to him by her "fuss-budgety" boss, Mr. Mooney (Gale Gordon).

Ruta Lee, who had co-starred with Lucille in *Lucy's Substitute Secretary* (January 1967), was brought back. As Lucy eavesdrops on Lee and Berle,

Two views of "Uncle Miltie," (aka "Mr Television" aka **Milton Berle**).

Lower photo shows him with **Lucille** after a food fight in this scene from "Lucy Meets the Berles."

she (incorrectly) concludes that they're having an affair. *[Actually, they're discussing a love scene in a script.]*

She sets out with her usual perky but disastrous results to end this presumed affair.

Berle had last appeared on her show in December of 1965.

Evoking one of those silent screen comedy *schticks,* he gets a salad dumped on his head, the Thousand Island dressing covering his glasses. "Show biz is a tough way to earn a living," he told Lucille.

"You've had worse things dumped on you," she tartly responded.

In another episode, Lucille was cast with the French heartthrob, Jacques Bergerac, in an episode entitled *Lucy and the French Movie Star* (September 25, 1967) The strikingly handsome actor had been married to Lucille's friend, Ginger Rogers, from 1953 to 1957.

In June of 1959, he married the very talented actress, Dorothy Malone, in Hong Kong when she was on location filming *The Last Voyage.* They had two daughters before their divorce in December of 1964.

Jacques Bergerac with **Ginger Rogers**, his co-star and then wife, in this publicity photo for *Twist of Fate* (1954).

Long before this French matinée idol entered the life of Ginger, she had a torrid affair with a Cuban bandleader in the late 1930s. His name was Desi Arnaz.

Rumors circulated that he impregnated her in New York and drove her across the Canadian border to have an abortion.

Lucille had seen only one of Bergerac's films, *Gigi* (1958), starring Leslie Caron and Louis Jourdan. She had heard gossip from Rogers herself that *Gigi's* director, Vincente Minnelli, had maneuvered Bergerac onto a casting couch. That apparently happened several times during the final weeks of his marriage to Ginger. "George Cukor and Noël Coward, among others, had also "auditioned him up close and personal," Rogers had claimed.

"Louis Jourdan was once voted the handsomest man in the world," Lucille said. "If that competition were held today, Monsieur Bergerac would get my vote. What is there about French men that makes them so gorgeous and seductive?"

In *Lucy and the French Movie Star,* Mr. Mooney assigns Lucille to play secretary to Bergerac for the drafting of a legal agreement. As he delivers dictation, he gets her drunk on champagne.

***

In her next episode, telecast on October 2, in a studio-sanctioned push to attract younger viewers, Lucy was teamed with teen idol Frankie Avalon in *Lucy the Starmaker.* Avalon was cast as Tommy, the nephew of Mr. Cheever (Mooney's boss). As she's showing him around the bank, Lucy discovers that he's an aspirant singer. Kind-heartedly, she sets him up for an audition before a producer.

Avalon was born the year Lucille married Desi Arnaz. His glory years as a singer had lasted between 1958 and 1962 with such *Billboard* hits as "Venus" and "Why?"

She had been taken by her daughter to see only one of Avalon's movies, *How to Stuff a Wild Bikini* (1965).

"I tagged along to the show, hoping to see some hot guys in bikinis, but I didn't see a one," she later complained to Avalon.

"In the movie, only the girls showed off what nature gave them," he said.

"When will directors learn that we gals like to see how men stuff a bikini, too?"

In avid (some said "strained") pursuit of a youth-oriented theme, the next episode was *Lucy Gets Her Diploma* (October 9). The bank has adopted a new policy that demands that every employee has to prove that he or she has at least a high school education. Lucy is forced to confess that she had been bedded with an illness and was unable to finish her senior year. So she re-enrolls in an adult education program with the understanding that when it's completed, she'll earn a diploma.

Frankie Avalon & **Annette Funicello** in *Muscle Beach Party* (1964)

Lucie Arnaz took her mother to see Avalon's movie, *How to Stuff a Wild Bikini.*

Lucille's verdict: "The damn prop department should have done a lot more stuffing."

inset photo: portrait of **Frankie,** years later.

[Its scriptwriter, Milt Josefsberg, had obviously never screened an episode entitled Lucy's College Reunion, *originally broadcast during the 1963-64 season. In it, she was a full-fledged college graduate attending an embarrassing class reunion.]*

The episode reunited Lucille with Doris Singleton, who is best remembered today as Lucy Ricardo's nemesis and frenemy, Carolyn Appleby, in *I Love Lucy.* Lucy lends a helping hand to a troubled student played by Robert Pine.

He later admitted that he was twenty-six when he auditioned for the role of the high school senior. "I didn't look my age, and believe it or not, I passed for seventeen…well, maybe eighteen or nineteen. But I got the role."

"Lucille liked me so much, she recommended me as one of her kids in

Yours, Mine, and Ours, that movie she released in 1968 with Henry Fonda. But the director turned me down."

Because Pine was an expert horse rider, he often appeared in TV Western where he played villains and wealthy racists. His most controversial role was in the 1993 TV series, *Big Boys Don't Cry,* where he was cast as a pedophile who seduces his nephews.

In all, Pine had roles in at least 400 episodes of TV series, from *Gunsmoke* to *Lost in Space,* from *Barnaby Jones* to *Magnum, P.I.,* and in such soap operas as *Days of Our Lives.* He is also remembered for his performance as Sgt. Joseph Getgraer on the TV series *CHiPs* (1977-1983).

Lucille also cast her daughter, Lucie Arnaz, in a supporting role. There, she met one of the supporting players, actor Philip Vandervort.

On July 17, 1971, she would marry this divorced actor.

***

Scriptwriter Milt Josefsberg had previously written comedic monologues for comedian Jack Benny, a longtime friend of Lucille's. He devised a script, *Lucy Gets Jack Benny's Account,* that she liked very much. So did Benny. They began rehearsing it for an episode of *The Lucy Show,* one that was eventually telecast on October 16, 1967. In it, Mr. Mooney (Gordon) is ordered to bring in new accounts, and although "Stingy Benny" is suspicious of all bankers and all banks, Lucy schemes to get his business.

She tries to convince the comedian that the bank's vault is foolproof, and, of course, the usual disasters occur.

Believe it or not, in the final segment of this banking comedy, she and Benny are going down in quicksand (of all things).

One critic found that the script might have been better suited for a sitcom of Benny's instead of an episode of *The Lucy Show,* But the two old pros pull it off, in spite of all those sarcastic suggestions that they should retire to nursing homes.

When their filming was finished, before saying goodbye to Lucille, Benny asked her, "Why don't you bring Dennis Day onto your show? He can sing and act, a real talent. You surely know that if you've been watching my show, the greatest comedy on TV today."

She took Benny's advice and had Milt Josefsberg write a script in which she could co-star with Day. [Josefsberg had already writ-

There were three famous show-biz personalities named "Day": Laraine Day, Doris Day, and **Dennis Day** (photo above).

After working with this singer, Lucille said, "He was the most lovable man in show business, impossible to hate."

Either in radio or television, he worked with his boss, Jack Benny, from 1939 to 1974.

ten many scripts for Benny and Day during his long creative association with them.]

According to the plot, the owner of the chain of banks is coming to town, and Lucy is asked to be his date for the evening. Since she is sure he is eighty-five years old, she disguises herself as a woman of his era. To her dismay, she finds him to be the youthful-looking Day, who turns out to be "a wolf."

An Irishman, born in Throggs Neck in the Bronx, Day had changed his family surname of McHulty. He had first been on Benny's radio program in 1939, and he would work with him until the comedian's death in 1974.

When introduced to Lucille, he said, "I can impersonate anyone in show biz—you name him, Jimmy Durante, James Stewart, Ronald Colman."

"How about Desi Arnaz?" she asked.

Immediately, he morphed into her ex-husband, pretending he wants her back.

She later claimed, "If I had closed my eyes, I could have sworn that it was the real Desi, come to try to marry me again."

"Day is that damn good, and also the sweetest guy I ever worked with in a Tinseltown peopled by shitheads and bastards."

***

When Lucille read the next script of *The Lucy Show,* she was quite pleased. In this telecast, *Lucy and Robert Goulet,* set to be broadcast on October 30, 1967, she was to co-star with this handsome, talented singer who was married at the time to the actress and singer, Carol Lawrence.

In this rather unlikely plot, a truck driver (guess who?) comes into the bank seeking a loan from Mr. Mooney. *[At this point in the series, the plot device wherein an episode begins with a handsome stranger seeking a loan from Mr. Mooney was a bit shopworn and tired.]* Lucy spots the good-looking hunk and talks him into entering a Robert Goulet lookalike contest.

In supporting roles, she cast her longtime friend, Mary Wickes, and even her sixteen-year-old

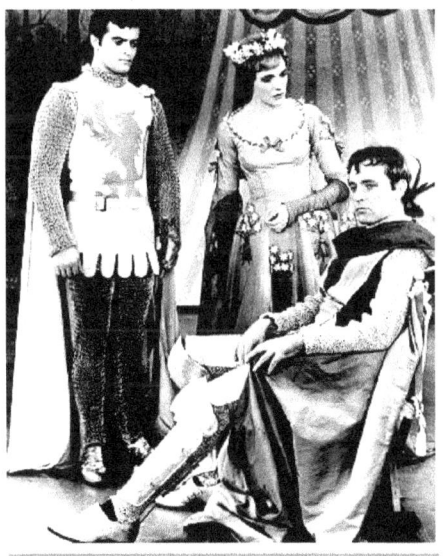

Robert Goulet (left) became famous overnight as the man who stole the Queen of (medieval) England's heart.

He appears above with **Julie Andrews** and **Richard Burton** in the original Broadway production of *Camelot*.

daughter, Lucie. Also in the cast was Sid Gould, a cousin of Gary Morton, who had by now become a regular on the show

A new face was Gould's wife, Vanda Barra, whom Lucille had first seen on *The Mothers-in-Law* series.

Privately, Lucille raved about Goulet's singing voice and his studly appearance. She'd been a fan of his ever since she'd seen him as Sir Lancelot in the original Broadway production (1960) of the musical *Camelot*. His co-stars had been Richard Burton as King Arthur and Julie Andrews as Guenevere.

"Bob's ballad, 'If Ever I Should Leave You,' was so powerful, it stopped the show," Lucille said.

For some reason, the dual casting of Lucille's TV episode didn't come off very well. Goulet photographed beautifully, and Lucille also looked good, but they just didn't seem to click in this weakly scripted episode. She later said, "Bob had a great presence on camera—and *that voice*—but I guess I just was not his Queen Guenevere."

In the Goulet episode, Lucille, however, liked the acting style of Vanda Barra so much that she cast her in the next episode, *Lucy Sues Mooney*, aired on November 27,. 1967.

This 30-minute comedy brought Lucille together again with the actor and comedian Jack Carter. He was the husband of Paula Stewart, Lucille's co-star in the 1960 Broadway production of *Wildcat*. Carter always took credit for introducing Lucille to Gary Morton.

In their episode, Lucy is doing bank work at the house of Mr. Mooney, and she falls and injures herself. She is talked into hiring a crooked lawyer to sue her boss.

"Lucille is my best friend and my worst enemy," Carter said. "She's wonderful when we have dinner together or go to a nightclub party. But on the set, she becomes Mussolini, a real dictator. No matter how you perform, it somehow doesn't seem right to her. Her favorite slogan to an actor is, 'You could have done better.' She and our real director were always at each other's throats with butcher knives. Jack Donohue was about the only one with balls big enough to stand up to her. I once heard that Desi Arnaz used to call his wife 'Miss Cojones.' I think that means 'balls' in Spanish."

***

Lucille reteamed with Carol Burnett, her friend and also her rival comedienne on TV, for two back-to-back episodes on *The Lucy Show*. The first was *Lucy and Carol Burnett, Part*

Buddy Rogers with **Mary Pickford** in 1927. A decade later, he married her...or at least he married her millions.

In the 1930s, when both he and Desi Arnaz were bandleaders on Miami Beach, Rogers tried to seduce the Cuban.

One (A.K.A. Coffee, Tea, or Milk?" which was aired on December 11, 1967.

After leaving her job at the bank, Lucy becomes an airline stewardess (flight attendant). On a flight of Trans Global Airways, her roommate and zany fellow stewardess (Burnett, of course) manages to shake up the passengers. Incidentally, on the show, Burnett's character is afraid of heights.

These telecasts marked some of the final episodes of *The Lucy Show*. Instead of featuring pre-scripted plots, as developed in episodes of *I Love Lucy*, to an increasing degree, *The Lucy Show* relied on loosely plotted improvisational skits. In this episode, Lucy and Carol, as stewardesses, put on a show for their passengers.

Buddy Rogers with **Clara Bow** in *Wings*.

Lucille later claimed, "I saw every movie Clara Bow ever made. Although we were vastly different in style, her zany movements and antics on screen later inspired my character of Lucy Ricardo."

The second episode, *Lucy and Carol Burnett, Part Two (A.K.A. Lucy and Carol Get Their Wings)*, was telecast on December 18, the last episode of 1967.

To celebrate getting their flight attendant wings, Lucy and Carol, along with Gale Gordon, put on a musical based on that silent film classic, *Wings* (1927). *[It had starred Buddy Rogers, Clara Bow (the "It" Girl), Richard Arlen, and a relatively unknown Gary Cooper. Wings became the first film to win an Academy Award as Best Picture of the Year.]*

At the time that they were cast on *The Lucy Show*, Arlen and Roger-

Arlen's spectacular success in Howard Hughes' 1927 production of *Wings* was long forgotten by the time he worked with Lucille Ball on a rather silly episode of *The Lucy Show*. He had fallen from grace in Hollywoodland, never regaining the early success of his very handsome youth.

Center photo illustrates the romantic triangle on which was based the emotional theme of *Wings*. Left to right, **Rogers, Bow,** and **Arlen.**

swere celebrating the 40th anniversary of the release of *Wings*.

Lucille enjoyed meeting and talking with Arlen. Like Humphrey Bogart, he had been born in 1899, as a century was dying.

In his career, he'd had many ups and downs, even working in the oil fields of Oklahoma.

"I, too, was a wildcatter in Oklahoma," she said. "Actually, that was my role on Broadway."

Before moving to Los Angeles, he'd been a sports writer. In 1921, he was in Hollywood, appearing uncredited in *Ladies Must Live* (1921).

Although he starred in a number of pictures, Arlen never topped his success in *Wings*. He eventually ended up working with Andy Devine, beginning in 1939, in a movie series loosely referred to as the *Aces of Action*.

During World War II, Arlen temporarily left Hollywood to become a flight instructor for the U.S. Army Air Force.

After the war, he was often seen on TV screens in such series as *Bat Masterson* and *Wagon Train*.

Lucille found Buddy Rogers more fascinating to talk to. He'd been married to Mary Pickford since 1937 and was once billed as "America's Sweetheart." Pickford had had that same title during her long-running gig as the most famous silent screen star in the world.

Rogers told her he had known Desi when they appeared as the leaders of rival bands on Miami Beach in the 1930s.

[Actually, Desi had spoken of Rogers in those days, claiming, "He once made a pass at me."]

Whether Pickford knew it or not (and she probably did), Rogers was bisexual. His most enduring affair was with Gene Raymond, the husband of that MGM singing sensation and operetta singer, Jeanette MacDonald.

Even if they didn't particularly like the oft-repeated *schtick* of Lucille Ball as she and her comedic rhythms aged, fans of vintage Hollywood remained endlessly fascinated by the old-timey talent she managed to haul onto the set with her.

The photos, left to right, show three eras in the career of **Jackie Coogan**, one of the rare Hollywood personalities who found roles after his success as a child star.

LEFT: in *The Kid* with **Chaplin**; middle as Uncle Fester in *The Addams Family*; and right with **Lucille Ball** in *Lucy Gets Involved*.

***

Vivian Vance bounced back into Lucille's life to launch the New Year of 1968 with Episode #148, *Lucy and Viv Reminisce.* It was aired on the first day of January.

On the show Lucy and Viv talked about the good old days when they had starred as Lucy Ricardo and Ethel Mertz, then a sadder-but-wiser woman with a most undesirable husband, Fred (William Frawley).

The plot, such as it was, has Lucy falling and breaking her leg. Mr. Mooney (Gale Gordon) becomes a nurse. He brings in Vance to take over her care and feeding, but Vance, too, falls and injures herself. Mooney finds himself nursing both of them.

The episode contains clips from old episodes of *I Love Lucy*. Desi hardly appears in any of them.

Two weeks later, *Lucy Gets Involved* has her and her entourage interacting with former child star Jackie Coogan and her future son-in-law, Philip Vandervort.

In contrast to her awkward collaboration with Robert Goulet, Coogan and Lucille seem a natural team, working in comedic harmony.

She had known the actor since the late 1930s when Coogan was married to Betty Grable, one of her best friends.

Coogan's film with Chaplin, *The Kid* (1921), is hailed today as one of the great classics of the silent screen.

In later years, after a noticeable aging and physical transformation, Coogan became famous to a new generation as the bumbling Uncle Fester in ABC's hit TV series (1964-66) *The Addams Family*.

By the time Lucille's episode #149 was telecast, TV critics hailed her stint with Coogan as one of the best in the entire series.

Her pairing with Coogan was immediately followed by *Mooney's Other Wife*, telecast on January 22, 1968. In this comedy, she was reunited with Edie Adams, the hardworking singer, actress, and widow of comedian Ernie Kovacs.

"Edie and Ernie" had once worked with Lucille and Desi in *Lucy Meets the Mustache,* an episode from "the old days" that first aired in 1960. Adams recalled the taping of that show as one of the worst appearances of her life. "Lucille and Desi—known

Edie Adams and **Ernie Kovacs** in 1960.

According to Edie: "My husband and I had appeared on Lucille's show before. I returned as a widow on her show. Reuniting with her, I realized at once that she missed the strong influence of Desi Arnaz, who, as her backup, made her the most famous woman in show biz. She had listened to Desi's advice. But poor Gary Morton. She wouldn't let him open his mouth."

at the time as 'the battling Arnaz's,' — were just weeks from their divorce," Adams said.,

In this latest Ball/Adams project, a woman shows up at the bank pretending to be Mooney's wife.

Lucy confronts her, claiming that she is the one and only wife of Mr. Mooney.

"Lucille was far more subdued when I worked with her years later," Adams said. "The years had been rough for her. She was wearing too much makeup and what looked like an entire tube of lipstick. Not only that, but her voice had changed, going from soprano to bass."

Edie's husband, Ernie Kovacs, a longtime cigar smoker, had died in 1962. Edie told Lucille, "I'm having to work day and night to pay off a mountain of bills, mostly to the IRS. I don't care how long it takes—I plan to pay off every cent."

Working tirelessly, Adams kept her vow, overcompensated, and ended up with millions. She launched a beauty empire, with products that included Edie Adams Cosmetics and Edie Adams Cut 'n' Curl.

She bought a 160-acre almond farm and became the TV spokesperson for Gun Giant Nuts. Even though Muriel cigars may have led to her husband's lung cancer, she became the pitch woman for those stogies, too.. In TV commercial after commercial, she sang "Hey, Big Spender, spend a little dime with me." *[At the time, that was the price for an individual cigar.]*

Her cigar commercials made her one of the top three most recognizable celebri-

In his appearance on *The Lucy Show*, **Buddy Hackett** was miscast. "The damn script doesn't give me much to work with," he complained to Lucille.

But she ignored his pleas for better lines, snapping back at him, "What do you want? For our writers to turn you into a sex symbol? Buddy, I hate to tell you this, but you are the unsexiest man in show biz!"

The photo above shows Hackett as he appeared in *The Music Man* (1962).

Comedian **Phil Harris** with his wife, **Alice Faye,** whom he married in 1941. It turned out to be one of the most successful matings in Hollywood. She was the reigning singing star at Fox until Betty Grable came along to replace her.

Lucille told her that two of her favorite movies had been *In Old Chicago* (1937) and *Alexander's Ragtime Band* (1938), in which Faye had co-starred with Tyrone Power.

"God, was he gorgeous," Lucille said. "Did you guys ever make it?"

"No," she claimed. "There were two reasons. First, he never asked me. Second, he liked boys too much."

ties on TV.

***

For her next three episodes of *The Lucy Show,* Lucille hired a trio of comedians: Buddy Hackett, Phil Harris, and Ken Berry.

With Hackett, *Lucy and the Stolen Stole* was telecast on January 29, 1968. Critics interpreted Hackett as miscast, his lines not very funny, and his role too small to make much of an impact. The plot has Lucy and Mr. Mooney purchasing a valuable fur stole for his wife, only to be arrested later for possession of stolen goods.

Although his humor in this episode wasn't particularly effective, in other appearances, Hackett had been a noted comedian. His slightly slurred speech was the result of the lingering affects of Bell's Palsy, a disease he'd suffered as a kid.

Offstage, he related far more to Gary Morton than to Lucille. Both Hackett and Morton had entertained at the Jewish Resorts of the "Borscht Belt," north of New York City in the Catskill Mountains.

On TV shows hosted by Jack Paar and Arthur Godfrey, Hackett became known for his brash, off-color jokes—and a lot of mugging. He was better served by his frequent appearances on Johnny Carson's *The Tonight Show.* In fact, he made more appearances with Carson than any other star in the history of television.

Lucille may have struck out with Hackett, but she had "high hopes" for her next episode, *Lucy and Phil Harris* (February 5, 1968).

At a cocktail bar, she meets a piano player and an aspirant songwriter played by Harris. He's having a love affair with the bottle, and she comes to his rescue, weaning him from alcohol and doing what she can to help him realize his dream as a songwriter.

Like Buddy Hackett in her previous episode, Harris (whose birth name was Wonga Philip Harris) was also miscast. As

For an episode of *The Lucy Show* entitled *Lucy and the Lost Star,* Lucille thought the temperamental silent screen diva, **Gloria Swanson**, would be ideal.

After all, she'd already made "the ultimate statement" of a psychotic has-been in *Sunset Blvd.,* for which she was nominated for a Best Actress Oscar in 1950.

Because of a sudden illness, however, Swanson bowed out.

Eventually, in Lucille's (and Desilu's) search for the quintessential diva, **Joan Crawford** won.

Vivian Vance said, "The pairing of Joan Crawford with Lucille Ball was a match made in hell. She found Crawford even worse to work with than Tallulah Bankhead."

"At one point before the episode was finished, Lucille fired Crawford but later hired her back."

155

a veteran bandleader, comedian, actor, and singer, he was too old for such an aspirant role, and far too talented.

In 1941, he'd married actress Alice Faye, a union that lasted until his death in 1995. For eight years, they had starred together in a hit radio show.

The son of circus performers, Harris told Lucille that his unusual first name ("Wonga") derived from a Cherokee word that translates as "fast messenger."

"Sounds like a pet chimp," she said.

When Lucille co-starred with him, his latest gig was as the voice of "Baloo the Bear" for the soundtrack of an animated movie, *The Jungle Book* (1967).

The highlight of the Ball/Harris show was the song, "But I Love You."

After hearing it, both Frank Sinatra and Perry Como phoned Lucille, telling her that they'd like to record it.

Yet another music-themed episode, *Lucy Helps Ken Berry* was telecast on February 19. Berry was known as an actor/singer/dancer. In time, he was seen on TV series such as *The Andy Griffith Show*, *Mayberry R.F.D.*, and *Mama's Family*.

During his heyday as a dancer, he'd been favorably compared to two of the best, and called "Another Fred Astaire" and "The next Gene Kelly."

Berry was one of Lucille's favorites, and she employed him for six months in the "talent pool" of Desilu, until it was dissolved.

In her episode with Berry (#153), he arrives at Mr. Mooney's bank seeking a loan for the expansion of his dance school.

The highlight of that episode was a Berry dance number configured as a tribute to Astaire called "Stepping Out With My Baby." He and Lucille performed their rendition of "Lucy's Back in Town."

***

Near the end of the run for *The Lucy*

8:30pm, CBS⑤ 5,12,13

In the late 1920s, in silent pictures, **Joan Crawford** had been the best Charleston dancer in Hollywood.

At one point during the filming of *Lucy and the Lost Star*, she was called upon to dance it again.

But when **Crawford** attempted to replicate it for a new generation of television viewers, **Lucille** called "*CUT!*," then stalked over to her and said, "I can't believe you launched yourself in the flickers dancing the Charleston. Now all you can do is a granny two-step. What's the matter? Your bones too brittle?"

In tears, Crawford ran to her dressing room, where she remained in seclusion for two hours. When she returned, Lucille solved the problem by ordering the cameraman to photograph the great diva only from the waist up, and for only ten seconds.

Show, Milt Josefsberg presented her with a script called *Lucy and the Lost Star,* set to be telecast on February 26. After reading it, she told him, "It would be perfect as a vehicle for Gloria Swanson. But after she starred as Norma Desmond, the fading silent screen star in *Sunset Blvd.* (1950), she claims she'd been inundated with scripts about faded stars, and that she accepted none of them."

When she was presented with the script, Swanson agreed to do it, but became ill two nights later and announced that she was no longer available.

"Well, we could have hired that bitch, Bette Davis," Lucille said, "but I'll never tangle with her again."

"How about Joan Crawford," Josefsberg asked. "I hear she's taking anything offered."

"I've never liked her—not at all—but since it's only a 30-minute episode, I guess I can control my temper. My biggest fear is that she'll show up drunk."

In the plot Lucy, re-teamed with Vivian Vance, is in a car that breaks down. In search of help, they knock on the door of the nearest house, which turns out to be the one owned and occupied by Crawford herself. She has sent her furniture out to be re-upholstered, refinished, or restored, and the house looks curiously devoid of furnishings. That leads Lucy and Vance to think she's fallen on bad days. The zany pair plot to get Mr. Mooney to use his influence to get her a well-paying gig.

The first days of rehearsal went badly, as Crawford appeared to be sneaking "overdoses of vodka." Apparently, she carried around small bottles of vodka in her purse.

One brief scene called for Crawford to do the Charleston. In the 1920s, she'd been hailed as "The Queen of the Charleston," and her ability was amply on display in *Our Dancing Daughters,* a Pre-Code silent film released in 1928.

Regrettably, time and age had taken their toll, and Crawford couldn't get the steps right.

In a loud, sharp voice, Lucille scolded her: "I thought you knew how to dance,"

When Lucille joined the all-star cast of *The Jack Benny Hour: Carnival Nights,* she had a reunion with comedian **Danny Thomas**. When Thomas signed a contract with ABC to headline his own sitcom (originally titled *Here Comes Daddy*) he chose Desilu as the place to film it.

In one of their meetings, they recalled the many times they'd worked together. Lucille said, "My most fun was when I got to play a chorus girl on *The Lucy Show* in November of 1965. I was middle-aged and all the other starlets were young."

Director Maury Thompson claimed, "Working with both of them was hell. Each wanted to direct. I remember how in one scene Lucy had to hook Danny's long nose on an umbrella. There was a lot of cursing before that scene was finally shot."

"I do, but it's taking me a while to get the right steps."

"Let's try it again," Lucille barked.

Crawford made two more attempts. Each of them failed.

"All right, god dammit," Lucille said. "We'll have to cut the scene." Then she turned to Crawford: "Are you drunk?"

In tears, Crawford ran to her dressing room. It took two hours to lure her back onto the set.

She never did get the Charleston right.

After the taping, Lucille invited Crawford, along with key cast and crew members, to dinner at Don the Beachcomber's.

Crawford sent word back to the set: "Tell Miss Ball to go fuck herself. I'm sure, when faced with this witch, that Gary Morton can't get it up anymore. Ball is a bigger bitch than I am."

***

Lucille might have launched *The Lucy Show* with a blast during its first season in 1962, but she ended it in 1968 with a whimper.

As the series was about to go off the air, except for re-runs, Bob O'Brien presented his latest script, *Lucy and Sid Caesar* (telecast on March 4), to her. In it, the audience learns that the comedian is a large depositor at Mooney's bank, and some imposter, a lookalike, is forging his name to withdraw cash.

At this point in his life, when he worked with Lucille, Caesar was mired in alcoholism, addicted to barbiturates, and in a career slump. He had had his heyday in the 1950s as the host of a massively popular weekly TV series, *Your Show of Shows* (1950-54). It had attracted an audience of sixty million viewers.

In the past, his writers had included Mel Brooks, Carl Reiner, and Woody Allen. O'Brien did not have the talent collectively represented by that trio, so it was a weak show with Lucille.

"It's not like the old days," Caesar told her. "Back then, they called me the Charlie Chaplin of Television."

"I'm not exactly gangbusters myself," she admitted to him.

It seemed that Caesar had not been able to handle the pressures of superstardom. "Working with Sid aroused a fear in me that I might, too, enter a career abyss," she confessed to Morton and O'Brien.

With Gary Morton, she sat in her living room watching the episode she'd taped with Caesar. When it was over, she turned to him. "It was merely okay. Let's face it: Neither Sid or myself are what we used to

The scriptwriter Bob O'Brien recalled the final teaming of Lucille with comedian **Sid Caesar**.

"In the 1950s, they had reigned as King and Queen of the Golden Age of Television., Sid with his hit *Your Show of Shows.*"

But years of alcoholism had taken its toll on he legendary comedian. Lucille was still holding in there, but poor Sid had seen a better day."

be."

If she found the episode with Caesar less than winning, she was horrified at the last show of the season, which ended the series on March 11, 1968. It was entitled *Lucy and the Boss of the Year Award*. She schemes to have the fussbudget portrayed by Gale Gordon designated as president of the San Francisco branch of their banking chain. "That way," as she told her co-stars, Jack Collins, and her husband, Gary Morton, "I can wash Mr. Mooney right out of my hair."

At this point in its broadcasting history, *The Lucy Show* had begun to receive more and more critical attacks, unfavorably compared when stacked up against the *I Love Lucy* series of the 1950s. In a review that appeared in *TV Guide,* a writer said, "What *The Lucy Show* needed was Desi Arnaz."

***

Lucille rounded out the spring of 1968 by making highly watched appearances on the TV shows of other (veteran) hosts. On March 17, she appeared on *The Ed Sullivan Show* mainly to promote the movie she'd made with Henry Fonda, *Yours, Mine, and Ours.*

It was a great promotional success for her, as Sullivan screened clips from several individual and iconic episodes of *I Love Lucy* dubbed in different languages, including Japanese.

She followed that three nights later with a guest appearance on *The Jack Benny Hour: Carnival Nights.* Heavily bewigged, she emerged as "Luscious Lucy," singing "It's So Nice to Have a Man Around the House." She appears before a bevy of musclemen who evoked the impression that they'd been shoplifted directly from Mae West's stage act.

Benny's show was a star-studded event that included appearances by George Burns, Johnny Carson, Bob Hope,

"I had no great love for **Ed Sullivan**," Lucille recalled. "He had the charm of a large bed bug. But over the years, he sure knew how to book talent—everybody from a young Elvis Presley (shot from the waist up) to the Beatles."

"My resentment of him stemmed from professional jealousy. Desi and I were No. 1 with *I Love Lucy* until we fell to third place, beaten by *The $64,000 Question* and by Ed's variety show."

Lucille's first appearance on **Mike Douglas'** syndicated daytime talk show, shot in Philadelphia, was in April of 1968. As a surprise to her, Vivian Vance suddenly appeared next to her, on camera, for a reunion, as the audience hooted and hollered.

"Going Indian on us, are you, Lucy?" Vance asked. Her former co-star was attrired in a black Nehru suit.

Dean Martin, The Smothers Brothers, and Danny Thomas, among others.

On April 13, she was invited onto *The Mike Douglas Show*. Since its inception in Philadelphia in 1965, the show had become quite popular. Over time, Douglas hosted guests ranging from Richard Nixon to Truman Capote, and helped introduce singers such as Barbra Streisand and Aretha Franklin,

When Lucille appeared on his show, she was seen by six million viewers.

Other guest stars that night included Ozzie and Harriet Nelson. A surprise came in the form of a visit from Vivian Vance. With Lucille, she talked about their glory days of portraying Lucy Ricardo and Ethel Mertz.

About five weeks later, as a keynote moment of that spring's TV lineup, the Twentieth Annual Emmy Awards were broadcast through NBC on the evening of May 19. Hosts Frank Sinatra and Dick Van Dyke welcomed Lucille. To her surprise, and for the second consecutive years, she walked off with another Emmy for "Outstanding Continued Performance by an Actress in a Leading Role in a Comedy Series."

In accepting her award, she beat out Elizabeth Montgomery *(Bewitched)*, Marlo Thomas *(That Girl!)*, Barbara Feldon *(Get Smart)*, and Paula Prentiss *(He & She)*.

***

In 1968, as Lucille neared the dangerous age for an actress, on the road to becoming a performer in her sixties, writers began to look back on (and evaluate) her career.

Alert to her widespread fame and the critical reviews her TV *schtick* had recently generated, she spoke to a reporter from *Variety*: "For the last five years, I've been announcing my retirement from television," she said. "After that, I signed on for another season, like I'm doing this year. What the hell? I predict that my new series, *Here's Lucy*, will be my last hurrah. As you know, it'll be a family affair, since both Lucie and Desi Jr. will co-star with me."

She might have been America's funniest mom on TV, but she didn't emote

Ozzie and Harriet Nelson were married in real life and also as the co-starring characters in their family-friendly show. They were sometimes described as "the Vanilla Versions of Ricky and Lucy Ricardo."

Appearing with them on camera were their real-life sons, David and Ricky Nelson, in a style perhaps inspired by Lucille and Desi, who likewise employed their son, Desi Jr. and daughter, Lucie.

During Harriet and Lucille's appearance on *The Mike Douglas Show*, they reminisced about the era when they were underpaid contract players struggling to survive at RKO.

Harriet said, "Who in hell could have known that one day, you'd end up owning the studio?"

that way at home. Her kids found her "a super-strict and demanding taskmaster."

During rehearsals for their joint appearances on TV, she constantly reminded them of any mistakes they made.

Reportedly, her children called her "a control freak," and "the most domineering mother in Hollywood."

Her friend and sometimes co-star, Mary Wickes, said, "I came to love her dearly as a friend, but only after I accepted the fact that she had to be in control 24 hours a day, every day."

Having escaped from her orbit, divorced from her, and re-married, her ex-husband had already formed Desi Arnaz Productions. Most of its success centered on the TV series it had created and launched, *Mothers-in-Law,* starring Eve Arden and Kaye Ballard.

Following Desi's example, his former wife launched Lucille Ball Productions early in 1968.

It came as no surprise to the industry that she made Morton her vice president and executive producer. Together, with a lot of help, they set out to launch yet another series, trading once again on the long-standing affection of the TV-watching public for the comedic *shtick* of their favorite redhead. The newest series was named *Here's Lucy.*

More and more, she had come to trust Morton for the day-to-day operations of business interests, a policy that allowed her to invest more time as a performer.

Commenting on his new and more prestigious role, Morton said, "Lucille is a diamond, and my principal reason for living is to see that that diamond is kept polished and sparkling, enough so that it even glows in the dark."

Originally, the new series would be taped at Paramount Television in studios she once owned. But when she feuded with Gulf + Western, which had bought her out, she moved her operations in a complicated legal maneuver to Universal, which became the new home for Lucille Ball Productions. "They welcomed me, and even decorated my dressing room to my specifications," she said.

As symbols of domestic bliss, **Lucille Ball** and **Gary Morton** pose for this publicity photo at Lucille Ball Productions.

Although she made the final decisions, beginning with the First Season (1968-69) of *Here's Lucy,* she made him Executive Producer.

According to Morton, "My job was to get what Lucille wanted, and that varied day to day. Mostly, I lined up guest stars, everyone from Jack Benny to Wayne Newton."

Elvis Presley asked him, "You want me on a show with Lucy Ricardo? You gotta be kidding."

To line up the first shows of the season, she turned to familiar "war horses," who included Tommy Thompson, who was called back to produce the shows, and Jack Donohue to direct them. She retained Milt Josefsberg as her script doctor. The new series would be broadcast on CBS, a partnership destined to last until 1974.

Doris Singleton, who had been cast as Carolyn Appleby on the *I Love Lucy* series, was tapped as a regular on the new show. However, at the last minute, Lucille decided to morph her seventeen-year-old daughter, Lucie Arnaz, and her fifteen-year-old son, Desi Jr., into her co-stars.

In a discussion about salaries paid to her children, Lucille frankly admitted, "I'm no Santa Claus. Each will receive a salary of $17,600 for the first year, rising to $20,000 for the second year, and $25,200 for the third year—that is, if *Here's Lucy* is still being aired. Forty percent will get set aside for the IRS, and twenty percent will go into government bonds 'for their future.'"

She gave some advice and drew up some agreements with her kids: "Sign up for only one season. If you don't like it, we can write you out for the second and, if there is one, the third. Also, if the critics pan one of you, or both of you, you're toast."

Her favorite actor, Gale Gordon, was retained as her co-star, but no longer would he be Mr. Mooney, and no longer would he be a banker. In his latest incarnation, he'd remain as her boss, but now in the role of Harrison Otis Carter (i.e., "Uncle Harry"), he was configured as her (bachelor) brother-in-law. He ran Carter's Unique Employment Agency, charged with finding "unusual employees to fill unusual jobs."

Mary Jane Croft, cast in the role of "Mary Jane Lewis," would be a "semi-regular" in the new venue. Character actress Vanda Barra, who had worked with Lucille in previous seasons of *The Lucy Show*, would have her role upgraded.

The always-reluctant Vivian Vance would make six guest appearances as "Vi-

Lucille poses with her children for the cast line-up of her new TV sitcom, *Here's Lucy*. As in real life, they would play her son and daughter.

"I played Craig, who I thought was a bit of a nerd," Desi Jr. said. "In private life, I viewed myself as very hip. At that time in my life, I didn't really know who I was., So why not play up a false front as her TV son, Craig?"

Lucie said, "The only thing that was light about my mother was that hair of hers. She was a tough task master on the set, trying for perfection, but, of course, rarely finding it."

Jack Benny, whom Lucille knew better than the rest of the cast and crew, appeared on several episodes of her show. She seemed aware of his sexual proclivities. Director Jack Donohue heard her warn Benny, "Don't you dare make a pass at Junior."

vian Jones," although audiences nationwide still remembered her (and referred to her) as Ethel Mertz.

In this new series, although Lucille would retain her (by now virtually trademarked) name of Lucy, no longer was she Lucy Ricardo or Lucy Carmichael, but Lucy Carter, the widowed mother of Kim Carter (Lucie) and Craig Carter (Desi Jr.). Together, they live in a high rise in Encino, in California's San Fernando Valley, where the real-life Desi Sr. and Lucille had lived in the 1940s, in a then-isolated ranch house.

In Lucille's newest incarnation, she appears ready, willing, and able for an eligible bachelor to come into her life.

In addition to co-starring as Craig, Desi Jr. would be a busy performer. He was still a teen idol with his pop band, Dino, Desi, and Billy.

As a change of pace for Lucille, it was clearly decided that the new series' scripts would address the generation gap that parents were facing (and suffering from) across America. Lucy Carter would deal with ferociously independent and rebellious teenagers. Themes would include conflicting views about civil rights, rock music, the sexual revolution, and shifting gender and lifestyle mores.

Although her associates loudly maintained that the new series was clearly unrelated to its predecessors, Lucille was nonetheless threatened with a lawsuit from Jess Oppenheimer, who claimed that Lucy Carter, as presented in *Here's Lucy*, was a warmed-over version of the character he had originally devised for *I Love Lucy*. After threatening to sue her in court, she paid him $220,000 in a private settlement.

Before the first telecast, Lucille met with Morton and the other members of her creative team to announce the names of the guest stars she wanted to invite. Of course, she didn't know if any or all of these stars would accept.

At the top of her list were Carol Burnett and Vivian Vance. Other stars might include Dean Martin, George Burns, Johnny Carson, Petula Clark, Eva Gabor, Liberace, Helen Hayes, Ann-Margret, Ginger Rogers, Tony Randall, Buddy Rich, Joan Rivers, Vincent Price, Danny Thomas, Dinah Shore, Lawrence Wells, Flip Wilson in drag, Shelley Winters, and Danny Osmond.

The first episode of *Here's Lucy*, telecast on September 23, 1968, was entitled *Mod, Mod Lucy*. In it, she valiantly tried to connect with the younger, "mod" generation.

Uncle Harry (Gale Gordon) has announced his intention of hiring some musicians (real cheap) to entertain at a Sweet Sixteen party.

Consequently, Lucy lines up her son's band, with her daughter, Kim, slated to play what Lucille defined as "The Janis Joplin role" as its lead singer. At the last minute, her daughter falls ill, and with the intention of replacing her, Lucy disguises herself as a "Modster" to take her place. *[Of course, a 57-year-old woman in a miniskirt and a "mod wig" doesn't quite pull it off.]*

Carole Cook was brought back to dub Lucille's singing voice. "Even back in the 1940s, no one ever accused me of being Jo Stafford," Lucille quipped. "And my children didn't set the critical world shouting their praises, either."

Critics took a dim view of Lucille's new series.

Women's Wear Daily was not impressed, claiming, "Lucie and Desi Jr. have no talent, and *Here's Lucy* is pure treacle."

The Hollywood Reporter interpreted the new series as "one giant marshmallow."

The New York Times was kinder: "Desi Jr. and Lucie Arnaz know how to trade lines with the veteran redhead. Miss Ball should have a ball trying to bridge the generation gap."

In reference to the then-blowsy former bombshell, **Shelley Winters**, Lucille said, "You never knew what was going to pop out of the mouth of that one!"

Burt Lancaster had said, "Shelley was a fine specimen of a woman. Then she got fat."

After some drinks, Winters was especially outspoken in reviews of her lovers: "Lancaster's dick wasn't big enough. Neither was Clark Gable's. Errol Flynn's wasn't as big as he claimed. Neither was Marlon Brando's self-styled 'noble tool.' John Ireland was the biggest I've ever known. My buddy, Farley Granger, would have preferred his dick in a man than in me. Sterling Hayden had a whopper. Howard Hughes was strictly oral. The best in the boudoir? Sean Connery, 007 himself."

***

Many public figures (including Rock Hudson, Charlie Chaplin, Marilyn Monroe, and Frank Sinatra) have faced charges of having a daughter or son whose existence was concealed from the public.

Such was the case with Lucille in 1968. Scandal magazines, in "Second Coming" headlines, revealed that in May of 1947, she gave birth to a daughter, Madeline Jane Dee.

[In 2003, when she was 56, Madeline Jane Dee was hit by a bus and killed. After her death, her daughter, Cassandria Carlson, revealed her own status as the granddaughter of Lucille Ball, alleging that her mother (Madeline Jane) had been the result of an adulterous affair, citing the father as Desi Arnaz, who had been married to Lucille since November of 1940.

Cassandria even produced a court document, notarized on June 24, 1947, granting permission for an adoption of Madeline Jane. Of course, Cassandria could not have known for certain who her mother's father had been. In the late 1940s, Lucille was having a number of affairs—including with such actors as George Sanders and William Holden—and Desi at the time was committing adultery almost daily.

"My mother never had a job, and my father was a low-wage blue collar worker," Cassandria claimed. "But if we needed something, my mother always seemed to have the money to buy it. Also, I learned that on occasion, my mother met with a "Mrs. Morton."

At the time of Madeline Jane's birth, Lucille, hoping to revive a sagging film career, was getting ready to embark on a nation-wide tour with a play called *Dream Girl*. Her tour began in June, about a month after that alleged birth.

Cassandria told reporter Jim Nelson that she was coming forward with these revelations "as a voice for my mother, but not as an attempt to extract money from the Arnaz family."

It was reported that Lucie Arnaz told the press that she did not believe the allegations of either Madeline Jane or Cassandria. Lucie cited that her mother and Desi struggled for years to have a child, and that Lucille suffered through miscarriages. *[Of course, Desi could have fathered a child with another woman.]*

As far as it is known, Lucie Arnaz, born in 1951, is the first child Lucille Ball ever gave birth to. There was some unconfirmed rumor that dated back to her starlet days in the 1930s — that she had had a child aborted.

***

Agitated and nervous, Lucille moved into the First Season (1968-69) of *Here's Lucy* questioning everything and everyone.

In reference to Episode #2 (*Lucy Visits Jack Benny,* telecast on September 30, 1968) of the *Here's Lucy* series, its producer, Tommy Thompson, said, "All of us liked Gary Morton, who, as executive producer, was my boss. But the cast and crew resented the fact that Lucille consistently mistreated him — not in private but in front of all of us. He was more like her manservant than he was her husband. She even tangled with Jack Benny when he was a guest on her show."

Milt Josefsberg wrote the script for that episode. It depicts her and her kids arriving in Palm Springs for a vacation. They rent rooms from Jack Benny, who always appeared on the air in his own show as a penny-pinching miser. He charges the Carter family for every item, even if it's only a Dixie cup.

Lucille shocked Thompson and the rest of the cast when she started to boss Benny around, giving him (unwanted) pointers about how he could sharpen his comedic techniques.

He could no longer stand for that, and after about three minutes, he lost his normally benign façade and shouted at her: "Just who in hell do you think you're talking to? I'm Jack Benny, King of Comedy."

"After that, Lucille shut up and let Benny do it his way," Thompson said.

Before he left the set that night, Benny met with Thompson, relating a story of what happened once when he met with Desi and Lucille for dinner. "Things went smoothly at first, and they were like lovebirds," Benny said. "But later, after they'd had a few drinks, Lucille accused Desi of bordello-hopping. Things got so fraught that he eventually punched her in the face. That led to her picking up a wine bottle and knocking him in the head. After he came to, all seemed forgiven before the end of the evening. Right after dinner, I made a speedy exit, but only after thanking them for a lovely evening."

***

Hoping to hold onto her Nielsen rating, Lucille set about, over the next few months, to appear with name stars.

A notable example was in Episode #4, *Lucy and Miss Shelley Winters* (October 14).

In reference to Winters, Lucille said, "The gal has *chutzpah*. Ever heard her interviewed on TV? She'll say anything."

In the script, a film producer has told a rather *zaftig* Shelley Summers (i.e., Winters) to take off fifteen pounds before shooting begins on her next picture.

Lucy is enlisted as her watchdog to keep her from pigging out. In rehearsal, she found Winters more amusing and provocative off-camera. They met at the end of the first day of rehearsal, as Winters changed into her street clothes. The subject was husbands.

"My first husband, Captain Mack Paul Mayer—I married him in 1942—was Jewish like your Gary Morton. That meant he was circumcised. Actually, I prefer uncut men like Burt Lancaster, although I once had a fling with John Garfield who is cut. My other two husbands, both of them actors (Vittorio Gassman and Anthony Franciosa) were uncut. I think every woman should marry an Italian man, at least once, but not for long—maybe a year. Howard Hughes and Anthony Quinn were uncut."

"Men are so different in bed," Winters asserted. "Going to bed with Ronald Colman was nothing at all like bedding Marlon Brando." Then Winters turned to Lucille as if demanding the truth: "Did you find Bill Holden as satisfying in bed as I did?"

"I did, indeed," Lucille said, "except for one thing: He showers before sex and after sex. Before the day is over, he has five or six showers."

The next morning, Lucille told Thompson, "You never know what's going to pop out of Shelley's mouth, and I mean that literally and figuratively. She told me that one

Above, the glittering "bygone and baroque" world of that trio of seductive sisters, **Eva, Magda, and Zsa Zsa Gabor** live again in Blood Moon's widely reviewed romantic biography, *Those Glamorous Gabors, Bombshells from Budapest.*

Their marriages were A-list and profitable and their seductions were newsworthy, men who included John F. Kennedy, Tyrone Power, Glenn Ford, Frank Sinatra, Nicky Hilton, Richard Burton, Mario Lanza, Sean Connery, and the Dominican playboy with the massive endowment, Porfirio Rubirosa.

night at Errol Flynn's house, she shacked up with both Clark Gable and him. She also claimed that in their early days, she and Marilyn Monroe were roommates. Her exact words, 'When we hadn't lined up a man for the night, Marilyn and I bumped pussies.'"

Months later, Lucille heard that Winters was in San Francisco, hanging out with (of all people) Janis Joplin.

For Episode #7, *Lucy and Eva Gabor* (November 11), Lucille starred with a very different blonde, this time Eva Gabor, the Blonde Bombshell from Hungary. She was a bit provocative, but far more ladylike than Shelley Winters. She was also becoming more famous than her celebrated sister, Zsa Zsa, because Eva was starring in the hit TV series, *Green Acres* (1965-1971). In that series, although she loved Park Avenue, she had opted—always dressed in diaphanous gowns and jewelry—to live on an isolated farm because her lawyer husband, Eddie Albert, wanted the rural life of a farmer.

Meeting with Lucille in private, Eva was not quite as provocative as Zsa Zsa, but gossipy and entertaining nonetheless.

"Marriage is too intriguing an experiment to try it only once," Eva claimed.

In their sequence, Eva was cast as Eva Von Kirsten, a novelist seeking a quiet retreat so she can finish her novel, *Valley of the Puppets,* a send-up of Jacqueline Susann's *Valley of the Dolls.* Lucille offers her home as a place for her to hide out and write.

Rehearsing together, Eva shared some confidences with Lucille, claiming that she'd had an affair with Frank Sinatra. "Zsa Zsa turned him down, but he got her anyway. He raped her."

At the time, Eva was married to Richard Brown, a textile manufacturer. However, she admitted she was still on occasion having a fling with Glenn Ford, an affair that had begun in 1957 when they'd co-starred in *Don't Go Near the Water.*

The "Latin from Manhattan," **Cesar Romero**—never without his mustache—became known in Hollywood for fellating his leading men—that is, if they would allow it.

He was such an expert, he was named "The King of Fellatio" among Tinseltown gossips. Lying on his sofa while he did all the work were the likes of John Payne and Tyrone Power.

During Romero's gig in the Coast Guard during World War II, he was one of the most popular men in the barracks. But his lifelong passion was reserved for Desi Arnaz.

***

Episode #22, *Lucy and the Matchmaker* (December 16, 1968), was memorable in that it marked the return of Vivian Vance. The moment she appeared before the live audience she was greeted with such thunderous applause that it disrupted the taping.

In this episode, Uncle Harry (Gale Gordon) needed a date to attend a gala affair. Lucy becomes matchmaker. Guess who she fixes him up with? None other than Vance herself.

Wally Cox, another familiar face from a former show, co-starred with Lucille again in *Lucy and the Ex-Con* (January 13, 1969).

In the plot, Cox plays a former safecracker who is released from prison. Working with Uncle Harry at their employment agency, she manages to get him a job as a security guard. When the premises he's guarding is robbed, Cox becomes the prime suspect. In disguise, he and Lucy set out to track down the real bandit.

Before the shoot, she asked him if he were still close to his best buddy, Marlon Brando, whom he had known "forever and a day."

"We'll be friends even after one of us dies," Cox said.

Indeed, when Cox died and was cremated, Brando kept his ashes in his bedroom until his own death.

***

In *A Date for Lucy* (February 10), she had a reunion with her longtime friend, the gay actor Cesar Romero. He had often appeared on screen in the 1940s as a Latin lover.

In the plot, her kids, Kim and Craig, fix their mother up on a date. At first, the character that Cesar plays, a good-looking bachelor, seems ideal as Lucy's escort. But, as it turns out, he is a jewel thief.

For more than twenty years, she had known that Romero was madly in love with her ex-husband. When she encountered him again, she bluntly asked, "Are you still in love with Desi?"

"Maybe we both are, after all these years," Cesar confessed.

"I never got over him, and I suspect that you haven't either," she said. "He was the only man I ever really loved. But life must go on."

Over the years, she had never expressed any jealous rage about Romero. In fact, when Desi was away and she needed an escort, she sometimes called on him to take her out. He became known as a proper and "socially correct" escort for a bevy of other aging female stars, including Jane Wyman, Ann Sheridan, Barbara Stanwyck, Linda Darnell, Ginger Rogers, and Joan Crawford.

Lucie Arnaz was quoted as saying, "Every star knew they could trust Cesar, and that there would be no funny business when he drove them home."

***

In Episode #22, *Lucy's Safari* (March 3), Lucille looked forward to co-starring with Howard Keel. He was cast as a big game hunter, Stanley Livingston. He and Lucy, along with Kim and Craig, set out to recapture "Gorboona," an ape which had escaped from the local zoo.

For some reason, during the taping, nothing seemed to work, and TV critics reviewed this episode as the worst of the season. The tall, handsome

Keel, with his rich bass-baritone singing voice, was in the wrong script. It should have been more of a musical, as that was the genre in which he had excelled within such hit films as *Annie Get Your Gun* (1950) with Betty Hutton, and *Seven Brides for Seven Brothers* (1954) opposite Jane Powell.

***

After Desi faced the cancellation of the series he'd helped create, *The Mothers-in-Law*, he learned that his bank account was dwindling, mainly because of his lavish lifestyle and gambling losses. Once, he possessed a few million dollars, but he'd gone through a huge hunk of it already.

Along with his second wife, Edie, he divided their time among four (expensive to maintain) residences. They included a resort hotel he owned in La Paz, Mexico; villas in Palm Springs and Del Mar, near the race track; and a high-maintenance horse-breeding farm in Corona, California.

"One morning, after watching Lucy on TV the night before, I decided that I, too, could cash in on the fame we still enjoyed from those *I Love Lucy* series," Desi said. "She seemed to be cleaning up in a life after Lucy Ricardo. Hell, what about life after Ricky Ricardo? Without me on *I Love Lucy*, it would have failed. Dozens of people have told me that."

Three days later, *Variety* ran an item announcing, "Desi Arnaz has announced a comeback, both as an actor and a TV producer, the dual jobs he had as President of Desilu Productions. Future TV series will be produced under his new banner of Desi Arnaz Productions."

He told a reporter, "I got tired of watching all those movies starring the talentless Ricardo Montalban and my former-friend-no-more, Fernando Lamas. Time for Desi Arnaz to make a spectacular comeback."

What he didn't tell *Variety* was that because he could no longer afford it, he had to sell his thorough-

In the late 1940s, after wartime service in the Army, **Desi Arnaz** had returned to Hollywood, hoping to become its latest Latin Lover.

"I wanted to be adored like Valentino, but Fernando Lamas and Ricardo Montalban assumed the lover roles—not me. I was bitterly disappointed."

"My attempts at becoming a screen actor after I co-starred with Lucy bombed."

Such was the case when he appeared (both photos above) in *The Man from Shiloh*, a spin-off of the popular TV Western series, *The Virginian*.

bred breeding farm at Corona.

He signed a contract to appear as a player in the TV series, *The Man from Shiloh*. Launched in September of 1970 and surviving for only a year, until 1971, it was the ninth and (radically reconfigured) final season of the hit Western series, *The Virginian*. Set in the late 19th Century, and loosely based on a 1902 novel by Owen Wister, it starred James Drury in the title role, and Doug McClure.

The series revolved around the tough foreman, as portrayed by Drury, of the Shiloh Ranch. His key man and associate was Trampas (McClure). Both stars would remain with the series for its entire run, 249 episodes airing on NBC from 1962 to 1971.

The Virginian had been the network's third-longest-running Western series, trailing *Bonanza* and *Gunsmoke*. *The Man from Shiloh* was a sort of sequel to *The Virginian*, set in the 1890s, a decade after the times slot for *The Virginian*.

In this new series, Shiloh Ranch, a featured locale within the previous series, has been purchased by an Englishman, Col. Alan Mackenzie (Stewart Granger).

Desi met with Granger, who confided in him that he "hated working in television—it's all rush and dash, throw it together and put it on the air. No time for quality. We're not turning out a very good show, since everything happens too quickly, not like it was when I was a big-time movie star."

The episode in which Desi appeared was entitled *The Best Man*. Trampas (McClure) travels across the Mexican border in his capacity as the best man at his friend's upcoming wedding, only to learn that the bride knows nothing about the plans underway for her upcoming wedding. Featured in the telecast was the song, "Take a Look Around."

According to Desi, "The cast, including Granger, had heard that I had cancer. During the past two years, I had had two operations, one for hematoma, another for diverticulitis. I had gained some weight, probably because I drank eighteen cans of *cerveza* every day."

Later on, Desi would make another stab at crafting his comeback as an actor. He worked to develop a pilot, *Doctor*

The English actor, **Stewart Granger,** once married to actress Jean Simmons, was past his prime when he co-starred with Desi Arnaz in *The Man from Shiloh*.

In his heyday, his love affairs included both Grace Kelly and Michael Wilding, who later married Elizabeth Taylor.

Columnist Dorothy Kilgallen said, "I have never seen anything like the way ladies with high boiling points and high intelligence fall to pieces before Gorgeous Granger."

During his seduction of Hedy Lamarr, she warned him "not to come on too fast."

Granger told Desi, "I had many lovers, but I had to say no to a love-sick Cary Grant."

Domingo, which was conceived as a spin-off of the hit TV series, *Ironside* (1967 to 1973). Its star was to have been the gay actor Raymond Burr, who played a consultant to the San Francisco police. On that show, his character was paralyzed from the waist down.

Desi knew he needed help in matching his in-development pilots with a corporate sponsor, so with that in mind, he turned to Lew Wasserman, a talent agent called "the last of the legendary moguls," and "the most powerful and influential Titan in Hollywood."

According to Desi, "Lew, too, had a wife named Edie, and my Edie and I were invited for dinner at his home. We were surprised that he had invited two other guests, namely, Bette Davis and Ronald Reagan. Both of them had starred in *Dark Victory* (1939). Bette could have been nice to Ronnie, but she didn't seem to care for him at all. Each of them had been clients of Lew."

No sponsor could be found for *Doctor Domingo,* so Desi enlisted Wasserman's help for a new pilot, *Chairman of the Board.* As its star, he had cast Elke Sommer, a star attraction in the films of the 1960s and '70s, including a sequel to *The Pink Panther* entitled *A Shot in the Dark* (1964).

As a producer, Desi Arnaz Sr. launched several pilots, hoping for corporate sponsors to turn them into full-fledged TV series.

He had especially high hopes for one of them, *Dr. Domingo.* It would have starred Raymond Burr, already well known for his portrayal of Perry Mason.

Lew Wasserman (photo above) was the most powerful agent in Hollywood, but even he could not sell any of Desi's pilots. He finally had to tell him, "Desi, my man, your time on the stage has come and gone. It's time to exit."

In spite of his influence, Wasserman never found a sponsor for Desi's projected TV series.

"He was itching to get back in the game," Wasserman recalled. "But without Lucy as his co-star, he was a dud on the Hollywood slave market. He was no longer highly regarded—in fact, he was considered an *I Love Lucy* has-been. News of his temper and heavy boozing had virtually destroyed his reputation as an actor and certainly as a TV producer."

***

As the 1970s advanced, Desi co-hosted a TV event starring Mike Douglas, which was broadcast out of Philadelphia. Desi had been impressed when he saw Lucille perform on Douglas' show, which was telecast in April of 1968. Ozzie and Harriet Nelson appeared, and the audience applauded wildly when Vivian Vance walked out onto the set on stilts.

Desi also appeared as a guest on the *Kraft Music Hall.* [*That was an umbrella title for several TV series telecast by NBC. Actually, it had originated in*

1933 as a radio series, and over time both Al Jolson and Bing Crosby had been its hosts. In 1958, Kraft Music Hall *came back with Milton Berle ("Mr. Television") as its host.]*

Desi was among the many stars who appeared on the show: Alan King, Don Rickles, Mitzi Gaynor, Bobby Darin (singing "Mack the Knife"), Wayne Newton, Johnny Cash, and that singing duo, Simon & Garfunkel. Sometimes, a husband-and-wife team was featured, including Steve Lawrence and Eydie Gormé. For the kiddies, Roy Rogers (The King of the Cowboys) came on with his horseback-riding wife, Dale Evans (The Queen of the Cowgirls).

Even though they were long-ago divorced, Desi devised what he called "a spectacular idea: Bring Lucy on for a reunion of the Ricardos. NBC will see the ratings soar." But when he phoned Lucille about it, she rejected the idea.

In 1976, Desi published his autobiography, entitling it *A Book.* To publicize it, he agreed to be a guest host on *Saturday Night Live. [Premiered in October of 1973, it was a late-night live TV sketch comedy and variety show that presented a parody of contemporary culture.]*

Desi Jr. played the drums, and his father sang "Babalu" and another favorite ("Cuban Pete") from his dance band days.

He ended the broadcast by leading the entire cast in a raucous conga line through the SNL studio.

Desi also popped up again in an episode of CBS's long-running (1976-1985) TV sitcom, *Alice,* in which Linda Lavin had the title role, portraying a widow who moves with her young son to Phoenix, Arizona, where she finds work as a waitress at a roadside diner.

One of the hallmarks of the series involved bringing on celebrities playing themselves. Desi carried on that tradition, following in the footsteps of such performers as George Burns, Robert Goulet, Jerry Reed, and Art Carney. The TV series had been based on the feature film, *Alice Doesn't Live Here Anymore* (1974), starring Ellen Burstyn and Kris Kristofferson.

Desi would have cast the fading actor, **Sonny Tufts**, in a new detective series, *Land's End*, but the deal fell through.

A native of Boston, Tufts was ruggedly handsome, big, blond, and tough. He set out to be an opera singer, but ended up in Hollywood, cast in *So Proudly We Hail*, a wartime movie released in 1943.

Stardom was on the way. But alas, it was not meant to last. In time, "Sonny Tufts" became a crude punchline for comedians.

***

In an attempt to relaunch himself as a televison producer, Desi had high hopes for *Land's End*, a series that focused on the adventures of a former Los Angeles police officer who quits the force for a job as a private investigator in Cabo San Lucas, Mexico. Procter and Gamble agreed to finance its pilot.

Mart Briskin was hired to help Desi get the series launched. A showbiz veteran, Briskin had done everything from managing Mickey Rooney to writing such TV series as *The Sheriff of Cochise*. In a lifetime, he would create more than three hundred scripts.

Desi also reunited with Daniel ("Dann") Cahn, whose major credential had been his stint as the film editor of both *I Love Lucy* and of Desi's other hit series, *The Untouchables*.

"I called Cahn and told him to quit chasing after all those exotic birds and get his ass over to my office. Did I have a job for him! I also summoned Briskin for our confab."

After Desi outlined his vision of the series and its main character, both men were in agreement that the role "Just called for Victor Mature as its star."

The gay "casting couch" talent agent, the notorious Henry Willson, discovered **Rory Calhoun**, a former prison convict, and made him a star.

He took these early beefcake photos of Calhoun and sent them out to movie producers and directors.

Over the years, Lucille expressed a desire to make him her leading man, but no deal was ever worked out. "Actually," as she told Vivian Vance, "I wanted more to do with him that co-star with him."

Desi immediately nixed the idea, reminding them that as executive producer, he had the final say on casting. "The male lead goes to Rory Calhoun. I've already talked to him, and he'll sign on."

He insisted on the handsome, rugged actor, who had a prison record, even though he suspected that many years ago he'd had an affair with Lucille.

Desi then set about casting the other key roles. He mentioned that Martin Milner had played the good guy in the hit TV series *Route 66*, aired on CBS from 1960 to 1964. "I like going against type. Therefore, I want Milner to start playing a bad guy."

As the tough cop, he had chosen Gilbert Roland, a Mexican-born actor whose career would span seven decades.

[Roland had once been married to Constance Bennett back in the days when Lucille, as a Hattie Carnegie model, had paraded before the star decked out in the latest fashions.

As a film star, Roland had once been engaged to Clara Bow, "The 'It' Girl," and he had also been romantically involved with Norma Talmadge, playing Armand opposite her Camille.]

"I could have played all of Roland's roles except I'd be better," Desi boasted to Briskin, "but he'll be perfect for our pilot."

As yet another key character, an aging movie star, Sonny Tufts, was an odd choice for Desi. Tufts was notorious, often arrested for public drunkenness, and was considered something of a joke around Hollywood. In an incident that had become a "darling of the tabloids," one starlet had sued him for biting her left thigh.

By the time Desi hired him, Tuft's career had been massively downgraded. He had recently starred in one of the worst movies ever made, *Cottonpickin' Chickenpickers* (1967).

The female lead of *Land's End* went to Leigh Chapman, a beautiful actress and scriptwriter from North Carolina.

Months later, she had nothing but bitter memories about having worked with Desi. "I hated his guts. After the pilot, I had to retire to Hawaii for a year. He drove cast and crew crazy and was drunk all the time. He falsely accused me of taking drugs. Once, at dinner, he got so mad at me, he threw a plate of spaghetti at me. He pulled that same stunt with Cahn one night. I think Arnaz thought he was directing *Gone With the Wind*, insisting on creating scenes to film that would run way overtime, since the pilot was only thirty minutes, less if you figured in commercials."

Finally, the time came to screen the pilot, as financed by Proctor and Gamble, before the William Morris Agency and other brass from the network.

The pilot was ninety minutes long, and before it was over, viewers were squirming in their seats. "It just didn't work, and Desi had insisted on shooting all sorts of detours, and refused to let me edit them out," Cahn said. "Then, when the brass complained about the length, he not only blamed me, but called me a cocksucker in front of everybody. I was humiliated. I'd always loved Desi, but he was no longer the man I'd worked with back in the 1950s. This reincarnation was a pure bastard."

Cahn, Briskin, and Wasserman all seemed to agree on one point: Desi Arnaz had reached his last hurrah.

The ironies of aging
Desi Arnaz Sr. and Jr.

CHAPTER SEVEN

HERE'S LUCY

As Cameras Roll and as TV Tastes Change, Lucille Copes With Her Kids & Maneuvers Her Way Through an Armada of Star Guests

As the revolutionary 1960s came to an end, and as the turbulent 1970s were about to begin, Lucille looked back on her past with fear for her future. She had recently signed a contract that made her the focal point of the second season (1969-1970) of *Here's Lucy*.

Although she retained Gary Morton as her executive producer, she fired Tommy Thompson as her producer, replacing him with her cousin, Cleo Smith, with whom she had always maintained a close bond. ("She's like a sister to me.") Milt Josefsberg remained her script consultant.

She also fired Jack Donohue as her director, replacing him with George Marshall, previously a veteran of feature films. Ironically, his first experience directing material for the "little black box" would be the first episode of *Here's Lucy's* Second Season.

Born in 1891, Marshall—an actor, screenwriter, producer, and native son of Chicago—would emerge as a key player in six decades of entertainment history.

[Lucille had worked well with him when he'd directed her with James Craig (a rugged lookalike for Clark Gable) in the 1942 Western romantic comedy, Valley of the Sun.*]*

[Although he wasn't in that movie, Desi Arnaz had made such a nuisance of himself during its filming that Marshall had banned him from the set. To amuse himself, Desi had given Conga lessons to several hundred Indians in Taos, New Mexico, who somehow managed to form a Conga line despite the 110-degree heat.]

John Houseman said that "Marshall never became one of the old maestros of Hollywood, but he held a solid and honorable position in the industry."

Throughout his long involvement in the industry, Marshall got involved with almost every type of film imaginable, beginning with silent

Westerns. Eventually, he'd direct one of the most iconic classic Westerns in history, *Destry Rides Again* (1939), starring Marlene Dietrich and James Stewart.

He could also helm a classic film noir such as *The Blue Dahlia* (1946), the Raymond Chandler *film noir* starring Alan Ladd and Veronica Lake.

Lucille had first admired Marshall's comedic skills as a director when he had made a trio of comedies starring Laurel and Hardy.

In addition to his work with Lucille, Marshall directed half a dozen films, each with Bob Hope and Jerry Lewis, and he also helmed Will Rogers, W.C. Fields, and Jackie Gleason.

***

The Second Season of *Here's Lucy* called for Lucille to repeat her role of Lucy Carter alongside her predictable co-star, Gale Gordon. Lucille's daughter, Lucie Arnaz, was cast in the series as her daughter, Kim, and Lucille's son, Desi Jr., played her onscreen son, Craig.

Lucille continued to insist that she should not be assigned a "husband" for her TV character to interact with. "My fans would not accept it. Every week, I get dozens of letters, urging me to bring back Desi. He certainly would be convincing as the father of Lucie and Junior, but somehow, I just could not bring myself to talk over such an idea with him. He seemed to have settled, comfortably ensconced, with his second wife, Edie, a woman I liked, although I never got over my case of jealousy."

"I did, however, try to bring Vivian Vance back onto the show," Lucille said. "Fans still wrote me that they missed Ethel Mertz, a perfect foil for me, but Viv kept turning down my overtures, preferring to live with her gay husband in Connecticut."

The Senior Desi was very supportive of both his son and daughter co-starring with Lucille. When they made their debuts on *Here's Lucy*, he took out full-page ads in both *Variety* and *The Hollywood Reporter* praising their talents. He went on to give TV and press interviews, welcoming his kids into show biz. He jokingly told a reporter, "Work-

Like a schoolteacher dealing with unruly students, **Lucille Ball** cracked down hard on her children, **Lucie** (left) and **Desi Jr.**

As her age progressed, she continued to feature her family in her show-biz orbit, sometimes with uneven results, and sometimes with inordinate amounts of pain and stress.

In later years, Lucie and Desi Jr. assured her that they were grateful.

ing with my son and daughter will be this red-headed showoff, a real zany dame whose name escapes me at the moment."

Critics within the corps of Lucille's cast and co-stars were increasing in numbers with every season. She became widely known as a tyrant on the set, an unforgiving matriarch who was said to "come down hard" on her children, seeking a kind of perfection in their performances, in spite of their young ages.

Many potential co-stars rejected her offers to appear in telecasts with her. When approached, Jack Lemmon said, "No way, José!"

Tony Randall thought he could deal with her, if asked. Joan Rivers phrased it differently, "I've worked with bigger monsters than Lucille Ball."

Jack Carter, the comedian and TV presenter, said, "Directing Lucille is like trying to flag down the Super Chief with a Zippo lighter."

One reporter who visited the set of *Here's Lucy* wrote: "She might have been America's funniest mom on TV, but she was tough on her kids, a super strict and hard-nosed taskmaster. She was a workaholic, very demanding. She seemed to crack down harder on her offspring than she did on the rest of the cast. She admired Gordon and never gave him a hard time, or so I was told."

In 1970, Desi Jr. admitted, "All this pressure and tension may have led to my turning to drugs in 1970. I started drinking and experimenting with drugs as an alternative to dealing with my fears and resentments from childhood."

Lucie Arnaz was quoted as saying, "My mother was a control freak who had to be in charge 24 hours a day."

Many of Lucille's neuroses and tensions were justified: Stacked up against her cast and crew, Lucille was under more pressure than anybody at the studio. Gossip reached her that CBS executives were disappointed with the First Season of *Here's Lucy*. Word spread that many of the episodes were dull, and some of the plots had been recycled from old episodes of the *I Love Lucy* shows, including ones which had starred Desi.

William S. Paley, the chairman of CBS, dispatched Fred Silverman to fly to Los Angeles to meet with Lucille.

A tough-talking New Yorker whose Jewish father had been a radio and TV service repairman, Silverman was defined by *Time* magazine as "The Man with the Golden Gut," which was the magazine's way of praising his instincts,

Introducing the (fictional) Carmichael family: **Lucille** lays a hand on **Lucie**, who plays her TV daughter Kim. Lucille faces problems of the Generation Gap with her son Craig (actually, **Desi Jr.**)

skill, and success in TV programming.

He brought about major changes in television programming in attempts to reach younger audiences. To boost viewership and widen the demographics of TV audiences, especially with younger viewers, he canceled such country-oriented series as *Green Acres, Hee Haw, The Beverly Hillbillies,* and *Petticoat Junction,* even though they still maintained high Nielsen ratings. He also shut down TV variety shows starring Red Skelton and Jackie Gleason.

Silverman was the sparkplug who ignited a new wave of classics specifically engineered to appeal to Baby Boomers. These included the controversial *All in the Family, The Mary Tyler Moore Show, M*A*S*H, The Waltons,* and *The Sonny & Cher Comedy Hour.*

Meeting Lucille for the first time in the Paramount commissary for lunch, he bluntly got to the point of his visit: "I've jotted down any number of suggestions about how you can save *Here's Lucy* from its creeping dullness."

She listened to all of them with a seeming politeness. Then she excused herself to make an urgent phone call.

She immediately got through to Paley at CBS headquarters in Manhattan. Since she was still high in the Nielsen ratings, he took her call. "Bill, so good to talk to you. I want you to do me a big favor."

"Anything for you, gal," he said.

"I want you to order Fred Silverman's dingleberry-coated ass off the Paramount lot and send him flying back to New York. Will you do that for me?"

There was a long hesitancy on the other end of the line. Finally, Paley said, "Done…your wish, my command."

Silverman later told Paley, "Lucille is aging, and her face looks like a pile of shit. She's hanging on to the past, even though I suspect she knows how creaky her episodes are. She belongs to yesterday, not tomorrow. I've sat through several of her episodes, each one more inferior than the one before."

In spite of these suggestions and/or attacks, *Here's Lucy* remained more or less the same.

Author Tom Gilbert offered an ex-

Over the course of many years, **Fred Silverman** was a top executive at each of the major networks: CBS, ABC, and NBC.

At each of them, he campaigned to cancel long-running shows that he considered pitched for the older generation and replace them with sitcoms focused on a younger demographic.

When he flew to meet with Lucille in California with plans to "update" her old format, she got rid of him quickly, telling him, "I've dealt with bigger shits than you!"

planation: "Lucille Ball, as she admitted herself, had no intention of changing her formula. She was quoted as saying, 'I want some place on the dial you can turn to and know what to expect. I haven't let changing times affect my writers. I'm trying to stay in the same old rut. My audiences are three generations in every home. I want it to stay that way. Out of all those millions, there must be a couple who want things to stay as they are. Me? I still like *Amos 'n' Andy.*"

***

In July of 1969, Lucille was saddened to learn of the death of Barbara Pepper, her longtime *confidante* and oldest friend. Throughout her adult life, Pepper had been the confessor who knew more about Lucille's love life than she remembered herself.

For years, Pepper had battled the bottle and fell into alcoholism, although she sometimes pulled herself together if she got a much-needed acting job, often uncredited.

At the age of fifty-four, she died of coronary thrombosis in Panorama City, California. Lucille helped arrange her funeral at the Hollywood Forever Cemetery in Los Angeles. Pepper's one and only marriage had been to the handsome actor, Craig Reynolds, in 1943, which, of course, was in the middle of World War II. After producing two sons with her, Reynolds died in a motorcycle accident in 1949 in California.

The loss of the man she loved so much led to more heavy drinking, as

HOMAGE TO **BARBARA PEPPER**:
HOW TO HANG IN IN SHOW BIZ:

Left: **Pepper** as a glam queen in the early 30s

Center: Already looking a bit puffy, she's seen here with **Fred MacMurray** in *Murder, He Wrote* (1945)

Right: Wryly self-deprecating, and not very well-preserved, she's seen here in the mid-60s as Doris Ziffel, the eccentric neighbor of Eva Gabor and Eddie Albert in that ode to country life, *Green Acres*. In this sitcom, that ran for 170 episodes from 1965-71, Barbara appeared only for the first three (1965-68) seasons.

she struggled to raise their young boys and find work in the film industry. Time and time again Lucille had bailed her out of financial emergencies.

A New Yorker, Pepper, like Lucille, had started out in Hollywood as a Goldwyn Girl, appearing with her in *Roman Scandals*. Both were cast as nubile sex slaves garbed only in floor-length blonde wigs and naked underneath. In those days, without the wigs, both Pepper and Lucille had dyed their hair "Jean Harlow blonde."

Back when she was fully functional and still retained her figure, Pepper appeared, sometimes uncredited, in forty-three movies between 1937 and 1943. She worked with Lucille again in *Moulin Rouge* (1934), in *Kid Millions* (also 1934), and in *Winterset* (1936). More often, she was uncredited as, for example, when she appeared in *Anna Karenina* (1935) opposite Greta Garbo.

Today, she is best known for playing Doris Ziffel (from 1965 to 1968) in the TV sitcom *Green Acres* opposite Eva Gabor and Eddie Albert.

On *Green Acres*, her porcine co-star was "Arnold the Pig," who often knocked her down.

In the midst of World War II, Barbara Pepper married the dashingly handsome "B-Picture" actor **Craig Reynolds**, with whom she had acted in live theater productions.

When he died in a motorcycle accident in 1949, she went into a downward spiral of depression and alcohol, becoming a bloated caricature of her former beauty.

Before that, she had played the Ziffel role in *Petticoat Junction* (1964). Her last feature film role was as Jerry Lewis' secretary in *Hook, Line, & Sinker* (1969), shortly before her death.

Pepper was often cast as an aging blonde floozie in bar scenes. "Any time a director wants a broken down old whore, I get a call."

She also filled a niche among casting directors as a middle-aged and snoopy next-door neighbor, or perhaps a belligerent landlady.

When casting the original *I Love Lucy* series in the 1950s, Lucille had campaigned for her as Ethel Mertz, but Desi refused. "I've already hired one drunk, William Frawley. I don't need a second booze hound."

Writing of her death, a reporter for a site called *Hollywood Forever* claimed, "So, you see, you do know Barbara Pepper—you know her work, you feel the joy she exuded on the big and small screens. Sometimes the name might not jog the brain, but the images live on and conjure up memories."

Moviegoers saw her in *The Women* (1939) with Joan Crawford and Norma Shearer; in *My Favorite Spy* (1942) alongside Bob Hope; in *Once Upon a Time* (1944) with Cary Grant; in *The Snake Pit* (1948), in which she played a mental patient opposite Olivia de Havilland; in *Auntie Mame* (1958) with Rosalind Russell; in *The Music Man* (1962) with Robert Preston;

and in *My Fair Lady* (1964) as Doolittle's dancing partner.

At her funeral, Pepper was cited as "the closest friend of a television legend, Miss Lucille Ball."

***

Here's Lucy, The Second Season (1969-1970), was launched on September 22. An aging Lucy Carter, in association with her children, Kim and Craig (portrayed by Lucille's biological children, Lucie Arnaz and Desi Arnaz Jr.) and Uncle Harry (Gale Gordon) decide to visit Colorado to see the Air Force Academy there. By now, any devotee of the series knows that she will create chaos within this tightly disciplined military institution.

For the filming of this zany episode, Lucille secured the cooperation of the U.S. Air Force, which configured real life pilots as extras. This episode marked the first contribution of George Marshall, a veteran director of dozens of feature films, to "the little black box."

Desi Jr. later said that most of the cast, except perhaps Lucille and Gordon, enjoyed filming scenes at the Academy and in the Colorado River, with Lucy in a wet suit. Marshall liked action in his movies and took his love of that with him during his filming of *Lucy Goes to the Air Force Academy: Part One*.

Beverly Garland, a native of Santa Cruz, California, is seen briefly playing a secretary. Her main gig was her casting as Barbara Harper, the woman who marries widower Steve Douglas (Fred MacMurray) during the latter months of the sitcom *My Three Sons* (1969-1972).

In Part Two of the Air Force Academy episodes, Desi Jr., for the first time, was ordered by Marshall to appear shirtless. Although he was actually in good physical condition, he needed his confidence bolstered. Marshall told him, "You look great. The gals will go for you."

"I thought I looked a little dumpy, but apparently, my baby fat had disappeared," Desi said.

Episode Three, *Lucy and the Indian Chief*, has a rather far-fetched plot by Gene Thompson. Leaving Colorado, Lucy drives south for a stopover in Arizona.

There, she meets a Native American chief (Iron Eyes Cody), who takes her back to his Navajo encampment. When she accepts a piece of jewelry from him, it means that they are married. As a wedding present, he gives his squaw an unusual gift: The entire state of Utah.

"After I won them over, the Navajos in our picture looked great on camera,

Gale Gordon, a time-tested staple with genuine comedic timing, appears here in this publicity photo for *Here's Lucy*, between **Lucille Ball** (left) and **Lucie Arnaz.**

In it, Gordon was cast in the role of Harrison Otis Carter. As one reviewer wrote, "Uncle Harry's parsimony and meanness were never explained."

but they took a lot of convincing," Lucille said. "I had to assure them that I was not a friend of that Indian killer, John Wayne."

Lucille found "Iron Eyes" fascinating to talk to. With a movie career that graced half a century, he was America's most famous film Indian. He had already starred in some two hundred movies directed by everyone from Cecil B. De Mille to John Ford.

"I broke in a screen newcomer named Gary Cooper, and I rode with guys like Tom Mix, Hoot Gibson, and Tim McCoy," Iron Eyes said.

Lucille was fascinated by his stories of working with Errol Flynn. "Flynn had a helluva sex drive, and the equipment to put it to constant use. He was famous all over Hollywood for being well-hung. I worked with him in some films where a new director sometimes asked him to take it out and show it to him, especially if he was a homo. Happy to settle any lingering doubts about his dimensions, Errol would unzip and set the record straight, regardless of who was present, even a lady, especially a lady, although he also like to plug boys, too."

"If you find this a bit much," Iron Eyes told Lucille, "There was another fellow named Freddie Frank. Casting directors used to keep him on salary for the purpose of servicing the needs of their female leads. His piece, which I understand he charged a pretty penny for, was colossal. Amazing!"

"He and Errol, when the latter was drunk (which was most of the time), used to have a 'stretch-and-measure' contest. Always an inch or two short, Errol never conceded defeat, but blamed his drinking for his inability to match Freddie's size and stretching capabilities. Ah, Hollywood!"

Hollywood's most famous "Native American," movie star **"Iron Eyes" Cody** (aka Espera DeCorti, the son of two first-generation immigrants from SIcily) is seen presenting a Native American headdress to **President Jimmy Carter** in the Oval Office in Washington on April 21, 1978.

He also gave the former peanut farmer an Indian name: "Wamblee Ska."

In his memoirs, "Iron Eyes" devoted space to Errol Flynn's penile dimensions, most unusual in a bio written by a male.

Olivia de Havilland and **Errol Flynn** are seen above in *Dodge City* (1939).

Cody described Flynn's attitude during filming as "reluctant, half-pissed, and only paying cursory attention to a half-baked script."

"It sounds to me that I missed out on a lot of fun not getting cast in other westerns," Lucille quipped.

***

To close the four-episode location shoot, George Marshall sent Lucille and her kids to the Grand Canyon and the banks of the Colorado River. Hapless Lucy Carter spots a raft and decides to take a ride. She soon realizes that it's headed directly for the rapids.

Marshall later recalled, "Timing and safety were of the essence. I think I spent more time planning this shoot than Ike did for the D-day landings."

Technicians at both the Glen Canyon Dam and the Hoover Dan had to be alerted about water control. In a wet suit, Lucille spent four or five hours in the cold waters.

Her children, also in the shoot, had to wear wet suits, too. The entire shoot took four days , and many of the crew, including Lucie Arnaz, caught the flu. In contrast, Desi Jr., said, "I had a ball." *[Obviously, that was not an oblique reference to his mother.]*

***

Lucille's favorite episode from Season Two was *Lucy and Harry's tonsils* (October 20, 1969). For the "guest star" cast, she engaged some of her best friends: Jack Collins, Paula Stewart, and the always faithful Mary Wickes. In the sequence, Uncle Harry (Gale Gordon) goes to the hospital to have his tonsils removed.

Collins was cast as his doctor, Wickes as his day nurse, and Stewart as the sexy night nurse. Collins had previously appeared at frequent intervals in guest spots on *Here's Lucy*, and Stewart had been Lucille's co-star in her Broadway production of *Wildcat* (1960). She was still married to comedian Jack Carter. The couple was said to have introduced Lucille to her present husband, Gary Morton.

***

Lucille cast Gary Morton in her next episode, *Lucy and the Andrew Sisters* (October 27).

Patty had been the youngest of the Andrew Sisters when the trio became an overnight sensation in the 1940s, crooning in perfect harmony "Bei Mit Bist Du Schoen," a melancholy but upbeat tune originally written for the Yiddish theater. Patty quickly emerged as the trio's star.

The sisters became forever linked to the entertainment orbits of World War II, when their music—often sung to troops heading overseas, many to their deaths— soared to the top of the *Billboard* charts.

They often joined Bob Hope on his USO tours, singing their signature "Boogie Woogie Bugle Boy," later revived for younger audiences by Bette Midler.

At the time that Patty worked with Lucille, LaVerne had died, but Maxene was still living.

Lucille told Patty that her two favorite songs were "Apple Blossom Time" and "Pistol Packin' Mama," which she sang to wild applause from the studio audience.

In the plot, Patty comes into the Unique Employment Agency, hoping to find two singers to replace her (unavailable) older sisters in an appearance in front of a fan club. Lucy grabs the assignment for herself and her daughter, Kim (Lucie Arnaz).

Disaster erupts. She manages to accidentally shatter all the vinyl LPs which were to have been used as background for their lip-synchs. Lucy tries to imitate the voice of LaVerne.

Patty found Lucie (daughter Kim) very talented. Lucie defined the fading singing star of yesterday as "a great old broad."

The fabled singers and morale-boosters of World War II, **The Andrews Sisters**, (left to right, **LaVerne**, a contralto; **Maxene**, a soprano; and **Patty**, a mezzo-soprano) are seen here in 1941, at the height of their fame, after the release of :"Boogie Woogie Bugle Boy," later revived by Bette Midler.

***

On another episode, "Lucy's Burglar Alarm," (November 3), she had a reunion with Actor Elliot Reid, who played a handsome detective who investigates an armed robbery at her home from the previous night.

She and Reid had maintained a friendship that dated back to work they'd produced during the Golden Age of Radio, when he appeared on her hit show, *My Favorite Husband*.

Regardless of his many gigs, Reid never topped his memorable role—that of Jane Russell's love interest in *Gentlemen Prefer Blondes* (1953), with Marilyn Monroe.

When Uncle Harry (Gale Gordon) refuses to give Lucy the money to buy a burglar alarm, he lives to regret it.

For a November 17 telecast, *Lucy and the Car Dealer*, she had another re-

A 1969 reprise of The Andrews Sisters starred **Lucille** (left), **Patty Andrews**, and, the tallest of the trio, **Lucie Arnaz**, on the right.

LaVerne Andrews was dead at this point, and Maxene was alive but unable to attend. Lucie was cast instead.

Patty later asserted, "This was my favorite TV appearance."

union, this time with Milton Berle. They had remained friends over the years, ever since their brief fling in the late 1930s.

"Uncle Miltie" said he really enjoyed this episode in which he got to spoof all those used car dealers who hype their automobiles on TV.

In the episode, Lucy's kids, Kim and Craig, are taken in by a sleazy used car dealer who sells them a piece of junk unfit for the road. Angered, Lucy seeks revenge. "It's payback time for the crooked dealer."

***

Lucille and Johnny Carson did not really click as co-stars or even as her TV interviewer. However, she would appear frequently with him on *The Tonight Show* in the late 1970s.

In *Lucy and Johnny Carson* (December 1), he agreed to guest star in her show with his sidekick, Ed McMahon.

The script by Milt Josefsberg is a bit silly. Lucy and Uncle Harry (Gail Gordon) crash *The Tonight Show* and manage to win a free meal at the celebrity-frequented Brown Derby. Carson goes to dinner there after his show is off the air. He is accompanied by McMahon.

The episode, entitled *L.A. at Last,* is a less well-written reprise of telecast #114 from the *I Love Lucy* show in which William Holden was her guest star. This was the celebrated episode where Lucy Ricardo dunks her putty nose into Holden's coffee.

In the episode with Carson, it is he upon whom drinks are spilled.

She and Carson met for drinks after the show, and both of them talked about other stars who had the greatest influence on them. She cited Carole Lombard in those screwball comedies of the 1930s. He told her he'd

Johnny Carson and **Lucille Ball** made a number of television appearances together, although she admitted, "I was never comfortable with him." Previously, at a Friars' Roast, he had introduced her as "Lucille Testicle" because of her reputation as a "ball-breaker."

One night, Carson invited Lucille to the Cocoanut Grove for a sort of business dinner. Flip Wilson showed up dressed as a Playboy bunny. He kissed Lucille on the cheek, but gave Carson "a wet one" on the lips before inviting him onto the dance floor.

had many influences, citing Jack Paar (an obvious one), Red Skelton, Fred Allen, Jack Benny, and even Groucho Marx.

She found Carson hard to relate to, even though she would appear with him again and again. "He was very introverted, very closed off, even shy," she said.

Dick Cavett had called him "the most private public man who ever lived. I felt sorry for Johnny that he was so socially uncomfortable." She shared Cavett's assessment.

Later, George Alexrod gave his opinion of Carson. "Socially, this son of Carning, Iowa, born in 1925, just doesn't exist. The reason is that there are no TV cameras in the room. If human beings had little red lights in the middle of their foreheads, Carson would be the greatest conversationalist on Earth."

She once invited Carson to dinner at her Beverly Hills home, and he had a strong response: "I will come but only if you promise not to serve kumquats. I hate kumquats."

He accepted her invitation for dinner on a Tuesday night, in which Gary Morton would be present. But Carson phoned on Sunday afternoon and canceled. He told her he had a conflict in his schedule and was meeting with a writer who was offering to ghost-write his autobiography, to be called *Toads and Tarantulas*.

Ed McMahon, a son of Detroit, would go on to become famous for his thirty-year gig as Carson's sidekick, his announcer and "second banana" on *The Tonight Show* from 1962 to 1992.

Lucille was long gone from the world when McMahon began facing enormous financial woes, falling behind on mortgage payments for his $4.8 million dollar home. A certain real estate mogul, Donald Trump, offered to buy it to prevent foreclosure. In Beverly Hills, McMahon became desperately ill from a toxic mold that spread through his home. A few months later, he sued the insurance company for $20 million, settling the suit for $7.2 million, rescuing him financially. McMahon's health, however, never recovered, and he died at the age of 86 in 2009 at the Ronald Reagan Medical Center.

In the wake of his death, a Hollywood reporter, whether true or not, revealed that he made several attempts to become a regular on Lucille's *Here's Lucy* series, but she consistently turned him down.

***

In addition to her own show, Lucille liked to make guest appearances on the telecasts of other celebrities, sometimes making joint deals with a TV host like Carol Burnett.

Lucille was flattered when she received news that Ann-Margret wanted to co-star her in *The Ann-Margret Show: From Hollywood With Love*, a sixty-minute revue set to be telecast on December 6, 1969.

Ever since she'd seen Ann-Margret perform in *Bye Bye Birdie* (1963), Lucille had admired her talent as an actress, singer, and dancer. Admittedly, she was also jealous of her sex appeal.

At the first private screening of *Bye Bye Birdie*, actress Maureen Stapleton approached her, saying, "I'm the only person in the room who doesn't want to fuck you."

Ann-Margret had been born in Stockholm, Sweden, in 1941, but her family had moved to the northern Swedish province of Jämtland, a village of lumberjacks and farmers, with a very short summer season, near the Arctic Circle.

Before Lucille met her, the star's reputation had preceded her. She was said to be shy and reserved in person, but wildly exuberant and sensuous on stage. In her autobiography, she claimed, "I go from Little Miss Lollipop to Sexpop Banshee once the music starts."

She was known as "The Female Elvis Presley." Their affair began when they co-starred in *Viva Las Vegas* (1964). At the peak of their affair, he had a round, pink bed made especially for her.

An affair with Steve McQueen began with their co-starring performances in *The Cincinnati Kid* (1965). He told the press, "She's a lady, every man's wet dream."

Ann-Margret with **Elvis Presley** in *Viva Las Vegas* (1964), four years before her show with Lucille.

Elvis later told his buddies, "Don't tell anyone, but I think Nancy Sinatra found me sexier in the movie than Ann-Margret."

When Lucille and Ann-Margret worked together, the actress had married Roger Smith, one of the most successful unions in Hollywood, lasting until his death in 2017.

"In my hopeless goal to look as sexy as Ann-Margret, I ordered makeup to make me glamourous," Lucille said. "I knew I would never be as enticing as she was. She comes through dirty no matter the role."

In their joint appearance, Lucille and Ann-Margret perform a duet, "Autograph Annie and Celebrity Lucy." Usually, Lucille's voice is dubbed, but this time, viewers get to hear her actual voice, which isn't all that bad.

One opening scene is at the door of Paramount Studios, which used to be the entrance to Desilu Productions.

In her final meeting with Ann-Margret, the charismatic star told Lucille, "When a guy tells me I'm sexy, he is paying me the greatest compliment I could ever get."

***

Episode #37 of *Here's Lucy*, called *Lucie and the Bogie Affair*, was telecast on December 15, 1969. It did not star Humphrey Bogart, but a sheepdog, named "Lord Nelson," whose mug was said to have evoked the legendary star.

The plot was rather routine, not one of the best of the season. It revolved around Craig and Kim (Desi Jr. and Lucie) finding a sheepdog in a rainstorm. They nickname him "Bogie."

However, when Lord Nelson delivers a litter of puppies in the Carter family's kitchen, the kids realize that Bogie is a female.

What made the episode special was that it had a new director, Herbert Kenwith. He wasn't new to Lucille, having formed a friendship with her back in 1948, when he'd toured the country with her in Elmer Rice's play, *Dream Girl*. [It had played to standing room audiences wherever it opened. The patrons were drawn to the star power of Lucille more than to the Rice play.]

Disappointed or else feuding with her previous directors of *Here's Lucy*, Lucille had called Kenwith, asking him if he'd like to meet with her and talk over helming her latest TV series.

The following afternoon, he drove to her home in Beverly Hills, where DeDe, Lucille's mother, greeted him. Lucille, he was told, would be down in about fifteen minutes.

As he talked to DeDe, she asked him, "Are you sure you want to direct my daughter? She's a real bitch!"

"You forget, I've directed her before when we went on the road with that Elmer Rice play, *Dream Girl*, in 1948," he answered. "We had a few minor arguments but, for the most part, pulled it off without gouging out each other's eyes."

"You know then, that she views herself as a perfectionist, and demands that everything be done her way or the door."

"The mark of a true artist!" he said.

"Okay, if you think you have the *cojones* to handle her," she said. "That means balls, a word Desi taught me."

"I'm sure he's an expert on *cojones*."

After a long afternoon of talking, Kenwith agreed to take over *Here's Lucy* as its director, beginning with *Lucy and the Bogie Affair*, although he was not impressed with its lackluster script. After one day of working with the sheepdog, Lord Nelson, he said, "She's no Lassie. Why is she called Lord Nelson? Should it not be 'Lady Nelson?'"

His first argument with Lucille began on the first day at a script meeting of the cast. She ordered him where to sit, and he defied her, seating himself in the middle of the table and not at its far end. "I immediately showed her I was not to be ordered around."

From that day forth, they got along reasonably well, although having minor arguments day to day. "She was always full of suggestions, one or two for every scene, and, I have to admit this, in most cases, she was right. But when she was wrong, she was way off-base."

A son of New Jersey, Kenwith—a director, writer, and producer— was six years younger than Lucille, but with vast experience. He had begun his career as an actor on Broadway, appearing as a bellboy in the 1944 play, *I Remember Mama*, in which Marlon Brando made his stage debut.

In time, Kenwith rose to become the youngest producer on Broadway, noted for such plays as *Me and Molly* (1948), named as one of the best plays of the Broadway season.

He'd also built up his reputation when for six years he was the director of the McCarter Summer Theatre at Princeton University. He managed to hire screen legends for his plays, notably Mae West, Gloria Swanson, Miriam Hopkins, Charlton Heston, Jeanette MacDonald, and Lucille Ball. He eventually gravitated to Hollywood, where, on TV, he directed such stars as Danny Kaye and Sidney Poitier, even Rose Kennedy, the matriarch of the Kennedy clan.

One writer claimed, "Although of the same physical appearance and height as Napoléon Bonaparte, Kenwith—a nonsmoker and teetotaler—was known for his charming personality, a tremendous sense of humor, and a friendly disposition that put any performer at ease during a guest appearance."

During Kenwith's tenure as director of *Here's Lucy,* Gary Morton and Lucille often visited him for dinners at his luxurious home, which looked down on a southwestern panorama of the Los Angeles cityscape. At one time, the house had belonged to Grace Kelly. Her husband, Prince Rainier of Monaco, stayed there during his visits to California, preferring not to stay at a hotel.

After leaving *Here's Lucy,* Kenwith would also direct numerous other TV shows, including such hits as *The Mary Tyler Moore Show* (1970) and *Sanford and Son* (1972).

***

As one of the subplots of *Lucy and the Bogie Affair,* she appears in a skit with Jack LaLanne. One scene is set in his gym, where she's jumping up and down with him, doing an exercise designed to take some of the flab off her "caboose."

Wanting to get rid of one of Lord Nelson's puppies, she brings the little dog to the studio to present as a gift to LaLanne. Unknown to her, he, too has a dog named Happy, who has also delivered a litter. To her dismay, instead of getting rid of the pooch, she ends up with one of Happy's offspring, too. At the end of the episode, she stands holding both pups before the camera, look-

Fitness guru and motivational speaker **Jack LaLanne** promoted physical exercise and proper nutrition to millions of television viewers as "the salvation of America."

After demonstrating some of his exercises with his dog ("Happy") and a comically bewildered Lucille (lower photo), she approached him and asked if he'd pose for a frontal nude of himself and send it to her, saying, "Gary (Morton) is getting out of shape, and I think your nude would inspire him to exercise."

LaLanne laughed it off, later making it clear to his associates, "I didn't expose my junk to Lucy."

ing bewildered.

She liked and admired LaLanne, one of the nation's main advocates of exercise, health training, and physical fitness.

She discussed filming another episode with him. Her "brainchild," had it come to fruition, would have involved about eighteen of the fattest women in Los Angeles, none weighing less than 300 pounds, who arrive *en masse* for an exercise class. He told her he thought that might be a "hoot," but they soon dropped the plan.

He revealed that as a teenager, he had been a "sugarholic" and a "junk food junkie," but soon switched to physical culture and good nutrition. He was years ahead of other celebrity health advocates such as Jane Fonda and Richard Simmons. The gym he opened in Oakland, California, became the model for dozens of other fitness centers across the country.

At the age of 54, LaLanne beat out 21-year-old Arnold Schwarzenegger in a bodybuilding contest. Movie hunk Steve Reeves credited LaLanne for helping him win the title of Mr Pacific, Mr. America, Mr. World, and Mr. Universe. Reeves also made a number of Hercules pictures, his *kitsch* and beefcake earning him several million gay fans around the world.

***

In the cast of *Lucy and the Bogie Affair* was actor Steve March. *[He later changed his name to Steve March-Tormé. His father had been Mel Tormé, a friend of Lucille and a guest on her telecast. Steve was born during the course of his father's marriage to actress Candy Tuxton. After her divorce, she wed another friend of Lucille's, Hal March, who adopted Steve as his bona-fide son.]*

A native of San Francisco, Hal March, like Tormé was also a friend of Lucille's, having co-starred with him in such telecasts as *Lucy Is a Matchmaker* (March 1953).

Hal, for years, worked on television shows that, among others, had starred George Burns and Gracie Allen.

His real fame came when he hosted the $64,000 question from 1955 to 1958, a show watched by millions, including Lucille, who viewed it as one of her favorites.

At the height of its popularity, the show devolved into a scandal when it was revealed that a few contestants, going for the big prize, were supplied with the answers before going on the air. A Federal probe was ordered, leading to the cancellation of the show and the firing of Hal. For the next decade, he floundered about, trying to restore his career.

Ironically, the year that Lucille worked with his stepson, Hal was trying for a comeback, having signed to shoot the TV show, *It's Your Bet.* His doctor revealed to him that he had developed advance lung cancer, and he died shortly before his 50th birthday in 1970.

As a footnote, the future girlfriend of Desi Jr., Patty Duke, as a child star appeared on the quiz show. She was later forced to testify before a congressional investigators, breaking into tears when admitting she'd been coached before the show went on the air.

***

To launch the year of 1970, Lucille came up with the idea of adding glitz, glitter, and lots of campy humor to some of her newest episodes in the form of Liberace, "Mr. Showman" himself. At this point in his flamboyant career, his custom-designed costumes, his giant candelabra, and his extravagant showmanship were more famous than his piano playing. When she got through to him, he surprised her by agreeing quickly. The deal was set for a telecast on January 5 of *Here's Lucy #40, Lucy and Liberace.*

He told reporter after reporter, "I come out like the burst of dawn in baubles, bangles, and shiny beads, perhaps with 200 pounds of fur capes. Perhaps I'll play Chopin's 'Minute Waltz' in less than a minute—thirty-seven seconds, to be exact."

This plot on *Here's Lucy* was by screenwriter Fred S. Fox and was a bit far-fetched. Craig (Desi Jr.) arrives at Lucy's house with a very valuable gold candelabrum, all part of a "scavenger hunt" he's conducting with other kids. *[Actually, Liberace has lent him the candelabra, but Lucy fears he'd stolen it.]* She plots to break into Liberace's mansion and return it. Of course, she's "caught in the act."

When Liberace arrived at the studio for the first day of rehearsal, Lucille met him for a late breakfast. With such sympathetic women as Lucille or Debbie Reynolds, the entertainer could be quite outspoken in speaking about his private life. But to maintain a certain public image, especially to blue-haired elderly ladies across America who adored him, he stayed deep in the closet.

When he published his autobiography four years from the date of that breakfast with Lucille, he claimed he was writing about "The women in my life."

He was attired that day in a gold *lamé* jacket, similar to a model which he'd given to Elvis Presley.

The flamboyant, often overdressed **Liberace** appears in a somber moment, as depicted by Allan Warren.

He was notoriously described by London's *Daily Mirror*, as "winking, sniggering, snuggling, chromium-plated, scent-impregnated, luminous, quivering, giggling, fruit-flavored, mincing—an ice-covered heap of mother love."

Late in his career, **Elvis Presley** frequently appeared onstage in variations of this costume inspired by Liberace.

"Elvis bombed during his first drab appearance in Las Vegas," Liberace said. "I took him home that night and showed him how to dress like a show-stopper. He was very grateful, if you get my drift. I could have done the same for Desi Jr. if Lucille Ball didn't hover over him like a protective hen."

As he told her, "When Elvis first appeared in Las Vegas, he dressed like a country boy," he told her. "I attended his first show and invited him home that night. There, I convinced him that he needed a drastic change of wardrobe to succeed in glittery Las Vegas. It took some convincing, but he finally went for it."

"I proceeded to strip him jaybird naked and put a sequin jockstrap on him to hide his goodies as he shook his pelvis before the gals. I dressed him flamboyantly. We got along so well that we've stayed in touch for years. I even sent him some custom-designed outfits to wear on stage."

"Did you seduce him?" Lucille asked provocatively.

"Do flowers bloom in the spring?" he answered. "I've had bigger and better, but he is one beautiful boy. A bit untamed, though."

Then a truck with his grand piano, candelabra, and a selection of costumes arrived. He told Lucille that he was leaving at least $100,000 worth of wardrobe at the studio overnight. You'l need a security guard to protect my valuables."

For some reason, the new director, Herbert Kenwith, was not free to helm the episode with Liberace, so the task went to Jack Baker. He met with the flamboyant pianist the following morning. "Let's face it," Mr. Showman told Baker. "I was television's first matinee idol. My show was carried by more stations than *I Love Lucy*, but you don't have to tell the redhead that. I don't want to make her jealous."

"I'm sure with her keen mind, that she's very aware of the ratings," Baker said.

During the next three days, Lucille and Liberace bonded, and she was delighted by his humor and accepted his dinner invitation.

"I'm the greatest chef in the world," he said. "I also grow orchids, with purple being my favorite color: I'm also an inventor, working on perfecting my invention of the disappearing toilet."

"Are you joking?"

"Not at all. Tomorrow night I'll demonstrate it to you. A toilet is a hideous thing to remain in view all the time. With my new invention, and after you've finished your business, you can press a button and the toilet will disappear into the wall."

"I'm also a painter," he continued. "Right now, I'm hand painting ties for the studly players of the Minneapolis Lakers basketball team. I've invited them over this Saturday afternoon for a pool party and barbecue. They'll be mandated to take off all their clothes before swimming in my pool—which is shaped in the form of a grand piano."

He told her he had to take elaborate precautions at times to conceal his sexuality. "One must be discreet."

He claimed that when he dated a man in public, going to a restaurant or night club, he also invited a "female beard" to conceal what was really going on. "Do you know who my constant beard is?" he asked.

"I haven't a clue," she said.

"Betty White."

He showed her his latest creation for a costume, an Edwardian tuxedo jacket that lights up in the dark. The spectacular jacket made its debut on

Lucille's show, and he would forever use it in his stage appearances after that.

Desi Jr. was cast in the same show with Liberace. When the teenager showed up at the studio, Liberace asked him to try on his "self-illuminating in the dark" jacket, and the boy agreed. After he put it on, Liberace fondled its lapel affectionately, complimenting him on what a good-looking stud he was.

Baker looked on while this was happening. "Liberace looked like he could devour the flesh of this handsome young man. I felt that Desi was very uncomfortable. I really think Liberace wanted to go to bed with the kid, but he could dream on. Liberace was smart enough to know if he made a pass at Desi, Lucille would become Lizzie Borden with her axe and come after him."

Years later, at a Hollywood party, Lucille and Liberace were seen gossiping in a corner. The magazine *Playgirl*, featuring male nudes, had recently been launched.

"I'm its most faithful reader," Liberace confessed. "It's become a great source for me to meet young men. After the release of every edition, one of the editors supplies me with the phone number and address of whatever model I'm interested in. I tear a thousand-dollar bill in half, and send one of the halves to the model, telling him that if he wants to retrieve the other half, he has to fly to Las Vegas or wherever I'm staying at the time. Of course, I provide transportation and pay all the expenses."

Perhaps jokingly, she added, "What a novel technique to meet studs, and you already know what you're getting from seeing them nude in the magazine. Of course, I could only do this when Gary Morton is out of town."

"Of course," he answered. "As I've said before, one must be discreet."

***

Vivian Vance flew in from her home in Connecticut to appear in *Here's Lucy*, Episode #41, entitled *Lucy and Lawrence Welk*, to be telecast on January 19, 1970.

"It would be the acting challenge of my life," Vance claimed. "I was supposed to have a powerful crush on Lawrence Welk, of all people. He was perhaps the unsexist man on Planet Earth, topped only by William Frawley in person or that Fred Mertz role in *I Love Lucy*."

Before Vance arrived to stay with Lucille at her home in Bev-

Vivian (left), **Lucille**, and bandleader **Lawrence Welk** (aka "The Polka King') appear in this publicity photo from CBS, advertising their trio as an ode to wholesome, some said "relentlessly cheerful" entertainment.

erly Hills, a script conference was taking place with Lucille and her director, Herbert Kenwith. For reasons known only to herself, she was demanding that cuts be made to Vance's dialogue.

After she arrived and settled in, and after she and Lucille had discussed "the good old days," Vance received a copy of the (revised) script.

"She flew into a fit," Kenwith said. "She demanded that each of her lines be restored, and if they weren't, she threatened to get on the next plane flying east. When her demands were presented to Lucille, she gave in without much objection, since she knew that Vance had delivered no idle threat. I think Vance was about the only person alive who could challenge 'Our Little Redhead, Frau Himmler' and get away with it and force her to give in."

Although Lawrence Welk would be forgotten by newer generations, he had once been one of the most famous men in America. People in any state knew who he was, even if they were unaware of the name of their Senator or the Vice President of the United States.

Born one cold and windy March day in 1903 in the wilds of North Dakota, he was the sixth of eight children.

His parents had emigrated to the United States from Odessa, then part of the Russian Empire (now Ukraine). As he was growing up, his interest turned to music, and he became an accordionist. Later in life he formed his own band, entertaining a growing number of usually older fans with what was known at the time as "champagne music."

In 1951, during the early days of television, he launched what became the longest-running variety show on television, *The Lawrence Welk Show*. It stayed on the air until he retired in 1982, a decade before his death in Santa Monica.

He was known for saying, *"Wunnerful, wunnerful!"* which became the title of his 1971 autobiography, which he published one year after appearing on television with Lucille.

Critics called it an "an uncontroversial, mostly vanilla read."

To his credit, Welk did not remain rigid in his musical style, forever emulating the big band flair of Tommy Dorsey and Harry James. He tried in his way to keep abreast of changing musical tastes, as he did when he incorporated material from The Beatles or from a young composer like Burt Bacharach.

Throughout the course of his long career—he lived until the age of 89—he was never associated with any scandal. In 1931, he'd married Fern Veronica Renner, and she was by his side when he died in 1992.

Vance, according to the plot, was said to have a powerful crush on Welk, viewing him as her male idol. From her home in Connecticut, she often received phone calls from Lucy, who bragged of her close friendship with Welk.

Based on this weak and unbelievable script by Martin Ragaway, Lucy panics when she learns that Vance is planning to visit her in California, and the main purpose of her trip is to be introduced to Welk. Knowing that Vance is near-sighted, Lucille comes up with a scheme. She goes to sculptor, Lowell Grant, and has him create a plaster of Paris replica of Welk.

At the dinner table, the dummy will be seated at the opposite end of the table from Vance, whose glasses have been stolen by Lucy. For his dialogue, his voice is imitated saying nothing but *"Wunnerful, wunnerful!"*

Before the deception is exposed, the real-life Welk appears to Vance's staged delight.

Privately, she told Lucille, "If Welk were the last man on earth, I'd turn dyke. I doubt if Welk's own wife is turned on by him. How could she? To me, he's a holdover relic from the dawn of the century."

"Don't be too harsh on him," Lucille warned. "In some quarters you and I are regarded as dinosaurs of yesterday, too."

Kenwith had his own personal story to relay about Welk years later: "He kept inviting me to visit his dressing room, claiming he had a gift for me. He kept doing it so many times I thought he was coming on to me."

"Surely good, wholesome and devout Roman Catholic Welk wasn't a closeted gay! But Desi Arnaz—senior, that is—once told me that many Catholic priests are gay, and that two priests sexually approached him when he was just a boy growing up in Cuba."

"I wasn't used to having men come on to me," Kenwith claimed. "If I ever entered a gay pick-up bar, all the boys would flee at the sight of me. Still, Welk kept insisting on that dressing room visit. Finally, on the last day of the shoot, I mustered enough courage to go to his dressing room, thinking that I could make a hasty retreat."

"Lucille had told me that Welk wasn't very bright, so we had simple lines written for him. It's true he couldn't act. But she was wrong about him being stupid—far from it."

Welk was a successful businessman and a shrewd real estate developer. He was in a joint ownership of the tallest building in Santa Monica, rising twenty-one floors. Next to it he owned a luxurious sixteen-unit apartment building

He also was somewhat of a genius in music publishing. As he talked rather intimately with Kenwith, he held out the possibility that he might help him secure some deals in the music publishing industry. "He also suggested that if we teamed up, I might get this super deluxe penthouse apartment in Santa Monica rent-free."

"It all sounded fabulous," Kenwith recalled. "But not for me. I had to make my exit. He took my hand and held it tenderly, as he pressed his gift into my paw. I made my way out the door and as I passed a nearby wastepaper basket, I tossed the gift. I'd opened it to discover it was a little plastic violin with a nail file inside."

***

One of Vivian Vance's best appearances on the *Here's Lucy* series was part of an episode that was telecast on January 26, 1970. Simply called *Lucy and Vivian Vance,* it was directed by Kenwith, starring Gale Gordon as Harry, with a script by Milt Josefsberg, who had written so many other episodes for Lucille.

In the plot, Lucy and Viv decide they want to visit Tijuana across the border in Mexico. Harry agrees to drive them down, but charges them twelve cents a mile, which makes them resentful.

On the way there, they stop at a souvenir shop, selling dolls. The operator of the stand will give them two dolls for the price of one if Harry will deliver a third doll to his niece living in the Los Angeles area. A deal is struck.

At the border, they are searched, and it is discovered that the third doll contains contraband. Lucy and Viv, perhaps to get a mild revenge on penny-pinching Harry, tell the border guards they don't know who he is.

One critic, using a bit of indelicate language, claimed, "Those two old broads, Lucille Ball and Vivian Vance, the former Lucy Ricardo and Ethel Mertz, can still work that old magic. They seemed better when they are scheming together than when they are plotting against each other. Time marches on in their faces, but they still know how to entertain for those seeking harmless diversion from their daily woes."

As it turned out, Lucille and Vance did not go south of the border for their filming. Instead, the crew raided the prop department to rescue the sets used on the hour-long telecast of October 6, 1958, *The Lucille Ball-Desi Arnaz Hour*. Desi had been the host, and the legendary French performer, Maurice Chevalier, had been the guest star.

***

In November of 1969, Lucille had made a guest appearance on *The Ann-Margret Show: From Hollywood With Love*. To return the favor, the sexy, sultry Swedish star agreed to co-star with Lucille in Episode #44 of *Here's Lucy: Lucy and Ann-Margret,* hardly a poetic label. It was directed by Kenwith with a script by Josefsberg, and it was telecast on February 2, 1970.

In the plot, Craig (Desi Jr.) is an eager young musician, hoping to hit it big with his song, "Country Magic." He painfully learns that his promoter is a fraud.

By chance, he encounters the devastatingly beautiful Ann-Margret, upon whom he quickly develops a crush. She not only autographs his music but likes his composition enough to feature it as a number on her next special for her TV audience.

Ann-Margret appears with the then-teenaged **Desi Jr.** in an episode of *Here's Lucy.*

Would the aspiring young musician, known even then for his attraction to older women, get lucky, the way Elvis did when he co-starred with the Swedish star?

We think not.

Desi Jr. himself was on the way to exuding a new maturity and sex appeal. With his band, he'd been a teen idol. Now he has a scene with an older woman who is a "sexpot." He is shown, brimming with excitement, as he waits on a sofa in her living room.

She exits with the intention of "changing into something more comfortable," and his face seems to convey a hint of intimacies to come.

At that point in real life Desi Jr. was dating and presumably seducing (in some cases) some young women in Hollywood. So he's beginning to grow up on the television screen. The young man, as many critics noted, was tremendously talented—much more than just good looking and sexy.

But after this one telecast, the writers of future scripts of *Here's Lucy* didn't want her son to upstage Lucille's own antics in future telecasts.

For his duet with Ann-Margret, he introduced a very special guitar: Covered in patterns of pinkish paisley, it had been specially made for Jimmy Burton, the lead guitar player in Elvis Presley's stage appearances.

As Desi Jr. later admitted to the press, "Since I was a ten-year-old with a gleam in my eye, I had a crush on Ann-Margret. Here I was actually working with her. She could not have been more helpful to me, especially when I had to learn this dance number."

Perhaps word that Desi Jr. was "the youngest Casanova in Hollywood" reached Ann-Margret's husband, Roger Smith. At any rate, he showed up the next day and seemed highly protective of his wife.

After the broadcast, one reporter asked Desi Jr., "Did you get lucky?"

"Not with Roger Smith as her bodyguard," he said. "In other words, I did not invade the territory as 'The King' himself once did."

The "Country Magic" heard on the show was composed by Steve March, the son of Mel Tormé and the stepson of Hal March, the famed TV host of *The $64,000 Question.*

For Lucille, the making of *Lucy and Ann-Margret* was a very sad occasion. It marked the death of her long-time music director, Wilbur Hatch, who had arranged the musical scoring of not only the *I Love Lucy* series (all 156 episodes), but also for the radio programs in which she'd co-starred with Richard Denning in *My Favorite Husband.*

For years, Hatch had been devoted to Lucille and Desi, both of whom admired his skill as a composer. His days working on radio dated back to 1922, when he was a pianist for KYW in Chicago. On radio, he created background music not just for *My Favorite Husband,* but for *Our Miss Brooks, December Bride,* and *Meet Corliss Archer.*

The pianist and arranger, Mart Young (1917-2009), was called in to replace Hatch. Right from the beginning, Lucille knew she had selected the right man. After listening to his background music on the episode with Ann-Margret, she made his job as her musical director permanent. He worked on *Here's Lucy* until its demise in 1974.

He told Lucille that as a young man in Chicago, he set out to become a chemical engineer. "One morning, I woke up and told myself that chemical engineering could go to hell. I had a song in my heart."

Lucille became friends with Young and his wife, Margaret Mathews of Grinell, Iowa. She also met their three children, the oldest of whom,

Robert, was born in 1932, near the beginning of the Depression.

***

Two days after the *Here's Lucy* episode with Ann-Margret was telecast, Desi Jr. and Lucie Arnaz were cast in a production of the Kraft Music Hall. Telecast on February 4, 1970, it was called *The Kraft Music Hall Presents Desi Arnaz.*

Days before rehearsals, Desi Senior met with the director, Gary Smith, and demanded that the hour-long special feature both his daughter, Lucie, and his son, Desi Jr. Smith had also signed both Bernadette Peters and Vivian Vance to the cast.

A New Yorker, Peters was both an actress and a singer. In time, her career would span five decades, mostly in musical theater, but also in solo concerts and recordings. On Broadway, she would receive seven Tony Award nominations, winning two. In music circles, she was regarded as the foremost interpreter of the works of Stephen Sondheim.

Bernadette Peters on the front cover of the December, 1981, edition of *Playboy.* Alongside profiles of right-wing evangelist Jerry Falwell, author James Baldwin, and "the Sex Stars of 1981," she showed off "the lingerie that dreams are made of," but didn't actually get naked.

Some said that she bore a striking resemblance to Lucie Arnaz.

For the Kraft show, Desi Sr. was reunited with Bob Carroll Jr., and with Madelyn Davis, who had gained their greatest fame writing all those *I Love Lucy* scripts.

Missing from this "family reunion" was one person: Lucille Ball herself.

Beginning when his hair turned grey, Desi Sr. had began dying it jet black, as it was in his younger days. He had lost a lot of weight, cut back his heavy consumption of alcohol, and, as host of the show, looked better than he had in years.

After watching both of his kids perform, he said "My God, my son and daughter are really talented. I wonder where they inherited all this talent. Was it from Lucille? Or was I the one? Perhaps a combination of the best of Mama and Papa."

Lucie later spoke of her thrill of co-starring with both her father and her brother. Her only regret was that this was just a one-time gig and that it would not be repeated again. *[Both she and Desi Jr. would appear on other Kraft shows, but not Desi Sr.]*

He indiscreetly spoke to a reporter from *TV Guide.* "When my little girl (actually, she's not little any more) sang a duet with me, 'We'll Build a Bungalow,' she was far better than Lucy would have been. And if you print that, I'll take a razor blade and remove one of your *cojones.*"

The reporter did print that, and Lucille read it, but her reaction was not one of fury. Actually, she was in agreement. "Lucie is a better singer and dancer than I could ever be. I was never any good as a singer and dancer. In all my films, when I was called upon to sing, my voice was dubbed. As for dancing, Marjorie Main could dance better than me. That sounds like a joke, but I heard that the old buzzard herself, back in the 1920s, used to be a hoofer in vaudeville."

Lucie later claimed, "Vivian Vance was a real professional and theater trained. She always showed up on time, knew her lines, and was right on the mark. However, she never escaped the role of Ethel Mertz, that character from *I Love Lucy* would forever brand her, much to her regret. Desi Jr. and I only called her 'Aunt Viv' on TV. We would never do that in real life."

"There was a certain irony here. My parents were never Ricky and Lucy Ricardo, and Vivian was never Ethel Mertz. As for William Frawley, I suspected that as Fred Mertz, he was merely playing himself."

***

Here's Lucy, Episode 45, was telecast on February 9, 1970, and entitled *Lucy and Wally Cox.* He was one of Lucille's favorite guests. Directed by Jay Sandrich and written by Ray Singer, it cast Cox as "the meek and mild" Walley Manley.

His aging father fears he is "not man enough" to take over his detective agency when he retires. Cox doesn't seem to be able to walk in the gumshoes of such hard-boiled detectives as "Sam Spade" or any of those characters Humphrey Bogart and others played in the 1940s.

Scheming and teaming with Lucy, Wally sets out to prove his dad wrong. He and Lucy become night guards in a warehouse. Of course, you just know they'll have to confront a gang of thieves breaking in. Wally proves he's man enough for the job after all.

The cast also included Alan Hale Jr., son of the more famous Hale Senior. But on the current market, Junior had achieved fame as the Skipper in the hit TV series, *Gilligan's Island* (1964-67).

In addition, stuntman Chuck Hicks was considered the best and most daring in the business. Lucille had known him in the heyday of *I Love Lucy,* when he was involved with the Desilu Workshop.

Sandrich as director was a familiar face. Originally, he'd been the assistant director on *I Love Lucy.* In the year he worked with her again, he had signed to direct *The Mary Tyler Moore Show.*

Lucille had long been fascinated by Cox's relationship with Marlon Brando, dating from the early days in Manhattan when they'd been roommates. Admitting that he was bisexual, Brando had already uttered the widely printed statement: "If Wally had been a woman, I would have married him and lived happily ever after."

His latest statement was even more provocative. Fueled by too much marijuana, Brando had told writer/editor Beauregard Houston-Montgomery, "Wally and I have had a sexual relationship that has lasted for years—he is, in fact, the love of my life, both sexual and spiritual."

Cox confessed to Lucille that he was receiving a lot of homophobic hate mail.

Over the years, Brando was known for having a number of male lovers, but, judging from reports, only once was he maneuvered onto a casting couch. He traveled to meet Tennessee Williams and won him over, getting cast as Stanley Kowalski in the play, *A Streetcar Named Desire.* Other lovers included James Dean, who worshipped him; the African-American writer James Baldwin; the composer-conductor Leonard Bernstein; the French actor Christian Marquand; and author Gore Vidal. Mart Martin, known for compiling a list of movie star seductions, also cited singer Bob Dylan, but that was never verified.

Serialized to a vast international audience by the *Sunday Times* (of London), and written by one of the co-authors of this biography, it's **Brando Unzipped.**

Of course, Brando's list of female seductions is far more extensive. It included Vivien Leigh when she co-starred with him in the film version of *A Streetcar Named Desire* (1951). The list also featured Rita Moreno, Tallulah Bankhead, Ursula Andress, Joan Collins, Yvonne De Carlo, Bianca Jagger, Shelley Winters, and Marilyn Monroe.

"I've never been circumcised, and my noble tool has performed its duties through thick and thin and without fail," Brando boasted.

Cox told Lucille, "I love Marlon dearly, and have ever since we were roomies. He is the greatest actor in the world. If I have a criticism of him, it is that he can sometimes be indiscreet in what he says. He makes some pretty shocking statements which can be harmful to me."

Gossipy Lucille was aware of that notorious "up close and intimate" picture being circulated of Brando fellating Cox, a photo taken in their bedroom in 1952. He admitted that it was authentic, and he'd foolishly agreed to pose for it when "all of us, including the photographer, were high."

He claimed that Kenneth Anger was going to publish the picture in his first edition of *Hollywood Babylon,* but Brando threatened him with a lawsuit.

On another occasion, two years later, Brando also brought up the subject of fellatio, commenting on the bust he posed for, in character as Marc Antony, in the 1954 film, *Julius Caesar.* "It makes me look as if I'm about to suck every cock in Hollywood," he said.

The most complete dossier on the love life of Marlon Brando, including his long affair with Cox, appeared in the pages of Blood Moon's *Brando Unzipped,* published in 2005.

In spite of the rumors about Cox's sexuality, he married three times, first to Marilyn Gennero in 1954, and later to Milagros Tirado. Both unions ended in divorce. His final wife was Patricia Tiernan, whom he married in 1969. In February of 1973, he was found dead at his home in Hollywood. He was only 48 years old.

***

For her next episode (#46) of *Here's Lucy,* she told her director, Danny Dayton, "I want to book that Indian as my guest star."

"You mean Iron Eyes?"

"No, I've been his squaw in a former episode. I'm talking Wayne Newton."

"Newton's an Indian?" he said. "Hard to believe."

"He's a half-breed, part Powhatan, part Cherokee," she said.

Dayton, a native son of Jersey City, was younger than Lucille and had been an actor in the 1950s in both film and TV. He had a recurring role as Hank Pivnik in the hit TV comedy, *All in the Family,* and had had guest roles on such TV hits as *M*A*S*H* and *Charlie's Angels.* In time, he switched to directing.

Dayton called Newton in Las Vegas, and after some persuasion, he agreed to appear with her in the next episode of *Here's Lucy.* The show would be entitled *Lucy and Wayne Newton* and would be telecast on February 16. He had credited Lucille with giving his singing career a big boost when he had appeared with her on *The Lucy Show* in an episode broadcast in December of 1965 entitled *Lucy Discovers Wayne Newton.*

This newest episode was shot on location in the San Fernando Valley, where Lucille used to live during the early years of her ill-fated marriage to Desi Arnaz. It included her two kids.

The plot gets rolling when she discovers a midget horse outside Las Vegas and returns it to the ranch of its owner (guess who?) Newton himself. Just for fun, she asks him to hire her family as ranch hands for the summer.

Perhaps their father had taught Lucie and Desi Jr. how to ride a horse, but for

To many visitors, **Wayne Newton** was an "unlikely celebrity," but in Las Vegas, he generated LOTS of excitement, LOTS of publicity, and LOTS of bookings.

The upper photo dates from the mid-1970s, during the peak of his reign and the pinnacle of his allure.

this episode, trainer Glen Randall was hired to teach them some of the finer points such as "dressage" and more of the nuances of horseback riding.

The kids were fine on camera, as later reported, but the horses wouldn't cooperate.

The script called for them to step in time with the music, including the song, "I've Got the World on a String," but they were always out of step.

Newton is so impressed with the singing talent of Lucy's brood that he asks them to appear with him on stage at the Nevada State Fair.

Working with Newton again, Lucille noted that his former squeaky voice was much lower. She would never live to see his incredible success in Las Vegas, where he became a regularly appearing star on The Strip, performing some 30,000 shows, always ending with his signature song, "Danke Schoen."

The Lucy script featuring horses was dear to Newton's heart. He once told a reporter, "My two loves in life, from the time I was a kid, were music and horses. I could never decide which I loved best."

He'd bought his first horse when he was a sixth grader, selling his bike and his parents' movie camera to raise the money. He eventually specialized in Arabians, and began breeding them at his sprawling ranch, Casa de Shenandoah. At one time, he paid $150,000 for a single stallion, Naborr, the highest price ever for an Arabian horse at that time.

Lucille had a great affection for Newton and felt sorry for him when he was constantly ridiculed by Johnny Carson on *The Tonight Show*. At one point, Newton confronted Carson and slapped him. "He is a mean-spirited human being," Newton said on *Larry King Live*.

A decade after co-starring with Lucille, she read in *Variety* that he had become part owner of the Alladin in Las Vegas. That led to a number of lawsuits. His troubles mounted, with seemingly endless legal challenges.

In 1992, he filed for Chapter Eleven Bankruptcy in an effort to reorganize an estimated $20 million in debt.

Lawsuits with NBC on a charge of libel, battles with the IRS, property seizures, whatever, Newton could easily have written, had his lawyers not stopped him, an autobiography entitled *My Life in Court*.

***

Lucille ended the 1969-1970 season by appearing once again with Carol Burnett, this time in Episode #48 of *Here's Lucy: Lucy and Carol Burnett (A.K.A. Secretary Beautiful)* telecast on March 2, 1970.

Lucille enters a contest for the most beautiful secretary, competing with her "ugly duckling" friend, Carol Krausmayer (Burnett).

The judge of the pageant is Robert Alda, who appears as himself. Actually, the highlight of the scene occurs when Harry (Gale Gordon) teaches Lucy how to walk like a sexy woman. For this scene, Gordon gets campy in the best tradition of a drag queen.

Lucille had long admired the comedic talent of Burnett and tried to view her as a friend—not a rival. Since 1959, she'd been a mentor to the young performer and also kept her friendship alive without being too competitive. She had starred as a guest on the CBS-TV special, Carol + 2, and the younger star had returned the favor by appearing with her on *The Lucy Show* series.

Lucille even offered her a gig to star in her own TV sitcom, *Here's Agnes*, but Burnett turned it down. She was holding out for bigger stakes, and that happened in 1967, when she went on the air with the hour-long *Carol Burnett Show*, broadcast weekly.

Over the course of its long run, it would garner 23 Emmy Awards, with its regular ensemble cast of Harvey Korman, Tim Conway, Lyle Waggoner, and Vicky Lawrence, who looked so much like Carol that she could have been her sister.

At first, Burnett faced objections from executives at both NBC and CBS who doubted if a woman could pull off a weekly gig as a variety show host, something in the tradition of Ed Sullivan.

As Lucille later told Vivian Vance, "American TV viewers are divided into two camps: One group claims that I, Lucille, am the best *comedienne* on TV. Another prefers the antics of Carol."

She acknowledged Burnett's greater talent for parody. Both of them had parodied *Gone With the Wind*, Burnett pulling it off more effectively. Her musical numbers with song and dance were also better than Lucille's.

Burnett struck gold with a skit entitled, "The Family" starring Lawrence.

As Lucille lamented to Vance, "I was the First Lady of Television, as you well know. But now that the 1970s have arrived, I fear some of us older dragons from the early days of radio and TV shows are being de-crowned. Carol is now on her way to becoming First Lady of Television. Not only that, but she can do the Tarzan yell better than me. I tried to imitate it at home, but I sounded more like a bull getting castrated."

Carol Burnett (left) and **Lucille Ball** appeared together often on one or another of their respective TV shows. For this scene, they drifted back into the Roaring '20s.

In reference to their costumes, Carol said, "I was inspired by the 'It' Girl, Clara Bow, with Lucille taking a cue from Joan Crawford."

WOMEN WE LOVE
HOMAGE TO LUCILLE BALL'S COMEDIC COMPETITOR,
CAROL BURNETT

Seismic changes in America's perception of comedy: **Carol Burnett** is funnier (or at least more up-to-date) than Lucille? Could it be true?

Here she is with her cohort-in-comedy, **Tim Conway**.

Carol Burnett (left) with **Vicki Lawrence**. Through comedy, they pulled off, some critics said, "the most devastating and accurate satire of the American family ever conceived."

WENT WITH THE WIND: **Carol Burnett** satirizing Vivien Leigh playing Scarlett O'Hara from *Gone With the Wind*, clad in f*aux*-finery crafted from her (dead) mother's curtains salvaged from the faded grandeur of Tara after the Yankee ravages. **Harvey Korman** portrays "Rat" Butler.

Burnett's line in the photo on the right? "I saw it in the window and just couldn't resist."

CHAPTER EIGHT

CELEBRITY FEUDS

Raging Battles with Richard Burton, Elizabeth Taylor, & Jack Benny

Insecure and Aging, Lucille Becomes More Bossy

As Lucille launched *Here's Lucy: The Third Season* (1970-1971), she'd been a legend long enough to have accumulated appearances on a wide dossier of television shows. *TV Guide's* Terrence O'Flaherty listed many of the details in *The Lucy Book of Records*.

He concluded that until that point in her career she had starred in 495 television shows. One hundred seventy-nine of them had been episodes of *I Love Lucy*, and one-hundred fifty-six had been telecasts of *The Lucy Show*.

In her newest series, *Here's Lucy*, another 144 episodes would be added to the other shows. Along the way, she had starred in at least sixteen TV specials with other stars.

All in all, it would require even the most avid of television addicts at least two weeks, watching day and night, to sit through all these broadcasts.

O'Flaherty also wrote of crazy pratfalls or pitfalls Lucille performed as, for example, when she was coated with chocolate syrup; starched; soaked; plunged down a ski slope; slid down a fire pole; locked in handcuffs; and crowned with a loving cup atop her head. Getting her teeth blacked out as a hillbilly or getting hit with a custard pie in her face were common slapstick.

Although she would appear with major-league entertainers such as Joan Crawford and Jack Benny, her other co-stars had been sheep, tigers, penguins, porpoises, bears, cats, birds, pigs, dogs, and ferocious lions.

He also cited various roles she had played, including a grape trampler (one of her most famous episodes), a fight manager, a saxophone player, a nun, an Indian, a bricklayer, a pool hustler (*à la* Paul Newman), a fireman, a kangaroo, a Martian (with Vivian Vance), the front of a horse, an astronaut, and the most bizarre of all, a pickle.

To launch the third season of *Here's Lucy,* a show called *Lucy Meets the Burtons* was telecast on September 14, 1970. At the time, Richard Burton and Elizabeth Taylor were at the peak of their international glamour and fame. It had begun with their adulterous affair on the set of the ultra-expensive and scandal-soaked *Cleopatra* (1963) in Rome.

To direct the Burtons and Lucille, Jerry Paris was hired. A native of San Francisco, he'd served in the U.S. Navy during World War II, and later attended New York University and the Actors Studio in Manhattan.

In Hollywood, he'd first tried to become a movie star, but ended up mainly appearing uncredited in such high-profile films as *Battleground* (1949) starring Van Johnson. *[Paris was cast as a German sergeant.]* In José Ferrer's *Cyrano de Bergerac* (1952), Paris was a cadet. He played a scientist in *Monkey Business* (1952), starring Cary Grant, Ginger Rogers, and Marilyn Monroe.

As a movie actor with a career headed nowhere, he switched to television, a medium in which he became somewhat known playing Jerry Helper, the next-door neighbor of Rob and Laura Petrie on *The Dick Van Dyke Show.*

Once, Desi cast him in an episode of *The Untouchables,* starring Robert Stack.

Almost from the first day on the set of *Here's Lucy,* he and Lucille conflicted. "We absolutely despised each other," Paris said. "I expected to be fired, perhaps before we finished shooting the Burton thing."

Indeed, he was fired, but he bounced back in other venues, eventually directing 237 of the 255 episodes of *Happy Days* (1974-1984).

In attempts to make sure that the Burton/Taylor episode was a hit, Lucille rehired her former co-writers of most of the *I Love Lucy* series: Bob Car-

Lucille appeared on an episode of *Here's Lucy* with **Richard Burton** and **Elizabeth Taylor**, then at the height of their fame.

In the most epic scene, Taylor struggles to get her big diamond back after it gets stuck on Lucille's finger.

It filled only five seconds of the telecast, but was an endless struggle in rehearsals to get it right.

roll Jr and Madelyn Davis (formerly Madelyn Pugh).

The plot they concocted turned out to be rather silly and lacked any semblance of believability. As depicted, superstars Burton and Taylor are staying at the Beverly Hills Hotel, where they can't leave the premises without being "devoured" by mobs of fans. To escape detection, Burton disguises himself as a plumber, putting on a pair of overalls.

Lucille spots him and thinks he is indeed a "plumber" and orders him to repair the waterworks leaking into her hotel bathroom. Burton valiantly goes to work fixing her plumbing while (brilliantly) reciting lines from Shakespeare.

After repairing the leak, Burton leaves his overalls behind. While searching through the pockets, Lucille discovers the 69.42 karat gemstone known as "The Cartier Diamond" for which Burton had recently — with enormous news and tabloid coverage — paid $1.1 million. It is almost too big to wear on a human finger. Being Lucy, she has to put it on to see how it looks.

When Elizabeth learns that Lucy is wearing her diamond, she visits, but cannot remove it from her finger.

Both she and Burton are soon due at a reception. All the visitors want to see the diamond, so Lucille hides behind a curtain. It is her hand wearing the diamond that the guests all gape at.

According to the script, as it unfolded, the leading gossip columnists of Hollywood, including Joyce Haber, think they're looking at the diamond on Taylor's left hand, but it is Lucille's, emerging from behind the curtain.

It had been pre-arranged for Haber, after the reception, to conduct an interview with Lucille.

[Many critics who reviewed the show mistakenly wrote that the focal point of the episode had been the famous (33.19 karat) Krupp Diamond. Burton had paid far less ("only" $305,000) when he'd purchased this ring from the Parke-Bernet Galleries in Manhattan in 1968. The Krupp diamond (later renamed "the Elizabeth Taylor Diamond" was notorious, *having been a prize possession of the Krupp family, armaments manufacturer for the Third Reich.*

As Burton told the press when he bought it, "Vera Krupp and her gang of cutthroats made munitions that killed millions of Jews. How appropriate that it now adorns the finger of a nice Jewish girl like Elizabeth Taylor."

Actually, the 69.42 karat diamond ring depicted on TV ("The Taylor-Burton Cartier Diamond") was larger and more valuable than the Krupp Diamond. Burton had shelled out $1.1 million dollars for it in 1969. After its acquisition by Taylor & Burton, Taylor — after deciding that it was too heavy to wear as a ring — commissioned its reconfiguration into a necklace specifically designed to conceal her tracheotomy scar, an after-effect from her bout with near-fatal pneumonia in 1961.

TRIVIA: the diamond featured on Lucille's finger, through the curtain, in September of 1970 had previously belonged to Harriet Annenberg Ames, the sister of the billionaire publisher and close friend of Ronald and Nancy Reagan, Walter Annenberg. Harriet Annenberg Ames felt unsafe wearing it in New York City: "I found myself positively cringing and keeping my gloves on for fear it would be seen. ... It sat in a bank vault for years. It seemed foolish to keep it if one could not use it. As things are in New York, one could not possibly wear it publicly."]

Only after the episode aired did word leak out about the feud that escalated during rehearsals with Lucille and the Burtons. After he was fired, Paris discussed it with reporters.

Although Burton at the time was probably the most acclaimed actor in the world, Lucille tried to direct him, criticizing his every move. "You're off your mark!" she shouted at him. "Get back on your mark!"

"If you'll get out of my fucking way, I'll get on my god damn mark!" he shouted back at her.

Soon, she was attacking him again. "You're mumbling! I can't hear a fucking word coming from your mouth. If I'd wanted a mumbler, I'd have hired Marlon Brando!"

"That really infuriated Burton. He looked at Ball as if he wanted to kill her," Paris said.

"Burton kept throwing away his best comic lines," Lucille later asserted. "He kept that English drawing room drawl when it wasn't appropriate. He had some big laugh lines, and he screwed up every one of them with his dumb delivery."

Elizabeth Taylor poses here with the Taylor-Burton Diamond.

Elizabeth rarely agreed with Marilyn Monroe about anything, calling her a "slut."

But when it came to the theme of her most famous song ("Diamonds Are a Girl's Best Friend," from *Gentlemen Prefer Blondes*) they were in complete agreement.

When Paris tried to interfere to keep the peace, she called him "a horse's ass."

After the shoot, Burton told the press, "Ball is a manipulating, controlling bitch."

Burton, as he was getting into a limousine in which Taylor was already seated, was approached by a young man from the press. He wanted to know "what it was like working with Lucille?"

"The old bag of wrinkles looks eighty if she's a day and was furious when I refused to fuck her."

In his memoir, Burton wrote, "Those who had worked with Ball claimed she was 'very wearing' and they do not exaggerate. She is not 'wearing' to us because we refuse to be worn. She lives entirely on that weekly show, which she has been doing successfully for nineteen years. Nineteen years of double-takes and pratfalls and desperate upstaging and nervously watching the 'ratings' as she does."

Before Elizabeth appeared on the set, Burton had warned Lucille not to antagonize her. "If you do, be prepared to see a thousand megaton hydrogen bomb explode when its warhead is detached."

Lucille had known Taylor for years, beginning when both of them worked for MGM. She was never friends with her, and on sound stages, she referred to her as "Miss Taylor" or "Mrs. Burton."

But they tangled when Lucille began to criticize Taylor's delivery of her lines. "You're speaking in a whisper. I can't hear a fucking word coming out of your mouth."

Taylor exploded and from that moment on, she referred to Lucille as "The Cunt"—and right to her face.

The next day during rehearsals, Lucille did not back off and remained critical of Taylor's acting.

"How many Oscars have you won?" Taylor shouted at her, using a voice familiar to those who'd seen her film, *Who's Afraid of Virginia Woolf?* (1964).

It was later learned that Taylor's patience was wearing thin because she'd developed a painful case of hemorrhoids and would soon enter the hospital for surgery.

Burton, too, was in a bad mood because he

The dreaded "golden age" gossip columnist Hedda Hopper had always been a loyal supporter of Lucille. But when **Joyce Haber**, depicted above, tried to fill her shoes, she and Lucille conflicted.

"I don't know why, but Haber always seemed to have a grudge against me," Lucille complained. "Maybe she thought Hedda had been too kind, and she was determined to show the world that there was a new girl in town, writing the hottest and most scandalous column in Hollywood."

Jean Seberg was the American-born darling of the French "New Wave."

Lucille always claimed that Haber's *exposé* of Seberg led to her suicide in Paris. Missing for ten days, her decomposing body was found parked on a Paris street in a white Renault.

Seberg made her acting debut in director Otto Preminger's *Saint Joan* in 1957 (see left photo, above). To do so, she beat out 18,000 other aspiring actresses. Later, the temperamental director blamed her for the critical assaults on the film.

A New York critic bitchily suggested that Preminger should send his *protégée* back to the Iowa high school where he found her.

Time magazine claimed that the young actress was "like a honeybun that drugstore desperadoes like to nibble on with their milkshakes."

was on a severe diet. Before their temper tantrums, Taylor had told Lucille that "Sleeping with Burton these days is like bedding Mia Farrow."

After hearing that, Lucille nicknamed Burton "Mia," a reference to an actress whose figure was compared to a matchstick.

Even before the Burtons arrived for the first day of rehearsals, their agent issued demands. Taylor wanted the luxurious "dressing trailer" that Barbra Streisand used during her filming of *Funny Girl* (1968). Burton was more modest in his demand, asking, and getting, a dressing trailer that stretched forty feet.

The night of the telecast, it was estimated that at least half of all TV viewers tuned in to see the Burtons face off with Lucille. It became the top-rated Lucy show in TV history.

Variety reviewed the episode as "a great sockfest, a fine example of situation comedy played to the hilt. The broad comedy was laced with crackling one-liners. Burton matched Ball step-by-step in a parody of himself."

Aspiring actor **Phil Vandervort** appears in a *Here's Lucy* episode with **Lucie Arnaz**, his future bride.

Lucie would always remember the episode with Burton and Taylor becuse it was around that time that Vandervort gave her an engagement right. Set into a gold band, it featured a marquis-shaped emerald surrounded with tiny diamonds.

Elizabeth Taylor came over to look at it, suggesting that in the future, Lucie should use toothpaste to clean it.

After the episode aired, Burton wrote, "I loathed Lucille Ball, but now I merely pity her. I will make it a point never to see her again. She can thank her lucky stars that I was not drinking—or else I might have killed her."

As had been pre-arranged, Joyce Haber stayed behind to interview Lucille. Writing for the *Los Angeles Times,* she had become one of the most powerful gossip columnists in Hollywood, and, so it was said, "was capable of canonizing a film or destroying a star." She'd taken over the former job of Hedda Hopper, who had always been a loyal supporter of Lucille.

Lucille did not have any chemistry with Haber. In fact, during their first interview, "there was a chill in the air," Haber later claimed. At the time that Haber interviewed Lucille, she had been instrumental in an FBI "black-op," as it was called, that led to the suicide of actress Jean Seberg in 1979. Haber planted an unfounded rumor in her column to the effect that Seberg's pregnancy was the result of a sexual liaison with a leader of the Black Panther Party. On a request from J. Edgar Hoover of the FBI, this was done in retaliation for Seberg's support of the Black Panthers. Seberg had miscarried shortly after and therefore suffered from a deep depression that ultimately, it was alleged, led to her death.

***

There was another backstage drama involving diamond rings whirling around the set during the filming of the Burton/Taylor episode on *Here's Lucy*. The actor, Phil Vandervort, had presented an engagement ring to Lucie Arnaz. It was a marquis-shaped gold ring with a tiny emerald and a baby diamond.

Taylor wore the Cartier Diamond, nearly 70 karats, as she held up Lucie's hand to inspect her ring, as her own diamond sparkled provocatively as sunlight streamed down upon it.

"Elizabeth didn't gloat, and any comparison would have been odious," Lucie said, "Actually, she was most gracious, telling me what a lovely ring Phil had given me, and wishing me all the luck in my upcoming marriage."

Lucille, however, was not impressed, as she opposed Lucie getting married. "You're too young," she told her daughter, "and he's not right for you. I'm not convinced he's in love with you, and I've worked with him. He could be a golddigger. Since his acting career seems to be going nowhere, maybe he wants to be more of your kept boy than a husband. Beverly Hills is peopled with men like that."

This is an original press photo issued to the media on July 17, 1971. The blurb that accompanied it is replicated below:

Lucie Desirée, daughter of Lucille Ball and Desi Arnaz poses with her husband of a few minutes, **Phillip Vandervort Menegaux**, as they show their wedding rings following their marriage in Beverly Hills today at the home of her mother.

Today was also the bride's 20th birthday. The groom is a producer-director and they plan to live in the West Los Angeles area after a short honeymoon.

The wedding was scheduled for July 17, 1971, which would be the occasion of Lucie's twentieth birthday. She had been born in 1951, and her husband-to-be came into the world in September of 1942, during one of the darkest days of World War II.

Between 1964 and 1967, he'd been married to Deirdre McDermott. He met Lucie when both of them had appeared in an episode of *The Lucy Show*. His film credentials were slim, with appearances in *The Doctors* (1963), *Mannix* (1967), and *Maryjane* (1968).

Since the age of sixteen, Lucie had been trained as an actress by her multi-talented mother. "It was a great experience for me to co-star with her in the *Here's Lucy* series. My brother was in some of the early episodes, but he eventually dropped out. My mother expected three times more from us than she did from the rest of the cast. If we fell off our mark, she let us know that. We couldn't get away with anything. Only our best would do. We learned our craft and got better as the series continued. Working on *Here's Lucy* was like going to acting school, only two million people were watching."

When Lucie turned eighteen and was earning money as a performer, she announced to Lucille that she was renting her own apartment and moving out, despite her mother's very vocal objections.

After she moved out and established herself independently, Lucie knew she would be forever known as "the daughter of Lucille Ball."

"It didn't really bother me that much that my mother was the center of attention in any conversation about me," Lucie said. "I learned a lot from her."

"The best thing I remember from my childhood was playing at Desilu Studios, using it like my big backyard."

One of her worst memories was generated during her enrollment in the Beverly Hills Catholic School. "The teachers, at least some of them, were cuckoo-loonies. One nutcase insisted she was from Mars. In class, she was a chain smoker, when not pulling out strands of her hair."

"That was in the sixth grade. In the seventh grade, my teacher, a Sister Martha Ann, wasn't much better. She seemed to detest the sons and daughters of movie stars. Sometimes, she'd stand right over my desk, dripping snot without a handkerchief."

"At the slightest perceived infraction, she would humiliate me in front of the class, saying things like, 'Just because you're the daughter of Lucille Ball, you think you can get away with everything. But you can't—not in my class.'"

"By the time I was in high school, conditions improved," Lucie said. "I was enrolled in a Catholic school named Immaculate Heart. I had made up my mind to become an actress, and to be something more than the daughter of Lucille Ball."

Lucille, however, had her own views about parenthood, sharing them with such friends as Arlene Dahl: "Don't let your kids run your life. Go out into the world and lead your own life without giving in to the never-ending demands of your offspring."

Although they were often absentee parents, both Lucille and Desi loved their kids. Even when divorcing Lucille in 1960, Desi assured them that he would always be there for them if they needed him, and that they'd always be welcome to arrive on his doorstep. He also confessed that he still loved Lucille even though he was divorcing her.

Sometimes, Lucille spoke of the upcoming marriage of her daughter. "She met this guy in high school. Personally, I give their marriage a year at the most. She's only nineteen, and she has a lot of growing up to do before settling into marriage with an actor, no less."

But she was forced to accept the marriage, and she offered her future son-in-law a good-paying position as the assistant to Gary Morton, his new father-in-law.

Around this time, Lucie was quoted as saying, "My brother and I came along rather late in our mother's life, as she'd experienced miscarriages. When Desi Jr. and I came into the world, she was wandering into that nightmare for an actress, middle age. She always had been overly protective of both of us."

After Desi divorced Lucille, his kids continued to visit Del Mar and to stay with him and his new wife, Edie. They'd known Edie some time before their father married her.

Lucie recalled the good times, often evenings, when the trio of them would sing together, having a lot of laughs.

As time went by, and as Desi consumed more alcohol, his temper flared. Sometimes, he'd act violently, slamming doors in the house and shouting. At those times, Desi Jr. and Lucie visited him less frequently than before.

Desi responded to criticism by saying, "I was never trying to be named Father of the Year."

On the late afternoon of Lucie's wedding to Vandervort, the sun was setting in the west as three hundred guests arrived for the ceremony at 1000 Roxbury Drive in Beverly Hills, creating a traffic jam. Neighbors turned on their sprinklers to keep people from trampling across their lawns.

Among the invited guests were Carol Burnett and the actor Lloyd Bridges, whom Lucille once cited as "The third-sexiest man in Hollywood, after William Holden and James Craig."

Even Jimmy Durante followed his long nose into the house, trailed by comedian Buddy Hackett.

Comedian Jack Carter, who had introduced Lucille to Gary Morton, thought she should have hosted a catered affair, since she'd just made a deal that netted her seventeen million dollars.

"Lucille must have gone to three delis and bought up all their bologna and salami and sliced ham. She then purchased about 350 paper plates. Even a church social in some backwoods town would have better food than that."

Desi Sr. drove north with Edie to attend the wedding and give the bride away. A family friend, Wanda Clark, said to be like a mother to Lucie, was the Matron of Honor. Richard Gautier, Vandervort's best friend, was Best Man. Desi Jr. served as an usher.

After the wedding, as Desi Sr. and Lucille were dancing to music of a Cuban band he'd hired, Gary Morton cut in.

In response, in a loud voice, Desi said, "This is the second fucking time you've cut in on me."

***

As regards *pizzazz* they lent to her show, Lucille was fully aware that Elizabeth Taylor and Richard Burton would be a tough act to follow. Since she couldn't match them, she turned instead to two talented performers she had long admired, Sammy Davis Jr. and drummer Buddy Rich.

But first, she agreed to appear on a special episode of *The Ed Sullivan Show* specifically choreographed for the presentation of "The Georgies," telecast through CBS on September 20, 1970.

When she met with Sullivan, the TV host and newspaper columnist, she found him filled with dread: "The heyday of the variety show is coming to an end," he predicted, ominously. "It'll be so sad to see it go. But, while it lasted, it was a hell of a run."

For his sixty-minute CBS special, Sullivan had booked an array of talent, including Milton Berle, Bob Hope, Barbra Streisand, Danny Thomas, and (with the hopes of attracting a younger audience), Blood, Sweat, and Tears.

The American Guild of Variety Artists, an organization noted for honoring night club performers, would be presented with not Oscars or Emmys, but with "Georgies," named in honor of the fabled Broadway producer and showman, George M. Cohan.

During negotiations in advance of the show, it was clearly understood that Lucille would present a Georgie to Carol Burnett, thereby honoring her as "Best Comedienne of the Year."

As a gag, Lucille "spoon feeds Burnett her lines, ending the skit with the suggestion that it should be herself walking off with the Georgie. The event was publicized as "The Battle of the Redheads."

***

The very next day, a telecast of her latest *Here's Lucy* episode was aired. It was entitled *Lucy and the Skydiver*. Since her children, Kim and Craig (Lucie and Desi Jr.), are pursuing what she views as dangerous sports (motorcycling and skin diving). Lucille, therefore, decides to outdo them by becoming a sky diver.

Her director, Herbert Kenwith, faced the logistics of one of the most ambitious stunts of any Lucy episode. He therefore worked closely with his crew and cameramen to make Lucille's dive from an airplane look authentic. They designed and built an intricate platform with the equipment to make it look like she was actually jumping out of an airplane. A parachute opened to suggest she's plummeting earthward in red-headed glory.

"What in hell will you and those hack writers think of next for me to do?" she asked Kenwith. "For my new episode, I'll probably be at the bottom of the Atlantic, boarding the wreckage of the *Titanic,* trying to find the safe where the jewelry of all those rich passengers was stored."

He patiently explained to her the layouts of several cleverly designed sets, including a sky blue background that would help simulate her fall to earth.

"I'll probably end up in the hospital with not two, but three broken legs, not to mention my brittle arms."

At that point, she had not read the script. When she did, she exploded in anger. She came face to face (some said "nose to nose") with Kenwith as she denounced him. "I knew all the vulgar names, but she'd learned some horrible ones in Spanish, no doubt from Arnaz," Kenwith said. "But eventually, she pulled herself together, and the next day she performed that stunt with nothing broken."

After that, she approached Kenwith with a remarkably different demeanor, inviting him to dine with Gary Morton and herself at Matteo's, a chic, celebrity-haunted bistro in Beverly Hills.

Mr. and Mrs. Morton were already ensconced in a red-leather banquette when Kenwith arrived at the restaurant. As she spotted him heading toward their table, she yelled out in a voice loud enough for the other diners to hear, "What a pair of *cojones* you have!"

As he was seated, she said, "You sure do have a pair of balls on you. You're the only director who has dared stand up to me. You must be a tiger in bed."

"After that dinner, Lucille was fairly tame for a while," Kenwith said. "I expected her next outburst to match the bombing of Hiroshima."

***

Lucille and director Herbert Kenwith had declared a truce by the time he had to helm her in Episode #51, *Lucy and Sammy Davis Jr.,* telecast on September 28, 1970, near the beginning of the autumn lineup of *Here's Lucy.*

As backup players to the named stars, the director hired Steve March-Tormé (the son of Mel Tormé), Elliot Reid, Buddy Hackett. He also cast Gary Morton.

The script had been heavily doctored by Milt Josefsberg, who was not pleased with the two writers he'd hired. When he presented their script to Lucille, she evaluated it as "a piece of shit." Kenwith quickly convinced her otherwise, assuring her that with her brilliant talent and the antics of "that marvel," Sammy Davis Jr., they could pull it off.

Lucille and Davis had been friends for years, ever since Frank Sinatra had introduced them in Las Vegas.

The script called for the African American star to wander into the office of Harry Carter (Gale Gordon), where he meets the secretary, Lucy. Davis had injured his nose in the elevator, and Harry fears a lawsuit.

Lucy is ordered to follow him around to see that he keeps his nose out of trouble and doesn't further endanger himself. Of course, expect the usual Lucy disasters.

A surprise visitor to the set was Desi Sr., who was very encouraging to the blossoming career of his only daughter. He and Lucille still frequently greeted each other, after prolonged absences, with a tight embrace and a lip-smacking kiss right in front of Morton, who always managed to conceal his jealousy.

Desi had come over from the Universal lot, where he was appearing in the TV Western series, *The Man from Shiloh.*

The episode in which Desi was starring was part of an year-long extension (*The Man from Shiloh*) of *The Virginian,* a hit TV series telecast on NBC from 1962 to 1971, a total of 249 episodes.

As he told Lucille, "I'm reduced to spaghetti westerns."

Desi was just one of the name stars featured in *The Man from Shiloh* and *The Virginian*. So, too, had been Harrison Ford, Charles Bronson, Lee Marvin, Ryan O'Neal, George C. Scott, and Bette Davis.

Since his hair had mostly turned grey, Desi showed up on the set with it dyed jet black—the color it had been when he was twenty, when it looked believable.

He laughed and joked with Sammy Davis. At one point, Desi revealed that he'd arrived unannounced on the doorstep of Marilyn Monroe as part of a "social call," and that her housekeeper had turned him away. "In contrast, I hear you scored with her. Perhaps she has a fondness for black dick. Mine is merely brown."

Davis neither confessed nor denied an affair with her. Desi had kept abreast of all the gossip about Davis' alleged affairs with white movie stars, even the doomed actress, Jean Seberg, a supporter of the Black Panthers.

Davis had also had an affair with Ava Gardner, Frank Sinatra's former wife. *[That liaison almost got him kicked out of the infamous Rat Pack.]* Davis had also seduced Tempest Storm, one of the most famous strippers in America, who had assured him, according to Davis, "that he was ten times better as a lover than Elvis Presley."

To Desi, Davis admitted that he was addicted to porn. Having already befriended and seduced Linda Lovelace, star of *Deep Throat* (1972), he'd also bedded both Marilyn Chambers and Georgina Spelvin, other porn actresses. "I make no bones about the fact that when they started making explicit sex films, I became their best customer. I think my collection is the biggest in America."

[The strange and "only in Hollywood" details of Sammy Davis Jr's. involvement with Linda Lovelace is fully documented in Darwin Porter's award-winning biography and exposé, Inside Linda Lovelace's Deep Throat, *published by Blood Moon Productions in 2013.]*

Singer Kathy McGee claimed, "Sammy had the stamina of a bull. You couldn't be alone in a room with him for five minutes without him demanding a blow job."

At one point in their talk, Davis had to go to the men's room, and Desi followed, claiming, "I have to take a leak too. I've been drinking."

The life and sorrows of **Linda Lovelace**, star of the ground-breaking porn film, *Deep Throat*, is explicitly exposed in Blood Moon's award-winning *Inside Linda Lovelace's Deep Throat*.

Uncensored, unapologetic, and ultimately tragic, with tie-ins to the complicated national politics swirling around her, it empathetically shows the fellatio star as a victim of her era's confusion about sexuality, censorship, and feminist liberation.

When *Deep Throat* opened at the Pussycat Cinema in Los Angeles, Sammy Davis Jr. was in the audience. He later told friends, "I'm in love with this Lovelace chick. I've got to get into her throat."

At the urinal, as both men displayed their equipment, Davis quipped, "Liberace would freak out if he could see us now. He'd think he had died and gone to penis heaven."

Unlike Burton, Lucille got on extremely well with Davis, praising his show-biz savvy. His response? "If God took away my talent, I'd be a nigger again. I'm probably the ugliest star you ever appeared with."

"Not at all," she answered. "In some photos I've seen of you, you look rather handsome."

"That's because complete ugliness, like mine, is attractive. I'm convinced I'm an ugly man, really ugly, so much so that in the end, it seems attractive. Of course, that jerk columnist, Robert Sylvester, doesn't agree. He wrote, 'God made Sammy Davis as ugly as he could, then hit him in the face with a shovel.'"

At the time that Lucille worked with Davis, he had divorced his wife, May Britt, the beautiful, Swedish-born actress. Much of America, especially in such southern states as Mississippi and Alabama, had been outraged by the interracial aspect of that marriage. Since 1948, although interracial marriage had been legal in California, "miscegenation" was still illegal in twenty-three states. In 1964, Lucille had gone to see Davis when he starred on Broadway in *Golden Boy*, in which his character was locked in a romantic relationship with a white woman. When she visited him in his dressing room after the show, she noticed a pile of letters overflowing from a wastebasket near his dressing table.

"Hate mail," he announced. "It arrives daily."

Sammy Davis Jr. and **May Britt** met and fell in love. When she told him she wanted to have "little brown babies," he married her.

According to May, "From the beginning, my chief trouble with him was that he treated me like a sex object rather than as a person."

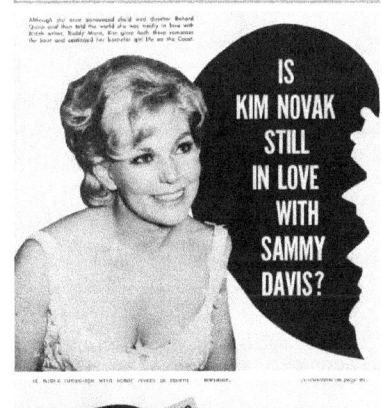

Sammy Davis Jr. heavily dated Kim Novak, but he had a lot of competition, notably Cary Grant, Prince Aly Khan, Frank Sinatra, and Peter Lawford.

Davis had a knack for seducing beautiful women. "I never made it with Lucille Ball," he later said, "not for lack of trying. I turned the Rat Pack not into a color picture, but one that was black and white."

After performing their first scene together for *Here's Lucy,* she noticed that one of his fingernails was painted a bright red. "Did you run out of nail polish and couldn't finish the job?"

"Not at all," he answered. "I'm a Satanist. A painted fingernail is how we identify ourselves as devil worshippers. Of course, I'm not a devoted Satanist—the type that likes to drink virgin blood. I joined the cult just to get a lot of poontang, which is readily available from women within its ranks. I got Frank Sinatra to attend one of our orgies. Would you like me to invite you to one of our secret gatherings? Satanists worship redheads even more than blondes."

"I can't wait for an invitation," she quipped, sarcastically.

Davis had also been splashed across the tabloids during his torrid affair with Kim Novak, the "lavender blonde" of Columbia. Harry Cohn, the czar of that studio and a tyrant known to Lucille, wanted to put a stop to this burgeoning romance.

Once night in Las Vegas, mobsters had been ordered by Cohn to kidnap Davis, drive and "unload" him in the desert, and threaten to put out his one good eye if he didn't drop Novak at once.

"If I'd been a gossip columnist like Hedda Hopper, Sammy would have given me a load of material," Lucille said.

He told her that in 1960, he had supported John F. Kennedy, but turned against him when he refused to allow him to perform at his inauguration. Robert Kennedy feared that his marriage to a white woman might cause political harm to his recently elected brother.

"I turned to support Richard Nixon," he confessed, "although I didn't really like his stated political beliefs. But I fared better with him. After my marriage to Altovise Gore, Nixon invited us to spend a night in the White House. I became the first African American to sleep in the Lincoln Bedroom."

[In 1970, Davis had married Altovise, a dancer he'd met while they were both performing on Broadway in Golden Boy. *The union would last until Davis's death in 1990. After decades of smoking four packages of cigarettes a day, he developed a fatal cancer of the throat.]*

***

Desi Jr., a talented drummer himself, was looking forward to starring as Craig, Lucy's son, in Episode #52, *Lucy and Buddy Rich,* which was telecast on October 5, 1970. "For me, it would be like working with God, I admired him (Buddy Rich) so much," Desi Jr. said.

Brooklyn-born, Rich, also called "the Drum Wonder," and a major-league rival of the more famous Gene Krupa, and known for his virtuoso technique, power, and speed, was hailed as one of the most influential drummers of all time. Amazingly, he'd never learned how to read sheet music.

He'd begun playing the drums at the age of two. Only two years later, he was on Broadway, cast as "Baby Traps, the Drum Wonder," and playing

"Stars and Stripes Forever." He also knew how to sing and soon, he'd become skilled at tap dancing. Later, he claimed, "You could call me the male version of Ann Miller."

At the age of fifteen, he'd become the second-highest-paid child entertainer in America, ranking right behind Jackie Coogan.

By 1937, he was appearing with such legends as Harry James, Count Basie, and Tommy Dorsey. In time, he'd work with Louis Armstrong and Ella Fitzgerald.

After serving in the U.S. Marines during World War II, he returned to his life as a musician, forming the *Buddy Rich Orchestra* with financial support from Frank Sinatra.

The crooner and the drummer became life-long friends, although they were each hot-tempered and often got into public brawls with one another. Rich usually emerged as the winner, as he had a black belt in karate.

Rich was a familiar face on television in the 1950s, as he frequently appeared as a guest on shows that included *The Tonight Show Starring Johnny Carson.* An amateur drummer himself, Carson became a longtime friend of Rich.

Before working with Rich, Lucille had learned of his reputation for sudden outbursts. She decided to give him wide berth and more or less turn him over to her son. She was not anxious to embark on another feud with a celebrity, as she was still recovering from her appearance with Richard Burton and Elizabeth Taylor.

During their time together, and meeting privately, Lucille learned of Rich's deep troubles. He confessed that two years before, he had run into trouble with the IRS for not reporting $50,000 in income from back in 1961. He was convicted and given five years' probation. A few months before he began working with her, the IRS had billed him for $140,000 in back taxes, which he could not pay, forcing him to declare bankruptcy. The agency eventually seized his home in Las Vegas.

"Poor Buddy came to a sad end," Lucille lamented. She was still alive in April of 1987 when she read that the musician had died of a malignant brain tumor.

"I agreed with Gene Krupa: Buddy was the greatest drummer of all time. Even Desi Sr., no mean drummer himself, agreed with me."

"Working with the great drummer, **Buddy Rich,** was like starring with God," claimed Desi Jr., who appeared with him on an episode of *Here's Lucy.* "He taught me to exercise control and not go crazy mad like Gene Krupa."

Rich later said, "I'm sorry the boy didn't work harder trying to be a drummer instead of getting sidetracked, hoping to become a movie star."

***

During rehearsals of their skit for *Here's Lucy*, Desi Jr. later admitted that "Buddy taught me a lot. I was too tense playing the drums, and he showed me how to appear more relaxed."

Rich later told the press, "Lucille's boy had a real talent, and I think could have become the next Gene Krupa. But he wasn't dedicated enough. He wanted to be a movie star.

The appearance of Desi Jr., on *Here's Lucy* marked one of his last presentations within the series. He would soon say *adieu* to television to become a film actor.

Before shooting the Buddy Rich episode, director James Goldstone had cast Desi Jr. as the third lead in *Red Sky in the Morning* (1971), a dramatic film based on the 1968 Richard Bradford novel of the same name. Richard Thomas and Catherine Burns had the lead roles, with Richard Crenna and Claire Bloom in supporting parts. It follows the saga of the Arnold family during World War II, when they relocate to New Mexico. The head of the family has died during the war, and mother and son struggle to readjust to their new circumstances.

The film drew mixed reviews, the *Daily Telegraph* in London claiming, "It has the right ingredients, only everything is overly done."

Desi Jr. earned a Golden Globe as "New Star of the Year—Actor" in 1972. Many critics predicted a bright future for him in feature films, based on his good looks and more importantly, on his acting talent.

***

In September of 1965, Lucille and Charles Nelson Reilly starred together on *The Steve Lawrence Show* and vowed at the time to appear on a *Lucy* show together. That came to fruition in Episode #53, *Lucy the Crusader*, telecast on October 12, 1970 under the direction of Herbert Kenwith. Her friendship with Reilly grew closer as a result of their shared experience.

The director also cast Carole Cook and Bob Hastings in that episode, with eventually emerged as one of the best and most lauded of the season.

It its plot, Lucy buys a stereo for her son, Craig (Desi Jr.), but it doesn't work.

She takes it back to the manufacturer and hands it over to the clerk (Reilly) who sold it to her and enlists his help in holding accountable the firm that's turning out these bogus appliances.

Casting Brooklyn-born Bob Hastings catalyzed potentially violent problems. He was known as a voiceover for animations, and also as a character actor ("Little Leadbottom" or "Carpy") in ABC's then-popular TV series, *McHale's Navy*.

In the wake of her fiasco with Richard Burton and Elizabeth Taylor, Lucille had managed to control her temper, but during the filming of this episode, she lost it again.

Hastings was having trouble with one of his props, a malfunctioning squirt gun concealed within the "body" of a rag doll. *[As a slapstick gag, it was supposed to squirt water into the face of Gale Gordon.]* Hastings failed to operate it correctly until Lucille grabbed it from him to demonstrate how it should be done, but she, too, couldn't manipulate it in the way demanded by the script.

Lucille then berated Hastings, accusing him of breaking the moving parts within the doll. "You're the most incompetent actor I've ever employed. What a lousy piece of shit…a real fuckup."

Hastings, too, had a short fuse. He had never been talked to that way before, and he lunged toward her to attack before being blocked by members of the crew.

After he was restrained, Lucille yelled at him again: "You son of a bitch! I'll see that you never work another day in this town!"

Carole Cook posed with **Lucille Ball** as part of this press and PR photo, and later autographed it.

Cook was originally named Mildred. Shortly after she met Lucille, the redhead told her, "I hope you don't mind, but the name Mildred reminds me of that movie, *Mildred Pierce*, starring that awful Joan Crawford. I'd like you to change your name to Carole, in honor of my late, lamented friend, Carole Lombard."

***

Carole Cook, Lucille's *protégée*, had been cast in several episodes with Lucille over the course of many years. Lucille had been impressed with her during her involvement in the Desilu Workshop, and for a while, she had occupied the Arnaz family's guest house.

Cook had been an eyewitness to the breakup of the Arnaz/Ball marriage. "They were the perfect couple, deeply in love. But sometimes perfection is not enough."

On a happier note, Lucille bonded with Reilly during rehearsals. "She was always gay-friendly," he said. "She never put gay people down, and thought they were a vital part of both the television and the film industry."

"A great contributor to the arts," she once said about him.

"I will forever be grateful to her for putting some fine touches on my own sense of comedy," Reilly claimed. "She really knew how to pull off a stunt. Once at a conference table, she interrupted us, saying, 'Great joke—but wrong place!' She was right. When we put the joke in another scene, it got a big laugh."

Born in the Bronx, Reilly was an actor, comedian, and eventually, a director during his long career in show biz. Although a personality in the theater himself, he could never sit through a show with the audience. If he watched a play, it was only from the standing room only section, close to an exit. He had been traumatized for life, after having survived the scandalous 1944 Hartford (Connecticut) circus fire that killed 167 people.

In 1957, he'd made his film debut in an uncredited role in *A Face in the Crowd*, starring Andy Griffith.

From that meager beginning, he went on to great acclaim, appearing in the Pulitzer Prize-winning musical, *How to Succeed in Business Without Really Trying*. He won a Tony Award in 1962 for Best Featured Actor in a Musical. Even bigger success came and another Tony, when he starred as Cornelius Hackl (Horace Vandergelder's young and enthusiastic chief clerk) in *Hello, Dolly!*, the hit Broadway musical starring Carol Channing.

Charles Nelson Reilly, who morphed his status as an "out and proud' character actor, later leveraged himself into a regular contestant on game shows, in some cases with Lucille.

When the actor appeared on *I've Got a Secret*, Lucille told a friend, "Charles has a secret all right, but I don't think he's hiding his gayness from the public all that well. What's the real truth about Burt Reynolds and him?"

Reilly became even better known for his appearances on television, especially on *The Tonight Show Starring Johnny Carson*. He appeared on that show one hundred times, an always reliable guest.

On *The Match Game*, he became a regular panelist, peppering his dialogue with a homosexual *frisson*, testing the TV boundaries of censorship in the 1970s.

For this latest episode of *Here's Lucy*, she and Reilly were hailed for a performing one of the best shows of the season.

The got to know each other much better and became *confidants*. In the future, she would visit his home in Beverly Hills. In time, he would become the lover of Patrick Hughes, a set decorator and dresser.

Battlestars was the game show that aired on NBC in the 1980s, featuring a six-celebrity panel on which Reilly sometimes appeared. Its host, Alex Trebek, would go on to greater TV glory.

Early in their relationship, Lucille was eager to know about his relationship with Burt Reynolds, who was on the dawn of becoming one of the biggest box office draws of the 1970s. In some circles, they were known as "The Odd Couple."

Rumors were rampant that Burt let Reilly "service" him. Lucille wanted to get to the bottom of this "scandal" *[if indeed, it were a scandal at all.]*

Reilly confided in her that he and Burt had begun their long friendship in 1957 in New York, when both of them were trying to break into television. Although Reilly became an almost permanent fixture on the tube, he had faced prejudice.

One executive at NBC told him, "We don't allow queers on television."

Despite different tastes, Burt and Reilly remained close friends for life.

In time, Burt invited Reilly to stay with him at his home in Jupiter,

Florida. Before he left to become an actor, Reynold's father, the homophobic Burt Reynolds Sr. warned him that New York and Hollywood "were full of fags. If you ever bring one of those sissy boys back to Florida, I'll shoot him and make a rug out of him for your mother," Burt Sr. threatened.

But after his arrival at the Reynolds' home in in Florida, Reilly won over a skeptical father the first day of their meeting. Soon, they were the best of friends, spending all day together. As he told Burt, "Charlie is the only person in the world who ever made me laugh."

"Didn't you guys at least make out some lonely night?" Lucille asked. "Surely he let you blow him?"

"It never happened," Reilly insisted. "We shared a bedroom together, and he often paraded around nude. One night, we slept together when we were both drunk. In the middle of the night, I desired him but didn't move in on him. The closest I ever came was waving my left hand over his genitals in a kind of butterfly effect. He moved slightly but didn't wake up."

Burt Reynolds, the most profit-generating actor of the 1980s, made his feature film debut in 1961 in a Southern Gothic film about rape, a woman who cannot speak, faith healing, and the rural American South. Depicted above is a scene from *Angel Baby*, with **Salome Jens** (right), a purported short-term sexual partner of John F. Kennedy.

Although Burt and Lucille randomly discussed it from time to time, especially whenever they shared time with their mutual friend Dinah Shore, they never actually appeared together in any episode of any of Lucille's series.

At Burt's theater in Jupiter, Florida, he hired Reilly to direct seventeen of his stage productions over the course of many years. On Broadway, he had directed Julie Harris as Emily Dickinson in *The Belle of Amherst* (1976).

Burt became so close to Reilly and such good friends that he gave him the beachfront house in Florida where he had lived with actress Sally Field during her time in Florida.

On the day Burt presented him with the lavish gift, he parked outside and gave Reilly the keys. "Go on a self-guided tour. The house brings too many memories of my times with Sally, I never want to enter the place again."

Although it had been talked about, Lucille and Burt did not perform together in any of her episodes. He did show up, however, at an event called *An All-Star Party for Lucille Ball* in 1984.

He was seated on the left of Gary Morton, who was placed next to Lucille. On her left were Sammy Davis Jr. and Dean Martin. Burt did not speak publicly, but attended in his capacity as a previous Variety Club Honoree.

As advertised, the event honoring Lucille was, indeed, star-studded: Among the guests were James Caan, Lloyd Bridges, Sammy Cahn, Farrah Fawcett, Raquel Welch, and Betty White.

***

When the director/choreographer Jack Baker told Lucille he'd cast Marilyn Maxwell in Episode #54, *Lucy the Coed,* she strenuously objected.

Actually, Baker had already signed Maxwell, and she was due any minute at the studio to begin rehearsals.

Lucille relented: "Bring on the whore," she finally said. "I hear the bitch is falling apart." *[She'd already been informed that Maxwell had not married since she'd divorced her third husband, writer/producer Jerry Davis.]* "At least I'll get a good look at her. I bet her phone is no longer ringing, certainly not from my ex-husband, Mr. Desi Arnaz. Bob Hope and Frank Sinatra moved on years ago, too."

Lucille had last worked with Maxwell in *Forever, Darling* (1956), a feature film that had starred Desi and Lucille. "Right in front of my eyes, Desi and Maxwell were carrying on. I'll never forgive that."

The affair sustained by **Bob Hope** and **Marilyn Maxwell** was so long-running that insiders in Hollywood sometimes referred to them as "Mr. and Mrs. Bob Hope." In the photo above, they appear together in a scene from *The Lemon Drop Kid* (1951).

Frank Liberman, a studio publicist who worked for Hope in the early 1950s, received instructions from his boss: "Your job is to keep all news of my fucking and sucking from the public, especially from my wife, Dolores."

Lucille detested Maxwell because of her affair with Desi Arnaz.

On the set, Lucille noticed that makeup on Maxwell could not disguise how she'd aged. As it turned out, she was suffering from hypertension and pulmonary disease.

During rehearsals, the two stars spoke to each other only when necessary. The script called for Harry (Gale Gordon) to stage a musical event for the Class of 1928 at Bullwinkle University. Instead of the usual Lucy episode, Baker wanted to turn it into a musical comedy.

The tension on the set was relieved somewhat by the co-star, actor, singer, and dancer Robert Alda. Lucille got along with him. She'd been an admirer ever since he'd co-starred as a handsome bachelor on *Lucy Goes to Art Class* back in January of 1964. She liked working with him so much that she eventually invited him back for another episode of *Here's Lucy.*

At the end of the shoot, Lucille and Maxwell departed without a farewell.

That would mark Maxwell's last appearance on television. In March of 1972, at the age of fifty, she was found dead, apparently from a heart attack.

Lucille called Desi and asked him to decline being designated as an honorary pallbearer at Maxwell's funeral, and he agreed. The task went instead to Frank Sinatra, Bob Hope, Bing Crosby, and Jack Benny.

***

On October 19, 1970, *Lucy the Coed* was broadcast on CBS immediately before *The Carol Burnett Show* in which Lucille was a guest star.

She joined the cast of Burnett's regulars, including Harvey Korman, her friend. Mel Tormé was the other guest artist.

This show was not one of Lucille's finest hours, and she underperformed, allowing Tormé and Burnett to steal the thunder.

Before agreeing to do the show, she had met with its director, Dave Powers, informing him that at no point should it be conveyed that she was older than Burnett. Also, she demanded that all her physical movements be outlined in specific detail within the script. "I will not improvise."

The night marked Lucille's last appearance on Burnett's comedy hour.

In the classic film, *Laura* (1944), **Vincent Price** was cast as **Gene Tierney's** weak-willed playboy fiancé who ends up getting slugged by the more rugged Dana Andrews. Price's greater fame would come in horror movies.

***

Ever since she'd seen *Laura* (1944), the *film noir* starring Dana Andrews and Gene Tierney, Lucille had been fascinated by Vincent Price. In that classic, he'd played a suave Southern gigolo, with Clifton Webb cast as the obviously gay, very cynical columnist, Waldo Lydecker.

At a party one night, Tierney said to Lucille, "How could I possibly draw attention to myself when caught in a scene between two of the campiest gay actors in Tinseltown?"

Price later made a name for himself in such horror films as *House of Wax* (1953) and *The Fly* (1958), which still enjoys a cult following today.

Price was married three times, once in 1974 to the Australian-American actress Coral Browne, although Lucille knew him to be bisexual.

Their marriage lasted until her death in 1991. Price himself had only two more years to live, when he died of lung cancer at the age of 82.

Lucille's friend, actor Roddy McDowall, once

Displayed above is a press promotion for the release of **Vincent Price**'s cookbook (*A Treasury of Great Recipes*). As an ironic reference to his status as a purveyor of horror, Price poses with a knife about to attack a piece of meat. He also cooked for Lucille.

told her that he kept Price supplied with a string of male hustlers, often out-of-work actors.

During the time Price worked on an episode with Lucille, he was accompanied to the set every day by Steve Lundigan, a nineteen-year-old "hotshot" who had won a muscleman contest.

Lucille was eager to get to know Price better. In 1999, his lesbian daughter, Victoria, would write a memoir of her father, calling him "a man of glorious contradictions. He was a Renaissance man in an age of specialists, a Victorian aesthete who mastered 20th Century media."

She also wrote, "I am certain as I can be that my dad had been physically intimate with men."

During the era that Lucille got to know Price, he was a liberal. But as a young man, he had been an early admirer of Adolph Hitler. As his daughter explained it, "When Hitler came into power, instead of seeing him as a dangerous force, my dad got swept up in this whole idea that the *Führer* was going to restore Germany's pride after its defeat in World War I."

However, later in the 1930s, Price became a liberal, hanging out with the likes of author Dorothy Parker and playwright Lillian Hellman. He'd later denounce racial and religious prejudice as "a form of poison."

Price was more than just an actor, as was a noted art expert and collector and a gourmet cook. By 1977, he would release a twelve-cassette boxed set entitled *Beverly Hills Cookbook — Cookbook of the Rich and Famous*.

On the set one day, he brought all the ingredients and prepared an elegant lunch for the director Herbert Kenwith. Lucille was the honored guest, and her close friend and co-star, Mary Jane Croft, dined with them.

In her episode with Price, Lucy purchases a vintage painting that she figures might be a valuable work, perhaps by an Old Master. She decides to take it to the home of Price for his evaluation. That's when trouble sets in, as it always does in one of her zany episodes.

Unknown to her, the actor had renovated a part of his home, turning it into the laboratory of a mad scientist for use in an upcoming film. When he discovers Lucy, he assumes she is an aspirant actress trying to audition for the role of his victim in his upcoming movie, *Scream and Scream Again*.

During the course of their work together, Lucille and Price bonded, and he put her on the guest list of his chic parties. At one of these events, she might encounter Boris Karloff, who had once appeared with her in a movie, *Lured* (1947). Lucille was having an affair at the time with her leading man, George Sanders, whom she had to share with Zsa Zsa Gabor.

One night, Lucille almost encountered Joan Crawford whom she detested ever since they'd feuded during their appearance in an episode together. At another party, she spotted Olivia de Havilland and Joan Fontaine, who were two feuding sisters, each standing in a opposite corners of the same room, keeping as much distance between them as possible.

***

During the remainder of the Third Season of *Here's Lucy* (1970-71), Lucille often worked with stars familiar to her. Such was the case when she reteamed with Wally Cox, Marlon Brando's best friend and lover, in *Lucy and the Diamond Cutter,* telecast on November 16. This marked Cox's third appearance on one of her telecasts.

In the current episode, Ruth McDevitt, cast as Mrs. Whitmark, wants a tranquil location to have a large diamond split. The diamond cutter is Cox, and Harry (Gale Gordon) selects Lucy's home as the venue for the delicate work. Bad mistake. Expect the usual disaster.

Ruth McDevitt, a beloved character actress who struggled with the rigors of aging, as everyone on the set of a Lucille Ball project knew—loud and clear.

Not all the trouble was filmed. Much of it occurred off screen.

The episode seriously strained the relationship between Lucille and her director, Herbert Kenwith. An argument broke out over her treatment of the longtime character actress Ruth McDevitt, who had been born in 1895. She'd appeared in numerous roles on TV in the past, everything from *The Alfred Hitchcock Hour* to *Bewitched.* But her control was fading because of her age, and she just could not seem to get on her mark or remember her lines.

Time and time again, she failed, as Lucille was growing more angry by the minute. Completely exasperated, she kicked the old woman's foot into place, not once but twice. McDevitt broke down and began to sob.

Replace this old relic…or else!" Lucille demanded. Then she stormed toward her dressing room.

Exasperated at the thousands of decisions he had to make, Kenwith trailed Lucille to her dressing room to confront her over her treatment of the aging actress. "I felt on the verge of tears myself, trapped between these two women," he recalled. "Lucille was driving me crazy. Week after week, she was throwing temper fits. A lot of it had to do with her own aging, and she was fighting valiantly—maybe not all that valiantly—to look youthful on the TV screen. I had first directed her in the traveling stage play, *Dream Girl,* in 1947, so we knew each other very well…perhaps too well."

"I'd had a lot of experience with bad-tempered actresses," Kenwith said. "Before Lucille, I'd directed Gloria Swanson. Talk about a bitch! She won the prize. Many stars were easy to work with, my favorite being starlet Nancy Davis (later Reagan). In the late 1940s, she was known as 'The Fellatio Queen of Hollywood,' so I got a great blow-job every day at lunch."

In Lucille's dressing room, Kenwith found her on the sofa, crying and bursting with anger.

"If you keep up this shit, I'm walking off the set, and I'll never direct you again," he said. "Get back on the set and finish the job after you've apologized to Ruth. Have some sympathy, goddammit!"

She rose from the sofa and lunged toward him, hitting him in the face. He struck her, and she fell back onto the sofa.

Then, to his surprise, she jumped up again and wrapped her arms around him. "I love you," she shouted at him. "Desi used to knock me down like that."

He barged out of the dressing room, as she stood in the doorway, calling out to him, "Considering your height, you'd be great cast as Napoléon!"

Deep down, both Lucille and Kenwith were professionals. When they cooled down, each of them finished the episode, and McDevitt pulled off the scene.

There would be a few more episodes that Kenwith would direct to fulfill his contract, but, from that afternoon on, the star and the director would give each other wide berth.

**

Before Lucille appeared on another episode of *Here's Lucy*, a call came in from her longtime friend, Jack Benny. He wanted her to appear in a cameo on his *Twentieth Anniversary Special*, to be telecast on November 16.

She would show up briefly as a French maid, the type usually called "Fifi," serving Mary Livingston, Benny's wife, who was also cast, as herself, in the episode.

In return for Lucille's appearance on his show, Benny agreed to appear in an upcoming episode of *Here's Lucy*, also in November.

Benny's anniversary special would also feature such stars as Phil Harris, Dinah Shore, Red Skelton, Frank Sinatra, and Benny's always reliable sidekick, the rotund Don Wilson.

She would recall November 16 as being "the busiest, most overscheduled television work day of my life." On that date, she had not only starred with Wally Cox, but also appeared as the maid to Jack Benny's wife, and also showed up on a *Bob Hope Special* on NBC.

With her on the Hope show were such stars as George Burns, Danny Thomas, and the Welsh singer, Tom Jones. "His pants were so tight you could tell he was uncut," Lucille told Mary Wickes.

"That's the way I prefer my men—that is, if I ever got one," Wickes said.

On the Hope show, he played a hypnotist, who goes into the audience seeking a volunteer. Guess who? HERE'S LUCY!, of course.

Jones hypnotizes her into thinking she's Cleopatra, Queen of the Nile, and that he is Marc Antony, her studly Roman warrior and lover.

In another skit on the same show, she appears with Hope and Thomas spoofing child movie stars.

**

Jack Benny kept his commitment to Lucille and starred in *Lucy and Jack Benny's Biography*, telecast on November 23. Still the director, Herbert Kenwith also cast George Burns with some lesser-known actors.

In the sketch, Benny hires Lucy Carter as his secretary, with the intention of dictating his autobiography to her.

Kenwith, working with veteran scriptwriter Milt Josefsberg, decides to tell the comedian's life story in flashback. It concentrates on the women in his life, with Lucille changing costumes and starring as each of the females who came and went, romantically and emotionally, from his life.

Lucille and Benny had known each other for years and had even co-starred together. They were also neighbors in Beverly Hills. Benny and his actress wife, Mary Livingston, were often guests at the Ball/Morton home or vice versa.

Kenwith later claimed, "Lucille was changing, and in my opinion, I think the lady was beginning to lose it. She seemed more insecure than ever. Gary Morton was her rock, the Prince Philip to her Queen Liz. She still wasn't accepting the fact she had lost Desi Arnaz. The chemistry they shared on *I Love Lucy* was a thing of the past. She had become more and more difficult. The cast and crew often privately complained about 'the boss lady.' Even some old friends were changing from 'I Love Lucy' to 'I Hate Lucy.'"

In this 1960 publicity photo from CBS, **Jack Benny** appears with his wife, **Mary Livingston.**

"Lucy and I were friends...of a sort, you might say," Benny told Gary Morton. "She was always jabbing me with a provocative question. One day she asked me if I'd seduced James Dean when he was a Hollywood hustler."

Benny was not his usual self. After an amazing career in films, radio, and TV, he was obviously slowing down and had only four more years to live.

Kenwith later related that Lucille kept "coaching" Benny until his patience with her wore thin. At one point, he turned on her in anger: "Listen, kid. I've been doing comedy before you were born. So don't tell me how I should deliver a line. Got that?"

"Your pauses are just too damn long," she charged.

"My pauses are what made me a legend as a comedian," he shot back.

In one unlikely scene, Lucille and Benny were supposed to perform a scene with a romantic twist. Attired in a white wig, she was to pull off one leg of his pants (which had been altered so that they could be detached easily). He had previously arranged a nearby prop as something he could hold onto to steady his balance, but she had had it removed. When the scene came, he fell onto the floor and could have seriously injured himself.

As more and more Hollywood insiders began perceiving their dynamic as a feud, Gary Morton denied it. "I was on the set every day, and at no point did I see Lucille mistreating Benny."

Kenwith countered, "Of course, Morton would say that. He was his wife's brown nose."

"I never saw my mother engage in any conflict with Jack Benny," Lucie

Arnaz claimed. "She is a perfectionist and may have been a bit tactless in striving to get everything letter perfect—but that's all there was to it. No feud."

Whatever the truth, Benny and Lucille would work together again. However, as he was leaving the studio with his work on the episode completed, he was overheard saying, "I think that redheaded cow belongs in a nuthouse."

***

The Third Season of *Here's Lucy* had more episodes that needed to be filmed before it would go off the air in February of 1971. But at this point, Lucille and her sponsors were not certain that there would ever be a Fourth Season.

On the home front, she was suffering through the kind of problems that most mothers have when their children start to leave the nest and become involved in tangled romantic trysts.

Such was the case with Lucie and Desi Arnaz Jr.

As a mother, Lucille wanted to be in control…but she was losing that control…fast.

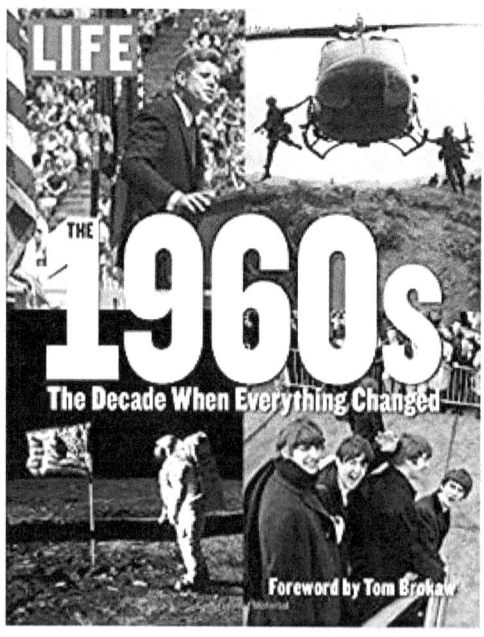

CHAPTER NINE

LUCILLE CONFRONTS THE GENERATION GAP

Sex, Drugs, Rock & Roll, and Her "Babe Magnet" Son

From the moment he was barely beyond puberty, Desi Jr. became what is known today as a "Babe Magnet," developing a following of screaming teenage fans evocative of Elvis Presley. In contrast, he also became involved with women older than himself.

In 1964, when he was twelve, he formed a rock band, a trio called "Desi, Dino, & Billy."

Its members included Dean Paul Martin ("Dino"), the son of singer and entertainer Dean Martin and his second wife, Jeanne Biegger. He was the fifth of Martin's eight children, and Jeanne's eldest son.

The third and oldest member of the rock group was Bill ("Billy") Hinsche. All three aspiring musicians had met in grammar school.

One of their first auditions was for Frank Sinatra, a tough sell. He was no fan of rockers—in fact, he'd gone on record as saying, "Rock 'n Roll is the most brutal, ugly, desperate, vicious form of expression that has been my misfortune to hear."

Sinatra had agreed to hear the boys because of his friendships with Dean Martin, a fellow "Rat Packer," and Desi Sr. Those two had made up after a feud over Desi Sr.'s TV crime drama, *The Untouchables*, which Sinatra felt portrayed Italian Americans in unfavorable terms.

Sinatra was impressed with their music and assigned them a slot to cut a disk at Reprise Records, which he had founded.

"**Desi,** my son, please *please* don't grow up," **Lucille** seems to be asking (or praying about) her young son, a creature who would enter the southern California maelstrom at almost any minute.

When Lucille heard their record, she predicted a glorious future for the trio.

Two weeks later, Desi Jr. came home bursting with hope and excitement, informing her that a new agent for the group had booked them on a tour. He'd be leaving home and heading out onto the road without any parental or adult supervision.

The following day, Lucille lunched with her longtime friend, Marcella Rabwin, sharing her anxiety about her son going out, on the road and into the "wilderness" of the music industry. "Sex and drugs and rock 'n roll...that's all I hear these days about young people."

"My husband and I in the medical profession know that many teenage girls are being driven south and across the border where they have abortions in Mexico," Rabwin said. "I only hope Desi, a darling boy, is careful."

"I've got to trust him to be responsible," Lucille responded.

A week later, she met with Dean Martin, sharing her concerns with him. But he was more confident than she was, claiming that the boys would manage quite well on their own.

Lucille encouraged her young son, **Desi Jr.**, to pursue sports such as baseball, considering it as a healthy pursuit.

"Who knows?" she asked. "He might become a budding Joe DiMaggio without the baggage of a future Marilyn Monroe."

Like millions of other mothers, Lucille became almost obsessively apprehensive about the drug culture and sexual revolution sweeping across America at the time. Many sources have claimed that her son had begun to drink at the tender age of eleven.

In addition to her other worries, Lucille was also concerned with his education. He had not adapted well to school, especially at the military academy to which she'd sent him. Also, she didn't see him studying very much when he attended Beverly Hills High.

"I love the boy dearly," she told Rabwin. "He's breaking my heart. I pray he doesn't become a drug addict or an alcoholic like his father. I fear the worst."

Screaming teenaged girls greeted them during key moments of their tour, and many made themselves available like groupies.

Dino was well built and handsome, loved music, but told his father and Desi Jr. that his real dream was to become a pilot. At the age of sixteen, he obtained a pilot's license and often invited his friends to fly with him. Later, he became an Air National Guardsman, eventually rising to the rank of captain.

Although the trio was popular with their teenaged fans, they were often attacked by music critics. The reviewer for *Allmusic.com* wrote, "The teenage boys never have an ounce of credibility and are innocuously bland in the extreme."

After Desi Jr. returned from his tour, Lucille met with Rabwin and confessed, "My fears were right. He left home a sweet boy, but he came back from the tour a changed young man, asserting his independence. He'd obviously gone out into the world like never before, and apparently tasted many of its pleasures — or dangers."

"I fear when he's away from me, he's getting either high or drunk," she continued. "He's got money of his own now, and I can no longer threaten to cut off his allowance.

DINO, DESI AND BILLY

DINO, DESI & BILLY reveal their hates & loves

To Lucille's horror, Desi Jr. was thrown into the music industry's publicity grinder.

The upper photo shows the trio (left to right, **Dino, Desi, and Billy**) as part of a press and publicity photo widely circulated to DJs and radio stations at the time.

The lower illustration shows abbreviated biographies of **Dino Martin** (left) and **Desi Jr.**, each aimed at audiences of teenaged "scream queens."

The question on every adult's mind seemed to be, "Unless it's already happened, which of them will lose his virginiity first?"

Once I locked him in the pool house, hoping to keep him away from his drug pusher, but how long could that ridiculous attempt last?"

Desi Jr. was impatient to grow up so he could go out on dates and pilot his own automobile. A car would give him the independence he so desperately needed. He couldn't wait until he was old enough to get a driver's license.

For one so young, he was growing up fast. His sister Lucie seemed fully aware of that fact, saying, "My kid brother has been thirty-four ever since we were kids."

On the road, as Lucille feared, Desi began to experiment with drugs. Like many other members of his generation, he became familiar with mescaline, LSD, marijuana, cocaine, and quaaludes.

His mother began to fear that he was becoming an addict. Their arguments became louder and more intense, and on occasion, Desi Jr. fled to the home of his father and his new wife, Edie.

Of course, Desi Sr. was not a very good role model, having a long record of too intimate a knowledge of alcohol and a notorious reputation as a philanderer.

Desi Sr. was relatively tolerant (some said, "amused") of his son's drinking and his attraction to older women. He told Edie, "I'd rather have my son date an older woman than getting a thirteen-year-old gal pregnant. Mature women can teach him a lot."

With bemused humor, he once told a reporter, "I know my son on occasion dates up the age scale. I did the same. After all, Lucille snatched me from the cradle when I was still in diapers. With my wife I experienced my first orgasm."

Of course, he was joking. He'd married Lucille, who was six years older than him, in 1940 when he was 23.

When Desi Jr. began staggering home as dawn broke across California from interludes with women who changed from month to month, he regularly encountered an irate mother. "I'm in love," he'd tell her. "And I can take care of myself. I earn my own money. I want my freedom after all. I'm no longer in nursery school. I'm sixteen years old. I want to move into my own apartment like Lucie did.

Although he surely knew his mother loved him dearly, he found him-

"**Cuban Pete**," (otherwise known as **Desi Arnaz Sr.**) serenades his son, **Desi Jr.**, on the occasion of his 21st birthday.

His dream had come true. As a little boy growing up in Cuba, Desi Sr. had been urged by his father to have a son who would "carry on the Arnaz name."

self drifting farther away because of her strict parental attitude, and her wanting to control his life.

***

Lucille had to put aside her excessive parenting of Desi Jr. long enough to continue with the filming of *Here's Lucy*. In many of the upcoming episodes, based on her hopes for higher ratings, she'd rely, to an increasing degree, on guest appearances from famous celebrities.

Here's Lucy (Episode #60), *Lucy and Rudy Vallee,* was telecast on November 30, 1970.

This time around, she got to know Vallee better than when she'd first appeared with him. In November of 1957, he had guest starred on an episode of the *Lucille Ball-Desi Arnaz Show* as it continued its Seventh Season in the *I Love Lucy* format.

In the current episode, Phil Vandervort, her son-in-law, was cast. She gave him wide berth, not wanting to hear or discuss any details about his failing marriage to her daughter. Predicting its early demise, she had opposed the union from the very beginning.

Gary Morton had asked her to cast Vanda Barra in both the Vallee episode and in the upcoming one with Art Linkletter, and she'd agreed. Barra was married to Morton's cousin, Sid Gould, who had become more or less a regular on previous sitcoms with Lucille.

At this point, Lucille faced a new director, Coby Ruskin, and oldtime vaudevillian. He had worked on *The Andy Griffith Show,* but was relatively new to directing. In rehearsals, as her director and as a performer himself, he would act out whatever scene Lucille was about to film as an indication of what he wanted. She was not impressed with this methodology, feeling that she knew more about performance comedy than he did.

Jane Greer, in this *film noir* photo from 1946, figuratively aims a gun at the centerpiece of her short-lived first marriage, bandleader **Rudy Vallee**.

During its early weeks, Greer objected when her new husband wanted to bring handsome, hung, and well-built young men into their bed.

In this latest episode, Lucy and Harry (Gale Gordon) dine together at a restaurant, where they discover the once-famous singer, Rudy Vallee, working as a waiter. *[Actually, he's doing this only as a lark, as he owns not only the restaurant but the entire block.]*

Unaware of that, Lucy takes it upon herself to

help him bring his music up-to-date.

The crooner, once known as "The Vagabond Singer," had been one of the first modern pop stars to develop a fan base as a teen idol. All of that had happened back in 1933 on *The Fleischmann's Yeast Hour*. He always signed on by saying, "*Heigh-ho, everybody*," a line which to Lucille seemed very old and very outdated.

Lucie Arnaz quickly ascertained that Vallee had a foul mouth and blamed anybody else—even if he were responsible— if something went wrong.

Early in the time she spent working with Vallee, in an encounter at which the crooner was not involved, Lucille met his ex- wife, the wide-eyed *film noir* beauty, Jane Greer. She had married him in 1943 in the middle of World War II. To the surprise of almost everyone in Hollywood, they separated after only three months.

When gossipy Lucille wanted to know why, Greer confessed what went wrong: "He rounded up handsome, well-built men, often out-of-work actors, and paid them to go to bed with him. He wanted these guys to join us in bed for an ongoing series of *ménages à trois.* He got voyeuristic pleasure in watching. No way! I fled from his bed and from the marriage, too."

Many newcomers to his legend were shocked by Vallee's foul mouth. George Ansbro, an NBC announcer, in a memoir, wrote: "Vallee has quite a temper and a very foul mouth. Every third word is a curse word. He takes out his nastiness on his orchestra. His outbursts are mean-spirited."

These sentiments had been backed up by his second wife, Fay Webb, in the divorce court. She charged that he "possesses a violent, vicious, and ungovernable temper, and is given to the use of blasphemy and intemperate, vile, and vituperative language, especially when applied to me."

Webb also accused him of being a serial adulterer, having sex with other women, citing Alice Faye in particular. She made no mention of any homosexual liaisons.

Lucille later said, "I was glad I survived the episode without getting a black eye. I was told that Vallee usually ended an argument by giving his opponent a black eye. She advised Gary Morton, "Let's not put him on the show again. Besides, he's past his expiration date."

She had worked with Art Linkletter, the Saskatchewan (Canada)-born TV personality before. He was host of *Art Linkletter's House Party,* which had survived, with many changes in venue and format, from 1945 to 1967.

Based on her ongoing search for celebrities to appear with on her show, Lucille co-starred with him on *The Lucy Show* (Episode #100) telecast on January 10, 1966.

Herbert Kenwith returned to direct her in *Lucy Loses Her Cool* (telecast on December 7, 1970), along with her frequent co-stars Mary Jane Croft and Vanda Barra.

In this episode, Lucille is about to appear as a guest on *The Art Linkletter Show*. She is challenged not to lose her temper for a whole day and night. Conspiring against her are her kids, Lucie and Desi Jr., as well as Harry (Gale Gordon) and Mary Jane Croft. They will do almost anything to get her to explode.

Desi Jr. was alleged to have admitted that his drugs and boozing negatively affected his performance as an actor. He didn't have cue cards like his mother. They seemed strategically placed at every point in her line of vision, but she didn't seem to need them. They were placed there "for insurance," the director said.

Lucie Arnaz weighed in years laer. "If Desi had a drug problem, I was not aware of it. To me, he always seemed on the mark."

During the Depression, Linkletter rode trains like dozens of other hoboes, looking for odd jobs whenever he could find them. Later, he attended what is now San Diego State University, earning a bachelor's degree in 1934.

A year later, he met and married Lois Foerster. Their marriage was later hailed as the most successful in the history of Hollywood, lasting until his death in May of 2010, when he was 97.

After the filming of the episode was wrapped, he invited Lucille and Morton to join his wife and himself to dine with his close friends, Ronald Reagan and his wife, a former MGM starlet named Nancy Davis. As Lucille remembered it, "All the talk was about politics. At that time, you could never have convinced me that Reagan would become president one day, and that as I was nearing the end of my own life, Nancy had to take over and run the Free World herself, because of his obvious decline."

Linkletter and Lois produced five children. Lucille wanted to share her concerns about her own son with him, since he had recently faced a grave tragedy in his life.

On October 4, 1969, his 20-year-old daughter, Diane, committed suicide by jumping out of

Calls Death Murder

LSD Killed Diane, Linkletter Charges

Art Linkletter (top photo) ran the cleanest, most family-friendly show on television.

So when news reached Lucille that his daughter, **Diane**, had jumped from the balcony of a high-rise after a dose of LSD, her anxieties soared with its implications for her son, Desi Jr., who was heavy-experimenting with it at the time, too.

In the wake of his daughter's death, Linkletter embarked an a widely publicized anti-drug crusade that virtually dominated the remainder of his life.

Although Lucille was horrified by LSD's potential dangers for her son, she refrained from a public position against drugs as extreme as Linkletter's.

a sixth-floor window. He claimed her suicide was spontaneous, euphoric, drug-related, and not based on any innate depression or conscious willingness to die. In the aftermath of his loss, he spoke out about the drug plague haunting American families and urged Lucille to try "everything possible" to persuade her son to refrain from recreational drugs.

The TV host would live to see two more of his offspring die, first Robert in a car accident in 1980, Another son, Arthur, died from lymphoma in 2007, just three years before Linkletter's own death in 2010.

On a happier note, Lucille attended a banquet honoring Linkletter. No one mentioned his tragedies but kept the mood light. She spoke of her friendship with him, chiding him for refusing to become a partner with Walt Disney in the development of Disneyland.

"Art didn't think it would go over with the public. However, in the 1950s, he did give America one of its greatest joys...The Hula Hoop."

[*Although its origins go back thousands of years, with documented use, for medical reasons, in England's 13th Century, the plastic version of the Hula Hoop was popularized in 1958 by the Wham-O toy company and became a staggeringly profitable instantaneous fad. Among the "copycat" business entities which began manufacturing them was a company associated with Art Linkletter, who helped publicize the swivel-hipped craze by showcasing it on his TV show.*]

***

In the entertainment industry, the offspring of famous stars have been unlikely to replicate the success of their famous parents, although dozens of them tried.

In rare instances, though, it has, in-

Lucille liked **Ronald Reagan**, although during his presidency, she did not agree with his politics.

In contrast, she had always been skeptical of his wife, former starlet **Nancy Davis**, whom she had met at MGM.

At the time, Davis was privately mocked by her many detractors as "The Fellatio Queen of Hollywood."

The **Hula Hoop Craze** that swept America in the 1950s was not only featured on the cover of *Life* magazine, but was taken up by Lucille herself.

"I find it was the best way to keep my hips trim so I wouldn't turn into a big-assed old broad."

deed, happened: The son of Kirk Douglas, Michael, became a big star on his own merits. Another, the multi-talented Liza Minnelli, escaped from the long, sometimes destructive shadow of her mother, Judy Garland, to become a world-class actress and singer.

Even in his wildest dreams, Desi Jr. must have known he'd never equal the success of his two famous parents, especially Lucille, who became a movie star in the late 1930s and 1940s and later enjoyed spectacular success as "The Queen of Television."

Yet despite the slim chances of world-class stardom for its members, 1965—the year of their greatest success—looked ever so promising for Desi Jr.'s singing group, "Dino, Desi, & Billy." Their concerts were marked by screaming teenaged girls who grabbed up copies of the group's hit records, "I'm a Fool" and "Not the Lovin' Kind." Although "D.D.&B" would go on performing for the next five years, never again would they top 1965.

Desi Jr. maintained his friendship with Dino long after the group broke up. He'd watched in admiration as Dino got his pilot's license when he was only sixteen. In 1980, Dino become an officer in the California Air National Guard. He also entered active duty for officer training in the U.S. Air Force. He eventually rose to the rank of captain as an Air National Guardsman.

Desi Jr. was said to have double-dated with Dino, who—like his famous father—was also a "Babe Magnet." He was seen out with such "in the news" cult icons as Candice Bergen and Tina Sinatra. *[Later, Desi Jr. would also date Tina.]*

In 1971, Dino married the English actress Olivia Hussey. *[Hussey had become famous throughout the entertainment world for her performance three years before as Juliet in Franco Zeffirelli's film version of Shakespeare's* Romeo and Juliet *(1968).* The couple produced a son, Alexander.

In 1978, Dino divorced her and didn't remarry until four years later, this time to Dorothy Hamill, the Olympic gold medalist ice skater. That union was far less successful than the first. After a few months of incompatible co-habitation, they divorced in 1984.

Olivia Hussey appears here with **Leonard Whiting** in the title roles of Franco Zeffirelli's *Romeo and Juliet* (1968).

Lucille went to see the movie, later predicting major stardom for its charismatic male star.

"I thought Leonard was one of the handsomest, most charming young actors to come along in a decade. I'm usually right about this, and I don't know what went wrong. Stardom can be so elusive."

Tragedy struck on March 27, 1987. In Dino's F-4 aircraft, he and his co-pilot, Captain Ramon Ortiz, departed from California's March Air Force Base as part of a routine training mission. After encountering a violent snowstorm, their plane went down in the San Bernardino Mountains. Dino, who was only thirty-five years old at the time, and his weapons systems officer were instantly killed.

Desi Jr. was greatly saddened by the horrible death of his longtime friend. Lucille phoned the dead man's father, Dean Martin Sr., and expressed her condolences. She later said, "I don't think Dean ever got over the death of his beloved son."

The tragedy only increased Lucille's anxiety over the fate of her own son.

Meeting once again with her friend and confidant, Marcella Rabwin, Lucille said, "In addition to drugs, I think Desi has developed a sex addiction, an attraction to older women."

Someone (unknown) had told Lucille that her son was having an affair with the mother of one of his friends. As a mother, Lucille was infuriated, accusing the woman (who was never named) "of seducing jailbait. There are laws against such things," she told Rabwin.

The accusation, whether it was true or not, traveled along the Hollywood grapevine, and Lucille quickly learned the identity of the culprit.

One day, or so it was rumored, Lucille packed many of her son's belongings, threw them into her Rolls-Royce, drove over to the alleged seducer's home, and dumped the baggage onto her front lawn. Coincidentally, it was Mother's Day.

Many young men, even teenaged boys, have a history of being seduced by older women. Sometimes, a female movie star *[a good example is Gloria Grahame, marrying her much younger stepson, Anthony Ray, in 1960)* would even marry a much younger man., Lucille herself had followed that example with Desi Sr.

Many male movie stars later revealed details of themselves having been seduced at a relatively young age by older women. Sean Connery once claimed that he was only fourteen when an attractive older woman in military uniform accosted him while he was walking down a street in London and escorted him back to her apartment, where she "stole" his virginity. That happened long before he seduced everyone from Zsa Zsa Gabor to Brigitte Bardot.

Orson Welles, Lucille's former lover, had confided to her that when he was only nine years

Dorothy Hamill appears on the cover of the February 2, 1976 issue of *Time* a few years before her unhappy marriage to Dino Martin.

Dino told Desi Jr., "Dorothy may be great on ice—maybe the greatest—but does a hot-blooded man like me want an ice queen in his bed?"

Dino Martin appears in this photo snapped shortly before his death.

His father, Dean Martin, told Desi Sr., "My son had everything to live for. He was talented, handsome, charming, . During his short life, he did not find happiness. If only he'd found the right wife. His choice of women filled him with despair."

old, he'd been seduced by two of his older female cousins.

No doubt about it...Desi Jr. was a budding young Casanova. In some ways, he was repeating the pattern of Desi Sr. At the age of fifteen in his native Santiago, Cuba, his father had escorted him on an inaugural visit to the local whorehouse, so he could hardly criticize the affairs of his own teenaged son.

As a rock star and also as a co-star on *Here's Lucy* with his mother and sister, Desi Jr. generated a lot of fan mail. No longer pudgy, he had developed into a handsome, well-built young man with large amounts of personal charm and charisma. He also generated fan mail (and "love letters") from gay teenaged males, too.

One sixteen-year-old boy wrote to a gay magazine claiming, "The thrill of my life would be to spend just one night in the arms of Desi Arnaz Jr."

The former "child star turned (gay) adult actor," Roddy McDowall, continued to maintain a friendship with Lucille. As Hedda Hopper once claimed, "Roddy knows more about the 'After Dark' antics of Hollywood than anybody else. He even knows when a cockroach crosses Hollywood Boulevard. He never reveals secrets to the press, but among his friends, he was a fountain of gossip."

McDowall became a close observer of Lucille and her son. "Ozzie and Harriet Nelson, as a family sitcom, was a big hit on TV. They presented an idealized look into an American family in the 1950s. In some way, I felt that Lucille wanted to replicate that ideal family. But the Nelsons weren't what they appeared on TV. I knew Ricky Nelson quite well. As a teenager, he posed for frontal nudes and fell in love with Elvis Presley."

McDowall was among the first to spread the rumor that Desi Jr. had fathered a child when he was only fifteen years old. Even Wikipedia, years later, reported as a fact that "Julia Arnaz" was conceived during an affair between Desi Jr. and the American model Susan Callahan-Howe. At the time, Callahan-Howe was said to have been only fifteen years old.

"At least my son turned out to be straight," Desi Sr. asserted. "Dozens of the sons of famous stars living in Beverly Hills were having a gay old time. Of course, Lucille and I never wavered in our love and devotion to our son. If he turned out to be

The young British star, **Roddy McDowall,** had known Lucille for years, since their days together at MGM in the 1940s.

Lucille, a devotee of gossip, considered him a font of information. Every time they met, he had some enticing detail to contribute, even "telling tales" on Desi Jr.

One explosive shocker he relayed involved his friend, Elizabeth Taylor, who was caught down on her knees at the age of fourteen servicing Mickey Rooney in his dressing room.

a gay blade, we would have kept loving him with all our hearts, maybe feeling even more protective of him because of homophobia. Both my son and daughter are confirmed heterosexuals, but they, too, have their own romantic problems. Being straight doesn't always come with having a happy life. Not at all. Just ask Lucy and me."

Unknown to both parents at the time, Desi Jr. was on the dawn of his most controversial affair with an older woman. It created a tabloid frenzy.

***

Here's Lucy Episode #62 (*Lucy, The Part-Time Wife*) was telecast on December 14, 1970 and directed by Ross Martin. For a number of years, he'd been a friend of Lucille's, and was widely known for portraying Artemus Gordon on the CBS Western series, *The Wild Wild West,* broadcast from 1965 to 1969.

The son of Polish Jewish parents from the Ukraine and born in March of 1920, he had emigrated to New York with his father and mother when he was six months old.

Lucille had worked with Martin in 1968 during his rebound from a terrible accident. *[A few minutes after falling from a scaffold and breaking his leg, he suffered a nearly fatal heart attack. The director of The* Wild Wild West *had to replace him in the series.]*

After Martin recovered, and shortly before teaming with Lucille, he landed a gig as a guest, playing Alexander Hamilton in *Swing Out, Sweet Land* (1970), a musical tribute to America hosted by John Wayne with other celebrities.

In the *Here's Lucy* script that Martin was assigned to direct, Harry (Gale Gordon) is alarmed that his college sweetheart is arriving in town for a reunion. He fears she wants to hook up with him again, so he recruits Lucy to pretend to be his pregnant wife. The plot thickens after "the college sweetheart" arrives and decides to nurse Lucy up until the day of her delivery. Lucille*, throughout the episode, belted a pillow to her stomach, concealing it with a maternity smock.]*

Lucille asked Martin to cast her longtime favorite, Carole Cook, in the episode, and he did.

Although Lucille had "discovered" Cook, she never elevated her to a full-fledged "regular" on either of her TV series, *The Lucy Show* and *Here's Lucy.* Lucille even served as matron of honor at Cook's 1964 wedding to actor Tom Troupe. *[Skeptics, however, often conclude that Lucille never paid Cook very much, and could have done far more for her career than she did.]*

Eve Arden suspected that Lucille was a bit jealous of the younger star, who could play some of her scenes almost as well as she could. "I think Lucille feared the competition," Arden claimed.

Without any help from Lucille, Cook eventually set out on her own, finding work in other TV series such as *Charlie's Angels* (1976-1981) or in such feature films as *American Gigolo* (1980). She also became another actress, after Carol Channing, to play Dolly Levi in the stage version of *Hello, Dolly!.*

In more recent years, 2018 to be exact, Cook received a lot of press attention, both good and bad, relating to President Trump. In a television interview, a reporter from TMZ asked her opinion of someone in the audience of the stage play *Frozen,* who had interrupted the performance by holding up a large TRUMP 2020 sign.

"Where is John Wilkes Booth now that we need him? Cook said.

"So we need to kill the President?" the reporter asked.

"Why not?" she replied.

Listening in, a bystander said, "If Lucy were alive tonight, she would have been proud of Carole."

***

Jealous or not, Lucille, a week later (also in December), welcomed the return of her director, Herbert Kenwith. She asked him to cast Carole Cook in her latest episode of *Here's Lucy,* entitled *Lucy and Ma Barker.*

[Unknown to younger generations, Ma Barker, a native of Missouri and born there in 1873, became the most notorious female gangster in America during the period (1931-1935) of her greatest notoriety. J. Edgar Hoover, then-director of the FBI, defined her as "The most vicious, dangerous, and resourceful criminal brain in America," and plastered WANTED posters with her photo and those words in post offices across the country. As the "mastermind" behind the criminal careers of her four sadistic sons, Ma Barker's age and so-called "respectability" allowed her to hide out disguised as a family matriarch.

At the age of 61, she was shot down in a gun battle in Ocklawaha, Florida.

Her bloody and sociopathic saga inspired the two scriptwriters assigned to create the latest episode of Here's Lucy. *As it was being rehearsed, she also provided the inspiration for a feature film—*Bloody Mama *(1970)— that played across the country.]*

In the *Lucy* script, Ma Barker with her son and daughter have become the Carter's new neighbors. Her kids are portrayed by male and female midgets, one with Shirley Temple curls evoking the child star in *Heidi* (1937); the other dressed like Freddie Bartholomew as he starred in *Little Lord Fauntleroy* in 1936. Either of the two characters, in those outfits, would have attracted unwanted attention in 1970.

Soon, Lucy becomes suspicious of her new neighbors, and through a series of schemes, gets them arrested.

In spite of its potential, this episode became the most critically ridiculed of the season. Critics found it impossible to believe that this so-called boy and girl would not be recognized as aberrational.

[Actually, the theme of midget crooks as con artists had already been developed in the 1925 silent film, The Unholy Three, *starring Lon Chaney. Hailed at the time as "The Man of a Thousand Faces," Chaney was known for his depictions of tortured, often grotesque characters and for his groundbreaking artistry with makeup.]*

***

In 1970, seventeen-year-old Desi Arnaz Jr., fell in love with the twenty-three-year-old actress Patty Duke when he saw her interviewed on *The Merv Griffin Show*.

The next day, he phoned her agent and got her private number. Later, he placed a call to her, but not before littering her apartment with flowers from a nearby florist. He was anxious for a face-to-face encounter with what he was dreaming of morphing into his "Sweet Irish Leprechaun."

After talking to her, he told her he wanted to meet with her to discuss a possible recording deal for his newly formed record company. She agreed to meet with him the following night.

Their first encounter evolved into more of a date than a business meeting about a record deal. *[If he felt like singing a song, it might have been "Zing! Went the Strings of My Heart."]*

Soon, they were dating and were spotted around Hollywood. At the time, he told her he was nineteen. She should have known not to believe him. His birth on January 19, 1953 had been the most widely publicized in television history. The day that the real-life Lucille gave birth to him in a hospital was the same night that the fictional Lucy Ricardo gave birth to "Little Ricky" on TV.

The front cover of the first issue of *TV Guide* ran a photo of the newborn lad with the headline, "Lucy's $50,000,000 Baby."

As Duke and Desi began to date, the tabloids were quick to focus on their blossoming romance, comparing it to the early dating of Eddie Fisher and Debbie Reynolds before Elizabeth Taylor stole him away. Patty Duke was at the peak of her fame in that era, although hardly remembered today.

[Whereas "Debbie and Eddie" enjoyed a brief but intense reign as America's Sweethearts, that label never applied to "Patty and

The real **Ma Barker** (1873-1935) was a notorious crime matriarch who was accused by J. Edgar Hoover and his FBI of orchestrating the murderous careers of her four sons.

Carole Cook was quoted as saying, "Powerful women like Lucille Ball and Ethel Merman could devour you...I mean, 'eat you alive.' It's not because that was their intent. They come on so strong and threatening that you give in to their demands."

"Either Lucille (Ball) or Ethel (Merman)," she continued, "could have played Ma Barker."

Shelley Winters, as Ma Barker, comforting her murderous son, as portrayed by **Robert de Niro**, in *Bloody Mama* (1970).

Desi." Most reporters remained skeptical, citing their age difference and his age of only seventeen.]

Patty's real name was Anna Marie Duke, born on December 14, 1946 in New York City. Her early career as a child actress had been orchestrated by her managers, John and Ethel Ross. She later confessed that "they made my life a living hell."

When she started dating Desi, Patty had just survived a marriage (1965-1970) to director Harry Falk, who was thirteen years her senior. He had married her when she was eighteen during his stint as the assistant director of *The Patty Duke Show* (1963-1966). That marriage had at last freed her from the supervision of her childhood guardians, the Rosses.

The marriage had been rocky. Even at her early age, she was drinking heavily and enduring dangerous mood swings. Her condition was later diagnosed as a bipolar disorder, a term not in vogue at the time. She also became anorexic and overdosed on pills a number of times, which appeared to have been several failed attempts at suicide.

For one so young, she'd had an amazing career. At fifteen, she portrayed Helen Keller in *The Miracle Worker* on the Broadway stage and in the film, both co-starring Anne Bancroft. When the film was released in 1962, Bancroft won the Academy Award, beating out Bette Davis for her performance in *What Ever Happened to Baby Jane?* and Katharine Hepburn for her performance in *Long Day's Journey Into Night.* To infuriate Davis, Joan Crawford, Davis' co-star in *Baby Jane,* walked on stage and accepted the Oscar for Bancroft, who could not leave a stage show she was involved in that night in Manhattan.

Also for her role as the young Helen Keller, Duke won the Best Supporting Actress Oscar, beating out such competitors as Mary Badham for *To Kill a Mocking Bird;* Shirley Knight for *Sweet Bird of Youth;* Angela Lansbury for *The Manchurian Candidate;* and Thelma Ritter for *Bird Man of Alcatraz.*

The following year, Duke gained a nationwide audience when she was cast in the dual role of "identical cousins" on *The Patty Duke Show* (1963-1966)

Her first mature role also became her most notorious. Jacqueline Susann had recently written

Anne Bancroft (left) with **Patty Duke** in *The Miracle Worker* (1962).

According to Patty, "My first beau was Frank Sinatra Jr. As a date, I moved on but we remained friends. I fell into the arms of Desi Arnaz Jr., a relationship that became serious. It was a romance the tabloids could not get enough of."

one of the best-selling novels in American history. A campy, tabloid-inspired classic published in 1967, it was *Valley of the Dolls*, a soapy tribute to pill addiction among the young, the beautiful, and the wannabees of Hollywood. The role of the insecure and flamboyantly unstable actress, Neely O'Hara, went to Duke. Critics found it hard to accept this "All-American teenager" as an alcoholic, drug-addicted movie star, popping "dolls" (i.e., pills) at very frequent intervals.

Actually, Patty Duke was perfect for the Neely O'Hara role. Its script seemed to mirror her own troubled boozing, pill-popping, and suicide attempts.

Mark Robeson, the director of the film version of *Valley of the Dolls,* later said, "I wanted to cast a girl whose nerve endings were exposed and ready to fly out before your eyes. That was Patty Duke. She was chain smoking an amazing four or five packs of cigarettes a day. Not only that, but she was biting off her fake fingernails before feasting on the real ones, right down to the quick.

Lucille's picture had appeared on the cover of *TV Guide* more than that of any other actress.

Above, editors celebrated the 20th anniversary of Desi Jr.'s birth, when as a newborn, he, too, had been celebrated—in his case as as "The $50,000,000 Baby."

Right before beginning her romance with Desi, Duke had starred in *Me, Natalie* (1969), in which she played "an ugly duckling," a Brooklyn teenager struggling to find a life for herself in Greenwich Village, home of the hippies and the so-called Bohemians of Manhattan. For her effort, she won the Golden Globe Award for Best Actress (musical or comedy).

Only months before hooking up with Desi, she starred in the made-for-television film, *My Sweet Charlie*, in which she portrayed a pregnant teenager on the run. The plot, ironically, would soon begin to mirror her own life, as she, too, became pregnant. (The identity of the father was uncertain at the time.)

Duke won her first Emmy for for *My Sweet Charlie*. But during the Emmy Awards presentation ceremony, the world became aware that something was wrong with her, as her acceptance speech was rambling and disjointed. Many in the audience and on TV thought she was either drugged or drunk, perhaps both.

Lucille—who had admired Duke for her brilliant performance as the blind and deaf Helen Keller in *The Miracle Worker*—was horrified by Duke's condition at the Awards ceremony. But what caused Lucille far more *angst* was the knowledge that her son was engaged in a torrid affair with the troubled actress.

Author Charles Higham summed up a mother's reaction: "For Lucille, this was the final straw. She had enough problems coping with her son's drinking and drug taking. Now he was running around with an older woman who had a reputed history of mental instability. Lucille threatened to kick her son out of the house, disinherit him, and get the law after Duke for corrupting a minor. She referred to Desi as 'jailbait.'"

In desperation, Lucille at one point angrily phoned Duke and threatened to bring a statutory rape charge against her.

"You wouldn't dare," Duke shot back. "You'd make all of us fodder for the tabloids. Your son's future might be ruined in Hollywood."

Right from the beginning, Lucille had never approved of the dates either her daughter, Lucie, or her son, Desi Jr., chose as partners. She compared them to "fish heads."

She later learned that on his first date with Duke, Desi had invited her to the disco, Daisy, a club that had a certain notoriety because most of its clientele was drugged.

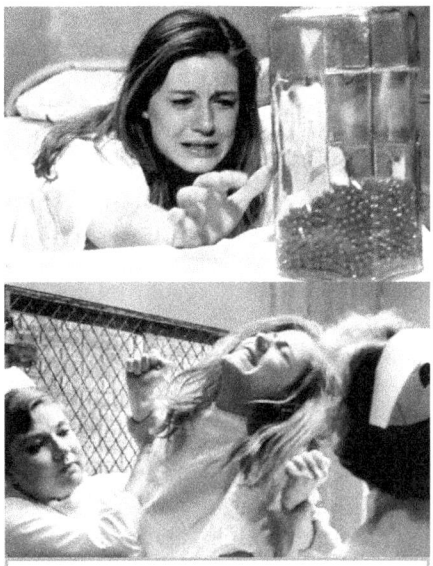

Two views of **Patty Duke** in Valley of the Dolls.

"I still believe that the novel Valley of the Dolls, trash though it may be, was far superior to the film, and that it did a real service in the pop psychological approach to exploring what it was in the lifestyles of the characters that drew them into addiction," Duke said. "And Nelly [the role assigned to Duke], was the best part of the book."

The pink streaks of dawn were usually breaking across the California sky, as Desi Jr. returned home after one of his nights on the town with Duke.

Thanks to subsequent high-profile dates, it didn't take long for the tabloids to discover the romance. Lucille failed to break up the relationship. She had threatened to fire Desi Jr. from *Here's Lucy*, although she'd continue with Lucie in the role of her child on TV. The script would be rewritten with the understanding that "Craig" was away at school.

Then, she persuaded Desi Jr. to join her on a vacation in Hawaii, hoping to break up the affair. But after his return to Los Angeles, his romance with Duke resumed.

To make matters worse, the unmarried Duke announced that she was pregnant, catalyzing even more scandalous headlines.

"The news was humiliating for me," Lucille said. "I just knew my son was the father, and that I was about to become a grandmother. That nasty girl could have had a discreet abortion like so many other unwed stars in Hollywood, But NO, not her. The bitch seemed to want the publicity. In many ways, I viewed the news of this pregnancy as worse than the *exposé* of my Communist Party membership back in the 1930s."

Desi turned eighteen on January 19, 1971, and his father rented a celebrity-frequented restaurant, Luau, for a big bash. He announced to the press, "My boy is now a man, all grown up. I'm proud of him. He's also very talented, and Patty is not only a beautiful gal, but one of the best actresses in Hollywood."

Desi Jr. showed up at the watering hole with Patty, as did a number of friends, even Gary Morton with Lucie Arnaz. Only one of the invited guest did not make an appearance—Lucille herself.

The following week, Lucille, at her son's urging, did invite Duke to dinner at her home in Beverly Hills. As Duke remembered it, she was "as glacial as the ice cream cake she served for dessert."

Duke, in 1987, published a memoir, *Call Me Anna,* a reference to her birth name of Anna Marie Duke. In it, she described her meeting with Lucille. "She felt she was in a crisis situation with her son and me. Her attitude was cold and efficient, with barely a veneer of politeness."

Duke later asserted that the stories being spread about Desi Jr. and her were "sleazy, slimy, and scurrilous. I suffered a great deal from them. My crime during that time—and it was indeed a crime—was that out of fear, I allowed people to assume that the baby was Desi's when I knew otherwise. In fact, there were times when I would nod in agreement without straight-out declaring, 'This is Desi's kid.'"

For reasons of her own, Duke left Lucille's home that night, giving the distinct impression that Lucille was about to become a grandmother. Actually, Duke didn't really know who the father of her unborn child was, as she was sharing intimacies with three different men at the time the baby might have been conceived.

In an angry confrontation, one afternoon

The headlines were relentless—and to Lucille, horrifying.

after Duke had been drinking heavily, she demanded that Desi marry her and announce that he was the father of her yet-to-be-born child, as they had routinely engaged in unprotected sex.

Duke later confessed, "In truth, I thought of marrying Desi as a way out of my dilemma, if nothing else. But he specifically said that he wasn't interested, that he never wanted to get married to anyone. I'm sure there were times when he thought the baby was his, as well as other times when he was convinced it wasn't. Either way, he definitely didn't want any part of the whole scene. It had been a great game for a while, but it was getting too real. That is probably how he felt. He didn't want to play anymore."

***

Patty Duke suddenly announced she was flying to Chicago to star in a play, an event that never happened. Before leaving Los Angeles, she sublet her apartment to a young man, Michael Tell, a writer, music promoter, and publisher—with his father—of a newspaper, *The Las Vegas Israelite.*

At once, he seemed attracted to Duke. He was said to have phoned her every day during her stay in Chicago. He even proposed marriage to her, even though he'd encountered her directly for fewer than fifteen minutes.

Tell contacted a Chicago florist and ordered him to deliver flowers every day to Duke's hotel suite.

Patty was rather drugged at the time and was rumored to have accepted Tell's proposal of marriage after he'd extended it to her four or five times.

Back in Los Angeles, she moved in with Tell. When Desi Jr. called, she invited him over. When he got there, she told him that she was going to marry Tell. There was no violent confrontation, but harsh words were exchanged. Desi was seen leaving the lobby of her apartment building in tears, perhaps with a broken heart.

The following night, Tell and Duke flew to Las Vegas, where they were married on June 2, 1970. Their honeymoon night was spent in a $450-per-night Las Vegas luxury hotel.

Tell later revealed that their marriage was consummated at 4AM in the hotel's swimming pool. When she appeared in court four days later to have the marriage annulled, she told the judge that the marriage was never consummated.

Tell was said to have asked for a settlement of $30,000, but later withdrew his request. To heal his wounds, he headed for the ski resort of Snowmass,

in retrospect, **Patty Duke** insisted that she had married **Michael Tell** during a "manic moment."

Here she is, shown with him on the occasion of their (disastrous) wedding.

near Aspen. Coincidentally, Lucille had also discovered this resort, and was buying real estate there.

To complicate matters, yet another man, John Astin, emerged in Duke's life, as part of a "love triangle." An actor, he was married and thirteen years her senior when they began a torrid affair.

He became better known when he played Gomez, the Addams family patriarch, on television.

In a phone call to Anne Bancroft, Duke revealed she was going to marry Astin after his divorce and announce to the world that he was the father of her (yet unborn) child.

Indeed, although her son was born February 25, 1971, and named Sean Astin, she wouldn't marry Astin until August of 1972. Yet, contradicting that, in a late night phone call to Desi Jr., she is alleged to have told him that he was the biological father anyway.

The press was confused, and rightly so. There seemed to be some agreement, at least a powerful suspicion, that Desi Jr. was the dad. It appears that Lucille, even though publicly denying it, felt that the newborn child was, indeed, her grandson. Morton teased her, calling her "Granny Lucy."

Later, it was learned that Duke's doctors had been disturbed by the infant's heartbeat and had delivered a five-pound baby boy by Caesarian. The newborn child spent his first three days in an incubator.

When the baby was born, Lucille did not go to the hospital, but Desi Sr., with his wife, Edie, did, announcing, "I'm a proud grandpapa." He also proclaimed, "The kid looks just like me!"

Also visiting were Gary Morton and Lucie Arnaz. Weeks before the birth, Lucie had been seen shopping with Duke in Beverly Hills buying a wardrobe for the as-yet-unborn infant.

The Hollywood Reporter claimed, "Lucille Ball and her divorced husband, Desi Arnaz Sr., are reported to be privately celebrating the birth of their first grandchild. The infant was born illegitimate, and teenaged Desi Jr. is rumored to be the father."

When the announcement was made, and when news of the annulment of Duke's marriage to Michael Tell was revealed, many Hollywood insiders expressed their feelings that Desi Jr. should marry Duke and that his mother,

For Lucille, the pregnancy of Patty Duke became even more surreal when one of the contenders as father of the unborn child was **John Astin.**

Astin is depicted here as the artfully creepy Gomez Adams with **Carolyn Jones**, portraying Morticia Addams, in 1974.

Perhaps Lucille was afraid that her fans would think her family was almost as dysfunctional as the Addams clan, but with fewer comedic lines.

"with all her millions," should provide for the boy, securing his future and his education.

When asked about this, Desi Sr. said, "I would be proud to add the name of Sean Arnaz to my family tree. My father in Santiago, long ago, urged me to carry the Arnaz name into future generations. I would welcome Patty into our extended family, as she is a beautiful young woman and a talented, award-winning actress."

When the infant was two months old, Lucille agreed to see the baby. At the urging of her son, she invited Patty and her child to her home. She later told a reporter, "I cuddled the baby in my arms because it was so adorable. I even changed its diaper. However, I do not for one moment believe that Sean is my grandson."

"As for Miss Duke, I am not happy that she has brought a certain notoriety to my family. She seems to be living in some haze, a kind of dream world. She has made my son a victim of her reported mental disorder. Desi Jr. was only seventeen when he met Miss Duke, far too young to get involved in such a complicated mess. My son told me he never wanted to marry Miss Duke."

Herbert Kenwith, Lucille's director on the *Here's Lucy* series, coincidentally had an apartment on the same floor as Duke. One day, as he was waiting for the elevator, the door opened to reveal Lucille herself. She was only slightly disguised with a heavy black veil. It was obvious to him that she'd come to see the baby, and "I felt that in spite of her protestations, she did indeed feel that Sean was her grandson."

On seeing Kenwith, she said, "What in hell are you doing here?"

"I might ask you the same question," he said. "I live here."

After his marriage to Duke, John Astin officially adopted Sean and legally changed his name to Sean Astin.

After her marriage in 1973, Duke gave birth to another son, Mackenzie Astin, who later became an actor.

When Sean turned fourteen, Duke told him that Desi Jr. was his real father, and the young boy developed a kind, loving relationship with him. However, he later met a relative of Michael Tell, who told him that Tell was his biological father.

The Duke/Astin marriage lasted until 1985, when they divorced. She then married Mike Pearce in 1986.

"I can call any of them on the phone any time I want," Sean said. "I have four dads…John, Desi, Mike, and Papa Mike."

Finally, to solve the mystery, Sean underwent genetic testing. It was revealed that his real father was Michael Tell.

Even so, Sean said, "Desi Jr. loves me, and I love him. We are so close. But science tells me he's not my biological father."

Sean later became an actor, producer, and director, and appeared as the loyal hobbit, "Samwise Gamgee," in *The Lord of the Rings* trilogy (2001-2003).

In *The Lord of the Rings*, Sean cheated death, fought dreadful enemies, and helped to bring a "gold ring" permeated with thousands of evil curses to its destruction.

He later spoke about the traumatic childhood that he and his brother experienced with a mentally ill mother: "She was so emotionally unstable that we helped her survive suicide attempts. There were fights followed by forgiveness. There was so much trouble, but in time, love won out. Life is, after all, about survival. That's what I love most about Patty. Ultimately, she was a survivor. I think through it all, she wanted to love. She's on this earth because she wants to be—and that's a good thing."

In spite of her mental health problems, Patty Duke was the president of the Screen Actors Guild from 1985 to 1988, a post once held by Ronald Reagan when he was a Democrat.

Death came to Duke on March 29, 2016. Before her death, she said, "I don't care what the tests reveal. I know for sure that Desi is the father of Sean."

A son to make a mother proud:

With humor, wisdom, and style, **Sean Astin** overcame the parental confusion of his childhood and emerged as a famous character actor (upper photo) in *The Lord of the Rings*, portraying the loyal best friend of the protagonist (Frodo), a stalwart but not-very-bright Hobbit named Samwise Gangee.

In the lower photo, he poses with his spectacularly talented, emotionally fragile mother, **Patty Duke**, before her death at the age of 69 in 2016.

***

Lucille put her personal problems aside to return to work on her *Here's Lucy* series. She reteamed with her former director, Jack Donohue, for a December 28, 1970 telecast, *Lucy Stops a Marriage*. He had directed her many times before, when not helming Frank Sinatra, Red Skelton, or Dean Martin, among others.

Its guest star was Jayne Meadows, married to Steve Allen, the famous TV host and friend of Lucille. The elder sister of actress Audrey Meadows, Jayne was a familiar figure on TV, especially when she became one of the regular panelists on the long-running (1952-1967) TV game show, *I've Got a Secret*. She'd also appeared with big-name stars in feature films alongside Katharine Hepburn, Gregory Peck, Susan Hayward, and Robert Montgomery.

In spite of the talent it had assembled, this was a weak episode to end the year. A rich old flame (Jayne Meadows) of Harry's (Gale Gordon) appears, informing him that she wants to invest $100,000 in his company, Carter's Unique Employment Agency. Lucy erroneously assumes Harry is going to marry her for her money, setting in effect an outrageous act of sabotage to ensure that he doesn't.

"Lucille was a friend of Steve and me," Meadows said. "She even apologized for having cast me in such a weak script, her excuse was that her budget had been severely cut because of over-the-budget spending on earlier episodes."

***

To launch 1971, on January 4, Lucille starred in Episode #65, *Lucy's Vacation*.

To his face, she harshly criticized the episode's co-author, Fred S. Fox. "I'm paying you a lot of dough, and all you guys can come up with is some old crap that's been done too many times before. How often have I faced a script where I'm trying in vain to get a raise or to get myself fired? Can't you come up with a fresh idea now and then? Is that too god damn much to ask?"

In this latest version, Harry (Gale Gordon) is so stressed out with Lucy as his secretary that he has to seek out a psychiatrist, Dr. Cummingham. The actor who played the doctor was Parley Baer, who had made five previous appearances on Lucille's previous series, *The Lucy Show*. He was better known for his recurring role as Doc Appleby on the hit TV series, *The Dukes of Hazzard (1979-1985)*.

In a secondary role, actress Kimetha Laurie was making her ninth (and final) appearance on TV. She played a friend of Kim (Lucie), whose rich parents have a home in Palm Springs.

Although Desi Jr., in the role of her Lucy's son, Craig, does not appear in this episode, he receives screen credit in the opening title sequence.

***

Lucille agreed to host *The Super Comedy Bowl* for a January 19, 1971 telecast, bringing in a new year of sports broadcasts. Producer and director Marty Pasetta lined up a dazzling cast of celebrities, none of them more famous than John Wayne. Also in the cast were such stars as Carol Burnett, Charlton Heston, Joe Namath, and Charles Nelson Reilly at his super-campy best.

Lucille sought out the English actress, Judy Carne, who had just completed her run on *Rowan and Martin's Laugh-In* (1968-1970). On that series, she became famous for her phrase, "Sock it to me!" Lucille explored the possibility that Carne might appear on a *Here's Lucy* episode in the future.

Lucille was fully aware that Carne had married and divorced (1963-1965) Burt Reynolds. When Lucille met her, she was in

Judy Carne during her marriage to **Burt Reynolds**, a photo of a relatively happy time in her otherwise tormented life.

She published it on the occasion of the release of her autobiography, *Laughing on the Outside, Crying on the Inside*.

the process of divorcing producer Robert Bergman, whom she had wed in 1970. That marriage would crash into pieces within just a few months.

What Lucille didn't know was that her own daughter, Lucie Arnaz, would also begin an affair with Reynolds.

As time went by, Lucille was saddened to learn about Carne's addiction to drugs, especially heroin. In 1986, she was arrested at London's Heathrow Airport and convicted of narcotics possession, which led her to prison for two months.

Only the year before, Lucille had read Carne's very frank biography, *Laughing on the Outside, Crying on the Inside: The Bittersweet Saga of the Sock-It-To-Me Girl*. In it, she detailed her bisexuality, providing juicy details of her marriage to Burt Reynolds. *[He tried, without success, to block its publication.]*

Also in the cast of the Super Bowl Comedy was footballer O.J. Simpson, nicknamed "The Juice." The football running back, two years earlier, had won the Heisman Trophy. At the time of his meeting with Lucille, he was playing for the Buffalo Bills, which had signed him before he came on her show. His contract lasted for eleven seasons.

Lucille was among the first to realize that Simpson's good looks and personal charisma could be exploited. They discussed a possible two-part series on *Here's Lucy* where she would play his football coach, giving him all the wrong advice. She noted that Hertz was one of the first companies to recognize his appeal, depicting him running through airports at record speed to the slogan of "Go, O.J., Go!"

In time, Simpson would star in films, such as *The Naked Trilogy* (1988, 1991, and 1994). For a while, director James Cameron considered starring him in *The Terminator* (1994) but changed his mind and cast muscleman Arnold Schwarzenegger instead.

Lucille died before Simpson's disgrace. In 1994, he was tried on a charge of murdering his former wife, Nicole Brown Simpson and her friend, Ron Goldman. After a sensational trial that had much of America glued to TV sets, he was acquitted. However, he wasn't that lucky in a subsequent civil trial, where he was found guilty of the deaths of the two victims. A $33.5 million judgment was leveled against him, but to escape liability, he moved to Miami.

In 2007, he was arrested in Las Vegas on charges of armed robbery and kidnapping. This time, he was convicted and sentenced to 33 years in prison. He

It seemed funny and lighthearted at the time...UNTIL IT WASN'T

Here's a newspaper ad promoting the 1973 appearance, on an episode of *Here's Lucy*, of the gridiron star and alleged double murderer, **O.J. Simpson.**

was granted parole in July 2017.

The days when *People* magazine had described him as "a bonafide, loveable media superstar" were a faded and very ironic memory.

***

In January and February of 1971, Lucille concluded the third season of *Here's Lucy*. For the most part, the episodes had been lackluster. Her friend, Jack Carter, the comedian, was given a chance to direct. He had been married to Paula Stewart, Lucille's co-star in the Broadway production of *Wildcat* in 1960. They had since divorced. But at the time Lucille worked with Stewart, she and Carter arranged a double date between Lucille with Gary Morton, who soon became her second husband. She always thought highly of both of them and was sorry to hear that their marriage had not worked out.

The year Lucille worked with Carter, he was to marry Roxanne Wander, divorcing her in 1977 but remarrying her again in 1992, a union that lasted until his death in 2015.

Carter had much success as a comedian and was sometimes compared to Milton Berle because of his rapid delivery. But Lucille thought he also might have talent as a director.

Carter made his directorial debut on January 11, 1971 telecast of Episode #66, *Lucy and 20-20 Vision*. Its plot was hardly worthy of either of their talents. Lucy has decided that her boss, Harry (Gale Gordon) needs glasses and arranges a visit with an eye doctor. Once he begins wearing those glasses, he sees more than Lucy wants him to.

Before signing on as her director, Carter had heard that Lucille was difficult to direct. "But I found her smooth sailing, and we got on real fab. At the end, it was hugging and kissing goodbye time."

After Carter departed, Lucille decided to co-star with a familiar face, Danny Thomas, on a January 21 telecast of an episode of *Make Room for Daddy* entitled, *Lucy Carter, Houseguest*. This was part of a less successful "rehash" of the comedian's hit TV sitcom, *The Danny Thomas Show*, *Make Room for Daddy*, which had a long run from 1953 to 1964, beginning when Eisenhower was president and ending around the time when Lyndon Johnson won the White House.

Marjorie Lord had the third lead, and she seemed to know from the beginning that the episode did not work. She played

Comedian **Jack Carter,** depicted above, claimed, "My greatest achievement was introducing Lucille Ball to Gary Morton."

"Morton was motor-mouthed, known for his rapid-fire delivery of one-liners, and impressions from Cary Grant to Bogie—and a dancer's light footedness."

Kathy Williams, an old friend of Lucy Carter, who stays with her in New York. There, she meets Kathy's beau, Danny Williams (Danny Thomas), who returns and seems to be coming on to Lucy. Kathy had told her that Danny is attracted to very feminine women, so Lucy dresses up like a man to turn him off.

"Lucille's voice had gotten quite deep at the time, and she could certainly impersonate a man," Lord claimed. She and Thomas had been working together ever since she'd replaced Jean Hagen on his TV sitcom *Make Room for Daddy*. A sequel, *Make Room for Granddaddy*, had bombed, however, lasting only one season.

***

Lucille took time off from *Here's Lucy* to make a guest appearance on *The Pearl Bailey Show*, telecast on January 23 for 60 minutes. When she hooked up with Bailey, an African American actress and singer, she had recently reached a high point in her career with the win of a Tony Award for the all-black production of *Hello, Dolly!* in 1968.

As a revered icon, and a loyal fan of the New York Mets, Bailey sang the national anthem at Shea Stadium prior to Game 5 of the 1969 World Series, and again prior to Game 1 of the 1981 World Series at Yankee Stadium, again in New York City.

Nonetheless, her series, *The Pearl Bailey Show* (January to May of 1971), was falling off in ratings. To save the show, she turned to big name guests, not only Lucille, but Bing Crosby and Louis Armstrong, in one of his last appearances before his death.

Bailey was a Republican, and, before working with Lucille, President Richard Nixon had appointed her as "Ambassador of Love." In that capacity, she attended several meetings of the United Nations.

On the set, Lucille learned that Bailey was compiling a cookbook, which would be published in 1973 under the title of *Pearl's Kitchen*. In it, she detailed how she'd served some of her favorite dishes, such as "Lamb Chops Sumpin' Else" to celebrity friends who had included Bing Crosby, Tony Bennett, Carol Burnett, and Burt Reynolds.

For lunch one day, Bailey, with her maid, arrived with some food she had prepared early that morning.

Pearl Bailey appears above with **Robert Wagner** in 1960 in a promotional photo for *All the Fine Young Cannibals*.

"That good-looking white boy tried to impersonate Harry James. But 'blow, boy, blow' he couldn't make it. If he reaches Heaven, Gabriel might use him as a stand-in."

"We're having my own special spareribs," she told Lucille. "The secret to cooking pork is to keep it on the stove a long time until the meat is falling off the bone. I always serve my spareribs with what I call 'My Ma's cabbage,' which I cook in fatback."

At the end of the shoot, Lucille had an awkward (and accidental) encounter with Joan Crawford, who had appeared on the set to meet with Bailey. Lucille was unaware that they were close friends.

Crawford walked by Lucille without speaking, still remembering the troubled time when they'd worked together in February of 1968 in an episode of *Here's Lucy*. Later, Lucille witnessed Crawford disappearing from the studio with Bailey. Then Lucille turned to her director, Dean Whitmore, claiming, "Why shouldn't Pearl make out with Crawford? She's already had Marlene Dietrich."

***

Lucille liked Jack Carter, the comedian who had directed her in a recent episode, so she hired him again. This time, he was to helm her and Carol Burnett in a February episode of *Lucy & Carol Burnett: The Hollywood Unemployment Follies*.

The weak plot has Harry (Gale Gordon) once again firing Lucy, sending her to stand in the unemployment line. There, she encounters Carol Krausemeyer (Burnett). They decide to produce a musical show to raise money.

Burnett saves the show by performing her own stunts and songs, evoking her own TV variety show. Lucille's singing voice was dubbed by her faithful regular, Carole Cook.

Carter later recalled, "I had heard that Lucille was Dr. Jekyll and Mrs. Hyde, but I had never seen that part of her personality. Directing her the second time around, I met Mrs. Hyde in person. The first episode had been a piece of cake. This time around, she was like something you might taste if you devoured a can of Red Devil lye. She rescinded every one of my directions, and I knew why."

"At the time, I was engaged in a bitter custody battle with Paula Stewart, her close friend, over our son, Michael. She took Paula's side—not mine. Working with her was one of the most humiliating experiences of my career, and I decided to give up directing. My god, I felt I was tangling with Bette Davis and Joan Crawford morphed into one body."

***

Lucille's longtime director, Jack Donohue, was brought back to helm two back-to-back episodes of *Here's Lucy*, which would bring an end to the 1970-71 season. The first episode was entitled *Lucy Goes Hawaiian, Part One (on CBS February 15)*.

It was like old home week as scriptwriter Milt Josefsberg was rehired to create a plot. He'd been the script consultant on *The Lucy Show*.

On the set, she had a reunion with Vivian Vance, and they talked a lot about their heyday as Lucy Ricardo and Ethel Mertz. "We'll never escape those characters," Vance said.

She was worried about her health, so Lucille tried to get her to accept an appointment with her doctor. Vance refused.

However, by 1973, she was diagnosed with breast cancer, which she survived.

Around this time, Vance was assigned a high-paying gig as a spokesperson for Maxwell House Coffee, touting its merits during commercial breaks on TV.

In the plot, Harry (Gale Gordon) is working as the cruise director aboard a luxury liner. Even though he should have known better, he employs Lucy as his onboard associate. Aboard the ship, she and "Viv" fall for the same man, Captain McClay, played by Robert Alda. He had once co-starred with Lucille in an episode that also teamed her with the blonde beauty, Marilyn Maxwell, who had once sustained an affair with Desi Sr.

In Part Two of *Lucy Goes Hawaiian,* Donohue found himself once again in charge of directing Lucille, Vance, Robert Alda, and Lucille's two biological children. Donohue himself was spotted briefly on the February 22 telecast.

Harry orders Lucille to put on a show for the passengers with the help of Vance—and she does just that. The episode was one of the better ones of the season, and Vance does a good rendition of "Yellow Bird."

In Episode #72, Desi Jr. worked with his sister, Lucie, in what would become his last appearance as a regular on his mother's series. He no longer had a pudgy figure and went shirtless in a musical number where he wore a grass skirt.

The Hawaiian two-part series marked the end of the 1970-71 season at a time when ratings were falling off. Nonetheless, CBS signed Lucille for yet another (the Fourth) season of *Here's Lucy.*

***

That spring, before her summer vacation began, Lucille also signed to appear on three specials, beginning with the March 10, 1971 telecast of *Everything You Always Wanted to Know About Jack Benny But Were Afraid to Ask.*

Benny brought in several of his fellow comedians, including George Burns, Phil Harris, and Bob Hope.

Even John Wayne made a surprise appearance as a chorus boy named "Marion Wayne." *[The Duke's birth name was Marion Michael Morrison when he entered the world in 1907.]*

The most embarrassing scene occurs when Benny, as a 76-year-old Romeo, attempts to seduce "chorus girl" Lucy, age 60. At one point, Lucille evokes her chorus girl days. *[Lucille, as readers of Volume One of this two-part biography probably remember, had played an artfully undressed slave in* Roman Scandals *way back in 1933. It had starred "Banjo Eyes," Eddie Cantor.]*

Another TV special, *Swing Out, Sweet Land,* was telecast on April 8, starring John Wayne as the host. Lucille no longer referred to him as "The Duke," preferring instead his girlie name of Marion.

In this "Salute to America," she avoided any comic overtones and made a patriotic speech. Ann-Margret provided the sex appeal; Bob Hope and Jack Benny the comedy; and Johnny Cash, Bing Crosby, and Dean Martin the songs.

Before taking her vacation, Lucille appeared at the 23rd Annual Emmy Awards, telecast May 9 from the Hollywood Palladium. Johnny Carson was the host.

Lucille and Jack Benny were assigned the role of announcing the winner of the Best Supporting Actor Award. When Benny and Lucille appeared together on stage, the show came to a stop until the standing ovation ended.

Gale Gordon was up for an Emmy for playing Uncle Harry in that season of *Here's Lucy*.

Lucille hogged all the cue cards for herself, until Benny reached over and grabbed one of them. Then he turned to the audience and said, "She won't let me do anything."

That brought a big laugh at her expense.

The Emmy was not awarded to Gordon but was carried off instead by Ed Asner for his role in *The Mary Tyler Moore Show* (1970-1977).

***

Two of the most widely publicized affairs in Hollywood during the 1970s centered on Desi Jr. and two older movie stars, much to the consternation of his mother. Lucille was enraged at the tabloid headlines generated.

After breaking up with Patty Duke, and before he got involved in a torrid romance with another big movie star, he reportedly had two other romantic interludes with starlets.

Right after Patty Duke married Michael Tell in Las Vegas, Desi Jr., it seems, spent very little time in mourning a lost love affair. He was seen dating an aspiring young actress, Kim Darby.

He'd met her when he was starring in the 1971 film, *Red Sky in the Morning*. In it, Darby had an uncredited role.

As he soon learned, she was the daughter of two professional dancers, known in show biz as "The Dancing Zerbys." At the age of fifteen, Darby had begun her acting career, appearing in the hit musical, *Bye Bye Birdie* (1963), a picture that Desi Jr. had seen. She'd also appeared on television in episodes of such hit Western series as *Gunsmoke* (1967) and Bonanza (1969). His wife, Pilar, in her autobiography, *My Life With John Wayne,* accused Darby of being rude to "The Duke" during the making of that film. Wayne referred to Darby as "that spoiled brat."

Before she started dating young Desi, Darby had gone through two failed marriages. For a year, she was wed to James Stacy beginning in 1968, during which the couple had a daughter, Heather Elias. After her divorce, Darby married another James (Westmoreland, in this case), but that turbulent union lasted for less than two months.

She was later quoted as saying that her career eventually went into decline because she had become addicted to amphetamines.

Like her marriages, her affair with Desi had a short life span. It didn't take him long to get involved with another "hot date," even more beautiful than the first.

He had gone to a screening of *The Sicilian Clan (le clan des Siciliens)*, a 1969 French gangster film starring Jean Gabin, Lino Ventura, and Alain Delon, who had been voted the handsomest actor in French cinema. At the time, Delon was involved in a scandal known as "The Markovic Affair." His former bodyguard, Steven Markovic, had been found murdered in a scandal that involved the President of France, Georges Pompidou, and his wife, Claude.

The movie didn't interest Desi Jr. for very long, and the *Los Angeles Times* had claimed, "It winds up seeming more corny and contrived than witty and ironic."

He was far more interested in the appearance of starlet Judy Brown, seated a few feet away. Their eyes met, and some signal was sent.

He later invited her for a drive to La Costa, near San Diego, a resort known for its champion tennis courts. There, they were the guests of Dino, son of Dean Martin, who at the time was married to the English actress, Olivia Hussey.

The next day, Desi drove Brown to the home of his father, Desi Sr., at his villa at Corona Del Mar, where he lived with his second wife, Edie. His son and his date were warmly welcomed.

The next day, they joined Dino and Olivia for a game of mixed doubles on one of the courts at La Costa. That following weekend, they returned to watch the La Costa Tennis Tournament.

Like his previous romance, Desi's affair with Brown had a short life span.

As a starlet, Brown deserves a footnote in Hollywood history, not just for her films, but for the men she dated: Warren Beatty, Ryan O'Neal, and Christopher Jones. This trio of studs was known for their charm and sex appeal. As one columnist reported, "The line of willing females formed on the right."

Warren Beatty was known as "The Casanova of Hollywood." Over the course of his romantic involvements, his star list would include both Jacqueline Onassis and Madonna.

Ryan O'Neal became quite well known in 1964 when he played Rodney Harrington on the

Kim Darby and **John Wayne**, as they each appeared in the cult Western, *True Grit (1969)*.

Alas, the tenacity her character showed on celluloid did not apply to her marital or romantic allegiances.

ABC soap opera, *Peyton Place*. He achieved worldwide success when he starred in the film, *Love Story* in 1970, for which he received an Oscar nod. He would later marry the blonde goddess Farrah Fawcett, but that union was troubled by his infidelity and volatile behavior. Notable on his list of affairs were Barbra Streisand, Liza Minnelli, Diana Ross, Joan Collins, and Margaret Trudeau, the errant and sometimes unstable wife of Pierre Trudeau, the Prime Minister of Canada.

When Desi Sr. heard that his son had joined this lineup of Hollywood studs, he said, "I'm real proud of my boy. He's a champ in the major league of Hollywood studs. Obviously, he takes after his old man."

A son of Tennessee, actor Christopher Jones also dated Brown. He bore a striking resemblance to James Dean, to whom he was often compared. Major stardom was predicted for him, but predictions often are wrong, especially from so-called fortune tellers.

As a young man, Jones had joined the U.S. Army, but was later sent to a military prison for going AWOL.

After his release, he began an acting career, and was given a small role on Broadway in December of 1961 when he appeared in *The Night of the Iguana* in tight pants. He was seduced by both its playwright, Tennessee Williams, and by its star, the buxom, blonde-haired survivor of all those *films noirs,* Shelley Winters.

Winters later introduced Jones to the actress Susan Strasberg, the daughter of Method acting progenitor Lee Strasberg at the Actors Studio. Their unsuccessful and turbulent marriage produced a daughter but was marred by his addiction to drugs.

It was reported that at the time of Desi's involvement with Brown, she was making a women-in-prison drama, *The Big Doll House* (1971). Cast as "Collier," she is sent to jail after having been found guilty of murdering her husband. The movie follows six female inmates, one cellmate being a lesbian. Some of them are victims of torture from a sadistic female guard.

This was one of the first B movies made by Roger Corman, "The Pope of Pop Cinema" and a trailblazer in the world of independent filmmaking. *The Big Doll House* had cost $125,000 but made ten million at the box office.

Corman once considered contacting Desi Jr. with the idea of starring him as the romantic lead in a number of films but was told that he was "too expensive" for his limited budgets. However, Corman became a key player in launching the careers of Peter Fonda, Dennis Hopper, Jack Nicholson, Diane Ladd, William Shatner, and Sylvester Stallone. He also was a sparkplug for directors such as Francis Ford Coppola, Ron Howard, Martin Scorsese, James Cameron, and Peter Bogdanovitch. Corman even impressed Lucille Ball herself.

That same year (1971), Corman also cast Brown in yet another prison drama, *Women in Cages,* where she had to face a sadistic lesbian guard hellbent on torturing her inmates. One critic found the movie "harsh, harsh, and harsh, full of devastating despair."

For a brief time, Brown became known as an almost universal "sexpot" in Corman's woman-in-prison movies. She would go on to star in *A Woman for All Men* (1975) with actors Keenan Wynn and Andrew Robinson.

COCKS OF THE WALK

aka: **Testosterone Kings Strutting Their Stuff** for the then-most-talked-about short-term seductress of her era, **Judy Brown.**

Judy Brown as she appeared in the title role of *A Woman for All Men* (1975), and (right) in publicity materials marketed by the studio.

In her personal life, "All Men" included four of the hottest studs of her era, each depicted on this page. One of them included **Desi Arnaz Jr.**

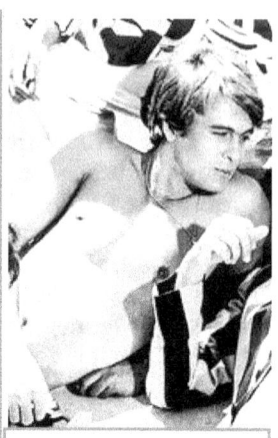

Members of **Christopher Jones'** four gay fan clubs (in Chicago, New York, San Francisco, and Los Angeles) saw a secretly snapped male nude of him and pronounced him "the Sexiest Man Alive."

Ryan O'Neal with his daughter Tatum, as a child.

After she grew up, Tatum claimed that alcoholism and drug addiction were in her DNA.

It was true that three generations of her family had been ravaged by weakness for addictive substances.

Warren Beatty as he appeared in *Bonnie & Clyde*.

Opinions varied about him. Madonna called him "a wimp and a pussy."

His sister, Shirley MacLaine, claimed, "Sex was his hobby.":

Desi Jr. at an age that invited sexual comparisons to his male peers.

He said, "I take after my dad. He loved sex and couldn't get enough."

The tangled plot involves a grouch millionaire (Wynn) who marries a young beauty (Brown). One of his sons, played by Robinson, falls in love with dad's trophy wife.

Robinson had become widely known for his portrayal of "The Scorpio Killer" in *Dirty Harry* (1975) starring Clint Eastwood. His role was based on the real life "Zodiac Killer."

Later, Robinson portrayed everyone from President Kennedy in an episode of *The Twilight Zone,* to Liberace in a biopic. "It was a lot of fun wearing Liberace's furs and jewelry and getting to sing 'I'll Be Seeing You.'"

When Lucille became fully aware of Corman's star-making talent, she told director Herbert Kenwith, "Maybe he could have made a movie star out of my son after all."

***

The tabloid press had gone wild with news of the latest romance of Desi Jr. When he launched an affair with Liza Minnelli, it was hailed by gossip columnists for merging "two houses of Hollywood royalty." She was the daughter of Judy Garland and director Vincente Minnelli, and Desi Jr., of course, was the son of Lucille Ball and Desi Arnaz.

For his latest love, he had certainly chosen a bundle of talent, as she was dedicated to singing, dancing, and acting.

Like Desi, she'd started performing in her teens, and was so good, she aroused jealousy in her own mother. Judy had instilled in her daughter the fierce idea that "the show must go on."

"I think it is the memory of Judy that drives Liza so relentlessly," Desi said. "That forms a bond between us, as I, too, have a legendary mother urging me ever onward. When I met Liza, she had suffered the devastating early death of Judy and had not gotten over it yet. In some way, Liza and I have the same problem: Both of us need to escape the lingering shadows of our mothers and emerge into our own sunshine."

Keenly aware of the difference in their ages, Tinseltown tongues wagged. Desi Jr. was only nineteen and barely out of high school. Liza, in contrast, was a very experienced twenty-six-year-old veteran of numerous affairs.

When asked about the age difference, Desi Jr. said, "Love doesn't confine itself strictly to age. Not all twenty-year-olds fall in love with other twenty-year-olds. Love is something you feel in your heart when you meet the person of your dreams. One look in those saucer eyes of hers, and I was a goner."

Actually, when she was only seven years old, she'd bounced him on her knee when he wasn't even six months old. When Vincente Minnelli directed Lucille and Desi Sr. in *The Long, Long Trailer* (1954), he had cast his daughter, Liza, in a cameo. *[The footage ended up on the cutting-room floor.]* But when Lucille appeared with her infant on the set, she let Liza hold her son.

The years went rushing by from that day forth until September of 1971, when Desi went backstage to congratulate Liza for her concert at Griffith

Park in Los Angeles. From that night on, their romance blossomed, even though she hadn't yet divorced Peter Allen, her gay husband, whom she'd married in 1967.

From that moment on, Desi was on Liza's trail, following her to her gigs in Las Vegas and Lake Tahoe.

Through a long life of ill-fated romances, disastrous marriages, an out-of-control mother, a gay father, Liza had known enough turmoil to populate a ten-part TV series. She found beaux around the world, as documented below. One of her biographers, George Mair, claimed, "She was a sexual revolution."

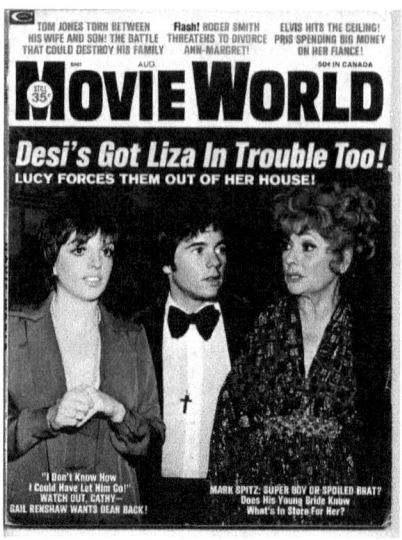

***

Liza had been linked romantically to a wide assortment of friends and/or lovers. Noteworthy on her list was Charles Aznavour, the French-Armenian singer, lyricist, and actor known for his distinctive tenor voice. During the course of his widely heralded 70-year career, he recorded more than 1,200 songs in nine languages, selling some 200 million records. Jean Cocteau once said, "Before Aznavour, despair was unpopular."

During one of her sojourns in Paris, Liza had launched an affair

Desi Jr. and **Liza Minnelli** were tabloid fodder, with Lucille lurking, disapprovingly, in the background.

"I can't understand how Liza and I can be in love one day and out of love the next," Desi Jr. was reported as saying. He was referring to how she had dumped him for Peter Sellers.

Her relationship with Sellers did not endure. She crept up behind him at a dinner and snatched off his toupée.

Sellers was not amused. Liza was shown the door.

with Aznavour, who told the press, "I gave up Edith Piaf for Liza. The young lady and I have a friendship, yet it is more than a friendship. Could it be called love? Who knows what love really is? Perhaps it is a mere illusion."

Another of Liza's high-profile romances was with Mikhail Baryshnikov, the Russia-born ballet star and choreographer. Emerging from the Kirov Ballet in Leningrad, he defected to Canada in 1974 and later became celebrated for his masterful performances at the American Ballet Theatre.

Martin Scorcese, who helmed Liza in *New York, New York* (1977), also had a fling with her. The film director and producer is hailed as one of the towering figures of "New Hollywood." Many of his movies are noted for their dependence on violence and a liberal use of profanity.

Bob Fosse, the dancer, choreographer, and filmmaker, directed Liza both on and off screen in her most memorable film, *Cabaret* (1972).

An unusual choice for Liza was Sir John Gorton, prime minister (1968-1972) of Australia. He was an ardent liberal, supporting such causes as the decriminalization of marijuana and prostitution. He once said, "*Cabaret* is my all-time favorite film, and my favorite movie star of all time is Liza Minnelli."

Edward Albert, son of the famous actor Eddie Albert and Mexican actress "Margo," also is on Liza's list of beaux. He starred in more than 130 films, including *Butterflies Are Free* (1972), for which he won a Golden Globe Award.

Actor Joe Pesci, no beauty, was an odd choice for her as a sexual or romantic partner. He was known for portraying tough, volatile characters and for his collaborations with Robert De Niro and Martin Scorsese in such films as *Raging Bull* (1980).

In Paris, Liza dated Alexis von Rosenberg, Baron de Redé, a socialite, banker, and aristocrat. He was known for his opulent costume balls. Never in her life had Liza gone out with a better-dressed suitor, as he was hailed as one of the best-dressed men on the planet.

At the peak of their affair, **Desi Jr.** and "that older woman," **Liza Minnelli,** were captured by photographers as they arrived at Heathrow Airport in London.

Her first husband, entertainer Peter Allen, said, "Dear silly Liza. She holds a press conference to announce she is in love and the next to complain that the press broke it up."

Minor flings in Paris included intervals with two French actors, including Jean-Claude Cassel, who had been discovered by Gene Kelly as he tap danced on the stage. He later cast him in his 1967 film *The Happy Road*. One of Cassel's most notable roles was in *Oh! What a Lovely War* in which he played a French military officer singing "Belgium put the kibosh on the Kaiser."

Liza's charm was not lost on Jean-Claude Brialy the French actor and director. Born in French Algeria, he became a star in the 1950s, one of the most prolific actors of the French "*nouvelle vague,*" working with such great filmmakers as Roger Vadim, François Truffaut, and Luis Buñuel.

Among Liza's more bizarre romances was with Gene Simmons, known as "The Demon" when he was onstage as the bassist and lead singer for the rock band Kiss.

In another momentary fling, Liza was also involved with Adam Ant, the lead singer of the rock band "Adam and the Ants," and later a solo artist scoring top hits in the UK from 1980 to around 1983.

What did Liza think of his music? "Glitzy glam pop."

An unusual romance developed between Liza and the African American performer Ben Vereen, the actor, dancer, and singer. He is still remembered for his Broadway performance in *Jesus Christ Superstar,* for which he received a nomination for a Tony Award, and for his success in *Pippin,* for which he actually walked off with a Tony.

Years after dating Liza, he was accused of sexual harassment, beginning when he directed *Hair* in Florida in 2015. *Variety* reported that while directing it, Verene is alleged to have invited female cast members to his apartment and goaded them into sex acts. A lot of cast members had to strip naked for a show that since its original opening on Broadway has been associated with a full cast nude scene.

Verene has since apologized for his misconduct.

***

Vigilant reporters soon learned of the Minnelli/Arnaz affair and followed the pair everywhere. The saga of two golden children of Hollywood legends made good copy, especially in tantalizing details, either real or imagined. There was a strong emphasis on Liza being a "child molester," although Desi Jr., of course, was of legal age.

At one point, they showed up for a romantic tryst at the Arnaz family's beach house in Del Mar, California, where Desi Sr. warmly welcomed them.

Liza began having fun with the press by confusing them. She might describe Desi Jr. as her *fiancé* one minute or else suggest, "He's too young for me." Often, she dismissed their age difference. "Desi is much older than his age. He understands my need for calmness. He knows I hate abrupt changes of emotion."

Right before hooking up with Desi Jr., Liza was emerging from a messy love affair with Rex Kramer, a young man from Arkansas, part of the musical group "Bojangles." Regrettably, both of them were married at the time their affair began.

As their romance deepened, he took her to the backwater (Smackover, Arkansas) where he grew up and introduced her to his parents.

She hired Bojangles as her musical backup when she starred in the Empire Room at Manhattan's luxury hotel, the Waldorf Astoria, early in 1970.

Months later, Kramer's wife, Peggy Kulbeth, sued Liza for alienation of affection, demanding half a million dollars. The *New York Post* referred to Liza as a "homewrecker."

Not wanting a lot of bad publicity, Liza settled the case out of court for an undisclosed amount. She finally decided that Rex didn't love her and that he was "merely using me." Shortly before launching her affair with Desi, she broke up with Kramer.

In the middle of her affair with Desi, she abruptly left him in California as she flew to Paris and into the bed of her former flame, Baron Alexis de Redé.

When she returned to Los Angeles, she resumed her affair with Desi.

With Liza back in his arms, Desi announced the next day, "I want everybody to know that we are deeply in love. We feel we've been married all our lives, and it would be wonderful if she had my baby. I want her to have my baby—in fact, I want her to be the mother of all my kids. I don't care if we're married or not. Just the picture of her pregnant with my child gives me the goose pimples. Of course, she'll have to divorce Peter Allen."

"Mother doesn't want me to be living with Liza out of wedlock, and she opposes the idea of Liza becoming pregnant before her divorce comes through. It's a struggle between what I want and what my mother wants for me. Liza and I don't know what to do—please ourselves or please my mother."

In spite of her objections, Lucille put up a good front to the press. "I think Desi and Liza are good for each other. I could not be happier. Because Judy Garland was not always a reliable parent, thirteen-year-old Liza had to be a kind of mother to her half-sister, Lorna Luft and her half-brother Joey. Based on those experiences of early parenting, Liza looks after Desi like a protective mother hen."

Although that was what she said publicly, privately Lucille complained that "cocaine and marijuana fuel their love affair far too much. I also object to her jet-setting lifestyle. She's known for having numerous lovers."

At an early age, Liza had asserted her independence. "I prefer to be Liza Minnelli onstage and offstage. I'm not just Judy Garland's daughter. I'm me. I've made it on my own."

During the run of their affair, Desi and Liza might pop up anywhere, no appearance more notable then when he accompanied her to the 1973 Academy Awards ceremony, where she won an Oscar for her performance as Sally Bowles in *Cabaret*.

After that, they were met by fans, photographers, and reporters as they departed from Los Angeles for Tokyo. Desi was set to co-star with Zero Mostel in a film, *Marco,* based loosely on the life of Marco Polo.

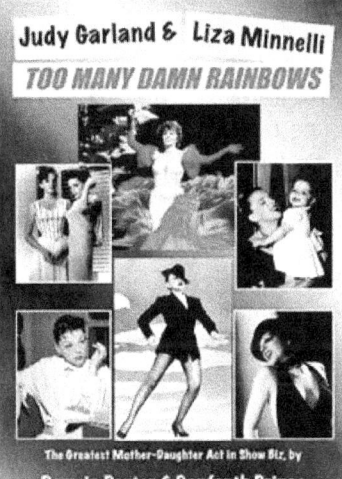

Judy Garland & Liza Minnelli
TOO MANY DAMN RAINBOWS

The Greatest Mother-Daughter Act in Show Biz, by
Darwin Porter & Danforth Prince

Uncovering the secrets of famous mothers and their famous daughters is a task which **Blood Moon Productions**, with finesse, has handled many times.

Actually, the fame of **Garland** and **Minnelli** eclipsed the fame of Lucille and her handsome, sexy, and often errant son, Desi Jr.

The movie bombed at the box office.

Lucille grew increasingly concerned that Desi Jr., like his father, would never achieve his dream of becoming a big movie star. Her son would spend most of the 1970s and into the 1980s in made-for-TV films.

Desi Sr. announced to the press that the marriage of his son to Liza would take place at his home in New Mexico.

It never did. On a trip to England, she fell in love with the 47-year-old English actor, Peter Sellers.

Soon after, she notified Desi that their affair was over.

Desi's competition, the English actor Peter Sellers, born in 1925, isn't as famous today as he was. He became known to an international audience when he portrayed the humorously offbeat Chief Inspector Clouseau in *The Pink Panther* series of films. He was nominated three times for a Best Actor Oscar, especially for his performance in *Dr. Strangelove or How I Learned to Stop Worrying and Love the Bomb* (1964).

Desi did not waste a lot of time mourning over lost love. It's hard to keep a Hollywood Lothario down. Soon, he was seen dating Victoria Principal in her pre-*Dallas* days and Tina Sinatra, whom Frank called "my little girl."

Liza Minnelli: Sexy, talented, and brilliant evoking Sally Bowles, a cabaret entertainer in "between the world wars" Weimar Republic..

CHAPTER TEN

As Hollywood's Aging Stars Fade and
Begin to Die, Like Troupers,
the Few Who Remain Attempt to
Boost Ratings for

HERE'S LUCY

Helen Hayes, David Frost, Flip Wilson,
Joe Namath, Dinah Shore, & Tony Randall

JIM BAILEY

A Cross-Dressing Man Who Wears Wigs and
Dresses with More Flair than Many Women
Enters the Lives of Lucille and Lucie

To launch the Fourth Season of Here's Lucy (1971-1972), Lucille retained most of her faithful crew. In Coby Ruskin, she'd found a compatible director. He never challenged her, even when she wanted to direct the episode herself. "Keep him on the payroll," she ordered Gary Morton, still her executive producer.

Her cousin, Cleo Smith, backed up her decisions, faithfully carrying out her orders. Milt

Josefsberg was retained as her script doctor, and cast regulars were Lucie Arnaz, her daughter, cast in the role of Kim, and the always-reliable Gale Gordon as Harrison (Harry) Otis Carter. Many of their episodes were written by Bob Carroll Jr., and by Madelyn Pugh (now Davis), who turned out some of the best scripts of *I Love Lucy* from the 1950s.

Lucille had long admired the talent of Flip Wilson, and she called on him to be her guest star. He signed with her, and an agreement was made that she would follow with a guest appearance on his hit TV series, *The Flip Wilson Show.*

At the time, he was at the peak of his national acclaim. Born in New Jersey, he'd had a troubled childhood, one of ten children. When Flip was seven years old, his father abandoned his brood. His mother, who could not support her kids, farmed them out to foster homes. Flip, in time, turned into a juvenile delinquent and was sent away to reform school.

When released at the age of sixteen, he lied about his age and joined the U.S. Army. He quickly became known for entertaining his fellow soldiers, and word reached his superiors, who sent him on tours of military bases to entertain other soldiers.

Out of the service in 1954, he was seen working as a bellhop at the Manor Plaza Hotel in San Francisco. The manager learned of his talent to entertain and started to let him appear to amuse between acts of the stars he had booked.

By the end of the decade, Flip was touring America, entertaining a black clientele on what used to be called "The Chitlin' Circuit."

Greater fame came to him when he was a big hit at the Apollo Theater

Like Bill Cosby, **Flip Wilson** was one of America's most popular comics in the late 1960s and early 1970s, known for frequent appearances on *The Ed Sullivan Show.*

He often appeared in his "Geraldine" drag, portraying a sassy black woman. From that gig emerged a hit record, "*Geraldine, Don't Fight the Feeling.*"

His variety show earned him a Golden Globe and two Emmy Awards. *Time* magazine hailed him as "Television's First Black Superstar."

in Harlem: When comedian Redd Foxx told Johnny Carson on *The Tonight Show* that Flip Wilson was the best comedian in America, he was soon booked on the show, entertaining millions of Americans. Stardom was around the corner.

In the September 13, 1971 episode with Lucille, called *Lucy and Flip Go Legit,* she played a Southern Belle, Scarlett O'Hara, and he was the mentally challenged "Prissy," the character in *Gone With the Wind* portrayed by Butterfly McQueen.

Although **Lucille Ball** (as Scarlett O'Hara) and **Flip Wilson** (as Prissy) were no competition for Vivien Leigh and Butterfly McQueen in *Gone With the Wind* (1939), "Lucy and Flip" were a riot as a comic latter-day satire.

Ironically, more than three decades earlier, Lucille had (unsuccessfully) auditioned for the role of Scarlett in David O. Selznick's iconic motion picture opposite Clark Gable.

The screen role of Melanie, as essayed in the movie by Olivia de Havilland, went to Lucie Arnaz.

Coincidentally, Lucille in the late 1930s had auditioned for the role of Scarlett, even though she knew she was wrong for the part. "At least I would have been more convincing than that baritone babe, Tallulah Bankhead," she said.

Three days after *Gone With the Wind* spoof aired, Lucille appeared on *The Flip Wilson Show* on NBC with fellow guests, The Osmond Brothers, and talk show host Ed Sullivan.

In spite of his dour personality, Sullivan had been a distant friend of Lucille for many years. But when he showed up on the set, she sensed that something was terribly wrong with him. He was showing signs of early Alzheimer's Disease.

In one skit, Lucille played "Lucy," the comic strip character in the cartoon *Peanuts.* In another skit, the high point of the show, she was a man-crazed carhop working in the drive-in restaurant with "Geraldine," Flip's drag persona.

From 1970 to 1974, *The Flip Wilson Show* was the second-highest-rated show on TV. He became the first African-American to host a hit TV variety show. Putting his picture on its cover, *Time Magazine* named him "Television's First Black Superstar."

His Geraldine, performed in drag, was hailed as one of the great comic characters ever seen. Because of his brilliant impersonation of a woman, Flip was rumored to be gay. Perhaps he was, at least during off moments, although he did marry twice—first to "Peaches" Dean and later to "Cookie" MacKenzie.

On his variety show, he featured many black artists, notably Redd

Foxx, The Supremes, and The Jackson Five. His most famous laugh line was, "The Devil made me do it."

Displayed above is a CBS Press photo for *The Odd Couple*.

Left, **Jack Klugman** overwhelms (right) **Tony Randall** with cigar smoke as part of their artful and deliberate mis-matching.

***

For her next episode on September 20, Lucille teamed with guest star Tony Randall in a telecast, *Lucy and the Mountain Climber,* one of her lesser efforts.

He had heard that she was difficult to work with, but he later claimed, "I didn't mind being bossed around by her, because she knew what she was doing."

The silly plot cast Randall as her partner in an employment agency. Somehow, the script gets around to having them compete in a mountain-climbing contest.

Randall shunned personal publicity, telling her, "The public needs to know only one thing about me. I don't smoke."

He told her that a frontal nude, for which he'd posed when he was a young man, was being circulated in the underground gay world.

Before working with Lucille, the Tulsa-born actor became a household name when he appeared as the "fuss budget" Felix Unger in *The Odd Couple,* a hit TV sitcom. In a career spanning six decades, he'd receive six Golden Globe nominations and six Primetime Emmy Award nods, winning only one.

In 1938, Randall married his high school sweetheart, Florence Gibbs, a union that lasted until his death in 1992. He remarried in 1995 when he was 75 years old, his wife only 25. However, he never escaped the gossipy rumors that he was a closeted gay. Lucille felt he was trying to conceal his homosexuality by attacking gay people.

One TV critic claimed that Randall always played it gay, most definitely as Felix Unger in *The Odd Couple*. "If Felix isn't a gay man, I don't know who is. Those prissy characters he played were a 1950s and 60s version of Edward Everett Horton or Franklin Pangborn, most definitely Clifton Webb. In fact, Randall was following in Webb's footsteps. Webb lusted after that beautiful Robert Wagner, and Randall went for that handsome hunk with the super-sized dick, Rock Hudson."

***

Kaye Ballard had remained friends with both Desi and Lucille even after their divorce. She was closer to him than his former wife because he had cast her in the hit TV sitcom, *The Mothers-in-Law* (1967-1969), starring

Eve Arden, more famous for *Our Miss Brooks.*

After a phone call from Lucille, Ballard agreed to appear on a September 27 telecast, *Lucy and Harry's Italian Bombshell.*

Ballard played Donna, Harry's long-lost girlfriend back during World War II. She is coming for a visit, and Harry works out at the gym, trying to get into shape, since he no longer looks like the soldier she used to know. And according to the script, she no longer looks like a late 1950s version of Sophia Loren.

Early in Ballard's first day on the set, Gary Morton gave her the bad news: For her role, she would have to be padded. *[Evidently, the once svelt and successfully seductive character of Donna had eaten a lot of pasta over the years, and the director wanted Ballard's waistline to show it.]* At first, Ballard refused the extra padding, until Lucille managed to cajole her into appearing as a relatively dumpy middle-aged woman.

After the telecast, Ballard received "a ton of mail," both from her fans and from her friends. Many assumed that she was pregnant; others that she had not dieted in years. Still others feared she might be ill. "You looked really bad," wrote Bob Pearle of Tampa, Florida. "Just plain gross."

Ballard claimed that she never watched the telecast. "I could not look at myself on that small screen. I just couldn't."

***

Lucille had long admired the acting talent and physical appeal of Mike Connors, watching him on every episode she could of his hit TV crime drama, *Mannix* (1967-1975), in which he played a hard-hitting private investigator.

During her comedic heyday, **Kaye Ballard** (left) appears with **Jane Powell** (right) in *The Girl Most Likely* (1958).

Desi Arnaz Sr., her producer for *The Mothers-in-Law*, claimed, "Kaye Ballard, that great old dyke, was always good for a laugh."

Lucille bonded with **Mike Connors**, who told her that early in his show-biz career, he'd been known to producers and casting directors as "Touch" Connors (a name he hated) because of his skill as a basketball player. Years later, he ruefully told Lucille, "I fear a lot of horny women and gay men took that name too literally."

Connors and the character he played (Joe Mannix, in a series developed by Lucille Ball at Desilu) was an Armenian-American. He spoke Armenian and in some of his episodes, he quoted (translated) Armenian proverbs.

She ordered scriptwriters Bob Carroll Jr. and Madelyn Davis, to create a script called *Lucy and Mannix Held Hostage.*

Fearing that Lucy is in trouble because she spotted bank robbers in the act committing a crime, Harry (Gordon) assigns her a bodyguard. Regrettably, when Connors, cast as "Joe," arrives at her home, she thinks he is one of the robbers and knocks him out. The real bandits show up and kidnap the pair, intent on doing them harm.

The episode telecast on October 4 was significant in her life, not only for her getting to co-star with Connors, whom she defined as "my kind of man," but because it was the first episode of *Here's Lucy* shot on the Universal lot. She had moved to the new studio from Paramount.

The men at Universal gave Lucille a grand welcome to her new grounds, even naming a roadway "Lucy Lane." Her dressing room was her most elegant yet, and it had been beautifully decorated. She was assigned a personal hair stylist, makeup artist, and wardrobe mistress.

She had not seen any of his early movies except one, and that was a soapy drama called *Where Love Has Gone* (1964), starring Susan Hayward and Bette Davis. It was based loosely on the real-life story of the murder of gangster Johnny Stompanato within the home of Lana Turner.

Connors always credited Gary Morton and Lucille for getting him his hit role in *Mannix.* One day, he'd parked his antique automobile right in front of Morton's office. *[Morton shared Connors' love of vintage cars and emerged from his office to inspect it.]* He met Connors and invited him for lunch in the commissary. He soon realized that the actor might be ideal as the character of Mannix and managed to get him cast in the series as its focal point.

The first season had gone poorly, with fairly low ratings. As such, CBS planned to drop it from their lineup of the following season. But Lucille still had a lot of power at CBS, and she prevailed on studio executives to let *Mannix* remain for a second season. She was right: After that, the series took off and became a big hit, staying on the air for the next eight years.

During her time co-starring with Conners, she confided to him, "If I were twenty years younger, you'd have landed on my casting couch."

***

On October 25, *Someone's on the Ski Lift with Dinah* was telecast. In it, Lucille was teamed with her longtime friend, the singing sweetheart, Dinah Shore, who had risen to fame during World War II as a Big Band singer.

In this episode, she was the spark that saved the telecast, especially when she sang, "Don't Let the Good Life Pass You By."

After the first rehearsal, Lucille lunched with Dinah, telling her, "I almost cried when I heard that song, since I fear it reflects my own life today."

"That's how I felt, too, when George Montgomery divorced me in 1962. We had met during the war, back in 1938, when I had to steal him from Hedy Lamarr. As you know, she was stiff competition, having been voted the most beautiful girl in the world."

"George was a most desirable man, but life went on. When he started sleeping around, I, too, did the same. In the 1950s, I had this secret affair with Frank Sinatra that lasted on and off for several years."

Lucille was aware that in the late 1960s, in the wake of her divorce, Dinah had sustained a brief marriage to Maurice F. Smith before ending up in the bed of comedian Dick Martin, singer Eddie Fisher, and actor Rod Taylor.

In the early 1970s, she'd begun a highly publicized affair with Burt Reynolds, twenty years her junior.

In the script by Bob Carroll Jr. and Madelyn Davis, Harry (Gale Gordon) takes Lucille and her daughter for a vacation at Snowmass, Colorado, near Aspen. They stay at the lodge where Dinah is also in residence. At one point, Lucy gets trapped on the ski lift with her.

Ever since she'd become a famous singing star, Lucille had followed Dinah's career and had collected her recordings. Her favorite songs were, "Baby, It's Cold Outside," "Shoo-Fly Pie and Apple Pan Dowdy," and "Buttons and Bows."

The love affair of **Dinah Shore**, an older woman, with a younger man, **Burt Reynolds**, became one of the most widely publicized romances of its day.

Here, they appear together on the April 1972 edition of *Photoplay*.

Reynold's statement replicated in the headline ("I'll never let her go") was a lie: He eventually dumped her for Sally Field.

Gossipy Lucille was eager to know the details of Dinah's affair with Burt Reynolds, who was on his way to becoming the leading box office star in America. The unlikely romance with Dinah would last for four years, as extensively documented in Blood Moon's biography, *Burt Reynolds, Put the Pedal to the Medal: How a Nude Centerfold Sex Symbol Seduced Hollywood*.

Little could Lucille imagine that after Reynolds dumped Dinah, he would take up with both Lorna Luft, the daughter of Sid Luft and Judy Garland, and her own Lucie Arnaz.

Because her last name began with an "A," Lucie leads the list that author Mart Martin compiled as an archive of movie star seductions.

Names that followed Lucie's on Martin's notorious list included Adrienne Barbeau, Kim Basinger, Candice Bergen, Catherine Deneuve, Lesley-Anne Down, Chris Evert, Farrah Fawcett, Marilu Henner, Lauren Hutton, Madeline Kahn, Sarah Miles, Florida cocktail waitress Pam Seals, Cybill Shepherd, Mamie Van Doren, and Tammy Wynette. "I was dating high on the hog when I had a brief fling with Elizabeth Taylor," Reynolds said.

Sally Field, whom he later defined as "the love of my life," lay in his future.

Dolly Parton, with whom Reynolds made *The Best Little Whorehouse in Texas*, was also on the list. But she later claimed, "Burt and I were too much alike to get involved. We both wear wigs and high heels, and we both have a roll around the middle."

The English actress, Sarah Miles, later reflected on Reynolds and her involvement with him: "A toupee and lifts—the man is an imposter."

***

A rather ridiculous pilot, *Lucy and the Celebrities*, telecast on November 8, teamed her with Rich Little and Jack Benny. She and Benny had known each other for years, and had worked together, not always successfully. This time around he told her that he would be his own director and would "not take any marching orders from you."

In the episode, Kim (Lucie Arnaz) is dating the impressionist Little, nicknamed "The Man of a Thousand Voices."

Lucy's boss, Harry (Gale Gordon), orders her to round up a list of celebrities for his agency so that he can compete with a rival employment agency.

She does not succeed but comes up with a scheme she hopes will fool Harry. She persuades Little to talk to Harry on the phone, his voice disguised as ones belonging to various celebrities.

It seemed that Little could impersonate anybody, be it Jackie Gleason, Rudy Vallee, James Mason, Ed Sullivan, Mike Douglas, and others. He was noted for his impressions of Richard Nixon, even acting out his impersonations in front of him. "The President didn't realize I was imitating him, and he wondered why I was talking in 'such a funny voice.'"

After the telecast, Lucille invited Benny and Little for dinner. Over the meal, Benny told him, "With Bob Hope doing my walk and you doing my voice, I can be a star and do nothing."

***

Rich Little appears above in a 1976 publicity shot for *Hawaii-5-0*.

In the episode of *Here's Lucy* in which he was featured, the script made clear that Kim (played by Lucie Arnaz) was romantically involved with the character he played.

"In my private life," Lucie said, "my mother objected to me dating older men. But in that TV series, Lucy, as the mother of Kim, the character I played, uttered no protest with my on-screen involvement with Rich."

"Gee!" Lucie was quoted as saying. "Rich Little is so much older than me. How come mother didn't mind that age difference on TV?"

This episode also marked the fourth time that Jack Benny made an appearance on one of her shows. But as was her custom, Lucille approached him, somewhat "disconnectively" as if it were for the first time.

For a November 15 telecast, *Ginger Rogers Comes to Tea*, Lucille and the fabled movie star had a reunion. They had known each other since the late

1930s when Rogers was known as "The Queen of RKO," a studio Lucille would later purchase in the 1950s. But back then, Lucille was only an extra in some of those Astaire/Rogers movies such as *Top Hat* (1935).

It was also during the late 1930s that Rogers had an affair with a young bandleader named Desi Arnaz.

The plot for the *Here's Lucy* episode was thin. In disguise, the star attends the Ginger Rogers Festival, but departs early, leaving her purse behind.

The next day, Lucy calls and invites her to her home for tea, where she can retrieve her purse.

Rogers did not enjoy working on the episode because it was "rush, rush, rush," as Lucille feared a union strike. Based on a tight schedule, she was hustled through the episode in ways she found annoying. There was no talk between the women of her former seduction of Lucille's future husband.

"It was work, work, work, with no time off," Rogers complained. "We hardly had time to rehearse the dance routine. Where's Fred Astaire now, when I need him?

***

Near the end of 1971, Lucille made two appearances with David Frost, the English TV host, journalist, comedian, and writer. She had been impressed with him since she'd first seen him on the satirical TV program, *That Was the Week that Was* in 1962.

A skilled interviewer, he, in time, grilled eight English prime ministers and seven American presidents, most notably Richard Nixon. When Lucille co-starred with him, he was engaged to the African American actress, Diahann Carroll.

Lucille had read many glowing tributes to Frost. Prime Minister David Cameron said, "He could be—and certainly was with me—both a friend and a fearsome interviewer." Since he was so versatile, Frost often was labeled "Television's Renaissance Man."

Lucy Helps David Frost Go Night-Night was telecast on November 29. In

Although Lucille always considered the English talk show host, **David Frost**, a bit "frosty," she appeared several times with him on TV.

She popped up on his American talk show (on the air from 1969 to 1972), and again on his TV variety show (1971 to 1973).

Lucille had heard about Frost's affair with Diahann Carroll and, like everyone else in Hollywood, she was aware of the punitive interracial trauma faced by Sammy Davis Jr. during his marriage to the Swedish actress May Britt. She had also followed the fury faced by Peter Lawford during his interracial liaison with Dorothy Dandridge.

Nervous, and trying to be funny, and with the brusque, jive humor for which she was increasingly well-known, Lucille said to Frost, "So you go in for black poontang."

He was not amused.

the plot, she is hired to accompany him on a flight from Los Angeles to London. Her job is to keep annoying fans from bothering him. Being Lucy, she ends up annoying the hell out of him.

For his appearance on *Here's Lucy,* she agreed to be a guest on *The David Frost Show,* which was telecast during the upcoming week. She didn't like the skits she'd been given, but, being a trouper, she worked hard to pull them off.

"David's budget must have been lean," she said. "Since the other guests were hardly on the A-list. The comedian, Jack Guilford, was the only known name. He was such a nice guy on TV or on the screen, but in person, he was a real jerk, making sarcastic remarks to me."

He asked her, "When are you going to think about retiring from all this Lucy shit? It's getting boring with all those recycled plots."

Lucille ended the rest of December of 1971 with four more episodes of *Here's Lucy* that she would rather forget. Each telecast seemed weaker than the one that preceded it, causing Gary Morton to wonder why she continued to employ Fred S. Fox as a scriptwriter.

"Want a dull script?" Morton asked. "Sign Fox. Even Bob Carroll and Madelyn Davis aren't what they used to be in the heyday of *I Love Lucy.* Many of their scripts today are tired, even boring. Sometimes, I feared there would be no Fifth Season, but there was."

In the meantime, Lucille had seven more episodes to complete in January and February of 1972 to bring the Fourth Season of *Here's Lucy* to its finale.

***

Continuing in his manifestation as a "Babe Magnet," Desi Jr. was seen around Hollywood with the actress Victoria Principal on his arm. Three

In the words of his mother, "My son was dating high on the hog. He even had a fling with **Victoria Principal**."

An image of **Desi Jr.** is "sandwiched" between two depictions of her, an actress who became famous in nine seasons of the long-running prime-time TV drama, *Dallas.*

The image on the right shows Principal on the cover of an issue of Hugh Hefner's *Playboy.*

years older than Desi, she could hardly qualify as one of the older women he'd tended to date.

She had an exotic background, having been born in Fukuoka, Japan, in 1950, where her father, Victor Rocco Principal, was a U.S. Air Force sergeant.

Based on his career in the military, he moved his family around a lot, anchoring in such different locales as Puerto Rico, London, Georgia, and Massachusetts.

At the age of five, Victoria was featured in TV commercials. Originally, she planned to study medicine, but her schooling was temporarily halted when she was injured seriously in an accident wherein a car was piloted by a drunk driver who was, in the wake of being convicted for negligence, sent to prison.

After months of recovery, she moved to New York, where she planned to pursue acting. For a time, she also studied at the Royal Academy of Dramatic Art in London, but relocated to Los Angeles, with hopes of breaking into the film world.

Around the time that she was dating Desi, John Huston cast her in *The Life and Times of Judge Roy Beam* (1972), starring Paul Newman. For her performance, she earned a Golden Globe Award as "Most Promising Newcomer." After appearing in *The Naked Ape* the following year, she was featured nude in Hugh Hefner's *Playboy*.

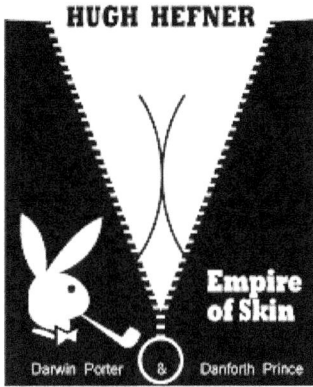

What was one of the most enduring after-effects of the eventful life of **Playboy's Hugh Hefne**r?

According to a biography published by Blood Moon Productions in 2018, it involved de-accelerating the shame factor of exposure in his magazine for dozens of mega-celebrities, including Victoria Principal.

For three years, she gave up acting to become a talent agent. After that, she returned to acting, this time on television, when she landed the role for which she is best known. She was cast as Pamela Barnes Ewing in CBS's primetime TV "soaper," *Dallas* (1978-1991). She would spend the next nine years of her life as Pamela, until she departed from the series in 1987.

The hit TV drama revolved around the affluent Texas family, the Ewings, oil tycoons and cattle ranchers. They were feuding and sworn enemies of another Texas family, the Barnes clan. The families were horrified when Pamela Barnes (Victoria) married one of the series' principal characters, Bobby Ewing (Patrick Duffy).

The show's principal character was J.R. Ewing, cast with Larry Hagman. His schemes and dirty business deals became the show's trademark. A cliffhanger, "Who Shot J.R.?" was the second-highest-rated prime time telecast ever.

Despite the intensity of their dating, it seemed that as a couple, Desi and Victoria were mere passing fancies. By the end of the 1970s, both of them would marry other people.

A multi-talented woman, Victoria also became a producer, entrepreneur, and author of books on beauty, skincare, fitness, and health.

Also in the early 1970s, Desi was seen dating Tina Sinatra, the daughter of Frank Sinatra and Nancy Barbato, who had divorced when Tina was only three years old. Born in 1948, Tina was five years older than Desi.

Like Victoria, she was also a woman of achievement, although she did not seem to want to be a singer like her sister Nancy or her father or her brother, Frank Jr. "We have enough singers in the family," she is reported to have said.

Around the time that Tina started dating Desi, she broke off, in January of 1972, her engagement to Robert Wagner, who had been married to Natalie Wood.

Two years later, Tina would marry the musician, Wes Farrel, at her father's apartment at Caesars Palace in Las Vegas. Their union survived only two years.

Upon the death of her father, Tina took control of his film and music legacy.

Her memoir, *My Father's Daughter,* was published in 2000. It seems that by then, Desi had devolved into only a footnote in her remarkable life.

***

By 1972, Lucille had become terrified of an "up-close-and-personal confrontation" with the "Big 6-0. As she told Gary Morton, "If I remember correctly, when I was born, a lot of American women were dying at the age of sixty. Men lived even less, perhaps expiring on average at the age of fifty-two.:"

She said she desperately needed and wanted a vacation, but had seven more episodes of *Here's Lucy* to complete before ending the Fourth Season for telecasts in January and February of 1972. It was determined that in this case, the Season would not extend until March or April, as it had in previous seasons.

Ever since the 1930s, Lucille had admired the stage and screen performance of Helen Hayes. She had become one of only sixteen performers to win an Oscar, a Grammy, an Emmy, and a Tony.

Born at the dawn of the 20th Century, Hayes had made her stage debut at the age of five at the Belasco Theatre on Lafayette Square, across from the White House.

As she grew into womanhood, she married playwright Charles MacArthur in 1928, a successful union that lasted until his death in 1956.

When he moved to Hollywood to write film scripts, she abandoned her stage life and went with him. There, producers were eager to cast her in feature films with some of Tinseltown's most famous male stars.

She made her sound debut in *The Sin of Madelon Claudet* (1931), for which she won an Academy Award as Best Actress.

She followed that by appearing in the screen adaptation of two more novels, beginning with Sinclair Lewis' *Arrowsmith* (1932), in which she portrayed the wife of physician Ronald Colman. That was followed in the same year by Ernest Hemingway's *A Farewell to Arms,* co-starring screen heartthrob Gary Cooper. Other roles included a leading part in *The White Sister* (1933) with Clark Gable.

Hayes later admitted that she never wanted to be a movie star, and by 1935, she was back on Broadway, cast in *Victoria Regina,* a role that immortalized her on stage as Queen Victoria. In that production, Vincent Price was cast as Prince Albert.

She competed with Katharine Cornell as "The First Lady of the American Theater." A critic wrote, "Cornell played every queen as if she were a woman, and Hayes played every woman as if she were a queen."

In the 1950s, Hayes was back in Hollywood appearing in *My Son John* (1952).

With Ingrid Bergman in *Anastasia* (1956), Hayes won another Oscar, this time for Best Supporting Actress. Lucille managed to get Hayes to sign for an episode of *Here's Lucy* at a strategic moment of her life. She co-starred with Lucille in *Lucy and the Little Old Lady,* telecast on January 3, 1972.

It was another of Fred S. Fox's silly plots and was hardly worthy of Hayes. She plays an elderly Irish lady who arrives at the employment agency run by Harry (Gordon) with Lucille employed as his secretary and receptionist. Hayes is impoverished and needs to sell some land in her native Ireland. The plot evolved into just who is swindling whom? A ridiculous and unbelievable *séance* was inserted into the plotline.

The question remained: Why would a legendary and distinguished actress like Helen Hayes accept such a stupid role? Right before appearing with Lucille, Hayes had been desperately ill. Her doctor diagnosed her with a violent allergy to stage dust, and declared that she'd no longer be able to work in the legitimate theater.

She was heartbroken to hear that diagnosis. Around this time, the offer to appear with Lucille emerged. "Why not?" Hayes asked her friends. "I was a movie star, a

In the upper photo, mega-diva **Helen Hayes,** as she appeared with **Gary Cooper** in *A Farewell to Arms* (1932). Coop later said, "Making love onscreen to Miss Hayes was like kissing my mother."

In the lower photo, Hayes appears at a theatrical dedication in 1982.

stage actress. Why not this new medium of television? No dust, please."

***

After two more lackluster episodes, a January 24, 1972 telecast, *Kim Moves Out,* spotlighted Lucie Arnaz. Those durable scriptwriters from *I Love Lucy,* Bob Carroll Jr. and Madelyn Davis, created the episode wherein Kim, now twenty, moves into her own apartment. She also has a boyfriend, Tim Matheson.

Kim wants to be free of her protective "mother hen" and chart a more independent life. However, in her apartment over a garage, she lives near her mother, who is reluctant to untie her from her apron strings.

As her beau, Matheson was already known to Lucille, since he had been cast in *Yours, Mine, and Ours* (1968), that family-friendly feature film she had made with Henry Fonda.

In his future, he would go on to carve out a career in television.

By this point, the backers of *Here's Lucy* realized that the very talented Lucie Arnaz might need to be showcased in roles that were more complex and more challenging.

ANCILLARY FAME

Lucie Arnaz, on the cover of the April 25, 1971 issue of *TV Week,* from around the time she appeared in *Kim Moves Out.*

The (barely legible) headline beside her photo announces, "Lucie Arnaz: She'll Stick with Lucy."

No one was surprised.

***

At last, Fred. S. Fox, aided by fellow scriptwriter Seaman Jacobs, came up with a good telecast, *Lucy's Punctured Romance* (February 20). Her guest star was Bob Cummings, cast as a handsome, good-looking bachelor who captures Lucy's amorous eye.

She didn't know Cummings well, and had last worked with him in 1959 in a skit, *Lucy Goes to Japan.*

In this current episode, Kim (Lucie) hears a rumor that Cummings is a boozer and entertains a lot of girlfriends. She schemes with Uncle Harry (Gale Gordon) to break up any burgeoning romance. The rumor they spread to the bachelors is that Lucy is actually "a drunk, a harlot, and a wench whose favorite food is hot peppers."

From 1955 through 1959, Cummings had his own hit TV sitcom, *The Bob Cummings Show,* in which he starred as a World War II pilot who becomes a professional photographer in civilian life after the war ends.

The actor reunited with Lucille during a troubled interlude in his private life. He was undergoing the ordeal of separating from his third wife, Mary Elliott, a former actress. She was accusing him of adultery and charging him with being a drug addict with fondness for methamphetamines, which caused him to lose control of himself during wild and often violent mood swings. She also alleged that he relied on astrologers and numerologists for financial decisions—often with fiscally disastrous results.

In 1972, the year he worked with Lucille, Cummings had ben charged with fraud for operating a pyramid scheme involving his company, Bob Cummings, Inc., which sold vitamins and food supplements. Although a health food advocate in public, he had allegedly been a drug addict since the mid-1950s.

He was also known for receiving regular injections from "Dr. Feelgood" (Max Jacobson), who had a lot of celebrity clients. He always lied about these injections, claiming they consisted only of "vitamins, sheep sperm, and monkey glands." In fact, these "feel good" shots contained a substantial amount of methamphetamines.

Lucille had learned from Betty Grable secrets about Cummings' closeted private life. He had co-starred with her in her last film, *How to Be Very, Very Popular* (1955).

Grable had also co-starred with Dan Dailey in a number of musicals for

AGE IS CRUEL, EVEN IF YOU'RE ALREADY POPULAR :

At the time (1955) that this saucy and frothy film was made, **Betty Grable,** once the most famous pinup girl of World War II, was considered a wee bit "over the hill." It was her last screen performance.

As such, the producers opted to focus heavily on the seductive allure of her "replacement," **Sheree North**, shown in her first leading role, as the right-hand figure in the *lower left* photo where she's being supported, along with Grable, by **Bob Cummings.**

As it turned out, movie audiences more readily related to Grable, who's shown with Cummings in the *lower right* photo.

Fox during the late 1940s. Lucille had met the dancer and actor when they had co-starred in a 1971 episode of *Here's Lucy* entitled *Won't You Calm Down, Dan Dailey?*

Grable claimed that during her working relationship with Dailey, since he liked to dress in drag, he had sometimes stolen (or "borrowed") her gowns. Grable also maintained that he and Bob Cummings had long sustained a secret homosexual affair.

"I learn something about people I know every day," Lucille told Gary Morton. "You work with them and think you know them, but you really don't. There are always surprises lurking in the background."

Before departing from Lucille, Cummings told her, "I've made dozens of films, from *Princess O'Rourke* in 1943 to *Dial M for Murder* in 1954, but I never felt I was particularly good in any of them. Hollywood producers never had the hots for me as an actor. I used to say to my estranged wife, Mary, that for me to get a role, some other actor who'd previously been cast had to suddenly take ill. Bill Holden, for example."

***

For a February 14 episode, *With Viv as a Friend, Who Needs an Enemy?*, Lucille reteamed with Vivian Vance, her co-star during the heyday of *I Love Lucy*. *The Hollywood Reporter* headlined it as LUCY RICARDO AND ETHEL MERTZ TOGETHER AGAIN.

In the plot by Carroll and Davis, Vance arrives from the East Coast, planning to relocate to California. Lucy invites her to move in with her, and then the trouble begins.

Once again, Harry (Gordon) fires Lucy and rehires Vance in her place. Based on a theme of "a friend who becomes a rival," the plot bubbled on.

The script evoked an old-time episode of *I Love Lucy*. Vance had made herself up to look glamourous, always struggling to escape the Ethel Mertz caricature.

Her appearance was misleading. During the months ahead, she would experience a minor stroke and undergo a mastectomy after being diagnosed with breast cancer.

This episode represented a footnote in television history, marking the last time Vance would appear as a regular on a Lucille Ball television production.

***

The Fourth Season of *Here's Lucy* had a most unusual ending, *Kim Finally Cuts You-Know-Who's Apron Strings*. Written by Bob Carroll and Madelyn Davis, it was telecast on February 21.

Instead of being a *Here's Lucy* episode starring Lucille herself, it featured Lucie Arnaz as a showcase of her burgeoning talent. As it turned out, it became a spin-off of *Here's Lucy*. Hopefully, the pilot would be picked up by a sponsor and go on the air in the autumn as *The Lucie Arnaz Show*.

The cast featured her co-star, Susan Tolsky, as well as actors Lloyd Battista and Alan Oppenheimer.

Now living in her own apartment, Lucie takes a roommate, Susan Tolsky. The apartment building is owned by a Mr. Oppenheimer, the brother of Lucy, who seems to keep an overly protective eye on Lucie. However, when an amorous race car driver (Battista) becomes too aggressive, she shows she can take care of herself by delivering a karate chop.

In the plot, Tolsky is so wacky she almost steals every scene she is in. As Lucy's brother—no mention was ever made of him before—Oppenheimer is rather undistinguished.

Two views of **Susan Tolsky**, part of a new generation of young *comediennes*, as she appeared (*right photo*) in 1973 and (*left photo*) in 1971.

Lucille was fast realizing that her time-tested (some said "running out of steam") *schtick* was facing stiff competition.

The role of the amorous race car driver could have been better cast, as Battista is anything but romantic.

Looking at the episode years later, Lucie remembered that she'd liked it the first time it was screened for her, but later, wiser and older, she viewed it as dreadful. She lamented, "I was Susan's straight man."

A Texan, Tolsky was born during the middle of World War II. Growing up, she planned a career in medicine, but in time, her career goal switched to acting, and she headed for Hollywood, where one can dream big.

Her first big break came when she was signed for *Here Comes the Bride,* a TV series that aired from 1968 to 1970 on ABC.

Right before working on the Lucie episode, Tolsky had appeared in the comedy mystery, *Pretty Maids All in a Row* (1971), cast as Miss Vraymire, the secretary to the character played by Rock Hudson.

The picture was directed by a Frenchman, Roger Vadim, who became famous for his love affairs (or marriages) to three of the most desirable women in the world, beginning with Brigitte Bardot and going on to Catherine Deneuve, once voted the most beautiful woman in the world. He was also to marry Jane Fonda.

Vadim's friends ranged from André Gide to Marlon Brando, from Frank Sinatra to Jeanne Moreau.

Battista was a minor actor, and he also wrote "Spaghetti Westerns." He had roles on and off Broadway, notably in *Sexual Perversity in Chicago.*

Oppenheimer was a voice, film, and stage actor, whose range could go from playing a Nazi in *Hogan's Heroes* to an Israeli agent in the other hit TV series, *Get Smart*. When he worked with Lucie, he also appeared that year in a feature film, *The Groundstar Conspiracy*.

In spite of Lucie's talent, the pilot failed to find a sponsor and was dropped. She would reappear on *Here's Lucy* for its Fifth Season after embarking on a medically disastrous vacation in Colorado with Lucille.

***

At the base of Snowmass Mountain, near Aspen, in Colorado, an emerging ski resort attracted Lucille as both a part-time resident and as an investor. At her age, she wasn't much of a skier, but she liked the fresh air and the sense of freedom there, where she could walk around shopping or getting her hair styled without being mobbed by fans.

She purchased three condos, each stacked on top of each other. Collectively, they'd provide ample room for her family on vacation. Her son and daughter could even invite their friends.

To furnish her condo, she had purchased the stage furnishings from her ill-fated Broadway musical, *Wildcat* (1960), after the end of its run.

After shooting the final episode of *Here's Lucy*, for the Fourth Season, she headed to Colorado with DeDe, her mother, Lucie, and Desi Jr., who was still dating Liza Minnelli at the time. She would regret that decision for the rest of her life.

Her husband, Gary Morton, didn't like ski resorts, preferring the golf courses of Palm Springs, so he remained behind.

Like a madcap episode from *I Love Lucy*, an accident seemed inevitable. One afternoon, she was standing with friends beside a ski slope when an out-of-control woman skier crashed into her. As Lucille recalled, "I could hear the cracking of my brittle bones. That damn bitch seemed to come out of nowhere to ruin my life."

As doctors later discovered, medics were called to the scene and carried Lucille down the slope to a waiting ambulance, its red dome lights flashing. To the sound of a siren, the vehicle took her wounded body to the local hospital, whose trained staff was familiar with skiers with broken arms and legs.

After an examination, he doctors determined that her right leg had been fractured in four different places, an injury referred to as a butterfly "spiral" or "shatter."

Lucie recalled that day, as she, Desi Jr., and Liza Minnelli followed her into the hospital. Lucille was screaming in pain. After she was anaesthetized, an operation was performed. When she regained consciousness, she found a plaster cast on her leg that stretched all the way to her waist.

She immediately burst into hysterical sobbing, telling her doctor, "I'm crying not just for myself, but this injury means I will put five hundred of my cast and crew out of work. I don't see how I can ever recover enough to appear on TV again."

In the days ahead, she admitted that the plaster cast was driving her mad. When no nurse or doctor was present, she grabbed the detachable handle used for raising and lowering her mattress and struck the cast several times, eliminating a quarter of it to allow herself more freedom of movement. "It was still living hell, but without the burning of fire."

Liza Minnelli with Desi Jr. arrived with an energy drink (in this case, a mixture of orange juice, coconut milk, and bananas) for Lucille. Liza assured Lucille that the drink would also prevent hair loss. In no time at all, the concoction became Lucille's favorite drink for life.

After the plaster cast was removed, four pins were surgically implanted in her legs, allowing her to walk slightly, although she would still need a brace.

Gary Morton had flown to her side and, after three weeks, he transferred her to Palm Springs, where she could rest and recover, at least partially. She knew she would never regain her old mobility—in fact, when she first arrived at the desert resort, she thought she would never appear on television again.

After several weeks, a decision was made that she would continue with a Fifth Season of *Here's Lucy,* but with a difference. In the coming months, she would appear in a wheelchair, and her skiing accident would be woven into the plot. That meant that her creative people, notably Bob Carroll Jr. and Madelyn Davis, would have to toss out the old scripts and write new ones. In the upcoming season, Lucie would play a greater role, the slapstick scenes so familiar to Lucy fans being assigned instead to her daughter.

It was agreed that in the upcoming series, "I would allow myself to age a bit. After all, time was marching on for Lucy Ricardo."

Although Lucille might have had qualms about **Jim Bailey's** motives *vis-à-vis* her daughter, Lucie, she found his cross-dressing impersonation skill breathtaking.

Top row, left to right, shows Bailey imitatiing **Phyllis Diller** and **Judy Garland**. *Upper row, right photo*, shows **Liza Minnelli** with Bailey as he imitates her mother, Judy Garland, once again, with an almost eerie accuracy.

Lower photo shows "the real" Jim Bailey with "the real" Phyllis Diller, mugging for the camera and self-satirizing.

***

After divorcing her gay husband, Peter Allen, Liza Minnelli had had a brief fling with Jim Bailey, the famous female impersonator. That fizzled soon enough when she'd turned to Desi Jr.

To Lucille's surprise, she soon learned that her daughter, Lucie, was also dating Bailey. She had taken up with him during the dying stages of her marriage to Phil Vandervort. It is said that she began her relationship with Bailey after she and Vandervort attended a performance of his act at the Century Plaza Hotel. After the show, she and her estranged spouse had an argument, and he stormed off. She remained behind and was seen departing from the showroom that night with Bailey.

Lucille admired Bailey and was awed by his talent, but she found it hard to believe that her daughter would take up with a man who wore heavy makeup, female wigs, and gowns. She reasoned that Judy Garland must have felt somewhat the same emotions when Liza had dated Bailey.

She especially admired his impersonation of Phyllis Diller and Garland herself, although he was equally adept at his "illusions" of Peggy Lee and Barbra Streisand.

One night at the Riviera Hotel in Las Vegas, the showroom began to oddly resemble a Ball family reunion. Lucille showed up with Gary Morton, Morton's cousin, Sid Gould and his wife, Vanda Barra (who had become a regular on *Here's Lucy*), and Lucie, who was accompanied with Jim Bailey.

In the casino, it became quickly obvious that it was Lucille's lucky night, as again and again she emerged as a winner. Ironically, when a Keno ticket stuck to her shoe, she cashed it in for $3,000.

After her divorce from Vandervort, Lucie and Bailey began seeing each other frequently. To her, it was somewhat of an amusing diversion in the wake of the failure of her marriage. She found him charming, witty, and always amusing.

"There is not big romance," she was quoted as saying. "At least not what the tabloids are suggesting."

Lucille feared that Bailey was dating Lucie for the publicity value such a union generated. She wanted to put a stop to it.

Coincidentally, Bailey, also a stage performer, toured in summer stock, performing with Gale Storm in *Wildcat*, a reprise of the Broadway musical in which Lucille had starred in 1960 with Keith Andes.

Bailey became quite a familiar face on television, appearing on shows hosted by Dean Martin. Carol Burnett, Joan Rivers, David Letterman, Mike Douglas, and Merv Griffin.

Lucille heard gossip, never really knowing whether it was true or not. But Lucie, glamorously attired in a gown, was seen dating Bailey, who was wearing heavy makeup, a wig, and a glamorous gown too.

***

Lucille had been signed to appear in the feature film, *Mame,* set for release in 1974, but since she had broken her leg, she could not do the picture. Amazingly, its producers agreed to postpone shooting for a year until she was more fully recovered.

After much self-styled "soul searching," she signed for the Fifth Season of *Here's Lucy* (1972-73). Ratings were still high enough to keep it on the air, although hardly what they used to be.

She kept Morton as her executive producer; her cousin Cleo Smith as producer; Goby Ruskin as the main director. *["He knows how to take orders from the boss," she claimed.]* Regulars again included the ever-faithful Gale Gordon, Lucie Arnaz, and Mary Jane Croft. Sid Gould and his wife, Vanda Barra, would appear in several episodes, as would Lucille's friend, Mary Wickes.

In the plot by Bob Carroll Jr. and Madelyn Davis, Lucy is in the hospital recovering from a broken leg, the result of a ski accident. Here, the fictional episode resembled reality.

She is visited by her loving family. When they are away, a handsome doctor visits a patient in the adjoining bed, and Lucy's scheme begins.

> **HERE'S LUCY**
> Starring
> Lucille Ball
> Co-Starring
> **Season 5**
>
> **MORE LUCY!! BECAUSE WE WANT LUCY!**
>
> Although by now **Lucille Ball**'s *shticks* and *spiels* were a bit tired, and although she needed more aggressive prepping from studio makeup artists, she still looked pulled together, well-preserved, and at the appropriate, carefully choreographed moments, oh so very glam.

The role of the doctor went to Lloyd Bridges, a native son of California, who was only two years younger than Lucille. For many decades, she had considered him one of the most ruggedly handsome and most macho film stars in Hollywood. "He comes onto the screen and I swoon," she told Croft.

Over the course of his career, Bridges would star in some 150 feature films, even having a small role in Gary Cooper's *High Noon* (1952).

Over lunch with Lucille, they shared memories of how hard it had been to rise to stardom. "When I started out," Bridges confessed, "I didn't have enough of a mature look to become a leading man. One director told me I was too broad in the shoulders, yet too much like a kid. At Columbia, the boss, Harry Cohn, paid me no attention. He focused on beautiful dames. All the roles I wanted went to William Holden or Glenn Ford. I drifted from one B picture to another."

"Tell me about it," Lucille responded, with irony. "At RKO, I was called the Queen of the B's. I even did a *Three Stooges* short, and sometimes I'd be in two or three films in just one week. Call it tough sledding."

After his stint in the Coast Guard during World War II, Bridges returned to Hollywood, where his career began to improve. "One of my best roles was in *The Goddess* (1958), starring Kim Stanley and based on the life of Marilyn Monroe. I played a character obviously based on Joe DiMaggio."

Like Lucille, he, too, drifted into television with *The Lloyd Bridges Show* (1962-1963). "That series was special to me because it also starred my two sons, both Beau and Jeff, who also wanted to be actors."

"The biggest mistake of my career was turning down the role of Captain Kirk on *Star Trek*," Bridges said. "That lucky shit, William Shatner, eagerly accepted my reject, and the rest is history. To be in a comedy scene with Lucy is a rare detour for me."

"Any stunts," she told Ruskin, "will have to be performed by either Lucie or Mary Jane. Also, in my condition, it would be too harsh for Harry (Gordon) to yell at me. Make him more sympathetic for this season."

The series marked the farewell of her long-time script doctor, Milt Josefsberg.

Lucy's Big Break was telecast on September 11, 1972, marking the debut of the season.

She was surprised to see Desi Sr. show up unannounced. The year had been hard on his body, and she was shocked by his appearance. He looked puffy and ill and had undergone a colostomy. No longer was he the sexy Cuban bandleader of the late 1930s when he had seduced such screen legends as Betty Grable, Lana Turner, and Ginger Rogers.

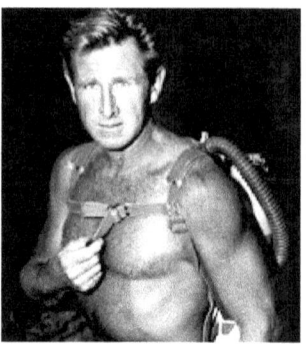

Lloyd Bridges strapping on his equipment in *Sea Hunt*.

The patriarch of an acting family, Bridges' real stardom did not come until the advent of TV.

Lucille said, "American housewives would be far more content with their husbands if all of them looked like Lloyd Bridges and were as well-equipped, if you get my drift."

He was still smoking four packages of cigarettes a day, but she could not fault him for that, since she was doing the same. Behind their backs, Ruskin called them "the smokestacks."

Over a break in rehearsals, Desi said to Lucille, "Remember sometime back in the early 1960s, I told you I wanted to retire and just grow old and fat. Well, I sure have achieved that goal. My days are either spent at the racetrack or spent doing nothing. "

"Except gambling," she interjected.

Watching her as she worked, he was all too aware of how bossy and controlling she had become, more so than ever. She didn't suggest: Instead, she barked orders and expected everyone to obey.

Over lunch, she shared her concerns about their son and daughter, finding their love lives objectionable to her. She feared that Desi Jr. was still into heavy drinking and drug taking. "You should talk to him. After all, he is your son."

Before leaving that afternoon, he told her, "I'm growing a bit tired of being television's forgotten man. Some people still think my real name is Ricky Ricardo. I'm thinking about making a possible comeback of some sort. I haven't decided yet."

"I wish you luck, Cubano," she said before turning away, as Morton approached to drive her home.

It front of Desi, she turned to Morton. "You remember Ricky Ricardo, don't you? In case you forgot, he was in that *I Love Lucy* series with me back in the 1950s."

"Oh yes, I remember you," Morton said. "You're Lucy's ex-wife."

As Desi turned to leave, he said, "If I were in better shape, a remark like that, even as a joke, would get you a bloody nose."

***

For her next episode, *Lucy and Eva Gabor Are Hospital Roomies,* she teamed with one of the glamourous Gabor Sisters, with co-stars Mary Wickes and Vanda Barra. The Hungarian star is in the hospital being treated for a broken foot, and gets huge amounts of rapt attention from the medical staff, who seem to ignore Lucy, who's laid up with a far more serious leg injury.

Lucille always found Eva amusing and easier to talk to than her more self-enchanted sister, Zsa Zsa Gabor. Lucille confessed to Eva that during the making of the picture, *Lured* (1947), she had an affair with Zsa Zsa's third husband, George Sanders, whom she had married after her divorce from hotel tycoon Conrad Hilton.

Eva, who would marry five times, admitted that her affairs with stars "are just a thimble compared to Zsa Zsa. My alltime champ in my bed was Glenn Ford, who's at the top of the list, followed by Frank Sinatra, John Hodiak, and Tyrone Power. Ty was the most beautiful."

"As for marriage, it is too interesting an experiment to be tried only once or twice. All a girl needs is simple black velvet and diamonds."

"I hear you are often mistaken for Zsa Zsa," Lucille said.

"That's true. Once, I was caught swimming in the nude late at night at the Beverly Hilton. When two men spotted me, one of them called out, 'Hi,

Although she was charming—some said "devastatingly so"— **Eva Gabor** was only one of three spectacularly alluring sisters.

Collectively known as "The Mad Hungarian Bombshells," they took the marriage chapels and divorce courts of California by storm.

A profile of **Eva**, the youngest of the three, appears in the inset photo, above.

She also appears on the left in the background shot, where she's *kibbutzing* with her sisters in a later-in-life reunion in Vienna.

The center figure is **Magda** (reputedly "The Countess of Warsaw"), who died the richest of the three in Palm Springs in 1997.

On the right is **Zsa Zsa**, our personal favorite, a name permeated with glamour, scandal, and a vivid sense of the courtship rituals of the glittering Old Europe from which she derived.

Eva!'"

"As I emerged from the pool, stark naked, and raced for my bath towel, I yelled back, 'No, *dah-link*, it's Zsa Zsa!'"

***

Two views of **Joe Namath**.

Upper photo: during his spectacular career with the New York Jets, and *(lower photo)* with **Desi Arnaz Jr.** on *Here's Lucy.*

After Eva Gabor, Lucille's next two episodes of *Here's Lucy* had no stars, only the familiar faces of Sid Gould and Vanda Barra, and Nielsen ratings fell off. For her next episode, she ordered Morton, "Let's Get Broadway Joe. We need some star power."

She used this nickname of footballer Joe Namath, the celebrated quarterback, "babe magnet," sex symbol, and celebrity athlete in both the American Football League (AFL) and National Football League (NFL). The peak of his fame as an athlete came when he starred with the *New York Jets*.

Lucille was not that interested in football but was impressed with Namath's celebrity status and his brash personality that in a way evoked Desi Arnaz Sr. of long ago.

She was delighted when Morton told her that Namath had accepted her invitation to be her co-star in *Lucy and Joe Namath* telecast on October 9.

At the time she hooked up with him, he had starred in *The Joe Namath Show* on TV in 1969. He had also appeared in a movie with Ann-Margret, *C.C. and Company* (1971). There were rumors, only rumors, of an affair.

He'd also made a guest appearance on *The Flip Wilson Show,* later saying, "I think Geraldine, Wilson's drag persona, actually wanted to take me to bed. He'd also been seen on such TV hits as *The Brady Bunch, The Dean Martin Show,* and *The Sonny & Cher Comedy Hour.*

At the time he came together with Lucille, he was yet to marry, but was alleged to have two or three affairs every week. At first, she thought, "Joe must be a terror in bed," but later wondered if that were true. At a party, singer Janis Joplin told her, "I've been to bed with both Joe Namath and Dick Cavett. Cavett is the better lover."

After his Super Bowl triumph in 1969, Namath opened Bachelors III, a night club on the Upper East Side of Manhattan. It was patronized by leading figures in the football world, movie stars, Broadway actors, even political figures. It also became rather notorious for attracting Mafia dons.

Lucille showed up one night with Frank Sinatra ("and some blonde"),

Sammy Davis Jr., and her husband, Gary Morton.

Namath's involvement in the club had a short life span. Because of the unsavory reputation of the club, NFL Commissioner (1960-89) Pete Roselle urged Namath to divest his financial interest in the night spot. When he refused, Namath, in tears, went on the air, announcing his retirement from football, shocking his fans.

He later recanted and sold his interest in Bachelor III, returning to the New York Jets, signing for the 1969-1970 season.

Before the next season and right before co-starring with Lucille, he once again threatened to retire from sports.

In an article in *New York Magazine,* a critic wrote, "Joe's retirement has become shallow and predictable. He claims he doesn't want to report to training camp, fearing bodily injury. Perhaps he can't retire because he needs the money since he made poor financial investments."

To TV audiences, he also became known—some claimed "notorious"—for his TV commercials. He surprised the women of America when he endorsed—and wore—Hanes Beautymist Pantyhose.

Among other products, he appeared in a commercial hyping Noxzema shaving cream. Shaving him was the future blonde-haired star, Farrah Fawcett, then an unknown. Again, there were unconfirmed rumors of an affair.

In *Lucy and Joe Namath,* telecast on October 9, Desi Jr. returned to the series after a long absence. He resumed his screen role as her TV son, Craig Carter, but he'd been away so long, some new viewers didn't even know that the character Lucy had been playing even had a TV son.

In real life, Desi Jr. was an expert tennis player, and he looked trim and firm on the court. He tells his mother that he wants to become a footballer, but she fears it is such a dangerous sport that he might injure himself. Namath is called in to get Lucy to change her mind.

***

Lucille had first seen comedian Totie Fields perform on *The Carol Burnett Show* in

Front and back of **Totie Field's** comic classic, *Totie Fields Live*.

Post-mortem, Totie and her *schtick* were reviewed by (online critic) Max Sparber as: "An oversized Las Vegas comic whose routines mostly dealt with her weight and the unliklihood of her fame."

At the peak of her success (and weight), she might have evoked a fat guy in drag. Alas, after she lost a large amount of weight as a means of calibrating her diabetes, some of her fans loudly asserted that she was no longer funny.

1971, and she urged Morton to book her for an upcoming telecast (October 23), *Lucy and the Other Woman.*

Fred S. Fox fashioned the somewhat lean plot wherein Lucy receives threats from the wife of her milkman, who thinks her husband is having an affair with Mrs. Carter. When Lucille read the script, she said, "I get it. The milkman is suspected of delivering the cream in more ways than one."

When the wife, played by the rather plump Totie Fields, confronts Lucy, she finds her very insecure. She convinces her that her husband is devoted to her and doesn't stray. It all ends well.

An almost forgotten figure today, Totie Fields became familiar to TV audiences in the 1960s and '70s, ever since she made her first appearance on *The Ed Sullivan Show.* Other TV hosts took notice of her comic talent, and she was booked by Johnny Carson, Merv Griffin, and Mike Douglas. She also became a regular guest on TV game shows such as *Hollywood Squares.*

In later years, Lucille would learn of the comedian's health problems. Among other ailments, she had a severe case of diabetes. Eventually, she had to have a leg amputated above the knee.

As she began to lose weight, she announced on TV one night, "I've waited all my life to say this, but now I weigh less than Elizabeth Taylor."

She even wrote a humorous "weight loss" book entitled *I Think I'll Start on Monday: The Official 8 ½ Oz. Mashed Potato Diet.*

A friend to both Lucille and Fields, Van Johnson claimed, "Totie isn't funny any more, now that she's lost weight."

In 1978, during the closing months of her life, Fields won awards from the American Guild of Variety Artists, which gave her two honors: "Female Comedy Star of the Year," and even more impressive, "Entertainer of the Year."

When Lucille learned of her death in Las Vegas, at the age of 48, she was saddened. Years before, she had to reject her request to become a regular co-star on *Here's Lucy.* "I could become your Ethel Mertz of the 1970s."

That, of course, never happened.

***

In general, Lucille liked the script of her frequent writer, Bob O'Brien, although he often recycled tired themes from previous episodes. Such was the case when he wrote *Lucy and Petula Clark* (October 30).

In this script, Lucy is hired by a pregnant Clark, who's in town to make a recording. As in previous episodes, Lucy becomes more and more of an annoyance than a help to the celebrated singer, actress, and composer.

In spite of its weak script, Clark rescues it when she sings. Her voice is at home in several languages, including French and Spanish.

Lucille wasn't the only star bidding for an appearance with Clark, as she was also sought by other hosts such as Ed Sullivan and Dean Martin. The singer had also revived her screen career by starring opposite Fred Astaire in *Finian's Rainbow* (1968) and co-starring with Peter O'Toole in a remake of *Goodbye Mr. Chips* (1969).

Weeks after working with Clark, Lucille encountered her at a party. She told Lucille that she and another singer, Karen Carpenter, had gone to Las Vegas to hear a performance by Elvis Presley.

"He flirted with us," she said, "when we went backstage to his dressing room. He said, 'Wow! Here I am in my jockey shorts with the two biggest girl pop stars in the country.'"

Although she didn't say so, Lucille interpreted the anecdote as Presley wanting a three-way.

"I never got a chance to go to bed with Elvis," Lucille lamented. "Just one of the many things I've missed out on in life."

Although his romance (or whatever it was) with Lucie Arnaz had cooled, Jim Bailey came back into Lucille's life to shoot a November 6 telecast, *Lucy and Jim Bailey*. In it, even Sam Yorty, the mayor of Los Angeles, made a cameo appearance. Scriptwriter Bob O'Brien was still in Lucille's favor, and he was tapped to come up with a coherent and believable plot.

The only high point of *Lucy and Petula Clark* was the singer herself. The script she was instructed to follow was staid, old, and recycled.

In January of 1965, **Petula Clark** scored her alltime biggest hit, "Downtown," selling three million copies and peaking at No. One in the nation. She followed that with other hits such as "My Love" and "Don't Sleep in the Subway."

Lucy Carter wins an agreement with comedian Phyllis Diller to appear at a charity benefit for the local Chamber of Commerce. However, at the last minute, she comes down with an attack of laryngitis.

Behind her mother's back, Lucie Arnaz, cast again as Kim, gets Bailey to fill in for Diller. Brilliantly imitating the mannerisms of Diller herself, Bailey fools most people in the audience, including Lucy, who thinks it is the comedienne herself.

When Lucy learns it is really a female impersonator (Bailey) performing on stage instead of the real Phyllis Diller, she says, "Jim does a better impression of Phyllis than she does of herself."

Lucie Arnaz seemed to dismiss all the "tabloid fodder" about a hot romance between Bailey and herself. "I made an attempt, but it just didn't happen. He is a very talented and amusing companion, and that was all it was. Even my mother liked him."

[Lucille did, however, tell her daughter that during her long career of dating many men, she had never gone out with one in drag.]

In a strange coincidence, before the show, Bailey had developed a case of laryngitis, and soon, Lucille learned that he, too, would not be able to go on. She called her doctor, and the two of them rushed to Bailey's aid to try to restore his voice, perhaps with an injection of cortisone.

Bailey's voice had come back in time for him to film the episode. He later said, "I will always be grateful to Lucille for giving my early career a boost."

***

Once again, Lucille turned to Bob O'Brien to fashion one of her better scripts of the fall. A November 13 telecast entitled *Dirty Gertie*.

Her co-star was Craig Stevens. Like Lloyd Bridges, the Missouri-born actor was one of the stars she considered among the most manly and sexiest in Hollywood. "No pretty boy like Tab Hunter or Robert Wagner," she said, "a real man's man."

She had "fallen for him" when she saw him on television as *Peter Gunn* 1958-1963), the hit TV drama in which he played a private detective.

MEMORIES OF VINTAGE HOLLYWOOD
Autographed press photo of **Craig Stevens** with **Alexis Smith**, during their respective heydays, long before Stevens agreed, decades later, to appear on *Here's Lucy*, Season Five.

Before World War II, he had only minor roles in films. When war broke out, he joined "the Culver City Commandos," a branch of the Army Air Corps' First Motion Picture Unit. They were based in Culver City, charged with the task of churning out training and propaganda films.

Right before America entered the war, Stevens had been cast in *Dive Bomber* (1941). During its filming, he met his future wife, Alexis Smith. In 1944, he married her, the union lasting until 1993, the year of her death.

Her film career advanced faster than his, and she was cast with leading men such as Clark Gable, Errol Flynn, and Cary Grant, and even a B picture actor, Ronald Reagan.

Throughout her career, rumors made the rounds in Hollywood that she was a lesbian. Gossips assumed her long link to Stevens was actually a "lavender marriage" to disguise their sexual orientations. The couple had no children during their decades-long union, and that also increased speculation.

"I knew Craig only briefly," Lucille said. "He was very good looking, very masculine. A lot of the public in the 1950s thought all gay men were effeminate. Quite the contrary…Some of the most masculine men in American, particularly bodybuilders, were gay."

In her *Here's Lucy* episode with Stevens, she is depicted cleaning her chimney, getting all dirty. A box of apples arrives from her doctor, who promotes the theory, "An apple a day keeps the doctor away."

Without cleaning herself up, she visits her hairdresser to share some of the fruit. *En route*, a bigtime gangster mistakes her for "Apple Annie," an apple vendor known for the transmission of good luck. He buys an apple from her, giving her a hundred dollar bill and telling her to keep the change. Eventually, Lucy collaborates with the police to help them entrap the mob leader and bring him to justice.

Character actor Bruce Gordon was also in the episode. Lucille had known him since Desi Sr. had cast him in his hit TV series, *The Untouchables.*

Lucille and her scriptwriter were obviously inspired by the Damon Runyan story of an apple vendor who provides "lucky apples" to gangsters. In a remake, Glenn Ford and Bette Davis starred in *A Pocketful of Miracles* (1961). This was the last film of the legendary director, Frank Capra. The movie also introduced sexpot Ann-Margret.

***

Fearing that her audience consisted to an increasing degree of aging Baby Boomers, Lucille turned to Donny Osmond for her November 20 telecast, *Lucy and Donny Osmond.* Her faith in Bob O'Brien, her scriptwriter, remained steady.

In addition to Donny, the episode also starred Phil Vandervort, her estranged son-in-law, and Eve Plumb. She was known to TV audiences for playing Jane Brady in the hit TV sitcom, *The Brady Bunch* (1969-1974).

Donny at the time was a teen idol, some of his fans calling him "Donny the Divine." Although viewed today as "campy" by more sophisticated audiences, he first gained fame by performing with his four older brothers in an act billed as "The Osmonds."

He broke from them to pursue a solo career, and later cultivated a variety series, *Donny & Marie,* which he performed with his sister.

It was rumored at the time that Donny developed a powerful crush on Lucie Arnaz, who was six years older than he was. "I heard that Donny had hot pants for my daughter, but I don't think it did him much good…at least that's what I think. Who knows what is going on these crazy days. Kids are going wild."

"As for his singing, I was not his greatest fan. I grew up loving Dinah Shore and Frank Sinatra. I hear Donny's music is called 'bubblegum pop and blue-eyed soul,' whatever in hell that means."

**The 70s:
ONLY IN AMERICA**

Two views of **Donny Osmond**.

Upper photo: Boy band teen idol Donny Osmond early in his career and

Lower photo, a mature entertainer primed for ongoing acts in Las Vegas.

During his appearance on her show, comparisons to Lucille's own children and their early fame became obvious.

***

Fred S. Fox was called back to write *Lucy and Prince Charming* for a November 27 telecast. Her co-star would be the Mexican actor, Ricardo Montalban, whose chief rival as the screen's premier Latin lover had been Fernando Lamas.

As she told the actor, "You and Lamas derailed Desi's dream of becoming the Latin Lover of the screen, swimming with Esther Williams and making love to Lana Turner."

"I know all about you Latin lovers, and even married one of you, as the world knows," she said. "Cesar Romero was actually in love with my husband. Now I get to try you out as my Prince Charming."

In the plot, Montalban plays a handsome prince who visits the Employment Agency run by Harry (Gale Gordon). He is seeking a beautiful American woman he can make his wife. If a suitable candidate can be found, he'll give Harry $250,000. Consequently, Harry pushes Lucy as a candidate.

In spite of his former rivalry with Desi, Lucille found Montalban a gentleman, full of charm and grace. As an actor, he had a wide range, no matter the genre—comedy, musicals, or crime dramas.

When Lucille teamed with him, he was enjoying box office success in films such as *Escape from the Planet of the Apes* (1971). Before that, he had played Khan Noonien Singh, a genetically enhanced human in the original *Star Trek* TV series (1967).

His greatest fame came when he starred as Mr. Roarke in the TV series *Fantasy Island* (1977-1984).

Over lunch with Montalban, Lucille told him that Desi had wanted to play the bullfighter in *Fiesta* (1947), opposite Esther Williams, a role that had gone to him. "Desi

Two views of **Ricardo Montalban** in his heyday.

Lower photo shows him with one of our favorite women, **Lana Turner**. The film they made was appropriately entitled *Latin Lovers* (1953)

DID YOU KNOW? that in 2017, Blood Moon produced history's most complete overview of **Lana Turner**, known during her heyday as both "The Sweater Girl" and "Hollywood's Ultimate Movie Star."

Lana was sometimes cited as a motivating spirit that helped win World War II. It was a reference to G.I.'s rushing into battle armored with a vision of Lana—a girl you might opt NOT to bring home to mother.

As this book reveals, Lana was, in her way, one of the most fascinating characters to ever come out of show-biz.

was so disappointed."

"That's why Hollywood is called the Boulevard of Broken Dreams," he answered. "Esther fell in love with me, and we made other pictures together."

"I don't want to brag, but many of my leading ladies fell in love with me," Montalban claimed. "But as you may know, I'm a faithful, devoted husband, married to a woman I love dearly."

"You married Loretta Young's sister, Georgiana Young, didn't you?"

"You nailed me! It was the best move I ever made. That meant I could reject unwanted or badly timed advances from Shelley Winters, Lana Turner, Van Johnson, Vincent Price, June Allyson, Anne Bancroft and Ann Miller."

In all my movies, I feel I have played Latin caricatures on screen. I should have had the courage of Dolores del Rio and returned to Mexico and made more true-to-life pictures. Actually, I accept any part that comes my way. I turn down nothing."

"You mean, you would do a frontal nude?" she asked.

"That's one thing I will not do. Not that I have anything to be ashamed of. But, as a Mexican man, I'm uncut. American mothers obviously prefer the circumcised penis, allowing doctors to whack off the foreskins of their screaming infant boys. I would not want to turn off those women fans of mine if they got a look at my uncut dick."

***

In her next episode, *My Fair Buzzi,* telecast on December 14), Lucille teamed with a fellow comedian, Ruth Buzzi. The Rhode Islander was enjoying the greatest fame of her career, starring in the hit TV variety show, *Rowan & Martin's Laugh-In* (1968-1973).

Lucille learned that at the age of nineteen, Buzzi had worked with Rudy Vallee. "I have, too," Lucille interjected. "And I was not all that impressed with the Vagabond Singer."

Buzzi had also worked with Carol Burnett, Barbra Streisand, Joan Rivers, Dom DeLuise, and Bernadette Peters.

Her most famous role was as the dowdy spinster, Gladys Ormphby, on *Rowan & Martin.* One reviewer wrote, "She was clad in drab brown with her bun hairdo covered by a visible hairnet knotted in the middle of her forehead. She used her purse as a weapon, in which she would flail away vigorously at anyone who incurred her wrath. She was most often the unwilling object of the advances of Arte Johnson's 'dirty old man' character, Tyrone F. Horneigh."

"It takes a lot of work to look this frumpy!"

—**Ruth Buzzi**, in reference to her character of Gladys Ormphby

Buzzi had read in *Variety* that Lucille would soon be filming *Mame* when her Fifth Season of *Here's Lucy* came to an end. Buzzi had played Agnes Gooch in a school production of *Auntie Mame,* and she felt she'd be ideal as a variation of the Gooch character in Lucille's feature film.

She promised she'd speak to the director about casting her. When she called George Saks, he told her that the role had already been cast with the actress, Jane Connell.

"Talk about a household name," Lucille snapped sarcastically.

***

Bob Carroll Jr. and Madelyn Davis were summoned back to co-write *Lucy Is Really in a Pickle,* telecast on New Year's Day in 1973.

An advertising agency wants Harry (Gale Gordon) to find an "average-looking," (i.e., not particularly beautiful) woman to appear in a pickle commercial. The script called for a dance sequence too, so Lucie Arnaz, as Lucy's daughter, Kim, was also cast.

In many ways, this latest episode evoked the 1952 episode from *I Love Lucy, Lucy Does a TV Commercial.* In it, she overdoses on Vitameatavegamin. In the new script, she can't really stand the taste of the sour pickles she's supposed to be hyping.

In the show, she also evokes her slapstick, "direct from the 1950s" Lucy Ricardo antics.

***

Bob Carroll Jr., and Madelyn Davis were called back to write a most improbable episode, *Lucy Goes on a Blind Date,* telecast on January 8.

She was teamed with Don Knotts in the role of Ben, one of Harry's (Gordon's) cousins. "No one ever came up with a less romantic partner for Lucille than Don Knotts," a critic for the *Hollywood Reporter* wrote.

Harry urges Lucy to date Ben, who, as Harry learns, is a millionaire realtor. Lucy is turned off by him.

In private, she tells Gordon, "Knotts has all the sex appeal of a dried apricot."

He was best known for playing the bumbling deputy sheriff, Barney Fife, on *The Andy Griffith Show* (1960-1968), which brought him five Emmy Awards.

The actor had starred in his own TV series, *The Don Knotts Show,* in the autumn of 1970, but ratings were low.

She read the best summation of Knotts by a critic: "The pulsing bundle of self-consciousness

Don Knotts, a talented comedian sometimes cited as "the least sexy man alive," appears here with **Andy Griffith** as the deputy sheriff of Mayberry on many seasons of *The Andy Griffith Show.*

expresses an infinite fury of emotion in a single turn of the shoulder, such is the intensity of his comedic characterizations. That intensity helps make Knotts something like all the Three Stooges wrapped into one unstable body: A panicked, pompous nitwit who displays the dweebish of Larry, the bullying of Moe, and the physicality of Curly."

Lucille told Carroll, "I read that Knotts' first wife, Kathryn Metz (1947-1964), divorced him because he was a ladies' man, often taking starlets to night clubs. That any red-blooded female would be attracted to him boggles my mind."

After working with Lucille, Knotts took a second wife, Loralee Czuchna (1974-1983). His final wife, whom he married in 2000, was Francey Yarborough, a stage actress, a union that endured until his death in 2008.

***

For several years, Charles Laughton had suggested that he and Lucille should star in a feature film, but that never happened. However, in *Lucy Goes to Prison*, telecast on January 22, she teamed with his wife, the English character actress, Elsa Lanchester, who had immortalized herself on the screen in *Bride of Frankenstein* (1935).

Lucille had worked with her before in a 1956 episode of *I Love Lucy*. She found Lanchester a delight and invited her to spend the weekend with her at her home.

According to the plot, Lucy Carter goes to prison as an underground spy, allegedly with the intention of learning enough information to collect a $30,000 award. She struggles to get secret information about criminal activities from a fellow prisoner portrayed by Lanchester. She fails to cough up any data until Lucy gets her "all boozed up."

During the course of a weekend with Lucille, Lanchester revealed some of the details of her life. Born outside London in 1902, she married Laughton in 1929, later insisting that she did not know he was a homosexual.

His greatest seduction was Tyrone Power when they appeared together in *Witness for the Prosecution* (1957). But for the most part, he had to rely on masseurs, chauffeurs for hire, barmen, and "rent boys" from Piccadilly Circus.

During his direction of Robert Mitchum, Lucille's former beau, in *Night of the Hunter*, Laughton told

Elsa Lanchester in the title role of *Bride of Frankenstein* (1935).

Her husband, Charles Laughton, said, "SInce I was the ugliest man ever to appear on the screen, I decided to marry the ugliest woman ever to appear on the screen. At least Frankenstein had the hots for her."

him, "Don't know if you know, and I don't know if you care to know, but there is a streak of homosexuality in me."

"Count me out," Mitchum replied, "even though I used to sell my goodies to Clifton Webb in my early years when I was struggling to make a living in Hollywood. That was before I moved up in the world, seducing everyone from Marilyn Monroe to Rita Hayworth."

Over lunch, Lucille told Lanchester she'd seen several of her films, beginning with *The Private Lives of Henry VIII,* in which Lanchester had been cast as Anne of Cleves. "Nothing ever equaled your singing a duet with Elvis Presley.

[One of the half-dozen songs he sang in one of his worst commercial failures, Easy Come, Easy Go (1967) was, indeed, an unexpected duet, "Yoga Is as Yoga Does," with a blowsy-looking "New Age" instructor, Elsa Lanchester.]

***

To complete the Fifth Season, Harry (Gordon) and Lucy dip into nostalgia in *Lucy and Harry's Memoirs.* They are seen packing up and closing down their employment agency, the venue that brought them so many adventures.

Before the final work on the episode was finished, executives at CBS persuaded Lucille to return for a Sixth (1973-74) Season. That prompted them to hastily attach a sign to the agency's door stating that the closure was only temporary.

As the Fifth Season concluded, *Here's Lucy* had fallen to #15 in ratings, marking the first time a series starring Lucille had dropped from the Top Ten.

But a tantalizing new project had appeared on the Hollywood horizon. Before she would appear again for another season of *Here's Lucy,* Lucille would finally get configured as the star of yet another (her last) major motion picture, the long-delayed *Mame.*

CHAPTER ELEVEN

> ### Defying the Odds,
> # LUCILLE EMERGES AS THE LAST SURVIVOR
> ### of Vintage, Golden-Age Television
>
> ### Lucille Plays *MAME*
> ### as a Flaming Drag Queen

After a long delay, Lucille was ready to star in the screen adaptation of *Mame*, with shooting beginning in January of 1973, and scheduled for a 1974 release. The studio had paid $3 million for its screen rights and had budgeted $12 million to shoot it.

Everybody, including Lucille, expected it to be a big hit. She told Gary Morton that "if all things go right, I might walk away with my one and only Oscar."

When Lucille shouldered the role of *Mame*, it already generated an impressive theatrical and cinematic history. Its legend had begun as a novel, *Auntie Mame: An Irreverent Escapade (1955)* by Patrick Dennis.

In chronological vignettes, the novel's narrator—also named Patrick—recounts his adventures growing up under the wing of his madcap aunt, Mame Dennis.

The first edition of his novel spent 112 weeks on the bestseller list, selling more than two million copies in five languages.

Despite its eventual spectacular success, its author had a hard time getting it published. Fifteen major publishing houses had rejected it, often citing, "It's just too campy and too gay."

In 1956, with the publication of *Auntie Mame: The Loving Couple (His and Her Stories,* and *Westward Ho!* a lighthearted romp about an urban family which relocated to New Mexico to operate a dude ranch), Dennis became the first writer in history to have three books on *The New York Times Bestseller List* at the same time.

In 1958, Dennis wrote a sequel, titled *Around the World with Auntie Mame.*

He also enjoyed great success in 1961 with a tongue-in-cheek "parody memoir" entitled *Little Me: The Intimate Memoirs of that Great Star of Stage, Screen, and Television, Belle Poitrine.*

[In 1962, Little Me was turned into a Broadway musical by Neil Simon. Sid Caesar was cast in all the male roles. At one time, Lucille considered playing the wacky Belle in a film adaptation.]

Dennis was married (from 1948 to 1976) to Louise Stickney. The couple produced two children. He also led a very active homosexual life and was seen frequently in the gay haunts of New York's Greenwich Village.

In 1956, *Auntie Mame*, starring Rosalind Russell, became a hit on Broadway. *[Russell went on to star in a 1958 screen adaptation.]* Regardless of which actress tackled the role of Mame, none was as "devastatingly good" as Miss Russell, who entered screen immortality with that role. She usually played classy and glamourous roles, but never became known as a sex symbol.

Rosalind Russell was the much-admired veteran of many golden-age classic films. In 1940, Lucille had lobbied for the role of the quick-witted ace reporter, Hildy Johnson, in the screwball comedy, *His Girl Friday*, directed by Howard Hawks and co-starring Cary Grant. Of course, Lucille lost and Russell was cast, the part having been rejected by a gaggle of A-list stars who included Katharine Hepburn, Claudette Colbert, Irene Dunne, Jean Arthur, Margaret Sullavan, and Ginger Rogers. Russell ran with it, and it became one of her biggest hits.

Later, Russell enjoyed huge success as Natalie Wood's stage mother in the 1962 musical film *Gypsy* an adaptation of the 1959 stage musical *Gypsy: A Musical Fable,* by Arthur Laurents, itself an adaptation of Gypsy Rose Lee's 1957 autobiography. Lucille had wanted the part for herself.

Russell could also play high drama, having been cast as a lady judge, a newswoman, and a psychiatrist.

Her 1941 marriage to the Danish-American producer, Frederick Brisson, lasted until her death in 1976, although there were repeated rumors of same-sex gender preferences for both members of that marriage.

Before agreeing to star in this most recent film adaptation, Lucille sat through the screening of Russell's *Auntie Mame* three times in one day. Lucille decided she would never equal the wise-cracking flamboyance of Rus-

---

BUILDING THE LEGEND OF EVERYBODY'S FAVORITE AUNTIE

Hipsters knew just from the cover of the first edition of **Patrick Dennis**'s *Auntie Mame* that it was gonna be campy. Its humor didn't come easily.

An alcoholic for many years, Dennis led a double life as both a husband and father and also as a closeted gay man. He attempted suicide three times and was once sent to an asylum, where he received electroshock therapy.

sell's rendition, so she opted for a less sophisticated approach.

Studly Forrest Tucker, Coral Browne, Roger Smith, and Peggy Cass had the supporting roles. Auntie Mame's most famous line was, "Life is a banquet, and most poor suckers are starving to death."

In 1966 in New York, Lucille and Gary Morton were seen attending the Broadway stage version of *Mame* starring Angela Lansbury. When they went backstage to greet her, Lansbury seemed thrilled that after the run of the play, she'd also be starring in its film adaptation.

However, in an act of something approaching betrayal, the producers eventually decided that Lansbury didn't have enough marquee value to carry this lavish and expensive movie adaptation and awarded the role instead to Lucille.

[Surprisingly, before Lucille got tapped, Elizabeth Taylor was invited to star in the musical, with the understanding that the role required her to sing and dance. Wisely, she rejected the offer.]

Rosalind Russell as Mame was a hard act for Lucille to follow

Here's Russell playing the fabulous, smart, clever, flamboyant, and "understanding" auntie to a closeted gay teenager, presumably someone like Patrick Dennis.

Before signing for the part, Desi Sr. sent his ex-wife an urgent telegram. *[He'd been unable to reach her on the phone.]* "Don't do it!" he urged. "It will end in disaster. After that ski accident, your body is not strong enough for such a demanding role. Do you want to break more of your notoriously brittle bones?"

Obviously, she chose not to take the advice of her ex-husband.

George Cukor, "a woman's director," was originally tapped to bring *Mame* to the screen, but in part because of the long pre-production delay, he "abandoned ship" (his words) and went off to make *Travels With My Aunt* (1972), a movie with a roughly equivalent theme. It starred Maggie Smith.

Gene Saks, a noteworthy stage and film director, was hired to direct *Mame*. Before the end of his illustrious career, thanks in part to a long-term professional association with playwright Neil Simon, he was nominated for seven Tony Awards for stage plays which included *Biloxi Blues*.

Since 1950, he'd been married to actress Beatrice Arthur, and he gave her the second lead in *Mame,* the role of Vera Charles, the acerbic and frequently "besotted" bosom buddy of the female lead. *[Bette Davis had originally wanted to be cast as Vera, but Saks turned her down since his wife, Bea Arthur, had virtually demanded the role. Arthur had wanted the lead role, but the producers preferred Lansbury instead. For Arthur's supporting stage role of Vera, she won a Tony for Best Featured Actress in a Musical.]*

A New Yorker, Arthur—as described by one critic—was "rather macho," having joined the U.S. Marine Corps Women's Reserve in 1943, where she became a truck driver, moving up to the rank of sergeant by war's end.

Before working with Lucille in *Mame*, Arthur had been invited by Norman Lear to guest star as Maude Finlay, Edith Bunker's outspoken cousin, in the hit TV sitcom, *All in the Family*. As such, she was the antithesis of the caricatured reactionary Archie Bunker.

Arthur later won her own TV series, *Maude*, which made its debut in 1972. For her personification of that character, she won her place in TV history as an icon of the women's liberation movement. The themes of the show addressed issues never seen on TV: Gay rights, mental illness, abortion, and spousal abuse.

Her greatest fame would come in 1985, when she signed at the age of 63 to play Dorothy Zbornak, a divorced mother and substitute teacher living in Miami with two widows played by Rue McClenahan and Betty White. *The Golden Girls* was a massive hit, running for seven seasons. In it, Estelle Getty was cast as Dorothy's mother, Sophia Petrillo.

Like so many other strong women in public life, the rather "butch" Arthur was accused of being a "part-time lesbian." She became a gay icon, embracing the homosexual community and taking up the cause of homeless gay youths. She helped raise money for the Ali Forney Center, housing young boys and girls who, because of their gender preferences, had been kicked out by their families.

Paul Zindel wrote the screenplay for *Mame*. In 1971, he'd won a Pulitzer Prize for his play, *The Effects of Gamma Rays on Man-in-the-Moon Marigolds*.

Bea Arthur in a 1973 publicity photo, promoting her television series, *Maude* in 1973

Bea Arthur with **Lucille** appear in this press photo from their cinematic morph, in 1974, of Patrick Dennis's best-selling novel.

Almost everyone said it was highly derivative, and not nearly as good, as Rosalind Russell's 1958 original.

Clad in the finery of the early 30s, and commiserating their woes at a fashionable luncheon, they're singing "Bosom Buddies."

Mame's composer and lyricist, Jerry Herman, had previously composed the score for the hit Broadway musical, *Hello, Dolly* (1964), starring Carol Channing. Herman's mother, Ruth Sachs, was a singer and pianist with some of the qualities which inspired that play's female lead. Years later, Herman told a reporter, "She had the wit of Dolly and the glamour of Mame."

The original production of *Hello, Dolly!* ran for 2,844 performances, the longest-running musical of its time, and was revived three times.

Herman's next big success was *Mame*, starring Angela Lansbury. It introduced such Herman standards as "If He Walked Into My Life," and that holiday favorite, "We Need a Little Christmas."

Later, Lucille was disappointed when she learned that Herman didn't want her to play *Mame* and that he'd lobbied unsuccessfully to have Lansbury cast in the film role instead.

Herman was openly gay. In 1985, although diagnosed as HIV-positive, he survived, dying in a Miami hospital at the age of 88 in 2019.

Hal King, who had been Lucille's favorite makeup artist since 1937, was assigned the task of preparing her face for *Mame*. To him (and anyone else who would listen), she expressed her fear that she would have to be shot in soft focus, "or else I'll look eighty-five years old."

To cover her wrinkles, which had become quite prominent, King painstakingly applied a liquid adhesive that made them less obvious, but which, when dried, was quite painful.

She complained loudly to him, and one of their arguments became heated. At one point, she picked up a blunt instrument on her dressing table and slammed it into his face, breaking his jawbone.

He screamed in pain and ran for the door, calling back at her, "You damn bitch!"

From outside her dressing room, an ambulance was summoned. Their long association immediately ended.

The leading male role in *Mame* was that of Beauregard Jackon Pickett-Burnside, a rich plantation owner from the Deep South. On a business trip to New York, he falls in love with Mame, marries her, and takes her back home. His family is horrified that he married a Yankee.

For that role, Lucille recommended both Rory Calhoun and George Montgomery, considering them as some of the sexiest actors on the screen. To her chagrin, her suggestions were overruled, and Robert Preston, a stage and film actor with a good singing voice, was shoehorned into the role instead.

Working with composer Meredith Wilson, Preston had originated the role of Professor Harold Hill in the Broadway musical, *The Music Man* (1957), and also brought it to the screen for its film adaptation of 1962, where it became a hit.

When Preston learned that Lucille had not wanted him as her leading man, he told Saks, "That often happens to me. When Jack Warner bought the rights to *The Music Man*, he wanted either Frank Sinatra or Cary Grant as its star."

When reporters "invaded" the film set of *Mame* to interview him, Preston refused. "My private life is my own, and I plan to keep it that way." At least three authors wanted to write his biography, but so little was

Press photo from 1968, celebrating the creative union of **Angela Lansbury**, who had played the title role in the Broadway version of *Mame*, with its composer, **Jerry Herman**, a friend, neighbor, and tenant of Darwin Porter, co-author of this book.

known about his personal life that the projects were dropped, since all the writers could do was review his public accomplishments as an actor.

Actress Jane Connell, a native of Berkeley, California, portrayed Auntie Mame's pregnant and unmarried secretary, Agnes Gooch. She had appeared as a key player in the original Broadway production and now replicated her role on the screen.

[Connell got her part in the film adaptation only after Lucille demanded that Madeline Kahn, originally cast in the part, be fired.]

At four feet, eleven inches, Connell was described as "a tiny woman, with a giant, squeaky voice."

Encountering her years later, Connell expressed her continued gratitude to Lucille. "I think I've been cast as everybody from Mother Goose to Queen Victoria, from Martha Washington to Queen Hepzibah."

It wasn't his first time at the "Musical Comedy Rodeo."

Photo above shows **Robert Preston** with **Shirley Jones**, musically "emoting" for *The Music Man* (1962),

The character of Mame's nephew, Patrick, called for two actors, one to play the boy and later in the play, the mature man. Boy Patrick was portrayed by Kirby Furlong, a son of Los Angeles, who has much to learn about life from his zany and very indulgent aunt.

Lucille found the boy version of Patrick (Kirby Furlong) adorable, and almost wanted to adopt him.

On *The Tonight* Show, she told Johnny Carson, "He was an unusual boy. When we started the movie, he was eight and a half, but he'd aged to ten when we finished the picture. It was hard to say good night to him because I fell in love with him and wanted to take him home. He was a darling on and off camera, a natural."

The older version of Patrick was played by Bruce Davidson, a son of Philadelphia who was 27 when he accepted the role. Standing more than six feet, he was described as blonde, clean cut, Ivy League handsome, and "with a Ready-Whipped smile evocative of JFK." When Lucille first met him, he had just co-starred with Burt Lancaster in *Ulzana's Raid* (1972).

Years later, Lucille recalled, "The next time I heard about Bruce, he was playing a child molester in some low-budget quickie, which I will not be attending."

Doria Cook was cast as Patrick's dim-witted girlfriend, Gloria Upson. Mame evaluates her as a snob and an insufferable bore. Even worse are her bigoted, narrow-minded parents, actors Don Porter and Audrey Christie, identified as "Mums" and "Dadums."

They live in a "restricted neighborhood," which—although never overtly expressed—meant "no blacks or Jews."

When Doria meets Vera Charles, she tells the actress, "I just adored you in *Mary of Scotland.*"

Vera responds, "That was Helen Hayes."

[Another memorable line uttered by Vera, a diva who's ferociously protective of her hard-won image? "I was never in the chorus. I was NEVER in the chorus!]

The world premiere of Lucille's version of *Mame* was held at Manhattan's Lincoln Center for the Performing Arts, before moving on for its big opening at Radio City Music Hall, which defined it as its Easter Attraction for 1974.

After reading the major reviews, Lucille painfully realized that *Mame* was going to be a colossal flop at the box office. "This is the end of my film career."

Pauline Kael in *The New Yorker* wrote, "After forty years in movies and TV, did Lucille Ball discover in herself an unfulfilled ambition to be a flaming drag queen?"

In a cruel jab, she was attacked in *The New Republic:* "Had Miss Ball shot *Mame* fifteen years ago, she might have been terrific. But she is now too old, too stringy in the legs, too *basso* in her voice, and too creaky in her joints." When she read that, Gary Morton claimed, "My wife went into a crying jag, feeling her life was over."

Newsweek quipped that she "looked like one of those seven deadly sins and a decorator wing chair."

Joy Cocks at *Time* observed "Bea Arthur is the only one who brings *Mame* alive."

The New York Times said, "It's all relentlessly good-natured, but unless you've been packed in storage somewhere, it's so familiar it puts a tremendous burden on its star. Miss Ball has some great moments, but she is not even a non-singer who fakes singing very well."

Gene Siskel of the *Chicago Tribune* lacerated Lucille's film version of *Mame* as "a total bust, devoid of joy, wit, good music, or decent dancing", adding: "Much ado has been made about the film's photographic treatment of Lucille Ball's face. Each time we see Miss Ball in closeup, it appears as though the camera lens has been smeared with Vaseline. This is no small matter. The goal of almost every film is to make you forget you are watching a movie. But the continual softening of focus each time Miss Ball's mug comes into view is at first distracting, then annoying, and, ultimately, offensive to our intelligence and to Miss Ball's strength as a performer."

In *Variety's* view, "Mame may not be perennial Lucy's theatrical screen capstone. She is great in the role. *Mame* is sometimes outrageously exaggerated like, say, a fashion layout in *Vogue*. To vary the metaphor, it's a case of, if you don't like chocolate éclairs, stay out

Despite the mixed reactions to her performance in *Mame*, *After Dark's* October 1973 edition dutifully placed **Lucille** on its cover.

of the bakery."

The New York Daily News found that "Lucille Ball provides *Mame* with the charm it does possess. In spite of the fact that *Mame* is a mess, she triumphs once again."

Mocking her age, the critic for the *Chicago Sun-Times* wrote, "When Lucille Ball confronts a photographer, she tells him to back up twenty feet."

Time's reviewer weighed in: "As Lucy Ricardo, Miss Ball had been molded over these many years into some sort of national monument. She performs like one in *Mame,* which, we predict, will be her *adieu* to the screen. Her grace, her timing, her vigor, have all vanished."

After its fiasco in New York, and to beef up *Mame* at the box office elsewhere, Lucille toured key cities. As part of her campaign, she stridently began supporting "family pictures," and often derided "the filth on the screen today." For special disdain, she singled out Marlon Brando's *Last Tango in Paris* (1972), speculating about why he had agreed to perform in Bernardo Bertolucci's "travesty, an example of sex gone wrong."

Mame would mark the end of Lucille's feature film career.

***

The Nielsen ratings for *Here's Lucy* were at their lowest ebb as she launched its Sixth Season (1973-1974), predicting, "It will be my last hurrah."

For her staff, she stuck to "the tried and true," meaning her husband, Gary Morton, as executive producer with her cousin, Cleo Smith, remaining in her post as producer. Gale Gordon returned as her boss, Harry, with her own daughter, Lucie, cast as her television daughter once again. Desi Jr. would remain out of the show. Mary Jane Croft, configured as "Mary Jane Lewis," would also remain, reprising the kooky, shrill-voiced character she'd already fine-tuned in previous episodes.

The season was launched on September 10, 1973, with an episode entitled *Lucy and Danny Thomas*. It included character actor Hans Conreid in a supporting role. She had worked with comedian Thomas many times over the years and had first performed with Conreid back in 1952 in the filming of an episode of *I Love Lucy*. Conreid had also played Uncle Tonoose on *The Danny Thomas Show,* and his latest appearance would mark the last time the two actors would work together.

Even before the premiere of Season Six, **Lucille**'s reign as "The Queen of the Sitcom" had ended.

Gale Gordon remained with her to the bitter end, as did her daughter, **Lucie**, who was ready and eager to strike out on her own.

In this episode, Bob O'Brien fashioned a script in which Lucy confronts Thomas, cast as a starving artist. He tells her that his paintings will be worth millions, but only after his death. Lucy, therefore, schemes to fake his death as part of a plot to bring in big bucks from the sale of his art. For the plot, O'Brien was inspired by the 1965 film, *The Art of Love,* a Technicolor comedy starring James Garner, Dick Van Dyke, plus two beauties, Elke Sommer and Angie Dickinson. In that feature, it was Van Dyke who fakes his death to increase the value of his paintings.

***

Lucille's *Here's Lucy* episode with Danny Thomas was followed by her migration to NBC on September 16 to co-star with Steve Lawrence and his singing wife from the Bronx, Eydie Gormé, in their TV special, *Steve and Eydie…On Stage.* It was shot at the chic Caesar's Palace in Las Vegas where earlier in the day, Lucille had had a chance encounter with Frank Sinatra in the lobby.

Onstage, and in front of TV cameras, Lucille sang "Bosom Buddies" from *Mame,* and was off-key. She was hardly a vocal match for Gormé, whose songs frequently morphed into hits on the pop and Latin pop charts. Lucille's favorite song from her repertoire was "Blame It on the Bossa Nova," for which Gormé had won a Grammy.

After the show, Lawrence told Lucille, "I fell in love with Eydie the moment I saw her and even more so the first time I heard her sing. I understand that Desi fell in love with you the first time you guys met."

"Something like that," she snapped, perhaps not wanting to remember.

***

O.J. Simpson was Lucille's co-star in the *Here's Lucy* episode entitled *The Big Game* (September 17, 1973). She had met him when both of them appeared on *Super Bowl Comedy* in January of 1971. Carol Burnett and others were also on that telecast. At the time, she had interpreted the football great, nicknamed "The Juice," as charming and attractive.

Based on another weak script by Bob O'Brien, Harry (Gale Gordon) is the president of the Beverly Hills Chamber of Commerce. He invites O.J. to address his fellow members.

The footballer generously provides him with two hard-to-get tickets to the game. Lucy, too, is given free tickets, so Harry decides to "scalp" them, later getting himself arrested.

Character actor Cliff Norton also had a small role. He was a regular face on TV, thanks to earlier appearances with such stars as Don Knotts, Sid Caesar, Dick Van Dyck, and Dave Garroway. He had recently worked with Eddie Albert and Eva Gabor on *Green Acres.*

Years later, he spoke to a reporter about working with O.J. and Lucille. "It all seems a bit eerie, in the light of the sensational murder trial of O.J. that happened later. I remembered him talking rather lovingly about his wife, Marguerite L. Whitley, whom he had married in 1967, leading to the birth of their two children. The couple later had a third child, a son born in 1977, but he drowned in the family's swimming pool."

"When Lucille and I worked with him, he was still the star tailback for the Buffalo Bills. He was just breaking in as an actor and was a bit stiff. He was far more lively in those Hertz commercials."

"One day during rehearsals, Lucille confided to me that Sammy Davis Jr. had told her that "A woman doesn't know what sex is really like until she's been seduced by a black man.'"

"As I remembered it, she gazed over at O.J., who was talking with Sid Gould, Morton's cousin, who was also on our show."

"I must say, that football player must be mighty tempting to a lot of women," Lucille said. "He's not only good looking and well built, but he's charming and such a gentleman."

"During rehearsals, word spread that Lucille and O.J. were having an affair," Norton said. "You know how gossip travels. There is no evidence whatsoever that they had sex, but that didn't stop people from gossiping. I personally believe they did not have an affair. Others disagreed with me."

[After his divorce from his first wife, O.J. went on to marry Nicole Brown, whom he had met when she was working as a waitress at a night club, The Daisy. When they eventually got married in 1985, he had been retired from football for some five years. Their volatile marriage produced two children. In 1989, Nicole filed for divorce, alleging spousal abuse and citing irreconcilable differences. The divorce came through in 1992, although there would be failed attempts at reconciliation.

In a murder that shocked the nation, Nicole Brown Simpson and her friend, Ron Goldman, were stabbed to death on the night of June 12, 1994.

Initially, O.J. did not turn himself in, but fled as a passenger in a white 1993 Ford Bronco SUV piloted by his friend, Al Cowlings.

As spectators across the nation shouted "GO O.J. GO!," his attempted flight from the police was televised by a helicopter flying overhead as his SUV sped along a California highway. It was later called "the most famous ride in America since the midnight ride of Paul Revere."

Charged with murder, O.J. was later found not guilty and freed. But that was only the beginning of his subsequent troubles.]

O.J. Simpson at trial in 1995, charged with the murder of Nicole Simpson and Ron Goldman.

Although he was acquitted by a jury, he was later arrested and jailed for armed robbery as part of an unrelated incident.

***

For her next episode, Lucy the Peacemaker (September 23), she teamed once again with Steve Lawrence and Eydie Gormé in yet another script by Bob O'Brien. According to the plot, Lawrence, separated from his wife, goes into Harry's employment agency, seeking domestic help.

Lucy maneuvers to bring the lovers back together again, but prospects look dismal. Lawrence is so angry at his wife that he even lets Lucy fill in for her at an engagement at Caesar's Palace in Las

Vegas.

Lucille uses the show once again to plug her failing musical movie, *Mame,* singing (badly) its most memorable song, "If He Walked Into My Life."

She later admitted, "I was no Eydie who made a hit record of my song."

***

In Episode #120, *Lucy, the Wealthy Widow,* she teamed with Ed McMahon, Johnny Carson's longtime sidekick on *The Tonight Show.* The plot (which failed to answer some basic questions raised by its premise) had been written by Bob O'Brien.

She sees a TV commercial that advertises a bank willing to give loans without a lot of personal investigation. She and Harry need $10,000 to renovate the headquarters of their employment agency. With the backing of Harry (Gordon), and Kim (Lucie Arnaz), Lucille pretends to be a wealthy widow as she approaches the bank for a loan.

Why did she need a loan if she were a rich widow? The script becomes unbelievable.

Lucille was aware of how weak the script was but went ahead with the telecast anyway. For her next two episodes, she turned to other scriptwriters before bringing back O'Brien.

Over lunch with McMahon, she found him in a sad mood. His marriage to Alyce Ferrell was coming to an end. They had wed right after World War II, when he was a flight instructor in the U.S. Marines. The couple had produced four children. Their divorce would become finalized in 1974.

"You must do what I did," Lucille advised. "If your first marriage does not succeed, try, try again."

"I may want to do just that," he asserted. "I've met this darling girl with a wonderful name: Valentine."

***

In *Lucy Gives Eddie Albert the Old Song and Dance,* telecast on October 15, she teamed with an actor who had once been her co-star in a feature film. In 1956, she and Eddie Albert had played the leads in a romantic comedy, *The Fuller Brush Girl.*

More recently, beginning in 1965, Albert had co-starred with Eva Gabor in the hit TV sitcom, *Green Acres,* a cult classic that ran for six seasons and encompassed 170 episodes. When Lucille met him again, he was set to play a sadistic prison warden in *The Longest Yard* (1974).

She told him, "I couldn't remake our *Fuller Brush* movie today. I would collapse on the set the first day. It was brutal. I sprained both of my wrists in all those antics we were forced to pull off, and I displaced three vertebrae. I also suffered two days of blindness from talcum powder sprayed on me from a wind machine."

In their current TV episode, a woman who looks like Lucy is stalking Albert. The real Lucy then meets Albert and wants to appear with him in a charity show. But he suspects she is his stalker. It ends happily with Lucy and with Albert doing a well-received song-and-dance routine.

Over lunch, the two stars discussed those troubled days during the McCarthy witch hunt in the early 1950s. At the time, Lucille was exposed for having joined the Communist Party in 1936 to fulfill the wishes of her left-wing grandfather.

Her career survived the exposure, but Albert had a rough time. Eventually, his career survived, but his Mexican wife, who billed herself as "Margo," didn't do as well.

Albert escaped censure because of his war record. As a lieutenant in the U.S. Navy, he had been awarded a Bronze Star for his heroic efforts during the invasion of the island of Tarawa in November of 1943. *[Under heavy fire from the occupying Japanese forces, he had rescued 47 Marines offshore and rescued another 30 civilians.]*

Top photo: **Eva Gabor** with **Eddie Albert** in a press and PR photo for *Green Acres*.

Although each of them was supremely sophisticated and adept in urban ways, their pose mimicked, much to viewers' amusement, the stern morality of Grant Wood's brilliant evocation of the American Midwest *(lower photo) American Gothic.*

***

Lucille had worked with actor Jackie Coogan before, but never in a script as weak as *Lucy's Tenant,* telecast on October 22. One of her previous writers, Fred S. Fox, was the "villain" who concocted its plot.

Beginning in 1937 and for two years, Coogan had been married to the blonde goddess, Betty Grable, who incidentally was one of the former lovers of Desi Arnaz. Coogan earned fame as a child actor in silent films, notably for *The Kid* (1921), co-starring with scene stealer, Charlie Chaplin.

In the 1960s, he'd become famous for playing the bumbling Uncle Fester in the hit TV sitcom, *The Addams Family.*

At their reunion, she congratulated him: "I hear that at last your marriage seems to be working out. The other day, I heard that you were once married to a gal named Flower. Is that true?"

"Yes, but she became a wilted rose after the first three weeks," he said. "You see, as Betty Grable widely promulgates, I require a woman to perform certain acts I learned in a San Francisco whorehouse when I was seventeen. I'm told there are some acts that even a wife refuses to perform on her husband."

"Believe me, I'm one of those women," she said. "Call me old-fashioned."

In the current episode, Lucille, to earn extra money, decides to rent out her daughter's bedroom, since she's away. The real estate agent sends over "a dud" (Coogan) as her tenant. She has signed a lease but wants to break it because she doesn't like his attitude about anything. As part of a campaign to get rid of him, she begins to make romantic overtures.

A critic for the *Hollywood Reporter* commented on the low register of her voice, which sounded deeper than he'd ever heard it. "If it gets any lower, Lucille Ball will become known as one of those 'baritone babes' like Tallulah Bankhead."

[Back then, "baritone babe" was a code word for "lesbian."]

***

Lucille had worked with the actor before, but never as intensely as she did in the October 29 telecast of *Lucy and Andy Griffith.* Bob O' Brien was rehired as its scriptwriter, and perhaps to hold onto his job, he came up with a better plot than his previous efforts.

Lucy is attracted to the Griffith character, a devout Christian, evocative of Elmer Gantry, who's dedicated to rescuing wayward youth.

The episode gave Lucie Arnaz a chance to show off her acting skills in ways that none of the other episodes had done. Aware of her mother's crush on Griffith, she disguises herself as a hippie in the emerging sexual revolution then sweeping across the land. She wants to know if he's "for real" or a fraud.

For most of the world, this famous son of North Carolina was known for playing Sheriff Andy Taylor in *The Andy Griffith Show,* a hit TV sitcom that ran from 1960 to 1968.

Set in the fictional town of Mayberry, North Carolina, it had been filmed at Desilu Studios, where both Desi Sr. and Lucille had gotten to known Griffith.

Griffith's talent had never been tapped as deeply as it had in his debut feature film, the very memorable *A Face in the Crowd* (1957). In it, he had delivered a performance that, in Lucille's view, was worthy of an Oscar. He played a far from innocent country boy and drifter who evolves into a cruel and manipulative TV host lusting for power.

Directed by Elia Kazan from a script by Budd Schulberg, it starred Patricia Neal, with support from Walter Matthau and Tony Franciosa. It marked the film debut of Lee Remick, cast as a sexy baton twirler who attracts the lusty eye of the Griffith character. Since its release, it had developed a cult following.

Since their inaugural meeting, he had divorced his first wife, Barbara Bray Edwards and was on the verge of marrying a Greek actress, Solica Cassuto. Again, that union was doomed to fail.

"I always respected Andy, both as a courteous gentleman and an artist of great talent," Lucille said.

In the spring of 1983, she heard about a bad turn in his health, and phoned him. He had been diagnosed with Guillain-Barré Syndrome, which had paralyzed him from the knees down. It took seven months of recovery before he could walk again.

***

Lucille might have viewed the Brooklyn-born comedian, Joan Rivers, as stiff competition, but, for the most part, was supportive of her. She was eager to work with her in a November 5 telecast, *Lucy and Joan Rivers Do Jury Duty.*

The episode was configured was a spoof of the taut 1957 drama, *12 Angry Men*. Although it had flopped at the box office, it had starred Henry Fonda in one of his favorite roles. It had already been spoofed in other sitcoms, notably *The Odd Couple* and *All in the Family.*

The Brooklyn-born Rivers became celebrated for her controversial comedic *persona*, regularly going—in Lucille's view—"where angels fear to tread." She often roasted celebrities, most notably Elizabeth Taylor, who once, according to Rivers, "ballooned up, becoming a fat mama."

He was a long way from Mayberry.

Andy Griffith appears during a key dramatic moment of *A Face in the Crowd (1957).* In it, he showed America that he was far more talented as an actor then he later appeared to be in his long-running sitcom, *The Andy Griffith Show* (1960-68).

He played a backwoods guitarist who reveals, with tragic consequences, his latent egomania and thirst for power.

It was the meatiest, most brilliant, and "most satisfying" (his words) role he ever played.

Johnny Carson on *The Tonight Show* did more than any other person to make Rivers famous across the country, even letting her host his show during his absence.

In 1986, she became the first woman to host a late-night talk show, *The Late Show Starring Joan Rivers*. After being designated as its host, she phoned Carson to talk the matter over with him, but he slammed down the phone on her.

Although Lucille was generally supportive of her, she may have felt jealous when TV critic Jack Gould defined Rivers as "quite possibly the most intuitively funny woman alive."

Rivers had married Edgar Rosenberg in 1965, which led to the birth of her only child, Melissa Rivers. She would later describe her marriage as a "total sham," even though it lasted for twenty-two years.

[*In August of 1987, Rosenberg, suffering from clinical depression and in a hotel room in Philadelphia at the time, committed suicide with an overdose of prescription medications. Nancy Reagan was one of the first persons to telephone*

Rivers with her condolences upon Rosenberg's death.]

Over the course of many years, Rivers consistently shocked her audiences, none more so than in 2012, when she told host Howard Stern that "back in the 1960s, my husband, Edgar, had a one-night stand with Robert Mitchum."

A young **Joan Rivers,** before she fine-tuned her *schtick*, poses here with the more experienced **Lucille**.

"She was actually my rival," Lucille confessed. "But I had to pretend to be her friend, fearing that she would turn on me like she did with that fatty pig, Elizabeth Taylor."

***

Still hoping to attract a younger audience, a November 19 telecast, *The Carters Meet Frankie Avalon,* teamed her with that singer and actor. Avalon, a major-league teen idol from 1958 to 1962, had 31 hit U.S. Billboard singles. Two of the best-selling had been "Venus" and "Why?."

Although he eventually got tired of them (who wouldn't?), he became famous for his "beach films." As justification for moving on to other artistic pursuits, he said, "Even a seagull leaves the beach from time to time, and I'm getting a little sick of sand."

Two of Lucille's scriptwriting "regulars," Bob O'Brien and Fred S. Fox, joined forces to fashion this comedy, where the Carters go to see Avalon's show at a nightclub. Kim (Lucie Arnaz), from her seat in the audience, is invited to come onto the stage and perform with him. She goes over so well that she's invited to perform with Avalon in the club's amateur contest.

In the song-and-dance number that follows, Lucie spoofs Cher, with Avalon pulling off an amazing impersonation of Sonny. Lucie recalled that Cher took the spoof with good-natured grace. She even lent Lucie her wig and was said to have laughed louder than Sonny when the episode was televised.

***

Lucille's appearance on *The Merv Griffin Show,* telecast in November for 90 minutes, quickly expanded to include other members of her family. She had always liked the gay host, and would appear with him several more times in the future.

On this occasion, she came on the air with Lucie Arnaz, Gary Morton, and Desi Jr., who had recently dyed his hair red for a movie role. Lucille's co-star in *Here's Lucy,* Gale Gordon, joined them, too.

Griffin allowed Lucille "to shamelessly promote" her film, *Mame.*

Bob Hope also showed up. Usually he had his gag writers create one-liners and quips for him in advance,, but on this occasion, he was "unscripted."

Before the end of 1973, Lucille did two more specials and some concluding episodes of *Here's Lucy*. First came *A Show Business Salute to Milton Berle* (December 4), celebrating his 60th anniversary as "Mr. Television." *[He and Lucille had had a brief affair in the late 1930s.]* Other guests on the show included Jackie Gleason, Kirk Douglas, Jack Benny, and Bob Hope.

That was followed by Lucille appearing as a guest on *The Bob Hope Christmas Show* (December 9). The occasion marked the first time that Lucille and Gary Morton had appeared as man and wife. As one TV critic noted, "Lucille and Gary Morton were anything but Lucy and Ricky Ricardo. What a contrast!"

Shirley Jones and Marie Osmond rounded out the cast, as did Doris Singleton, Lucille's longtime friend.

***

Before year's end, Lucille filmed two more episodes of *Here's Lucy*. First came a script by those *I Love Lucy* writers, Bob Carroll Jr. and Madelyn Davis.

In this latest caper, *Lucy and Chuck Connors Have a Surprise Slumber Party*, , telecast on December 17, Harry (Gale Gordon) has managed to rent Lucy's home to a film crew. Knowing what a trouble-maker Lucy is, Harry orders her to remain far away from her house until shooting is over.

With the mistaken belief that filming had ended, she slips back into her house to discover Connors asleep in her bed.

[At the time, Connors was astonishingly famous, worldwide. In June of 1973, Connors was introduced to the Soviet leader, Leonid Brezhnev, his fan, at a party hosted by President Nixon at the Western White House in San Clemente, California. As news cameras rolled, Connors presented the leader with a cowboy hat, a massive dose of show-biz razzmatazz, and a pair of Colt "Single Action Army Six-Shooters."

Later, as Brezhnev was boarding a plane for Moscow at the conclusion of his U.S. tour, he spotted Connors in the crowd which had gathered to say goodbye. Brezhnev moved through the crowd to shake Connors' hand, and then lunged into the actor's towering hug. Photographers went wild.

Coincidentally, very few U.S. TV shows were being broadcast in the Soviet

HEEEERE's MERV!

Merv Griffin began his career as a big band singer, moved onto a career as a romantic movie hero and eventually rewrote the rules of the entertainment industry.

In addition to maintaining a long-term "arm candy' relationship with Eva Gabor, he interviewed everyone, from Martin Luther King Jr. to Joan Crawford and brought drag queens, revolutionaries and gay activists into the mainstream. He also created the hit game shows *Jeopardy* and *Wheel of Fortune*.

In 2009, Blood Moon's Darwin Porter wrote (and Blood Moon published) the most comprehensive and most scandal-soaked biography of one of the richest and most notorious media moguls in entertainment history.

Union at the time, with the notable exception of Connors' The Rifleman, *which was Brezhnev's favorite TV series.]*

Weeks before appearing in her episode with Connors, Lucille had attended a mostly stag party hosted by her friend, the gay actor Roddy McDowall. As Gary Morton recalled, "It was in the early 70s, the heyday of porn. You could not attend a Hollywood party but what a porn flick was showing on a home screen and a bowl of cocaine rested on a coffee table."

As "entertainment" that particular night, McDowall had obtained a copy of a "blue movie" that Connors had made when he was a young man. In it, he emerged with a huge erection and sodomized a young man. That film was followed with a gaggle of other porn flicks, including a pirated copy of *Deep Throat* (1972), starring Linda Lovelace.

"I had heard that Chuck was a baseball star, but I didn't know he carried a bat that big in his pants," Lucille said.

Actually, Connors had enjoyed rousing successes as both a baseball and a basketball star. He was one of only 13 athletes in the history of professional sports to have played in both Major League Baseball (Brooklyn Dodgers, 1949; Chicago Cubs, 1951) and also in the National Basketball Association (Boston Celtics, 1947-48). But his greater fame came when he was cast as Lucas McCain, the gunslinging rancher turned single father in *The Rifleman* (1958-1963).

Chuck Connors appears above with **Doris Day** in *Move Over, Darling*, released in 1963 after more than its share of frenzy, rage, and upset. It was a remake of *My Favorite Wife* (1940) with Cary Grant and Irene Dunne.

Shortly before *Move Over, Darling* was conceived, an earlier attempt to revive its older role model was started but never completed. Entitled *Something's Got to Give*, it was Marilyn Monroe's last attempt to star in a feature film, one in which she would co-star with Dean Martin.

After endless delays on her part, often not showing up for for her scenes at all, she was fired by 20th Century Fox. Martin then turned down the "counterpart role."

***

Although those *I Love Lucy* writers, Bob Carroll Jr. and Madelyn Davis, had submitted many a weak script for the *Here's Lucy* series, they were in top form in their latest episode, *Lucy Plays Cops and Robbers*, telecast on the last day of December, 1973. During its filming, she enjoyed strong support from her two leading men, Dick Sargent and Gary Crosby.

As a response to a series of burglaries that had been plaguing nearby homes, Lucy organizes a Neighborhood Watch Committee supervised by two local policemen.

Every night since then, she has imagined that someone is trying to break in on her. It doesn't take a rocket scientist to figure out that one night it will be a real-life burglar. That role was winningly shouldered by character actor Gino Conforti.

Lucille's oldest friend, Mary Wickes, had the most humorous role, that of a hysterical housewife with a long-suffering, hen-pecked husband.

[Unknown to most viewers, Wickes had portrayed the first videotaped version of Mary Poppins, having beat out Julie Andrews by more than a decade.]

Richard Cox, who had grown up in California's Carmel-by-the-Sea, later changed his name to Dick Sargent, a name he stole from an illustrator for the *Saturday Evening Post*. His father, Col. Elmer Fox, had been the business manager for both Douglas Fairbanks Sr. and Erich von Stroheim.

After studying drama at Stanford University, Sargent broke into the movies, appearing in such pictures as *Operation Petticoat* (1959) shot in Key West, Florida. Sargent, along with the stars of that picture, Cary Grant and Tony Curtis, were said to have had "a gay old time" in the bars of this old seaport.

It was rumored that Sargent "developed the hots" for Elvis Presley during the filming of *Live a Little, Love a Little* (1968). Reportedly, the object of Sargent's affection (Presley), remained unresponsive.

Sargent enjoyed his greatest fame after becoming the second actor to portray Darrin Stephens in ABC's hit TV sitcom, *Bewitched* (1964-1972), starring Elizabeth Montgomery.

Lucille had long known Bing Crosby and his wife, the former singer and actress, Dixie Lee. Now, she was working alongside their son, Gary.

[Gary was an accomplished recording artist in his own right. As a teen, Gary had dueted with his father, releasing "Sam's Song" and "Play a Simple Melody." Both of these became hits, the first in recording history, for a double-sided record. In the 1940s, he had performed in a group called "The Crosby Boys," and before working with Lucille, Gary had appeared with the likes of Sammy Davis Jr., Louis Armstrong, Pat Boone, and Tennessee Ernie Ford. In 1965, he had appeared in Girl Happy *with Elvis, with whom he had been stationed in Germany during their respective stints in the U.S. Army.]*

Dick Sargent with **Elizabeth Montgomery** in *Bewitched*.

On National Coming Out Day, 1991, Sargent publicly revealed his homosexuality. Within a year, he evolved into one of the entertainment industry's leading advocates for Gay rights and a Grand Marshal in the Los Angeles Pride Parade. Riding beside him in an open convertible was his co-star in Bewitched, Elizabeth Montgomery.

There was a certain irony there. Her father, the legendary actor, Robert Montgomery, had been widely publicized as a notorious homophobe before his death a decade earlier.

***

At one point, Lucille had briefly considered booking "The Crosby Boys" onto *Here's Lucy*, but never followed through with her idea. She was not around to witness the tragic ending of two of the Crosby brothers.

After heavy drinking and many emotional problems, Lindsay, the youngest of the four sons, died on December 11, 1989 from a self-inflicted rifle shot to the head. The police revealed that he committed suicide in a Las Virgenes (California) apartment after learning that the inheritance he had relied on to support his family had "evaporated." He was only 51 years old.

A family spokesperson later claimed that Dennis never recovered from his brother Lindsay's death. He was 56 when he, too, shot himself to death on May 7, 1991. It was reported that he sat on a sofa, aimed a 12-gauge shotgun at his forehead, and pulled the trigger.

Tabloids later referred to the motivation for their suicides as "The Crosby Curse."]

> When Lucille worked in a telecast with **Gary Crosby**, she was shocked at the hatred he had for his father, Bing.
>
> Six years after his father's death, Gary wrote his autobiography, *Going My Own Way*.
>
> In it, he detailed his struggle with alcoholism and that of his mother, Dixie Lee, who suffered from the same addiction. But what shocked readers, and did much to damage the reputation of Bing Crosby himself, was what Gary revealed about growing up. He cited the physical and emotional abuse he suffered at the hand of his father.

***

Bob Carroll Jr. and Madelyn Davis turned in one of their better scripts, *Lucy Is N.G* (i.e., "No Good") *as an R.N.,* telecast on January 21, 1974.

Lucy designates herself as a nurse to Kim (Lucie Arnaz) when she comes down with a bad case of the flu. Shortly thereafter, Harry (Gale Gordon) suffers a wrenched knee, and Mary Jane Croft breaks each of her hands. In her eagerness to emulate Florence Nightingale, Lucy is kept hysterically busy.

As a regular on *Here's Lucy* (as she had been on *The Lucy Show*), Croft had developed a hard-earned reputation as an actress who could portray almost any character: old women, society belles, and back alley floozies.

Cast as a doctor, veteran character actor Roy Roberts made his last appearance on TV, capping a 40-year career in which he appeared in 900 productions on stage and on the screen.

Although viewers often did not know his name, his face was most recognizable.

In his last role, he had been cast opposite Lucy as a veterinarian.

***

During the filming of the episode entitled *Meanwhile, Back at the Office* (telecast on January 14), Lucille renewed her relationship with Don Porter.

He was far better known for playing Peter Sands, the boss and foil of

Ann Sothern's character on *Private Secretary,* a hit TV sitcom in the 1950s. A retooled version of the series, now entitled *The Ann Sothern Show,* appeared later.

In 1977, Porter was in Key West (Florida) co-starring as "The Commodore" with Eartha Kitt in the film version of *Butterflies in Heat* (also known as *The Last Resort)* based on Darwin Porter's best-selling cult classic novel.

In Key West, (Don) Porter spoke at length with Darwin Porter (no relation), author of this biography, about his experience working with Lucille. In early October of 1959, he had co-starred with both Ann Sothern and Lucille.

"Of course, I much preferred working with Ann," Porter said. "It was smooth-going with her. In contrast, Lucille barked orders coming from such a deep throat she could do voice-overs as a male. She was the boss, and she told you what to do and how to do it. She was a tyrant with her fellow cast members and crew. I felt sorry for hen-pecked Gary Morton. It was obvious to me, and to everybody, that she wore the pants in that family."

"If Morton at one time had *cojones,* he'd lost them by now. I have a suspicion that Lucille snipped them off. Desi showed up one afternoon looking a little worse for wear. No, that's not true. He looked a hell of a lot worse for wear. All those years of boozing had caught up with him."

"Lucille was quite open with me," Don Porter said, "telling me what I already know. Her series, *Here's Lucy,* was nearing its final curtain, as we say in the world of show biz. Her Nielsen ratings were plummeting."

"I had worked in a minor role on *Mame,* and both of us lamented the failure of that picture. She had had such high hopes for it, and she confessed that she'd cried when she read all those unfavorable comparisons to Rosalind Russell."

"At my age, I know there is no future for me in feature films," she admitted to him. "That might as well include TV. Instead of photographing me in soft focus from twenty feet away, a photographer will need to step back a mile."

Later, Porter claimed he talked to two executives from CBS. "I won't name them in case the network has a role to offer me. One told me that the expiration date of Lucille as a television star was long overdue. His exact words were, 'It's time for her to retire and spend the rest of her day accepting lifetime achievement awards.'"

Don Porter preferred working with Ann Sothern more than he did filming telecasts with Lucille.

"Long after we worked together," he said, "my agent told me that Lucille might want to meet with me about appearing with her in a pilot for TV," Porter said.

"The meeting never happened. If I was informed correctly, I heard that she had financed five pilots starring herself. No networks and no sponsors were interested. In the pilots, she brought back her faithful lapdog, Gale Gordon, and also developed husband-and-wife roles for Gary Morton and herself."

"I don't think she wants to make horror movies like Joan Crawford or Bette Davis," Porter said. "No one would believe Lucy Ricardo as a female Frankenstein."

Porter himself faced dwindling prospects, making his last TV appearance in 1988 in the *CBS Summer Playhouse*.

He'd married actress Peggy Converse in 1944, and she was at his bedside at their home in Beverly Hills when he died at the age of 84. The couple had a daughter and a son.

It was reported that on the day before he died, he'd watched a screening of the 1965 ABC-TV sitcom *Gidget* in which he'd played the widowed father of 15-year-old "Gidget" Lawrence (Sally Fields).

Many obits identified him as having been born in Miami, Florida. *[Whereas it's true that he was born in Miami, it was in "the other Miami," this one in Oklahoma.]*

***

Lucy the Sheriff, telecast on January 28, 1974, looked smooth on the screen, but off screen, during its filming, it was a different story. Lucille had worked well with her director, Coby Ruskin, but one afternoon, they got into an argument about lighting.

In a fit of anger, she ordered him off the set, giving him only fifteen minutes to pack his possessions and leave. If he remained after that, she threatened, two of her studio guards would forcibly evict him.

After ridding herself of him, she designated herself as the episode's official director. *[Actually, she'd been not only its star, but the director, too, even before she fired him.]*

According to the plot, Lucy is invited to Cartridge, Montana, for a festival. The local townspeople had learned that she's the great-granddaughter of Flora Belle Orcutt, the first female sheriff of this Western outpost.

Lucy hits town and becomes not only the chief law enforcement officer, but the queen of the festival too. As in all Lucy plots, she gets into trouble. This time around, she has to deal with some real bank robbers.

Her long-time friend and frequent co-star, Mary Wickes, appeared in the episode. So did Ross Elliott, who had played the director of her TV commercial for *Vitameatavegamin,* the episode telecast back in May of 1952 on *I Love Lucy.*

Lucille liked the name of Flora Belle, and would use it again in *Stone Pillow,* her last made-for-TV movie.

***

Unofficially, Lucille referred to her next show (Number 139, telecast on February 11), as "Old Home Week." It was formally entitled *Milton Berle Is the Life of the Party.* Written by Bob Carroll Jr. and Madelyn Davis, it reteamed her with "Mr. Television."

[Lucy had often proclaimed, "Uncle Miltie is the biggest thing on TV," an informal reference to his legendary sexual endowment.]

In this current episode, Berle offers his comedic talents to the organizers of a charity event. For just $7.50, Lucy secures his services.

Berle wasn't the only performer making this episode something akin to "Old Home Week." Several other familiar faces would be appearing with Lucille for the final time. One of them was actor Elliot Reed, who had once been cast with Lucille on *The Lucy Show* back in 1965 in an episode called *Lucy the Stockbroker*.

For the telecast with Berle, she brought back Jack Donohue, her previous director. She always called him "John Francis," his first and middle birth names.

Starting out as a choreographer for the Ziegfeld Follies in the 1920s, Donohue became, in time, an actor, a screenwriter, and a producer. Once, when asked to name the biggest stars with whom he had worked during the long course of his career, he cited Lucille Ball, Dean Martin, Frank Sinatra, Mickey Rooney, and Red Skelton.

In their next script, both Donohue and Lucille decided to better showcase the talents of Mary Jane Croft in *Mary Jane's Boyfriend* (February 18). In Fred S. Fox's plot, Mary Jane has a boyfriend, but he falls for Lucy instead. She has to come up with ways to make herself less appealing.

***

After filming that, Lucille took time out to attend a *Dean Martin Roast* of Jack Benny on February 22, when the longtime comedian suffered insults not only from Lucille and Martin, but from George Burns, Johnny Carson, Rich Little, and other celebrities.

It was back to work again on an episode telecast on February 22, *Lucy and Phil Harris Strike Up the Band*. Donohue stayed on as director, ordering a script written by Bob O'Brien, who had had more misses than hits in previous *Here's Lucy* telecasts.,

Phil Harris is trying to put together a new band, and he turns to the employment agency run by Harry (Gale Gordon) with Lucy as his assistant.

She rounds up musicians from minority groups. However, that doesn't satisfy women's "libbers," who demand that a woman be added to the band. Harris ends up designating Lucy as its girl singer.

Harris, a veteran actor and comedian, was still married to Alice Faye when he worked with Lucille. Faye had been the reigning musical star at Fox in the 1930s until she was replaced by Betty Grable.

Lucille had known Harris for years and called him by his first name ("Wonga"), which in the Cherokee language meant "messenger."

In the 1970s, she and Gary Morton had seen Harris and his band perform in Las Vegas. At one time, he was sought after with the same fervor as Harry James (who had been married to Betty Grable) and his band.

***

Donohue accepted another script from Bob O'Brien, *Lucy Carter Meets Lucille Ball,* telecast on March 4. She used this episode to promote *Mame,* her most recent (and last) feature film.

Kim (Lucie Arnaz) enters a Lucille Ball lookalike contest but is quickly eliminated for how different she looks from Lucille herself. Then Lucy schemes to enter the lookalike contest herself.

One critic wrote, "This episode of *Here's Lucy* turns out to be just one prolonged commercial for *Mame."*

Lucille and one of her co-stars, Carole Cook, were coming to an end of their long professional association. She had even given Cook her first name of Carole, a moniker inspired by Lucille's long-ago friend, Carole Lombard. *[They were indeed close: At Cook's 1964 wedding ceremony to actor Tom Troupe, Lucille had been the matron of honor.]*

Cook recalled, "Lucille looked sad. She knew she was in the final days of *Here's Lucy* and had decided not to try to get CBS to produce another season of the show.:"

She told Cook, "I don't know where I'm going from here. I'm used to reporting to work every day. Perhaps I'll take up knitting."

***

The director, Jack Donohue, tapped himself as a guest co-star on the March 11 telecast, *Where Is My Wandering Mother Tonight?*. In preparation, Madelyn Davis and Bob Carroll Jr. did their final work on a *Here's Lucy* script.

The plot contained a touch of realism—something akin to a chapter drawn from the actual life of Lucille and her daughter, Lucie Arnaz.

Through the intervention of Harry (Gale Gordon), Kim (i.e., Lucie) invites her mother for a weekend at her apartment. Eavesdropping, Lucy hears her daughter talking to a friend and learns she is not a welcome guest. Devastated, Lucy then arranges to disappear.

To end the 1973-74 season of *Here's Lucy,* Donohue came back to helm a final telecast, *Lucy Fights the System* (March 18). Co-stars were Mary Treen and Jack Collins.

At Harry's employment agency, Treen was depicted as a middle-aged waitress who has been fired because of her age. Vengefully, Lucy plots to get even with the owner and sends over her daughter Kim (Lucie) to wait tables in her place. Of course, Lucy's mission is to drive the restaurant owner "wacky."

Kim quickly evolves into the worst waitress in the history of the food and beverage industry. Clearly, this episode belongs to her daughter, who steals the show.

An actress from Missouri, Treen never made it into the major leagues, but she worked steadily in character roles, becoming a familiar face to Americans, even if they didn't know her name. She made her first movie in an uncredited role in 1930, and most of her films have been forgotten. On rare occasions, she would appear in a celebrated picture. Such was the case when she got a role in *Kitty Foyle* (1940), starring Ginger Rogers. Treen was also seen in the 1946 movie, *It's a Wonderful Life,* starring James Stewart. Her longest-running gig was as Hilda, the baby nurse and housemaid in 64 episodes of the sitcom, *The Joey Bishop Show,* which ran from 1962 to 1965.

Brooklyn-born Jack Collins also appeared in the final episode. He'd starred on the previous series, *The Lucy Show,* but was better known for playing Mike Brady's boss, Mr. Philips, on the hit TV sitcom, *The Brady Bunch* beginning in 1970.

The telecast also marked the *adieu* of a married couple in real life, Vanda Barra and Sid Gould, the cousin of Gary Morton. They would eventually divorce.

Gale Gordon, after years of being cast with Lucille, ended on a sad note. He gets a pie thrown into his deadpan face. "I suspected it would end like this," he said. "In TV history, I think I took more physical abuse, even more than The Three Stooges."

The telecast marked the end of Lucille's twenty-three years of weekly television.

"It's the end of an era," she proclaimed.

***

As television moved deeper into the 1970s, Lucille went off the air with a #29 in the Nielsen ratings.

CBS, along with the other networks, was reinventing itself, telecasting such programs as the controversial *All in the Family* or *The Mary Tyler Moore Show. The Bob Newhardt Show* and M*A*S*H were drawing wide audiences, too. *Gunsmoke* still hung around for one more season.

In 1974, Lucille remained as the sole survivor of the Golden Age of Vintage Television. She still had a contract with CBS and would fulfill it by doing a number of TV specials.

A very profitable new source of money was opening up for her, and she didn't have to entertain in person anymore. She delayed turning *Here's Lucy* over for syndication because reruns of both *I Love Lucy* and *The Lucy Show* were being telecast first by Telepictures and later by Warner Brothers Television.

When *Here's Lucy* did go into syndication, it attracted low ratings and was, in 1985, withdrawn. Throughout most of the 1980s and the first part of the 1990s, it was largely forgotten. However, reruns came back on the air in 1998.

Somewhere around the world today, reruns of all the Lucy shows are being shown on TV sets.

Facing a rather bleak summer of 1974, Lucille told Gary Morton, "Should I try for yet another series? Both Desi Jr. and Lucie have gone off to pursue careers of their own. I can cast another 'son' and 'daughter,' perhaps just two boys, or maybe two girls?"

Morton offered some worthwhile and very timely advice: "Give it a rest, kid."

CHAPTER TWELVE

After the Lingering, Long-Awaited Death of *Here's Lucy,*

Lucille Forges Ahead
With a Frenzied Campaign to Re-Invent Herself

Lucille's mother, DeDe, was strongly opposed to seeing her daughter giving up on her TV series. Along with a group of her aging girlfriends, she had frequently attended live performances, laughing and cheering Lucille on in whatever episode she was crafting.

At a CBS board meeting, while discussing Lucille's decision to ease herself out of her trauma-soaked TV series, one executive said he was relieved that Lucille "had gone into that good night voluntarily. It would be hard having to tell a living TV legend that it was time to sit home like grandma."

Board members generally agreed, however, that Lucille was not altogether washed up. It was suggested that she should probably be showcased as a guest on other hit shows, and that she should be configured as the centerpiece of occasional star-studded anniversary tributes every now and then.

On Monday nights, Lucille's venues were replaced with the sitcom *Maude,* starring Bea Arthur, the strong-willed actress who had previously appeared with her in *Mame.*

It was no secret that Lucille found *Maude* "perverse." Making things worse was the fact that she also strongly objected to *All in the Family* for its bluntness in handling sensitive issues like race. Her favorite sitcom at this point was *The Mary Tyler Moore Show,* which she considered relatively inoffensive.

Lucille, however, could not resist the spotlight forever. Eventually, she agreed to appear with Dinah Shore on one of her specials, *Dinah!,* which was slated for an October 13, 1972 telecast.

She had long been one of Lucille's favorite singers, and she liked working with her. Together, they performed a duet, "Bosom Buddies" from Lucille's recently released, tepidly reviewed film, *Mame.*

After its telecast, Dinah invited Lucille to join her for a weekend in Palm Springs, an invitation she willingly accepted.

Dinah seemed to have recovered from being dumped by Burt Reynolds and was seen out with other men, some of them even more enticing than the nude centerfold.

But for personal reasons, it was Reynolds that Lucille wanted to talk about. Her daughter, Lucie, had started dating him, and he was fast emerging as a top box office attraction and one of the most desirable men in America.

How did Lucie's romantic link with Reynolds begin?

Its origins lay with Liza Minnelli, the half-sister of Lorna Luft, who was also involved with Reynolds. Coincidentally, Lucille's son, Desi Jr., had enjoyed a prolonged and rather torrid affair with Liza.

The ins and outs of these unusual and closely intertwined matings were detailed in history's most comprehensive biography of Burt Reynolds, published by Blood Moon Productions in 2019. It was subtitled *Put the Pedal to the Metal; How a Nude Centerfold Sex Symbol Seduced Hollywood.*

***

After Liza Minnelli's great success as Sally Bowles in *Cabaret* (1972), she said, "I was sent 400 scripts before I found one I wanted to do." It was *Lucky Lady* (1975), a 20th Century Fox release, a Prohibition-era saga about bootleggers who hauled, by boat, their illegal cargoes from the Pacific coast of Mexico into San Diego. Liza (as Claire) romances her two male counterparts and smuggles black-market liquor.

The film's producer, Michael Gruskoff, was fully aware that there were only two "bankable" female stars who might portray Claire: Liza Minnelli and Barbra (Streisand). Streisand rejected the part, but Liza went for it after reading the script by Willard Huyck and Gloria Katz. *[As a writing team, they had scored big with their authorship of the script for* American Graffitti *(1973) directed by George Lukas. They were paid $450,000 for the script, which at the time was a record for an original screenplay.]*

In his second movie with Judy Garland's daughter, **Burt Reynolds** played a cop and **Liza Minnelli** was cast as a prostitute. She "rents" him, not for stud duties, but to protect her from killers out to do her in.

Alan Ladd Jr., the CEO of Fox Studios and son of the famous actor of the 1940s and '50s, turned to Stanley Donen and hired him as its director for $600,000.

As "royalty," i.e., the daughter of Judy Garland and director Vincente Minnelli, Liza had grown up appreciating the musicals of Donen, who had once had an affair with her friend, Elizabeth Taylor. Donen had helmed Fred Astaire in scenes where he appeared to be (effortlessly) dancing on the ceiling, and Gene Kelly in *Singin' in the Rain*.

Liza was disappointed when both Paul Newman and Warren Beatty rejected the script and were replaced by Burt Reynolds, for $500,000, and George Segal for $750,000. Segal later bowed out, his role going to Gene Hackman, who at first was reluctant to accept. However, when he was offered $1.2 million, he said, "It would have been obscene for me to refuse that figure."

For the shoot, which would last a hundred days, cast and crew were flown to Guaymas in Mexico, a site defined by the location agent for Fox as "a sleepy seaport on the Gulf of California." It was thought at the time that Guaymas would be ideal because of the calmness of its waters. But production was delayed on several occasions when harsh winds swept down from the north, threatening to capsize nearly a hundred vessels moored nearby.

As a sign of Burt's expanding popularity with women, he was literally mobbed when he showed up at a drunken wedding party. "The women were very aggressive," Donen said. "Once or twice, Burt got his crotch felt, and one woman exposed her breasts to him."

Soon, Burt and Liza were generating tabloid headlines that heralded their "torrid affair." That brought Jack Haley Jr., her husband, to the scene. To help calm things down, Dinah took time out from her busy schedule to fly in on weekends.

As Liza reportedly said, "Burt was not screwing me, but he *was* bedding my sister, Lorna Luft."

Liza had cajoled Lorna to fly down to the location shoot to meet Reynolds, although her half-sister was not that interested in him at first. Lorna later said, "As millions of tabloid readers knew, Burt was a disaster waiting to happen. Half the women in America were in love with him—but not me."

Lorna's affair with Burt seemed doomed from the start. When she first met him, she had not seen any of his movies, not on the big screen or on television.

And "in the flesh," he didn't impress her all that much, either. She was twenty years old, and he was more than a decade older than her—and he wore a *toupée*. But when they returned to Los Angeles, he began to pursue her with an aggressive campaign, sending flowers, telegrams, messages, and letters, just as he would later in his pursuit of Lucie Arnaz.

Soon, Lorna read unwanted tabloid headlines—GARLAND'S KID STEALS BURT FROM DINAH.

"I suddenly found myself in the position of the woman who had stolen the man of America's Sweetheart," Lorna said. "Months later, those same rumors would swirl around Lucie."

FAMOUS MOTHER, FAMOUS DAUGHTER

Liza Minnelli (left) poses with her legendary mother, **Judy Garland.**

"Both of us had poor judgment when it came to picking husbands," Judy claimed.

***

News of Dinah Shore's romantic troubles with Burt Reynolds had been traveling for weeks along the Hollywood grapevine, but on April 17, 1975, reports about it began moving across the wire services. Fans across America were shocked when gossip columnist Joyce Haber announced in her column that Dinah's affair with Burt had ended.

Friends sided with one party or the other. Farrah Fawcett denounced Burt in the press. "I think Reynolds revealed the news to reporters because he was too much of a coward to face Dinah himself. Don't expect her to give any interviews about the breakup. She's too busy crying."

Burt's press agent, David Gershenson, rushed to his defense. "They were never married, so it's not like they're getting a divorce. They also have no kids to worry about, so it's a much easier break. There are hundreds of couples in Hollywood who hook up with each other, and then later go their separate ways. It's no big deal. Burt and Dinah were just going together. There will be other women for Burt and, I'm sure, other men for Dinah, who is most attractive and charming. Of course, for Burt now, the world is his oyster, as he is just entering his glory days as a movie star."

In the months leading to their breakup, Dinah had flown to Mexico where Burt was shooting *Lucky Lady* with Liza Minnelli. "She lit up the place whenever she was around," Liza said, "especially Burt's eyes. He seemed to adore her. She'd fly back on Sunday night, often with Burt's dirty laundry."

During the final weeks of the shoot, Burt was out of touch, and Dinah could not get through to him on the phone, thinking first that the phone wires were down. He finally sent word to her that he would see her when he got back, but "I'll be staying at my own place."

To Dick Clayton, he confessed, "Thanks in part to you, my career is soaring. Women are literally throwing themselves at me. I want to enjoy the fruits of my fame. I've worked so hard to get where I am, and I hope to enjoy the reward that comes with being a box office champ. More than that, I want a kid of my own, and Dinah can't give me that. But I still love her, and I guess I always will."

The following night he phoned Dinah, telling her that he had returned from Mexico and was coming over. "I'll remember it always. She was sitting in her living room listening to an album by Frank Sinatra. She had a hanky in her hand as if she was prepared for what I was about to tell her. I never sat down but stood before her. I wanted to make it quick before she could melt my resolve."

The more the affair of **Dinah Shore** *(right)* with **Burt Reynolds** was publicized, the more agonizing and embarrassing it became when it (inevitably) ended.

"When I told her I was leaving her, she was very composed. She took the news with all the dignity I had come to expect of her. I knew I had to be striking a blow to her heart, but I had to go through with it. I was the second fella who'd walked out on her. The first was the love of her life, George Montgomery, her longtime husband. George broke her heart, just what I was doing. But I also knew that heart of hers would mend—the lady, after all, is a survivor."

Dinah confessed to Lucille that weekend in Palm Springs, "What Burt didn't tell me was that he was getting more deeply involved with Lorna Luft. I had to learn that from the tabloids."

After moving on and away from Lorna, daughter of a famous mother, Judy Garland, Burt in time began to date Lucie Arnaz, daughter of yet another famous mother, Lucille Ball.

At first, Lucie did not find life with Reynolds all that compatible. "He was a homebody and I liked to go out every night. But I really came to care for him. Behind that *bravado* façade, there actually lived a sensitive, loving man."

Unknown to Lorna at the time, Burt was reassessing his former relationship with Dinah.

To Lucille, sitting by Dinah's swimming pool, Dinah revealed what happened next.

***

According to Burt, "I began to miss Dinah the moment I walked out the door. For weeks, I could think of nothing else but Dinah. I had promised I'd be her friend forever—and meant it. But that wasn't the same as turning over in bed at night and finding her there."

Throughout their relationship, Dinah had always tried to be accommodating, rearranging her schedule to fit his needs and wants. She would come home from the studio after enduring a heavy work schedule and prepare him a gourmet dinner.

"I'm sure Burt came to miss Dinah, but I didn't feel that sorry for him," Clayton said. "He was having an affair with Lorna Luft but didn't seem to want to talk about it."

When confronted by the press, Lorna said, "Burt and I like each other very much. We go out together and have a lot of fun. He has a great sense of humor. Don't blame me for his breakup with Dinah. When he started going out with me, he had already decided to split with Dinah. If it hadn't been me, it would have been some other girl."

"The press came down hard on me." Burt said. "Leaving Dinah was like breaking up with the Stars and Stripes. First in any relationship comes the fireworks. Then you ease into the next stage. Passion can die, and you settle in together leading a more subdued life. By then, it's a different kind of love. The final curtain can be that you grow old together, sitting around watching television."

"Dinah once told me she didn't want to grow old in my arms, and I understood that. I guess I wanted to put that first-stage passion back into my life. I wasn't ready to settle down into domestic bliss, at least not now."

"The breakup was awfully hard on Dinah," said Jane Brolin, wife of Jim Brolin, the *Marcus Welby* star. "Dinah gives, gives, and gives some more. She's low right now, but I feel she'll bounce back. That's what she does."

Peter Marshall, of TV's *Hollywood Squares,* was a friend of Dinah's. "She puts up a good front, even though her heart is breaking. Of course, that good ol' Southern boy has upset her a lot. Many people like Esther Williams told me she thinks Dinah is getting too old to start another passionate relationship with a man."

Actually, Dinah was seen going out any a number of dates, notably with Ron Ely, best known for portraying Tarzan on the 1966 NBC TV series. This was one tall Texan, standing 6'4" with an athletic build. He was younger than Burt by two years.

He was the same age as Frank Langella, who also was spotted going out with Dinah. A stage and film actor, that Italian American from New Jersey would win four Tony Awards.

Dinah was also seen out with Frank Gifford, the American football player, actor, and TV sports commentator. For twelve years, he'd been a halfback and flanker for the New York Giants.

For a while, Dinah also dated Wayne Rogers, the film and TV actor known for playing the role of Captain "Trapper" John McIntyre in the CBS TV series, M*A*S*H.

An incongruous beau was Iggy Pop. Burt had been born in 1936, but the "Godfather of Punk" entered the world in 1947. Often appearing on stage bare-chested with long hair, he was the vocalist of the proto-punk band, "The Stooges."

One afternoon in October, a mass of flowers was delivered to Dinah's door without a card. At around midnight, she got a call from Burt. Without asking for an invitation, or even inquiring to see if she were with some "gentleman caller," he announced he was coming over. An hour later, he arrived with a suitcase. "I brought my toothbrush," he said as an indication that he planned to spend the night.

Actually, he was moving back in.

The following morning over breakfast, he told her, "I'm back for good. This time, it's forever."

It had taken a while, but eventually Lorna appeared to be falling in love with Reynolds. It then came as a total surprise when she confronted the headline—BURT AND DINAH BACK TOGETHER. Reportedly, Lorna was devastated.

Months later, when he encountered Lorna, he admitted, "I was a complete asshole."

Later, Lorna was quoted as saying, "The guy is a self-admitted schmuck."

***

To celebrate Reynolds' re-entry into her life, Dinah leased a luxurious beach house in Malibu. During their residency there, Dinah had her elegant Beverly Hills home redecorated, more to his taste than hers. Occasionally, they went out together, but never to a gala or premiere, preferring an intimate dinner at their favorite restaurant, The Saloon, in Beverly Hills. When a reporter asked him if he had reconciled with Dinah, he answered, "We're just good friends."

Their romance continued even during his gig in Valdosta, Georgia, for the shooting of his latest movie, *Gator,* released in 1976.

When friends asked him about Dinah, he said, "She's my very best friend. I see her often. I visit her place in Malibu." He left out mention of the fact that he was living there, too. "I see her on occasion when we have something to talk over."

"Dinah's in a kind of limbo," said Frank Sinatra. "I talked to her about Burt. He's back, but she can't count on him staying."

Around the end of December, Burt moved back into Dinah's redecorated Beverly Hills home. When asked by the press, he said, "My relationship with her is better and more romantic than ever. She has the body of a 25-year-old and the mind of a mature woman."

But in a few weeks, without warning, he suddenly stopped living in her beautiful home—and didn't even call.

Disillusioned for being "dumped" a second time, Dinah said, "There's one thing I've learned about men. You can't trust them, no woman can. They're adorable creatures, but more gamesmanship than trustmanship."

As time went by, their friendship remained, but the love affair was over.

Burt had fallen in love with another singer: Tammy Wynette.

***

Burt confessed one night to his best friend, actor James Best, "I still have this thing for older women. For years, I thought I might seduce Lucille Ball. I think she could go for me bigtime. But instead of turning my macho charm on Lucille, I've directed it at her daughter, Lucie Arnaz. That's Lucie with an 'IE' at the end. She goes ballistic when she sees her name misspelled in the paper as 'Luci.'"

[Lucie was born in 1951, Reynolds in 1936. Burt began his affair with Arnaz in 1976, near the end of her marriage to actor Phil Vandervort, whom she divorced in 1977.]

Burt had first seen Lucie when she'd appeared briefly in walk-ons on her mother's TV series, *The Lucy Show.* She appeared again with her mother in *Here's Lucy* (1968-1974). In 1975, she played a murder victim in the NBC telefilm, *Who Is the Black Dahlia?*

"I'm realistic about show-biz," Lucie said. "Being the daughter of Lucille Ball is like being the son of Frank Sinatra. Sinatra Junior and I know we'll never come within miles of equaling the fame of our parents."

One night she told Burt, "Thank you for not asking what it's like to have super famous parents. Everybody I meet asks me that same question. I don't know how to answer it because that's the only life I've known. When my parents used to take me out, they were mobbed by autograph seekers. In spite of her fame, Lucille was never a flamboyant movie star like Joan Crawford. She was a wife and mother first and second, and a star in third place."

"As a kid, I got used to walking into our living room and seeing Elizabeth Taylor, Richard Burton, Bob Hope, or Milton Berle. Henry Fonda might drop in, or Katharine Hepburn."

"I was devastated when my parents divorced, and now, I'm getting my first divorce. I know I might marry again someday to someone."

"Why not me?" Burt asked flirtatiously.

"Just make that a serious proposal, and you'll see me walking down the aisle," she said. "It seems you get off dating the daughters of famous stars."

"Yeah," he said, jokingly. "That's true. Actually, instead of the daughters, I'd have preferred the mothers."

"Well, there may be some truth in that. After Dinah, I wouldn't be surprised."

"I was glad when you agreed to go out with me," Burt said. "But at first, I was afraid I'd have to show up in a dress."

"Please don't kid me about that," she protested. "I've taken enough ribbing."

[She was referring to her affair, beginning in 1971, with Jim Bailey, a cross-dressing "illusionist" known for his stage appearances as Judy Garland and Barbra Streisand.]

"I adore Jim, and we've remained best friends," she said. "Lucille didn't understand him. She told me she was shocked when I started dating a man who prefers dresses to pants. Jim impersonates women on stage. The rest of the time, he wears pants. He likes women."

"Too bad," Burt said. "I was hoping you might hook me up with him."

"Are you always joking?" she asked.

"It seems I have something in common with your brother, Desi Jr." Burt said. "He's involved in a serious affair with my recent co-star, Liza Minnelli. He's dating the daughter of Judy Garland, and I'm going for the daughter of Lucille Ball. Junior and I should get together and chew the fat."

"It's hot and new now with Liza, but it won't work," Lucie said. "My brother learned from a psychic that he and Liza, in former lives, were Louis XVI of France and Marie Antoinette. For them to get married, they might be doomed as they were in their previous lives."

As stated by Burt Reynolds, "First, I dated the daughter of Judy Garland, Lorna Luft. Then I turned my attention to **Lucie Arnaz** (depicted above), the daughter of Lucille Ball."

"Do you know who I was in a previous life?"

"I haven't a clue…perhaps Bluebeard."

"Not at all. Henry VIII. Of course, I weighed more back then."

"Obviously, I get off on Hollywood royalty."

"As I said, always joking. At least you amuse me."

"I do more than that," he said.

On another night, she told him, "It's marvelous we get on so well, since we come from totally different backgrounds. I'm a true daughter of Beverly Hills. My mother, my dad, and my brother are all in show business in one sense or another. Lucille prefers television while dad likes to work more in the background. Junior is breaking into the business of movies and television, too. But I prefer the stage. If I succeed there and become famous, it will be something totally different from my mother."

When queried about her then-romance by the press, Lucie said, "Burt is a lot of fun, and I enjoy being with him. There is no talk of marriage. He's endlessly repeated that he's not the marrying kind. I'm in the throes of a post divorce and not anxious to rush into another bondage. Burt has a roving eye. For all I know, he'll fall in love with his next co-star."

She was right. Her love affair with Reynolds ended moments before he met and fell in love with Sally Field, the co-star of his next film, *Smokey and the Bandit* (1977). According to Lucie, "When it ended, I really cared for the big guy. Sally's a lovely girl. If he dropped me and ran off with some dummy, I might have cut my throat. As it is, I accept it. He got a gem in Sally."

"Of course, Burt will be missed. But he's not completely gone. We've vowed to become friends. He could have done worse than marrying me. But I can't live in the past when there's today and tomorrow to worry about. Didn't Judy say it all in that song about the man who got away?"

***

With Lucille as executive producer and her husband, Gary Morton, as producer, she moved ahead for a big telecast special to be aired on CBS on November 10, 1974. The hour-long show was entitled, *Happy Anniversary and Goodbye*.

She worked with director Jack Donohue in selecting the guest stars who included Art Carney, Nanette Fabray, Don Porter, and—surprise of surprises—Arnold Schwarzenegger.

The plot centers on Malcolm and Norma Michaels (Carney and Lucille), a middle-aged couple who have grown bored with each other. Finally, they separate, hoping to carve out new lives for themselves. Since this is a feel-good special, expect a happy ending after some bumps in the road.

Schwarzenegger makes his television debut as Rico, a masseur, whom Lucy hires to "service" her.

The only scene that evokes slapstick comedy, like that depicted on the *I Love Lucy Show*, is when a lusty Don Porter chases after her. In high heels, she races across a waterbed, puncturing it.

Shot in Las Vegas, the episode featured Lucille looking much older than she had ever allowed herself to be photographed before. Of course, that was appropriate to the role she was playing, that of a middle-aged housewife who is no longer turned on by her husband.

This TV event dealt with more serious topics (pre-marital sex, birth control, and alcoholism) than any of her previous shows. Only the topic of abortion was avoided.

Actor Peter Marshall joined the cast at the last minute. The brother of actress Joanne Dru was better known as the host of *The Hollywood Squares*, a role he had been assigned in 1966 and one which would not go off the air until 1981.

At first, he had been reluctant to sign on, since the last time he had worked with Lucille had been a disaster, back in January of 1963, for an episode of *The Lucy Show*.

[Although that long-ago episode had been "officially" directed by Jack Donohue, Lucille had interfered, rejecting his direction and changing it to suit her own tastes and desires. As Donohue and Lucille argued, Vivian Vance stopped forward to tell Marshall how to play the scene.

Finally, Marshall stormed off the set, shouting, "Who in the fuck is the director, Donohue, Ball, or Vance? Reluctantly, he was finally persuaded to return and finish the scene.]

During rehearsals for the TV special of 1974, he met with Carney over lunch and asked him if he had ever worked with Lucille before. Marshall later told a reporter, "Carney said this was his first time of working with her, and he asked me to give him some pointers."

[Marshall seemed to have gotten it all wrong. Carney surely did not say that. In the feature film, A Guide for the Married Man *(1967), Carney had played Lucille's "cheating heart" husband. Of course, Carney had immortalized himself playing Ed Norton, Jackie Gleason's upstairs neighbor, a sewer worker, on the hit TV sitcom, The Honeymooners.*

Before signing on, Carney had starred in Harry and Tonto (1974), for which he'd won both the Best Actor Oscar and a Golden Glove for his performance as Harry Coombes, an elderly man going on the road with his pet cat.]

For some reason, during filming, Carney was not in his usual good form, and he consistently flubbed his lines. In exasperation, Lucille sarcastically asked him, "Have you ever done comedy before?"

That did it for him. He called her "a fucking bitch," and stormed off the set. It took all of Marshall's persuasive powers to lure him back.

Nanette Fabray had a similar experience during her own conflicts with Lucille. A native of San Diego, she became widely known as an actress, singer, and dancer. In the 1950s, she was Sid Caesar's comedic partner in *Caesar's Hour*, for which she'd won three Emmy Awards. In 1953, she had co-starred with Fred Astaire in *The Band Wagon*.

She, too, did not perform as Lucille demanded. Finally, Fabray shouted at Lucille, "To hell with you"

Art Carney *(upper photo)* and **Nanette Fabray** *(lower photo)* had to bear the brunt of Lucille's attacks on their acting.

They fought back.

and headed for her dressing room to pack her belongings for a hasty departure. This time, it was Donohue who persuaded her to stay.

"Lucille agreed to back off and let me direct her in the final scenes," Donohue said. "Fabray returned to the set, finished the shoot, and made a hasty departure with no farewell."

It was cast member Arnold Schwarzenegger who drew most of Lucille's attention. Nicknamed "The Austrian Oak," he had previously appeared on *The Merv Griffin Show*, which was watched by both Lucille and Gary Morton. She found Schwarzenegger seductive, charming, handsome, and amusing, and asked Morton to phone him the next day to see if he'd join the cast of her special.

After a brief conversation with Morton, Lucille came on the line. In reference to his appearance on Merv's show, she said, "You were fabulous, just great! We'll see you later, right? Come on over. We love you."

She was among the first to realize that the body builder wanted to become an actor, since he knew that muscle men, like ballet dancers, do not tend to have prolonged careers.

Actually, he had already acted in the 1970s film, *Hercules in New York*, for which he'd been credited as "Arnold Strong." *[It had been hailed in some quarters as the worst film ever made. Schwarzenegger's accent was so thick, his lines had to be dubbed. He had also played a deaf-mute mob hitman in* The Long Goodbye *(1973).]*

Lucille soon learned that he had begun lifting weights when he was fifteen years old, back in his native Austria. By the time he was twenty, he was named Mr. Universe, and by 1966, he held the title of "Best Built Man in Europe." His greatest acclaim had come in 1970 when he was named Mr. Olympia, a title he held for seven years.

Over lunch with Lucille, he discussed his dream of becoming an actor, but revealed how difficult it was. "I was told by agents and casting people that my body was 'too weird.' My so-called funny accent was mocked. I was also urged to change my name. It was too long and the 'negger' part sounded too much like a racial slur. Whatever it was about me, I was ordered to change it. Everyone warned me that I could never make it as an actor. I was advised to open a gym in Los Angeles when I grew too old to compete as a bodybuilder. Then you entered my life."

She guided him through his role as the masseur, Rico, who would make Art Carney, her estranged husband, jealous. She would be depicted half-naked and receiving a sensual massage from him, and he would be stripped down, wearing only tight "shorty-shorts" and a tank top, thereby showing off his chest, arms, and bulging legs.

In one scene, Lucille is depicted gasping at his stunning muscular frame.

"How did you get like this?" she asks.

"I actually came from Italy, where I was a truck driver," he claims. "I then became a masseur guy, and I'm very happy to be here today to massage you."

He made up one line of his dialogue: "Lie down so I can work you over."

As Lucy, she got a big laugh when she seemed mesmerized by this "living god" before her, a true Hercules descended from Mount Olympus. She says, "Oh, y..yes...won't you come in. Oh, you're in" Then she rushes to shut the door behind him.

His next line was, "Where do we do it, here or in the bedroom?"

In his memoirs, Schwarzenegger recalled that Lucille followed his career in the years to come. "As tough as her reputation was, she was a sweetheart to me, loving and kind. In the future, after every one of my movies, a letter arrived from her praising me for my work. She told me she saw *Pumping Iron* (1977) three times, and that I had a body for which God had thrown away the mold after creating me, his finest specimen. I thrived on that flattery. She also raved about my breakthrough role in 1982 when I starred in *Conan the Barbarian*, that sword-and-sorcery movie that became a bit hit."

In her employment practices, Lucille was stalwartly gay-friendly, and one day she talked with Schwarzenegger about the large gay following he had developed since early in his career.

"I've never been bothered by homosexuality," he told her. "I'm never annoyed by it because in bodybuilding, a lot of gay men come into the gym, and, as we shower, we are checked out by them. If they tell me how much they like looking at my body, that's fine with me. I'm actually flattered. Of course, they love my body. I worked so damn hard to create it. If I were Sophia Loren, straight men would love my body."

"*Hercules in New York* was a low-budget spoof on the big sword-and-sandals epics," **Arnold Schwarzenegger** said.

"The idea was that Hercules gets bored living on Mount Olympus and rides a stray lightning bolt to present-day New York, even though his father, Zeus, forbids him to leave."

"There's a certain feeling I've always had about freedom. If somebody wants to go out and fuck six chicks at the same time, then that's what he should do. If somebody wants to fuck six guys, then more power to him. It absolutely makes no difference to me."

Lucille's excessive attention to Schwarzenegger raised gossip and speculation among cast and crew. Some claimed that she was having an affair with him, a sort of May/December mating. *[Whereas she'd been born in 1911, he entered the world in 1947.]*

Don Porter, who had recently appeared with Lucille in *Mame,* later discussed those rumors.

"She never admitted to me directly that she had sex with Arnold, but she certainly suggested it," Porter said. "I swear that she was at least giving it consideration, as she was really turned on by the Greek god. She was known for preferring very masculine men. She told me that producers such as Harry Cohn in the 1930s or Louis B. Mayer regularly put starlets on the casting couch."

"I think it only fair that a woman producer like me should have the power to place an attractive male on my own casting couch," she told Porter. "It's happening all over the world between rich women and young men. Take, for example, the *beaux* of Woolworth heiress Barbara Hutton, or the tobacco heiress Doris Duke. Dozens of other rich bitches follow the example set by those two lusty old broads."

She confessed to Porter that she'd already shared some sexual banter with the charming Austrian. "He told me that he was ready and willing, if summoned, to do his duty. His exact words were, "God knows I'm able to perform.'"

"I jokingly suggested to him that I would have to be on top, since all of his 250 pounds of muscle would crush my brittle bones."

Years later, Schwarzenegger claimed, "I never had as devoted a fan as Lucille. She marked a turning point in my career, and her encouragement led to my breaking into the movies. However, if she had been around when I became governor of California (2003-2011), she would have been amazed."

[A few years later, In 1980, Schwarzenegger starred as Mickey Hargitay in The Jayne Mansfield Story. *Loni Anderson played the big-bosomed blonde goddess, performing sexy love scenes with "Ah-nold."*

Hargitay himself showed up on the set and talked to the actor portraying him. In 1956, eleven years before Schwarzenegger, he too had won the title of Mr. Universe.

After hearing about it, Lucille confessed to Joan Rivers, "I had the wet dream of my life. I dreamed I was in bed with Mickey as he looked in 1956 and with Arnold as he looked in 1970. What a setup for a ménage à trois! *In my dream, at least, Mickey, Arnold, and I were still going at it when the sun rose over Los Angeles."]*

***

The Sullivan Years: A Tribute to Ed, was an hour-long telecast from his home studio of CBS. Hosted by Dick Cavett on February 2, 1975, it featured footage from his long-running variety program, *The Ed Sullivan Show.* Film clips from old footage was included, including sequences from *I Love Lucy* in the 1950s that teamed then husband-and-wife, Lucille Ball and Desi Arnaz.

During the peak of his career, Sullivan was hailed as "The Starmaker," since so many of his performers went on to find stardom.

At first, he had resisted booking Elvis Presley because of his "bad boy" image. But the growing popularity of the singer forced him to invite him onto his show. He ordered his cameramen to shoot him from the waist up.

"I don't want him to be caught shaking his thing at my audiences. We are a family-fare show."

Later, like the rest of America, Sullivan became aware of "Beatlemania," sweeping the land. Considering them the next greatest musical sensation after Elvis, he invited the "Fab Four" to appear on his show for a February 9, 1964 broadcast. It became one of the most-watched programs in TV history.

Sullivan came under fire, especially in the South, for booking many African American artists. One of the executives of his sponsor, Ford's Lincoln dealers, was shocked when he kissed Pearl Bailey on the cheek and warmly shook the had of Nat King Cole.

A Lincoln dealer in Chicago phoned him: "I realize you have to have niggers on occasion on your show. But do you have to put your arms around them, as you did with Bojangles after his dance?"

Sullivan was also among the first TV hosts to feature Nashville performers such as Glen Campbell and Johnny Cash.

Sullivan always liked episodes of *I Love Lucy* and *The Lucy Show*, relating to her brand of zany humor. She had appeared with him before. In February of 1956, she and Desi joined the cast of *The MGM Story*, a salute to that studio's 30th anniversary. There would be other appearances, including one star-studded night when she and Desi appeared to celebrate Sullivan's eighth anniversary on TV.

In September of 1974, Lucille learned that the TV host had been diagnosed with an advanced stage of esophageal cancer. Doctors gave him only weeks to live, but his family did not want him to know, informing him that his ailment was caused by his long battle with gastric ulcers.

At Lenox Hill Hospital in Manhattan, Sullivan died on October 13, 1974, two weeks after his 73rd birthday. On a cold rainy day, his funeral was held at St. Patrick's Cathedral and was attended by 3,000 fans.

"I'm told that most bodybuilders are deficient in one department," said **Jayne Mansfield** (right).

"Not so my husband, **Mickey Hargitay**. He's big all over!"

It was perfect casting: **Loni Anderson** as Jayne Mansfield, and **Arnold Schwarzenegger** as Mickey Hargitay in *The Jayne Mansfield Story* (1980).

At the end of filming, Loni told Arnold, "If I ever get divorced, I'll look you up. What a kisser!"

***

The Dean Martin Celebrity Roast was a series of TV specials that developed a wide audience in 1974 and continued for a decade. Its format was modeled after the "roasts" at the New York Friar's Club.

A coven of celebrities, most often friends of a star, turn up at a long table to pay tribute to the "victim." Instead of praising him or her, they roast the star with a series of insults, evocative of Don Rickles' nightclub act.

The telecasts emanated from the Ziegfeld Room of MGM's Grand Hotel in Las Vegas. The telecasts were halted temporarily in 1980 because of the fire that swept through this luxury property.

Lucille was one of the first celebrities to be mocked, appearing in a telecast on February 7, 1975. Guests included Phyllis Diller, Totie Fields, Gale Gordon, Bob Hope, Rich Little, Don Rickles, Ginger Rogers, Rowan & Martin, even Henry Fonda, her former beau and co-star. The telecast marked the last appearance of Jack Benny on TV. The roast was aired six weeks after his death.

Vivian Vance showed up to ridicule Lucille for 'henpecking' Desi Arnaz throughout the run of the *I Love Lucy* series.

Even Gary Morton climbed to the podium to deliver a series of jabs.

***

On March 11, 1975, CBS telecast *Timex Presents a Lucille Ball Special: Lucy Gets Lucky*. Jack Donohue was brought back as her director, and he also appeared in a cameo on the show.

She still had faith in the script-writing abilities of Bob O'Brien, although he'd been responsible for the bland boredom of some her previous episodes.

This time, he turned to the mothballed scripts of yesteryear, recycling material from the *Here's Lucy* series. It was obvious he'd also seen Jerry Lewis perform in *The Bellboy* in 1960. Brittle-boned Lucille took a chance by performing some of her own stunts, including driving a car down a series of steps.

In the plot, Lucy Collins (Lucille) arrives in Las Vegas to attend the opening night of Dean Martin, her longtime favorite entertainer. She has booked eight tickets to make sure she gets a seat, but, when that is discovered, she ends up with none.

She learns that Martin is going to stage a special show to entertain the staff, so as a vehicle to get inside, she is hired as a cocktail waitress in a skimpy "chorus girl" costume.

Also on the show was Jackie Coogan, Lucille's former co-star, as well as her "regulars," Vanda Barra and Sid Gould. Even Gary Morton appeared in a cameo.

***

Dinah Shore and Lucille had remained friends, and for an April 29,

1975 telecast, the singer invited Lucille back for another performance on her show, an event simply entitled *Dinah!*. Vivian Vance also agreed to be on the show.

Before rehearsals began, Lucille talked privately with Vance, learning details about her breast surgery.

Vance was in recovery after discovering she had developed breast cancer. To conceal the surgery, she was attired in a tunic that was loose-fitting around her chest.

On the show, the two former stars of *I Love Lucy* wandered down memory lane. Lucille appeared in a black wig, claiming that she was abandoning her red hair and going back to her natural hair color. Vance tugged at the wig while delivering, with sarcasm, the line, "Natural color, my eye!"

In a surprise move, Vance complained that she had to gain twenty pounds to play Ethel Mertz and that she wasn't allowed to wear false eyelashes. She also ridiculed the frumpy clothes she had to wear.

The banter between the two women seemed to steal Dinah's show right from under her.

***

Lucille later recalled that in May of 1975, she'd made the mistake of her life by appearing on the ABC game show, *Password*, telecast for thirty minutes on ABC. Gary Morton appeared on the show with her.

Originally aired on CBS, *Password* had been bought by ABC in 1971. Its host, Allen Ludden, had become one of the most familiar faces on television. He was also famously married to an even more familiar face on TV, Betty White.

On the show, two teams, each with a celebrity guest and a contestant, entered a contest with a similarly composed team. Each contestant could use only one word to convey the correct answer to their partner.

Before the show, Lucille had spent a night experiencing pains in her chest. Apparently, she came on the show just after the full effects of having overmedicated herself took effect. She appeared bewildered and confused, and Morton chimed in, trying to rescue her to the degree he could.

Many viewers believed that she was either intoxicated or else was showing the beginning signs of Alzheimer's Disease.

Ludden later said, "Lucille Ball was the worst celebrity guest I ever had on my show. Something was seriously wrong with her. In real life, she was as dumb as her Lucy character on TV."

***

If Lucille regretted her appearance on *Password*, she embarrassed herself far more when she was a presenter at the Twenty-Sixth Annual Emmy Awards. They were telecast on ABC on May 19, 1975. As one reviewer said the next day, "Last night's ceremony shocked millions who saw Lucille Ball in the most embarrassing moment she ever had on television."

Five minutes before she was to go on, a telephone call came in for her.

To her horror, a voice on the phone during an "emergency call" told her that her son, Desi Jr., had been involved in a fatal car accident while driving drunk and drugged, and that although an ambulance, with its dome light flashing, had rushed him to a hospital, he was Dead on Arrival (DOA). "It was too late," the voice, pretending to be a policeman, informed her.

She screamed and burst into tears. Gary Morton took her in his arms and comforted her.

Minutes later, she was informed that she'd been the victim of a crank caller. Desi Jr was not on the road, and he had been reached within the safe confines of his apartment. "He's fine," the stage manager said.

As Lucille was about to be announced for her appearance before millions of viewers, Morton helped her with her makeup. "Do you really want to go on? We could get Milton Berle, who's waiting out in the wings, to replace you. He could make your presentation for you."

"No, god dammit," she hissed. "Haven't you heard that the show must go on? If nothing else, I'm a trouper."

She stumbled awkwardly onto the stage, appearing unsteady on her feet. Morton watched in horror at what happened after the applause for her ended. She didn't announce the category of the award she was about to present, and then she dropped the envelope onto the podium, where other discarded envelopes lay in disarray, left there by the presenters who had gone before her.

Then it became obvious that because of the confusion and emotional pain that preceded her appearance, she had forgotten her glasses and couldn't see clearly enough to find the pertinent envelope. Stunned, the audience looked on in disbelief, wondering if the act might have been one of Lucy Ricardo's stunts.

Milton Berle, waiting in the wings, realized what was happening, and he stepped out onto the stage accompanied by loud applause.

Somehow, from the jumble of debris on the podium, he managed to find the missing envelope and read both the category and the name of the winner. Then he helped Lucille exit from the stage, where she rushed, sobbing, back into Morton's arms.

***

It was with a certain sadness that Desi Sr. watched the last episode of *Here's Lucy*. When it ended, he turned to his wife, Edie. "It's all over for Lucy, certainly as a star of a regular series. Maybe a few guest appearances on the show of another star like Dinah Shore…but then, oblivion."

As he made clear to her, "I'm not ready to wander down the road to oblivion." In spite of his poor physical condition and declining health, he had been trying to relaunch his career.

He'd appeared in an episode of *Ironside*, the television crime drama that was first telecast on NBC in 1967, where it would run for eight seasons. In a wheelchair, Raymond Burr was its star. He played Robert T. Ironside, a consultant for the San Francisco police who was paralyzed from the waist down after having been shot while on vacation.

Desi had been impressed with Burr's acting talent ever since he'd seen Alfred Hitchcock's thriller, *Rear Window* (1954), a celebrated classic which had co-starred James Stewart (also in a wheelchair) and the very elegant Grace Kelly.

On the set, Burr introduced Desi to his domestic partner, Robert Benevides, a Korean War veteran who had been production consultant for twenty-one of Burr's *Perry Mason* TV crime dramas.

Desi found that together, the two men seemed like ideal partners. They invited Edie and him to visit their vineyards for the weekend. According to Burr, "I'm a great cook. Just ask Bobby."

Their home was in Dry Creek Valley, California. Desi and Edie considered the invitation but never got around to actually pursuing and accepting it.

Anxious for another gig, hopefully as producer of a hit TV show, Desi encountered Lew Wasserman, the former agent, at a Hollywood party. By then, this son of Ohio was being hailed as "the last of the legendary moguls of Tinseltown," and "the most influential and powerful Hollywood figure in the four decades following World War II."

During Wasserman's discussions with Desi, he was head of MCA Universal. Carrying the dialogue into the following day, Wasserman eventually suggested that Desi open an office, and he did so, in a building around the corner from Lucille Ball Productions.

After getting settled in, Desi phoned Lucille, who accepted his invitation for lunch at a nearby bistro. She would later detail to Vivian Vance how the reunion went.

Lucille had had another engagement at the time it had aired, and had not seen Desi in his role of Dr. Domingo on *Ironside*. "Who were you impersonating?" she asked.

"Dr. Domingo, a small-town doctor,"

"Where's the drama in that? An unwanted pregnancy? Perhaps an abortion quack on the side?"

"Cut the shit, Lucy. It's a strong character, and I'm asking Wasserman if he can turn Dr. Domingo into a series. I would play a cross between Marcus Welby and Columbo."

"That would be an uphill climb," she predicted. "But I wish you luck with it. Certainly this is new territory for you. Ricky Ricardo was no god damn brain surgeon."

"Thanks for the good wishes," he said. "I'll need it." As it was nearing the time to leave, he told her that Edie would be in Beverly Hills the following week and that she wanted to have lunch with her.

"Sure thing," Lucille said. "I like Edie. She and I can compare notes on what kind of lover you are."

That made him switch the subject to his present physical condition. "In 1971, I had my most serious attack of diverticulitis. I'm in august company. I hear President Johnson also suffers from this condition. I went from 205 pounds to 175, so I'm back at my fighting weight. I'm even back to my old seven handicap on the golf course."

"Good for you, *Cubano*," she said. "Hang in there."

His face turned sad as he confessed to her he had not been smart with the money he'd earned from his sale of Desilu stock. "Mounting medical bills, great losses at the racetrack and gaming tables of Las Vegas, a lavish lifestyle… It all adds up. I might have to ask you to send me another three-million dollar check if money gets too tight."

"Sure, any time," she said, glancing at her watch. "I gotta go. An appointment."

"Oh," he said. "Before you hop off, one final question. Is my replacement, Gary Morton, still able to get it up?"

"Funny you should ask. The other night, he asked the same question about you."

"Also, I didn't ask about our kids. How are they?"

"Why don't you visit them and find out for yourself? Our boy is having a drug problem. Why don't you see him and give him some fatherly advice?"

"Yeah, I'll get around to that."

Desi Sr. with **Raymond Burr** in an episode of *Ironside*.

"As everyone knew, Burr was gay," Desi said. "To relaunch my career, I was willing to lie on his casting couch. But he never asked me."

Lucille kept the lunch date with Edie, the details of which she would later relay to Vance: "I know he might not show it, but Desi is still in love with you and the kids," Edie claimed. "That's true even if he doesn't see much of you guys. He talks often of you, always claiming what a rotten husband he was."

"Is he still hitting the bottle?" Lucille asked.

"Against doctors' orders, he drinks far too much, damaging his health," Edie said. "There's nothing I can do about that. There's another problem too…but one that I'm handling. He's taken up with this bleached blonde floozie. She looks like that starlet, Barbara Nichols, who was better at playing a whore than any actress on the screen."

"I know," Lucille said. "Desi used to bang her."

"He's stashed this gal at his villa at Las Cruces," Edie said, "and he goes back and forth between our two houses."

"He's following in the tradition of his grandfather in Santiago," Lucille answered. "His dad was a whorehouse regular, too. Are you filing for divorce?"

"I don't intend to," Edie said. "I'm no longer burning to have a man pounding away. Desi will soon retire from it. Frankly, he's almost too old now to be cutting the mustard. We have a decent marriage. After a day or so away with his *puta*, he comes back, we have dinner, watch TV, and go to bed early."

"As for me," Lucille said, "I keep Gary on a tight leash. He's busy all day at work, and he comes home with me for dinner. We have separate rooms. But I have this big bell. I clang it whenever I need servicing, and

Gary comes running to perform his husbandly duties."

"Gary is also getting rid of what he calls 'the spongers' in my life," Lucille continued. "All except for my mother, DeDe. She'll stick around for the duration. Fred Ball, my brother, was given a motel to run in Cottenwood, Arizona. Cleo, my cousin, is living with her third husband, Cecil Smith, in Mexico. He's retired from his job as a TV critic for the *Los Angeles Times*."

"As for our boy and girl," Lucille said, "they're trying to become big-time stars, hoping perhaps to outrace Desi and me."

"I hope they're not kidding themselves," Edie said. "Where your stardom and that of Desi is concerned, it's a bridge too far, far beyond the reach of mere mortals like Lucie and Junior."

"It's been swell, Edie," Lucille said. "Let's do this again sometime."

"Yeah," Edie answered. "Sometime."

***

As a former producer, Desi Sr. lived through what he called "a long, dry spell." He now found himself on the road to becoming seventy in three years and felt the need to "do something…and now!"

The Mothers-in-Law, his hit TV sitcom and one of his greatest successes, had faded from the air in 1969, and his crime drama, *The Untouchables*, was a distant memory.

Now, with the help of agent Lew Wasserman, he hoped to be back on television again as Dr. Domingo. He also wanted to put on his producer's hat and launch a new TV drama, *Chairman of the Board*. It would be different from other dramas in that it would feature a woman in a power position in the business world. "It will be a definite winner with women libbers, but I think it could attract a far wider audience, especially with the gorgeous Elke Sommer as its star," he predicted.

[He had been a fan of hers ever since he'd seen A Shot in the Dark, *a film in which she'd co-starred with Peter Sellers. The blonde Berlin-born beauty had been born in 1940, "the most glorious year" of the Third Reich, when Hitler's Nazis had taken over large parts of Europe, even getting France to surrender.]*

To his great disappointment, Desi saw his hopes and dreams fade. It seemed that no network and no sponsor were interested in either of these projected series. One executive at CBS privately said, "Desi Arnaz is a bit of yesterday's cheese."

Without much fanfare, Desi's dream of appearing in his own TV drama eventually collapsed. He was also forced to tell Elke Sommer that their the deal was off. He need not have worried about her, as she went on to be featured in nearly a hundred TV and feature films until 2005.

Ironically, Desi soon got another offer instead. William Morrow, that prestigious publishing house in Manhattan, wanted him to write his autobiography, and they were willing to send an editor west to aid him in the project.

For the next two years, working on that story of his life would consume him.

***

The 1975-1976 season of Lucille's professional life was meager, as she no longer had a regular series. She brought an end to her appearances in 1975 in a 60-minute special for CBS entitled *Three For Two*. In it, she was teamed once again with one of her favorite performers, Jackie Gleason, nicknamed "The Great One."

She had first worked with Gleason and with Desi Arnaz back in June of 1958 on *The Ed Sullivan Show*. In other shows, Lucille and Gleason had co-starred in *Lucy Visits Jack Benny*, the second telecast of her *Here's Lucy* series.

The director of her latest special was Charles Walters, a former dancer and director of MGM musicals. He had also helmed some episodes of her *Here's Lucy* series. He later said, "I shouldn't be surprised at anything Lucille was likely to do, but I found the sexual banter between her and Gleason a bit much."

"Why didn't you let me get in your panties back when I could still get it up?" Gleason asked her.

"I didn't think you were man enough to handle a wildcat like me," she shot back.

"I heard you were a real *Wildcat*. No wonder your Broadway show had that title."

Their latest special consisted of three "playlets," the first of which was called *Herb and Sally*. "Both of my stars bombed with this one," Walters said, "and they weren't helped along by a weak script by James Eppy. It just didn't work."

In a black wig, Lucille played a middle-aged housewife who can't generate any passion from her husband (Gleason).

Faced with a weak script, Gleason improvised, reverting to his familiar role of Ralph Kramden in his hit TV sitcom, *The Honeymooners*.

"At any moment, I expected Gleason to shout, 'To the moon, Alice...to the moon.'"

As a change of pace, the next playlet, *Fred and Rita*, featured Lucille in a blonde wig and showgirl feathers, a floozie in a sleazy night club who is supposedly sustaining an affair with Gleason. "I don't think they convinced any viewer that they were actually doing it," Walters said.

Fortunately, the failed segment lasted only six minutes before moving on to the next playlet, *Mike and Pauline*. Lucille dons another wig, this one a shade of dirty blonde. "She plays a control freak, one who's been obviously inspired by an old Joan Crawford movie." Walters said. "Gleason once again is her hapless spouse."

To the horror and chagrin of CBS executives, the TV special bombed. It generated a low Nielsen rating and was attacked in newspapers by TV critics. In its aftermath, a high-placed executive at CBS told board members, "In my view, Lucille Ball is through on television."

Gary Morton privately expressed his displeasure: "Lucille depended on a live audience, and in this case, a sound track was used. All the laughter came from the sound track and not from (live) viewers. Yet in spite of this latest fiasco, I still think Lucille and Gleason are two of the best performers on TV."

***

For years, Lucille had been pushing Gleason to appear with her in a script based on the fabled Gilded Age celebrities, Diamond Jim Brady and his consort, Lillian Russell.

Born into poverty in 1856, Diamond Jim became one of the richest financiers in the United States. He had a taste for diamonds, some of which he presented to Russell. His jewelry would be valued at $65 million in 2022 dollars.

As part of his claim to fame, he became the first New Yorker to own an automobile.

Applauded for his gluttony, he was vastly overweight. Restaurant owner George Rector told the press, "Diamond Jim is the best 25 customers I have."

Lucille Ball performs with "the great one," a rotund **Jackie Gleason**.

For five years, she had held a script about the lives of Diamond Jim Brady and Lillian Russell. She presented it to Gleason, telling him she wanted to produce a made-for-television movie about them.

He wasn't at all interested.

Lucille told Gleason, "You are not quite fat enough to play Diamond Jim. We'll have to do some padding."

The script was to have depicted him eating one of his traditional suppers, beginning with three dozen raw oysters, six crabs, two bowls of turtle soup, seven lobsters, two canvasback ducks, a double portion of terrapin, one large sirloin steak (rare), served with a large helping of creamy mashed potatoes. Dessert was a platter of French pastries, followed by two pounds of chocolates.

Gleason assured Lucille that if that scene was actually filmed, he would devour the entire supper, and it would not have to be faked.

Lucille had long wanted to play Lillian Russell, a singer and actress who emerged from the cornfields of Iowa at the beginning of the Civil War, later growing up in Chicago.

In New York, she became one of the most famous actresses and singers of the late 19th Century. At the beginning of the 20th Century, she was the foremost singer of operettas and Broadway musicals.

With scandalous consequences, Brady supported her extravagant lifestyle throughout the course of her four marriages.

Lucille was aware the Diamond Jim and Lillian Russell had been depicted on the screen before. The 1935 film, *Diamond Jim* had been written by Preston Sturges. In the 1940 movie, *Lillian Russell*, Diamond Jim was portrayed by the corpulent Edward Arnold.

"Although the part was perfect for Gleason," Lucille said, "I just could not get him to commit to it."

***

Although her star power had faded by the mid-1970s, Lucille still had fans loyal to her since her debut on *I Love Lucy* in the early 1950s.

Yet in defiance of their support, the powers at CBS decided not to take a chance on her as a "stand-alone" figure within her next special. A decision was therefore made to team her with Shirley MacLaine in an hour-long song-and-dance "personality tribute," *The Gypsy in My Soul*.

"I thought they'd make an ideal pairing," said Cy Coleman, the special's co-producer and (with Fred Ebb) co-author, "but they were anything but ideal. For a dramatic comparison, it would be like teaming Bette Davis in a dance with Joan Crawford. They got along fine off-screen. I'd see them in a huddle, laughing and gossiping, no doubt comparing notes on the men they'd seduced over the course of many years in Hollywood."

Diamond Jim Brady with **Lillian Russell.**

Russell (1861-1922) was a fabled entertainer, the toast of New York.

Corpulent Brady, a high-rolling financier, railway supplier, and gourmand, kept her supplied "with rocks that don't lose their shape."

The very overweight Edward Arnold had portrayed Brady in *Lillian Russell*, a 1940 film that had also starred Alice Faye and Henry Fonda.

Shirley was an established star when she worked with Lucille—successful, controversial, iconoclastic, unpredictable, and endlessly fascinating. She was the sister of an equally famous star. She and Warren Beatty were the hottest sibling co-stars in Hollywood. He was a Tinseltown Lothario, seducing everyone from Jacqueline Kennedy Onassis to Vivien Leigh, with whom he'd co-starred in Tennessee Williams' *The Roman Spring of Mrs. Stone*.

One of the first questions Shirley asked Lucille was, "Have you gone to bed with Warren?"

"Not yet," Lucille answered. "He hasn't gotten around to me yet. Tell him I'm still waiting for his midnight call. I'll come running."

It was alleged that Shirley came running whenever either Dean Martin or Frank Sinatra called during the filming of *Some Came Running* (1958).

One of Lucille's favorite films was one in which Shirley had co-starred with Jack Lemmon in *The Apartment* (1960). "There were rumors of an affair, but it didn't happen. I adore Jack, but he reminds me of my Aunt Rose."

When Lucille had last worked with Martin, he'd gossiped about Shirley: "I love her dearly, but her oars don't touch the water."

Privately, as was natural for an aging star, Lucille was jealous of the younger actress, especially because of her ability to dance. Shirley was twenty-three years Lucille's junior.

She had married film producer Steve Parker in 1954, but he lived in Japan. "I don't have to worry about Steve growing tired of me because I never see him. We have an open marriage."

Lucille was often horrified at Shirley's frankness with the press. Once, she was quoted as saying, "I have only one vice, and that's fucking. One time I had three men in just one day."

When she wasn't talking about sex, Shirley sounded off on spirituality, reincarnation, and metaphysics. "I'd rather play backgammon in my off hours than listen to that shit," Lucille said.

At the beginning of rehearsals, Lucille warned Shirley, "I'm no Ginger Rogers, and I've got a bad leg, so I'll have to fake it."

Their joint appearance evolved into a tribute to the girls who labored, often thanklessly, in the chorus lines of Broadway.

Shirley told her, "It's a page from my own life. I was the understudy to the singer-actress Carol Haney. I was told she'd never missed a performance, but on the third night of *The Pajama Game,* I had to go on in her place. She'd broken her ankle or something. It just so happened that producer Hal Wallis was in the audience that night. He later, over dinner, offered me a seven-year contract in Hollywood. In no time at all, in his office, he was chasing me around the desk."

Shirley discussed other men, too. "Now that Frenchman, Yves Montand, is a great lover. Marilyn Monroe must have taught him well. But Jack Nicholson….Forget it! He is just too much for me to deal with. I like dangerous chemistry in a man, but Jack is too much. He is not in control and therefore authentically lethal."

Even though she was no dancer, Lucille made an impressive appearance in a top hat like the one worn by Fred Astaire in those 1930s musicals in which Lucille had been an extra. She also wore a tuxedo jacket and black hosiery evocative of Judy Garland.

As Coleman noted, "Lucy had trouble lip-synching, and although she got along with Shirley off camera, there was a lot of tension between them as performers. Shirley wanted to do it one way, Lucy another. I had to be the peacemaker on several occasions."

Lucille preferred a live audience but didn't get one. The laughter was canned. Nonetheless, the stars pulled off such numbers as "Bouncing Back for More" and "Bring Back Those Good Old Days."

At one point, Shirley asked Lucille if she still got fan mail, and Lucille assured her that she did, although not in the same volume as during the heyday of *I Love Lucy*.

"Here's one I got today," Shirley said. She

The very outspoken **Shirley MacLaine** appeared in the title role of *Irma La Douce*, a popular prostitute in this *Belle Époque* romance released in 1963.

"I danced the Can-Can for Nikita Khrushchev during his visit to Hollywood. He later denounced me for flashing my ass at him, but I think he wanted to plug it."

read its oblique and rather sinister contents to Lucille.

"Your time is drawing nigh, Shirley. Spread your garbage as long as you can, because the day is soon coming when you'll reap every morsel that you sowed."

After working with Shirley, Lucille ended up agreeing with producer Martin Rackin: "Shirley MacLaine is a disaster, a fucking ovary with a propeller who leaves a trail of blood wherever she goes. A half-assed chorus girl, a pseudo-intellectual who thinks she knows all about politics, and a coat hanger who wears clothes from the ladies of a church bazaar."

Despite its drawbacks, their show got good ratings when it was telecast on January 12, 1976.

***

At long last, Desi Arnaz Sr. released his autobiography, which he entitled simply *A Book*. The subhead was more intriguing: *The Outspoken Memoirs of Ricky Ricardo—The Man Who Loved Lucy.*

It was published early in 1976 by William Morrow in New York. At the time, Desi promised readers he would continue his life story "in a second autobiography, *Another Book,* but he never finished it.

Lucille was among the first to read a copy, hot off the press. She did so with great trepidation, fearing he might reveal many of her affairs within the context of their marriage. But after reading it, she said, "Desi treated me with respect."

He promised readers, "It's all here—the good, the bad, the beautiful, the unbelievable lucky breaks, and the heartbreaking failures."

Although he was rather candid in some pages, in the opinion of those who knew him well, he didn't deliver all the dirt. He left out the more sordid aspects of his life, yet he did admit that he was a favorite patron of Polly Adler's *putas*. *[Adler ran the most famous bordello in America.]* And although he mentions Betty Grable, he skims over descriptions of his affairs.

He's quite a name dropper, touching on personalities who include Lana Turner, Eleanor Roosevelt, Louis B. Mayer, Bob Hope, Judy Garland, and Doris Day.

With a great deal of honesty and a noteworthy degree of pain, he wrote, "The irony of it all is how our undreamed-of success, fame, and fortune turned into hell."

Judging from their reactions, most of his readers, he concluded, were fans of *I Love Lucy*. Desi himself admitted that his autobiography was "mainly for aficionados."

A reader from Chicago, Mary Beth Marshall, praised Desi's "wit, charm, luck, and brains." Ronald Wise asserted, "Desi doesn't mince words when describing personal memories. At times, I felt he was trying to shock readers."

Deborah Skillman summed it up: "Desi Arnaz owns his life, warts and all."

Privately, to friends, he admitted, "I didn't expose a lot of the bad stuff. As a young man, I was mixed up in some weird sexual shit. I just couldn't let fans of Ricky Ricardo know some of the things I did, struggling to make it big. I did teach America how to Conga."

Largely to promote the book, Desi—with his son—agreed to appear on NBC's *Saturday Night* (its title was later changed to *Saturday Night Live),* a late-night sketch comedy and variety show that had premiered in October of 1975. Desi's telecast was slated for airing on February 21, 1976. The series was a hit and became known for parodying contemporary culture and politics.

Also in the cast lineup were Dan Aykroyd, Chevy Chase, John Belushi, and Gilda Radner.

Although Lucille was missing, her Lucy Ricardo *persona* was brilliantly impersonated by Radner. At the time, Radner was set to play Lucille, as Lucy Ricardo, in a projected Broadway comedy that never came off.

Lucille claimed, "Gilda plays Lucy Ricardo better than I did."

Emerging from Detroit, Radner would become a regular on *Saturday Night,* specializing in parodies of stereotypes such as news anchors and lovelorn newspaper columnists.

To the surprise of viewers of that show, Desi Jr. delivered a brilliant impersonation of his father, Cuban accent and all.

The Arnaz father and son were greatly aided by Chevy Chase, who became one of the key cast members in the first season of *Saturday Night*. He later became even more famous for playing the bumbling Clark T. Griswold in five National Lampoon *Vacation* films.

The script included a sketch that focused on *The Untouchables,* that hit crime drama that Desi had produced during his stewardship of Desilu Productions. Aykroyd was tapped to play Ness, the crime fighter.

As might be expected, Desi Sr. sang his ever popular "Babalu," but the cameras seemed to have been cut off before he finished his trademark, high-energy song. He also sang another one of his favorites, "Cuban Pete."

It became embarrassingly obvious that Desi Sr. had lost that spark of yesterday, and he wasn't in top form. Even without being told, he seemed to know that, and he never sang in public again.

Aykroyd often worked in partnership with John Belushi. A son of Chicago, he was born two years before *I Love Lucy's* first-ever telecast. He was one of the seven original cast members of *Saturday Night.* Both Belushi and Aykroyd would eventually team to make a hit movie, *The Blues Brothers* (1980).

When he starred on the show with Desi and Junior, Belushi had already become a heavy drug user. At the time, Desi Sr. cited him to his son as an example of what could go wrong if he didn't change his drug-abusing ways.

Desi Sr was right. At the age of 33, Belushi was found dead from a heavy drug intoxication.

***

A most unusual script, a sort of quasi-autobiographical memoir, was presented to Lucille as a special entitled, *What Now, Catherine Curtis?* Set for a March 10, 1976 telecast, it was to be produced by Lucille herself, with Gary Morton assisting her.

After she met with her director, Charles Walters, she said to him, "I know where your writers (Sheldon Keller and Lynn Roth) found inspiration for this little drama? You got it from my life."

Her co-stars were Art Carney and Joseph Bologna.

Her character of Catherine had been married for almost a quarter of a century, living in the suburbs. But after her divorce, in search of a new life, she moves to a luxurious apartment on the Upper East Side of Manhattan.

In the first episode, Lucille delivers a monologue of her past married life, and photographs from her actual life and career are flashed across the TV screen.

Although the plotline ends in tears, she is fashionably attired. Wearing a darkish wig, her hair is beautifully styled by Irma Kusely. She still looks glamourous, but seems to have put on a few pounds, as befits a woman of her age.

Into her new life emerges the handyman for the apartment, cast with Art Carney. The veteran comedian had clashed during their previous appearance together, but all seemed to have been forgotten, and they worked smoothly together during this shoot.

Her affair with the handyman was not destined to last. Soon, she is attracted to a younger and much sexier man. That role was cast with Brooklyn-born Joseph Bologna.

Actually, he was twenty-three years younger than Lucille. As she told her director, jokingly or not, "Joe is my kind of guy, a real masculine hunk. If it were another day—say, Lucille Ball back in the 1950s, I would have invited him to my dressing room. He's hot!"

Regrettably, Bologna wasn't available for stud duty. After serving in the U.S. Marine Corps, he had married the actress Renée Taylor in 1965. They had worked together on a film script, *Lovers and Other Strangers* (1970), about the complications of staging a "culturally clashing" wedding in which an Italian clan tries to blend with a traditional Jewish family. Both Bologna and his wife were nominated for an Oscar for Best Adapted Screenplay.

Her hair a mess, **Gilda Radner** as she looked in 1980.

In a TV broadcast that later became known as *Saturday Night Live*, she did an impression of Lucille Ball performing as Lucy Ricardo.

"So that's how I acted?" Lucille asked after watching it.

The doomed **John Belushi** as he appeared on the cover of *Rolling Stone*.

A talented comedian and the star of *The Blues Brothers* (1980), he would be found dead from a drug overdose at the age of 33.

Lucille had their latest film, *Made for Each Other* (1971) screened for her.

Greater numbers of actors were showing increasing amounts of flesh in the films of the 1970s, and Bologna was no exception. His last film, *Blame It on Rio* (1984), co-starring Michael Caine, had featured nudity.

Lucille was mildly surprised when she overheard a heated discussion between Bologna and the director. At the time, many actors, even Clint Eastwood, were being photographed in jockey shorts. Bologna wanted a scene inserted of himself in tight-fitting jockeys. He told Walters, "It will spark a lot of interest among women and a lot of gay men to see me stripped down. After all, I'm playing a stud."

Walter nixed the idea, telling him, "Lucille is strongly opposed to porn in the movies."

When the special was released, some viewers thought the depiction of Lucille with a younger man derived from a chapter in her own life. After all, she had been the older member of her marriage with Desi Sr., and when that had ended, she had moved into a second marriage with the (younger than herself) Gary Morton.

In some respects, the Catherine Curtis role made up for a lot of previous bad scripts. Walters predicted that Lucille would be nominated for an Emmy, but that did not happen.

To everyone's dismay, many of her Lucy Ricardo fans didn't accept this "new" portrait of Lucille. Letters of protest arrived. A typical one was from Claire Powell of Louisville, Kentucky. "What are you guys trying to do? Turn Lucy Ricardo into a whore?"

***

To end her 1975-1976 season on television, Lucille once again agreed to be a guest star on *Dinah!* for a 60-minute telecast on June 4. She had admired the work of George Segal and was pleased that he would be their guest star.

A versatile actor Segal seemed equally at home in drama or comedy. She complimented him on his star role in Edward Albee's *Who's Afraid of Virginia Woolf?*, in which he had appeared with Elizabeth Taylor and Richard Burton cast as her henpecked husband. *[The roles were originally intended for James Mason and Bette Davis. In that memorable and "emotionally violent" film, Segal is married to Sandy Dennis, but is seduced during the course of that long, drunken night by Elizabeth Taylor, who portrays one of the most frightening harridans in film history.]*

"In that movie, Elizabeth didn't think much of you in the sack, but you're a good-looking guy," Lucille said. "I bet you deliver between the sheets."

"You've got that right, lady," he shot back. "No complaints in that department."

For his performance in *Virginia Woolf*, Segal was nominated for a Best Supporting Actor Oscar.

Morton also complimented the actor, but for a very different reason. Segal was one of the first leading American film actors who refused to change his Jewish name, setting an example for other Jewish actors in the future.

"At least you weren't born with the name of Issur Danielovich Demsky, who never attained any credit as an actor until he changed his name to Kirk Douglas," Morton said.

"I can't make up my mind," Segal told Morton and Lucille in a moment of reflection. "Do I want to act in films or settle for being a banjo player?" *[At the time, he was part of a group called The Imperial Jazz Band, which two years earlier had released an album,* A Touch of Ragtime. *He presented Lucille and Morton with a copy.]*

The same year he worked with Dinah and Lucille, Segal was seen by millions throughout TV land when he hosted the Academy Awards with Gene Kelly, Walter Matthau, Robert Shaw, and Goldie Hawn.

***

After the taping of *Dinah!*, Lucille once again was invited to spend the weekend with Dinah in Palm Springs. To her surprise, she found that Dinah—having long ago recovered from having been dumped by Burt Reynolds—had a new beau,.

"He is a living, breathing Greek God," Lucille later told Glen Swanson, who had directed the *Dinah!* telecast.

He was Ron Ely, a lanky, 210-pound, 6'4" Adonis. At the age of 38, he was "one of the world's sexiest and most charismatic stars" as Lucille later noted. "How do you do it, Dinah?" she asked. "You have some magic formula to get all the good-looking studs."

Ely had thrilled women and an array of gay fans when he'd appeared wearing only a loincloth in *Tarzan's Deadly Silence* and *Tarzan's Jungle Rebellion*, both released in 1970.

Ironically, in the *Deadly Silence* jungle adventure, he had co-starred with Jock Mahoney, who had played Tarzan himself in 1963.

Before the feature films, Ely had played the Ape Man in a television series for the 1966-1968 seasons, a total of 57 episodes, in which he had built up a large base of salivating fans.

His Tarzan series was noted for its roster of movie stars who included

In this quasi-autobiographical TV drama about the romantic liberation of a prosperous widow, **Lucille Ball** is depicted getting cozy with her co-star, **Joseph Bologna**, a much younger man.

As its producer, she nixed the idea of a scene depicting him in his jockey shorts, although suggesting she wouldn't mind a private viewing. Was she joking...or serious?

James Whitmore, Russ Tamblyn, Julie Harris, Sam Jaffe, James Earl Jones, Geoffrey Holder, Diana Ross, and Fernando Lamas. In a surprise to her fans, even Helen Hayes, then the First Lady of the American Theater, had co-starred in one of Ely's Tarzan episodes with her adopted son, James MacArthur, also an actor.

It had escaped Lucille's attention, but her friend, Ethel Merman, had also appeared in a two-part series with Ely entitled *Mountains of the Moon* in 1967. The "Broadway Belter" appeared in it as Rosanna McCloud, the leader of a fervent religious cult, members of which have been falsely lured into "The Promised Land" in Africa.

At one point, Lucille and Ely talked about the bones they had broken while performing their own stunts. "I suffered two dozen injuries," he said. "They included two broken shoulders and various lion bites."

Before retiring for the night during that weekend in Palm Springs, Lucille jokingly warned Dinah, "If I get desperately horny in the middle of the night, you might suddenly hear the Tarzan yell. That will be me, calling out into the night, 'Hey Tarzan! Me Jane!'"

[Lucille was not alive to hear of a horrid chapter in the life of Ron Ely when he was in his eighties. In 1981, he had married Valerie Lundeen, Miss Florida USA. The couple had three children: Kirsten, Kaitland, and Cameron.

On October 15, 2019, Cameron took a knife and fatally stabbed his mother several times at their home at Hope Ranch, a suburb of Santa Barbara.

Sheriff Deputies summoned to the scene encountered an enraged Cameron, who threatened them. He was fatally shot on the spot, dying instantly.]

Playing flirtatious drunks, **George Segal** and **Elizabeth Taylor** made screen history when they co-starred with **Richard Burton** *(who is aiming a gun at them in the photo above)* and Sandy Dennis in the 1966 film adaptation of Edward Albee's *Who's Afraid of Virginia Wolff?*

As a slatternly, provocative Martha, she takes Sandy's young husband to bed, later suggesting he was a lousy lay.

In this historically existential role, she allowed herself to be "fat and forty," letting the boozing and bloodletting flow.

Depicted in both photos, sexy **Ron Ely**, a stud from Texas, brought *Tarzan the Ape Man* to television in 1966. He was immediately deluged with fan letters from horny women and gay men.

Partly because of his preference for executing his own stunts and animal fights, he suffered 16 serious wounds and injuries. Nevertheless, in her boudoir, Dinah Shore found him "in great shape," sparking envy in Lucille Ball.

CHAPTER THIRTEEN

LUCILLE'S CAREER DECLINES

As It Falters, Her Children Struggle for Industry Recognition

Lucille was not jealous of her fellow *comedienne*, Phyllis Diller, because their styles were so different. The Ohio-born performer, six years younger than Lucille, was known for her eccentric stage persona, her self-deprecating wit, her gigantic clown-like hairdo, her baggy dresses, and her exaggerated cackling laugh.

In her routine, she often referred to a made-up husband she called "Fang." The fake husband sprang from an appropriation of elements from the comic strip, *The Lockhorns.*

Originally, Diller was influenced by such comedians as Sid Caesar, Milton Berle, and Jonathan Winters. In time, she would have a great influence on future women performers, notably Joan Rivers and Rosanne Barr.

With machine-gun precision, Diller was celebrated for delivering one-liners: One chestnut? "I once wore a peekaboo blouse. A man would peek and then would boo."

In the early 1960s, Diller performed at the *Bon Soir* in Greenwich Village, where a future singing sensation, Barbra Streisand, was her opening act. Both performers developed a wide circle of gay fans, who never deserted them.

One afternoon, Diller made a call to Lucille Ball Productions, wanting to speak to the "bossy lady." She was put through right away to the red-headed president.

Diller wanted to have dinner with her to present her with a proposition: "Don't panic," Diller warned Lucille. "My proposition is not sexual. Your vagina can stay under lock and key. It's about the idea for a sitcom starring the two of us. If anyone needs a new theme for a sitcom, it's you, right now— something completely different from *Here's Lucy.*

"This I've got to hear," Lucille said. A time was arranged for a Saturday night at Lucille's Beverly Hills home.

Diller told Lucille not to prepare any main dish, since she would arrive with a cannister of her celebrated "Phyllis Diller chili."

On her show, she mocked her inability to cook, although during one episode, she admitted, "Fang likes my rhino soup."

Actually, she was a good cook, and had licensed her chili recipe.

After tasting it, Lucille proclaimed, "It's the best chili I ever ate, even better than Desi made. But I've got to warn you: Chili makes me fart. Prepare yourself for a blast-off to make light of that bomb dropped on Hiroshima."

Other than Lucille, Diller was Bob Hope's favorite co-star in movie roles. He described her as "a Warhol mobile of spare parts picked up along a freeway."

Their first picture together in 1966, *Boy, Did I Get it Wrong!* was a hit. Their other two movies, *Eight on the Lam* and *The Private Navy of Sgt. O'Farrell*, were critically panned, but did well at the box office. At the height of the Vietnam War, Diller accompanied "ski nose" to that war-torn country.

After dinner, both stars put on their business caps and talked seriously about

Phyllis Diller showing off her "funny hausfrau" act on the cover of *Gentleman's Quarterly*. The *comedienne* made self-deprecating humor the main motif of her act.

Bob Hope hailed Lucille Ball and Diller as his two favorite co-stars. "Of course, I didn't put them in sarongs like I did Dorothy Lamour."

Although Carol Channing was most frequently associated with the role of Dolly Levi in *Hello, Dolly!*, many other (aging) actresses took on the role too.

Phyllis Diller was one of them. She appears above, clad in the opulent finery of the "horse and buggy era" outside the **St. James Theatre** in Manhattan.

The Broadway version of *Hello, Dolly!* made **Carol Channing** a household name and brought her a Tony Award. The role propelled her to television fame, too.

Nonetheless, Hollywood ruled against her playing Dolly Levi on the big screen, awarding the part to Barbra Streisand, who failed miserably in the movie role.

Diller's grand plan for a sitcom. It would co-star both of them as fast-aging former rivals for the same roles on stage and in feature films.

At the time (the 1970s), her idea for the sitcom was revolutionary. Diller used Carol Channing as her role model, a star who was married to a homosexual. She modeled the role that Lucille would play on Mary Martin, with Lucille cast as a closeted lesbian.

At first, Lucille seemed horrified at the idea, feeling that it was too controversial for any network or sponsor to greenlight it. But slowly, in her imagination at least, the project began to grow.

Playing a character named "Alice Wiggins," Diller would be married to a gay husband, a page drawn from her own life as well as that of Channing. In 1965, Diller had married Warde Donovan, who soon confessed that he was bisexual. She planned to file for divorce after three months, but they reunited, their marriage lasting until 1975.

Channing had married Charles Lowe, her manager and publicist, in 1956, and was still married to him when he died in 1999. He was a dedicated homosexual with a fondness for chorus boys. She spoke of him years later. "I don't recall if he ever visited my bedroom. I was just the wrong gender for him."

Both Lucille and Diller had followed the career of Channing ever since they'd seen her in *Gentlemen Prefer Blondes* in 1949. Diller later imitated Channing when she, too, took over the role of Dolly, as did Betty Grable, Pearl Bailey, Martha Raye, Ginger Rogers, and even Ethel Merman.

For Lucille, Diller acted out how she intended to play Alice in the projected sitcom. "I'll come on like an overgrown kewpie, singing like a moon-mad hillbilly. My dancing will be crazily comical, like Ruth Buzzi imitating Ginger Rogers. I'll keep my eyes wide open to suggest those saucer-like blinkers of Carol, but behind those eyes will be a gentle sweetness, a woman calling out for love."

Then Diller surprised Lucille by revealing how she would draw another, perhaps more controversial page from the secret life of Channing: "I want my character of Alice, like Channing herself, to be concealing her black ancestry."

Before Channing went away to college, her mother, the former Adelaide Glasser, warned her, "If you get pregnant, don't be surprised if a black baby pops out of your womb. George, your father, had a mother (your grandmother) who was black. He himself was German, so as regards your ancestry, you're part Hun, part African American , a combination of which Hitler would definitely not approve."

It would not be until 2002 that Channing publicly revealed her African American roots. "I know it's true every time I sing and dance. I'm proud of my black ancestry. It's one of the great strains in show business. My father was a very dignified man and as white as I am."

After listening patiently to Diller, Lucille butted in. "And what am I in all this fatty suet pudding?"

"You'll play Myrtle Lawnmow, a once towering figure on the Broadway stage, known for her musicals. The actress you're portraying would be brilliant at Peter Pan, Mary Poppins, or Maria Von Trapp in *The Sound of Music."*

"Like Mary Martin herself, the character you're modeled after, you'll be a classy broad from Texas," Diller said. "Although you used to dance like Ruby Keeler, your bones are now brittle. You used to sing like a female Bing Crosby, but now you're in competition with a croaking frog. On one episode I've conceived, you'll do an impersonation of Fanny Brice. We'll bring in a dance instructor to teach you Mary Martin's famous 'waltz clog' number. You'll even have a mentor based on Oscar Hammerstein II. He'll be tall and craggy, looking like a mountain. I see your character as an actress who can even play butch dames like Annie Oakley or Calamity Jane."

"I want you to come across as a secret lesbian, although you'll have a husband and a son," Diller said. "Perhaps there's a role in it for Desi Jr."

"Your lover on the sitcom (I've named her Zita Taffin) will be modeled on Janet Gaynor. As you may know, Mary Martin and Janet Gaynor were secret lesbian lovers for many years."

[Closeted lesbian or not, in 1930, Martin had married Benjamin Hagman, who she would divorce in 1936, but not before giving birth to Larry Hagman.]

For the time being, at least, Diller drew a blank about the right actress to play the Gaynor-based lesbian character.

[Gaynor's career had recently dimmed. A former WAMPAS Baby star, she shared an early link to Joan Crawford, also a WAMPAS star. But in time, she

> Janet Gaynor's longest-running lesbian affair was with Broadway's singing sensation, **Mary Martin.**
>
> Hollywood gave her only a few film roles, but Broadway audiences adored her in hit musicals such as *South Pacific* and *The Sound of Music.*
>
> Above, in 1954, she is depicted in one of her most memorable roles, "the boy who never grew up," *Peter Pan.*

> In Janet **Gaynor**'s (left figure in photo) heyday, she was a much-beloved figure, a box office draw, and the first person to win a (then newly minted) Best Actress Academy Award. In the 1930s, she easily transitioned from silent film to talkies, achieving her biggest success in the first version of *A Star Is Born* (1937), starring opposite Fredric March.
>
> Although a closeted lesbian, she married three times, most notably to the gay costume designer, Adrian. Her union with him became one of the most famous "lavender marriages" of its era.
>
> She is seen above with actress **Margaret Lindsay** (right), one of her first lovers. In *Jezebel* (1938), Lindsay stole Henry Fonda from the arms of Bette Davis.

gravitated to Mary Martin and began a life-long and very close-knit relationship with her.

Forty years before, Gaynor's star had risen rapidly over Hollywood, never shining as bright as when she won the first Academy Award for her performances in three films: 7th Heaven (1927), Street Angel (1928), and Sunrise (also 1928). That was the only time in the history of the Academy that an Oscar would be awarded for a trio of movies.]

For the next few weeks, Lucille pondered how to develop a pilot. Gary Morton was adamantly opposed to the sitcom. "You've got to be kidding. Your fans still see you as Lucy Ricardo, not some god damn dyke, like Ethel Merman."

As it turned out, Lucille could find no sponsor or network willing to take a risk an such an avant-garde theme. It was surmised that if the sitcom had been launched, it would have been a role model for gay-themed dramas to come. Gay liberation and marriage were around the corner, but in the early 1970s, they had not yet arrived. The projected Diller/Ball sitcom died a slow, homophobic death.

Coincidentally, author James Kirkwood Jr., whose script for the Broadway musical, *A Chorus Line,* eventually won a Pulitzer, later wrote a play entitled *Legends!* about two aging (female) stage stars. It contained few, if any, homosexual overtones. Into the roles of its leading ladies, he cast the real-life Mary Martin and Carol Channing.

In 1986, *Legends* toured successfully across the country, with an im-

Lovers **Mary Martin** (left) and **Janet Gaynor** did not conceal their lesbian affection for each other.

Tragically, in San Francisco in 1982, they were seriously injured in an automobile accident that killed Martin's manager. She suffered pains from the accident's aftereffects until her death in 1990.

Gaynor never fully recovered either, ultimately dying of pneumonia in 1984.

In 1976, playwright **James Kirkwood Jr**. won both a Tony Award and the Pulitzer Prize for his hit Broadway musical, *A Chorus Line.* He hoped to repeat his success in 1986 by teaming two aging divas, **Mary Martin** (left) and **Carol Channing** (right) in *Legends.* Its plot focused on two aging but ferociously competitive film divas.

Although it was never a critical succes, its tour through America played to packed houses, in part because of the fame of its legendary stars. It closed before reachng Broadway.

Kirkwood, shortly before his death, wrote a memoir about his tour with Martin and Channing entitled *Diary of a Mad Playwright.*

pressive box office mostly generated by power of its two legendary stars. Regrettably, it never made it to Broadway.

In 2006, Joan Collins and *Dynasty* star Linda Evans also toured with the play.

In 2009 in New York, Lypsinka (aka the cross-dressing *artiste* John Epperson) would transform *Legends* into a vehicle for two men in drag. His co-star was Charles Busch, one of the leading female impersonators in America at the time.

As the 21st Century rolled in, Diller lamented that "No producer had the *cojones* to produce my version of Mary Martin and Carol Channing. It would go over big today, but I've never been able to interest anyone. What is show biz? It's about broken dreams of what could have been."

In the 21st Century, the Diller/Ball series might have found a more welcoming home.

Lucille died before 1998, when *Will & Grace* became a hit sitcom for NBC. It focused on the friendship between best friends Will Truman (Eric McCormack), a gay lawyer, and Grace Adler (Debra Messing). *Will & Grace* became one of the most successful TV series with gay principal characters.

A decade and a half into the new century, Netflix released *Grace and Frankie,* a series of telecasts starring Lily Tomlin and Jane Fonda, the co-stars of *9 to 5* (1980).

This time around, the third member of *9 to 5 team,* Dolly Parton, was missing.

Its plot deals with two wives married to men in their seventies (Sam Waterson and Martin Sheen), who decide to "come out," and reveal to their families, friends, and clients that they are gay.

Pumped by the star power of its actors, *Grace and Frankie* was the latest in shows attempting to tackle LGBT issues in a way that mainstream TV still desperately wanted to avoid.

***

In the early 1970s, Larry Hagman, the son of Mary Martin, would also appear in Lucille's life.

Almost every day, a hopeful screenwriter sent a script to Lucille

Two views of **Larry Hagman** with his mother, **Mary Martin.** Left photo was snapped in 1949, when Hagman was 17 and his mother a Broadway star; right photo, during his *Dallas* years, as he wears his trademark "oil baron's Stetson."

Something about their *amitié* inspired Lucille to (unsuccessfully) develop a new TV series that vaguely mimicked their mother-mentor dynamic.

Ball Productions, often either with a possible "older woman" role for her or, more frequently, with the draft of a proposed TV series, a sitcom or a crime drama. The memory of her *Lucy* series lingered as an impressive benchmark in Nielsen ratings, as did her former husband's hit TV drama *The Untouchables,* starring Robert Stack.

Incoming scripts were usually forwarded directly to Gary Morton for him to read. He discarded most of them, but every now and then, he sent a proposal along to his "boss lady," Lucille herself. The final decision always rested with her, and she was a hard woman to please.

She tossed most of them into the trash after reading the first two or three pages.

One afternoon, because of its theme, a proposed feature film script captured her imagination. Entitled *The Son Also Rises,* it told the story of a screen legend, an older actress who was finding it harder and harder to find suitable vehicles for a woman of her diminished health, stamina, and beauty. *[Think Bette Davis, Joan Crawford, Ginger Rogers, Tallulah Bankhead, Vivien Leigh, and/or Lucille herself.]*

As her career fades, that of her only (biological) son rises. Whereas the mother character had shot to stardom after years of struggle, including time spent on the chorus line, her son hit box office paydirt with his first film role—the story of a returning G.I. who finds his errant wife, who had promised to be true, shacked up with another man.

[In some way, its plot evoked Dana Andrews and Virginia Mayo in The Best Years of Our Lives *(1946). It also evoked* A Star Is Born, *where an actress wife sees her career zoom ahead as her husband, a former matinee idol, fades into oblivion.]*

[Mother/daughter jealousies had played out before in the lives of Judy Garland, whose career faded as that of her daughter, Liza Minnelli, was rising. In another real-life drama, Debbie Reynolds took a career backseat to her own daughter, Carrie Fisher. Debbie, in fact, in her night club appearances, started to introduce herself to audiences with, "Hello, everyone, I'm the mother of Princess Leia."]

Lucille began to strongly promote the idea of herself in the role of the mother, a Hollywood legend with a fading film career. For some reason, her thoughts of the actor who would play her son turned to Larry Hagman. As a man roughly twenty years younger than she was, he was the right age.

She'd watched every episode she could of his hit TV sitcom, *I Dream of Jeannie* (1965-1970).

In the sitcom, he played a befuddled astronaut, Major Anthony Nelson, in 130 episodes broadcast over the course of five seasons.

Lucille placed a call to Hagman, who invited her to his home the following afternoon to discuss the deal. She was met at the door by his Mexican maid, Rosita, who praised Lucille for her long-running stint as Lucy Ricardo.

She followed Rosita to the terrace of Hagman's swimming pool. Wearing a bikini, he was resting in a lounge chair. As she later related to producer Greg Garrison, "The mound was impressive, but what enchanted me even more were his legs. He surely has the best set of gams that God ever created on man."

Hagman expressed great interest in his possible role. He feared a problem: In 1973, his stepfather, Richard Halliday, died, which brought about a reconciliation with his mother, Mary Martin, after months of estrangement.

He felt that by accepting the role, one so closely distilled from his own mother's character, their alienation would begin all over again.

Like most projected film scripts in Hollywood, this one never got off the ground. Lucille went through four scriptwriters, finding that none of them had turned out a shootable film script.

Within a short time, Lucille and Hagman each drifted on to other projects.

She was impressed when Hagman proved his acting credentials as the ruthless oil baron, J.R. Ewing, in the primetime soap opera, *Dallas*. Watching him perform, she regretted that the two of them never got to work together.

After hearing of her death in 1989, Hagman told the press, "Lucille Ball was a tough old broad but a helluva woman. If we'd even found the right script for that mother-son pic she wanted us to do, both of us might have carried home Oscars. The movie would have been made even more shocking with just a hint of incest."

***

Even more than Lucille herself, Vivian Vance had many long career talks with Lucie Arnaz whenever they weren't due on the set of one of the *Here's Lucy* episodes.

The older actress encouraged the younger one to forge a separate career—and not just play "straight man" to her mother's zany on-screen antics.

"Touring in summer stock is the way for you to break out," Vance suggested. "It will be a great experience. You'll learn a lot and perhaps build up a fan base of your own."

Lucie decided to take Vance's advice and by the summer of 1974, she was on a nationwide tour of the musical play, *Seasaw*. With a book by Michael Bennett and music by Cy Coleman, it was based on a comedy drama *Two for the Seasaw*. Authored by William Gibson, it had originated in 1958 as a non-musical play on Broadway starring Henry Fonda and Anne Bancroft.

The plot centered on a character, Jerry Ryan, a young lawyer from Nebraska, who arrives in New York. There, he becomes involved with Gittel Mosca, a kooky, streetwise dancer from the Bronx, accent and all.

At the end of the Broadway run of the musical version of *Seasaw*, Lucie went on the road with John Gavin and Tommy Tune. Gavin had played the role on Broadway for seven months as a replacement for Ken Howard. Gavin had fan clubs, and some of his most ardent admirers called him "the handsomest actor in the world."

In its review of the musical, *The New York Times* wrote, "*Seasaw* is less a musical than a play, less a play than a musical—and not enough of either. The saving grace, to the extent that it has any, was the choreography of Michael Bennett (who also served as director and partial librettist). The high point of the production is Tommy Tune's long-legged high-kicking dance up a set of stairs on a stage filled with balloons."

Perhaps not even known to her daughter, and artfully concealed, Lucille developed a fascination for *Seasaw's* male lead, John Gavin, similar to the feeling she'd had for Larry Hagman. When she met him, Gavin had just finished his term (1971-1973) as president of the Screen Actors Guild, a post once held by Ronald Reagan.

Ever since she'd seen *Imitation of Life* (1950), in which Gavin starred with Lana Turner, she was mesmerized by his screen presence. He'd even had a role in Alfred Hitchcock's *Psycho* (1960) starring Anthony Perkins as the crazed motel keeper.

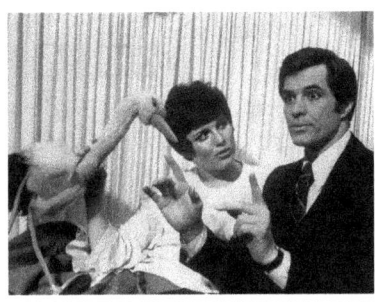

Gavin, Lucille learned, was the biological by-product of a Mexican mother and an Irish father, a mining engineer.

During the Korean War, he was commissioned in the U.S. Navy, where he was an air intelligence officer.

Gavin told Lucille that he had never planned to be an actor, but was offered "so much money, I couldn't say no. What I didn't expect was that when I started appearing on the screen, I was besieged by autograph seekers. By the hundreds. Fans seemed to think I was Rock Hudson."

Lucille arranged for Gavin's star-making film, *A Time to Love and a Time to Die* (1958) to be screened for her twice. The Douglas Sirk film was based on the novel by Erich Maria Remarque.

After *Imitation of Life,* wherein Lana Turner seduced him offscreen, Gavin appeared opposite such leading ladies as Doris Day, Sophia Loren, Susan Hayward, and—in *Tammy Tell Me True* (1961)—with Sandra Dee.

Gavin revealed to Lucille that he had almost been designated as Secret Agent 007 in the James Bond film *Diamonds Are Forever* (1971) after George Lazenby left the role. But David Picker, head of United Artists, insisted on Sean Con-

Two views of **Lucie Arnaz** in the theatrical production of Seasaw: *Upper photo*, with **John Gavin,** lower photo, a poster of show biz razzmatazz interacting with **Tommy Tune.**

Vivian Vance had urged Lucie to chart a theatrical career of her own: "You don't want to spend the rest of your life being known only as the daughter of Lucille Ball," she had bluntly told her.

nery. Gavin claimed he might have been given the role of Bond once again in *Live and Let Die* (1973), but producer Harry Saltzman insisted on a British actor instead, assigning the part to Roger Moore.

In 1974, shortly before their first meeting, at Lucille's home, Gavin had married the stage and screen actress, Constance Towers, a union that would last until his death in 2018.

Lucille had choreographed and made ready six scripts, each similar in theme. Her idea involved merging and melding the best aspects of each into a coherent whole, and then use that as the basis for a TV pilot in which Gavin would be cast with an on-screen wife, who'd helped him solve crimes at great danger to both of them.

As she pitched the possible deal to Gavin, he immediately saw that the project might be a 1970 version of all those *Thin Man* movies of the 1930s in which William Powell and his screen wife, Myrna Loy, solved crime mysteries from within the confines of their (very witty) marriage.

Like the proposed script with Larry Hagman, the detective series in which she'd co-star with Gavin never got off the ground. "My ex *(a reference, of course, to Desi Sr.)* shared common ground. We projected one TV series after another, and most of them went the way of all flesh," Lucille said.

Two views of **John Gavin**. Upper photo: with **Lana Turner** in *Imitation of Life*, and lower photo: as Julius Caesar (right) with (Lord) **Laurence Olivier** (left) as the sexually predatory Crassus in *Spartacus*.

Henry Willson, the gay talent agent of the casting couch, found Gavin so handsome, sexy, and seductive that he got him a screen test and, ultimately, a contract with Universal.

During the Reagan administration, Gavin served as U.S. Ambassador to Mexico for five years.

Lucille's idea, not very original, of having a rich couple, man and wife, cast as amateur detectives, was also a success on NBC. In 1971, Rock Hudson, to whom Gavin was often compared, launched *McMillan & Wife*, and it became a hit with Susan Saint James cast into one of the title roles.

As time went by, the same basic plot became yet another hit TV series. That heartthrob of the 1950s, Robert Wagner, starred in *Hart to Hart*, a mystery series that went on the air in 1979, with his co-star Stephanie Powers. They played a rich couple who lead a glamourous life and often find themselves working as unpaid detectives in order to solve crimes in which they often accidentally become embroiled.

***

In her most unusual role, Lucie Arnaz starred in the NBC-TV crime drama, a made-for-TV movie entitled *Who Is the Black Dahlia?* In just 120 minutes, that question could not really be answered, since her murder was the most notorious and controversial of all Hollywood murders, involving a savage butchery and blood draining.

With almost no time to rehearse, Lucie was given a choice between two black wigs and three black dresses, each reflecting the fact that the real-life murder victim on which the film was based always dressed in black. An aspiring actress, she had worked part-time as a waitress and occasionally as a prostitute.

The mutilated body of the Boston-born Elizabeth Short, aged 22, was discovered in a vacant lot near Leimert Park in Los Angeles on January 15, 1947. It was later determined that the body had been placed there about ten hours before.

The identity of the sadistic murderer has never been discovered, and the case remains one of the most famous unsolved mysteries in the history of Los Angeles.

Over the decades, her brutal murder has fueled many wild rumors, including allegations that she had a lesbian affair with Marilyn Monroe (then Norma Jean) shortly after MM's arrival in Hollywood.

For the Lucie Arnaz TV drama, director Joseph Pevney lined up an impressive cast, the lead going to Efram Zimbalist Jr., cast as detective Harry Hansen. Also cast as members of the police force were Ronny Cox and Macdonald Carey. A trio of fairly well-known actresses were also assigned key roles, Gloria DeHaven, Mercedes McCambridge, and June Lockhart.

At her office at Lucille Ball Productions, Lucille obtained a copy of the script and, after reading it, strongly objected to her daughter playing such a grisly role. "Who is this gal?" she asked. "A hard-as-nails chick? An easy mark to any man in uniform? A party girl? A whore?"

Lucie defied her mother and went ahead and starred in the TV drama anyway.

With the understanding that there were almost no rehearsals, Lucie did a creditable job. "She gives a sympathetic performance," wrote one critic, "playing a young woman who arrives in Hollywood in the Post-War era, dreaming of stardom as did thousands of other hopefuls. Instead of stardom, a brutal death

Left Photo: **Elizabeth Short,** a failed actress who, because of the circumstances and mysteries surrounding her grisly murder, became more famous than she might have become as a successful actress, and...

Right Photo: An unexpectedly vulnerable-looking **Lucie Arnaz** portraying Elizabeth Short in the made-for-TV movie, *Who Is the Black Dahlia?*

awaited her."

Another critic wrote, "Lucie Arnaz's restrained performance succeeds in presenting Elizabeth Short as a young woman of thwarted ambition, floating in a vacuum of failure, just hanging on by a thread. Lucie Arnaz should have won an Emmy."

Another reviewer wrote, "For years, I have watched Lucie Arnaz play the daughter of Lucy in rather bland comedies on TV. I had no idea what a powerful actress she was until I saw her cast as the Black Dahlia. I think her acting career has been seriously stifled because of her famous mother."

In his role of a detective who's trying, but failing, to uncover who murdered Short, Zimbalist Jr. was also praised for his performance. He reflected, "The police never found anyone who saw Elizabeth Short in the last six days of her life. As far as I know, there has never been another murder in Los Angeles quite like this one….ever! In the files of the L.A. Police, the case is still open."

The critic for the *Los Angeles Times* reviewed the telecast as "One of the best TV movies ever made."

Coincidentally, Lucie's next made-for-TV role, also in 1975, involved yet another murder of a young woman—this time one named "Judy."

It was loosely based on a real-life incident of a young victim whose murder was witnessed by fifteen of her neighbors They not only stood by and watched her be killed, they later refused to help the police in their pursuit of the killer.

When filming began, the TV drama was entitled *Homicide*. Later, it was switched to *Death Scream*. In some re-runs, the title was changed to *The Woman Who Cried Murder*. For such a low-budget drama, a remarkable cast was assembled, with three actors (Raul Julia, John F. Ryan, and Philip Clark) cast as detectives.

The supporting cast starred Ed Asner, Cloris Leachman, Art Carney, Diahann Carroll, Kate Jackson, Tina Louise, Nancy Walker, Sally Kirkland, and Helen Hunt.

The telecast was broadcast on the ABC-TV network on September 26, 1975.

***

"Against my better judgment," Lucille admitted to Gary Morton, "I've become fascinated by Elizabeth Short, the Black Dahlia.

A made-for-TV movie, *Death Scream*, teamed two talented stars, **Ed Asner** with **Cloris Leachman** as they appeared in the poster above.

Lucie Arnaz was cast as Kitty Genovese, the historical subject of a brutal 1964 murder who was slain in front of her Queens apartment building as 38 onlookers refused to help her.

Lucie chose the script's shorter but more crisis-oriented role rather than one which would have given her more screen time.

So was half of America."

She came up with an idea for a motion picture different from any she had ever made before. "Why not make *The Black Dahlia* into a feature film? Many major motion pictures originated from TV dramas or comedies."

She kept her burgeoning idea from Lucie, fearing that she might insist on repeating her role of The Black Dahlia. "I don't want my own flesh and blood, even in a movie, being subjected to such a brutal death where her blood is drained and her body butchered. No way!!"

Lucille ordered three members of her staff to compile a huge dossier on Elizabeth Short's murder, which she would read the following weekend in the privacy of her home. As she was to find, it was a complicated story, filled with lies, false confessions, and contradictions.

Amazingly, during the murder investigations, sixty persons, most of them men, but a few women too, had confessed to the murder. By the time Lucille read the dossier, 500 people had come forth, claiming that they had killed Short, even though some of them were not even born at the time of the murder.

Morton claimed that Lucille wanted to be taken more seriously as a producer of drama, not just of sitcoms. "I think she hoped to show the world that she was far removed from Lucy Ricardo."

One night in a screening room, she showed him two *films noirs* she made in the late 1940s, which she presented with the belief that they proved her own abilities as a dramatic actress. One was *The Dark Corner* (1946) with co-stars Clifton Webb and Mark Stevens. Another was the melodrama, *Lured* (1947), in which her co-star was George Sanders. Even Boris Karloff had had a small, scary role in it.

Morton estimated that during the weekend, both of them studied the dossier on Short. *[During the course of their brainstorming, Lucille proposed that Morton himself might be cast into the role of a detective investigating the grisly murder.)* Lucille suggested at least a dozen actresses—but pointedly avoided adding her daughter to the list.

Lucille learned that Short had been born in Boston in 1924 and was last seen in Hollywood on the night of January 9, 1947.

During various stages of the investigation, 150 suspects had been brought to police headquarters for questioning. But none of them were ever charged because there was no strong evidence linking any of them to the crime.

Historians claimed that Elizabeth Short's murder became the first of the post-war era to capture the lurid imagination of millions of Americans.

A medical report was issued in reference to Short's mutilated body. It stated, "The body had apparently been washed by her killer. Her face had been slashed from the corners of her mouth to her ears, creating the effect known as a 'Glasgow smile.' She had several cuts on her thighs and breasts, where entire portions of her flesh had been sliced away. The lower half of her body was positioned a foot away from her upper half, and her intestine had been tucked neatly behind her buttocks. The corpse had been 'posed,' with her hands over her head. Her elbows at right angles, and her legs spread apart."

In the mid-1970s, after years in Hollywood, Lucille did not shock easily. However, as she was reading through the thick dossier on Short, she called out to Morton, "Bring me a god damn drink and make it a stiff one. You'll never guess what I've just learned. At the time Franchot Tone was fucking me, he was also plugging Elizabeth Short. He was one of the guys rounded up for questioning about her murder. His name, address, and phone number were found in her little date book."

Morton was almost as astonished as his wife was.

She had first met Tone when he was "heavy dating" his future wife, Joan Crawford, late in 1933. He was Constance Bennett's co-star in *Moulin Rouge* (1934), in which Lucille appeared as an extra, one of the girls in the chorus.

Lucille's affair with Tone didn't begin until they co-starred as a married couple in *Her Husband's Affairs.*, a 1947 release from Columbia Pictures.

Tone had been born into a wealthy family in 1905 at Niagara Falls, a place usually known more for honeymoons than births.

When Lucille was first introduced to him, he had also made *Today We Live*, in which he had the third lead after Joan Crawford and Gary Cooper.

She was on the rebound in the wake of her divorce from Douglas Fairbanks Jr. She was also involved in a long-enduring affair with Clark Gable, although the two stars would never marry.

Louis B. Mayer at MGM believed that "Tone makes a perfect foil for our dynamic diva, Miss Crawford." He would go on to cast them together in a number of pictures, following with *Dancing Lady* (1933) in which Tone co-starred with both Crawford and Gable.

The following year (1934), Tone reteamed with Crawford to make *Sadie McKee*, this film also starring Gene Raymond, who made several sexual advances toward Tone.

Later, without Tone, Crawford reteamed with Gable for *Chained* (1934), followed by another Gable/Crawford picture in 1934, *Forsaking All Others*. Tone, however, was back with Crawford again for the filming of *No More Ladies* (1935), in which Robert Montgomery was the leading man.

Tone was also in her next picture, *The Gorgeous Hussy*, in which the male star was Robert Taylor. He, too, made sexual ad-

Years after the fact, Lucille learned that **Franchot Tone,** her leading man in *Her Husband's Affairs*, had been conducting an affair with her at the time he was dating Elizabeth Short, the notorious "Black Dahlia," the victim of one of Hollywood's most gruesome murders.

Tone became a suspect in the murder of Short, but no evidence was found that he was the killer.

A "devil-may-care" leading man in movies of the 1930s, he was once married to (and frequently cast with) **Joan Crawford,** who appears with him in the amorous scenario above.

vances toward Tone.

Although Tone was no male beauty, Crawford was largely responsible for making him attractive to gay or bisexual men. She spread the word that he had a thick, ten-inch penis, which she'd named "Jawbreaker."

As Gable said, "Tone gives Joan class, and she gives him ass."

In 1935, Tone co-starred with Crawford's screen rival, Bette Davis, in *Dangerous,* and launched a torrid affair with her. Word soon reached Crawford, marking the beginning of their ferocious, decades-long feud.

In spite of his having betrayed her, Crawford married Tone on October 11, that same year of 1935. Their tumultuous union would last until April 11, 1939, when she filed for divorce.

Even after their marriage, Mayer continued to cast Tone in Crawford's movies. In 1936, he rejoined Gable and Crawford for *Love on the Run.* In 1937, Tone became her leading man in *The Bride Wore Red,* in which Robert Young had third billing.

The Tone/Crawford marriage was marked by adultery, heavy night clubbing and partying, and many violent arguments. Sometimes, Crawford showed up at MGM badly bruised, requiring great effort from her make-up artists.

As Lucille found out, it was because of Tone's violence against Crawford that he had come in for intense questioning about the brutal death of Elizabeth Short. He was known for excessive drinking which often exploded into violent confrontations. The TV host and newspaper columnist Ed Sullivan referred to him as "a vodka zombie."

By the time Lucille learned the contents of the police department's files on her former lover, he had been dead since 1968. A heavy smoker, he had died of lung cancer.

According to the dossier that Lucille read, Tone had first been attracted to Short in 1946 when he'd encountered her at the Formosa Café near the MGM Studios. At that time in his life (1941-1948), Tone was married to the actress Jean Wallace.

Apparently, he invited Short back for an afternoon on the couch in his dressing room at MGM. He later confessed to police that he gave her all the money he had in his wallet, about two-hundred dollars, and sent her on her way. As he also told the police, "She told me that she'd been ill and had some sort of operation on her chest. I had the feeling that I wanted to be far away from her—that I did not want her near me again. Sex with her had been a strange, unsettling experience for me. It had something to do with the aura she gave off. I wanted her gone from my life forever."

It appeared to Lucille that initially, he had lied to the police, because, as mentioned, his address and private phone number were found in her address book. He was rumored to have taken her for an off-the-record weekend in Palm Springs.

The blonde actress, Jean Wallace, was also questioned by the police, and she confirmed that Tone had continued his affair with Short, at least until two months before her death.

At the time, she also told police that he was also having affairs with both Lucille Ball and with Zsa Zsa Gabor, and that this "blatant adultery" prompted her to divorce him in 1948.

After reading the dossier that weekend, Lucille stormed back to work on Monday morning. She told the staff that she was no longer interested in making a film about The Black Dahlia. "Let the poor victim rest in peace," she said. "One thing is clear to me: The more I know about Miss Elizabeth Short, the less I know about her. Case closed."

Privately, she told Morton, "I had no idea that my name even came up in the investigation of the death of Short. That Jean Wallace, the former wife of Franchot, was a bitch. She had a lot of nerve to introduce me as the woman that Franchot was messing around with at the time he was seeing Short."

"Do you think he was the murderer?" Morton asked.

"Not at all," she answered. "He was violent and had this explosive temper, and he could beat up on women. But I don't think he would kill anybody. Besides, Franchot wouldn't have the surgical skill to do all that butchering. She must have been killed and cut into pieces by a doctor."

***

In 1976, after her role ended in the musical *Seesaw*, Lucie starred in the West Coast premiere of *Vanities* at the Mark Taper Forum in Los Angeles. Lucille and Gary Morton attended the opening. It had premiered that January at the Playwright's Horizons in Manhattan, with music and lyrics by David Kirshenbaum and a book by Jack Heifner.

The plot centered on the lives and friendship of three cheerleaders from Texas whose high school days dated back to 1963. They continued their links on to college, where they became sorority sisters, but by 1974, they were ready to go their separate ways. Whereas one of them had become very conservative, another, the owner of an art gallery, is exploring sexual liberation.

Privately, Lucille told a few select friends that she believed that her son, Desi Jr., was more talented than his sister and that he'd go much farther in the theater, feature films, or TV drama.

After leaving the premier of *Vanities*, Lucille was accosted by reporters wanting a quick review of her daughter's performance. Rushing to her limousine, she gave only a cursory answer, "She was perfect. Gary and I are proud of her."

While seated in the limousine, she faced a reporter who stuck his head in through the open window. "Do you think Lucie is talented enough to escape the long shadow of her mother?"

Not answering, she ordered Morton to raise the window.

A year after she starred in *Vanities*, Lucie also appeared in a feature film, *Billy Jack Goes to Washington* (1977), a loose, very loose remake of Frank Capra's *Mr. Smith Goes to Washington* (1939), a vehicle that James Stewart morphed into a classic.

It was the fourth in a series (the "Billy Jack" series) of films written and directed by its star, Tim Laughlin, but whereas the first three had been hits, this one failed at the box office and had only limited screenings. Laughlin's two male co-stars included E.G. Marshall and John Lawler. Lucie, portraying a character named "Saunders," had the fourth lead.

As anticipated, the reviews were bad. *Variety* wrote, "By comparison with the spine-tingling emotionalism and technical brilliance of the Frank Capra 1939 movie, the picture is much flatter and largely devoid of visual nuances. Most of the humor is gone, and the characters are thinned out, replaced with a theatrical and rhetorical talkathon interspersed with a few cop-socky sequences."

Writing in *The Washington Post*, Gary Arnold described the movie as "a talky, static, and derivative picture that seems to run on forever. Laughlin relies so heavily on the original plot and dialogue of *Mr. Smith Goes to Washington* that one may feel a little embarrassed on his behalf. It's obvious that he's used the Capra movie as a crutch rather than an inspiration."

Without a doubt, Tom Laughlin would be the most controversial actor with whom Lucie would ever appear.

A son of Wisconsin, he was multi-talented, not only as an actor and director, but as a screenwriter, author, educator, and activist. He co-produced and acted in four Billy Jack films, centering on a character of the same name, beginning with the film *Born Losers* in 1967.

Three hip metrosexuals, (left to right) **Lucie Arnaz, Sandy Duncan,** and **Stockard Channing**), portray ambition-crazed Texas cheerleaders in *Vanities*.

This motorcycle-gang exploitation film became a surprise box office hit, leading to three more sequels. He attracted the attention of Marlon Brando, Jack Lemmon, Candice Bergen, and director Robert Wise, all of whom were willing to finance his next film, a documentary focusing on the life of Martin Luther King Jr., but the deal fell through.

In 1971, *Billy Jack*, the sequel to *The Born Losers*, ran into distribution troubles and conflicts with American International Pictures. The movie was not only politically explosive, but Laughlin insisted on appearing in it frontally nude. After deciding to release the movie himself, the youth of America embraced it.

He told the press, "Young people in this country have two heroes, Ralph Nader and Billy Jack." Adjusted to inflation, the movie became the highest-grossing independent film in movie history.

Its sequel, *The Trial of Billy Jack* (1974), was a huge box office hit, and became known for its casting of Native Americans such as "Sachen Littlefeather" and other counter-culture figures.

However, in 1977, the fourth installment, *Billy Jack Goes to Washington,* in which Lucie Arnaz co-starred, failed at the box office.

Lucille Ball herself was seen at a private screening, sitting next to the daughter of Walter Cronkite, the fabled newscaster.

In 1995, the actor began to work on a fifth Billy Jack movie, *The Return of Billy Jack,* but suffered a neck injury, the effects of which halted production. The movie, which depicted Billy Jack fighting child porn in Manhattan, was never completed.

In time, Laughlin's interest turned to politics. In 1992, as a political activist, he sought the Democratic Party's nomination for U.S. President, losing to Bill Clinton. He told the press, "I am the least qualified person I know to become president, except for George W. Bush."

Later, he attacked the Christian Right, calling them "False Evangelists," "Fake Prophets," and "Christian Fascists."

In later life, suffering ill health himself, he turned to the topic of domestic abuse, citing the murder of Nicole Brown Simpson as a key example. In a statement to the press, he said: "O.J. Simpson was my neighbor up the street on Rockingham. He lived at 300 Rockingham Drive, I lived at 100 Rockingham. I've known O.J. forever. This is one of the sickest, sorriest days in our culture, that he was found not guilty. Eight times Nicole cried out and eight times, because it was O.J. and it was woman-battering, it was dismissed. But now, with the trivialization, people are afraid to call because they don't trust that the system will work. The fact that he was found not guilty is going to make that ten times worse."

In 2013, Laughlin, firmly ensconced as an activist and crusader for human rights, died from pneumonia at a medical center in Thousand Oaks, California.

Ironically, although the first three **"Billy Jack"** movies had been successful and—in a cult way—very famous, the fourth installment in the film series—the one in which Lucie finally got a part, bombed.

***

In spite of his ongoing issues with drug addiction, Desi Jr. in the 1970s was the most employed member of the Arnaz clan, certainly beating out his father, who found most doors closed to him as an actor.

On television, at least, 1971 was a particularly busy one for Desi Jr. He started out cast as "Alan" in an episode of *Love, American Style.* His segment was named *Love and the Motel Mix-Up,* part of an anthology TV series from Paramount Television telecast between 1969 and 1974. Each week, an unrelated story was featured, most often with a comedic spin. The musical score of Charles Fox featured flutes, harp, and flugelhorn set to a contemporary pop beat that provided the "love" ambience which tied the different narratives together.

Desi followed that television appearance with a more substantial role in *The Mod Squad* (1971), where he was cast in the role of Victor Emory. This crime series ran for five seasons on ABC between 1968 and 1973. Its star was Michael Cole in the role of Pete Cochran. Its executive producers were Aaron Spelling (who would later work with Lucille) and Danny Thomas, who had a long association with her.

The counterculture police series earned six Emmy Award nods and four Golden Globe nominations.

Other than Cole, the other co-stars included Clarence Williams III and Peggy Lipton. Studio publicists promoted them as "one black, one white, and one blonde, the hippest and first young undercover cops on television."

More than a year before the release of *Easy Rider* (1969), starring Dennis Hopper, Peter Fonda, and Jack Nicholson, *The Mod Squad* was one of the earliest TV series to deal with the power of the hippy counterculture then sweeping across the land. Desi Jr. felt at home working with the young cast.

Stories dealt with student protest, police brutality, sex education, anti-Vietnam protests, and racism.

Also in 1971, Desi was given the starring role in a made-for-TV movie, *Mr. and Mrs. Bojo Jones*. He had the title role of Bo Jo in this controversial drama based on a 1967 novel written by Ann Head, a book credited with launching new realism into young adult literature. The theme dealt with the once-forbidden subject of teenage pregnancy. The telecast drew irate letters of protest from viewers who objected to its subject matter.

***

Joan Crawford, her heavily made-up face trying to defy gravity, made her last film appearance in a made-for-television movie called *Night Gallery*, a telefilm that launched a hit TV series in 1969.

In a cast that starred Gary Collins and Rod Serling, Crawford played Joan Fairchild, who stumbles upon a coven of ESP enthusiasts who

He was understandably jaded from too close a contact to show-biz, even at an early age, but to sitcom consumers, **Desi Jr.** was a perfect "bachelor prototype" for the frothy romances that had evolved into day-to-day entertainment for daytime and early-evening TV.

In this publicity photo from 1972 for *The Mod Squad*, **Clarence Williams** (in sunglasses) shields **Desi Jr** (a deaf-mute who has witnessed wrongdoings) from malefactors in "Feet of Clay."

decide to use their abilities to scare her to death.

Under the guidance of a sinister leader, the evil young people offer her shelter for the night. They intend to use their psychic abilities to telepathically send Joan distressing images of her deceased daughter. For her appearances, Crawford was generally panned, one critic citing the telecast as "1970s TV at its worst."

Another wrote, "Joan Crawford is keeping on until she can give no more. Any sane actress would have called it quits after this."

The concept of *Night Gallery* itself went on to become a hit TV anthology series aired on NBC from 1970 to 1973. Desi Jr. made his appearance in the role of Doran in one episode in 1971. Featured were stories of horror and the macabre, hosted by Rod Serling, who had gained fame from an earlier series, *The Twilight Zone*.

As previously mentioned, Desi Jr. at this point in his career, had long ago dropped out of *Here's Lucy*, where he had been endlessly cast and re-cast as her on-screen son. He went on to star in a "coming of age" drama, a feature film set in World War II, *Red Sky at Morning*. He followed that with a leading role in yet another feature film, *Marco* (1973). Set in "the mysterious Orient," it was the saga of the Venetian explorer, Marco Polo (1243-1324).

He returned to television in 1973, starring as Andy Reed in *She Lives!* His female co-star, Pam, was played by actress Season Hubley, the story based on a 1972 novel by Paul G. Neimakr.

The couple meet after Andy places a singles ad in his college newspaper. They are instantly attracted to each other, and soon they are living together.

Disaster descends when Pam discovers a lump in her neck. Tests reveal she has Hodgkin's Disease. She ponders suicide, but finds strength in the love of Andy. She undergoes experimental treatments

Consistent with the other roles he played (a young and handsome high school senior with a strong sex drive and good intentions) in the early 70s, **Desi Jr.** appears here with co-star **Julie Greher** in *Mr. and Mrs. Bojo Jones*. It's theme? Unexpected pregancies in the best of homes.

Who played one of the mothers? Dina Merrill (see photo below), one of the most sophisticated (and wealthiest) heiresses in Hollywood.

Dina Merrill as the pregnant teenager's frantic mother in *Mr. and Mrs. Bojo Jones*.

Formerly married to screen idol Cliff Robertson, she sold Mar-a-Lago to a real estate developer, Donald Trump, for $7 million.

that almost kill her.

In San Francisco, her disease goes into remission. Andy (that is, Desi Jr.) runs through the street shouting "She Lives!"

***

Desi's biggest career break came in the form of *The Voyage of the Yes*, a made-for-television film that cast him as Cal, a young skipper of his small craft, known as "Yes," during a hazardous transit from the coast of California to Hawaii.

Young **Desi Arnaz Jr.** had a featured role in *Red Sky at Morning*, a tense drama set against the backdrop of America at war in the 1940s.

His talent was widely praised by some critics, and major stardom was predicted for him.

Sometimes, Hollywood is known as the Boulevard of Broken Dreams.

The producer, Andrew J. Fenady, had high hopes for the movie, even talking about turning it into a TV series where he and his African American companion sail between various ports of the world, getting into one adventure after another.

The role of Orlando, Cal's sailing companion, was awarded to the very talented Mike Evans. A son of North Carolina, he would become better known as Lionel Jefferson in the hit TV sitcom, *All in the Family* and *The Jeffersons*.

At first, the two men have sharp exchanges, Desi calling him "a coon," and he shouting back that Desi, in his role of Cal, is a "honky."

Yet as the plot unfolds, they face life-threatening adventures, and a bond grows between them. It almost becomes a (non-sexual) love affair. The most touching scene is Cal's fight to keep Orlando alive after he is attacked by a shark.

Desi gives one of his best performances, some critics claimed. "At last, he has escaped from the shadow of his famous father and become his own man."

Today, this rarely shown movie, *The Voyage of the Yes*, is hailed as one of the lost treasures of 1970s TV. One critic hailed it as "the best movie on sailing and self-discovery ever made."

Della Reese is given only a small role as the mother of Orlando.

The screen mother of Cal is played by Beverly Garland. When she accepted the role, she had concluded playing the wife of Steve Douglas (Fred MacMurray) in the sitcom *My Three Sons*.

***

Both Lucille and Desi Sr. were impressed with their son's performance in *The Voyage of the Yes,* and even lobbied to get it made into a series, but the project never found a sponsor.

The parents' hopes for major stardom for their handsome offspring came when he was cast into a feature film in the title role of *Billy Two Hats,* a western shot in Israel. It cast Desi Jr. opposite matinee idol Gregory Peck.

Lucille, Desi Jr., and on occasion Lucie, had seen many of Peck's classic films: *Spellbound* (1945), *Gentleman's Agreement* (1947), *The Snows of Kilamanjaro* (1952), *Moby Dick* (1956), *To Kill a Mockingbird* (1962), and *Roman Holiday* (1963).

Peck's co-starring roles were usually reserved for formidable female talents such as Ingrid Bergman, Audrey Hepburn, Sophia Loren, Ava Gardner, Susan Hayward, or Lauren Bacall. Peck's directors had included such giants as Alfred Hitchcock, John Huston, Elia Kazan, Stanley Kramer, and William Wyler.

Desi Jr. with **Mike Evans** in this poster for *The Voyage of the Yes*, a tale about friendship, loyalty, and survival.

Desi met Peck after his visit to the White House. Peck told the younger man that Richard Nixon had praised his performances in such films as *Red River, The Quiet Man,* and *Sands of Iwo Jima.* "To my horror, I realized he had confused me with John Wayne."

In the role of *Billy Two Hats,* Desi was cast as Billy, a "half-breed" hero. Peck played Arch Deans, a Scottish outlaw. Before the beginning of shooting, he took diction lessons to get the accent right.

Peck wasn't really that fond of his role, complaining to director Ted Kotcheff and producer Norman Jewison, "I spend much of my screen time being hauled around by Desi." [Peck's character, Arch, had been shot from a long-range buffalo rifle. The shot killed his horse, and as the animal fell to the ground, Arch's leg is broken. Billy constructs a *travois* (a sledge consisting of two lashed-together poles pulled by a horse or dog), places Deans on it, and drags him off to a remote homestead where they encounter a frontiersman named Spencer (John Pearce), and his wife, Esther, whom he purchased as a mail-order bride. In the role, Sian Barbara Allen has this awful stutter.

When Deans pays Spencer a hundred dollars to take him to a frontier post where he can buy a horse, Billy stays behind to guard the farmstead and to protect Esther. They fall in love.

Everything ends tragically, at least for Spencer and Deans, who are ambushed by drunken Indians, some of the most grotesque ever to appear on film.

Deans dies of his wounds but Billy, according to Indian tradition, does not bury him in the ground but places his body atop a tree. He and Esther ride off together.

The movie was one of Peck's lesser efforts, and it did not bring stardom to Desi. *Variety* labeled the film "a fresh and different oater (the first filmed in Israel) that opens with violence and contains some throughout but never lingers lovingly on mayhem and gore."

Gene Siskel of the *Chicago Tribune* awarded the film two stars out of four. "When the action turns, as inevitably it must, to conversation between Peck and Arnaz, *Billy Two Hats* becomes vapid. And when young Arnaz strikes up a romance with a rancher's stuttering mail-order bride, the action and the dialogue become positively embarrassing."

Only a year after the release of *Billy Two Hats*, Peck's son, the news reporter Jonathan Peck, committed suicide by means of a self-inflicted gunshot wound. At the time, he was going through a broken relationship and suffering from arteriosclerosis and severe fatigue. Shortly before his suicide, he told his father, "When I wake up in the morning, I feel I have no energy to live through another day."

Gregory Peck, in the aftermath of his son's suicide, was unable to work for the next two years.

EQUAL BILLINGS FOR UNEQUAL STARS

Gregory Peck, right, co-stars with **Desi Jr**. left.

Sometimes defined as "impossibly handsome," Peck didn't look his best when he made *Billy Two Hats* for a 1974 release.

He was much more challenged by his role in *The Boys from Brazil* (1947) in which he played the first real villain of his career.

His co-star was Laurence Olivier in a story about a plot to breed a new race of Adolf Hitlers.

Peck later told the press that Olivier was "beautiful—a real darling, gallant,, funny, easy to work with, not at all intimidating."

***

After *Billy Two Hats*, Desi returned to appearing in established TV dramas, beginning with *Medical Story*, a short-lived anthology series on NBC. Focused on surgeons working at an unnamed university hospital in Los Angeles, it was inaugurated in September of 1975, but it was not a success and went off the air four months later, in January of 1976.

Desi Jr. appeared in only one episode, shown in 1975, joining an array of other, frequently rotating guest stars who included Diane Baker, Richard Basehart, Ralph Bellamy, Dane Clark, Beau Bridges, Broderick Crawford, Howard Duff, Vince Edwards, John Forsythe, Ruth Gordon, Hope Lange, Susan Strasberg, Carl Reiner, and a blowsy-looking Ann Sothern, who had put on a lot of weight. As a side note, an aspiring actress, Linda Purl, also appeared in an episode. In 1979, she became the first wife of Desi Jr.

[Medical Story *was sometimes confused with another, more successful and longer-running drama series,* Medical Center *(also known as* Calling Dr. Gannon*), which ran from 1969 to 1976. It starred James Daly as Dr. Paul Lochner, Chad Everett as Dr. Joe Gannon, and Audrey Totter, one of those hard-edged dames of 1940s-era film noir, as Nurse Eve Wilcox. At this stage of her career, Totter's career was in decline, but once she'd played opposite John Garfield, Robert Montgomery, Robert Taylor, and Clark Gable.*]

***

Desi Jr may never have known this, but he was once considered as a possible cast member for a feature film that never got off the ground.

If it had gone through, Desi might have ended up co-starring with a porn star in a non-porn motion picture. Its spark originated in the mind of XXX film star Jack Wrangler, who was tiring of porn and wanted to work in more legitimate film fare.

Wrangler's real name was Jack Stillman, the son of the A-list Hollywood producer Robert Stillman, who was one of the creative forces behind the long-running hit TV series *Bonanza*. Under his stage name of Jack Wrangler, he evolved into one of the leading porn stars of the 1970s, making eighty porn films, both straight and gay.

Edward Albert, Desi Arnaz Jr. (center) and **Meredith Baxter**, all professional-looking and lined up, in an episode of *Medical Center*.

Henry Winkler, (The Fonz) with **Linda Purl,** in a feature story entitled "AAAY! Meet the Girl Who Won Fonzie's Heart" appear together on the cover of *TV Guide*.

Later, in addition to winning The Fonz, she also won Desi and actually married him!

Jack had never set out to be a porn idol, but originally studied to be an actor. In 1969, he had appeared in a single episode of *Medical Center* as "Student #2."

Wrangler identified with Desi, claiming, "Both of us were born in the long shadow of our more successful fathers, and both of us were struggling to make it on our own, without coasting on the big names of our dads."

Most of Wrangler's porn fans never knew that as Jack Stillman, he had been a stage director, radio talk show host, songwriter, actor, and businessman. He also managed both Ann Sothern and Gale Storm when their careers started to fade, and each of them turned to touring on the dinner theater circuit.

Jack had appeared on stage with such fading stars as Betty Hutton, Ruth Roman, and the eccentric English actress, Hermione Gingold. She dared asked him, "Are you gay or straight?"

He answered, "My aim is to become a gay heterosexual jock."

Darwin Porter, the co-author of this book, had long been a friend of singer Margaret Whiting. He was somewhat stunned when she began dating Jack Wrangler, deep into his porn career, as part of a May-December mating. The "odd couple" would eventually marry

Whiting introduced Darwin to Wrangler because she wanted to recommend him for the role of Numie, the protagonist of the upcoming film adaptation of Darwin's cult classic, the novel *Butterflies in Heat*, which had sold a million copies. Its film adaptation eventually starred Eartha Kitt, Barbara Baxley, Pat Carroll, and Tom Ewell. *[Ewell had been Marilyn Monroe's leading man in* The Seven Year

Born a Hollywood child of privilege and wealth, **Jack Stillman** became the famous gay porn star, **Jack Wrangler,** in the late 1970s and '80s. He occasiionally also appeared in straight porn too.

He brought an image of gay macho to the screen in many profit-generating films, eventually becoming known as "The Robert Redford of Porn."

Margaret Whiting was a famous songbird, the daughter of composer Fred Whiting. She had many hit records, including "Springtime in Vermont."

For a while, she had a torrid affair with screen stud Hugh O'Brian, then shocked her friends when she married a porn star significantly younger than herself, **Jack Wrangler.**

Itch *(1955).]*

Wrangler ultimately lost the role of Numie because of the stigma associated with his background in porn. The part of the blonde hustler in *Butterflies in Heat* (aka *The Last Resort* aka *Tropic of Desire*) (1979) went to supermodel Matt Collins, who at the time had been voted the handsomest man in the world.

Darwin's friendships with Whiting and Wrangler survived because Wrangler wanted Darwin to write a novel about the sons and daughters of movie stars who, despite having been reared in environments of luxury and privilege, ultimately commit suicide. Wrangler wanted to adapt the nascent novel into a feature film that would star "two sons of privilege," Desi Jr., himself, and some as-yet unnamed actress.

Super model **Matt Collins** had been voted "the handsomest man in the world" before he graced the cover of *After Dark* in December of 1979.

Author Pat Pacheco wrote: "Matt Collins is the most well-known 'unknown,' in the world, since his face has stared out from countless magazine covers and grooming guides, particularly the best-selling *Looking Good*."

As the highest paid male model in the world, the former equestrian copped a role that producer Jerry Wheeler said had launched a talent search akin to the casting of Scarlett O'Hara."

It was the character of Numie in the film adaptation of Darwin Porter's bestselling (and most nihilistic) novel, *Butterflies in Heat*.

[EDITOR'S NOTE ABOUT SUICIDE AND THE CHILDREN OF STARS: For years, Darwin had been fascinated by the deaths of movie star sons and daughters and would continue to be in the future. Overcommitted, and regrettably, he abandoned the project after only three chapters because he had a staggering total of fifteen Frommer Travel Guides *to complete, each already contracted for by Simon & Schuster.*

Attempts were made to revive the film project but none ever showed much promise. Darwin, however, kept the idea alive in the years to come, continuing to investigate the tragic and deeply disturbing suicides of the children of Hollywood's most famous actors.

In time, he wrote about the suicide of Marlon Brando's daughter, Cheyenne, who hanged herself in 1995 at the age of 25. After becoming pregnant, the Tahitian-born model, along with the baby's father, Dag Drollet, moved into Brando's home in Los Angeles. Shortly after moving in in 1990, Cheyenne's half-brother, Christian, shot and killed Drollet.

After that, Cheyenne's mental state deteriorated, and she was diagnosed with schizophrenia.

Darwin also wrote about the suicide of Scott Newman, son of Paul Newman, who was an aspiring actor himself. At the age of 29, he was found dead in a hotel room after overdosing on pills and alcohol. On the night of his death, Scott mixed a lethal dose of Valium, and other drugs.

Michael Charles Boyer, the son of the French movie star Charles Boyer, in 1965 committed suicide at the age of 21 while playing Russian roulette after a bad breakup of a love affair. Thirteen years later, his father also took his own life with a lethal dose of Seconal.

At the age of 20, in 1968, Diane Linkletter, daughter of TV talk show host Art Linkletter, jumped from a window in her apartment in West Hollywood, plunging to her death on the sidewalk below.

Jenny Lee Arness, the daughter of James Arness, committed suicide by means of a drug overdose in 1975 just a few weeks shy of her 25th birthday. She was said to be despondent over the breakup with Greg Allman, her boyfriend.

The only child of French actor Louis Jourdan, Louis Henry Jourdan, committed suicide in 1981. He was 29 and had a long history of drug addiction and suffered from a manic depressive type of disorder.

Heiress Gloria Vanderbilt had two sons, Carter and Anderson, the latter becoming an announcer on CNN. However, at the age of 23 in 1988, Carter committed suicide by jumping from the 14th floor terrace of his mother's apartment in Manhattan.

In 1991, Billy Nelson, 33, the son of singer Willie Nelson, hanged himself in his family's Tennessee cabin following a period of financial woes.

Hugh O'Connor, the son of Carroll O'Connor, in 1995 committed suicide after a long battle with drug addiction. He was only 32. He called his famous father to tell him he was committing suicide and his dad phoned the police. They did not reach the young man's home in time.

Nikki Bacharach, the daughter of Burt Bacharach and Angie Dickinson, committed suicide in 2007 at the age of 40. She used a plastic bag and helium to kill herself. She had struggled with mental problems throughout her life and probably suffered from Asperger's Syndrome.

Lucille Ball was alive when many of these suicides occurred, and she would have understood the despair. Once she confessed to her mother, DeDe, that during her darkest days as a late teenager, she, too, had contemplated suicide.

DeDe once asked her if she feared that either of her children might take their lives.

"Not Lucie. She's far too strong," Lucille said. "But Desi Jr. with his drugs makes me fear for him."

"You and I both know my son and daughter will never become as famous and successful as the Cubano and myself. I think both of them can deal with lesser positions in show biz. But who in hell ever knows what a kid is going to do?"]

***

In 1976, Desi Jr. joined the cast of the TV crime drama, *The Streets of San Francisco*, portraying a character named P.J. Palmer. Filmed on location, the show had been on ABC since 1972, originally starring Karl Malden and Michael Douglas in the lead roles of two homicide inspectors.

The series had originated as a pilot starring Robert Wagner and Tom

Bosley, based on the 1972 detective novel, the badly named *Poor Poor Ophelia* by Carolyn Weston.

Michael Douglas, the son of Kirk Douglas, eventually left the series to produce the movie *One Flew Over the Cuckoo's Nest*, which won an Oscar as Best Film of 1975.

To beef up Nielsen ratings, the producers brought in a steady stream of successful movie stars and an occasional relatively unknown actor who later rose to fame. Patty Duke, Desi's former girlfriend, starred on the show as did Ricky Nelson, Eileen Heckart, Don Johnson, Nick Nolte, John Ritter, Larry Hagman, and Mark Hamill.

Desi followed that episode by appearing as Jay Vernon in two telecasts of *Police Story*, an anthology series that aired on NBCs from 1973 to 1977. Some critics called it "one of the most realistic police series to be seen on television."

Desi Jr. was no stranger to the lingos and demands of TV serials, thanks to his mother, whom some said was obsessed with every aspect of their production.

Even as Lucille herself struggled to reinforce her niche in the "New and Confusing Hollywood," Desi Jr. found multiple, usually small-scale roles.

In the press photo above, he's seen with **Karl Malden**, a Hollywood pro as experienced as his mother, Lucille herself, in an episode of *The Streets of San Francisco*.

Regardless of the story, the setting was always Los Angeles. The series dealt not just with homicides but covered a wide range of subjects such as women officers trying to fit into a male-dominated profession, marital difficulties, and alcohol addiction.

The series also became the testing ground for spin-offs. For example, the first season's episode, *The Gamble,* starring Angie Dickenson, led to her successful *Police Woman* (1974-1978).

Its array of guest stars was staggering: Chuck Connors, Mike Connors, Jackie Cooper, Larry Hagman, George Hamilton, Don Johnson, David Janssen, Hope Lange, Hugh O'Brian, Kurt Russell, Robert Stack, Steve Lawrence, Patty Duke, and Robert Goulet.

***

To conclude 1976, Desi starred as Frank Gorman in a TV drama called *Having Babies,* first airing in 1976. Three TV movies with that title were followed by an ABC network show retitled *Julie Farr, M.D.,* named after its lead character, played by Susan Sullivan. *[Before that, she had worked at the Playboy Club in Manhattan for three years, later becoming a Playboy Bunny.]*

Dr. Farr is a busy physician at the Lake General Hospital, where many of her patients are either expectant mothers or new parents. Dr. Blake Simmons (Mitchell Ryan) is her veteran co-worker and a mentor to the young Dr. Ron Danvers (Dennis Howard).

The show was the first U.S. hospital drama that featured a female character as its lead. Whereas medical dramas featuring males as their leads had enjoyed great success, going back to the Dr. Kildare films in the late 1930s. *[Many of them had featured Lew Ayres.]* This newer, series, *Julie Farr, M.D.* caused some concern in Hollywood that a female character as the lead in a medical story could not attract a wide audience. The not-particularly compelling story line probably contributed to its demise after a single season.

***

During the mid-1970s, Lucille's re-runs of *I Love Lucy* and *The Lucy Show* were being shown in seventy-seven countries. In some newly emerging African nations, mothers named their newborn girls "Lucy." As some grew older, mothers dyed their daughters' hair red.

A Gallup Poll in the mid-1970s listed Lucille as one of the ten most famous women on the planet. She beat out First Ladies Mamie Eisenhower and Patricia Nixon, and even ran ahead of Queen Elizabeth II.

Ironically, most of that fame was still based on yesterday and had little to do with her current standing in Hollywood or along Madison Avenue in New York.

Yet despite her undeniable acclaim, at CBS, William Paley told his executive board, "I have no interest in introducing yet another Lucy series. She's just too old to be in a vat stomping on grapes or having her face cov-

At this point in her career, although most of it derived from her original (by then long-ago) *I Love Lucy* series of the 1950s, Lucille was more famous, according to Gallup polls in the 1970s, than either **Queen Elizabeth II** (left photo); **Mamie Eisenhower** (seen with her presidential husband, **Dwight**); and **Patricia Nixon**, seen here at one of the inaugurations of her controversial husband, **Richard Nixon**.

ered in melted chocolate. Those zany pranks of yesterday are dead and gone. No old lady would be performing them. Also it would look horrible to see a boss like Gale Gordon tormenting her and barking orders. Actually, the way they look today, it would be more believable to have Lucille as the lady boss ordering fatso around."

Very rarely did Lucille ever speak to her former husband, Desi Sr. One day, he called to talk about their kids as well as what she labeled "the nadir of our careers."

"If that means rock bottom, I'll go for that," he said. "Most of my time is spent licking my self-inflicted wounds."

For her 1976-1977 TV season, she figured she would occasionally pop up on a TV special or perhaps as a guest on the shows of more current stars such as Dinah Shore.

Mostly, Lucille stayed home playing backgammon, which had become an almost all-consuming passion.

As she told Vivian Vance, "Yes, I'm reduced to backgammon. There's been a change in me. The new Lucille Ball is not preoccupied with what — say, William Holden — is carrying around in his jockey shorts."

After 1976's long hot California summer, autumn finally came, as did an offer for her to co-star with Danny Thomas in his latest TV series. It was faltering in the Nielsen ratings. He hoped her star power would increase audience interest.

Entitled *The Practice,* which quickly became pegged as a dismal flop, their joint appearance was telecast on October 13, 1976.

Lucille played an aging mystic who, through her crystal ball, envisions her upcoming death.

Thomas was cast as a gentle, kind doctor who comes to her aid, hoping to help her through her despair. The chemistry between them just didn't seem to spark.

One TV critic wrote, "Lucille Ball today looks like a dumpy Ethel Mertz revisited twenty years later."

In that same month (October 29), Lucille, for NBC, agreed to appear on the telecast *Texaco Presents Bob Hope's World of Comedy.*

Jack Haley Jr. was both the producer and director. He told her, "I hope I didn't break your son's heart when I married his girlfriend, Liza Minnelli,"

"Desi is young...oh so young, and it took him only one night in 'Broken Heart Recovery' before other Hollywood babes ended his period of mourning."

"I think Liza tired of all that young flesh and decided to settle for a father figure like me," he said. "At least I'm

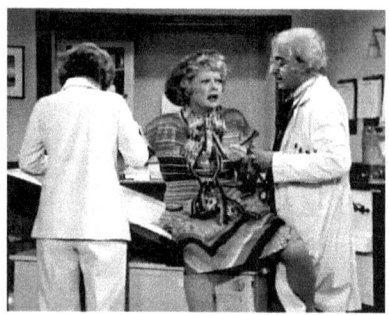

Lucille (center) as a confused geriatric being treated by a doctor (a much-aged **Danny Thomas**) in The Practice.

Reviewers and fans didn't find it particularly funny, nor endearing. Truth is, Lucille had lost some of her comedic touch.

better than her former husband, that Peter Allen fag. You see, I'm straight."

[Haley's father, Jack Haley Sr., had immortalized himself when he co-starred with Judy Garland in The Wizard of Oz. His son married "Liza with a Z" in 1974, but by 1979, she'd grown tired of him and filed for divorce.]

Also in a guest spot on the Hope special was Norman Lear, the writer and producer of so many hit TV sitcoms, including *Sanford and Son. Maude,* and *All in the Family.*

Lear was one of the wealthy Jewish Angelenos known as the "Malibu Mafia." In the 1970s, they were political activists funding liberal causes and sometimes very controversial progressive issues, too.

Also in a guest spot was that terrifying Don Rickles. In private, he and Lucille always greeted each other with X-rated banter. "I heard that on your wedding night with Barbara," she said, "you had your first sexual experience because no woman before would give you a tumble. I also heard that she had to ask, 'Are you in now?'"

"Oh, Lucy, Lucy, what a gal!" Rickles said. "You're at the age when women develop sagging tits. But that will never be your problem, because you never had any tits to sag. I was told you've had plastic surgery, not on your face, but below your belt. It seems that your plumbing down there had become such a gopher hole it had to be tightened."

Playwright Neil Simon also guest-starred on the Hope special. Unlike Lucille's obscene banter with Rickles, she and Simon did nothing but compliment each other. He called her "the greatest female *comedienne* who ever lived, and the only woman who could be called the female Chaplin."

"My God, you're our greatest living playwright," she said. "You name it, you can write it—farce, drama. My favorite is *Barefoot in the Park.*"

"You can trace the story of my life through my plays," he admitted. "Nearly all of them are semi-autobiographical."

"I could never appear in anything linked too closely to my own life," she said. "It would definitely be XXX-rated."

One night, she had dinner with Hope, and they talked mostly not about their previous triumphs, but lamented about the present dismal state of their careers.

He revealed that at a Thalian Ball, he'd had a reunion with Bing Crosby and Dorothy Lamour, who had last co-starred with him in *The Road to Hong Kong* in 1962.

Lucille had seen the film, which involved espionage and space rockets that predated *Dr. No* (1962) that famously starred Sean Connery as James Bond.

Hope gave Lucille some behind-the-scenes background on the making of their last Road picture. "You gals have it harder in Hollywood than we men do." Hope told her, a fact she already knew. "You're forced to retire long before we old geezers get the ax."

"Bing thought Dorothy—then aged 48—was too old to be the leading lady. He demanded that we cast bombshell Joan Collins, sometimes known as 'The British Open' because of her (allegedly) promiscuous sex life."

"That was insulting to poor Dottie, whom I still adored," Hope said.

"We once had an affair. A compromise was reached: Dottie was brought back for an extended cameo."

Hope carried around a review that Bosley Crowther had written in *The New York Times*. "Age may have withered somewhat the glossy hides of Bing Crosby and Bob Hope, and custom may have done a little something to steal their brand of vaudeville. But the old boys still come through with consecutive chucklers and frequent belly-deep guffaws."

"Let's face it," Hope told Lucille. "You're in the same sinking boat with me, Bing, and Dottie. That boat has sprung a leak, and all of us are sinking, with little hope for a comeback. I don't mean to sound gloom and doom, but we've got to face facts and adjust our lives accordingly."

He spoke of his most recent movie, *Cancel My Reservation*, a 1972 comedy whose co-star was Eva Marie Saint.

"The producer, Paul Bogart, dug up the grave of Ralph Bellamy and cast him as the third lead. In fourth spot, Forrest Tucker had to wear a heavy duty jockstrap to carry around those sagging goodies that had thrilled so many women...and some gay men, too."

"So just for old times' sake, I gave *Der Bingle* (Crosby) a cameo as himself, a favor I also extended to Johnny Carson, The Duke (John Wayne) and that gay black comic, Flip Wilson. I once saw you and 'Geraldine' perform together."

[*Cancel My Reservation bombed at the box office and was devastated by critics.*]

"Dolores and I attended its premiere at the Radio City Music Hall in Manhattan. Regrettably, the Musician's Union and the Rockettes were on strike. I later admitted to the press that I was getting too old to play a leading man again."

"Then *The New York Times* said what I was already god damn aware of: The asshole critic said that I, at the age of 68, was just too old to play a 42-year-old."

Lucille's own four-minute appearance on the *Hope TV Special* was hardly her most memorable. As one critic noted, "It was obvious to all that Miss Ball, not looking her best, was reading from cue cards. How much longer can Bob Hope and Miss Ball carry on before, like two former race-

The sometimes venomous **Don Rickles,** scourge of the late-night comedy circuit.

Bob Hope and **Dorothy Lamour** in *Road to Bali*.

On occasion, Lucille lunched with Lamour, often gossiping about Bob Hope.

Lamour discussed her early role as a beauty: "Glamour is just sex that got civilized. I never thought I'd be a movie star. My hips are too big, my feet aren't very pretty, and my shoulder blades stick out. I wish critics had said that not only did I wear a sarong beautifully, but gave a good performance as well."

horses, they're turned out to pasture?"

Actually, in 1977, a script, a sort of Monty Python type of picture, was being written as a farewell "Road Picture" that would reunite Hope, Crosby, and Lamour for a final celluloid *adieu*.

But on October 14, 1977, broadcasts around the word were interrupted to announce the death of Bing Crosby. His trademark warm bass-baritone voice had morphed him into the best-selling recording artist of the 20th Century, having sold more than a billion records before the age of 74.

Death caught up with him at Alcobendas, near Madrid, in Spain.

No pop singer in history has been as closely identified with Christmas (as in "White Christmas") than **Bing Crosby**.

***

Lucille seemed delighted when she was asked to appear on a December 1976 episode of *Van Dyke and Company*, a 60-minute short-lived variety series for CBS.

She had long admired Dick Van Dyke's talent as a performer, especially on *The Dick Van Dyke Show,* which ran from 1961 to 1996. She had also seen him in feature films, none more notable than when he co-starred with Julie Andrews in *Mary Poppins* (1964).

In his latest TV series, this son of Missouri was not doing so well. As he talked to Lucille, both of them admitted that "our glory days are behind us. Now begins the struggle to survive."

A scene within one of the skits struck a disturbing note with her: Van Dyke played a TV executive who confronts Lucille, cast as a big shot, to inform her that her series has been canceled.

In yet another skit, "Child Bride," she was cast as a gold-digger who marries a rich old geezer, perhaps hoping he'll soon kick off, leaving her with his fortune. He lives for another forty years.

Lucille often watched **Mary Tyler Moore**'s TV appearances with **Dick Van Dyke**, and later, her solo acts on *The Mary Tyler Moore Show.*

"I wish I had been younger," Lucille lamented. "I think Dick and I would have made a great team back in the 1960s, especially if Carl Reiner had written our material."

Lucille and Van Dyke had little time for rehearsal, and she was increasingly dependent on cue cards. She joined him to watch a screening before the telecast of the final cut. When it was over, he rose to his feet, reaching for her hand. "Where is Carl Reiner now that I need him?

Although Lucille became known for her longevity in show business,

Van Dyke's record of "hanging in there" would beat almost any other actor except for George Burns and a few others.

Born in 1925, and at the age of 95 in 2021, this frail legend was planning a one-man TV show as a kind of last hurrah in show biz. Insiders claimed that although he could barely walk, he became deeply committed to a final splashy bit of *razzmatazz* for his remaining fans.

As proof of his tenacity to live, he married Arlene Silver in 2012. A make-up artist, she was 46 years younger than him.

Someone close to him told the press, "Dick thinks he's still 39, and is even rehearsing a few dance numbers at his age. He'll probably end up injuring himself trying to put together a final show."

***

As executive producer, Gary Morton worked all day and into the nights putting together a tribute to Lucille. Telecast on November 28, 1976, it was entitled *CBS Salutes Lucy—the First 25 Years*. Released through Lucille Ball Productions, it was on the air for 120 minutes.

In addition to guest stars, Morton featured clips from long-ago episodes of *I Love Lucy* and *The Lucy Show*. For some reason, he did not include any of her on-screen appearances with Lucie Arnaz or Desi Jr.

Desi Sr. was invited onto the show, marking his first on-screen appearance with Lucille since 1960. He told her, "I never regretted selling out to you. I just didn't have it in me to go on and on forever."

In poor health and still recovering from breast cancer, Vivian Vance had aged considerably, and was hardly the wise-cracking Ethel Mertz of legend. She told Lucille, "I don't know how much longer I can go on. I feel dizzy a lot. But I just had to show up for this tribute to you, since I owe you so much."

A surprise guest was an aging Richard Burton. When he'd last appeared on television with her, he told reporters that he detested working with her, calling her "a real bitch."

This time around, however, he said, "I've buried the tomahawk, which is not a very Welsh expression. It's something I picked up in America. Morton practically begged me to come on, and I said what the hell. In show business, we often have to co-star with people we hate. What makes me ill is to have to make love on screen with a woman I loathe. But since I don't have to kiss Miss Ball, I came on."

Dick Van Dyke, with whom she had recently appeared, was also a guest. Both of them preferred not to mention their latest, deeply flawed, appearance together on TV.

Gale Gordon showed up, too, still praising Lucille and paying gratitude to her for giving him work over the decades.

Sanmy Davis Jr. was also a guest, as were Danny Kaye, the ever-faithful Bob Hope, and Duke Wayne, with whom she'd had some sort of bond despite their many differences in personality and politics.

At the end of the show, a lanky, fast-aging James Stewart appeared on screen to present her with an achievement award.

After the show, he whispered to her, "You and I would have made one of the great screen teams in film history. But, alas, it didn't happen. I remember meeting you back in the 1930s. You were one hot tomato. But Hank saw you first and went for it."

He was referencing, of course, his best friend, Henry Fonda.

Carol Burnett, also on the show, later claimed, "It should have been a greater tribute. Our star certainly deserved it. But most tributes never really hit the mark."

***

For her last television appearance of 1976, Lucille agreed once again to be a guest on *Dean Martin's Celebrity Roasts*. On December 15, Danny Thomas, her former co-star, would be the victim of barbs from his fellow celebrities. Lucille was still stung from the night "when I, too, went up in flames just like Joan of Arc."

Lucille and Dean Martin had long been friends, and she thought he deserved his nickname of "King of Cool" for his seemingly effortless charisma and self-assurance.

His variety program, *The Dean Martin Show* (1965-1974), had been one of the most successful on TV. By the time it went off the air, it was immediately replaced by these celebrity roasts, whose bantering and unexpected insults proved really popular with TV audiences.

The series was launched with a roast of Ronald Reagan, followed by the skewing of *Playboy's* Hugh Hefner. Over the years, other celebrities roasted included Bob Hope, Bette Davis, Johnny Carson, Don Rickles, Jack Benny, James Stewart, and even Frank Sinatra. (Of course, with the King of the Rat Pack, one had to proceed carefully as he took offense easily, often with dire consequences.)

When Lucille met privately with Martin, he brought up the subject of her son's close friendship with his son. He also told her that his third marriage to the much younger Catherine

From *The Dean Martin Show* in 1966, **Lucille** performs with **Dean Martin** and the fervently patriotic singer, **Kate Smith**.

"Dean and I went way back," Lucille said. "Over the years we kept appearing together. On our celebrity roast in 1976, I was seriously pissed. Most of what I had to say was cut out of the program by director Greg Garrison, who told me that the hour-long show ran over. Why in hell couldn't the bastard have cut Red Buttons or Orson Welles? Why me?"

Hawn had entered the divorce courts. Formerly, she'd been a receptionist at an exclusive hair salon in Beverly Hills.

To Lucille, Martin vowed that he'd never remarry. "I'm no good at being a husband," he confessed.

Although they would never remarry, he did have a reconciliation with his second wife, Jeanne Biegger (1949-1973), once the Orange Bowl Queen of Coral Gables, Florida.

Showing up to roast Danny Thomas were Gene Kelly, Don Knotts, Harvey Korman, Red Buttons, purse-swinging Ruth Buzzi, and even waist-expanding Orson Welles.

Before going on, Lucille ordered her makeup artist and hairdresser "to make me look lovely."

And so they did.

***

Over the holidays, Lucille and Gary Morton exchanged presents, and both of them gave a sigh of relief that they had survived 1976, unlike many of their friends and associates who had been hauled off to the cemetery.

She didn't have high expectations for 1977. "Things have been going too well lately, she said to Morton. "I find that whenever that happens, the shit is about to hit the fan."

Posing for the cameras: **Dean Martin** and **Lucille Ball.**

The public soon tired of Martin's celebrithy roasts. In some of them, he had appeared with Lucille.

Author Nick Tosches wrote: "It was a dais of despair. The guest celebrities sat at banquet tables at either side of the podium, the undead of dreamland and the fleeting stars of the television season, each rising in turn, at the beckoning of Dean or his bloated sidekick, Orson Welles, to deliver the moribund jokes consigned to them for the occasion."

CHAPTER FOURTEEN

AGING GRACEFULLY?

Lucille Becomes a Key Figure in Televised Odes to Vintage Hollywood

In 1977, Lucille Ball, Vivian Vance, & Gale Gordon Reach a Combined Age of 203 Years

Desi Jr. Makes a Splash as a Reliably Aimiable Straight Guy

"I've lost my greatest fan," Lucille mourned when she heard that her mother, DeDe had died of a heart attack. The date was July 22, 1977, and the frail woman was eighty-five years old.

Throughout Lucille's career, DeDe never missed one of her daughter's live shows. She'd show up with a group of women friends to lead the clapping. Positioned in a front-row seat, she was always the loudest in the cackle brigade, laughing uproariously, even when the comedy sketch didn't merit it.

"I'm not one of those demanding mothers, trying to run my daughter's life. I don't ask for anything. I don't have to. She is more than generous with me, always giving me a spending allowance and buying anything I need, such as a new air conditioner or refrigerator."

"Otherwise, I'm fairly self-sufficient,

Nicknamed "DeDe," **Desirée Hunt Ball Peterson** poses with her famous daughter, **Lucille.**

They'd had rough times when her daughter was young, struggling to survive. But Lucille saw that she spent her final years in the lap of luxury.

doing my own cooking and housekeeping. Of course, Lucille sends over a yard man. I live my own life and have my own friends, a set of girlfriends my own age. None of us are getting any younger."

"Lucille was the greatest daughter a mother could have," claimed Vivian Vance. "She bought this beautiful home in Brentwood for DeDe. On taping days for a Lucy show, she always sent her mother to the most elegant beauty parlor in Beverly Hills. A chauffeured limousine would take DeDe and her friends to the studio. Lucille also provided DeDe with an expensive wardrobe."

"At the death of her mother, I offered Lucille what comfort I could," Gary Morton said. "But it was not enough to chase away her depression and gloom."

Scriptwriter Madelyn Davis said, "On the first show Lucille did after her mother's death, she came on and, for a long and very awkward moment, she seemed lost. It was as if she'd completely forgotten the script. It was like she was scanning the audience, looking for her mother. Those two had been through a lot together, especially during their early days in Western New York State."

Months after her mother's death, Lucille told a reporter, "From beyond the grave, I still rely on DeDe's advice. I dream about her, and in my dream, she appears and answers my question."

Lucille had arranged for DeDe to be buried at Forest Lawn Memorial Park in the Hollywood Hills.

"I've set aside my own burial plot next to my mother's," she said. "I'll be joining her sooner than you might think."

***

Lucille, that spring of 1977, made her first appearance on TV on March 25, when she was a guest star on *Texaco Presents Bob Hope's All-Star Comedy Tribute to Vaudeville*. Fellow guests included the familiar faces of Vanda Barra and Sid Gould before their divorce. Lucille had worked with Bernadette Peters, also a guest, before.

The highlight of this fairly routine and rather lackluster tribute was Lucille doing her impersonation of "The Last of the Red Hot Mommas, Miss Sophie Tucker," who had died a decade earlier. She sang Tucker's signature song, "Some of These Days," although Bette Midler would later do it better.

Biographer Arthur Marx wrote: "One of the most amusing things about the Hope mystique is that after he agreed to Texaco to make a clean sweep of his writing staff and come up with a fresh format as part of his new deal, he did not. He led off with the same old material. Even more astonishing, the public bought it and would continue to buy it more or less for the next eighteen years, or until death do us part."

Another biographer, Richard Zoglin, wrote: "As for the Hope specials in 1977, he paid only minimal attention. He didn't even learn his lines. Most of his rehearsal time was spent worrying about where the cue cards would be placed. He liked to run through a routine only once—and that was that. He didn't want to lose spontaneity of the joke. He wasn't happy with Lucille Ball, who rehearsed obsessively and would often stop to make suggestions about how a scene could be improved. Grumbled Hope during one rehearsal, 'She thinks I just got into the business.'"

***

Lucille had yet another guest appearance before the spring of 1977 came to an end. On April 15, she appeared once again on the TV show, *Dinah!* with the shows host, Dinah Shore. Lucille sang, "Hey, Look Me Over," that time-tested song from her Broadway musical *Wildcat*, which she'd starred in seventeen years before.

Before Oprah, before Ellen, there had been Dinah Shore. Lucille and Dinah had long been friends, never rivals, at least between themselves.

Fans, however, divided into two camps: One calling Lucille "The First Lady of Television," others preferring to assign that honor to Dinah.

"I adore Dinah," Gary Morton said, "but I think my wife deserves the title of TV Queen, wearing the crown herself."

Lucille had remained Dinah's favorite guest. Her list of other stars had been amazing. Burt Reynolds was once invited onto her show and came on to her so strongly, right on the air, that they soon began an affair.

She even managed to get Boris Karloff, the "Monster Man," to appear as her guest. Occasionally, she would score a coup, as when she conducted the first post-White House interview with the former First Lady, Nancy Reagan.

A constantly changing array of top stars kept Dinah's Nielsen ratings high. Frank Sinatra, her former lover of the 1950s, might come onto her show and share his secret recipe for spaghetti sauce. Her guest list was wide-ranging, all the way from Bing Crosby to Pearl Bailey, from George Burns to Groucho Marx, from Peggy Lee to Mahalia Jackson.

Viewers never knew who might show up, perhaps the disgraced former Vice President, Spiro Agnew, sitting at the piano during a rendition of "So-

Every Baby Boomer in America who watched television in the 1950s could sing, "See the USA in your Chevrolet." In one of the most successful commercials in TV history, the singer of that jingle (**Dinah Shore**) was credited with selling a thousand Chevrolets a week.

In addition to her salary, the automobile company also saw to it that she was provided with (and seen driving) the brand's most expensive and most recent models.

Back then, it cost only $2,000 to produce one television commercial, unlike the huge amounts spent today.

phisticated Lady." Frequent guests were James Stewart and Bob Hope.

Privately, Lucille admired Dinah for her dating—"Dating is not the exact word I'd use," Lucille said—such desirable men as Eddie Fisher, Rod Taylor, Andy Williams, Ron (Tarzan) Ely, Wayne Rogers, and Dick Martin. Her most famous love affair, lasting four years, had been with Burt Reynolds, two decades her junior.

Once again, Dinah invited Lucille to join her for the weekend in Palm Springs. She surprised her by telling her that the former screen heartthrob, George Montgomery, was temporarily reunited with her. The couple had been married in 1943, divorcing two decades later.

Dinah assured Lucille that their getting together was only a temporary reunion—"for old times' sake,"—and not the beginning of a remarriage.

Dinah said, "George really wants to meet you. He says it's urgent."

"I have always considered him the handsomest actor in Hollywood," Lucille confessed. "Should I begin divorce proceedings against Gary?"

"No, hold off on that," Dinah cautioned with a smile. "I think he has something else in mind to talk to you about. I'll suggest to him that he should wear a very revealing bikini so you'll get a sneak preview of what I enjoyed for years and years and years. I think they grow them big in the Ukraine. Did you know that George was the last of fifteen children his mother had?"

"Believe it or not, George was both a champion boxer and an interior designer," Dinah said. "An unusual combination."

Up until the moment of their meeting, Lucille had no idea of why Montgomery wanted to see her. She suspected that he wanted her to pose for a sculpture. His sidelines included furniture making and sculpting portrait busts. He'd already managed to get Gene Autry, John Wayne, Clint Eastwood, Randolph Scott, and Ronald Reagan to pose for him.

Lucille remembered that when she'd first met Montgomery, Dinah had "to wean him away from the breasts of Hedy Lamarr, to whom he was engaged at the time."

Lucille called Hedda Hopper's former assistant, who had compiled a list of movie star seductions. She wanted the list of the actor's conquests read to her.

The names it included was A-list and long, including, as mentioned,

Two of the most famous women in America were also close friends—or so the story goes.

Here's a view of **Lucille** with **Dinah Shore** on *Dinah!* in June, 1974.

Lamarr as well as Carole Lombard, Lynn Bari, Tyrone Power, the doomed Carole Landis, Ann Rutherford, Merv Griffin, Gene Tierney, Ginger Rogers, Betty Grable, Robert Taylor, Audrey Totter, Van Johnson, and Randolph Scott.

"Well, George is certainly versatile in his tastes," Lucille said after hearing all the names on the list.

In Palm Springs, Dinah and Lucille were out beside her pool, talking about missed opportunities in their careers. Dinah revealed that Dore Schary at MGM had once tested her for the role of Julie in the remake of *Show Boat* (1951). Before that, the role had been briefly considered as a vehicle for Judy Garland, but she was viewed as too unreliable.

For the character of Julie, a romantic *chanteuse*, the script called for a woman of mixed blood, passing as white. In part because of her light skin color, Lena Horne wanted the role, losing it to her friend, Ava Gardner.

"MGM had had to dub Ava's voice," Dinah told Lucille. "With me, they wouldn't have had to do that."

Dinah confessed that another reason that she didn't get the role was because MGM feared the part of Julie, a woman of mixed races, would renew rumors that Dinah had faced all her life—that she was a mulatto herself.

Montgomery arrived late and hugged and kissed Dinah before embracing Lucille. Dinah asked him to change into the bathing suit she'd left for him on the bed in her bedroom and join them at poolside.

"When George emerged in that skimpy bikini," Lucille recalled to Vivian Vance, "his body was still in great shape. But surely that mound I saw in that bikini must have been fake. I think he'd stuffed a big sock in there. Very few actors had that much to reveal."

It turned out that Montgomery had never considered Lucille as a subject for one of his portrait busts. Instead, he wanted to present the script he'd written for a feature film which he wanted Lucille Ball Productions to produce.

Dinah Shore and "that handsome hunk" (her words), **George Montgomery** were photographed in the happier days of their long-running marriage.

She wasn't the only female (or male, for that matter) attracted to him. Everyone from Carole Lombard to Tyrone Power chased after him.

Here's **George Montgomery** invading King Solomon's Mines, alone and with a shotgun, in *Watusi* (1959).

It was a disturbing thriller torn from the pages of his own life. In the 60s, it had generated widespread tabloid coverage.

Montgomery's film career at the time was at low ebb. Since there hadn't been many film offers lately, he wanted to play the lead in the script he'd written, with the understanding that some actress in her twenties would be cast as his psychotic house maid.

In 1963, his private life had made headlines when it was revealed that his housekeeper had been charged in a failed attempt to kill him. Suffering from a fatal attraction to her employer, she'd plotted to shoot him before taking her own life. *[To some, it evoked a version of* Fatal Attraction *(1987), a film starring Michael Douglas and Glenn Close that Lucille would see two years before her death.]*

Montgomery revealed to Lucille that he had fired his housekeeper, Ruth Wenzel, when he discovered, quite accidentally, that she'd stolen and "archived" at least a hundred pairs of his dirty jockey shorts. She'd replace each of them with a freshly re-laundered new pair. Until the scandal broke, he had had no idea that the jockey shorts she regularly presented as used but laundered were, in reality, being worn by him for the first time.

Even after he fired her, she continued to stalk him as when he was with a touring company, perfoming in *Toys in the Attic,* in Ann Arbor, Michigan. According to Montgomery, "She broke into my dressing room and threatened to kill herself if I did not return her love. She claimed she wanted to 'lure me away from stupid glamour gals.'"

She also followed him to Yonkers, New York, where she broke into his hotel room. Once inside, she (threateningly) warned him that he'd never be able to elude her before making sexual advances.

Two days before Montgomery returned from his road tour, the 37-year-old Wenzel had broken into his home at 16531 Saticoy Street in Van Nuys, California. She waited for him there with a loaded pistol, ostensibly to kill him and later follow his murder with her own suicide.

On August 27, 1963, he entered his home with a blonde-haired stewardess who had waited on him in the first-class section of an airplane flying westbound to Los Angeles.

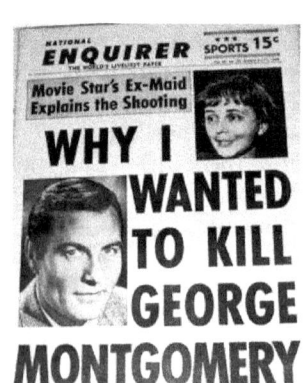

Months after the tabloids went crazy, Lucille "borrowed" the scandal-soaked "only in Hollywood" theme of **George Montgomery vs. his housemaid** for a (never actualized) TV serial of her own.

The airline attendant was alone in a downstairs bathroom when Montgomery went upstairs and entered his bedroom. There, he encountered Wenzel, who pointed her gun at him, insisting that she'd shoot him if he did not make love to her.

During a struggle, he tried to take the gun away from her, but she managed to fire one shot. The bullet whizzed past his left ear.

The Van Nuys police were called, and Wenzel was found tied up, awaiting her arrest. The stewardess had fled from the scene, not wanting to get involved.

Wenzel was hauled off to the main police station in Van Nuys to be charged. In her purse, the police discovered a letter she had written right before the shooting.

In that letter, the delusional housemaid revealed that Montgomery, in the weeks before he filed for divorce from Dinah, had had a sexual relationship with her. Dinah had been away, preoccupied with a singing engagement at Lake Tahoe.

Wenzel went on trial before Los Angeles Superior Court Judge Herbert F. Walker on charges of burglary and assault with intent to commit murder. Montgomery himself showed up to testify against her.

"The bitch got off light," he later told Lucille at poolside in Palm Springs. "She was was found innocent of trying to commit murder, and convicted only of a misdemeanor assault."

Later, the former housekeeper told reporters, "I still am in love with Mr. Montgomery, but I've learned my lesson. I won't go after him again with a gun."

Lucille was shocked but impressed with the story and moved ahead with pre-production for Montgomery's proposed script.

But, once again, as had happened with so many other projected films or TV plots unleashed into the maw of Lucille Ball Productions, this one, too, was lost in the dust.

***

After taking the summer of 1977 off for a much-needed rest, Lucille lined up a series of TV appearances scheduled for telecasting throughout the remainder of the year.

She led off with one of her best performances in recent memory on the ABC series, *Donny and Marie,* telecast on September 30.

Producer and director Art Fisher, aided by Annie Kogan, was determined to present the aging actress in her most favorable light, with soft camera work that took two decades off her age.

A clever wig designed by Irma Kusely made her look more glamourous than she had in months. Her wardrobe of sequined pants, inspired by Judy Garland, and a pink boa added extra allure. Within the context of this elaborate production number, she sang "I'm a Leading Lady."

In another sequence, she impersonated Mae West in her last good film, *My Little Chickadee* (1940). She also did an impersonation of Ethel Merman during her stint as Annie Oakley in the Broadway production of *Annie Get Your Gun.* (1946).

For her finale, Lucille teamed with the very talented Ray Bolger in a spoof of that classic *The Wizard of Oz* (1939). She impersonated "The Tin Man" as he repeated his role of "The Scarecrow."

After the skit, she asked him, "Do you get residuals from all those repeat showings on TV?"

"Not a penny," he said. "Only immortality. I'll settle for that."

Once again, Lucille came together with Paul Lynde, the comedian and game show panelist, who poked fun at his thinly veiled homosexuality. He detested Lucille, and the feeling was mutual.

"I hear you bought Errol Flynn's old Hollywood mansion," she said. "The orgies going on there today must be very different from those of that old swashbuckler."

"Yes, they are. Your former husband, Mr. Arnaz, is often our star attraction."

"That'll be the day," she said. "I hear you're not popular with the gay community. They seem to perceive you as a relic of their self-loathing era."

"I prefer the label of 'Liberace without a piano,'" he said. "Mel Brooks thinks I could get laughs by reading a phone book, a tornado alert, or a seed catalogue."

"I guess that's his way of saying you're a joke," she said, before walking on.

She got along far better with songwriter Paul Williams. The tabloids reported details of his struggle with alcohol and substance abuse. But in spite of that, he turned out hit after hit, including "We've Only Just Begun," "Rainy Days and Monday," and "An Old-Fashioned Love Song." At the time, he was also appearing in *Smokey and the Bandit* (1977), starring Burt Reynolds.

At first, Lucille had been surprised when invited on *Donny and Marie*, a hit variety show telecast on ABC from 1976 until its demise in 1979. "It was a generational mix I feared would not work."

Paul Lynde appropriately outfitted as a witch on his "Hollywood Special" (1976).

The secret to his success lay entirely with, concealed but in plain sight, being gay. He was also snarky, self-loathing, relentlessly bitchy, and a difficult-to-work-with alcohol and drug abuser.

He was known for his frequent cruelties, especially when he was drunk. Many other gays disliked him intensely.

She had never related to Donny Osmond as an entertainer, especially after his "teen idol" period when he was noted for his "bubblegum pop" and "blue-eyed soul."

He'd been born in 1957, just as the *I Love Lucy* sitcom was winding down. He was not only a singer, but a dancer, actor, and TV host who had started as a singing star with his older brothers. Later, as a solo performer, he scored top ten hit recordings.

He once told a reporter that gay people should be accepted into the church only if they remained celibate. Lucille certainly did not share his views.

She found his younger sister, Marie, much more liberal in her views. She once said, "I believe in civil rights for all people.'

Lucille and Donny Osmond would share a mutual problem as the 1970s came to an end, and a new generation emerged in the 1980s. To a newly emerging class of young people, both Lucille and Donny appeared as "unhip" or "not cool."

Donny's publicist—seriously, that is—once suggested that his client get arrested for cocaine possession as a means of changing his squeaky-clean image.

Lucille jokingly asked Gary Morton what she should do to be "'Hipper than Thou.' Have an affair with Burt Reynolds and pose with him for a double nude centerfold? Or perhaps inaugurate a lesbian romp with Liza Minnelli?"

"You should go on being Lucille Ball until you're carted off to Forest Lawn," her husband advised.

***

Following Lucille's appearance on the telecast with Donny and Marie Osmond, she agreed to appear on a special: *Dinah: The First Ladies,* for a 90-minute show with her friend, Dinah Shore, its host.

Elizabeth Taylor had agreed to be on the telecast, too, but her segment had been pre-filmed. She told Dinah, "I will not appear on live TV with Lucille Ball. Richard (Burton) and I have done so with disastrous results."

One of the many manifestations of former teel idols **Marie and Donny Osmond**.

Privately, Lucille said, "This singing duo are so sweet, they give me indigestion."

"I'd be delighted to do the show with two of my favorite singers, Ella Fitzgerald and Beverly Sills," Lucille claimed. "I'm a fan of both of them, even though their voices are as different as night and day. I'm versatile in my taste in music."

Lucille met Sills near the twilight of her operatic career, which had a long run on the stage. Lucille had heard her as Rosina in Rossini's *The Barber of Seville* and as Elisabetta in *Roberto Devereux.* Her voice had been described as "robust and enveloping," or "rich, supple, and silvery." *The New York Times* wrote that she could dispatch coloratura roulades and embellishments, capped with radiant high Ds and E-flats with seemingly effortless agility."

Sills confessed to Lucille that her voice was faltering and that within two years or so, she planned to retire from opera.

She carried through on her announcement. In 1980, Lucille read that she had retired to become General Manager of the New York City Opera.

A daughter of Virginia, Ella Fitzgerald seemed shy when introduced to Lucille, who soon put her at ease. As a jazz singer of renown, she had been called "Lady Ella," "The Queen of Jazz," and "The First Lady of Song."

Lucille was thrilled watching her perform a duet with Dinah.

One music critic wrote, "Miss Fitzgerald is noted for her purity and tone, impeccable diction, phrasing, timing, intonation, and a horn-like improvisational ability, particularly in her scat singing."

Lucille's alltime favorite of her recordings was, "It Don't Mean a Thing If It Ain't Got That Swing."

Fitzgerald won thirteen Grammy Awards as well as, eventually, in 1967, the Grammy Lifetime Achievement Award.

Once Lucille got her to talk, Fitzgerald was quite candid. "I married this guy, Benny Kornegay, in 1941—put the emphasis on GAY—but that union was annulled in 1943. Later, I married this guy, Ray Brown (1947-1953), but it didn't work out. However, my son, Ray Brown Jr, emerged from that union."

"Many guys have come on to me from Louis Armstrong to Duke Ellington. One drunken night, even Frank Sinatra made a pass at me. As a woman, I have found I can live without some man tagging along behind me. Besides, I'm too old to think of such things these days."

"How does that make me feel?" Lucille asked. I'm older than you."

***

After the telecast of *Dinah!*, Lucille and Dinah Shore agreed that they'd spend ten days together in Palm Springs. Gary Morton would tag along, mainly to spend his days on the golf course.

Lucille and Dinah had hours and hours to get to know each other better, and to speak of their status as aging entertainers. Dinah was only five years younger than Lucille, but many of her fans considered her "ageless" based on her youthful appearance.

Lucille told her, "When people talk about you to me, it is not to speak of your thirty years on television, urging people to see the U.S.A. in a Chevrolet. They don't cite your gold records of such big hits as 'Whatever Lola Wants.' They don't even ask if Tony Martin got to bed you long before Frank Sinatra

Operatic soprano **Beverly Sills** could grace a record album or a magazine cover.

Lucille Ball claimed, "Beverly truly deserved her title of 'America's Queen of Opera.' That lyric *coloratura* voice of hers thrilled me and millions of her fans. She was one classy dame, and I felt out of my league talking to her."

Lucille was an ardent fan of **Ella Fitzgerald**. Unknown to most fans, **Marilyn Monroe** was an even more devoted fan.

The singer revealed, "I owe Marilyn a real debt. She personally phoned the Mocambo and told them to book me. If management would do that, she said, she'd show up at a front row table every night.

"The owner agreed, and the press went overboard. After that, I never had to play in a small jazz club again."

"Marilyn was an unusual woman—a little ahead of her time—and she didn't know it."

had the privilege. They don't even cite that on the latest Gallup Poll, you emerged as one of the top ten most admired women in the world. What they speak of is how you have defied time and that you appear as fresh as a spring daisy. Of course, a few catty bitches claim that you get blonder every year."

"Personally," Lucille continued, "I admire your joy of living and your vitality on the golf course or the tennis court. You're a real girl athlete."

In response, Dinah said, "When asked about my birth date, I claim I was born in 1937 like Jane Fonda," Dinah said. "I then tell a reporter if he dares to print that, he can come up and see me sometime."

Dinah also claimed that she was tiring of her long-running talk show: "It's talk, talk, talk. I'm a singer. I want to sing more. If a singer doesn't keep at it, she starts to lose her voice. It's like a cook who stops cooking."

"Speaking of cooking," Lucille said. "You're a better cook than Pearl Bailey—and that's stiff competition. That cookbook of yours, *Someone's in the Kitchen with Dinah*, has gone into its 18th printing, or so I read."

"I eat pretty much what I want, and I never go on fad diets," Dinah claimed. "I've got a five-foot, six-inch body, and I never let it go beyond 132 pounds."

She admitted to Lucille that she never had undergone plastic surgery. "I've considered it on several occasions. I'm not Phyllis Diller or Betty Ford admitting that they had undergone the knife. If I do get plastic surgery one day, I don't see any reason I have to announce it to the entire world. The next time I came on TV after surgery, and talked about it, people would be staring at me. They'd say, 'My god, what did you look like before?'"

At one point, Dinah discussed her failed attempt to become both a movie star and singer like her rival, Doris Day. "I bombed as a singing film goddess making love to Rock Hudson. I'm just not photogenic."

Although she talked about Burt Reynolds and his long affair with her, she rarely spoke of her short marriage, in 1963, to tennis pro Maurice Smith. She did confess, however, that "my marriage seemed to be heading for the divorce courts on our wedding night."

She suspected that she might marry again: "If I do, it'll be to a much younger man. Burt was nearly two decades my junior. My third husband, if there is one to be, will be about thirty years younger. What difference does age make anyway? I know so many people 32 years old who are older than men I see who are 54. And some men of 54 are younger than guys who are 32. It has to do with how you feel emotionally about yourself. Love is so hard to find that you must cherish it at any level."

"Of course, some hustler husbands—young men, that is—marry women who are multi-millionaires, but there are certain young men who are genuinely attracted to women older than themselves."

"If I do snare one of those young men, I want to be a Jane to his Tarzan, responding to that Tarzan love call three times a day."

Lucille thought that was an obvious reference to Ron Ely, her former lover who had starred as the "Ape Man" in both Tarzan-themed feature films and on television.

Before Morton returned home from the golf course, Dinah asked Lucille how her own marriage was holding up.

"Gary is always there for me when I need him," Lucille confessed. "Of course, the white heat of passion has flickered out. It's not 1940 anymore, and he's no Desi Arnaz."

***

Lucille brought together a lot of familiar faces for her next special, *Lucy Calls the President,* a 60-minute telecast through CBS on November 21, 1977. Its director was Marc Daniels, who had helmed the first episode of *I Love Lucy* in the series' First Season (1951-1952).

Gary Morton, always dependent on his wife to get him a job, produced the show, along with co-producers Madelyn Davis and Bob Carroll Jr., who also wrote the script, as they had for so many episodes of *I Love Lucy.*

Steve Allen, one of its guest stars, had a reunion with them. *[Back in the late 1940s, when they were in their twenties, they had worked for him as scriptwriters for his radio program.]*

"Lucille and I went way back," Allen said. "I once worked with her when she and Richard Denning were starring together on radio in *My Favorite Husband.* Once, in 1954, when I was a panelist on *What's My Line?,* she appeared as a mystery guest before my fellow panelists, who were blindfolded."

"Since I hadn't seen her in a long time, I was shocked by her heavily made-up appearance," Allen recalled. "The years had toughened her. She more or less told Daniels how to direct. That good-looking Baby Doll of yesterday had turned into a powerhouse, dictating to her guest stars how to act, where to move, and where to stand."

"I had always admired her talent, but the 1980s were around the corner, and she seemed locked in some time capsule, still pulling some of the same stunts she did back when Harry S Truman was president."

"Frankly, I don't think she was ever as good as when she worked with Desi. That pairing was never matched. As her on-screen husband, Ricky Ricardo, he was perfectly cast. All of Hollywood knew that he was a total failure as a husband, a whoremonger and a drunk. Of course, nobody's perfect. Just ask my own wife, Jayne Meadows."

Talk show host and arts entrepreneur **Steve Allen** in 1959.

"I've known Steve for years and have appeared with him on television," Lucille said. "But he's just not my kind of guy. If I were a casting director, I would put him in the role of a college algebra professor."

When Allen had worked with Lucille back in the 1940s, he claimed that she was "a great woman of beauty, with a cute, babydoll visage about her."

But in later years, he soured on her. "She was not a cutesy dollbaby anymore, but a harsh taskmaster who told everybody what to do."

"She often knew what worked for her, but didn't give good advice to other performers. By the 1970s, she could have entered a (male) drag queen contest."

In subsequent Lucy shows without Desi, the producers didn't dare give Lucy a husband, since Desi, as Ricky Ricardo, was so imprinted on the public mind. However, for *Lucy Calls the President,* the producers broke with tradition and assigned her a husband, played by Ed McMahon, Johnny Carson's longtime sidekick on *The Tonight Show.*

Gale Gordon was cast as her father-in-law, Omar, a change of pace for him, since he usually played her boss, Mr. Mooney. Vivian Vance returned to the set to star as Lucy's next-door neighbor. Also on the show were Lucille's regulars, Mary Wickes and Mary Jane Croft.

Incidentally, who was the President of the United States in this latest episode? He was that peanut farmer from Georgia, Jimmy Carter. As Lucy Whittaker, Lucille calls on him during his weekly radio show, citing how he could help out with some local problems in Indiana. He informs her that he will soon visit her state and take up these urgent matters.

When Lucy extends an invitation to Carter for dinner, "friends and relatives came out of the woodwork, demanding an invite so they could meet the President."

When they weren't needed on the set, Lucille talked to Steve Allen, finding it amazing that he had time to write so many books. *[During the course of his lifetime, he penned an amazing fifty books—adult novels, children's books, and book of opinion.]*

He told her that on the day he retired, he was going to write and arrange for publication of his final book, "and you'll be featured heavily in it. I even have the title: *Vulgarians at the Gate: Trash TV and Raunch Radio."*

"Sounds like I'm in good company," she said.

Amazingly, Allen lived to keep his promise, and such a book was indeed published in 2001, a year after he died.

Like Lucille herself, **Eve Arden** had been a radio *comedienne* before becoming a big hit in TV sitcoms. Here she's seen holding an Emmy for her hit 1954 sitcom, *Our Miss Brooks*, in which she played an (inspirational) school teacher.

"Eve and I shared a friendship and weren't the rivals many critics made us out to be," Lucille said. "There was only one big difference between us: I liked the boys, and she went for the girls."

***

At the start of filming for *Lucy Calls the President*, Lucille experienced a sort of emotional breakdown, since she still had not recovered from the death of her beloved mother, DeDe. As she looked at the seat once occupied by her mother at every show, she almost burst into tears.

This time, in that time-worn seat, sat her friend, Eve Arden. The actress rose and embraced Lucille, comforting her so she could go on with the show.

Regaining her confidence, Lucille continued, apologizing to the audience for her mini-breakdown.

Although *Lucy Calls the President* was rather mediocre, it became a landmark in Lucille's television career. It would be the last time she co-starred simultaneously with Vivian Vance, Mary Jane Croft, and Mary Wickes. One TV critic mourned it as, "The end of an era."

Wickes had appeared on television almost from its infancy. She had also starred as *Mary Poppins* long before Julie Andrews stamped her brand on the role.

Wickes had been the original choice for the role of Ethel Mertz. Even though she decided not to accept that part, she was seen on and off on *I Love Lucy*, *The Lucy Show*, and *Here's Lucy*.

She also appeared in other sitcoms such as *Make Room for Daddy* and *Dennis the Menace*.

After finishing off her career with Lucille, Wickes continued to work until near the time of her death. She was cast as the mother of Shirley MacLaine's character in *Postcards from the Edge* (1990). Before she became ill, she appeared in *Little Women* (1994).

Her final months were plagued with numerous ailments. She fell and broke her hip, prompting surgery. At the age of 85, she died of the complications that followed.

Her final film role, voicing Lavern in Walt Disney's animated feature, *The Hunchback of Notre Dame*, was released posthumously in 1996. Wickes left only one recording session unfinished when she was rushed to the hospital and died. Jane Withers was hired to finish her last six lines of dialogue.

Although only a supporting player, never a star, Wickes had been clever in saving her money and investing it wisely. She left an estate worth millions.

"The other Mary," Mary Jane Croft, also delivered her *adieu* to Lucille, whom she had first worked during an appearance on her radio show, *My Favorite Husband* in the late 1940s. She later appeared in episodes of each of the various *Lucy* series, becoming a familiar face to TV viewers, and getting added exposure frequently on *The Adventures of Ozzie and Harriet*.

Her first marriage in the 1950s to actor Jack Zoller survived for only a few months before

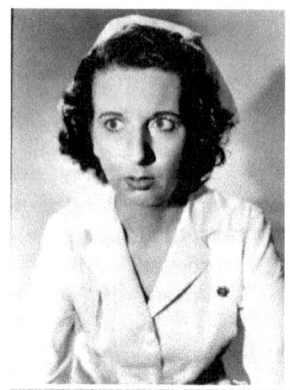

A stalwart and reliably funny cohort of Lucille through many episodes of whatever series she was doing at the moment: **Mary Wickes.**

A regular on various Lucy sitcoms, **Mary Jane Croft** was called "the blonde face with the blonde voice." Opposite Lucille, she often played kooky, shrill-voiced dames.

She always felt she should have gotten better billings and more recognition in the Lucy series.

On the surface she maintained a friendship with the star, while "seething inside my skin.":

Eventually, she faded into seclusion until her death.

she divorced him. She had a son, Eric, with that husband, although he was killed in action during the Vietnam War, causing her endless grief.

In 1959, she remarried, this time to Elliott Lewis, and was still wed to him at the time of his death in 1990. Devastated, she retired from acting and went into seclusion in an apartment at Century City in Los Angeles.

At the age of 83, Mary Jane Croft died quietly on August 24, 1999. She had expressed a desire to witness the birth of a new century.

For Lucille, it was a sad ending to see Vivian Vance in declining health, too. Vance had never escaped from the shadow of Ethel Mertz, the role she first played on *I Love Lucy* in 1951. "At least I don't have to work with that old geezer, the late William Frawley. I couldn't stand the drunken slob."

Frawley, alias Fred Mertz, had suffered a massive stroke on March 3, 1966, while strolling down Hollywood Boulevard.

Although hailed as "bosom buddies" over the decades, Vance and Lucille had had their differences, often disputes over money and billing.

Even though their friendship would sometimes go into the deep freeze, they always managed to come back together again.

"One of my biggest problems with Lucille was in her insisting on keeping me dumpy-looking forever, even though she knew I was fighting hard to look glamourous—and not remain as Ethel Mertz forever."

In reference to Lucille, Vance was once quoted as saying, "I knew that I had to learn to love the bitch. In spite of our occasional differences, we made a great comedy team."

TV critics hailed them as the female equivalents of Laurel and Hardy, Abbott and Costello, and Martin and Lewis.

In 1973, Vance, age 64, discovered she had a cancerous tumor in her breast, and underwent a mastectomy at Columbia Presbyterian Hospital in New York.

She had hoped that the cancer would not return, but her health continued to deteriorate. While working with Lucille on *Call the President,* Vance kept complaining of pain in her hip and her left leg. Lucille arranged for her to see her doctor at once.

When Vance showed up the next day, her face was one of horror. "Your god damn doctor told me the fucking cancer has spread through my body. I'm doomed."

Two views of **Vivian Vance**, upper photo with her frenemy and comedic cohort, **Lucille Ball**.

Lower photo with a jar of a product she endorsed frequently: Maxwell House Coffee.

Then she flew back to San Francisco, where she suffered a stroke that left her partially paralyzed.

Responding to that, Lucille and Mary Wickes flew to San Francisco, where they spent a final afternoon talking to their longtime friend. In spite of Vance's pain, they sometimes laughed, as they remembered the good times of their long association with each other.

En route aboard an airplane back to Los Angeles, Wickes comforted Lucille as she occasionally sobbed. "She's dying. She knows that. We know that, too."

At the age of 70, on August 17, 1979, Vance died of bone cancer.

After her death, Lucille told the press, "I've lost one of the best friends I've ever had. The world has lost one of its greatest performers on the stage, on television, and in films. I will miss her terribly."

A reporter was able to reach Desi Arnaz. "It's bad enough to lose one of the great artists I had the pleasure to work with. It's even harder to reconcile the loss of one of your best friends."

***

An annual TV special broadcast on CBS, *Circus of the Stars* featured celebrities performing circus-derived acts. Launched in 1977 and running through 1994, it was star-studded. The list of performers is long: Bea Arthur, Lauren Bacall, Carol Channing, Sammy Davis Jr., Phyllis Diller, Peter Fonda, Whoopi Goldberg, Merv Griffin, Rock Hudson, Burt Lancaster (a former circus performer himself), Angela Lansbury, and Jerry Lewis.

Barbara Walters was one of the most famous tele-journalists of her era. Above, she's seen with then-president **Gerald Ford.**

Barbara Walters didn't limit her interviewees to political figures. Her 1976 interview with **Lucille Ball** was widely advertised in advance in both TV and print.

Barbara Walters, whenever she could, focused on the private lives of the *glitterati* she interviewed.

This publicity photo shows her in the backyard of Lucille's house in Beverly Hills, with **Lucille**, a housepet, and (left) a diplomatic, charming, and very photogenic **Gary Morton.**

Both Lucille and her daughter, Lucie, appeared on the second broadcast of the series, which ran for 120 minutes on the night of December 5, 1977. Having outfitted herself as a Barnum and Bailey ringmaster, Lucille was attired in a top hat and red hunter's jacket.

She introduced a third of the acts, and worked with such entertainers as Telly Savalas, Michael York, Robert Conrad, Jack Klugman, David Nelson, Betty White, and songwriter Paul Williams.

Before the year's end, Lucille, along with her husband, Gary Morton, appeared in yet another special, and it turned into a disaster. Billed as *A Barbara Walters Special*, it aired for sixty minutes on ABC.

Walters, a working journalist since 1951, had begun her TV career on *The Today Show* in the early 1960s. She had interviewed every sitting president or First Lady since Richard and Pat Nixon occupied the White House. Her last presidential interview was with Barack Obama in 2013. Even before they became president, she had invited both Joe Biden and Donald Trump onto her show.

Her segment with Lucille and Morton was filmed in the backyard of their Beverly Hills home. To fill out the show, Walters also invited the big-busted Dolly Parton and Henry Winkler, who was still playing the greaser, "Fonzie," on the hit TV sitcom, *Happy Days* (1974-1984).

Lucille got to meet Parton, who had made her debut album, *Hello, I'm Dolly,*" a decade before. As they talked, Dolly informed Lucille that she had rejected Hugh Hefner's offer for her to pose nude for a centerfold in *Playboy*, which Lucille called "the tits-and-cunt mag."

For some reason, the talk shifted to plastic surgery, as Lucille was considering going under the knife. "When my time comes, and I need it, I will submit to the body butchers, if I see something saggin', baggin', or draggin'. I'm gonna git it nipped, tucked, and

Barbara Walters, noted nationwide for her fascination with fame, appears here with **Dolly Parton**, also in 1976.

When Lucille met Dolly, she said, 'Hi, Big Tits, meet Little Tits."

If anything, the Walters' interview highlighted the **Lucille** and **Gary Morton** marriage as viable, functioning, intimate, and enduring. Middle photo shows theim answering pointed and sometimes embarassing questions from Walters,

A RICH MAN'S HOBBY: Lower photo shows the license plate of one of his (vintage and highly collectible) cars.

sucked," Dolly declared.

Lucille would meet Dolly again after she'd seen her perform with Burt Reynolds in *The Best Little Whorehouse in Texas* (1982).

"Did you and Burt hit the hayloft, as they say in Tennessee?" Lucille asked.

"No, we didn't," Dolly said. "We're too much alike to get involved. We both wear wigs and high heels, and we both have a roll around the middle."

For Walters' interview with Lucille, she led off with a provocative question:

"What's the difference between your two husbands, Mr. Desi Arnaz and Mr. Morton, who's sitting here beside you?"

Instead of being kind to both men, Lucille, in the words of the program's co-producer and director, Don Mischer, decided to rip the flesh off the Cuban bandleader she'd married in 1940.

According to Mischer, "Maybe she was overly medicated, but something was seriously wrong with her that afternoon."

"Desi was a damn loser," Lucille claimed. "He did found Desilu, but then he fucked it up. He started showing up for work drunk by ten in the morning after spending the night in a whorehouse at one of those bordellos in Los Angeles. He was a terrible father, ignoring his children, but mostly ignoring his wife, creating a philandering trail from Manhattan to Hollywood. He could not keep it zipped up. He called his thing his 'Cuban Salami.'"

At this point in her career, Walters did not shock easily. She lured Lucille into calmer waters before filming a segment that she could actually air.

Mischer reportedly said, "The part of the tape that was dangerous was later destroyed. We didn't want some producer in the future to discover it and air it...ever. That would have finished off Ricky Ricardo to his last remaining fans, and it would not have helped Lucille's image at all. Believe it or not, in 1977, much of America still believed that feuding pair were still Ricky and Lucy Ricardo."

Some viewers thought that **Desi Jr.** wasn't well cast (too appealing, they said) as the unscrupulous manipulator and predator in *Black Market Baby*—an alarmist and tear-jerking "call to arms" against the "baby trades."

Does Life Really Imitate Art?

He eventually married **Linda Purl**, his co-star, of this not-very-well-rated made-for-TV movie.

The marriage lasted about a year.

***

Desi Jr. continued to be the most employed member of the Arnaz clan throughout the latter half of the 1970s.

In *Black Market Baby,* a made-for-TV movie, Desi took second billing to actress Linda Purl. However, before the end of the decade, she would have a second billing title of Mrs. Desi Arnaz Jr. Their romance was heading up.

The original pre-airing title was *A Dangerous Love,* but when *Black Market Baby* was shown in Europe, the title was changed to *Don't Steal My Baby.*

Robert F. Day directed a supporting cast that included Jessica Walter, David Doyle, Tom Bosley, and Bill Bixby.

In this teleplay by Andrew Peter Marin, a young college woman (Purl) becomes pregnant. She and the father-to-be (Desi Jr.) are sucked up in a feverish struggle with a black market adoption ring out to take the baby and sell it. At its initial airing on ABC on October 7, 1977, the film was praised by the *Los Angeles Times* as "outstanding in all respects." It was the 36th-highest-rated show of that autumnal week.

Desi again took the lead in his next feature film, *Joyride* (1977), which some TV critics hailed as his alltime best movie. Distributed by American International Pictures, it opened in June of 1977. After Lucille watched it, she told Gary Morton, "The kid is headed for major stardom."

Cast as Scott, Desi links up with a couple, John and Suzie, played by Robert Carradine and Melanie Griffith. Quitting their jobs in California, they take a car ferry to Alaska, with the hope of making good money fishing for salmon. After a fight in a bar, they discover that their car has been broken into, and they've been robbed of all their dough. Their adventure begins.

Scott and John get low-end jobs on the maintenance crew of an oil pipeline, and Suzie is hired to wait on tables. Trouble and more troubles await them as they face hazards in the Far North. At one point, with no funds at all, they survive by eating dog food.

Two promising "Stars of Tomorrow," **Desi Arnaz Jr.** with a very young **Melanie Griffith** in *Joyride* (1977).

It was a "coming of age' story about nihilistic despair, the importance of friendship, and survival in the rough-and-tumble "frigid north" (i.e., hardscrabble Alaska).

In one provocative scene, the two men win enough money in a "pissing contest" to buy a 1957 Pontiac. At another point, they shoot a bear for food. In yet another episode, they break into a house and get naked together in a hot tub.

Tension rises between John and Scott when he catches him showering with Suzie.

Despite a daunting series of hazards, the trio seems headed for a brighter future as the credits roll.

The film was shot at Roslyn and Granite Falls in Washington State. And although it got good reviews, it didn't launch Desi into the feature film causeway that Lucille had predicted.

The only star who emerged from *Joyride* into stardom was Melanie Griffith, who rose to mainstream success in the mid-1980s after appearing in several independent thrillers during the 70s. The role that brought her the most attention was her portrayal of a porn actress in Brian De Palma's *Body Double* (1984). Her star role in *Working Girl* (1988) earned her an Oscar nod for Best Actress. She would later marry the actor, Antonio Banderas.

***

Desi followed *Joyride* in a rarely seen movie, *Flight to Holocaust*, also released in 1977. Its plot revolved around an airplane that nosedives into the top of a skyscraper. Engineers work desperately to figure out how to remove the passengers without making the plane fall to the sidewalk. One critic called it "an edge-of-your-seat" film. Another referred to it as "good, suspenseful, but faintly cheesy."

What interested many reviewers was that the three stars of the film were each sons of Hollywood icons. Desi was cast in the third male lead, the other roles going to Patrick Wayne and Christopher Mitchum.

Patrick has been born in 1939 as the second son of John Wayne and his first wife, Josephine Alicia Saenz, the daughter of Panama's Consul General in the U.S. Throughout his career, he made forty films, including eleven with his father, most notably *The Quiet Man* (1952), in which The Duke played opposite that flame-haired Irish beauty, Maureen O'Hara. In one American Civil War film, *Shenandoah* (1965), Patrick had been cast as the son of the character played by James Stewart.

Desi worked with Patrick during his career peak when he also starred that year in the popular matinee fantasy, *Sinbad and the Eye of the Tiger* (1977), followed by *The People That Time Forgot* (also 1977). Wayne also tested for the role of Superman but was rejected.

Born in 1943, Christopher was the second son of Robert Mitchum and his wife, Dorothy. In time, he would appear in 60 films distributed in 14 countries. He even appeared in three films with his famous father: *Chisum*

Although it wasn't particularly successful or well-reviewed, **Flight to Holocaust** was noteworthy for employing the sons of three famous legends of Hollywood's most "golden" eras: Patrick Wayne (son of John Wayne); Christopher Mitchum (son of Robert Mitchum), and Desi Arnaz Jr. son of "You know who."

(1970), *Rio Lobo* (also 1970), and *Big Jake* (1971). At this time, although *Box Office* magazine predicted that Christopher would become "one of the top five male stars of the future," that never happened.

As a Republican, he also failed in 2021 when he ran for a seat in the U.S. House of Representatives.

Flight to Holocaust also included some famous faces among the cast, including Sid Caesar. Like Desi Sr. and Lucille, the peak of Caesar's career had occurred in the 1950s when he was watched by some 60 million TV viewers for his live TV series, *Your Show of Shows* (1950-1957) and later *Caesar's Hour* (1954-1957).

Critics hailed him as television's Charlie Chaplin, and *The New York Times* referred to him as "the comedian of comedians from TV's early days."

Caesar later wrote that the pressure of his success, "which came all too fast," caused him to descend into alcoholism and an addiction to barbiturates.

Also in the cast was Rory Calhoun, who had known Lucille for years. "She once told me that I was her kind of man," he claimed. A rugged, former lumberjack, he was discovered by bisexual actor Alan Ladd and also spent time on the casting couch of the gay talent agent, Henry Willson, before hitting it big. He had an affair with Marilyn Monroe when he starred in two of her movies: *How to Marry a Millionaire* in 1953, and *River of No Return* in 1954, in which Robert Mitchum also co-starred.

Also in the cast was Lloyd Nolan, who became better known for originating the role of private eye Michael Shayne in a series of 1940s B movies. He also worked with major stars such as Mae West, Dorothy McGuire,

Within the cast of *Flight to Holocaust*, Desi Jr. was not the only raised-in-Hollywood progeny of famous show-biz parents.

One of his co-stars was **Chris Mitchum**, the hardworking son of **Robert Mitchum**, shown above (left) with his very famous father.

As is obvious in the photo, Chris inherited the good looks of his father, who had long ago lost his sex appeal.

Robert Mitchum knew his star had set in the Hollywood sky when a girl approached him and asked, "Are you the father of Chris Mitchum?"

Another famous scion of a "complicated Hollywood childhood was **Patrick Wayne**, son of John ("The Duke") Wayne, shown with **Jane Seymour** in *Sinbad and the Eye of the Tiger*.

Lana Turner, Rock Hudson, Barbara Stanwyck, and Humphrey Bogart.

Nolan was well known to Lucille. He had played a detective in pursuit of her and John Hodiak (playing con artists) in the 1946 film, *Two Smart People (1946)*. Nolan also reteamed with Lucille in *Easy Living* (1949), in which the male lead was Victor Mature, cast as "King Football."

***

During his acting heyday, Desi Jr. moved from heavy drama into comedy when he played the male lead in *How to Pick Up Girls!*, a made-for-television film first aired on the ABC network on November 3, 1978. It was loosely based on a bestselling book published in 1968 by author Eric Weber. It was promoted widely at the time as a guide to what "today's women" are looking for in "today's men."

For his research, Weber interviewed women to learn what it would take for them to hook up with a complete stranger. His research was published in a hot paperback that was marketed through *Playboy*, *National Lampoon*, *GQ*, and *Esquire*. It sold more than three million copies and was translated into 20 languages.

Desi's co-star was Fred McCarren, a TV and film actor who later starred in the TV series *Amanda's* (1983) and *Hill Street Blues* the following year. [*Amanda's* was a short-lived sitcom starring Bea Arthur.]

The year before working with Desi, Bess Armstrong had made her CBS debut as Julia Peters in the sitcom *On Our Own*. She had also appeared opposite Richard Thomas in her first TV movie, *Getting Married* (1978). She later co-starred with Thomas again in a 1981 stage production in Seattle of Neil Simon's *Barefoot in the Park*, from which a video was made for an HBO broadcast.

Armstrong's biggest success would come in the 1980s when she starred in such films as *The Four Seasons* (1981) with Alan Alda; in *High Road to China* (1983) with Tom Selleck; and *Jaws 3-D* (also 1983) with Dennis Quaid.

Rory Calhoun. Turning a rough and tumble past and a stint in prison into a successful movie career.

How did he get his start in Hollyhood? The bisexual actor Alan Ladd fell in love with him, and he ended up on the casting couch of the gay talent agent, Henry Willson.

Like Lucille herself, *film noir* veteran **Lloyd Nolan** found himself straddling the peak years of both of "between-the-wars" classic film and pop entertainment of the 70s.

Depicted above is a print ad for Nolan's performance as a mastermind detective in a radio episode originally broadcast on December 15, 1952, "The Man With Two Faces." It was about a three-year-old corpse found in a package case planted with many false clues. Radio audiences found it riveting.

Three other well-known actors were also cast in *How to Pick Up Girls!:* Polly Bergen, who played an editor, and Richard Dawson, a photographer of beautiful models. Alan King, the executive producer, had a cameo appearance as a cabbie.

The plot, the work of four writers, depicts ingenu Donald Becker (McCarren) arriving in Manhattan from Grand Island, Nebraska.

He's been invited and introduced to the Big Apple by his former childhood chum, Robby Harrington (Desi Jr.). Robby is a promiscuous playboy taking full advantages of the Swinging Seventies. Robby coaches Donald, who emerges as runner-up in a John Travolta look-alike contest.

Donald (McCarren) falls for Sally (Armstrong), who is having an affair with a married man. But he'll straighten her out in the end, as true love triumphs.

How to Pick Up Girls!, released early in 1978, marked the busiest year of Desi Jr.'s life as an actor, as one TV role was quickly followed by another.

Provocative, heady, firmly rooted in the 1970s, and very very forgettable. In its film adaptation, **Desi Jr**. got to play a promiscuous, drug-abusing, heterosexual hedonist.

His frenemies scoffed, dismissing his involvement as "type casting."

***

Fantasy Island, created by Gene Levitt, was a TV fantasy drama series that was telecast on ABC from 1977 to 1984. Desi Jr. appeared as Barney Hunter in one of the early episodes of 1978.

The star was that Latin heartthrob, Ricardo Montalban, who had once beat out Desi Sr. as one of the screen's most in-demand Latin Lovers, a moniker that Arnaz Sr. had once coveted but didn't get.

Montalban starred as the mysterious Mr. Roarke, His assistant, Hervé Villechaize, played "Tattoo." Guests were granted so-called "fantasies" on the island, for a price.

The fantasy might be a reunion with a long-lost love, or the arraignment of a cold-blooded killer who had murdered a loved one.

In one episode, Mr. Roarke had to face the devil, played by the gay actor Roddy McDowall. Satan himself had come to Fantasy Island to challenge Mr. Roarke for a guest's immortal soul or else his.

"My dear guests," Mr. Roarke would say to arriving guests. "I am your host. Welcome to Fantasy Island."

Mr. Roarke was a fantasy himself. His age was unknown, except that he was said to have been friends with both Cleopatra and Helen of Troy.

Montalban had not been the first choice. Producer Aaron Spelling wanted to cast Orson Welles, but found him too cantankerous and demanding. In an early meeting, it was also suggested that instead of the dwarf, the sidekick role should be played by a sexy female.

Born in 1943 in Nazi-occupied France, Villechaize was a most unusual actor since he was born with dwarfism, the result of an endocrine disorder. In later years, he preferred to be defined as "a midget" and not be labeled as a dwarf. His small body became known to millions, as did his catch phrase, "Ze plane! Ze plane!" [That's what he called out at the arrival of each new aircraft carrying a passenger or passengers committed to living out their fantasies.]

Before Villechaize starred in *Fantasy Island*, he was seen by millions when he played the evil henchman, Nick Nack, in the 1974 James Bond thriller, *The Man with the Golden Gun*. He told Desi Jr. that at the time he was cast, he was so poor, that he was sleeping in his car. "I was working for starvation wages as a rat-catcher."

Desi learned that the pint-sized star was causing a lot of trouble with other members of the series. He aggressively pursued the female stars, making lewd propositions to them, and he was constantly fighting with the producers, demanding more money. Eventually, he was fired and replaced with Christopher Hewitt.

Desi, along with much of America, learned of Villechaize's suicide at the age of 50 on September 4, 1993. He shot himself after leaving a suicide note, claiming that he was suffering from chronic pain because he had oversized internal organs that increased pressure on the bones, ligaments, and tendons of his small body.

Ricardo Montalban, as the well-mannered conduit to hell on *Fantasy Island*. On the right is his assistant and protegé, **Hervé Villechaize**, as "Tattoo."

***

For another film released in 1978, Desi Jr. joined an all-star cast to shoot *A Wedding*, directed by Robert Altman, who also produced it as one of the four scriptwriters.

Altman, of course, was one of the greatest and most influential filmmakers in cinema history, comparable to such directors as Woody Allen, Martin Scorsese, Sidney Lumet, and David Lynch.

When he hired Desi, some of his greatest achievements were behind him, notably *M*A*S*H* (1970); *McCabe and Mrs. Miller* (1971); *The Long Goodbye* (1973); *Nashville* (1975); and *3 Women* (1977).

A Wedding takes place in a single day during a lavish ceremony that merges a *nouveau riche* Southern family to a rich clan from Chicago with possible ties to organized crime.

Never again would Desi Jr. appear with such a star-studded cast.

Among them were such notables as Carol Burnett (Lucille's longtime friend), Paul Dooley, Vittorio Gassman, Mia Farrow, Lillian Gish, Howard Duff, Geraldine Chaplin, Nina Von Pallandt, heiress Dina Merrill, Viveca Lindfors, Lauren Hutton, Amy Stryker, Dennis Christopher, and Peggy Ann Garner.

According to the plot, Dino Sloan Corelli (Desi Jr.) marries Muffin Brenner (Amy Stryker) and attends a wedding reception at the Corelli mansion.

Lillian Gish was cast as the bed-ridden Nettie Sloan, who is attended to by a disreputable doctor, Jules Meechan (Howard Duff).

As "Tulip" Brenner, Carol Burnett steals the show and was later nominated for a Golden Globe for Best Supporting Actress in a Motion Picture.

Vittorio Gassman was cast as Luigi Corelli, Dino's (aka Desi's) father.

Before Muffin and Dino go away on their honeymoon, the bride is rattled when a nude photo of her is discovered, and when Rita Billingsley (Geraldine Chaplin) makes a pass at one of the guests. That's not all. Dino, the groom, is discovered in the shower with Reedley Roots (Craig Richard Nelson), presumably having a sexual encounter.

Howard Duff's glory days were behind him when he agreed to portray the larcenous doctor. In the late 1940s, Duff sustained a highly publicized affair with Ava Gardner. Between 1951 and 1984, he was married to Ida Lupino, an actress sometimes known as "the poor man's Bette Davis."

During the era when he worked with Desi Jr., Duff had recently signed to play Dustin Hoffman's attorney in the Oscar-winning *Kramer vs. Kramer* (1979).

Geraldine Chaplin was the daughter of Charlie Chaplin, the first of eight children with his fourth wife, Oona O'Neill. Geraldine had achieved fame for playing Tonya in David Lean's *Doctor Zhivago* (1965).

Shortly after working with Chaplin, Desi learned Geraldine had become the victim of a failed extortion plot by kidnappers, who had dug up and stolen the corpse of her fa-

Desi Jr. showing his skill as an uncontroversial but likable "straight man," appears here with his bride, **Amy Stryker** in a calm, relatively "non-frantic" scene from Robert Altman's *A Wedding* (1978).

When Desi Jr. met **Lillian Gish**, she was one of the most enduring legends of the screen.

Born in 1893, she had made her film debut in 1912 with her sister Dorothy in D.W. Griffith's *An Unseen Enemy*.

She would make her last feature film, *The Whales of August*, co-starring Bette Davis, in 1987, seventy-five years later.

ther, Charlie Chaplin. She negotiated with the kidnappers for the body's return, and also faced threats to her infant son.

A Wedding marked the 100th film of Lillian Gish, once hailed as "The First Lady of American Cinema." Born in 1893, Gish was a major star from 1912 and into the 1920s and was particularly famous for working with the pioneering director, D.W. Griffith, including on *The Birth of a Nation* (1915).

After starring in the film with Desi Jr., she would, a decade later, star opposite Bette Davis in *The Whales of August* (1987). Gish was to die at the age of 99, just eight months away from becoming a centenarian.

Also in the cast was Lauren Hutton. This daughter of Charleston, South Carolina, became a top model in spite of that signature gap in her front teeth. In 1973, she'd signed a contract with Revlon, which at the time was the most lucrative in the modeling industry. She was also an actress, appearing in such films as *American Gigolo* (1980) with Richard Gere.

Like Ingrid Bergman, Viveca Lindfors emerged as another beautiful actress from Sweden. She moved to Hollywood right after World War II. In her heyday, she appeared on the screen opposite such stars as Errol Flynn, Charlton Heston, and Ronald Reagan. "Ronnie was not a big star," she told the press. "He didn't carry enough weight. To think that the guy became President is really kind of funny."

Dina Merrill, married at the time to actor Cliff Roberson, added a certain class to *A Wedding*. The daughter of Post Cereals heiress Marjorie Merriweather Post, she grew up at Mar-a-Lago in Florida, later selling the property to Donald Trump.

She could have lived in luxury all her life, but wanted to act. By 1959, she was hailed as "Hollywood's new Grace Kelly." That same year, she appeared with Cary Grant in *Operation Petticoat*.

Grant had been married to her cousin, Woolworth heiress Barbara Hutton. Merrill also starred in another notable film, *BUtterfield 8* (1960), which won an Oscar for its star, Elizabeth Taylor.

Popularly known as *Il Mattatore ("Spotlight Chaser")*, the Italian actor, Vittorio Gassman was once married (1952-1954) to the American actress, Shelley Winters. One of the greatest Italian actors, he could play almost any role, ranging from the title role of Shakespeare's *Hamlet* to Stanley Kowalski in Tennessee Williams' *A Streetcar Named Desire*. When Gassman starred opposite Elizabeth Taylor in *Rhapsody* (1954), he later told the Italian press, "She learned that Italian men make the best

Lauren Hutton, in her late 70s, as a skin care expert for StriVectin.

Some Hollywood insiders had speculated that her co-starring (with Richard Gere) role in *American Gigolo* (1980) should have propelled her into major motion picture stardom. But it did not.

One critic described it a "feeble morality play posing as a thriller. It is further undermined by neurasthenic acting and some of the worst sex scenes ever filmed."

lovers."

The eldest daughter of Australian director John Farrow and the Irish actress, Maureen O'Sullivan, Mia Farrow had been famously married to Frank Sinatra from 1966 to 1968. When Sinatra's former wife, Ava Gardner, heard of the union, she told the press, "I always knew Frankie would end up with a boy."

At the time of Farrow's marriage, she was 21 years old and Sinatra was 50.

When Desi worked with Farrow, she was on the road to divorcing her next husband, conductor/composer André Previn. Her tortuous relationship with Woody Allen lay in her future.

In *The New Yorker,* Pauline Kael reviewed *A Wedding:* "There's no way to get into the movie. It's like a busted bag of marbles. People are running every way at once."

Gary Arnold in *The Washington Post* claimed, "Musically and pictorially, Robert Altman can't hide his condescension. He has invented a wedding party, ostensibly as a misalliance between old but tarnished Midwestern aristocracy and new, uncouth Southern wealth, but that seems to inspire him to nothing but stale jokes and a complacent contempt."

Critic Gene Siskel wrote: "Altman mistreats us to one boob after another. He appears not to care for any one of the people involved here. He creates pompous straw men and women and then he ridicules them. It's a particularly mean-spirited movie likely to please no one."

***

In Desi Jr.'s next film, also released in 1978, he co-starred with Vince Edwards in *The Courage and the Passion* in a script by John Llewellyn Moxye. The made-for-TV drama focused on the lives and loves of a group of U.S. Air Force test pilots on a sprawling air base called "Joshua Tree." Actually, it was filmed at Edwards Air Force Base in California.

Produced by NBC Entertainment, the

Vittorio Gassman in the Italian romance, *Sorpasso (1962).*

During its filming, he told the press, "I'm confused. I don't know if I should promote myself as a sex symbol or as a serious actor."

"Actually, I'm both. Shelley Winters once used me to do a frontal nude scene in a movie. She said it would attract milloons of female admirers and an equal number of gay men."

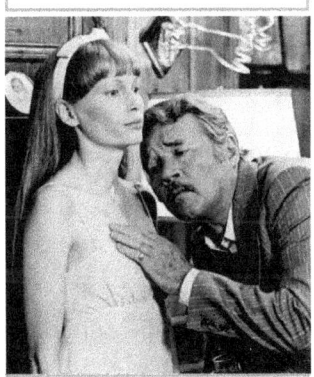

Mia Farrow colluding with **Howard Duff** in *A Wedding.*

Duff's greatest romantic involvement was with Ava Gardner, with whom he had a torrid affair with before she fell in love with Frank Sinatra, before he left her to marry (guess who?) Mia Farrow.

movie came and went without creating much of a stir.

Edwards played Colonel Joe Agajanian, with Desi cast as Sergeant Tom Wade.

Long before he ever met Desi, Edwards had encountered Lucille in a confab in his dressing room. She always remembered the occasion because he had shown her a frontal nude of himself.

The Brooklyn-born "macho stud" was best known for his TV role as Doctor Ben Casey.

Privately, he bragged about his conquests, having cited Grace Kelly and Anne Bancroft as two of his classmates he'd seduced when they studied together at the American Academy of Dramatic Arts.

His medical drama was on the air from 1961-1966. He also became known for a major role in the 1968 war drama, *The Devil's Brigade.*

Like Desi Sr., Edwards always was a compulsive gambler.

An older and perhaps wiser **Vince Edwards** (formerly known as *Dr. Ben Casey*), plays Desi Junior's commanding officer in *The Courage and the Passion.*

Once, while putting the make on Lucille Ball, Edwards had showed her a frontal nude of himself, a photo for which he had posed in the studio of a gay photographer.

The two female leads in *The Courage and the Passion* went to Trisha Noble and Linda Thompson (aka Foster).

Cast as Lt. Linda Rydell, Noble was an Australian singer and actress who had been a teenage pop star in the early 1960s. Since 1965 she appeared in such TV series as *The Mary Tyler Moore Show, Baretta,* and *Mcmillan & Wife.*

Early in her career, she fell for her fellow Aussie, Peter Allen. Her ardor cooled when she learned he was gay. He later married Liza Minnelli.

For most of her early singing career, she was billed as "Patsy Ann Noble," later changing it to Trisha.

In the fourth lead, cast as Captain Kathy Wood, Linda Thompson was a songwriter/lyricist, actress, and beauty pageant winner. But she is more famous for two romantic involvements with two very different men.

She had been voted Miss Tennessee in 1972 when she first met Elvis Presley. They began a love affair that lasted for four and a half years as his life was winding down. She was said to be not just a girlfriend, but a "nurse and mother" too. They developed their own language, calling it "baby talk."

During the course of their long affair, Thompson must have learned Elvis' secret. He wasn't all that fond of penetration, since he was not circumcised and had an extremely tight foreskin that sometimes

YESTERDAY'S GONE

Linda Thompson, "keeping The King's flame alive" at the Bad Nauheim (Germany) Elvis festival in 2019.

caused him to bleed during sexual intercourse with the likes of Ann-Margret, billionairess Doris Duke, Diana Dors, Jayne Mansfield, Nancy Sinatra, Barbra Streisand, Tuesday Weld, stripper Tempest Storm, Marilyn Monroe, and Natalie Wood, plus the 1,000 women and young girls he claimed to have seduced.

After a breakup with Elvis that occurred shortly before his death in 1977, Thompson began dating Bruce (aka Caitlin) Jenner, the former Gold Medal decathlete. They were married on January 3, 1981 in Oahu, Hawaii. The couple produced two sons, Brandon and Brody.

Bruce Jenner later became one of the most famous transsexuals in history, requesting and getting a gender change. When Desi Sr. learned of the Jenner/Thompson marriage, he told a reporter, "At some point in his life, Bruce must have had a dick."

To Kill a Cop

Louis Gossett Jr. with **Joe Don Baker** in *To Kill a Cop*.

This low-budget thriller was minor fare for Gossett, who became the first African American to win a Best Supporting Actor Oscar for *An Officer and a Gentleman*. He had starred in it with Richard Gere and Debra Winger.

***

Desi Jr's. next role on television came when he was cast as Martin Delahanty in *To Kill a Cop*, another telecast of 1978., It was a four-hour, made-for-TV movie that was presented in two parts, each on a different night.

Desi's co-star was Brooklyn-born Louis Gossett Jr. Only months before, in 1977, he had won an Emmy for his role as "Fiddler" in the ABC miniseries, *Roots*.

He would go on, in 1982, to win an Oscar for his role of Gunnery Sergeant Emil Foley in *An Officer and a Gentleman*. He was the first African American to win a Best Supporting Actor Oscar.

One reviewer wrote, "The plot about a cop killer gang overseen by a former black revolutionary and also an ex-inmate of Attica prison might seem far-fetched. The revolutionary was Everett Walker, played by Gossett, returning via Cuba from exile in North Africa. His wife and baby were killed in a

Now impossibly dated, **The Love Boat**, was a romantic TV series that thrived, pre-Covid, back when romance on the high seas, as part of cruise, was still considered desirable and chic. Portraying a well-adjusted, aimiable, and reasonably horny single man, Desi Jr. fit perfectly into the frothy and sometimes silly plots.

police raid in Chicago about a decade before."

The review continues: "Walker teamed up with Charles (Nathan George), and the dangerous duo form an army of 'street crazies,' recruited from the underbelly of the black world."

In opposition to these revolutionaries stands Earl Eischied (Joe Don Baker), the hefty, growling chief of New York City Detectives. He is constantly at odds with the ambitious Police Commissioner, cast with Patrick O'Neal in the role.

The plot allows time for some love angles, as when Desi Jr. and Christine Belford, two new police partners, fall in love.

A native son of Florida, O'Neal was the best-known of the supporting cast. After serving in the U.S. Air Force during the Korean War, he moved to Manhattan and studied at the Actors Studio. He later won acclaim on Broadway for starring in Tennessee Williams' *The Night of the Iguana*. Although he wanted the film role, it went to Richard Burton. For four decades, O'Neal was a guest star on various TV shows.

The Texas-born character actor, Joe Don Baker, a lifetime member of the Actors Studio, usually played cowboy drifters, deputy sheriffs, Mafia hitmen, and police detectives. In 1967, he had a supporting role in *Cool Hand Luke* starring Paul Newman. He was often seen on such TV series as *The Big Valley* and *Mod Squad*.

A minor actor, Nathan George launched his stage career in 1969 by winning an Obie for *No Place to Be Somebody*, the Pulitzer Prize-winning play by Charles Gordone. In time, George popped up in several famous films such as *Klute* (1971) with Jane Fonda and *One Flew Over the Cuckoo's Nest* (1975) with Jack Nicholson.

The script of *To Kill a Cop* was by Ernest Tidyman, who won a screen-writing Oscar in 1971 for *The French Connection*.

***

Desi Junior's last appearance in 1978 was in the role of Steve Hollis on two episodes of *The Love Boat*. This romantic comedy/drama was telecast on ABC from 1977 to 1986, often using celebrities as co-stars.

Desi was one of the first stars to be a passenger aboard the luxury passenger cruise

"This is your captain speaking."

Gavin MacLeod, the handsome star of *The Love Boat*, presents a smiling face in this photograph. But much of his early life was marred by depression, alcoholism, and near suicide attempts. He also went through some painful divorces.

His biggest loss was not getting the role of Archie Bunker in *All in the Family*.

In his memoirs, he wrote of his encounters with such stars as Marilyn Monroe, Frank Sinatra, Ronald Reagan, Steve McQueen, Bette Davis, and Robert Redford.

In the end, he claimed he found true happiness in his Christian faith.

ship, *MS Pacific Princess.*

Overseeing the action is Merrill Stubing, played by the actor Gavin MacLeod, the ship's captain. He was a Christian television host and author whose career would span six decades.

In films, he had starred in such fluff as *The Sword of Ali Baba* (1965), before getting down and gritty in *Kelly's Heroes* (1970), a war drama.

MacLeod also had continuing success alongside Ernest Borgnine in *McHale's Navy* (1962-1964), playing " Happy Haines." He also starred as Murray Slaughter on *The Mary Tyler Moore Show* (1970-1977).

As MacLeod related years later in a memoir, he braved some rough seas personally on *The Love Boat,* suffering through alcoholism and divorce before "sailing through to discover faith and Christianity."

***

Desi's TV career slowed down considerably in 1979 as he starred in only one drama *Crisis in Mid-Air,* a made-for-television film that was telecast on CBS in color on February 13.

Unlike other airplane disaster movies of the 1970s, this one concentrated on the stresses of air controllers. Shooting was at the Los Angeles International Airport (LAX), the major air traffic hub of the West.

Director Walter Grauman assembled an unusual cast, co-starring George Peppard and Karen Grassle. Desi Jr. was the third lead as Tim Donovan, a young air controller posted at LAX with Nick Culver (Peppard) as his instructor.

As Nick, Peppard suffers recurring nightmares in which he causes collisions in the air. He often wakes up terrified, and is comforted by his wife, Betsy (Grassle).

Supporting players included Martin Milner and even Fabian.

Dr. Eric Denvers (Milner) a psychologist,, arrives on the scene, but he causes more stress, as the controllers fear they are

In the inset photo, **Desi Jr.** seems to be "giving the eye" to his co-star, **George Peppard.**

In *Crisis in Mid-Air*, Desi played second lead to Peppard, who is known today for scoring big heat in *Breakfast at Tiffany's* (1961) with Audrey Hepburn.

Peppard was a good performer even though some had suggested that he could get by "just on those blue eyes and blonde hair."

From 1966 to 1970, he was famously married to actress Elizabeth Ashley, who wrote about him in her memoirs.

being too closely monitored, which makes them nervous.

Singer Fabian had a most unusual role, that of Billy Coleman, an airport worker at LAX. He loses his mind after a cab driver kills his child and he becomes a killer himself. While trying to escape from the police, he rams a bus into the radar installations, thereby destroying the airport's radar when many planes are in the air.

In general, the movie garnered a warm reception, one critic found it "Most authentic in its realism and accuracy." Another reviewer noted that the traffic scene at LAX "was very impressive and well shot."

Desi Jr. might have considered Peppard an actor to envy, as he'd been assigned the choice role of the struggling writer, Paul Varjak, in the 1961 film, *Breakfast at Tiffany's*, starring Audrey Hepburn and written by Truman Capote, who had intended the role for Marilyn Monroe.

Peppard also played a Howard Hughes-like character in the provocative *The Carpetbaggers* (1964). Both Desi and Peppard had at least one trait in common, as both of them had struggled with alcoholism and drug addiction.

At the time, Desi was struggling to cure himself from his heavy drinking. He later recalled, "I knew I had to stop...and I did. Looking back now, I'm ashamed of some of the things I did when I was drinking."

In reference to Peppard, critic David Shipman wrote, "He is tough, assured, and insolent—in a way that recalls Dick Powell more than early Bogart. His bright eyes, blonde hair, and boyish face suggest the all-American athlete, perhaps going to seed."

As Peppard told Desi Jr., "Being a movie star never interested me. Stars, *per se*, are a pain. To me, stars are in the sky, the important question is, 'How good an actor are you?'"

Cast as the wife of Peppard's character, Karen Grassle had the second lead. At the time she worked on *Mid-Air*, she was also starring as Caroline Ingalls in *Little House on*

George Peppard with **Audrey Hepburn** in *Breakfast at Tiffany's*, one of Hepburn's most iconic roles.

As a backwoods girl turned prostitute, Hepburn as Holly Golightly was praised for delivering a brilliant performace. Nonetheless, the author, Truman Capote, of the short story on which the film was based said he was disappointed. "I wrote the role of Holly for Marilyn Monroe."

Karen Grassle was widely known for her role as a mother to many children in *Little House on the Prairie*.

"Hollywood is not a world I would choose for my own children."

the Prairie, a TV series that ran from 1974 to 1983.

Don Murray, a son of Hollywood, had a small role as Adam Travis. He had co-starred as the innocent cowboy, Bo Decker, in William Inge's *Bus Stop* (1956), opposite Marilyn Monroe.

[The role of the loud, boisterous, and naïve cowboy was one that Elvis Presley wanted to play. That proposal was nixed, with horror, by Elvis's sometimes larcenous and always short-sighted manager, Col. Tom Parker, much to the latter-day regret of Elvis & Marilyn fans.

As it happened, on the set of Bus Stop, *Murray, cast as Bo, the rambunctious cowboy, met and later married Hope Lange, cast as Elma Duckworth, the empathetic waitress in the diner where most of the characters huddle throughout the duration of a road-blocking snowstorm.]*

Murray followed *Bus Stop* with such high-profile roles as *A Hatful of*

ONCE UPON A TIME, IN HOLLYWOOD

Fabian (aka Fabiano Anthony Forte) in the late 1950s. He is still remembered by Baby Boomers for his heyday as a pop star. In 1959, alone, he crafted three "Top Ten" hits: "Turn Me Loose;" "Tiger;" and "Hound Dog Man."

Lesser known is his career in pictures. Although he was mocked by many critics, he created a niche for himself during the months when Elvis was in the Army.

He later claimed that when his career was at a low ebb in the 1970s, he made "the mistake of my life" when he posed nude for *Playgirl's* September, 1973 edition.

During the Vietnam War, it was alleged that he was rejected for military service when he presented a note from a doctor stating that the Army might cause him to develop homosexual tendencies.

Depicted is the cover of September, 1973 edition of **Playgirl** in which Fabian posed "vanilla nude."

The sight of Fabian without clothes generated curiosity and some degree of scandal, but didn't win him many new fans.

Even so, he began singing again, but without equaling the sales of his heyday. Despite his widely publicized "retirement' in 1977, he began recording again four years later.

In time, he appeared with other fading stars of the "Baby Boomer" generation, Bobby Rydell and Frankie Avalon, delivering live performances to grown-up audiences, many of whom had been "Teenagers in Love" in the late 1950s.

Rain (1957), in which he played Johnny Pope, a morphine-addicted Korean War vet. He also starred as a blackmailed U.S. Senator in *Advise & Consent* (1961), a film version of the Pulitzer Prize-winning novel by Allen Drury. It was directed by Otto Preminger and starred, among others, Henry Fonda.

Martin Milner, as Dr. Eric Denvers, was best known for co-starring with George Maharis in the hit TV series, *Route 66,* which ran from 1960 to 1964). Milner returned to television in 1968, performing as an LAPD Police Officer, Pete Malloy, in *Adam-12*, the series telecast until 1975.

Billed as Billy Coleman in *Mid-Air*, Fabian had risen to national prominence as a teen idol in the 1950s and 60s on Dick Clark's *American Bandstand*. Eleven of Fabian's recordings reached *Billboard's Hot 100 Listings*.

Fabian was also cast in feature film roles, But, as his career began to wane, he began drinking heavily.

In 1971, he agreed to pose frontally nude for *Playgirl*. He later said, "I knew it was a mistake the minute I saw the thing sold in a paper bag. I could barely live with myself for posing nude for that skin rag."

Fabian would never reclaim the glory he had enjoyed as a young man. The height of his popularity was of another day.

The same thing could be said about Desi Arnaz Jr.

***

Although her son was working steadily on television shows, Lucille's own career in 1978 and 1979 fell into a black hole. She was still seen on the tube, but most often as a tribute to seasoned but fast-aging performers such as Bob Hope or Milton Berle. The theme of many of them were retrospective accolades of vintage Hollywood and the early days of television.

Indeed, her first TV appearance in 1979 was on March 3, a 90-minute telecast for NBC called *TV—the Fabulous Fifties*. Her co-stars included David Janssen, Mary Martin, Dinah Shore, and Red Skelton. The stars, especially Skelton and Dinah, were familiar

Don Murray during his heyday as a gauche, horny cowboy in love with Cheri, the stripper (as portrayed by **Marilyn Monroe**) in *Bus Stop* (1956).

Elvis Presley wanted the role, but his manager, Col. Tom Parker, nixed the idea. "I don't want you starring in a role created by that fag writer, William Inge."

Desi Jr. wasn't TV World's only heartthrob. Here's **Michael Landon** as he appeared driving piles in 1975 on *Little House on the Prairie*.

faces.

Michael Landon was new to her. The handsome young actor had appeared on the cover of *TV Guide* twenty-two times, second only to Lucille herself. He was a household name, having starred as Little Joe Cartwright in *Bonanza* (1959-1973) and as Charles Ingalls in *Little House on the Prairie* (1974-1982). The actor would marry three times and father nine children.

Lucille had long admired the husky voice and rugged masculine appeal of David Janssen. That young man had emerged from the cold winters of Nebraska to become a big hit in television, the star of such series as *Richard Diamond—Private Detective* (1957-1960); *The Fugitive* (1963-1967); *O'Hara: U.S. Treasury* (1971-1972); and *Harry O* (1974-1976).

When he worked with Lucille, he had just starred with Angie Dickinson in *A Sensitive, Passionate Man* (1977), in which he played an alcoholic. In 1978, he also starred in *Nowhere to Run*, in which he was cast as an engineer who devises an unbeatable system for blackjack, with co-stars Stefanie Powers and Linda Evans.

After appearing with Lucille in that tribute to the 1950s, Janssen hugged and kissed her goodbye.

Within two years, he would be dead at the age of 48.

When Lucille came together with Mary Martin, the former leading lady on Broadway, she said, "I fear my glory days are behind me. Today, I'm introducing myself as the mother of Larry Hagman."

Then Lucille chimed in: "My glory days are over, too. And your son, Larry, is a living doll."

Martin, a daughter of Texas, had originated many leading roles in plays which had included *South Pacific* (1949); *Peter Pan* (1954), and, as Maria von Trapp in *The Sound of Music* (1959).

She told Lucille that she and her husband, Richard Halliday, lived on a vast ranch in Brazil. "The locals call me Dona Maria."

[*Martin and Halliday often traveled with Janet Gaynor and her husband, Paul Gregory. On September 5, 1982, they were involved in an automobile smash-up in San Francisco, victims of a drunk driver. Mar-*

Lucille Ball and **Henry Fonda** had been on-again, off-again lovers both on the screen and in private life.

For years, Lucille had asserted that her performance as Gloria Lyons (photo above) in *The Big Street* (1942) had been "the most stimulating to that point in my fledgling career as 'Queen of the Bs.'"

Displayed above are replicas of U.S. Postage stamps issued in honor of (and showing younger, heyday-era likenesses of) **Henry Fonda** and **Lucille Ball.**

tin's manager, Ben Washer, was in the car with them at the time, and he was killed instantly. Martin herself suffered broken ribs and a broken pelvis. Gayner's husband suffered two broken legs, and Gaynor herself died two years later from complications associated with that car wreck.]

Skelton and Lucille talked about the time both of them co-starred in *Du Barry Was a Lady*, released by MGM in 1943.

They had kept in touch over the years, and she found him amazing.

He told her he rarely slept more than four hours a night. Rising early, he would write short stories, compose music, or paint pictures. In time, he would compose 8,000 songs and symphonies.

He was also an avid photographer, always taking pictures of celebrities. In addition to doing all that creative work, he tended his Japanese and Italian gardens in Palm Springs and became known locally for his cultivation of bonsai trees.

He sold prints and lithographs of his paintings, earning $2.5 million annually on sales of lithographs alone. At the time of his death in 1997, his art dealer told the press that Skelton earned more money through his art work than he had from his films and TV career, one which was dedicated "to making people laugh."

Also on the salute to the Fifties was Dinah Shore. She told Lucille, "If you and I don't stop appearing so often together, people will talk. In spite of our heterosexual credentials, they'll think we might be another Mary Martin/Janet Gaynor-style love affair."

For her part in the 1950s salute, Lucille appeared quite glamourous as she narrated the introduction to a segment focusing on hit TV sitcoms of the 1950s. Makeup and wardrobe spent a lot of time on her, "removing [in her words] a decade or two." She appeared in a chic midnight black gown and an artfully designed wig.

Ten nights later, Lucille starred in CBS's TV special, *Gene Kelly...an American in Pasadena*. Decades before that, Kelly had been the co-star, with Skelton and Lucille, of *Du Barry Was a Lady* (1943). To honor Kelly, the director brought on not only Lucille, but some of the leading ladies Kelly had worked with, including another dancing sensation, Cyd Charisse, along with Gloria DeHaven, Betty Garrett, Kathryn Grayson, Janet Leigh, and Liza Minnelli.

Frank Sinatra, another of Kelly's dancing partners, also starred on the show.

He told Lucille, "I heard it was devoted to Gene's leading ladies. When I was invited to join the cast, I asked the director, Mary Pasetta, if I needed to undergo a sex change."

"Well, if you had your much-used genitalia removed, I'm sure the package would have been donated to the Smithsonian, to be preserved for posterity in alcohol," Lucille quipped.

Two nights later, again on CBS, another retrospective was telecast— *The American Film Institute's (AFI) Salute to Henry Fonda*. Whenever Lucille encountered her former lover, they always warmly embraced and kissed "with whatever passion we had left" (Lucille's words).

On the telecast, she discussed the time the two of them had co-starred in a serious drama, *The Big Street,* released in 1942 by RKO. Lucille played a showgirl who is injured and spends her life in a wheelchair. Fonda didn't like his character's name of "Little Pinks."

He told Lucille, "No man wants to be called Little, much less Pinks."

A lot of Fonda's friends and co-stars also appeared on the show, including his daughter, Jane. Among others, the cast also featured the aging Lillian Gish, who claimed, "I invented the close-up.:"

James Garner appeared, as did Jack Lemmon, Fred MacMurray, Gregory Peck, Barbara Stanwyck, and Hank's longtime friend and former "roomie," James Stewart.

Before March came to an end, Lucille, on the 26th, signed with NBC to join the cast of *A Tribute to Mr. Television,* Milton Berle. She and Berle had had an affair in the late 1930s, and they'd remained friends and appeared together over the years.

Before the broadcast, Berle filled Lucille in on some of his legend "Believe it or not, when I was six years old, with long yellow curls, Charlie Chaplin cast me in *Tillie's Punctured Romance* (1914)."

Actually, I first appeared on TV in 1929, performing on a closed-circuit experimental broadcast."

He also told her that the actor, Stephen Boyd, who had played the evil Messala in *Ben-Hur* (1959), died in his arms at the Beverly Hills Hotel.

"You don't have to tell me, but what was that gay stud doing in your arms?" Lucille asked. "Of all your lovers, excluding me, who were the most memorable?"

"Actually, the evangelist, Aimee Semple McPherson."

"Who was the worst?" she asked.

"Marilyn Monroe. She had bad breath and a certain lack of hygiene that even Chanel No. 5 could not disguise."

Others in the tribute to Berle included Joey Bishop, Kirk Douglas, Bob Hope, Johnny Carson, Gregory Peck, Don Rickles, and Frank Sinatra.

Most TV critics found the show lackluster. "Mostly all that the stars did was come on and read a tribute to Berle in honor of his thirty-years on television," wrote one critic.

A day after saluting Milton Berle on NBC, Lucille was invited back by CBS for the studio to celebrate itself. After all, she'd been the star of its biggest hit sitcom, *I Love Lucy.*

The telecast was called *CBS on the Air — A Celebration of 50 Years.* Her co-stars included Bea Arthur, George Burns, and

Stephen Boyd as Messala at the baths in *Ben-Hur.*

One reviewer said: "If there was an Academy Award deserved by any cast member of *Ben-Hur*, it belonged to Stephen Boyd, playing the villainous Messala who turned his boyhood friendship into a vendetta of hate. Boyd was a near absolute personification of the power which corrupts."

Arthur Godfrey.

Clips of the TV shows of the past were shown, including scenes that featured Desi Arnaz and Vivian Vance. The highlight of the telecast was when Arthur and Burns joined Lucille for a rendition of "What's So Funny About Monday?"

Lucille had long maintained her friendship with Dean Martin, and on May 10 for NBC, he invited her back to appear on one of his *Celebrity Roasts*. She had once been the victim of a "Roast" herself, but this time, the subject roasted would be James Stewart.

Joining Lucille and Martin was an array of celebrities: June Allyson, Eddie Albert, Milton Berle, Red Buttons, George Burns, Orson Welles, Mickey Rooney, and Don Rickles.

Lucille had long been intrigued by the legend of Stewart, whom she first met on a double date. His belle that evening had been Carole Lombard, who later married Clark Gable. *[Lucille's date that evening had been had been Henry Fonda.]*

Right before Stewart entered the air corps in World War II, a Hollywood columnist estimated that during his early heyday in the 1930s, the lanky, homespun actor had seduced 263 different glamour girls of his era.

The biggest names on the list included June Allyson, Olivia de Havilland, Diana Barrymore, Jean Harlow, Rita Hayworth, Katharine Hepburn, Ginger Rogers, Grace Kelly, Lana Turner, Loretta Young, and Norma Shearer.

He'd lost his virginity to actress Margaret Sullavan, the wife of his "best pal," Henry Fonda.

When Stewart made *Destry Rides Again* (1939), co-starring Marlene Dietrich, he made her pregnant, forcing her to have an abortion.

Before the roast, Lucille visited with Stewart. "Why in hell didn't you slip around Fonda's back and add me to that incredible list of your seductions?"

"I promised, after doing Hank's wife,

Milton Berle's list of "unforgettables' included **Aimee Semple McPherson** (1890-1944), the most influential (and notorious) evangelist in America.

McPherson transformed her pulpit into a theater, sometimes dressing as an Indian princess or a motorcycle cop, with an orchestra and stage sets. One of her early lovers, Charlie Chaplin, taught her how to stage these elaborate productions, each presumably a Christian revival.

Aging titans of the film and television industries, **Lucille Ball** and **James Stewart**—brittle in bone but still beilieving that the show must go on—make a final appearance.

Margaret Sullavan, that I wouldn't plug any of his girlfriends, at least while he was dating them. I'm a man of honor, and I kept my oath to him."

***

"All I'm doing these days is celebrating all great performers except myself," That was Lucille's reaction when NBC included her, on May 29, in a star-studded tribute to Bob Hope. The show was called *Happy Birthday Bob: A Salute to Bob Hope's 75th Birthday.* Sponsored by the USO, it was telecast from Washington, D.C.

Lucille was asked to introduce some of Hope's leading ladies over the years, notably Dorothy Lamour, with whom he'd made all those Road pictures co-starring Bing Crosby.

A galaxy of stars signed on to appear, including Pearl Bailey, Johnny Carson, Redd Foxx, Fred MacMurray, John Wayne, Red Skelton, and Danny Thomas. Also present onscreen was Hope's "very understanding" wife, Dolores, who always seemed to forgive him for his many infidelities.

At this point, Lucille still kept Lucille Ball Productions going, but, as she told Hope, it had become for the most part a vehicle to keep Gary Morton employed. "His main job is handling my fan mail, which I still get from around the world. He also handles all these requests I get for appearances at charity events."

"I wish I could find just one more script which I can do," she continued, "even as an old lady. It's my last chance to win an Oscar."

"Those things are hard to come by," Hope said. "I never appeared in any picture that had Oscar written on it."

When filming was over, and before they parted, he came up with a suggestion to keep Lucille Ball Productions in business.

"Why don't you do a series of three specials, perhaps each running an hour long, for three nights in a row? I think these specials should be devoted to me, the star of stars, as

Margaret Sullavan: Some of her casual cruelties will be described in Blood Moon's upcoming biography of *Henry and Jane Fonda, To Each His (or Her) Own.*

Early in their respective careers, Sullavan, Fonda, and Stewart each met in acting school in Falmouth, Massachusetts.

For decades after that, they remained entwined in a confusing rondelay of love affairs and breakups, each interspersed with caustic and highly quotable bitcheries from Sullavan.

NEARING THE END

Lucille, disguising her age with multiple layers of makeup, with **Bob Hope**.

She told him, "I keep appearing on TV to show fans that I'm still alive."

well as to Frank Sinatra and Sammy Davis Jr."

"That's not a bad idea," she said. "It would be something for me to do other than appear on TV in a wig and overly made up."

"Instead of the usual tributes, I suggest you present detailed portraits of all of our lives—the scandals, the failures, the triumphs, plus little-known facts about us that the viewing audience hasn't heard a million times already."

"I'll keep in touch, but I think I'll put what writing staff I still have left to give it hell. But it might be embarrassing to you guys."

"I can take it," he said "And Frankie and Sammy are used to attacks. It might go over. Let me know how it's going."

In 1968, before (fully justified) protests from Animal Rights activists made fur unfashionable, even contemptible, **The Great Lakes Mink Association** inaugurated an award-winning ad campaign to sell more mink. Their campaign focused more on WHO was wearing it than it did on the garment itself. Dozens of glamourous celebrities signed on, many photographed by Richard Avedon. For a while, at least, many received a furpiece of their choice, and the satisfaction of knowing that they were "instantly recognizable," even without spelling out their names, to millions of consumers.

In 1979, **Lucille Ball,** with the help of a team of stylists, pulled herself together and joined the ranks of equivalent celebrities (Sophia Loren, Marlene Dietrich, Judy Garland, Catherine Deneuve and dozens of others), who plugged **Blackglama** with the "addictive" catchphrase, "What Becomes a Legend Most?."

Since then, Blackglama has been written about in history books as the sponsors of one of the 20th Century's most successful ad campaigns, and perhaps, the precursors of the end of an era.

CHAPTER FIFTEEN

LIKE MANY MOTHERS

OF THE 1970S AND EARLY '80S, LUCILLE STRUGGLES WITH HER SON'S

DRUG ADDICTION

Lucille, who in 1979 learned that Desi Jr. had proposed marriage to Linda Purl, was not that surprised. She had suspected that the two of them were having an affair. It had originated during their joint appearances in such TV dramas as *Black Market Baby* (1977).

She set about finding whatever she could about her future daughter-in-law and ordered her staff to round up some films in which Linda had starred.

In the year they eventually married, Purl was starring in four separate television dramas.

Based on his previous affairs with Patty Duke and Liza Minnelli, Lucille had long suspected that her son might marry an older woman. But against her expectations, she soon learned that Purl was actually two years his junior.

She'd been born in Greenwich, Connecticut, the daughter of a chemical industry executive, Raymond Charles Arthur Purl. Her mother was named "Marshie," and she also had a sister, Mara. Their grandmother, Beatrice Saville, was a founder of Actors' Equity Association.

At the age of five, Linda and her family moved to Japan, where Raymond Purl was employed by Nippon Unicar.

Linda didn't return to the United States until she was fifteen. She would go on to enroll at Finch College and later study at the Lee Strasberg Theatre and Film Institute, where she seriously pursued her goal of becoming an actress.

Lucille's staff arranged for her to see Linda's performance in Jonathan Demme's action comedy, *Crazy Mama* (1975). The film starred Cloris Leachman and Stuart Whitman, and it marked the movie debut of Dennis Quaid. Lucille's friend, Ann Sothern, had been cast as Sheba, the mother of Linda's character, Cheryle.

Lucille also sat through a screening of *W.C. Fields and Me* (1975), based on the memoirs of Carlotta Monti, the aging actor's last mistress. Linda joined a cast composed of Rod Steiger, Valerie Perrine, Jack Cassidy, and

Bernadette Peters, with whom Lucille had previously starred.

At the time Desi Jr. and Linda were arranging their wedding, the bride-to-be also starred in a TV movie, *Women of West Point,* which was shown on CBS-TV at eight o'clock one night.

In reference to that TV movie, *The New York Times* wrote, "Linda Purl plays a plebe destined to go to the head of her class, though the road to success is predictably rocky. Miss Purl, who seems sensible and serious, makes it easy to understand why a young woman would not want a career in the military. Having fun is out of the question, and so is lying down on one's bed between *reveille* and taps. Looking at anything but the table at mealtimes is a serious violation. This is a great hardship for Miss Purl's character because a handsome upperclassman, played by Andrew Stevens, is intent on winking at her. Their romance, though charming, is off limits."

In 1979, the year of her marriage to Desi Jr., Linda also starred with Shaun Cassidy, the rock singer and teen idol making his dramatic debut in a TV movie, *Like Normal People* (1979). *[Shaun was the son of Shirley Jones and Jack Cassidy and the half-brother of another teen idol, David Cassidy.]*

The drama was about a pair of "developmentally challenged" young adults who face angry resistance when they decide to marry. *[In reference to the dynamic between Linda Purl and Shaun Cassidy, one tabloid got it all wrong, writing that Shaun and Linda were embroiled in a torrid romance and would soon marry. Actually, in 1979, Shaun was getting ready to marry his first wife, Ann Pennington, a model and former Playboy "playmate."]*

Linda was far better known for her work in television than for her ap-

As a devoted mother neurotically (some said) obsessed with the well-being of her children, Lucille quickly got word that the woman Desi Jr. had married seemed, at the time, to have serious star potential of her own.

Here are two widely circulated newspaper ads promoting **Linda Purl** as the female lead of (*left photo*) a saga about the manhandling of female recruits at West Point; and (*lower photo*) her key role in a soapy romance about unlikely and unexpected love.

pearances in feature films. Year after year, at least until 2018, she went from one role to another, sometimes appearing in such series as *Happy Days* (1974-1984) and *Murder, She Wrote* (1984-1996).

She had launched this amazing string of television roles from the foundation of the character she'd created on *The Secret Storm* (1973-1974), a daytime soap opera.

Christina Crawford, the adopted daughter of Joan Crawford, was a regular on that series, appearing in the role of Joan Borman Kane, a character about 24 years old.

When Christina became ill, Joan Crawford herself, then in her sixties, convinced the producers to allow her to fill in for her daughter until she recovered. At the time, this created a certain amount of notoriety and in some quarters, extreme embarrassment.

After Joan's death in 1977, Christina published a memoir entitled *Mommie Dearest,* the supreme hatchet job of a mother-daughter relationship. In it, she alleged child abuse, even though many of its (devastating) allegations were disputed. The book forever tarnished the reputation of Joan Crawford, the ultimate diva of Golden Age Hollywood,

Its widely promoted movie adaptation starred Faye Dunaway hysterically impersonating Joan after Anne Bancroft rejected the role. In one scene, the movie depicted Dunaway, as a narcissistic Joan looking demented, standing in for her daughter in *The Secret Storm.*

Lucille went to see *Mommie Dearest* with Gary Morton, later asking him, "Do you think Lucie, after my death, will publish a tell-all about me?"

"She wouldn't dare," Morton assured her.

Two views of **Joan Crawford** in actions associated with her bitter and according to some, dysfunctional daughter, **Christina.**

Lower photo: Joan, filling in for Christina on *The Secret Storm*

***

In January of 1979, Linda Purl and Desi Jr. were wed, having already had babies born to them in TV dramas. Neither the bride nor the groom were Jewish, yet they were married at the Simon Weis Temple in Bel Air. That was the only house of worship which would allow them to draft their own version of a wedding service. Reportedly, at least five churches, including two Catholic ones, refused to allow that break in their traditions and liturgies.

As his best man, Desi Jr. selected his stepbrother, Greg Hirsch. As her maid of honor, Linda chose her sister, Mara. Dino Martin, the son of Dean Martin, was one of the ushers, as was Tony Martin Jr. the son of the singer, Tony Martin Sr. Lucie Arnaz was designated as a bridesmaid.

Since Desi Sr. pleaded "poverty," Lucille financed the expensive reception at the exclusive Le Bistro in Beverly Hills, a haunt of resident movie stars.

Outside the temple, Lucille faced reporters. "I'm glad to see my son settle down. He did not marry an older woman, as so many members of the press have suggested. In fact, Linda is young enough to be a child bride. Gary Morton calls her a living, breathing, Barbie Doll. I prefer to call her a talented young actress."

Desi Sr. was also interviewed. "I think Linda was a great choice for my son. She's smart, and I hear she knows how to keep the show on the road. Our poor boy is so disorganized, he has a hard time getting out of bed in the morning. I think she will help get his life better organized."

***

The much-anticipated marriage of Linda Purl and Desi Jr. had the lifespan of a sickly butterfly. At the time, the groom had not yet freed himself of his addiction to drugs and alcohol, or so it was reported.

Almost immediately, the marriage ran into trouble, and it was characterized by frequent breakups and reconciliations, caused allegedly by her unhappiness over his fast-lane lifestyle."

On January 3, 1980, Linda filed for divorce, citing "irreconcilable differences." She did not want to embarrass him by referring to any addiction.

After his divorce, Desi Jr. was rumored to have gone on a "real bender."

On hearing of the divorce, Desi Sr. said, "As a baseball fan, I would say that my son and my daughter Lucie are batting zero in their marriages. Maybe the next time around, they'll hit a home run. Divorce is awful. Just ask Lucy."

Linda would marry three more times. On November 5, 1988, she wed screenwriter William Broyles Jr., whom she later divorced. On July 23, 1993, she wed British screenwriter and producer Alexander Cary with whom she had a son, born two years later.

They later divorced. On July 15, 2006, she wed James Vinson Adams, but that union also led to divorce.

***

Throughout 1978 and 1979, Lucille sank to a new low point in her television career. Although she was rarely seen on the tube during the course of that season, on September 29, 1978, she did sign with producer Paul Keyes to appear as a guest for CBS in a 120-minute variety show called *General Electric All-Star Anniversary*, to be hosted by John Wayne.

Although relatively unknown to the general public, Keyes, an award-winning comedy writer and producer, was well known in the entertainment industry, especially for such productions as *The Jack Paar Tonight Show, The Dean Martin Show,* and *Rowan & Martin's Laugh-In.*

During the course of his career, he was nominated for an Emmy ten times and won three of them. His gift for humor won him such friends as John Wayne, Frank Sinatra, Carol Burnett, Clint Eastwood, Jack Lemmon, Ingrid Bergman, and Ronald Reagan Even a U.S. President, Richard Nixon, once asked him to produce a White House dinner show for heads of state.

Despite his credentials, the variety show with Lucille and John Wayne was not one of Keyes' better efforts. The aging stars began an on-air chat that went nowhere. Perhaps viewers used the moment to get up for visits to the toilet.

Lucille picked up some steam when she appeared as a showgirl floozie, perhaps from the 1920s, doing a dance number. It wasn't memorable: She had never been a dancer, even during her heyday, and the fact that she had injured her leg in a ski accident didn't help matters.

At least the show gave her a chance for a reunion with Henry Fonda, Bob Hope, Henry Winkler, Donny and Marie Osmond, and Red Skelton, each of whom she had worked with before.

Also on the program was Elizabeth Taylor. Off camera, she passed Lucille in the hall without speaking. Their oldtime feud had not been forgotten.

James Stewart made up for Taylor's snub when he encountered Lucille. He grabbed her in a bear hug and kissed her. "I'm trying to make up for not having seduced you in the 1930s," he announced.

***

Lucille's biggest TV moment that autumn came with a distinctive Southern accent after she signed as the star of *A Lucille Ball Special: Lucy Comes to Nashville.* A sixty-minute, nostalgia-soaked variety show, telecast on November 29, 1978, it was produced by Jack Donohue, who had helmed her so many times in the past.

Lucille had recently turned sixty-seven years old, and she looked it—that is, if you stared through the heavy make-up. Otherwise, despite looking slightly puffy, she was glamourously attired.

Although she wasn't exactly "home, sweet, and at home" on the stage of Nashville's Grand Old Opry House, the other performers, most of whom were from the South, were most gracious to her.

As part of the somewhat silly plot, Lucille finds herself functioning as conductor of the

"The legs are always the last to go," **Lucille** said, perhaps with a drawl, before posing for this press and PR photo commemorating her appearance on *Lucy Comes to Nashville.*

Nashville Philharmonic. As one critic put it, "Viewers tuning in must have thought that Lucy Ricardo had accidentally wandered into a scene from *Hee Haw.*" [*Hee Haw* thrived in its original run (1969 to 1971) and continued in syndication for another twenty years or so after that. Inspired by Rowan & Martin's Laugh-In, *and set in "Kornfield Kounty," it featured "grits and chitterlings" conepone and lots of scantily clad "farmer's daughters" (the Hee Haw Honeys) with big hair and shorty-shorts. "What?" her fans asked, "was Lucille doing?"*]

In one of the televised sequences, Lucille and Barbara Mandrell collaborated (and competed) in an evergreen rendition of "Glow Worm." *[Known as "The Sweetheart of Steel," Mandrell, a daughter of Houston, Texas, became famous in the 1970s and 80s when she was one of the country's most popular vocalists. One of her big hits was "I Was Country When Country Wasn't Cool."]*

Also on the show was Ronnie Milsap, a native son of North Carolina, who, like Mandrell, was one of America's most popular country music singers. His peak popularity was also in the 1970s and 80s.

As a "crossover singer," he could sing both country and pop, one of his biggest hits being "Smokey Mountain Rain." Milsap went on to win six Grammy Awards and record more than three dozen #1 country hits.

When Lucille chatted with another performer, country singer Mel Tillis, she was surprised at his awful stutter. He struggled to complete just one sentence. *[Amazingly, when he sang, he had no stutter at all.]* He told her that he was part of the "outlaw country movement," but didn't define exactly what that meant.

His biggest hit recordings were "Good Woman Blues," "Coca-Cola Cowboy," and "I Ain't Never." She learned from him that his Coca-Cola song was going to be a feature in the upcoming Clint Eastwood movie, *Every Which Way But Loose.* Tillis was also set to have a role in *Smokey and the Bandit II* (1980), starring Burt Reynolds.

That did not surprise Lucille. What did was Tillis' revealing that he was preparing to make "duet recordings" with Nancy Sinatra.

To Gary Morton, Lucille admitted that "although they treated me like a lady," she didn't feel at home in Nashville around "all these country boys. I think they'd rather be working with Dolly Parton. When it came to the war of the bosoms, Parton needed a heavy-duty brassiere to hold up those jugs. I was never noted for Jayne Mansfield breasts, as those topless photographs I posed for back in the 1930s reveal."

During production. she met The Oak Ridge Boys, former gospel singers, who also recorded *doo wop* and pop. They were on the verge of turning out such future hits as "Elvira," "Bobbie Sue," "and "American Made."

After watching a screening of the show she'd just appeared in, Lucille said, with wry humor, "The Queens of Country Music have nothing to fear from me. They can sleep peacefully in their beds at night. I don't plan to ever invade the cottonfields of the South again. Maybe Miami, but that's not the real South."

***

Lucille agreed to appear on *The Mary Tyler Moore Hour* for a 60-minute telecast on CBS on March 6, 1979. She came into Mary's life as her spectacular career was winding down.

Mary Tyler Moore had launched herself in Show Biz as "Happy Hotpoint," a tiny elf dancing on Hotpoint appliances in TV commercials. But when she became pregnant, the elf gig abruptly ended.

She later unsuccessfully auditioned for the role of the elder daughter of Danny Thomas on TV, but he rejected her. "No daughter of mine would have such a small nose."

After appearing on such failed series as *The Tab Hunter Show* (1960), Mary got her big break. In 1961 when Carl Reiner cast her as the female lead on *The Dick Van Dyke Show* (1961-1966). She became a household name, and often wore tight Capri pants on the show. "I got the idea from Jackie Kennedy," she claimed.

That hit TV series led to Mary's biggest break when she was configured as the lead of her namesake comedy, *The Mary Tyler Moore Show* (1970-1977), a half-hour newsroom sitcom featuring Ed Asner as her gruff boss. After her character became a symbol of independent (and single) working women everywhere, the show became a landmark in the women's liberation movement. On the air for seven seasons, it won 39 Emmys.

When Lucille joined Mary, she was struggling with a lukewarm spinoff, *The Mary Tylor Moore Hour*. In its ongoing battle with low Nielsen ratings, and configured as part situation comedy, part variety show, it was broadcast only from March to June of 1979. Mary played a TV star putting on a variety series, but only eleven episodes were filmed before the show was canceled.

The big number from these two seasoned performers involved a skit which depicted them getting drunk on Irish coffee, but it didn't come off. Another comic highlight (at least that was what it was supposed to be) had Mary and Lucille trying to eat such Japanese delicacies as eel and octopus. Critics attacked their joint appearance, citing "a feeble script and canned laughter."

In yet another scene, Lucille reverted to her

When **Lucille** met **Mary Tyler Moore**, depicted in the upper photo on the cover of *TV Guide*, Mary fully understood the sometimes scary impositions her recent sitcom success inflicted on her privacy.

In 1995, *Entertainment Weekly* wrote "TV's most famous bachelorette pad" was in a real house (*lower photo*) in Minneapolis.

Once fans discovered its location, the house morphed into a popular tourist destination. Its occupant became overwhelmed by hundreds of fans who showed up asking if Mary were at home.

chorus girl roles from back in the 1930s, struggling through a number called "The Girlfriend of the Whirling Dervish."

Mike Douglas, who had his own TV show, also made a guest appearance, but even he couldn't save the day.

Even her most loyal fans tuned Lucille out that night, switching channels.

***

Lucille was hesitant about signing for her next gig, the last of that spring, fearing that she and the show's star, Cher, "The Queen of Pop," would have no chemistry. Nonetheless, with no other offers available to her at the time, she agreed to appear on *Cher and Other Fantasies*, telecast on NBC on the evening of April 3, 1979. Elliott Gould would be the show's male co-star.

The wobbly plot depicted Cher living out her fantasies. Perhaps borrowing a routine from her friend, Carol Burnett, Lucille played an old cleaning woman. "I looked like shit," was her own review.

If the show had any saving grace, it came from Cher, a real trouper, even though this was one of her weaker efforts.

Best known for her distinctive contralto singing voice, Cher had gained popularity in 1965 as one half of the folk rock duo, *Sonny & Cher*. Their song, "I Got You Babe," peaked at No. 1 on both the U.S. and U.K. charts.

After divorcing Bono in 1975, she married Greg Allman, the rock musician. Cher told Lucille that although she made the decision to divorce Allman only nine days after their wedding, their marriage drifted on until 1979, the year she worked with Lucille.

Lucille learned not to be surprised at any of the quips emerging from Cher's lips. "I believe in face-lifts," she said, "nips and tucks. You know, if I wanted to put tits on my back, I would."

"Tits on the back," Lucille said. "What a novel idea."

"My rule of thumb," Cher continued, "and it never fails me, is that if a man is a good kisser, he's also a good fuck."

In time, Cher's lovers would include Warren Beatty, Tom Cruise, Val Kilmer, and the exotic dancer, Marc Connelly. He later said, with perhaps deliberate ambiguity, "Cher straddled me and fed me whipped cream and strawberries that came from parts of her body."

She reportedly told Lucille that at

Cher, a scene-stealing trouper, was stiff competition for Lucille, her co-star in an episode they telecast in the spring of 1979.

As a self-satirizing contrast to Cher's extravagant glamour, Lucille played a dumpy-looking cleaning woman.

times, she regretted having shortened her name to Cher. "It might have been more exotic if I'd used my own name: Cherilyn LePiere Sarkisian. That might look more impressive on a marquee."

At the peak of her popularity, some thirty million viewers had watched Cher perform with Bono. Lucille's favorite of her numbers was "Gypsys, Tramps, and Thieves"

She advised Lucille to consider working The Strip in Vegas. "I've signed to do just that for $300,000 a week.

As for their male co-star, Lucille never considered Elliott Gould very sexy, but this Brooklyn-born actor intrigued her, mainly because of his former marriage to another Brooklyn-born performer, Barbra Streisand. The couple had married in 1963, divorcing in 1971. During their union, they had a son, Jason.

Lucille had seen Gould on the screen when he co-starred in the comedy, *Bob and Carol and Ted and Alice* (1969), for which he'd received an Oscar nod as Best Supporting Actor.

"Babs and I were the 'it' couple of the 1960s," he told Lucille. "We eventually went our separate ways because we did not grow together. Of course, she became a superstar, and I did not."

Before Streisand eventually married James Brolin, she impressed Lucille with the number of men with whom she was linked: Warren Beatty, Richard Burton, Sidney Chaplin, Don Johnson (she urged him to get circumcised), Kris Kristofferson, Liam Neeson, Anthony Newley, Ryan O'Neal, Robert Redford, Tommy Smothers, Pierre (Prime Minster of Canada) Trudeau, Omar Sharif, and Elvis Presley.

After finishing *Cher and Other Fantasies*, Lucille began gearing up for the 1979-1980

"Four people in bed together are better than a twosome." Or so *Bob & Carol & Ted & Alice* attempted to prove. From left to right are **Elliott Gould, Natalie Wood, Robert Culp**, and **Dyan Cannon**.

Denounced as a "slick, whorey movie," it explored infidelity and sexual experimentation.

Nominated for four Oscars, it became the fifth-highest-grossing movie of 1969.

In 1935, Barbara Stanwyck showed the world she was butch enough to play the sharpshooter Annie Oakley in a movie with the same name.

But more people saw the zany **Betty Hutton** portray Annie in the MGM film, *Annie Get Your Gun.* (1950).

"Most of the cast and crew wouldn't speak to me except when they had to. They resented me for taking over Judy Garland's role after she was canned," Hutton claimed.

television season, a gloomy prospect that would begin that fall and extend into the spring.

***

Between marriages, Lucie Arnaz in 1979 became the sharpshooter, Annie Oakley, in a revival of the hit Broadway musical, *Annie Get Your Gun* at the Jones Theater in New York.

The original version of that play had opened in 1946 on Broadway and starred Ethel Merman. With music by Irving Berlin, it had run for 1,147 performances. Betty Hutton had starred in its film adaptation in 1950, after Judy Garland was fired.

The musical was a fictionalized version of the life of Annie Oakley, (1860-1926), part of *Buffalo Bill's Wild West Show*. It depicts her romance with another sharpshooter, Frank Butler (1847-1926).

Lucie would perform the hit songs from the show, including "Doin' What Comes Natur'lly," "You Can't Get a Man with a Gun," and "There's No Business Like Show Business."

As housing during that summer in Massapequa, New York, Lucie rented a villa next door to the Jones Beach Theatre. Before the summer ended, she would have been seen by some 750,000 people.

She told a reporter that she had longed to play Annie ever since she'd listened to the Mary Martin recording, "Why Mom didn't have the Merman album, I don't know."

She admitted that she was not impressed at how Hutton played Annie, and that she, Lucie, was giving the role her own distinctive interpretation.

She said that she had been trained by her mother, Lucille Ball, especially when she co-starred on the *Here's Lucy* series. "She expected three times more from Desi Jr. and me than she did from the other performers."

Critics noted that Lucie didn't seem afraid to take roles which other stars had made fa-

Lucie Arnaz was a real trouper, not afraid to take over hit roles made famous by other stars in other productions.

Take Betty Hutton in *Annie Get Your Gun* or Liza Minnelli in *Cabaret*.

Here, Lucie is seen with **Robert Klein** in the musical, *They're Playing Our Song*.

mous. A case in point was her playing the Liza Minnelli role in *Cabaret*. In fact, Lucie's first professional role had been as Sally Bowles in the San Bernardino Light Opera Production of that musical. Lucie had also worked at the Kenley summer stock productions of such hits as *Once Upon a Mattress, Goodbye, Charlie,* and *Bye Bye Birdie.* [*Kenley was an Equity summer stock theater company which presented television, film, and Broadway stars in plays at affordable prices to communities throughout the Midwest between 1940 and 1996.*]

Ruefully, she confessed to a reporter, "There used to be a time when all I heard was, 'I just loved your mother as Lucy Ricardo, and your father, too.' My mother is constantly the center of attention in every conversation I have. It's okay because I've learned a lot from her. But I would like people to come to see me because they like me—not just to see what Lucille Ball's daughter can do."

After going on a tour with *Annie,* Lucie that same year was picked to co-star with comedian Robert Klein in *They're Playing Our Song,* essentially a high-energy, two-character musical.

The show opened on Broadway in February of 1979, running for 1,082 performances. Book was by Neil Simon, lyrics by Carole Bayer Sager, and music by Marvin Hamlisch. The story was based on the real-life relationship of Hamlisch and Sager, depicting a wisecracking composer mating with an off beat lyricist. Lucie made her Broadway debut in this hit musical.

However, for the show the names of the two characters were changed to Vernon Gersch and Sonia. Walsk. Lucie won the Theatre World Award and the Los Angeles Drama Critics Circle Award for Best Actress in a Musical for her portrayal of Sonia.

In spite of her busy work schedule, she was also falling in love in real life—not just on the stage.

***

The 1979 fall season was a lean harvest for Lucille, but she did appear on *The Big Event: TV Guide, the First 25 Years,* a 120-minute tribute telecast on October 21 on CBS.

Its host was Phil Donahue, a media personality and the star of TV's *The Phil Donahue Show,* the first TV show to invite audience participation.

His controversial show was launched in Dayton, Ohio, in 1967

Marlo Thomas with **Phil Donahue** in Rome in 1979, the year before they married.

Donahue, a TV talk-show host, could be rough on a guest, asking tough questions, but he soft-pedaled it with Lucille when they appeared together on his show. In her tango red wig and glamour-girl make-up, she looked younger than she had in years.

and didn't end until 1996 in New York. During that time, Donahue earned the title of "The King of Daytime Talk." When Lucille worked with him, she was introduced to Marla Thomas, whom Donahue was dating and would wed in 1980.

As a talk show host, no topic seemed off-limits to him, and Lucille admired him for that. "The guy has guts," she told Gary Morton. Then she quipped, "For Marla's sake, I hope he has something else, too."

Donahue was the first to produce a show on widespread child molestation in the Catholic Church by priests. His exposé was widely condemned, but that didn't stop him from launching a "priest pedophile show" on St. Patrick's Day. He later admitted "I'm not a very good Catholic."

However, all was tame during Lucille's stint on his show as she reflected on her early days in television.

After a summer of rest and a lot of backgammon, she looked more glamourous than she had in years, and her appearance was enhanced by her attire and a flattering wig in "tango red."

Donahue could have moved in on her, perhaps with the intention of getting her to reveal what had really gone on in her marriage to Desi Arnaz, but he chose not to.

"For that, I was grateful that he soft-pedaled it," she said.

***

Paul W. Keyes had assembled a star-studded cast for an NBC telecast on January 30, 1980, marking Lucille's first appearance on television in the new decade. "Within an hour, I'd never been kissed by so many men," Lucille said. "What a welcome to a show."

The performers lining up to kiss her included the top-ranking star of the night, Frank Sinatra. The 120-minute telecast, *Sinatra, the First 40 Years*—was in honor of his 65th birthday and his 40 years in show business.

Welcoming Lucille with a kiss, often on the lips, were Tony Bennett, Milton Berle, Sammy Davis Jr. ("he fed me a foot of tongue"), Cary Grant ("too, too chaste"), Glenn Ford, bandleader Harry James, Gene Kelly, Rich Little, Red Skelton, Dean Martin, and Orson Welles.

The Sinatra offspring—Frank Jr., Tina, and Nancy—were also included, as was singer Dionne Warwick.

Filming took place at Caesar's Palace in Las Vegas. Gary Morton flew with her to Nevada to help her in any way he could. She was not called upon to do any comedic sketch. All she had to do was make some flattering remarks onstage about Ol' Blue Eyes.

The night was memorable in that after the taping, Sinatra wanted her to go with him for a late-night supper. He had heard that she had taken Bob Hope's advice and was researching a three-night special devoted to his (Sinatra's) spectacular career. Various facets of his life were being researched, including his turbulent marriage to Ava Gardner and his rumored ties to the mob.

Although Hope had suggested that it should be a "warts-and-all" portrait, she assured him that it would not be a hatchet job.

"Of course, I would like to get statements from such ladies as Angie Dickinson, Eva and Zsa Zsa Gabor, Anita Ekberg, Patty Duke, Mia Farrow, Hope Lange, Kim Novak, Lee Remick, Jill St. John, Elizabeth Taylor, Gloria Vanderbilt, Lana Turner, Grace Kelly, and Shirley MacLaine, to name a few," Lucille said.

In advance, and before granting permission, Sinatra wanted to hear some of the comments made about him from his friends and frenemies. Lucille, therefore, compiled some of the opinions learned by her research staff.

Over drinks, she read some of them to him:

WHAT FRENEMIES SAID ABOUT FRANK:

"When he gets to heaven, Frank's gonna give God a hard time for making him bald."
—Marlon Brando

"Mais oui...the Mercedes of men!"
—Marlene Dietrich

"He was no Joe DiMaggio"
—Marilyn Monroe

"He's the most fascinating man in the world, but don't stick your hand into his cage.
—Tommy Dorsey

"A complete shit."
—Lauren Bacall

"I was not impressed with the creeps and Mafia types he keeps company around him."
—Prince Charles

WHAT FRENEMIES SAID ABOUT HIS ENDOWMENT:

"Well, there's only ten pounds of Frank, but 110 pounds of cock."
—Ava Gardner

"More would be almost too much."
—Juliet Prowse

"Oh, hell, I've got to tell you, it's the biggest cock I've ever seen in my life. Warren Beatty, Raymond Burr, James Dean, Steve McQueen, Robert Wagner, Audie Murphy, and others, especially Elvis Presley, pale in comparison."
—Natalie Wood

"What are you trying to do, break my jaw, so your records will outsell mine?"
—Judy Garland

"It was like a watermelon at the end of a toothpick."
—Actress/model Jeanne Carmen

"Not bad for a white boy."
—Billie Holiday

Then, in a way Lucille found frightening, Sinatra slammed down his drink and ordered another one. "Don't go on. I don't want to hear any more. Some of it is flattering, some creepy. I've done a lot of things in my life I'm ashamed of, and I don't want them relived on television. Yesterday is dead and gone. You've got to call off this so-called special. It's not going to happen. Got that?"

She studied his face for a moment, later telling Gary Morton, "He frightened me."

She finally said, "Okay, Frankie, your wish, my command. Let's get on with our present lives."

Lucille Ball came on stage to talk about his early days as a singer with the Tommy Dorsey Orchestra, and the many bobbysoxer fans he attracted. She was followed by Gene Kelly remembering the musical films he'd made with Sinatra. Sammy Davis Jr. gave an emotional speech about "my best friend."

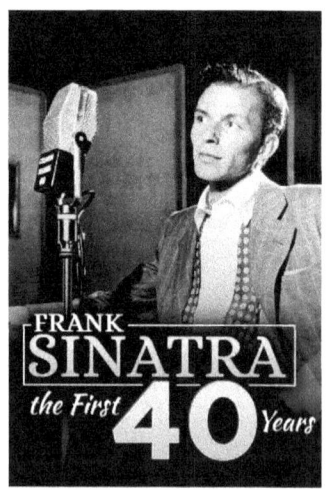

Frank Sinatra's self congratulatory, nostalgic, and relatively underpublicized retrospective was telecast on December 12, 1979.

It featured a brief testimonial about bobbysoxers and teen love from Lucille, but in a less flamboyant context than what had been originally conceived.

***

In the 1980s, Lucille appeared on television with Bob Hope more than with any other entertainer. Whatever the season, as a team, they always seemed to be starring in some TV special or celebration.

She could always rely on him for a wisecrack:

"Golf is my profession—show business pays my greens fees."

"You know you're getting old when the candles cost more than the cake."

"Bing Crosby and I weren't the type of men to go around kissing each other. We always had a light jab for each other. One of our stock lines used to be, 'There's nothing I wouldn't do for Bing, and there's nothing he wouldn't do for me. And that's how we went through life, doing nothing for each other."

"The other night, my wife Dolores asked me where I wanted to be buried. I told her, 'Surprise me!'"

***

Lucille was labeled a "turncoat," "a traitor," and a "betrayer," when she signed with (and switched loyalties to) NBC, the rival of her longtime studio, CBS. She agreed to produce and star in a 90-minute broadcast called *A Lucille Ball Special: Lucy Moves to NBC*, telecast on the night of February 8, 1980. She was designated not only as its star, but as its executive producer, assisted by Gary Morton. Her longtime director, Jack Donohue was imported to helm stars such as Bob Hope and Johnny Carson, not that either one of them needed (or wanted) much direction.

During rehearsals, Lucille became intrigued with a young African American performer, Gary Coleman. She had seen a few episodes of *Diff'rent Strokes* in 1978, in which he was cast as Arnold Jackson, one of two black brothers from Harlem who are adopted by a rich white widower in Manhattan.

Although Coleman evolved into one of the highest paid child actors in the world during the late 1970s and early 1980s, his life was living hell.

[Lucille learned that he suffered from a congenital kidney disease. He had to undergo a kidney transplant in 1973 (plus another one in 1984). Both were unsuccessful, and he required frequent dialysis. Corticosteroids and other medications stunted his growth and kept his height at four feet, eight inches. Lucille didn't live to see Coleman's bleak future, as he struggled with more emergency health issues, career fluctuations, financial hardships, and endless legal battles. At the age of 42, death came to him in Utah.]

Although **Gary Coleman** could put on a smiley face, his personal life was one of the most painful and disastrous in show biz. Few stars ever had to struggle with the physical horror he experienced, not to mention his money problems and attorney bills.

Also on the show was Doris Singleton. She and Lucille dated back to the late 1940s, when she'd first appeared on her hit radio sitcom, *My Favorite Husband*, with Richard Denning cast as her spouse.

Singleton frequently appeared on other shows, including Jack Benny's and *Perry Mason* (Raymond Burr), but she would be forever remembered as Lucy Ricardo's friend and nemesis, Caroline Appleby, on the *I Love Lucy* series.

Actor Robert Alda was also cast. Lucille and Carol Burnett had already co-starred with him back in March of 1970.

Lucille's most prominent co-stars on the night of February 8 were Donald O'Connor and Gloria DeHaven, portraying the owners of a music stor.

Lucille had known DeHaven since their days together at MGM in the 1940s, when she had portrayed every role from Mickey Rooney's sweetheart to Judy Garland's disagreeable sister.

Lucille had always considered O'Connor as one of the most brilliant and talented actors on the screen, but felt that Hollywood filmmakers had wasted his talent, especially when cast in those series of *Francis the Talking Mule* films.

She felt that only *Singin' in the Rain* (1952) had provided him with the proper showcase. In that movie, which co-starred Debbie Reynolds, O'Connor with his athleticism in dance even managed to steal the show from Gene Kelly.

After the special, NBC faced the same problem that CBS had confronted: What to do with a sixty-eight-year-old female *comedienne* whose heyday had come and gone? Fred Silverman, known as "The Wunderkind Prexy" of NBC, had originally hired Lucille in spite of their past conflicts when he had been the programming vice president at CBS. When he moved to NBC, executives there had softened his negative opinion of Lucille, noting that as "Queen of Television" she would bring prestige to the studio.

"My God, she's been in show business for six decades," Silverman

Like Lucille, **Doris Singleton** was a veteran star of radio entertainment, including an episode of Lucille's star-making radio vehicle, *My Favorite Husband*.

Originally aiming for a career as a ballerina, she eventually appeared in ten episodes of *I Love Lucy* as **Lucy Ricardo's** frenemy and nemesis.

When she died in 2012, she was the last surviving major recurring adult cast member from the "Lucy" shows.

Gloria DeHaven, the perky star of MGM musicals in the 1940s, is seen here with **Frank Sinatra** in *Step Lively* (1944).

She once said, "Into my bed popped Charlie Chaplin, Tony Martin, Gene Kelly, Mickey Rooney, and Glenn Ford...even Sinatra himself. But no man ever beat the boudoir skills of that hunk of flesh, my husband (1944-1950), John Payne."

said. "How long can she go on?"

Actually, as it turned out, Silverman didn't have that much for her to do at NBC, perhaps a few specials in the months ahead, but not a lot more. He rejected the pilots that she proposed in her capacity as head of Lucille Ball Productions. The one she seemed most deeply committed to involved starring Donald O'Connor in a sitcom, but that proposal was nixed.

Despite his fast-advancing age, Gale Gordon always "delivered the goods," in Lucille's words. In this special, he played her TV partner, rounding up celebrities to perform.

Ruta Lee, also in the cast, claimed, "Gary Morton tried to get me to work for almost nothing, claiming he had no budget." Lee had worked with Lucille before, including in an episode of *The Lucy Show,* where she played a curvaceous schemer plotting to take over Lucille's job as a secretary.

"I would have been perfect in the Gloria DeHaven role," Lee claimed. "Poor Gloria was horribly miscast."

After filming the NBC Special, Lucille would not work again on the tube for about six months, until the autumn of 1980.

***

Even as a little boy, Desi Jr. had faced an identity crisis. He was, of course, the son of Lucille Ball and Desi Arnaz (aka, Lucy and Ricky Ricardo). In the 1950s, because of their hit TV sitcom, *I Love Lucy,* they were the most famous couple on earth.

As he was growing up, Desi Jr. was called "Little Ricky." But that was not who he was. The Little Ricky portrayed on TV was an unrelated actor named Keith Thibodeaux, a son of Louisiana, who had his name changed to Richard Keith because Desi Sr. could not pronounce his last name.

Even as a pre-adolescent, he was a master drum beater. He was discovered by Horace Heidt at the age of three. From an early age, Keith toured with Heidt's orchestra, earning $500 a week.

In 1975, Keith's father took him to audition for the role of Ricky Ricardo Jr. on the *I Love Lucy* sitcom.

Lucille was the first to appraise him. "He's cute, but what does he do?" she asked.

"He plays the drums," his father said.

"Yeah, right," she said sarcastically. "This I gotta see." Then she motioned him to go over to where the band instruments were, and Keith started to beat a big drum with passion.

At that point, Desi Sr. walked onto the set and decided to join Keith in a drum concert.

"They were terrific," Lucille said. "We've found our little Ricky."

With the permission of his father, Keith almost became a member of the Arnaz family. "We practically adopted the kid," Lucille said. He became best friends with Desi Jr. and taught him how to be a drummer. Keith often spent weekends at the Arnaz home and traveled with the family in summer.

Of course, as might have been anticipated, there were some issues of jealousy, at least on the part of Desi Jr.

"I was watching *I Love Lucy* at the age of three," Desi Jr. recalled. "At home, my parents weren't anything like that couple on TV. They also called this little boy on TV their son. That was a lie! I was their son. He wasn't even my brother."

"My parents pretended they had a son on television. Why didn't they tell the truth and go on TV with me as their real son?"

"Early in his life, my son was confused about who he was," Lucille said. "I felt responsible for that, even though it was just show biz. Just play action. However, he and Richard—real name Keith—became good friends."

"When Desi Jr. started school, all his classmates called him 'Little Ricky,' and he told me he hated that name," Lucille said.

"I wanted to be myself, the real son of Lucy and Desi," he said. "At home, mom certainly wasn't Lucy—in fact, she hated that name. Her name was Lucille. If Keith (or Dick) was real cute on television, I wanted to be cuter. Millions of TV watchers were raving about what an adorable son he was. What about me? Didn't I count for something? Wasn't I even more adorable?"

He later blamed his "muddled self-image" as the reason that he turned to drugs and alcohol by the time he was only twelve. "My mom told me to be a good boy. To do that, I took drugs and drank at a very early age. I even got certain doctors to supply me with drugs, since I had plenty of money in my pocket. I could bribe the bastards into giving me what I wanted."

***

In time, as might have been predicted, Desi Jr. and Keith went their separate ways. As of this writing in 2021, Keith is the last living regular cast member from the *I Love Lucy* sitcom.

Keith continued to work with Lucille and Desi Sr. until their divorce in 1960. One day, when he showed up on the set, he was abruptly told that he was no longer needed. Desilu Productions had no more regular work for him, but he occasionally got a walk-on in a sit-

Whatever happened to Little Ricky?
Hint: Baby stars eventually grow up:

Having demonstrated undeniable talent as a toddler on the drums, **Keith Thibodeaux** (third from left in photo above) joined a Christian rock band, David and the Giants, and continued—no longer with a nationwide viewership—his development as an artist.

com being filmed on the lot.

In time, Lucille and Keith's father got into a bitter argument, and she ordered both father and son off the lot. Since they could no longer afford to live in Hollywood, they rode the train together back to their native Louisiana.

By 1969, Keith joined the rock group *David and the Giants*, and toured mostly in the South. In time, Keith, like Desi Jr., developed a drug problem, and the band broke up. After becoming a "Born Again Christian" in 1974, Keith reunited with the band, and the young men released albums, beginning in the 1980s, through Epic Records.

In 1976, he met and married ballet dancer Kathy Denton in Jackson, Mississippi. In 1990, he became executive director of his wife's *Ballet Magnificent*, the largest Christian ballet company in the world, often going on national and international tours.

In 1994, he published his autobiography, *Life After Lucy*.

***

Just as Keith moved on with his life, so did Desi Jr. Little Ricky was buried in their respective pasts.

At the age of twelve, Desi Jr. formed a rock band trio. His partners included the thirteen-year-old Dino, son of Dean Martin, and Billy Hirsche, who was also thirteen.

"At first, gigs at Hollywood parties brought us only five dollars for the three of us," Desi Jr. said. "But we rose quickly. Frank Sinatra heard us perform one night at Dean Martin's house, and he signed us to a contract with his Reprise Records. Our first hit was 'I'm a Fool.' Soon, we were getting $4,000 a week. Our greatest exposure came when we starred on *The Ed Sullivan Show*. We were seen by millions, and we soon developed fan clubs."

Desi Jr. found himself a teen idol, with dozens of girls screaming for him like they did for an even bigger star, Elvis Presley.

Around this time, Desi turned to drink and to drugs, like many other kids in America. He became a devotee of marijuana, Quaaludes, cocaine, LSD, mescaline, and liquor. This led to epic battles with Lucille. Often, the young man fled from his mother's home in Beverly Hills to join his father and his second wife, Edie, at one of their homes. He found his father far more understanding because he, too, had struggled for years with his own heavy drinking.

At the time, Desi Jr. was said to suffer from bouts of depression. His weight shot up and down, and he complained of severe headaches. Even so, he developed a reputation as a "teenaged Casanova," dating young women years older than himself.

"I'm sure he impregnated a few, as I did myself," Dino Martin later confessed. "We were not exactly experts at that time on safe sex."

"I desperately wanted my son to be happy," Lucille said. "Sometimes, I blamed myself when he went into one of his depressions. It wasn't his fault that his parents were the most famous people on earth. He started out in show biz when he was only twelve, but we knew he could never reach the fame of his parents. Neither could Lucie."

"Such fame that happened to Desi Arnaz and me rarely happens in a generation. My children should never try to top their father or me. If they harbored such ambitions, they were doomed for failure."

Desi Jr. later recalled, "I got tired of being me. I was killing myself slowly. Something was running my life. I was no longer in charge of myself."

On January 25, 1979, suffering from narcotics abuse, severe depression, and an upper respiratory infection, he checked himself into a Chemical Dependency program at the Cedars Sinai Medical Center in Los Angeles.

After treatment, he left the hospital on February 6, but soon reverted to drug taking.

As biographer Charles Higham noted: "Insecure as always, afraid of his mother, dreading her private criticism of him, and appalled at some of her remarks about him to the press, he plunged deeper and deeper into drugs."

In 1982, Desi Jr. checked into the Scripps Medical Center and began on the long road to recovery. This time around, he would finally succeed, later thanking his parents for their support and help.

During his recovery, both Lucille and his father participated in family therapy, joining the families of other sons and daughters who had succumbed to drugs. "I remember my mom and dad were always asked for autographs."

"I can't tell you how much my son's addiction hurt me," Lucille said. "I mean really hurt me like a stab in the heart. I tried to listen to him, to hear his hurt and pain. More important, I tried to understand what had driven him to drugs and alcohol. I also decided to be strong and tough through the ordeal. At the same time I wanted to be loving and supporting. I was being torn apart. Desi Sr. handled it better. In fact, he was in therapy himself for his heavy drinking."

Age and ill health had cut down on Desi Sr.'s philandering. "The therapy worked for my son, but not for my ex-husband," Lucille said. "Desi Sr. did not maintain his sobriety, even though I warned him he was committing a slow suicide."

"Mom was there for me," Desi Jr. said. "She understood my dilemma and helped me get my act together. She stood by me through every step of my recovery. When something was required from her, she delivered."

Actually, even though it didn't last, my father helped, too." Desi Jr. said. "He had to put aside his pride and stand up to tell a group, 'I am Desi Arnaz. I am an alcoholic.'"

"I cried when I first heard Dad say that," Lucie Arnaz claimed. "I have enormous pride that he had the courage to do that."

Years later, after his mother's death, Desi Jr. told the press, "Her commitment to my healing myself helped me through every stage of recovery. She was a crucial part of it. She spoke to other families about her own feelings of guilt at my taking the wrong path."

"I kept thinking that if I had done something differently, it would not have happened," she confessed. "Perhaps I was absorbed too much in my own career and neglected him when he needed me the most. I was terrified when I saw my son destroying himself."

"Hearing her talk like that made me realize how much pain and suffering I had inflicted on her," Desi Jr. said. "Realizing what I had done speeded me on the road to recovery."

***

Lucille's 1980-1981 season on television was not noteworthy or even memorable. Some critics even labeled it a disaster.

Her first and only gig that fall was on *The Steve Allen Comedy Hour,* broadcast on NBC on October 18, 1980.

During rehearsals, she met two of the performers, Steve Martin and George Kennedy.

Martin, a son of Waco, Texas, born in the dying days of World War II, was an actor, comedian, writer, and musician. In the 1970s, he had delivered his offbeat, absurdist comedy routines before packed houses on national tours. Fresh from his starring role in *The Jerk* (1979). he told Lucille he was planning to become a movie star.

George Kennedy was gracious to her. She'd first seen this New Yorker in the movie *Cool Hand Luke* (1967) starring Paul Newman. He'd won an Oscar for Best Supporting Actor.

She told him, "I must be the least known actor you ever starred with."

She was no doubt calling attention to his former co-stars: Kirk Douglas, Cary Grant Audrey Hepburn, Gregory Peck, Joan Crawford, James Stewart, and Dean Martin.

Lucille ate lunch that day with Louis Nye, an actor who had made many appearances on *The Steve Allen Show,* and with whom she'd perform in a televised skit. Survivor of countless television, film, or radio programs, Nye told her, "I'm a Jew but I ended up playing rotten Nazis on radio."

As she and Nye lunched, he discussed their mutual friend, Ann Sothern. He had appeared as a den-

Funny guy **Steve Martin** was a "wild and crazy guy" and an absurdist stand-up comedian in the 1970s.

He later became a top-rated film star, even daring to walk in the shoes of Spencer Tracy in the 1991 remake of *Father of the Bride.*

George Kennedy (*right*) punishing **Paul Newman** (*left*) in a key scene from *Cool Hand Luke* (1967).

If a director wanted a no-nonsense, cigar-chomping troubleshooter or a beefy, loutish heavy, he could call on Kennedy, the son of show-biz parents.

tist on several episodes of her sitcom.

"I went over big on *The Beverly Hillbillies*, but the producers later fired me, claiming that I came off as a fag," Nye said.

In time, he would not only work with Lucille, but with Bob Hope, Dean Martin, Walter Matthau, Robert Mitchum, Jack Webb, and Joanne Woodward.

Allen's writers had not yet come up with a suitable script for her, so, as the show's host, he wandered down memory lane and reformatted a sketch he'd written many years ago for his wife, Jayne Meadows, and Gene Rayburn. The action takes place in a hospital room, where the husband has broken every bone in his body. His wife enters. Even though his body should not be moved, she grabs him and violently tosses him about.

The original sketch, as interpreted by Meadows, had drawn a lot of laughs, and Allen felt it would be a good vehicle for two veterans like Lucille and Nye. In the revised version of the skit, she tosses him around in spite of his broken bones. But this time around, after it became obvious that the skit didn't generate any laughs, Allen ordered the sound engineers to insert canned laughter.

One TV critic, while praising the other performers, cruelly noted that "Lucille Ball, droopy eyelids and all, looked like she had just emerged from a 40-night drunk."

Louis Nye was one of the most talented character actors in Hollywood, but he had to admit that he and Lucille bombed in a sketch they did for *The Steve Allen Show* in the fall of 1980.

"I'm in a hospital bed with every bone broken and can't be moved. Lucy played my hysterical wife. She yanks me around and yells at me with almost no motivation. She also looked like shit. She was great as Ricky Ricardo's wife—but not as mine."

***

To launch the new year, Lucille, on January 18, 1981, agreed to be a guest on *Bob Hope's 30th Anniversary Television Special* on NBC. The aging comedian was also its executive producer, and he easily signed up familiar faces—not just Lucille, but Ann-Margret, Milton Berle, George Burns, Steve Lawrence, and his wife, Eydie Gormé. Sammy Davis Jr. also agreed to appear, as did Donny and Marie Osmond, Danny Thomas, Brooke Shields, and Douglas Fairbanks Jr.

Lucille introduced old clips of their previous films. She found herself laughing at some of Hope's stale jokes she had already heard so many times.

"I do benefits for all religions. I don't want to blow the Hereafter on a technicality."

"As for co-starring with Jane Russell, don't let that dame fool you. Tangle with her and she'll shingle your attic."

"I'm constantly asked why I don't run for President of the United States. Blame it on my wife, Dolores. She refuses to move to a smaller house."

"They say I'm worth $500 million. If this were true, I would not have visited Vietnam. I would have sent for it."

Brooke Shields was that "sexy Manhattan babe," who had started out as a pre-teen model. At the age of twelve, she'd been assigned the leading role in Louis Malle's film *Pretty Baby* (1978), in which she played a child prostitute in New Orleans.

When she came together with Lucille, she'd also shot *The Blue Lagoon* (1980) and would soon be filming Franco Zeffirelli's *Endless Love* (1981).

She seemed on the verge of major stardom, something Lucille envied, wishing such opportunities would come to her own daughter.

Shields, at the age of fourteen, in 1980, became the youngest fashion model to appear on the cover of *Vogue*. That same year, she posed for print and TV ads for Calvin Klein jeans. Her soon-to-be-famous tagline was, "You want to know what comes between me and my Calvins? Nothing!"

Brooke Shields rocketed to fame as a model wearing Calvin Klein jeans and no panties.

"I became famous as a sexy screen siren in such films as *Pretty Baby* and I was also a famous virgin. That was a real disconnect, hard to live with. I can't believe I survived those days and didn't turn into a train wreck."

While filming the Hope special, Lucille had a reunion with Douglas Fairbanks Jr. She'd had a supporting role with him in *Having Wonderful Time* (1938), released by RKO. In that picture, Fairbanks had co-starred with Ginger Rogers, and the movie marked Lucille's fifth and final time in which she appeared in a Ginger Rogers movie.

Off the screen, Lucille was having an affair with the movie's producer, Pandro S. Berman.

Fairbanks and Lucille recalled how they'd been driven to Bear Lake in California's San Bernardino Mountains for the location shoot.

As she lunched with Fairbanks, he, like her own son, both with a "junior" at the end of their name, were following in the footsteps of their incredibly famous fathers.

During his marriage to Mary Pickford, Fairbanks Sr. and his wife were voted the most fabled couple on the planet. That was also the case with Lucille and Desi in the 1950s.

"Dad was completely opposed to my becoming a movie star," he said. "His exact words to me were, 'There is only one Fairbanks!' He felt I was breaking into films by exploiting his more celebrated name."

"You certainly succeeded as a film star more than my son," she claimed. "I mean, you did get to appear in some classics, such as *The Prisoner of Zenda* (1937) and *Gunga Din* (1930) with Cary Grant. My son hasn't had any breaks like that, and I fear they will not come his way."

"It's said that lightning can strike twice, but I'm not sure that's the rule in the movie world," he answered.

"Let's face it: Most sons of famous fathers—not only in the field of acting—rarely make it as big as dear ol' Dad," he said.

"There's the exception set by Michael Douglas. But the example of John Barrymore and his tragic son, John Barrymore Jr., is more common. Of course, the father-son competition for movie stardom can lead to toxic jealousy. Your son should be careful. He'll never become as famous as his father. And Lucie Arnaz, talented though she might be, will never come anywhere near your fame."

The subject then shifted to Joan Crawford, who, in 1929, had married Fairbanks when he was only nineteen. Their turbulent union lasted until 1933.

"She spent more time in bed with the actor with the big ears, Clark Gable, than she ever did with me," Fairbanks Jr. said. "I heard that you and Joan didn't get along too well when she worked with you on one of your shows.:"

"We almost came to blows," Lu-

Douglas Fairbanks Jr., was a Hollywood Casanova, and an "entitled since birth" member of Hollywood royalty thanks to his father (swashbuckler and early film icon Douglas Fairbanks Sr.) and stepmother (silent screen diva Mary Pickford). He took an adulterous **Joan Crawford** as his first wife, and seduced from both the A and the B list. *Top tier*: Marlene Dietrich, Tallulah Bankhead, Gertrude Lawrence, and Loretta Young. *Lower rung*: Lupe Velez, ballerina Vera Zorina, and Coral Browne.

He became close friends with Laurence Olivier, and Noël Coward was also "Mad About the Boy," the title of one of his popular songs.

Years later, in reference to his spectacular early success as a film actor, Fairbanks Jr. said, "By sheer accident, I had four successes in a row in the early '30s, and although I was still in my 20s, I demanded and received approval of cast, story and director. I don't know how I got away with it, but I did!"

With cigarette in hand, **Tom Snyder**, hard-hitting host of NBC's late-night *Tomorrow Show* became the one of the brainiest and most controversial interview hosts on TV.

In the early spring of 1981, Lucille dared come onto his show, uncharacteristically appearing without a wig, showing her own hair. Her conversation with him was personal but not sexual. She revealed that when she was a passenger aboard an Amtrak run from Los Angeles to New York, she had to get off "because of the lousy berths...and I'm a major stockholder!"

cille said. "It was a case of two bitches going at each other."

***

Lucille slept by herself in a bedroom that joined that of her husband Gary Morton. Since she didn't have to get up anymore at four or five o'clock in the morning to report in RKO or MGM, she became a devotee of late-night television, keeping the volume low so as not to disturb her husband.

She'd become fascinated by the TV personality of Tom Snyder, who had become best known for his *Tomorrow* Show (1973-1982), telecast on NBC.

With cigarette in hand, Snyder asked hard-hitting questions from his guests, often delivering provocative personal observations that infuriated some of them.

The shows that stood out in Lucille's mind included Synder's interviews of John Lennon, Sterling Hayden, Ayn Rand, and the notorious Charles Manson.

[*The studly Sterling Hayden was once married (1942-1946) to the blonde goddess, Madeleine Carroll, and was known as "the Viking God" in Hollywood. He spoke with a distinctive, rapid-fire baritone and stood 6 feet 5 inches.*

As he once told a newspaper reporter, "When I served in the Marine Corps and had to go into the communal shower, a horde of young men would follow me. That didn't necessarily mean that they were gay, but perhaps wanted to see for themselves if all those rumors about my appendage were true."

Lucille had seen some of his movies, notably when he starred in John Huston's The Asphalt Jungle *(1950), in which Hayden had an off-screen affair with starlet Marilyn Monroe. Lucille also saw him as General D. Ripper in Stanley Kubrick's* Dr. Strangelove or How I Learned to Stop Worrying and Love the Bomb *(1964). Of course, she'd also viewed him in Francis Ford Coppola's* The Godfather *(1972), in which Hayden was cast as an Irish-American policeman, Captain McCluskey.*

A *noir* view of **Sterling Hayden** in *The Asphalt Jungle*.

"Marilyn Monroe was in that crime thriller with me," he said. "She rated men on a score of one to ten. I got a nine-and-a-half, which was actually another measurement of mine."

Tom Snyder appears here in this NBC newswire publicity photo with **Charles Manson.** Together, they were co-stars of the edgiest and most disturbing talk show the host had ever choreographed.

After Manson's devoted and crazed acolytes killed a pregnant Sharon Tate and her friends, Lucille hired bodyguards, fearing a break-in of her own home.

For a time, Lucille had contemplated playing the fallen movie star, Margaret Elliott in The Star *(1952) opposite Hayden.*

Writers Dale Eunson and Katherine Albert had once been employed by Joan Crawford, and it was clear that the role of Margaret had been inspired by her.

Somehow, it didn't work out for Lucille, and Bette Davis took over the role, at one point almost doing an impersonation of her nemesis, Miss Crawford.

Years later, when Lucille met Hayden at a Hollywood party, something he rarely attended, she talked about the lost possibility of having worked with him.

"Well, give me a ring some night, and you'll find out what you missed out on. If you want references, ask Crawford. We co-starred in Johnny Guitar *(1954)."*

"It's sad I missed my big chance," Lucille said.

"It's big all right." Then he turned and walked away.]

Lucille also watched as Snyder interviewed Ayn Rand, the controversial writer and philosopher known for her hit 1943 novel, The Fountainhead. It was later adapted into a film starring Gary Cooper and Patricia Neal, who became lovers at the time. [*Lucille had struggled through Rand's best-known novel,* Atlas Shrugged *(1958), but finally abandoned it.*]

One night at a party, Barbara Stanwyck told Lucille, "My biggest career disappointment was not getting cast in The Fountainhead."

"I was told that Rand supports rational and ethical egotism and rejects altruism. Just what in hell does that mean?" Lucille asked.

Far more controversial than Rand was the appearance on Snyder's *Tomorrow* show of Charles Manson.

When Manson came on the show, Lucille was half asleep, but she bolted up in bed when he began to talk.

After his discharge from prison in 1967, Manson attracted a group of followers, mostly young women. Soon, they became known as "the Manson family" or "the Doomsday Cult."

Manson became obsessed with The Beatles and claimed to be guided by his interpretation of their lyrics, adapting the term "Helter Skelter" to describe his vision of an impending apocalyptic war between blacks and whites.

A white supremacist, he also believed that African Americans would win the race war. He seemed to believe that since he felt they were not intelligent enough to survive on their own, they would turn to him as their "white master and leader."

Manson's appearance on Snyder created a storm of protest.

In July and August of 1969, Manson's followers choreographed a series of murders, including that of a pregnant Sharon Tate. The starlet was married to director Roman Polanski, who was in Europe at the time.

In the wake of the murders, fear swept across Hollywood's movie colony. Gary Morton hired security guards to protect Lucille and her son and daughter. Lucille later recalled, "I surprised myself when I agreed to go on the *Tomorrow* Show hosted by Snyder."

Appearing with her was Lucie Arnaz. Snyder's interview was telecast by NBC on April 5, 1981.

Lucille's appearance shocked fans as she wore very little makeup and appeared with her own hair (i.e., no wig), dyed, of course.

It was not the usually explosive Snyder-type show, however. There were no "bombshell questions" thrown at her. She did claim, "I'm tired of working. I think I've done enough. I'm no spring chicken anymore."

A great deal of her expression and emotions were hidden by a pair of sunglasses. She also talked about the death of her mother, DeDe, and how painful it was.

Lucie was a mere backdrop. If the interview revealed any news at all, it came when Lucille said, "I'm ready now to take on grandmother roles. Bring 'em on!"

Bungle Abbey was a 30 minute pilot for a hoped-for TV series about wacky monks in an abbey.

It was also one of the rare instances where Lucille got official credit as a director.

***

A TV critic once wrote: "Each year, networks produce dozens of pricy TV pilot episodes. In the end, only a fraction makes it on the air—and even fewer stick around for another season. It's no wonder that producers play it safe by casting familiar faces. However, a beloved TV actor at the top of the bill does not always equate success. Even small screen legends suffer from their share of failure."

Lucille was no exception. In 1981, a failed pilot, *Bungle Abbey,* represented her first-ever debut as a solo director. It starred Gale Gordon.

Long before his character of "Mr. Mooney" came along, Gordon was known as Lucy's banker. Even before that, he had had a long and full acting career, beginning in 1923 as an extra on a silent film, *The Dancers*.

Originally, Gordon had been slated to be Fred Mertz on *I Love Lucy,* but other commitments prevented that, the role going to William Frawley.

Way back in 1958, Gordon had played a judge in *Lucy Makes Room for Daddy,* an episode on *The Lucy-Desi Comedy Hour. The Lucy Show* solidified his partnership with Lucille for the rest of their careers. Gordon went on to play Harrison Otis Carter in *Here's Lucy* and Curtis McGibbon in *Life With Lucy.*

In addition to her status as solo director, Lucille was also the executive producer of *Bungle Abbey,* a thirty-minute telecast that was aired on NBC on May 31, 1981. Fred S. Fox, who had written many scripts for her before, was the chief scriptwriter. The plot depicts the misadventures of the monks of the Brothers of Benevolence at a San Francisco monastery founded by Brother Bungle. The brothers attempt to raise $5,000 to help the nearby children's orphanage by selling a valuable painting by Brother Bungle. Gordon had the lead role of "The Abbott."

Both critics and viewers clobbered the pilot. One wrote, "Brothers even had brown-hooded robes and sandals. There are many jokes about stomping grapes, wine-making, and Vows of Silence. The set is a large storeroom with an enormous fireplace and bulky wooden floors, something you'd expect in a monastery in the Middle Ages, but not in present-day California. The jokes in the show are as old as the monks, or as stale as the abbey wine. The pilot is incredibly awful."

Another reviewer wrote, "I've seen many terrible pilots, but *Bungle Abbey* is one of the worst."

Gordon was steadily employed as an actor but found time to have a life away from Hollywood. He and his wife, Virginia, lived on a 150-acre farm in Borrego Springs, California. He became one of the few commercial carob growers in the United States.

In 1995, at the Redwood Terrace Health Center in Escondido, he died of lung cancer at the age of 80. His wife, Virginia, married to him for sixty years, had died in the same facility one month earlier. The couple had no children. By this time, Lucille was not around to mourn the passage of her favorite actor.

***

Lucille was terribly disappointed by the failure of *Bungle Abbey*, but she took solace that many other pilots which had melded big-name stars into their plot premises had also bombed.

Among the many failures was Dick Van Dyke in *Harry's Battles*. In it, he co-starred with Connie Stevens in an adaptation of the British series *A Sharp Intake of Breath*. His character was a supermarket manager in Pittsburgh who struggled to keep his cool while cutting through the red tape of everyday life.

Telly Savalas bombed in *Hellinger's Law*. The hero of *Kojak* did not stray too far from formula here. He was cast as a gritty, swaggering criminal lawyer.

Andy Griffith in a pilot named *McNeil* was obsessed with turning the 1972 James Garner film, *They Only Kill Their Masters,* into his latest TV series. He would play a sheriff, solving crimes at a ski resort. No takers.

Among the many other actors who flopped in attempts to launch pilots for new TV series was Fred MacMurray, hoping to repeat the success of *My Three Sons* and the Chadwick family.

Sally Field had had a hit with *Gidget* and *The Flying Nun*. Not so with *Hitched*, wherein she and Tim Matheson would play teenage newlyweds in the Old West.

The list goes on and on, as more and more stars failed in pilots: Bette Davis, Elizabeth Montgomery, Robert Wagner, Don Adams, Alan

Self-help guru **Vernon Howard**, whom Desi Jr., credited with helping to rescue him from his chemical dependencies.

King, Adam West, William Shatner, Leonard Nimoy, and so many others. In other words, Lucille was not alone.

***

After his recovery from drug addiction, Desi Jr. came under the influence of Vernon Howard and his New Life Foundation, a self-help group. In time, he became a spokesman for the group, which was "dedicated to sharing true principles of self-understanding and success as a human being."

As he told various groups, "Howard's principles are for everyone who has run out of his or her own answers and have said to themselves, 'There has to be a key that unlocks the secrets of life.' Delightful feelings will arise as these powerful truths are absorbed."

Lucille attended one of these meetings and was later heard asking, "Just what in hell's name is all this crap about?"

Born at the end of World War II in Massachusetts, Howard had become a spiritual teacher, author, and philosopher, writing such books as *The Power of Your Supermind* and *Solved: The Mystery of Life*.

Desi spoke about "success without stress."

As Lucille told Gary Morton, "I obtained success, and it was nothing but stress."

Desi Jr.'s career peak was in the 1970s when, in spite of his personal struggles, he was seen frequently on television. However, by the 1980s, his gigs became scarce.

He launched the decade of the 80s by portraying the character of Robbie Reinhardt in the TV movie, *Gridlock* (also known as *The Great American Traffic Jam)*, a series of auto mishaps that lead to several miles-long traffic jams. Desi's character is desperately trying to get to his pregnant wife.

One review was headlined, "Love, *angst*, rock 'n'

Traffic Jam? Desi Jr.'s film documented, as an action adventure movie, something that everyone in Southern California knows: The horrors of L.A. traffic.

Desi Jr. appeared in a film with the engaging but widely ridiculed **Pia Zadora**. He had a chance to play a detective, but an updated version—definitely not the Sam Spade of the 1940s.

The film's original title was advertised as *Fake-Out*. Commercially, at least, it fared better after it was re-named *Nevada Heat*.

roll, baby born, all on the Freeway!" Another reviewer called *Gridlock*, "a guilty pleasure."

In 1981 Desi Jr. was seen briefly in *Advice to the Lovelorn*, a comedy/drama pilot that starred Cloris Leachman as "Maggie Dale," a syndicated newspaper advice columnist. In a column "Dear Maggie," she solves lovelorn dilemmas. Aired on November 31, 1981, the pilot did not find any sponsors.

It wasn't until the following year that Desi got another role, appearing as Detective Clint Morgan in *Fake-Out*.

Also released under the title of *Nevada Heat*, this crime drama starred Pia Zadora, Telly Savalas, Desi Jr., and Larry Storch. Mostly filmed in Las Vegas in the vicinity of the Riviera Hotel, and telecast on November 18, 1982, *Fake-Out* was just another B-movie about women in prison.

Reportedly, although Zadora found young Desi "extremely attractive," she was less than thrilled by the results of their joint effort. "It was a cops-and-robbers-and-nightclub-singer story, kind of like a long *Kojak*," she said. "The film has me singing a little, but it's nothing I'm terribly proud of."

Desi's biggest role came when he was cast as the lead in thirteen episodes of *Autumn* in 1983 and 1984. In them, he played a police officer and computer programmer who generated a hologram (Chuck Wagner) which is able to separate itself from the computers that generated it at night and fight crime.

Thirteen episodes were filmed but only a dozen were ever telecast on ABC. The series was later rebroadcast as reruns on the Sci-Fi Channel.

Autumn suffered from poor ratings and expensive special effects, going off the air on April 2, 1984.

The Night the Bridge Fell Down, a TV movie, had actually been filmed in 1979 but not released until February of 1983, the same night the final original episode of *M*A*S*H* was

Press interest centered on **Pia Zadora**. She had a brief reign as a tabloid queen, having married business tycoon Mashulam Riklis in 1977 when she was 23 and he was 54.

They bought the most famous residence in the area, Pickfair, the former home of Mary Pickford and Douglas Fairbanks Sr. They tore down the termite-ridden historic home, and in its place, built a new mansion.

Desi Jr. was cast in *The Night the Bridge Fell Down*, an action-adventure story that also starred **James MacArthur** and **Barbara Rush**. It was released, with disastrous results, on the night CBS telecast the final episode of *M*A*S*H*. (1972-1983), a series that had thrived for eleven seasons.

"No one saw us," Rush complained. "All but two or three viewers in American wanted to see the last episode of that Army comedy."

aired. Warner Brothers could not have picked a worse night. The last episode of *M*A*S*H* attracted the largest audience for any single show in television history.

In the plot of *The Night the Bridge Fell Down*, Engineer Cal Miller, played by James MacArthur, makes an unauthorized attempt to collapse the dangerously unstable Madison Bridge. But his attempt is foiled by a police pursuit of a robbery suspect.

The chase ends in a multi-car accident midway across the bridge, which begins to collapse under the weight of the ensuing chaos. Desi appears in the second lead as Johnny Pyle. Others in the cast included Leslie Nielsen and Barbara Rush.

MacArthur, who worked smoothly with Desi, was the adopted son of playwright Charles MacArthur and actress Helen Hayes.

A daughter of Denver, Barbara Rush first achieved fame in the 1953 sci-fi thriller, *It Came From Outer Space*. She later became a regular performer on the hit TV series, *Peyton Place*.

From 1950 to 1955, she was married to actor Jeffrey Hunter. As one critic at *The Hollywood Reporter* noted, "I can't decide who is more beautiful—Barbara or Jeffrey."

Desi had the fourth lead in *House of the Long Shadows*, a 1983 comedy horror film directed by Pete Walker. Its cast was notable because four well-known horror movie specialists—Vincent Price, Christopher Lee, Peter Cushing, and John Carradine—were cast together in the same feature.

Scriptwriter Michael Armstrong based the plot on the 1913 movie, *Seven Keys to Baldpate* by Earl Derr Biggers. That novel was adapted into a famous play that gave birth in turn to several film adaptations.

Its dynamics revolved around Kenneth Magee (Desi Jr.) a young, handsome, and rather arrogant writer who bets $20,000 that he can write a novel of the caliber of *Wuthering Heights* in just 24 hours. To immerse himself in the spirit of that Gothic romance, he books himself into a deserted Welsh manor. He soon discovers, to his horror, that the manor is already occupied.

James MacArthur, shown here as Detective Danny Williams on-*Hawaii-Five-O*, was—like Desi Jr.—the child of a very famous mother, Helen Hayes.

Unlike Lucille's boy, MacArthur had been adopted.

Desi Jr. with **Julie Peasgood** in *House of the Long Shadows*.

At this stage of his career, more and more of his roles had him playing a likable but not particularly complicated American bloke acting like a "regular guy" alongside, in this case, eccentric *glitterati* like Vincent Price.

Desi would have one final role before the decade ended. In 1987, he was cast as Michael Porter in an episode of *Matlock,* starring Andy Griffith as a folksy but cantankerous attorney.

The hit show was telecast on NBC from 1986 to 1992. Later, ABC picked it up and extended its run. The show's format was similar to *Perry Mason* at CBS.

Linda Purl, the former Mrs. Desi Arnaz Jr., was part of the original cast, playing Matlock's younger daughter and (for part of the series) his crime-stopping partner. Later, she leaves for Philadelphia to set up her own law practice.

The next time Desi Jr. was seen in anything new on the screen would be when he impersonated his own father in *The Mambo Kings* (1992). By that time, Desi Sr. had died.

In 1987, Desi Jr. worked with **Paul Reiser**, the comedian, actor, writer, and musician, who was a familiar face in such hits as *My Two Dads, Mad About You,* and *Diner.* Desi had seen Reiser play a detective in *Beverly Hills Cop* (1984).

As one reviewer wrote, "Paul Reiser brings his sophisticated observational humor to home video in this rare showcase of his acclaimed talent."

Cameo appearances were by Carrie Fisher, Elliott Gould, Teri Garr, Michael J. Pollard, Woody Harrison, and Carol Kane.

***

For Lucille, the 1981-1982 television season was listless and lackluster. It began on September 13, 1981 when she was a presenter at the *Thirty-Third Annual Emmy Awards,* broadcast on CBS. She joined two of her favorite stars, Dinah Shore and Ella Fitzgerald.

This time around, it was not Lucille who was named Outstanding Actress in a Comedy Series. At the Civic Auditorium in Pasadena, the award went to Isabel Sanford for her role in the hit TV sitcom, *The Jeffersons* (1975-1985).

On September 20, Lucille joined a cast of other stars for a telecast, *The Magic of the Stars,* hosted for an hour by Milton Berle on HBO.

Lucille was enrolled to make some on-camera introductions. The cast included purse-swinging Ruth Buzzi; Glen Campbell with his girlfriend, Tanya Tucker; and Melissa Gilbert, Harvey Korman, Dick Shawn, and "The Odd Couple," Walter Matthau and Jack Lemmon.

Off screen was marked by a confrontation between the usually mild-mannered Gary Morton and Berle. During rehearsals, "Uncle Miltie" was going around bossing everybody and attacking both their appearance and their performance. After he heavily criticized Lucille, she retreated to her dressing room.

From the bleachers, Morton called out, "Hey, Uncle Miltie, why in hell don't you let the stars do their thing without any stupid interference from you?"

Berle stormed over to confront Morton. "What in the fuck did you ever direct, you rotten son of a bitch?" The only thing you ever directed was what your wife gave you because she felt sorry for you, you no-talent piece of shit. Remember this, flunky. I banged that overripe snatch of hers before you fell in it!"

For this special, director Terry Williams had each guest perform a magic trick. Attired in black slacks and a gold *lamé* jacket, Lucille suddenly makes a cane appear out of nowhere. Later, wearing a top hat, she does a levitation trick. Several critics commented on how glamourous she looked, even at the age of "the big 7-0."

Later, in a private talk with Morton, she told him, "Glen Campbell is in bad shape. Rumors have it that he is struggling with alcoholism and an addiction to cocaine. He divorced his wife, Sarah Jan Davis, and is now involved in that affair with Tanya Tucker."

When Harvey Korman showed up to embrace Lucille, she asked him "Did Carol Burnett give you permission to do that?"

She told him that only recently, she had seen him in Mel Brooks' *Blazing Saddles,* even though it was made in 1974. In that movie, Korman had been cast as the villainous "Hedley Lamarr."

Lucille met and was impressed with **Glen Campbell**, that son of Arkansas best known for his hit songs of the 1960s and 70s.

He reached into American living rooms during his hosting of CBS's *The Glen Campbell Hour* (1969-1972). He also had released 64 albums, including a dozen gold ones.

She praised his music, and he asked her which, from among his repertoire, was her favorite

She told him, "By the Time I Get to Phoenix."

"I hear that the real Hedy Lamarr is suing you or else has sued you," Lucille said.

"I'll never tell," Korman answered. "You know, the real Hedy Lamarr, even at her age, may still be beautiful, but she's completely nuts."

Lucille lunched with Walter Matthau and his frequent co-star, Jack Lemmon.

"He's my greatest partner ever," Matthau said, reaching over to warmly embrace Lemmon. "Don't tell anybody, but off screen, we're lovers."

Lemmon quickly added, "You know this ugly mutt is a joker."

Matthau said, "In case you missed it, when *The Odd Couple* opened on Broadway in 1965, the fuss budget (Felix Ungar) was played by Art Carney and I, of course, played the slob, Oscar Madison. I made an enemy for life of Carney when I demanded that Jack (Lemmon) here play Felix in the screen version."

Lucille took out a package of cigarettes and offered Matthau one after Lemmon waved his hand in rejection. "I was a three-pack-a-day smoker," Matthau claimed, "but when Jack and I made *The Fortune Cookie* (1966), I had a very serious heart attack, slowing down production. I played

'Whiplash Willie' Gingrich."

"Walter had a nicotine problem," Lemmon whispered. "But alcohol was my demon, at least for most of the 1970s. I am so god damn insecure I think every job will be my last. Talk about high anxiety."

She told Lemmon that she felt that *Some Like It Hot* (1959) was the best screen comedy ever made, referring to the picture in which he and Tony Curtis were mostly in drag, appearing opposite Marilyn Monroe.

"Did Monroe seduce you?" Lucille asked.

"Hell, no!" Lemmon said. "I think if I took down my pants in front of her, she would have belly-laughed. Tony told me he frequently banged her during his early days in Hollywood, back when he was trying to make up his mind about his sexual preference."

"Orry-Kelly, that gay costume designer who used to support a young Cary Grant, caused a rift between Marilyn and Tony. He told her that Tony's ass was perfect compared to her flabby cheeks."

"That may be true," Lucille said, "but Marilyn had other assets, particularly upfront. When I saw that early nude photo Tony posed for in his teens, I could only hope he had a lot more growing to do."

"Oh, Lucille, don't be naughty," Lemmon said. "You know men don't like a dame commenting on the size and efficiency of their most prized possession."

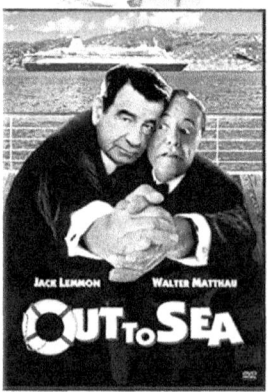

One of **Jack Lemmon's** greatest cinematic successes derived from his cross-dressing role in *Some Like it Hot*. In it, in the upper photo, he appears with **Tony Curtis** *(left, and also in drag)* and **Marilyn Monroe**.

In the lower photo—a poster for *Out to Sea* (1997), a comedy about ballroom dancing and romance on the high seas—Lemmon camps it up with **Walter Matthau**.

***

Because she had no other gigs on television, Lucille allowed herself to accept the role of a "visiting celebrity," someone qualified to comment on the life and distinguished career of the legendary director, Frank Capra. *[Born in 1897, he was in his late 80s during the filming of this tribute.]* She was to sit in the theater with other stars, make comments, and introduce clips from some of Capra's most classic films.

Functioning as the program's co-producer was Capra's son, Frank Capra Jr., President of EUE Screen Gems Studios in Wilmington, NC. Its director was Vincent Sherman. Since Lucille had nothing else to do except play backgammon, she set out to learn everything she could about both Sherman and Capra.

Her selection as someone who could (and would) comment on Capra came as a surprise even to her most dedicated fans. Lucille wasn't sure that Capra knew that he had directed her in the 1934 film, *Broadway Bill*. Her part (she portrayed a telephone operator) had been very tiny. The frontlining stars of that horse-racing movie were Warner Baxter and Myrna Loy. The plotline had remained a favorite of Capra's, and in 1950, he remade it, this time starring Bing Crosby.

Born in Sicily in 1897, Capra had immigrated to America when he was five years old, traveling with his family in "stinking steerage." During his rise to fame, he did a series of odd jobs such as processing the laundry of his fellow classmates during his university years, and cleaning the engines at the local power plant.

Somehow, he managed to get a college education and, after serving in the U.S. Army during World War II, he joined the film industry. After minor jobs, he was employed by producer Harry Cohn. In time, Capra wrote scripts for comedian Harry Langdon.

His first big job came at First National, where he helmed a budding starlet, Claudette Colbert, in *For the Love of Mike* (1927). The movie bombed.

Returning to Columbia, he worked his way up the ladder reel by reel. As time went by, he became ensconced as Cohn's most trusted director, making $25,000 a year. "I owed everything to Cohn," he later said.

Before filming began, Lucille told director Sherman, "I didn't owe Cohn all that much. I found him a lousy fuck."

Capra's big break came with his direction of *It Happened One Night* (1934), starring Clark Gable (who didn't want to do the picture), and, once again, Claudette Colbert. It became the first movie to win all five top Oscars—Best Picture, Best Director, Best Actor, Best Actress, and Best Adapted Screenplay. This "picaresque" movie was one of the earliest "road films," inspiring countless variations.

He followed that film with *Broadway Bill* (also 1934), a romantic screwball comedy about horse racing. That is where he directed Lucille, even if he didn't remember her.

He began to make films in which he tried to convey "fantasies of goodwill." The first of these was *Mr. Deeds Goes to Town* (1936), starring Gary Cooper and Jean Arthur. Capra won his second Best Director Oscar, although critic Alistair Cooke noted, "Capra is making movies about themes instead of people."

In 1938, Capra won a third Best Director Oscar for *You Can't Take It With You*,

Director **Frank Capra** helped Harry Cohn turn Columbia into a major studio. He was crucial in the crafting of some of the greatest films of Golden Age Hollywood, some of which have been credited with helping to define both the American Dream and The American Experience.

Since his heyday, "*Capra-esque*" has morphed into an oft-used adjective for the style he developed wherein "a little guy bucks the system."

which also carried home the Best Picture Oscar. Its stars were Jean Arthur and James Stewart.

Capra liked Stewart so much, he cast him in *Mr. Smith Goes to Washington* (1939), a film that expressed Capra's patriotism more than any other. He called it "a presentation of the individual working within the democratic system to overcome rampant political corruption."

Another controversial movie directed by Capra was *Meet John Doe* (1941) with Gary Cooper as a representative of the "common man."

After the war, Capra made his most celebrated movie, *It's a Wonderful Life* (1946) starring James Stewart. Once again, at first, the film failed at the box office, but in time, it became a classic, and is shown on TV every year.

As the years passed, and as he grew older, Capra became disenchanted with the film industry. In his 1971 autobiography, he wrote: "The winds of change blew through the dream factories of make-believe, tore at its crinoline tatters...The hedonists, the homosexuals, the hemophiliac bleeding hearts, the God-haters, the quick-buck artists who substituted shock for talent, all cried, *"Shake 'em! Rattle 'em! God is dead. Long live pleasure! Nudity? Yea! Wife-swapping? Yea! Liberate the world from prudery. Emancipate our films from morality! ...Kill for thrill—shock! Shock! To hell with the good in man. Dredge up his evil—shock! Shock!"*

Capra added that in his opinion, "Practically all the Hollywood filmmaking of today is stooping to cheap salacious pornography in a crazy bastardization of a great art to compete for the 'patronage' of deviates and masturbators."

***

The director of the Frank Capra tribute was Vincent Sherman. Lucille called him "one of the most fascinating men in Hollywood. Did he have stories to tell! He didn't spare anyone. Thank God I never got sexually involved with him. Otherwise, I bet I would have ended up in his tell-all memoirs."

For a little boy growing up in Vienna, Georgia, in the years before World War I, it's hard to imagine that he would end up directing and having affairs with some of the most legendary actresses of the silver screen.

Sherman became known as a "woman's director," a title he hated, pointing out that he'd also directed Errol Flynn, Humphrey Bogart, Richard Burton, and Paul Newman. In his crusty old age, he reflected, "Woman's director. That's bullshit. The last time I checked out their dicks, Errol, Bogie, Ronnie Reagan, that drunk, Richard Burton, and that Paul Newman boy with the baby blues were men."

Although at least by reputation, Southern gentlemen aren't supposed to kiss and tell—think Rhett Butler—Sherman did a lot of talking in both his memoirs (appropriately entitled *Studio Affairs*) and in interviews.

As he grew older, he adopted a "what-the-fuck" attitude and made additional, even more startling, revelations about Hollywood legends, going much farther than he did even within his "tell-all" memoirs.

You name the legend, and Sherman had plenty to say about the star.

Take, Humphrey Bogart for instance:

Sherman directed Bogie in such films as *The Return of Dr. X* (1939) and *All Through the Night* (1942). For the most part, these two strong egos got along well together.

"I really got to know Bogie when I directed *Crime School* (1938), in which he appeared with the Dead End Kids. Maybe the casting of Bogie as a do-gooder instead of as a villain was a mistake. The guy was not like his screen persona. He was not a swaggering macho—in fact, I think he was a coward. He was the kind of guy who would run from a fight."

"Because of that lisp, many people at Warners, but not me, thought he was a faggot. He wasn't. In fact, he was a ladies' man and had seduced many of the leading lights of Hollywood, including Joan Crawford, Bette Davis, Jean Harlow, and Barbara Stanwyck. Of course, he'd had his cock sucked a few times by a guy, I'm sure. But that could be said about nearly any actor in Hollywood. Getting your cock sucked comes with the business."

Near the end of his life, director **Vincent Sherman** wrote a kiss-and-tell autobiography. During his direction of *Old Acquaintance* (1943), Jack Warner became so impressed with his work that he decided to make Sherman "a woman's director—our answer to that faggot, George Cukor over at MGM."

"My most difficult star to direct," Sherman continued, "wasn't Bogie, nor even Ida Lupino, who wanted to take over the direction herself," Sherman said. "It was Miss Bette Davis. When we shot *Old Acquaintance* at Warner's, a picture released in 1943, I had not only to direct her, but act as referee between her and Miriam Hopkins. I was once told that Hopkins had lesbian designs on Davis and was bitterly rejected. Could that have been the cause of such animosity?"

At the end of the shoot, Davis, while having a hamburger with Sherman, told him she loved him. Stunned, Sherman claimed he was flattered.

At the time of this confession, Davis was married to her second spouse, Arthur Farnesworth, and Sherman was married to his long-devoted wife, Hedda. Although she knew about his many extramarital adventures, she obviously tolerated his dalliances. She remained with her errant husband for fifty-three years until her death in 1984.

Old Acquaintance co-starred two ferocious rivals, **Bette Davis** (*left*) and **Miriam Hopkins**, who hated each other and behaved spitefully throughout the shoot. Sherman, then aged 37, sustained a torrid affair with the 35-year-old-and-married Davis.

Later, he had an affair with yet another Davis rival, Joan Crawford. "It was very difficult to resist their charms, even though I was married."

Before the start of their next picture together, *Mr. Skeffington*, Sherman heard over the radio that Davis's husband, "Farney," had died, apparently of a brain hemorrhage he'd suffered while walking down Hollywood Boulevard. The report claimed that the hemorrhage may have come from an accidental fall he suffered that summer at the home he shared with Davis in New Hampshire.

When Sherman agreed to direct Errol Flynn in *The Adventures of Don Juan*, a film eventually released in 1948, Flynn was still Warner Brothers' biggest moneymaker. His star, however, was starting to flicker and die.

Alcohol, beautiful women—and sometimes teenage boys—had taken their toll on his once-fabulous face and physique. The script by George Oppenheimer was a bit too Walt Disney for Sherman's taste. Some of the brass agreed with the director. "In a Flynn film, he's got to be either fighting or fucking on the screen," Jack Warner told him. Other writers were called in "to toughen up" the Oppenheimer script.

On the first day of shooting, Sherman encountered trouble with Flynn in the wardrobe department. The costume department had designed jackets for the star that fell to a point three inches below his crotch line. Flynn did not like them, wanting the hems raised so that at least half of his crotch was exposed to view.

Sherman was leery about showing Flynn's celebrated endowment on screen. He suggested that he follow the custom of ballet dancers. "Pull your thing up and put a piece of tape across it, then put on either a jock strap or the cod piece."

"My dear, boy," Flynn said. "I've done many things for Warners over the years, but I'm damned if I'll tape up my cock for them."

The Hasty Heart, released on December 2, 1949, was directed by Vincent Sherman and starred Ronald Reagan, Patricia Neal, and the British actor, Richard Todd, a newcomer to the screen.

Although Sherman had known Reagan for a number of years, he became much better acquainted with him in London during the shooting of *The Hasty Heart*. "He was still heartbroken over his recent divorce from the Oscar-winning actress Jane Wyman," Sherman said.

Reagan admitted that he knew of Wyman's affair with her co-star Lew Ayres, during the filming of *Johnny Belinda* (1948), in which she played a deaf mute who is raped.

"I can overlook an affair here and there," Reagan said. "She's been very tolerant of me when I get *Leadingladyitis*. I'd heard

Errol Flynn, protecting his famous crotch in *The Adventures of Don Juan* (1948), directed by Vincent Sherman.

"I was just a goddamn phallic symbol to the world," the swashbuckler claimed.

about Lew and Jane. She very much needs to have a fling, and I intend to let her have it. If she'd stayed with me, we could have worked things out. I'm sure of that."

"Reagan told me he was stalking her, and that often, he'd park his car across the street from where she lived," Sherman said. "Sometimes, according to him, he'd wait in his car until two or three o'clock in the morning to see who she was bringing home.

When Vincent Sherman met Joan Crawford, he swore to himself that he would not get involved sexually with her the way he had with her rival, Bette Davis. Also, by his own admission, he wasn't that turned on by her. With a director's steely sharp eye, he noted, "there were lines in her face, crow's feet around her eyes, and her neck was beginning to show wrinkles."

Crawford, however, had other plans: She invited him to a screening of her 1946 movie, *Humoresque*, in which she'd co-starred with John Garfield.

"Midway through the movie, when I complimented her on a very sexy scene, she took my hand, held it against her breast, and soon followed it by placing her other hand on my knee and moving it up my leg. I was stunned but aroused."

Before he knew what was happening, she had pulled off her clothes, including a pair of red silk panties, and demanded that he take her on the carpeted floor of the projection room. "I confronted a female who went after what she wanted and was very masculine in her approach to sex."

When he seduced her again days later in the shower of her luxurious home, she told him, "The ideal wife is a lady in the living room but a whore in bed."

Rita Hayworth, screen goddess of the 1940s, was nervous facing the camera again after a long absence. But Columbia's primary honcho, Harry Cohn, who had constantly pursued her for sexual favors, convinced her he had a great property lined up for her.

The picture, which was released in the autumn of 1952, came to be

Ronald Reagan in this photo still from a late-night NBC rerun of *The Hasty Heart*.

During its filming in England, his co-star, Patricia Neal, offered him what comfort she could. He was trying to get over having been dumped by his first wife, Jane Wyman.

No one thought at the time that one day, he'd rule the Free World—least of all **Jane Wyman**, dressed here as a "snow bunny" with the actor she'd marry, **Ronald Reagan**, eventually the 40th President of the United States.

called *Affair in Trinidad*. Hayworth's return to the screen after three years caused worldwide anticipation, even though the actual movie didn't merit such press fascination.

The director she'd been assigned was Vincent Sherman. Her co-star was her former lover, Glenn Ford, who had created box office magic with her in *Gilda*. Cohn assured her that *Affair in Trinidad* would be greater box office than *Gilda* (1946), although after reading its script, she wasn't convinced.

She'd been a Princess during her ill-fated marriage to a real-life Muslim prince, the Aly Khan, but at this point in her life, their relationship was over. "I think he started fucking other women during our honeymoon," she later confessed to her former husband, Orson Welles, during their reunion.

Princess Rita had danced onscreen with both Fred Astaire and Gene Kelly. She'd had affairs with everyone from Howard Hughes to Victor Mature, from Robert Mitchum to Tyrone Power.

Vincent Sherman, in a "professional looking" stance with **Joan Crawford**.

It did not take long for him to be added to her long list of lovers. They stretched from Clark Gable to John F. Kennedy.

Vincent Sherman, flirting with **Rita Hayworth** in the era he was lowering her down onto a casting couch during the filming of the suggestively titled *Affair in Trinidad* (1952).

***

Once again, Lucille performed in a Television Special with Bob Hope. "We've been seen together so many times," she told him, "that people are beginning to talk."

"Don't worry about that," he answered. "No one will believe that I can get it up anymore. After all, I came into the world kicking and screaming in 1903, when Theodore Roosevelt was President."

In their latest telecast on February 28, 1982, the title was *Bob Hope's Women I Love—Beautiful but Funny*. For the most part, the show used film clips, some of which depicted Lucille and Hope during some of their many previous appearances on television.

Kip Walton, its director, had all the Hope/Ball feature films screened for him in advance of recycling any of the clips that might be pertinent—*Sorrowful Jones* (1949); *Fancy Pants* (1950); *The Facts of Life* (1960); *Critic's Choice* (1968); and *A Guide for the Married Man* (1967).

The night after the filming, Lucille met privately with Hope to discuss a business matter he'd proposed: Lucille Ball Productions would compile a trio of documentaries—each a 60-minute telecast—focusing on himself, Frank Sinatra, and Sammy Davis Jr.

Sinatra had already bowed out, not wanting his personal life to be inspected so closely. Hope, as he revealed that night, also didn't want his private life revealed. He preferred his series to concentrate on his razzmatazz public *persona*, especially anything associated with his entertaining of troops in wartime.

He told her he'd been under constant fire from the Soviet newspaper *Izvestia*. Russia's attempt to smear his reputation first appeared in the *Hollywood Citizen News* under the headline of REDS SAY HOPE TAKES NAKED GIRLS TO GIs.

Izvestia accused Hope of being "a Pentagon clown," and "a salesman for a dirty war."

In Moscow, a Soviet reporter claimed, "Hope's official reason for going to Vietnam was not to raise the morale of American troops. His actual purpose was to supply half-naked girls to the soldiers trapped in a hopeless war of aggression on the part of the United States. Hope is a comedian without principles."

The next day, after an intense talk with Gary Morton, Lucille decided to abandon the three-part series proposed by Hope.

A comedian himself Morton was no great admirer of Hope. "He is totally dependent on his staff writers, and he never rehearses. Instead, he reads all of his lines from cue cards His comedy is *passé*. It hasn't worked since back in 1942."

"Okay," she answered. "You've convinced me. That leaves only Sammy Davis Jr."

Then she skimmed through the research her staff had compiled on Hope. In 1970, an article by Mort Lachman, one of his former scriptwriters had appeared in the magazine of *The New York* Times. Lachman spoke candidly about Hope's limitation as a comedian: "He can't do faces or pantomime like his frequent co-star, Lucille Ball. He's the worst dialect stand-up comedian I've ever heard."

Phyllis Diller disagreed. "Lachman was wrong about Hope and dialects. He was brilliant at two dialects, fag and Negro. Only thing was, he didn't dare do either of those before an audience."

To Lucille's amazement, she learned that Spiro Agnew, Richard Nixon's disgraced vice president, sometimes supplied Hope with off-color jokes.

Hope's favorite of the Agnew jokes has him saying, "I used to play a little football, but I had to quit because I was ticklish. I played center, and I kept giggling when the studly quarterback put his ever-so-manly hands between my legs."

***

"John Ritter is a delight both as a man and as a comedian," Lucille said. The actor's co-star, Don Knotts, called this son of Burbank, "The greatest physical comedian on the planet."

Lucille tried to catch every episode of *Three's Company* (1974-1984) that she could.

Ritter became a household name portraying a struggling culinary student, Jack Tripper, living (non-sexually) with two female roommates. Originally, his character had appeared in the series with Joyce DeWitt and Suzanne Sommers. Their roles were later reassigned to Jenilee Harrison and Priscilla Barnes

Ritter pretends to be gay as a means of appeasing his old-fashioned landlord, originally cast with Norman Fell and later with Don Knotts.

The farce, based on the British sitcom, *Man About the House,* chronicles the trio's constant misunderstandings, social lives, and financial struggles.

Long ago, at a Hollywood party, Lucille had met John's father, Texas-born Tex Ritter, the singing cowboy and star of seventy movies. He had attracted attention for his rendition of "The Ballad of High Noon," which was heard during the opening credits of the classic Western, *High Noon* (1952), starring Gary Cooper and Grace Kelly.

Lucille was the host of *The Best of Three's Company,* a 90-minute event telecast on May 18, 1982. John Ritter was her co-star. Together, as it was broadcast to millions, they viewed a clip-loaded retrospective of the popular TV sitcom.

At the end of the show, Ritter planted a passionate kiss on her cheek.

She later told director Bill Hobin, "The kiss was disappointing. I had licked my lips, getting geared up for a sloppy wet one. He got my cheek instead of my luscious, overly painted lips."

Joyce DeWitt, John Ritter, and **Suzanne Somers** in a hit sitcom that Lucille never wanted to miss—"Not one episode."

***

One night from her bedroom, Lucille placed an urgent call to Gary Morton, who was working late and still in his office at Lucille Ball Productions.

"The shit has hit the fan," she told him in a very distressed voice. "I just learned from a friend of Lucie's that she's pregnant. That means I'm gonna be a grandmother—that is, if son Desi hasn't already made me so. Just think...*ME*, a grandmother! ME, the youngest person who ever lived."

CHAPTER SIXTEEN

LUCILLE GETS NOSTALGIC AND PATRIOTIC

(AGAIN AND AGAIN AND AGAIN)

WITH BOB HOPE

Bravely, They Morph Into Predictable, "Past Their Expiration Date" Television Fixtures & Icons of The American Century

Relics of "The Greatest Generation"

Because Lucille was one of the richest women in Hollywood, she felt that her daughter, Lucie Arnaz, might fall prey to a fortune hunter. At the time, she was dating Gary Pudney, a TV executive. One afternoon, Lucille met with him and offered him $3 million if he'd ditch Lucie. In response, he told her, "I'll marry your daughter for $3 million, or I will NOT marry her for #3 million—your choice."

Lucie herself dropped Pudney when she fell in love with, and would eventually marry, a fellow actor, Laurence Luckinbill.

Lucille had feared that Lucie might take up with some handsome stud, but Luckinbill was not exactly possessed with that kind of charm, and he was seventeen years older than she was. Whereas he had been born in Fort Smith, Arkansas, in 1934, Lucie had entered the world in Hollywood in 1951.

In time, Lucille would come to view him as both a mentor and husband to her daughter.

Lucie and Luckinbill first met on Broadway when both of them were performing in Neil Simon plays. She was appearing in *They're Playing Our Song,* the Neil Simon-Martin Hamlisch musical. A local critic claimed, "She has inherited the incomparable comic timing of her parents."

Luckinbill was also appearing nearby in another Neil Simon production, the autobiographical comedy, *Chapter Two.*

They were introduced at Joe Allen's, a restaurant in the theater district which was heavily patronized by actors. From that first night, they began to date.

From 1965 to 1976, he had been married to actress Robin Straser, with whom he had two sons, Nicholas and Benjamin.

Lucille had investigated Linda Purl before her son married her. Likewise, she set out to learn what she could about Luckinbill, this older actor her daughter was marrying. As it turned out, he was not only an actor, but in time, he became a playwright and director.

He'd made his film debut playing Hank in *The Boys in the Band* (1970). This was a landmark film, among the first motion pictures to revolve around gay characters. It became a milestone in the history of LGBT drama and was the first mainstream American movie to use the swear word, "cunt."

In a screenplay by Mart Crowley, *The Boys in the Band* starred Kenneth Nelson. A gay man himself, he had first achieved success in 1960 in the off-Broadway show, *The Fantasticks,* which became the world's longest-running musical with 17,162 performances.

The marriage took place on June 22, 1980 at the estate of Don Farber, Luckinbill's attorney, near the town of Kingston in New York State. Supreme Court Justice Aaron Klein officiated. The ceremony marked the last gathering of the Arnaz clan.

Luckinbill wrote his own marriage vows, saying, "I cherish you more than I can ever put into words." Following the ceremony, a lavish buffet was presented outdoors under the apple trees.

At the reception, a local Kingston reporter asked Desi Sr. his thoughts about giving away his daughter in marriage for the second time.

"It feels just great," he answered. "I'll keep giving her away in future marriages until she finds Mr. Right and settles down for the rest of her life, having my grandchildren."

At the wedding, he had sung, "Forever Darling," the title song of the feature film in which he had starred with Lucille for a 1956 MGM release. It had flopped at the box office, but the song remained a sentimental favorite of Lucille. It had been the last time the couple would co-star in a film. At the end of the song, Lucille, with tears in her eyes, approached Desi Sr. to hug and kiss him.

Instead of having a honeymoon, the newly married Luckinbills went

Press photo from 1991: **Lucie Arnaz** and **Laurence Luckinbill**.

She seemed determined to make her second marriage to this older actor work. In time, the Luckinbills would give Lucille and Desi three grandchildren.

With Gary Morton, Lucille bought a condo in Manhattan as a means of being closer to Lucie's ever-growing family.

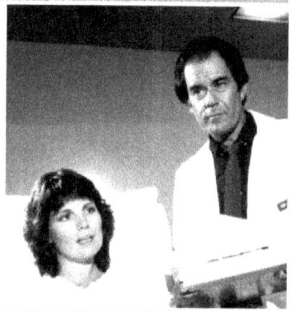

Here's a commemorative photo of a rehearsal of **Lucie** and **Laurence** for the Broadway production of *Whose Life Is It Anyway?* To show their diversity and stagecraft, they'd sometimes switch roles.

Lucille was pleasantly surprised to find that her new son-in-law was a talented actor on his own.

on a nationwide tour with a play entitled *Whose Life Is It, Anyway?* The stage version had premiered in 1978 at the Memorial Theatre in London and opened the following year on Broadway.

The subject was euthanasia. The action revolves around Ken Harrison, a sculptor who is paralyzed from the neck down, the result of a car accident. He is determined to be allowed to die. The argument is advanced that the government should not be allowed to interfere in the life (or attempt to end it) of a private citizen. In this case, Harrison wants to depart from his "useless body."

In their wildest imagination, Lucie and Luckinbill could only dream that they might become an acting team, perhaps the Alfred Lunt and Lynn Fontanne of the 1980s. To show their versatility, they sometimes alternated the roles, with Lucie playing the paralyzed patient,

As her pregnancy advanced, Lucie gave birth to Simon in December of 1980. Instead of being called Grandma, Lucille told her daughter that "Simon—or any children in your future—will be allowed to refer to me as 'Nana.'"

After Simon, Lucie gave birth to two more children, Joseph and Katharine.

Neil Diamond and **Lucie** in this publicity photo for *The Jazz Singer*.

The remake of Al Jolson's first "talkie" marked the acting debut of Diamond. Lucie's talent was recognized when she was nominated for a Golden Globe.

***

Not that fond of California, Lucie and Luckinbill settled into an apartment on Central Park West in Manhattan. Lucille, so that she could visit her growing family on a regular basis, had Gary Morton rent them a more fashionable residence on the east side of Central Park, where they lived in luxury.

In a period of his late life when he shouldered many "non-typical" acting parts, here's **(Lord) Laurence Olivier** playing a rabbi in Neil Diamond's (and Lucie Arnaz's) *The Jazz Singer*.

In November of 1981, Morton and Lucille were in Manhattan to celebrate a milestone, the 20th anniversary of her second marriage.

Morton told the press, "I have now been married to Miss Ball longer than that Cuban bongo player—you know...what's his name? I can never remember it. I've always referred to him as my husband-in-law, although we've never tricked."

In the early 1980s, Lucie still harbored a dream of movie stardom.

For a 1980 release, she co-starred with Neil Diamond and the great

Laurence Olivier in a remake of *The Jazz Singer*. Diamond made his acting debut in this classic, and Olivier signed on for $1 million, playing Cantor Rabinovitch for a shoot lasting ten weeks.

Of course, *The Jazz Singer*, as a pioneering "talkie" starring Al Jolson, had first been released as a film in 1927.

For the most part, the remake garnered negative reviews. And it made $27 million, having been filmed for $13 million. A critic for *The Chicago Tribune* wrote, "What the daughter of Lucy and Desi does so well is to perform quietly but confidently as Diamond and Olivier chew the scenery."

Lucie showed that she could be both a song-and-dance performer and a dramatic actress.

She demonstrated her emerging skill in the play *Second Thoughts* in which she is wooed by two very different men. In this curious love triangle, she is also impregnated. But can the audience really be sure which suitor is the father?

Lucie earned a nomination for a Golden Globe Award as Best Supporting Actress in a Motion Picture.

She followed with another film, *Second Thoughts* (1983), in which her co-stars were Craig Wasson and Ken Howard. As a lawyer, Amy (Lucie) finds herself romantically pursued by two very different men—her client, Will Wasson, a roguish street musician, and her old boyfriend John Michael (Howard). A curious triangle unfolds as Amy becomes pregnant by Will, but both men vie for her love.

Lucie chose to commit to this film instead of *Poltergeist* (1982), based on the belief that *Second Thoughts* offered a greater acting opportunity.

In addition to her overscheduled life as a wife and a mother, Lucie in 1986 agreed to tour with Tommy Tune in the national company of the musical *My One and Only* in 1986. *[For her performance, she won a Sarah Siddons Award.]*

With music and lyrics by George and Ira Gershwin, the plot, set in 1927, revolves around Captain Billy Buck Chandler, a barnstorming aviator, and Edith Herbert, an ex-swimmer known for swimming across the English Channel. All the tours had starred Tune, first with Sandy Duncan at the Kennedy Center in March of 1985. The tour also included six weeks in Japan. Lucie replaced Duncan on this tour.

My One and Only had opened on Broadway in May of 1983 and had run for 767 performances, featuring such songs as "Funny Face," "Strike Up the Band," and "How Long Has This Been Going On?"

Luckinbill also carved out a career for himself in his one-man shows based on the lives of former President Theodore Roosevelt, author Ernest

Hemingway, and the famous defense attorney, Clarence Darrow.

He also did a show based on President Lyndon B. Johnson. Lady Bird attended one night and came backstage to greet him. "Lyndon lives again!" she proclaimed.

Luckinbill was seen by far larger audiences when he starred as Spock's half-brother, Sybok, in the film *Star Trek V: The Final Frontier.*

Laurence Luckinbill portraying former U.S. President **Lyndon Baines Johnson** in the underpublicized TV drama, *Lyndon.*

Released in 1987, 18 years after LBJ's presidency and 14 years after his death, it was forceful, empathetic, emotional, and well-executed, a one-man show that should have been better and more widely known. Some viewers of the latter-day taped version attributed the public's aversion to LBJ as the only reason more people didn't see it.

***

In September of 1981, Lucille and Gary Morton signed a two-year contract with 20th Century Fox to develop sitcoms and feature films for television. From this new deal emerged a movie, *All the Right Moves,* set for a 1983 release, starring a handsome and emerging young actor, Tom Cruise, who was a bit short for a leading man. The movie was shot on location in Pennsylvania.

Morton was named executive producer, and Lucille read the script by Michael Kane, making several suggestions.

Cruise played Stefan Djordjevic, a Serbian-American high school student defensive back gifted in football. He wants to escape from his depressed small town and his dead-end job of working at the mill. His dream is to become an engineer.

At the time, both Morton and Lucille could not have possibly imagined that Cruise, though he appeared to have talent as an actor, would go on to become one of the highest-paid actors in the world. In time, his movies would gross more than $4 billion in North America and more than $10 billion worldwide.

With a budget of $5.6 million, *All the Right Moves* took in more than $17 million at the box office. Lucille devoured all the reviews, *The New York Times* defining it as "a well-made film but a sugar-coated working class fable about a football star."

TV Guide labeled it "cliché riddled" and attacked director Michael Chapman for not taking more risks.

After his involvement in the football-themed movie, *All the Right Moves,* **Tom Cruise** headed down the road to a fabled career in films.

"Boy, did Gary Morton and I miss out on the chance of a lifetime," Lucille said, ruefully. "We should have signed a long-term management contract with this boy wonder."

Richard Corliss of *Time* magazine called it "a naïve little movie that hopes to prove itself as the *Flashdance* of football."

That same year, Cruise, outside the orbit of Morton, had a breakthrough role in comedy, starring in *Risky Business* (1983). One of its highlights involved Cruise dancing in his jockey shorts, a scene later satirized on *Saturday Night Live* by Ron Reagan Jr. In 1986, *Top Gun,* an action drama, was released, and Cruise, after successfully jockeying his fighter plane through difficult landings on an aircraft carrier and a romance with Kelly McGillis (playing an attractive astrophysicist), was on his way to almost undreamed-of stardom.

***

Even though she had no more clout from studio executives maneuvering their ways through new feature films, Lucille still received scripts daily from hopeful writers. Most of them wanted her to finance and star in their offerings. Nearly all of them were rejected by Morton.

Tiring of daily backgammon, and with a limited number of upcoming television gigs, she learned from promoters that she'd be a big office draw if she toured America in a play. Her friend, Van Johnson, was thriving in dinner theater. More and more frequently, Morton assured her, "In towns and cities across America, people will shell out good money to see Lucy Ricardo in the flesh."

She had seen *The Solid Gold Cadillac* when it opened on Broadway in 1953 but was more impressed when she and Morton attended the 1956 film version starring Judy Holliday. [*Lucille had long envied Holliday for her brilliant success as a "kinda dumb and kinda smart" gun moll in* Born Yesterday *(1950), too.*]

Cadillac—a denunciation of big business and corrupt businessmen—had been crafted by writers who included George S. Kaufman. In it, Paul Douglas had been Holliday's co-star. One nail-chewing night, Lucille suggested that in the reprise she was toying with launching, Morton himself would be ideal as the character Douglas had developed (Edward I. McKeaver), opposite the character—to be portrayed by Lucille— of Laura Partridge.

Holliday was born in 1922, and therefore younger than Lucille by almost a decade. But in the original Broadway production, character actress Josephine Hull, then in her seventies, like Lucille, had played the role brilliantly to good notices. One review claimed, "Miss Hull knocks the role completely dead."

In the white heat of her early enthusi-

Judy Holliday appears above in a detail from a poster advertising a movie many viewers back in 1956 found both satirical and endearing.

Had Lucille opted to replicate Holliday's character as a vehicle for "Lucy," it would have been, her frenemies said, a hard act to follow.

asm, Lucille believed that she, too, would "knock 'em dead," but after thinking about it for five weeks, she dropped all plans for it, deciding that her fading energy and health would not sustain such a grueling cross-country tour.

Nevertheless, she continued demanding scriptwriters to develop an even more strenuous role for her: This time, a portrayal of the indomitable stage actress, Tallulah Bankhead. As she told Morton as part of a justification for her idea, "I already have Tallu's deep *basso* voice."

[Bankhead had died in 1968. Fear, therefore, of a libel suit was no longer an issue.]

In whatever script they might be able to devise, Lucille wanted the playwrights to include some of Bankhead's quotes, some of which were spectacularly off-color. Examples included: "*Cocaine is habit forming. I should know. I've been using it for years,*" and "*My father in Alabama warned me about men and booze when I headed off to New York. But he never mentioned anything about women and cocaine.*"

Lucille was then presented with a list of Bankhead's pansexual conquests, and told to "cherry pick" which of them should be included in the script. "Otherwise," Morton said, "the play would begin on a Saturday night and not end until Monday afternoon."

The "Tallulah Tales" that Lucille found particularly controversial was her affair with Hattie McDaniel, the first African American to win an Oscar—in this case, for her performance as Mammy in *Gone With the Wind*.

Among others of Tallulah's lovers considered for scenes inserted into Lucille's movie were John Barrymore, Marlon Brando, Gary Cooper, and Katharine Cornell. Johnny Weissmuller, ("Me, Tarzan") was particularly controversial, as was Sir Winston Churchill.

"Of course, Tallu was known for pulling off all her clothes at parties and doing cartwheels," Lucille said. "But at my age, and with my figure, we can have none of that."

There was one scene from Bankhead's life that particularly fasci-

Upper photo: **Lucille** (*left*) confronts the formidable **Tallulah Bankhead** in a 1957 episode of *I Love Lucy* entitled "*The Celebrity Next Door.*"

In the lower photo, Lucille (*right*) gets grand, failing to impress Tallulah (*left figure*) and infuriating Ethel (**Vivian Vance**) Mertz, who has been unwillingly pressed into service as a table maid.

Some viewers remember it as one of the very best episodes of any Lucy episode ever filmed.

After Tallulah's death, Lucille toyed with, but rejected, the idea of impersonating her in a stage drama based on her life.

nated Lucille, but she knew she couldn't emulate it on celluloid. Otherwise, she'd have depicted herself with the Prince of Wales doing a far-from-decorous Apache dance.

After a few months of debating the project's virtues and commercial potential, it was Gary Morton who nixed it with the justification that "public reaction in the hinterlands to Lucy Ricardo doing all these 'disgusting things' would set off a backlash, eventually damaging viewership of *I Love Lucy* reruns."

"Tallu bit the dust," Lucille finally said.

For her upcoming television season (1982-1983), that left a very limited repertoire consisting of only a few guest appearances, two of which would be with "old ski nose," Bob Hope.

***

Lucille launched her 1982-1983 season by appearing in a 90-minute telecast of *The Merv Griffin Show*. It was designed as a salute to the great Broadway stage star, Ethel Merman, then in the final months of her life. Two old (by now, some detractors said "ancient") friends of "The Belter," Ginger Rogers and Lucille, were to appear as surprise guests.

Gay and closeted, Griffin was the star of *The Merv Griffin Show*. Launched in 1962, it lasted, in various formats, until 1986. During its decades-long run, more than 25,000 guests were interviewed, including four Presidents [Nixon, Ford, Carter, and Reagan] and other celebrities who included Martin Luther King Jr., John Wayne, Judy Garland, Doris Day, Sophia Loren, Clint Eastwood, and Grace Kelly.

Trumpeter Jack Sheldon, a regular on Griffin's show, later said, "I was awed to be on the set with Miss Merman, Miss Ball, and Miss Rogers, each a show biz legend. When I wasn't appearing as Merv's sidekick, I did such gigs as the voice of 'Louis the Lightning Bug" in a series of animated public service announcements aimed at kids in the 1980s," Sheldon said. "Of all my songs, Lucille's favorite was 'The Shadow of Your Smile." That song brought an Oscar when it was

HEEEERE'S MERV!

An Irish-American from California, **Merv Griffin** evolved into TV's most powerful and richest mogul, earning 17 Emmy Awards for his *Merv Griffin Show*, a durable staple which attracted 20 million viewers daily.

He developed a reputation for interviewing "everybody who mattered" in contemporary American life, including Lucille Ball. He broke social barriers and aired interviews wih everyone from Martin Luther King Jr. (his first major TV appearance) to Joan Crawford (one of her last), to Lucille Ball. He also brought on drag queens, revolutionaries, gay activists, and "fringe elements" of the society in ways which at the time were considered radical.

Referring to whom he had interviewed during his long career, Merv, with his trademark merriness, said, "The only person who ever eluded me was The Pope."

introduced in *The Sandpiper* (1965), the movie that starred Elizabeth Taylor and Richard Burton. Liz loved it, Dick hated it."

"It was great working with 'The Merm,'" Sheldon continued. "I had followed her career for years. She was a chunky, aggressive stage star with a clarion voice, a brash personality, a shrewd comic sense, and steel nerves. Just ask Irving Berlin, Cole Porter, Jule Stein, or George Gershwin."

In 1966, Lucille had gone to see Merman in a revival of her former hit, *Annie Get Your Gun.* "Merm's voice was still powerful," Lucille said, "but it was a bit much seeing a woman turning sixty playing a lovestruck sharpshooter. Ethel told me that originally, Jerry Herman offered her the female lead in *Hello, Dolly!* But she turned it down, allowing Carole Channing to step in. But in 1970, Merman finally starred as Dolly Levi."

The appearance Merman made on Griffin's show in September of 1982 would be her last time on TV. She had undergone surgery for brain cancer. In 1984, at the age of 76, she would die.

After Merv's taping, Lucille joined Ginger Rogers and composer Jerry Herman for drinks. Ginger had taken over the Broadway role of Dolly Levi

THE MARCH OF TIME

Upper image shows **Ginger Rogers** interacting with **Douglas Fairbanks Jr**. in *Having a Wonderful Time* (1938) as a then-ingenue **Lucille Ball** looks on, hovering enviously as a "third wheel."

Lower image is a press photo from 1982. It promoted the reunion of **Ginger Rogers** (left), **Ethel Merman**, and **Lucille Ball**, each a senior citizen, after Merman received a Pied Piper Award.

in 1965, scoring a great popular success. Not only had Ginger starred in *Hello, Dolly!*, but she'd also appeared in Herman's *Mame*, in 1969. The movie role of *Mame* had gone to Lucille, and she offered Herman her apologies for turning it into such a disaster on the screen.

Herman told the two aging divas that he was working on a new show, *La Cage Aux Folles,* about a gay couple whose son is about to marry the daughter of a conservative politician. "I knew it's at the height of the AIDS epidemic, but it's my attempt to put gay life into the cultural mainstream at a time when many gay men are being stigmatized."

"It would be obvious even to a fool that anyone with a bloodstream can contract AIDS," Lucille said. "I heard that in Africa, babies are being born with it."

Ginger congratulated Lucille on the seeming success of her second marriage. "My final divorce—and it will be my last—came in 1969 to my fifth husband, producer William Marshall. He was a drunk who bankrupted our film company. I've had so many lovers: Fred Astaire being the worst, Howard Hughes strictly oral, George Montgomery the most proficient. But for the sweetest in bed, it was a tie: Jimmy Stewart or Desi Arnaz before you got him."

Lucille was saddened to learn in 1985 that Herman had been diagnosed as HIV-positive. "Jerry was a survivor, and he turned to experimental drug therapies and conquered the disease," Lucille said.

At the age of 88, the day after Christmas in 2019, Herman died in a Miami hospital.

Ginger herself would survive until 1995, dying at her home in Rancho Mirage, California, at the age of 83.

Griffin told the press, "Those old show biz broads—Merman, Ball, Rogers—are dying out. We'll never see the likes of them again."

***

After that appearance on *The Merv Griffin Show,* Lucille idled away most of the rest of 1982 until producer Paul W. Keyes tapped her as the host of *The All-Star Party for Carol Burnett,* telecast on December 12 on CBS for 120 minutes.

It would be a star-studded event peopled with performers she knew, at least casually, everyone from Bette Davis to Sammy Davis Jr. James Stewart and Burt Reynolds greeted Lucille, followed by the actress Glenda Jackson, Monty Hall, Jack Paar, and Beverly Sills.

Lucille arrived onstage on the arm of her longtime friend Carol Burnett, and was greeted by her "regulars," Vicki Lawrence, Tim Conway, and Harvey Korman.

The special was a retrospective of what had been hot on television in the year just passing. Lucille was asked to introduce clips from *I Love Lucy.* Of course, although that sitcom premiered in the 1950s, it had remained relentlessly popular in reruns in the year coming to an end, 1982.

James Stewart, also a guest, greeted Lucille with a passionate wet kiss. "That's to make up for not doing that back in 1939 when we double-dated," he said.

"Our dear friend Carole Lombard seemed to be satisfying all your needs at the time," she countered. "If you and I had made it, I'd be gal No. 264." She was referring to Stewart's claim that he had seduced 263 women in the 1930s.

"I just worked with Ginger Rogers," Lucille said. "She said you were very sweet in bed."

"I don't like that label," he said. "Sweet? Hell, I was a tiger. Just ask Marlene Dietrich, Grace Kelly, Lana Turner, or Loretta Young."

Between takes, when Lucille encountered Bette Davis, she got an icy reception,

"Dear girl," Davis said. "You made a foolish mistake in not casting me as Vera Charles in your movie, *Mame.* I could have saved that disaster."

"Granted," Lucille said, not wanting to break into hostilities. "That was just one of the many mistakes I've made in life."

"I, too, have made mistakes," Davis said. "One involved hitting my second husband, that innkeeper Arthur Farnsworth so hard over the head that it led to his death. Call it murder if you will."

This *All-Star Party* for Burnett was, indeed, structured, as the cameras rolled, like a black-tie celebrity-studded *fête*, in this case, a fund raiser for the Variety Clubs International. Its highlight involved Burnett singing, "I'm In Love with John Foster Dulles," which she had previously performed on *The Ed Sullivan Show*.

At the end of the telecast, Lucille threw a champagne party for the cast. She got to chat with her friend, Jim Nabors, and she complimented him on his amusing and frequent appearances on the Burnett Show.

He extended an invitation to her to take a vacation at his macadamia farm on Maui in the state of Hawaii. He told her he was very much in love with his new partner, Stan Cadwallader. "He was a fireman in Honolulu when I met him. I fell madly in love with him the first night we were together."

"I wish him luck in putting out your fire," she said.

Jim Nabors is shown here with a pre-teenaged **Ron Howard** during their "Gomer Pyle and Andy Griffith in Mayberry" era.

Most child stars fade into oblivion after they reach puberty. No so Howard. As he grew up, this red-headed, freckle-faced boy wonder became one of the most popular mainstream directors in America. Some films he helmed include *Splash* (1984) and *Cocoon* (1985).

Also appearing in the salute to Burnett was Jack Paar. In retirement, the former talk show host occasionally appeared as a guest on *The Tonight Show* with Johnny Carson and later with David Letterman.

"Are you still attacking gay men?" she asked. "Blaming them for the decline in the theater and in the movies?"

"I'm trying to convince all red-blooded men to rally to my new crusade to have girls look like girls again: If we show a strong determination, I'm sure that women will throw off the tyranny of fairy designers."

"Paar, I think you spend too much time labeling people as 'fags, dykes, and fairies.' Jonathan Winters, your former frequent guest, told me that you live deep in the closet." Then she turned her back on him and walked away.

Also at the "party," Lucille and Beverly Sills discussed their fondness for Dinah Shore and recalled appearing on television with her in October of 1977.

Burt Reynolds came over to Lucille, toasting her with a glass of champagne.

"Why didn't you marry my daughter, Lucie?" she asked him. "Wasn't she good enough for you?"

"She was too good for me," he said. "I'm not in her class."

"True, true," she said before kissing him on the mouth. "But if I'd been born in 1936, you'd now be looking at Mrs. Burt Reynolds."

Then Monty Hall, a Canadian American game show host, warmly greeted Lucille, expressing his admiration for her.

"It's you I admire," she said. "You took that hosting of *Let's Make a Deal* gig from one network to another. That game show seems to run forever. You and Alex Trebek are going to become immortal."

"Hosting a game show was better than going into my father's business. We're Jews but Dad, nonetheless, cuts off the heads of a lot of pigs to feed the Canadian love of pork."

At the Burnett show, Lucille "worked the room," greeting the other guest stars. Like most of Hollywood, she was awed by the sheer talent of Glenda Jackson, born in England to a maid and a carpenter, she had risen in fame and fortune and was the recipient of two Best Actress Oscars, one for *Women in Love* (1970), and another for *A Touch of Class* (1973). Lucille had preferred her in *Sunday, Bloody Sunday* (1971), in which she vied with Peter Finch for the love of a young man.

"The early 1970s was the busiest years of my life," Jackson told Lucille. "In addition to those Oscar winners, I did *The Music Lovers* (1970) with Richard Chamberlain cast as Tchaikovsky. In a nutshell, it was the saga of a homosexual who marries a nymphomaniac. For Queen Elizabeth I in that BBC serial, *Elizabeth R.*, I had to shave my head. Anything for my art."

"I've seen several of your films, and you were one beautiful woman," Jackson continued. "Not that you don't look 'handsomely well preserved' even today. I was never beautiful and as I age, I can only shudder at how future critics will describe me."

Jackson's fears were to some degree clairvoyant. *The New York Times* found her, with her helmet of hair and gashed features," akin to "a Cubist portrait of Louise Brooks." Other critics described her as "a Zelda Fitzgeraldesque neurotic," or "a rotting and spiteful middle-aged matron," even "a spent sphinx-like widow embracing extinction."

Jackson eventually distanced herself from the entertainment industry. Between 1992 and 2015, she threw herself into a career in British politics,

Starring **Monty Hall**, *Let's Make a Deal*, at its pinnacle, developed a cult following of 40 million devoted fans.

It became controversial, however, after scandals broke. The press revealed how far advertisers and network executives would go to achieve high ratings.

One former fan wrote, "The *exposé* of behind-the-scenes manipulations changed our relationship with daytime TV forever."

Contestants were faced with the option of either accepting a guaranteed cash prize or trading their winnings for the (unknown) contents of an offstage box. Sometimes it was an object of impressive value. Otherwise it was a worthless "zonk" prize.

getting elected as the Labour Party's MP from Hampstead and Highgate in North London. From 1997 to 1999, she was Tony Blair's Junior Transport Minister.

***

Sam Harris produced and directed *The Fourth Annual TV Guide Special,* telecast for 120 minutes on NBC on January 24, 1983.

It was a look back at the "TV Highlights of 1982." As such Lucille was asked once again to introduce film clips from *I Love Lucy.* In reruns that summer, her old sitcom had topped the charts.

With Bryant Gumble as host, it focused on stars who included Michael Landon, Carol Burnett, an aging George Burns, and Alan King. *Dynasty* had been the TV drama rage of 1982, so its stars, John Forsythe, Linda Evans, and Joan Collins were also honored guests.

Michael Landon had been included because of his star role in the hit TV show, *Little House on the Prairie* (1972-1982). He reminded Lucille of what she already knew—that he had appeared on the cover of *TV Guide* twenty-two times, a record topped only by her.

She was introduced to Bryant Gumbel, the television journalist and sportscaster. He'd broadcast numerous sporting events for NBC, including Major League Baseball games and gridiron battles among teams of the National Football League. When she met him, he was giving up sportscasting to spearhead *The Today Show.*

Lucille always enjoyed working with Burnett, who confessed, "I used to be so nervous about going on TV that I was near hysterical. My heart would beat faster whenever I heard the audience coming in to watch a live show. Butterflies danced in my stomach whenever the music began. Talk about stage fright. But that's all past now. I look in the mirror at myself and say, 'Kiddo, you've got it made.'"

Alan King was a Jewish comedian and satirist known for his biting wit and angry but humorous outbursts. He was often the opening act for such stars as Judy Garland, Nat King

Glenda Jackson (*appearing in both photos above*) never relied on her physical attributes to generate applause as an extraordinary actress. She had an exceptional talent for playing brainy, ferociously strong-willed women, many culled from the pages of English literature.

After a stint in British politics, where she served as a Member of Parliament, and after a 25-year absence from acting, she resumed her career in show-biz in the title role of *King Lear* in London's West End. The role won her her fifth Laurence Olivier Award nomination.

She later reprised the role on Broadway.

Cole, Patti Page, Billy Eckstine, Lena Horne, and Tony Martin. On occasion, he starred in feature films, most often as a gangster. When he appeared on *The Fourth Annual TV Guide Special,* he had just completed the film, *I, The Jury.*

Most viewers tuned in to see the trio of stars from *Dynasty:* Forsythe, Evans, and Collins.

Born in Brooklyn, Forsythe would enjoy a career that spanned six decades in both television and such feature films as *The Trouble with Harry* (1955) with Shirley MacLaine or *The Ambassador's Daughter* (1956) with Olivia de Havilland. For this moderately handsome, smooth-talking actor, his greatest fame came as a result of his stint as the patriarch, Blake Carrington in *Dynasty* (1981-1989).

Linda Evans had once been married to the 1950s heartthrob, John Derek (1968-1974), until he fell in love with seventeen-year-old Bo Derek and married her. In the 1960s, Evans played Andra Barkely, the daughter of Victoria Barkley (Barbara Stanwyck) in the Western television series, *The Big Valley* (1965-1969). Her greatest fame came when she was cast as Krystle Carrington in ABC's primetime "soaper," *Dynasty,* for its entire run. Her character was the wife of the millionaire oil tycoon.

The sexy British actress, Joan Collins, had been tapped to play Alexis Carrington, the ex-wife of the Forsythe character for the 1984-1985 season. She would help keep *Dynasty* number one, beating out its major competitor, *Dallas.*

Lucille had long been intrigued with Collins reputation and the gossip that swirled around her. Coming and going from her life were Warren Beatty, ("he wanted it day and night,") Harry Belafonte, Robert Wagner, Terence Stamp, Arthur Loew Jr., Dennis Hopper, Nicky Hilton, Marlon Brando, and producers George Englund and Roger Evans. *Vogue* magazine wrote: "Joan Collins displays her breasts on *Dynasty* as if bra-cup size

Bryant Gumble. the spectacularly outspoken (some said "outstandingly tactless") sportscaster and 15-year veteran co-host of NBC's *Today* Show.

In June of 2000, a CBS camera caught a disgusted Gumbel blurting out, "What a fucking idiot!"

He had just interviewed Richard Knight of the Family Research Council. Knight had defended the Boy Scouts' policy of excluding gays from becoming leaders.

Alan King in 1966, delivering a monologue about his pregnant wife on *The Ed Sullivan Show.*

Perhaps jokingly, King once said, "Lucy should have married me instead of that other stand-up comic, Gary Morton. I would be a much funnier opening act than Gary, with his stale humor of yesterday."

was a measure of personal magnificence."

Her sister, the novelist Jackie Collins, told the press: "Joan always lived her life like a man. If she saw a guy she wanted to go to bed with, she went after him, and that was unacceptable behavior at the time."

Collins told Lucille, "I've got a great body, and sometimes, if it's photographed right, it can look absolutely great."

Lucille found it amusing to chat with her. The sex symbol told her, "I can't make up my mind which title I prefer: 'The Most Beautiful Woman in the World,' or 'The World's Sexiest Woman.'"

***

Bob Hope was the executive producer of *Bob Hope's Road to Hollywood,* an NBC telecast of March 2, 1983. Lucille headed a list of stars that featured George Burns, Rosemary Clooney, Rhonda Fleming, Martha Raye, Jane Russell, Jill St. John, and Dorothy Lamour.

Beautiful and a native of New Orleans, Lamour had a special place in Bob Hope's heart because of all those "Road" movies she' made with him and Bing Crosby beginning with *Road to Singapore* in 1940.

During filming of the show, Lucille chatted with Hope about the movies they'd made together, remembering them to the audience but also privately gossiping about what went on off camera.

Both of them remembered *The Facts of Life* (1960) as a money-making classic. It had involved a middle-aged couple, bored with their spouses, who briefly consider having an adulterous affair.

He told her, "Too bad you and I didn't have that affair. You really missed out on something. I'm too old to cut the mustard now... well, almost. At any rate, adultery is very difficult, unless you're British."

Privately, and with nostalgia, Lucille and Hope recalled attending the New York premiere of the film they'd made together, *Sorrowful Jones* (1949), where they had stayed in separate accommodations at the Waldorf Astoria. He had brought along, she remembered, the blonde nymphomaniac, actress Barbara Payton.

Hope told Lucille that he preferred dignified sex more than he did "the

---

Survivors (and collusionists) of 1980s Hollywood's most celebrated on-screen feud: **Joan Collins** *(left)* and **Linda Evans**, chief combatants on *Dynasty.*

Exploring the oil-soaked corruption of Texas's most notorious (fictional) clan, it was the most-watched TV show in the nation by 1985. Lucille—no stranger to hit TV series and their politics—took note.

According to Collins in 2018, "Every single person on *Dynasty* was good-looking. You wanted to see rich, good-looking people fighting with each other."

In 2012, *The New York Times* credited Nolan Miller's costumes with "setting a trend for thick shoulder pads during a decade of power dressing". No one did that better than Joan Collins, with the possible exception, decades earlier, of Joan Crawford.

nasty kind" that Payton preferred. "So does Ingrid Bergman, Dorothy Lamour, Paulette Goddard, and Betty Hutton. Marilyn Maxwell is another slut in bed. If you don't believe that, ask Desi Arnaz, Senior, that is. I guess it could have been Junior. I hear he doesn't say no to older women."

Lucille considered the tragic saga of Barbara Payton worthy of a Hollywood film.

Payton, the blue-eyed, peroxide blonde sexpot, rose from a blue-collar background, emerging in Hollywood as a "drop dead gorgeous floozie" in a number of films. In addition to Hope, she also was known for seducing her leading men. They included Gary Cooper, her co-star in *Dallas* (1950) and Gregory Peck, who appeared with her in *Only the Valiant* (1951).

Caught up in the glitz and glamour of Tinseltown, Payton led a life of capricious romancs. She was briefly married to actor Franchot Tone, but soon returned to her much sexier and more muscular lover, actor Tom Neal.

In 1951, Neal attacked Tone in a deadly brawl that put Tone in the hospital with broken bones and a brain concussion.

As time went by, Payton sank deeper into the bottle. From 1955 to 1963, there were brushes with the law, including arrests for prostitution. In the end, she was forced to sleep on park benches. She was also beaten and bruised by her tricks, losing a lot of her front teeth in the process.

Novelist **Jackie Collins** and her sister, **Dame Joan Collins**, photographed by Terry O'Neill, as donated to the UK's National Portrait Gallery.

The novels of Jackie were dismissed by some critics as "romantic sleaze," and decades earlier, Joan had been irreverently nicknamed "The British Open" because of her multiple sexual conquests.

Nonetheless, today, both women are celebrated and on display at the National Portrait Gallery, alongside such crucial figures in British history as William the Conqueror

***

Before the end of spring—that is, on May 23, 1983, Lucille was asked by producer and director Don Mischer to be one of the guests on a 180-minute NBC telecast, *Happy Birthday: A Salute to Bob Hope's Eightieth Birthday.*

She was joined by George Burns, Phyllis Diller, Loretta Lynn, Barbara Mandrell, Tom Selleck, Brooke Shields, George C. Scott, and Flip Wilson. Hope's wife, Dolores, would appear to honor her husband, as would Kathryn Grant, the wife of the late Bing Crosby, who had died in 1977.

The "Ultra-VIP" guests of the evening were Ronald and Nancy Reagan, Hope's longtime friends. Their segment was taped in the White House.

Lucille still could not believe that Reagan had been elected President. Neither could much of Hollywood. Everywhere, Lucille went, she heard someone express an opinion about Reagan, particularly at parties she attended.

"His Presidency would never have happened if Hollywood had given him better parts," Lauren Bacall told her.

Richard Widmark said, "Of course, I never voted for Ronnie. I know him too well."

"I can't stand the sight of Ronald Reagan," said Gloria Grahame. "I'd like to stick my Oscar up his ass."

Jane Wyman, Reagan's former wife, warned Lucille, "Don't ask Ronnie what time it is, because he'll tell you how a watch is made. He's about as good in bed as he was on the screen."

Lucille thought Reagan's early reputation as a Hollywood horn-dog would work against him. "He was planning to marry Doris Day until he learned that Nancy was pregnant," Lucille claimed. "He did the honorable thing and married Nancy instead, although I don't think his heart was in it."

After Jane Wyman dumped him for Lew Ayres, her co-star in *Johnny Belinda,* Reagan proposed marriage to Adele Jergens, who at the time was appearing as the mother of Marilyn Monroe. Both of them had been cast as glamourous showgirls in *Ladies of the Chorus* (1948).

"Once Ronnie met Marilyn, he dumped Adele for her," Lucille claimed.

"His best friend at the time was my former beau, William Holden. Rumors persist on the Hollywood

TRAGIC HOLLYWOOD HOMAGE TO BARBARA PAYTON

By 1951, the career of **Barbara Payton** had sunk so low that she co-starred with **Lon Chaney** and **Raymond Burr** in the B-list horror film, *Bride of the Gorilla*. She also did a stint with Burr (*upper right-hand photo*) in an episode of his hit Perry Mason show on TV.

"I usually seduce my leading man:" she said. "but Burr was gay."

"Hoping to make a buck" (her words), Payton published her tell-all autobiography, entitling it *I Am Not Ashamed*. Perhaps she should have been. In May of 1967, she was found dead at the age of 39.

In 1981, during a remake of the Lana Turner classic, *The Postman Always Rings Twice* (1946), leading lady Jessica Lange read Payton's confessional. Somehow Lange found inspiration in what Payton had written, and used it to enhance her portrayal of Cora, the hard-luck, hard-bitten roadhouse waitress made famous by Lana in the original *film noir* from 1946.

grapevine that Ronnie and Bill had a three-way with Marilyn."

Reagan started early seducing his co-stars, including June Travis in *Secret Service of the Air* (1939). The list of actresses with whom he became sexually intimate is long: Penny Edwards, Susan Hayward, Evelyn Knight, Christine Larson, Piper Laurie, Monica Lewis, Doris Lilly, Jacqueline Park, Ruth Roman, Dorothy Shay, Ann Sothern, Kay Stewart, Peggy Stewart, Betty Underwood, and Selene Walters.

Lucille had known Nancy Davis in the 1940s when she was a starlet at MGM. She had the nickname, "The Fellatio Queen of Hollywood." Director George Cukor claimed, "If I had a nickel for every Jew Nancy was under, I'd be rich." Author Ann Edwards wrote, "Nancy was one of those girls whose phone number got passed around a lot."

Lucille said, "I heard she proposed marriage to Clark Gable. When he turned her down, she made a play for Reagan."

Just a tiny fraction of Davis's other lovers included Robert Walker, Peter Lawford, Yul Brynner, Spencer Tracy, Frank Sinatra, and Benjamin Thau, head of MGM casting.

Producer Pandro S. Berman, previously one of Lucille's lovers, told her, "Nancy just isn't star material."

According to Lucille, "Nancy overcompensated by nailing a better role than any of those other stars in Hollywood combined," Lucille said. "She became First Lady, the power behind the throne of Ronald Reagan."

***

In March of 1982, Desi Sr. flew to

After the release of *Johnny Belinda* (1945), **Jane Wyman** won an Oscar for her portrayal of a deaf-mute victim of a rape.

Here, she's seen with her leading man, **Lew Ayres**, the former husband of Ginger Rogers. Off screen, she fell madly in love with him.

To Wyman's horror, shortly after announcing to her then-husband, Ronald Reagan, that she wanted to divorce him and replace him with Ayres, Ayres dumped her.

Ronald Reagan made two pictures with **Doris Day:** *Storm Warning* (1951), a story about the Ku Klux Klan, and *The Winning Team* (1952), in which he played Grover Cleveland Alexander, one of the foremost legends of American baseball.

During filming of the baseball movie, Reagan fell in love with Day and proposed marriage. Unknown to her at the time, he was also dating starlet Nancy Davis on the side.

When Nancy told Reagan that she was pregnant, he did the honorable thing. He dropped Doris Day and married Nancy instead.

Miami, the city where he and his parents had forged a living during his teen years after they had fled from Cuba, where they had been rich, politically connected landowners, in the 1930s. "My early occupation in Florida was cleaning shit from canary cages," he remembered.

Now, half a lifetime later, he was the celebrated guest of honor at the Orange Bowl, where a "Carnival Festival" was being staged mainly for the city's enormous (and growing) Cuban population, many of whom had fled to Florida as refugees.

At sixty-five years old, and still recovering from minor surgery, Desi bounced out onto the stage as in olden days. A yelling, screaming crowd of some thirty thousand spectators roared its approval and welcome.

Soon, he was pounding a conga drum and singing "Babalu," followed by "Cumba, Cumba, Cumba, Cumbachero."

He was joined onstage by his children, Lucie and Desi Jr. Their lively number morphed into a nostalgia-soaked tribute to the legendary Tropicana Club in Havana once patronized by thousands of off-the-record *norteamericanos*, including Frank Sinatra.

Lucille had given her daughter, Lucie, the glittery Sally Sweet ("I'm the Girl from Delancy Street") costume she had worn during a duet with "Cuban Pete," a nickname used at the time for Desi Sr., and a reference to one of his hit songs.

Desi flew back to Los Angeles where an offer to appear in a feature film awaited him.

Francis Ford Coppola, who, a decade before, had helmed Marlon Brando in *The Godfather (1972)*, wanted Desi to accept a leading role in *The Escape Artist*, a 1982 movie starring Raul Juliá and Griffin O'Neal. The role Desi Sr. eventually accepted was that of a crooked politician Mayor Leon Quiñones.

Other stars included Teri Garr and Jackie Coogan.

The Escape Artist was the final film for both Desi and Joan Hackett. It marked the directorial debut of Caleb Deschanel, an American cinematographer who was later, during the course of his career, nominated six times for a Best Cinematography Award.

The cast also included Gabriel Dell and Huntz Hall, still remembered for playing

With their respective movie careers in steep decline, **Ronald Reagan** and **Nancy Davis** co-starred in *Hellcats of the Navy*, a 1956 release from Columbia. Critics defined it as "a jingoistic wartime potboiler."

In its final reel, he agrees to marry Nurse Nancy.

As she told director Nathan Juran, "It was easier to get Ronnie to propose to me on the screen than it was in real life."

493

the Dead End Kids in all those "street urchin" movies of the 1930s.

Young and self-confident, Danny Masters (Griffin O'Neal) is the son of the late Harry Masters, the greatest escape artist since Houdini. Danny himself is an accomplished magician and escape artist.

He soon finds himself embroiled with Stu Quiñones, the son of a corrupt mayor, Leon Quiñones (Desi Sr.) The quest for a missing wallet (pickpocketed by Danny) leads to the comeuppance of the crooked mayor and his vindictive and his out-of-control son (Juliá).

Desi met with the executive of Zoetrope Films and demanded that he be billed as "Desiderio Arnaz."

[His motivation for wanting himself billed with his full and formal name involved the hope that his son, Desi Jr., now in his thirties, would no longer have to relentlessly continue adding "Junior" as a suffix to the end of his name. Of course, for clarity, the news media didn't change any of their nomenclature, resulting in the fact that the Senior Arnaz continued to be referenced in many news outlets as "Desi Arnaz" until long after his death.]

Although *The Escape Artist* received fair reviews from fans and critics alike, it earned a pathetic $145,000 at the box office, and eventually contributed to the bankruptcy of Coppola's Zoetrope Company.

***

Lucille appeared only rarely on television throughout the course of 1984. Occasionally, she was spotted shopping in Beverly Hills. She later asserted that the questions she was most frequently asked from chance encounters with passers-by were:

"Did anyone ever tell you that you resemble Lucille Ball?"
"Didn't you used to be Lucille Ball?"

As she grew older, as many seniors do, she developed certain loudly pronounced eccentricities. One of them involved her refusal to drink water from California. Fearing that all water derived from there was polluted, she demanded that all the water she drank was to be shipped in from Florida.

Two views of **Desi Sr.**, each with **Raoul Julia**, in *The Escape Artist* (1982).

A box-office flop, it became Desi Sr.'s farewell film. Fans were shocked by his appearance.

"Ricky Ricardo," he said, "that cute, sexy Cuban, was a distant memory when I took this role. Seeing myself on the screen dramatized to me, as nothing else did, that I was ready to be turned out to the pasture, a race horse no more."

Gary Morton joked, "Lucille depends on these water shipments from Florida because she has discovered the Fountain of Youth there, something Ponce de Leon failed to do."

Her most publicly triumphant moment that year was her induction into *The Television Academy Hall of Fame*, a 120-minute ceremony that was telecast by NBC on March 4. 1984.

[John H. Mitchell, the former president of the Academy of Arts & Sciences, had founded the Television Hall of Fame with the intention of recognizing individuals who had made extraordinary contributions to the programming finesse of "the little black box." The event honoring Lucille and a half-dozen others (Milton Berle, Paddy Chayefsky, Norman Lear, Edward R. Murrow, William S. Paley, and David Sarnoff) marked the first of the many annual award ceremonies to come.]

After Carol Burnett introduced Lucille, Desi Jr. performed a live salute to his mother. In contrast, Lucie Arnaz, who was appearing at the time in a Broadway show—the aptly named *Your Mother the Star*—had videotaped a musical salute to "dear ol' mom" and arranged for it to be played during the televised ceremony.

Lucille was not exactly thrilled to be working alongside Milton Berle again, as she'd heard reports that he was increasingly cantankerous and difficult. She almost couldn't believe that in the late 1930s, she had actually contemplated marrying him during the peak of their affair.

Gossips were still evaluating his 1979 appearance as guest host on NBC's Saturday Night Live.

Rosie Shuster, one of that show's writers, compared his appearance "to watching a comedy train accident in slow motion on a loop. Never again would he be invited back. Why? Because of upstagings, camera mugging, inserting old-time comedy bits, and climaxing our show with a maudlin performance of 'September Song.'"

On the set of the "Television Hall of Fame" special, Berle informed Lucille that he was going to star on an episode ("Fine Tuning), of NBC's *Amazing Stories* created by Steven Spielberg. Its plot involved friendly aliens who are fascinated by the 1950s-era TV signals from Earth that they've been monitoring from outer space. "They will be traveling to Earth in search of their idols, you, Jackie Gleason, the Three Stooges, Burns and Allen, and yours truly, Mr. Berle himself."

Berle's autobiography revealed some of his sexual exploits, notably with Marilyn Monroe, Betty Hutton, columnist Dorothy Kilgallen, and evangelist Aimee Semple McPherson.

Many of the charter inductees were already dead. That included Paddy Chayefsky, a Bronx-born playwright, screenwriter, and novelist, and the only person to win three solo Oscars for writing both adapted and original screenplays. *[The awards were for Marty (1955), The Hospital (1971), and Network (1976). One of the great dramatists of the Golden Age of Television, Chayefsky wrote intimate, realistic scripts, providing a naturalistic style of TV drama. He had died in August of 1981, suffering from cancer. He was 58 years old at the time of his death.]*

Another charter inductee, Norman Lear, was a television writer and producer, who in the 1970s churned out an amazing number of hit TV sitcoms: *All in the Family, Maude, Sanford and Son, One Day at a Time,* and *The Jeffersons.*

Lear was also a key member of the "Malibu Mafia," a group of men funding liberal and progressive causes and politicians.

Born in 1891 in what is now Belarus, and also honored at the ceremony, David Sarnoff was a pioneer in both radio and television throughout most of his career. He led RCA in various capacities shortly after its founding in 1919 until his retirement in 1970. (He was to die a year later). He ruled over the ever-growing telecommunications and media empire that included both RCA and NBC, one of the largest companies in the world.

Also honored as a "Hall of Famer" was Edward R. Murrow, who had died in 1965 at the age of 57. A native son of North Carolina, he was a broadcast journalist and war correspondent. The peak of his fame came in World War II during The Blitz when his opening line, "This is London," was heard all over America.

During the war, he had fallen in love with Pamela Churchill (*née* Pamela Digby), the daughter-in-law of Sir Winston Churchill. Pamela wanted Murrow to marry her, and he seriously considered it, but finally rejected the idea when his wife gave birth to their only child, Casey.

Tallulah Bankhead claimed that she'd seduced both Murrow and Sir

Infuriatingly unpredictable and often cruel in her mockeries, **Tallulah Bankhead** was at times kind and gallant. She had a reckless spirit, often mired in alcohol and drugs, and was a lonely and wandering soul searching for a love she never found. One of the most dynamic personalities of the 20th Century, she became a legend in her own time.

Her list of male and female lovers was long. They included one of the most celebrated newscasters of World War II, **Edward R. Murrow** *(left)*. She never talked a lot about him, but claimed, "Let me tell you: This macho man could do more than announce the news."

The most famous of the men she seduced was **Sir Winston Churchill** *(right photo)*, who became her fan during her long runs on the London stage in the 1920s. On occasion, he would disappear with her after the curtain went down at the end of any of her performances. Once, he invited her for lunch with him in the House of Commons. Back in America, she spoke frequently of how "well hung" he was.

Winston, finding that both men "were well-hung, *dah-lings*."

William S. Paley, also an inductee who was honored that night, was still alive when the *Hall of Fame* was telecast. He is best known for converting CBS from a small radio network into one of the foremost radio and television network operations in America.

Although at first he was a bit leery of female comics, Paley played a key role in the Lucille's television career. She had to prove herself to him, and she did so by performing in a hit radio sitcom, *My Favorite Husband* alongside Richard Denning in the late 1940s.

He greenlighted her *I Love Lucy* debut but wanted Denning as her co-star. He strongly objected to the casting of Desi Arnaz but (reluctantly) relented after they toured the nation as a successful duo on the vaudeville circuit—or what remained of it.

Lucille claimed that although Paley was a notorious womanizer, he never seduced her. In 1932, he'd married Dorothy Hart in the wake of her divorce from John Randolph Hearst, the third son of press baron William Randolph Hearst. She later divorced him, charging him with infidelity.

In 1947, he married Barbara (nicknamed "Babe") Cushing Mortimer, who was consistently voted best-dressed woman in America and became a member of Truman Capote's inner circle, until they feuded. She infuriated Lucille when she was quoted as saying, "I think the former Mrs. Ricky Ricardo should be voted worst-dressed woman in America."

One of Bill Paley's most enduring affairs was with the silent film star, Louise Brooks, who had immortalized herself by starring in the silent film, *Pandora's Box* (1929). He provided a living stipend for her until the end of her life in 1985. Paley himself would die in 1990 at the age of 89.

Ball remained one of his favorite stars during her successful *I Love Lucy* heyday of the 1950s.

In time, however, and as she and her *schtick* aged, he told his executives, "Lucille Ball is beyond her expiration date." (She had heard that before.)

Nonetheless, he thought her achievements in television history should be honored. In 1975 he had launched The Museum of Broadcasting, later renamed the Paley Center for Media, in Manhattan.

For reasons known only to themselves, **William S. Paley** (*left*) and his wife, "**Babe Paley**," adored the effeminate author, **Truman Capote**. Here, they're hanging out together at Round Hill, an exclusive resort in Jamaica.

At the time, Paley was the chairman of CBS, which made him Lucille Ball's boss. Although she doesn't look it, Babe was consistently voted "Best Dressed Woman in America."

In April of 1984, he honored Lucille there, labeling her as "The Queen of Television."

The museum opened with two auditoriums and individual devices whereby the public, at long last, would have access to viewing TV programs since their inception.

Its original retrospective, *The First Lady of Comedy*, featured screenings of some eighty hours of Lucy telecasts.

For its opening night, Lucille and Gary Morton flew in for a gala, attended by 250 key players in the industry.

***

In one of their weaker presentations, Lucille teamed with Bob Hope again for an April 4, 1984 telecast, lasting an hour. It was entitled *Bob Hope in Who Makes the World Laugh: Part Two*, a sequel to an earlier special in 1983. This time around, Hope, as executive producer, hired George Burns and Mickey Rooney as backups to Lucille.

In this latest installment, Hope and Lucille engaged in their usual banter, but their interaction wasn't very funny. He didn't want a rehearsal, so both of them relied on cue cards. At one point, she read his cue card instead of her own, which angered him.

Privately, Lucille shared her latest opinion about Hope with Gary Morton: "My own career is in decline, but Bob is way past his prime. It seems that this new generation just doesn't get Hope's old jokes and a lot of his tired old references. Betty Grable might have been the pinup darling of GIs in World War II, but she has little recognition among today's kids."

When Lucille agreed to do the show with him, Hope was in the process of firing some of his scriptwriters. NBC had notified him that his specials would be reduced to four a year.

Over lunch with Lucille, Hope admitted, "I'm not only firing staff, but at my age, I've had to let all of my mistresses go—except one. No more presenting several ladies with a mink coat at Christmas."

"I've rented a small bungalow for my new gal at 212 North California Street in Burbank, not too far from where I live with Dolores. I've put her on my payroll so I can take a tax deduction."

Both Lucille and Hope were united in their ferocious determination to hold on until the end, never retiring until they had to, perhaps because of declining health.

Marlon Brando once joked that Hope "would go to an opening of a gas station in Ana-

Unknown to the tabloids, **Louise Brooks** was the long-time mistress of Bill Paley. Even after their affair ended, he continued to support her. Her most famous silent pictures were made in Germany, even though she was a daughter of the Midwest, in her case, from the fields of Kansas.

As Lulu, a nymphomaniac in *Pandora's Box* (1929), she became an overnight legend. The dark-haired girl with the bobbed hair developed a passionate cult following.

heim, providing there was a camera and three people watching."

If I weren't working, I'd need an applause machine to wake me up in the morning," Hope said to Lucille.

As he told the *Saturday Night Post*, "I want to have a long life, staying busy and hanging in there. Procrastination is the number one cause of tension. I don't just depend on those specials at NBC. My secretary gave me a list of my appearances over the past year: There were 42 charity benefits, 14 golf tournaments, 86 stage shows, 15 TV commercials, and about a dozen routine guest appearances."

In reference to George Burns, Lucille told Hope, "That guy will live forever. You probably will, too. George was born in Brooklyn in 1896 when Grover Cleveland was president. His wife, Gracie Allen, as you know, died in 1964."

Burns told Lucille that he kept in shape by following a strict regime of swimming, long walks, sit-ups, and push-ups. "Every year, I buy myself a new Cadillac, which I continue to drive. But pretty soon, I'll have to hire a chauffeur because my vision is not what it was."

"Every time I see you, you've got a cigar in your mouth," she said. "Too many cigars have damaged Desi's health."

"I've been smoking cigars since I turned fourteen," he responded. "It's been estimated that over the course of my life, I've smoked 300,000 cigars, but recently, I've reduced that to only four a day. I've never gotten any kick out of marijuana. What can weed do for me that show biz hasn't done?"

Lucille had encountered pint-sized Mickey Rooney on and off over the years, but by now, she was rather shocked at how badly he had aged. His "Between the Wars gig" as a box office champ was a distant memory.

He told her "I'm down to my eighth wife, Jan Chamberlin. I married her in 1978. My days of seducing the likes of Betty Grable and Lana Turner are long gone. Frankly, I'll never get over my first wife, Ava Gardner." *[Rooney had famously published, in his autobiography, years before, that her big brown nipples, when aroused, stood out like some double long golden California raisins."]*

Rooney told Lucille that he was contemplating a return to Broadway in a play entitled *Sugar Babies*. "There's a great part in it for a gal. Maybe you might consider being my co-star."

"Count me out," she answered. "I simply don't have the energy. Why don't you consider Ann Miller?

Eventually, Rooney did, indeed, star in it with tap-dancing Ann Miller, much to the delight of his nostalgia-soaked fans. For it, he received a Tony Nomination as Best Actor in a Leading Role in a Musical.

***

In that same month of April, on the 24th, Lucille was a guest star on *The American Parade,* an hour-long telecast by her former home studio, CBS. For this documentary series on American celebrities, she was flanked by newsman Bill Moyers, Charles Kuralt, and Bill Kurtis.

It was Kurtis who interviewed her, as she shared memories of her co-stars during their collective heyday on *I Love Lucy*. She had remained married to Desi Sr. throughout the entire original run of that series. She also discussed William Frawley and Vivian Vance, who'd played Fred and Ethel Mertz, their landlords. It was only during her evocation of Vance that she became teary-eyed.

Lucille was familiar with both Kuralt and Moyers, having seen them frequently on television.

Kuralt was widely known for his long career as a broadcaster for CBS. His "On the Road" episodes were telecast on *The CBS Evening News with Walter Cronkite*. Later, Kuralt became the first anchor in the *CBS News Sunday Morning*, a spot he'd occupy for fifteen years.

His *On the Road* Episodes were clearly inspired by John Steinbeck's *Travels with Charley*. Based on traveling in a motor home with a film crew, he followed the back roads of America for interviews with "everyday Americans" who never expected they'd end up on a national broadcast.

Moyers, a journalist and political commentator, had been best known during his stint (1965-1967) as White House Press Secretary during Lyndon Johnson's administration. He also worked for a decade in public broadcasting, producing documentaries and news journal programs.

Moyers was always outspoken as when he said, "The rich are getting richer, which arguably wouldn't matter if the rising tide lifted all boats. Instead, the inequality gap is the widest it's been since 1929. The middle class is besieged, and the working poor are barely keeping their heads above water."

CBS publicity photo of **Charles Kuralt** (*left*) and **Bill Moyers**.

These respected and world-famous broadcasters would appear with Lucille in *The American Parade*.

Her makeup expert, Robert Edmonds claimed, "She would do anything short of cosmetic surgery to look good. Before the show, she spent the entire day on her makeup and wardrobe. It was like she was trying to recapture the look of her RKO days in the 1930s."

"For me, at least, that was so long ago, that I was tempted to ask if her mother ever ordered her to wipe the dinosaur shit off her feet before going into the house."

***

Every day of her life, Lucille fretted over her career, and spent many a lonely weekend depressed as Gary Morton took to the golf course, later hanging out with male club members of whatever organization he'd joined. "Of course," he sadly said, "I could only join clubs that allow Jews. Many did not."

Lucille's ex-husband, Desi Sr. was devoted to the good life. To him, that meant sailing every weekend aboard his yacht to Catalina Island—often without Edie. Although she had threatened to divorce him in 1975, they had largely worked out their differences.

According to Edie, "I decided to hang

in there for the long run. I loved Desi, and I also understood—and tolerated—his weaknesses. He certainly had plenty of those."

Desi was also an expert fisherman, claiming that Ernest Hemingway would have labeled him as, "the old man of the sea." With two or three of his male friends, he would sail along the coast of Baja, California.

He also maintained his deeply ingrained fascination for raising what he called "blooded horses," and he never tired of watching them race at the track. Even though he'd gone through most of his millions, he still continued to lose at casinos and, more frequently, gambling at the races.

On Sunday afternoons, he often retreated to his kitchen, where he turned out Cuban specialties introduced to him in Santiago, Cuba, when he was a boy. "I challenge anyone to make a better black bean and rice casserole than 'yours truly.'"

One night at a party in Palm Springs, he told Dean Martin, "My Cuban salami is more or less in semi-retirement. But it was a noble appendage, carrying me in epic conquests through one boudoir after another. I hear Don Juan seduced 1,003 gals. I never bothered to count my seductions, but I'm sure I've got Don Juan beat."

"I'm sure you screwed Marilyn Monroe," Desi continued, "Perhaps for a final time when you were cast in that picture from which she was fired. I failed to get her honeypot, but, oh, there were so many others. My highlights were Betty Grable, Sonja Henie, Lana Turner, and Ginger Rogers. How about you?"

"Oh, it's hard to say," Martin answered. "Marilyn, certainly, but June Allyson ranks at the top of my list. That gal was mad for me. Lana, too, was a treat for me. But so was Catherine Deneuve. Actually, I think no one knows this, but there was this gal with a notorious past, Judith Campbell Exner. The world found out she was sleeping with both Jack Kennedy and with Sam Giancana, probably passing secrets and messages between them. What the tabloids never knew was that I was also bedding her. She assured me that my dick was bigger than JFKs and the gangster's."

In reference to his father's aging, Desi Jr. was later quoted as saying, "My Dad was happier when he no longer had to swim through the shark-infested waters of Hollywood as a studio boss. Today, he's found himself, and seems to be doing what he wants."

"If my grandfather hadn't been chased out of Cuba in a revolution, my dad would have been happier living the rich lifestyle they had in those days, visiting the local bordello on Saturday night, raising nine kids with a fat wife,

Desi Arnaz Sr. in May 1983, on *Late Night with David Letterman*.

Lucille watched the show with Gary Morton. "You've held up rather well," she told him, "but Desi has never looked this wretched. What happened to that sexy Cuban bandleader of long ago? I know all of us age differently, but he looks like some great grandfather who's been told he's on his way to the burial grounds."

and going through a box of Cuban cigars every day. I think his mother was linked to the Bacardi Rum people, so there would have been one *Cuba Libre* after another, beginning right after breakfast. What a life!"

Regrettably, Desi Sr. continued to be plagued by health problems, especially diverticulitis and "other crap going wrong in my guts."

He underwent operations and therapy, checking in and out of hospitals. His wife, Edie, continued to stand by him through the good times and the bad.

She was not successful, however, in getting him to abandon his habit of smoking four or five big Havana cigars every day of his life—"and ten stogies on Sunday."

***

Lucille ended her 1984 summer hiatus when Bob Hope called on her once again, this time to be his guest on *Bob Hope's Unrehearsed Antics of the Stars*. He had been designated as both its executive producer and host of the hour-long telecast that NBC aired on September 28.

Her fellow guests would include Milton Berle (again) with two additional new faces for her: Angie Dickinson and Lee Marvin. The show would feature outtakes from previous Bob Hope specials.

As regards the fast-fading marketability of other female comedians from the 1950s, Lucille told Hope, "I feel that I'm wandering in a graveyard, stomping over the burial mounds of Ann Sothern, Gale Storm, Eve Arden, Harriet Nelson, and Jane Wyatt."

Donna Reed was still working but not in a comedy. For a single season, she replaced Barbara Bel Geddes in *Dallas*, that prime time soap opera that became a hit after airing for the first time in 1978.

Lucille often watched it. *Dallas* configured Larry Hagman (Mary Martin's son) as the greedy, scheming oil tycoon, J.R. Ewing, within 357 episodes. Eventually, it emerged as one of the longest-running prime time dramas in television history. A cliffhanger, *Who Shot J.R.?*, remains the second-highest rated prime time telecast ever.

Reed's own sitcom, *The Donna*

In an interview in the Oval Office when he was President, **Donald Trump** attacked women reporters. "I can tell you this. They sure aren't **Donna Reed**."

He was referring to the film and TV star best known for her role of Mary Bailey, married to James Stewart in *It's a Wonderful Life* (1946). She later starred as the perfect 1950s mom in her eponymous family TV sitcom of the 1950s and '60s.

In reference to Trump's comment, a reporter for *The New York Post* wrote: "The levels of narcissism, sexism, and pure delusion in these statements is classic Trump. He manages to insult women and imply that they'd do better as archetypical '50s housewives. In other words, keep the house clean, the kids cared for, and dinner on the table when hubby comes home from work."

Reed Show, had aired from 1958 to 1966. She was still seen on the screen every Christmas alongside James Stewart in Frank Capra's *It's a Wonderful Life* (1946). She won an Oscar as Best Supporting Actress.

"An Oscar!" Lucille said. "that's one Golden Boy who has eluded me."

***

For years, whenever possible, Lucille had indulged in tasteless banter with one or more of her male co-stars. In this case, it was with Lee Marvin, a gray-haired actor with a distinctive, tough-sounding voice. He often played villains, soldiers, and other hard-boiled characters in such pictures as *Cat Ballou* (1965) with Jane Fonda, or *The Dirty Dozen* (1967).

One day, when Marvin invited her to lunch, Lucille accepted, having been intrigued by him for years.

"A long time ago," he told her, "you should have given me your private phone number whenever you were ready for a most satisfying fuck. I bet in the good old days, you had a sweet clittie."

"You nailed me," she said. "I have to admit it. What you say is true. Ask any man."

After directing Marvin in *Paint Your Wagon* (1969), director Josh Logan said, "Not since Atilla the Hun swept across Europe, leaving five-hundred years of total blackness, has there been a man like Lee Marvin."

During his heavy drinking years, Marvin's favorite form of entertainment involved donning a hairnet, putting on his bathrobe, grabbing his gun, and shooting up the mailboxes in his neighborhood.

On night in Hawaii during the filming of *Donovan's Reef* (1963), Marvin got drunk, pulled off all his clothes, and danced nude on top of the bar countertop of his hotel, a lurid hula, shaking what he called, 'God's gift to womanhood.'"

Lee Marvin on *The Twilight Zone* in 1961.

"Unlike so many of the Hollywood actors I've worked with, Marvin, I bet, would know what to do when confronted with a naked woman," Lucille said.

"I fell for him when I saw him as a psychopathic gangleader in *The Big Heat* (1953). He hurled scalding coffee in the face of his girlfriend, Gloria Grahame."

Angie Dickinson, who emerged from the cold winds of North Dakota, had distinguished herself in a number of films such as *Rio Brava* (1959) starring John Wayne. Although she had married Burt Bacharach in 1965, she was linked to many other lovers, including Frank Sinatra, Johnny Carson, and David Janssen. She became tabloid fodder when she became sexually associated with President Kennedy. She was rumored to have an autographed picture of JFK on which he had written: "Angie, the only woman I've ever loved."

The French director, Roger Vadim, who had helmed her in *Pretty Maids All in a Row* (1971), claimed, "She has more sex appeal than any woman I've ever directed."

That was a great compliment, since he'd married Brigitte Bardot and Jane Fonda, and was romantically linked with the French beauty, Catherine Deneuve.

***

"You know that you're washed up when your admirers start paying tributes to your career," Lucille told Paul W. Keyes when he wrote and produced *All-Star Party for Lucille Ball,* a 120-minute CBS special that was aired on December 29, 1984. Its music was by Nelson Riddle, whose long career stretched from the 1940s to the mid-1980s. He was to die a year after the telecast at the age of 64.

When Keyes hired Riddle, he said, "Why not? I've survived Frank Sinatra and Judy Garland. I even turned down Paul McCartney."

During a personal chat, he told Lucille, "My wives were not my greatest loves. It was Rosemary Clooney."

Keyes appropriately surrounded Lucille with some familiar cohorts, including Sinatra himself, James Stewart, John Ritter, Burt Reynolds ("she warned me not to get Lucie pregnant years ago"), Cary Grant, Dean Martin, and Joan Collins, with whom she had appeared before.

Monty Hall, the host, invited Lucille's son and daughter to perform, and he even brought Gary Morton into the lineup. A pregnant Lucie and her brother, in a duet, sang the "I Love Lucy" song.

Carl Reiner, the actor, comedian, and director, had once contributed sketch material for *The Show of Shows* and *Caesar's Hour* starring Sid Caesar. In its heyday, *The Show of Shows* (1950-1954) reached an audience of 60 million viewers. For the Lucille tribute, Caesar and Reiner, two old friends, performed a sketch that evoked their heydays in the 1950s.

Lucille met privately with Sammy Davis Jr. who was also in the cast.

"The two entertainers had long been friends. Bob Hope had once suggested that Lucille Ball Productions develop a three-part TV biography of Davis' life, but she told him that no sponsor could be found.

"Sammy, you're just too controversial for too deep a look into your private life," she told him. She was no doubt referring to his marriage to Swedish-born May Britt in 1960. Interracial marriage was legal at the time in California, but anti-miscegenation laws still existed in 23 states. A

Angie Dickinson, star of *Police Woman*, in 1961.

Lucille said, "She told me she dresses for women and undresses for men. I think she has more sex appeal than any dame I've ever worked with. I had to keep Gary Morton on a chain, and when his tongue hung out, I had to put it back in his mouth."

Gallup Poll at the time revealed that only four percent of Americans supported marriage between blacks and whites. From all over the country, Davis received tons of hate mail.

Lucille's researchers uncovered that he'd had affairs with two screen goddesses, Ava Gardner and Marilyn Monroe. He had also been romantically involved with Kim Novak, Jean Seberg, and the stripper, Tempest Storm.

Davis had also had a very controversial affair with Linda Lovelace, the pornographic centerpiece of *Deep Throat* (1972) fame. He was also rumored to have one of the largest collections of porn in the country.

"No hard feelings, Lucy baby," he said. "I didn't think any network would go for my story. But try it again to a sponsor in twenty-five years. America may have changed by then, and blacks who look like me may be popping up on the TV screen day and night."

An award for "humanitarian services" (her work to find a cure for juvenile diabetes) from **Gary Morton**, bestowed at the *All Star Party for* **Lucille Ball** in 1984.

***

Night of 100 Stars was telecast on ABC on March 11, 1985, lasting for 180 minutes. Staged at Radio City Music Hall in Manhattan, it was configured as a sequel to *Night of 100 Stars* (1982) and a benefit for the Actors Fund of America.. One of the highlights of the special was a salute to tap dancers.

Lucille, as a member of the largest and most glittering cast of stars ever assembled, did little more than provide an introduction. It seemed that all of Hollywood had flown in. To name-drop a bit, stars included Lucille's daughter, Lucie Arnaz, as well as Ann-Margret, George Burns, Joan Collins, Olivia de Havilland, Robert De Niro,

Press photo from *All-Star Party for Lucille Ball.* in 1984. **Gary Morton** places a protective hand over **Lucille's**.

One of the highlights of the show occurred when **Desi Jr.** and a pregnant **Lucie Arnaz** sang the "I Love Lucy" theme song as a loving ballad with specially written lyrics.

Linda Evans, Lillian Gish, Lena Horne, Van Johnson, Danny Kaye, Mary Tyler Moore, Jim Nabors, Sidney Poitier, Ginger Rogers, Dinah Shore, James Stewart, Lana Turner, and Dick Van Dyke.

***

Lucille would not appear on TV in a special again until September 17, 1985. Once again, she was teamed with host Bob Hope, this time in *Bob Hope Buys NBC*. Hope was also its executive producer, and he'd lined up a lot of familiar faces to join Lucille: Milton Berle, George Burns, Johnny Carson, Phyllis Diller, Michael Landon, Dean Martin, and Danny Thomas.

Lucille was seen chatting with Tom Selleck.

In Selleck, Lucille felt she was meeting the best example of the male stars of the 1980s. Rugged and masculine, he had launched his hit TV drama, *Magnum P.I.* in 1980. In it he portrayed a private investigator. One of the last feature films she saw was Selleck cast as a bachelor architect in *Three Men and a Baby* (1987).

The plot of the special has Hope staging a telethon to buy NBC. Even Gerald Ford made a special appearance. Hope and Ford had long been friends.

The Bob Hope Golf Classic had been founded in 1960, and Hope continued his interest in golf until he got too old. In the future (in 1995, to be exact), he even made history of a sort when his astonishingly prestigious foursome on the course included Gerald Ford, George H.W. Bush, and Bill Clinton. Hope told Lucille that in 1978, he putted against Tiger Woods in a TV appearance with James Stewart on *The Mike Douglas Show*. "I showed up Tiger big time. I beat his ass and made him look like an amateur. Of course, he was only two years old at the time, but what the hell."

Before the airing of *Bob Hope Buys NBC*, an offer came in during the spring of 1985 for Lucille to star in the last feature film of her long career.

Sexy **Tom Selleck** bares all—or at least his hairy chest.

Top stardom always eluded him, as he seemingly could not escape the image he'd developed in telecasts of his successful detective series, *Magnum P.I.* Set in Hawaii, and focusing on Selleck as a high-rolling sybarite, it ran for eight very successful seasons (1980-88).

One of his notorious movie roles included his portrayal of a handsome, amoral hunk in Gore Vidal's *Myra Breckinridge* (1970), co-starring the sexually suggestive 77-year-old, Mae West.

CHAPTER SEVENTEEN

LUCILLE'S LAST HURRAH

"Stone Pillow was my final feature film, made especially for showing on television, and the shoot nearly killed me," Lucille lamented. "No longer glamourous, I played a bag lady who takes her shits in an alleyway, using a newspaper as toilet paper. I played a character I named myself. Flora Belle was the name of my maternal grandmother."

As a homeless woman, with few resources and even fewer options, Flora Belle pushes a cart that contains all of her belongings. The plot revolves around her interactions with a social worker in disguise played by Daphne Zuniga cast as "Carrie Lange."

Lucille was seventy-three years old, and she did not disguise with heavy makeup what she really looked like. All memories of Lucy Ricardo were forgotten. She resembled a homeless crone, wandering pathetically (and territorially) through the harsh streets of Manhattan. The script called for her to wear heavy clothing to fight off the winter weather. However, shooting was delayed until late spring, when the city suffered an unusual hot spell.

"For six weeks, I had to wear about twenty-five pounds of heavy clothing. It was like I was in a steam bath."

During the shoot, she protested about almost everything, even the "sissy rats" from the prop department. "I wanted fierce rats to play opposite me."

Even though her face was among the most famous of the 20th Century, in her bedraggled costume, few of her fans recognized her,

Stone Pillow's co-producer and scenarist was Rose Leiman Goldenberg. She'd had a success by writing the screenplay for *The Burning Bed,* a made-for-television film telecast on NBC in 1984 starring Farrah Fawcett. It became NBC's highest-rated television movie. The script depicted a woman who suffered thirteen years of physical abuse at the hands of her husband. After setting his bed (with him in it) on fire, she goes on trial for murder.

Lucille noted that Fawcett's performance was hailed "as one of the finest of TV movies." She was hoping that *Stone Pillow* would duplicate the success of *The Burning Bed.*

The director, George Schaefer, had distinguished himself during the Golden Age of Television. Before that, he had earned fame on Broadway, helming Maurice Evans in Shakespeare's *Hamlet* and also winning a Tony for his production of *The Teahouse of the August Moon*. He later adapted for TV many Broadway plays for NBC's *Hallmark Hall of Fame*. He later won five Emmys from twenty-one total nominations.

On the first day of the shoot, he told Lucille, "Don't worry about how you look. You look better than some actors I've directed. Take Boris Karloff, for example."

Stone Pillow was telecast by CBS on the night of November 5, 1985. It ran for 120 minutes. Reviews were mixed, but ratings were high, a goodly percentage of them fans of Lucille wondering "What ever happened to Lucy Ricardo?"

The New York Daily News wrote, "There was always an uneasy feeling that this was Lucy Ricardo miscast as a bag lady. Still, credit is due to her for tackling such an offbeat project. It took guts for her to show her fans what she really looks like today."

Several film critics noted that *Stone Pillow* gave Lucille her most dramatic acting role since she'd appeared in a wheelchair in *The Big*

In 1984, perhaps as precursor to the "heightened realism" of Lucille's decision to play a bag lady, NBC showcased the then-spectacularly famous fashion icon, **Farrah Fawcett**, in a gritty and deeply disturbing depiction (*The Burning Bed*) of a domestic abuse victim, based on a real-life murder trial.

Vastly successful, it was reviewed as one of the best made-for-TV dramas ever made, and Fawcett received wild accolades for her lack of concern about her "beauty" and the intensity with which she handled herself as an actress.

About a year later, frustrated by the bad scripts she'd been assigned and eager to self-reinforce as a serious actress, **Lucille**, too, abandoned her preconceived notions of grooming in her bold and affectionate portrayal of an elderly homeless woman living "out, loud, and in your face" on the mean streets of NYC.

According to Lucille, "I hadn't worked in a long time because the scripts I was getting were so disgusting and all anybody really wanted me to do was Lucy all over again. So when CBS told me (that) director George Schaefer wanted to work with me, that and fascinating subject matter was what got me to do it. I don't care how I look on screen, so that was it."

In the photo above, Lucille, as the homeless Flora Belle, grabs some uneasy shuteye on a public bench in the City that Never Sleeps.

Street (1942), in which she'd co-starred with Henry Fonda.

The *Boston Globe* wrote, "Lucille has told us that she gave up on TV sitcoms because they are 'all filth—sex, sex, and more sex.' But there aren't many sitcoms as obscene as a TV movie that would exploit the plight of the homeless for the sake of ratings as envisioned from the resurrecting of a faded comedian's career."

The review in *The Washington Post* read: "What Lucille Ball does with the character of Flora Belle, a bag lady, qualifies more as an appearance than an actual performance."

John J. O'Connor in *The New York Times* wrote: "*Stone Pillow* is a carefully contrived concoction, earnest but not above being cute and nearly outrageous in its determination to jerk a few tears. Accepted on that level, the exercise works reasonably well. Miss Ball is in total control, from the opening scene in which, emerging from a cocoon bed of green plastic garbage bags, she takes one look at the world and proclaims, 'Well, I'm still here.'"

On her return to Los Angeles, she entered the hospital, where she was treated for dehydration, exhaustion, and heat prostration.

***

Since way back in the early 1960s, in addition to playing backgammon games at home, Lucille had been a devoted fan of TV game shows. Since it had first been first telecast in 1961, *Password* had been one of her favorites.

According to the rules of the game, two teams, each composed of a celebrity player and a contestant, attempt to convey mystery words to each other using only single-word clues, as a means of winning cash prizes.

For a May, 1964 telecast of *Password*, host Allen Ludden had invited not only Lucille onto his show, but included Gary Morton and her son and daughter (Desi Jr. and Lucie) too. This marked the first time Lucille's post-divorce and "reconfigured" family unit (i.e., with Morton and not Desi Sr.) had appeared on television together

---

The back side of this press photo issued by CBS in August of 1985 described **Lucille Ball's** role in *Stone Pillow* like this:

"Lucille Ball, who won numerous awards including four Emmys during her more than 30 years as one of television's foremost comediennes, stars in her first television drama as an elderly New York City shopping bag lady, existing on spunk, scraps and dead dreams, in 'Stone Pillow.'"

"The new motion picture-for-television filmed, in New York, will be broadcast on the CBS Television Network during the 1985-86 season."

A line from one of the drama's characters expressed the feelings of the real-life Lucille perfectly:

"You think there's something so different about the homeless? A few bad breaks, a few checks that don't come...We could all be sleeping on stone pillows."

Desi Jr., then eleven years old, seemed completely at home. Not so Lucie at age thirteen. It was suggested that with her short curly hair and braces, she could have been appropriately cast as a gawky and eccentric "caricature" adolescent.

During a later period of the game show's life, Lucille made several appearances on *Password Plus,* a revised incarnation of the original *Password,* this time (1980-1982) hosted by Kentucky-born Tom Kennedy after the death of the show's original host, Allen Ludden.

A few years later, Kennedy was hired as the host of yet another game show, *Body Language* (1984-1986), also a favorite of Lucille's.

Body Language featured celebrity players who each teamed with a "civilian" partner to act out, at manic speed, words that were part of a larger puzzle. Lucille was cast in two weeks of guest appearances. In one episode, she was featured with her gay former co-star, Charles Nelson Reilly. Their appearance was billed as "the game for the uninhibited." In one, she has to (silently) convey the memory of Groucho Marx, with whom she had starred in *Room Service* way back in 1938. In an attempt to evoke his memory, she does an imitation of Groucho stooped and holding a cigar.

In other installments of *Body Language,* Lucille teamed with exercise guru Richard Simmons, known for his flamboyant, campy, and energetic eccentricities. Simmons said that after years of watching Lucille on televi-

Press photo showcasing **Lucille Ball**'s ladylike and graceful contribution to the vaudeville slapstick of *Room Service* (1938) with the Marx Brothers. Decades later, in an era wildly different from the one in which it was produced, Lucille was called upon, within the context of a game show, to replicate the spirit, energy, and character of Groucho.

sion, he could hardly believe he was actually appearing with her on TV.

In one episode, Lucille has to conjure up the Mona Lisa. Coincidentally, she had twice been "Mona Lucy," her face stuck in the famous painting, on one or another of her television episodes. As part of the *schtick*, actor Robert Morse interprets her gestures as her attempt to convey to members of the audience that she's Grandma Moses, not the Mona Lisa.

Morse was an actor and singer, known for appearing in the 1961 original Broadway play, as well as in its 1967 film adaptation, of *How to Succeed in Business Without Really Trying*.

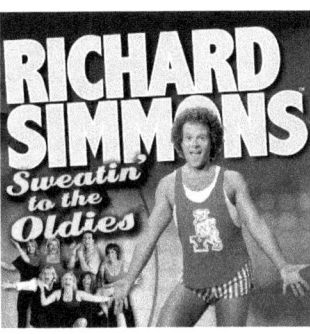

Loud, proud, and flamboyant, here's exercise guru **Richard Simmons**.

Lucille might have been worried that the title of this workout tape (*Sweatin' to the Oldies*) might have been a reference to her fast-advancing age.

Robert Morse in 1962 as a corporate climber in *How to Succeed in Business Without Really Trying*.

Isabel Sanford was another guest star who worked with Lucille. Born in Harlem, she was best known for her role of "Weezy" Mills Jefferson on the CBS sitcom, *All in the Family* (1971-1975) and later, as one of the leading characters in *The Jeffersons* (1975-1985). In 1981, she became the second black actress to win an Emmy. Later, she became the first and, to date, the only black actress to ever win an Emmy as the Outstanding Lead Actress in a comedy series.

Unknown to most viewers, Lucille played a key role in the staggering game-show success of Alex Trebek, a Canadian-American game show host and TV personality. Beginning in 1974, she had seen him on the game show, *High Rollers*, and was impressed.

She recommended him to her friend, Merv Griffin, the producer of *Jeopardy!*, and the TV talk show host hired Trebek for the show.

Isabel Sanford appears on the cover of *Jet* magazine with her screen husband, **Sherman Hemsley**, celebrating their survival as "The longest married couple (i.e., *The Jeffersons*) on TV."

Contestants were presented with clues in the form of an answer. According to the rules, they had to rephrase their responses in the form of a question, hoping that their partners would eventually hit the original answer.

By 1984, Trebek was drawing an average nightly audience of 51 million viewers on 200 stations.

Shortly before his death in 2020, he said, "I will always love Lucy."

***

At NBC, Bill Cosby had broken racial barriers to become "America's Dad" in his hit TV sitcom, *The Cosby Show*. [*Running for eight consecutive seasons (1984-1992), it was, according to TV Guide, "TV's biggest hit in the 1980s, and almost single-handedly revived the sitcom genre and NBC's ratings fortunes.*]

Also on NBC, the ongoing misadventures of some senior citizens, *The Golden Girls* (1985-1992), was a big hit, too. It starred Bea Arthur, Estelle Getty, Betty White, and Rue McClanahan.

According to a rumor at the time, the executive producers of *The Golden Girls* considered asking Lucille to play the star role of *divorcée* Dorothy Zbornak. The offer may never have actually been extended to Lucille. In any event, the producers later decided that Elaine Stritch would be more suitable for the role, but she bombed at her audition.

Producers then turned to Bea Arthur, who had been Lucille's co-star in the ill-fated feature film, *Mame* (1974). Arthur was ultimately persuaded to accept the role, which evolved into a spectacularly successful comeback vehicle for her.

It was Aaron Spelling himself who insisted no one but Lucille could handle the leading role in yet another spinoff sitcom, *Life with Lucy,* on ABC. He envisioned the venue as competition for rival shows being broadcast on Saturday nights through CBS and NBC. To entice her, he even agreed to name Gary Morton *as Life with Lucy's* executive producer, which more or less guaranteed that Lucille would accept his offer.

So confident was Spelling that *Life with Lucy* would be a success that he did not commission a pilot for the newest spinoff. Instead, sight unseen, ABC agreed to pay Lucille $150,000 for each episode, with Morton getting $100,000. She demanded that Gale Gordon come out of retirement to play once again her co-star. He would be paid $25,000 per episode. He went on to (successfully) demand that his contract would include payment in full for 22 episodes, even if the sitcom were canceled early.

As for his physical condition at the age of eighty, he assured Spelling,

Game show (*Jeopardy*) host **Alex Trebek** on the cover of *People* magazine.

For years, he credited his game-show breakthrough to Lucille.

Until **Bea Arthur** became deeply entrenched as the uber-matriarch and ringleader of spectacularly successful *The Golden Girls*, Lucille Ball was considered for her role.

Above is a commemoration of one of Arthur's most enduring lines from that long-running TV series, the sardonically intoned "Have a NIce Day."

"I can still turn a cartwheel."

Once called "The Boy Wonder," Spelling, a native of Dallas, seemed the ideal choice to inject new vigor into Lucille's fading career, which was on life support at the time.

Spelling, through his production company, Spelling Television, was already legendary as the most prolific producer in TV history, with 218 credits. His most breathtakingly successful productions included the TV series *Family* (1976-1980); *Charlie's Angels* (1976-1981); *The Love Boat* (1977-1986); *Hart to Hart* (1979-1984); and *Dynasty* (1981-1989).

Spelling became so rich that he acquired Bing Crosby's former home, tore it down, and on its site constructed "The Manor," a 123-room megamansion, the largest single family home in Los Angeles. In time, he would receive Jacqueline Kennedy Onassis, Prince Rainier, and Prince Charles as his guests there.

Lucille had known Spelling for years, as he had once appeared on Episode 112 ("Tennessee Bound") of *I Love Lucy*. She later said, "Aaron represents how far a poor little Jewish boy from the wrong side of the tracks can go in America."

As scriptwriters, Spelling offered to hire the creative team who had developed M*A*S*H, but Lucille rejected them. She turned instead to scriptwriters Bob Carroll Jr. and Madelyn Pugh (Davis), with whom she'd had a long (some say "tormented") history already. It was they who had written most of the *I Love Lucy* episodes and also many of the scripts for her radio show, *My Favorite Husband,* back in the late 1940s.

Aaron Spelling, best remembered for his enormous wealth and his development of *Gunsmoke* and *Charlie's Angels*, appears here with his then-wife, **Carolyn Jones** during their 12-year (1953-1958) marriage.

Like Lucille, Jones got a gig in a very long-running TV series, appearing as the original "Morticia": in the first incarnation (1964-66) of the spectacularly successful *The Addams Family.*

Over the years, the writing team of Davis and Carroll churned out 500 TV and radio episodes for Lucille, plus an occasional TV special.

Even before the first episode of *Life With Lucy* was filmed, Spelling assured Lucille that he felt her new sitcom would last for many years.

"My god," she answered. "I feel with my brittle bones that it might even outlast me."

Her previous sitcom, *Here's Lucy,* had gone off the air twelve years ago. She met with Carroll and Pugh, telling them that although she wanted to retain the first name of Lucy, she preferred the new last name of Barker. She also insisted on retaining many of the same characteristics she had spent decades developing and "perfecting." Consequently, each of the writers began developing various situations and plots into which a septuagenarian might suitably fit.

One wag suggested that *Life With Lucy* had been inspired by Desi Arnaz's *Mothers-in-Law,* in which Eve Arden and Kaye Ballard portrayed (bickering) in-laws. In *Life With Lucy*, Gale Gordon, since their offspring were married to each other, would be her in-law.

Carroll later recalled, "I wasn't really interested in writing the new series as envisioned by Lucy, but I went along for old times' sake. Madelyn and I, at least jokingly, wanted to call it *Granny of the Year*, but Lucille would have none of that. She detested the word 'grandmother.'"

"Although Madelyn and I always thought Gordon was a reliable performer, we didn't like the young actress cast as the offspring of Gordon and Lucille. After watching the first episode, I knew that Lucille had lost it. Her charm on screen was of another day."

Life With Lucy was telecast on ABC for only one season, lasting from September 20 to November 15, 1985. This was the only Lucy sitcom that did not air on CBS. Only eight of the thirteen episodes were actually aired before ABC executives pulled the plug on the series. Today, some TV historians list it as "the worst sitcom in broadcasting history."

According to the general plot, Lucy Barker is a widowed grandmother who has inherited her late husband's half interest in a hardware store in Pasadena, California. The other half of the store is owned by a widower, Curtis MacGibbon (Gordon). Lucy demands that she run the store with him, even though she knows nothing about hardware. Expect the usual zany mixups and disasters, the theme of which was already familiar to viewers of previous Lucy sitcoms.

Lucy moves in with her daughter, Margo (Ann Dusenberry) and her son-in-law, Ted MacGibbon (Larry Anderson) whose father is the Gordon character.

Margo and Ted also have two kids, Becky, (Jenny Lewis) and Kevin (Philip Amelio II) in the role of Leonard Stoner. Conovan Scott also became a regular on the sitcom.

Three different directors were hired, although Peter Baldwin ended up helming most of the shows. He was also an actor, having appeared in such films as *Stalag 17* (1953) starring William Holden. In the 1980s, he would

As she'd done during previews of earlier *Lucy* sitcoms, **Lucille** managed to get a lot of printed publicity for the rebirth of "The Lucy America Loved."

It was part of her "Last Hurrah," the short-lived (some said, "embarassing") fourth "Lucy" series, *Life With Lucy*. At the time, she was 75, and her co-star, Gale Gordon, was 80.

None of the publicity seemed to help, thanks in part to bad scripts and the fact that Lucy seemed tired and simply wasn't that funny any more. She had not managed to revitalize her TV *schtick*.

Life With Lucy bombed, closing after less than a full season and laying to rest, at last, a television character judged by latter-day critics as one of the most durable in entertainment history.

have the dubious distinction of directing both Lucille and Mary Tyler Moore in their failed comebacks on TV.

Marc Daniels was a longtime associate of Lucille's, having directed the first 38 episodes of *I Love Lucy*. It was he who had hired Vivian Vance as Ethel Mertz. He later bolted from *I Love Lucy* to accept a better-paying job, although he expressed regret for having done so. "Who knew at the time that we were creating TV history?"

Bruce Bilson would direct the last episode of *Life With Lucy* ever telecast. He was a director, producer, and scriptwriter with a long list of credits. He had been involved in another number of hits, ranging from *Bewitched* to *Hawaii Five-O*. His most notable work was on the spy spoof, *Get Smart,* which brought him an Emmy in 1967-1968 for Outstanding Directing in a Comedy Series.

The regulars in the cast were virtually unknown to most TV viewers. Arizona-born Ann Dusenberry, a very minor actress, appeared in both TV and feature film roles. Some viewers remembered her for playing Amory in *Stonestreet: Who Killed the Centerfold Model?* (1977). Or as Amy March in *Little Women,* a two-part miniseries on NBC in 1978. In one TV movie, *Elvis and the Beauty Queen* (1981), she was cast as Jeannie. *Life With Lucy* did not advance her career.

Larry Anderson was cast as Ted, Lucille's son-in-law. Critic Thomas C. Tobin wrote: "If you watched TV for the past three decades, your probably saw Larry Anderson, who starred in some thirty telecasts, including *The Six Million Dollar Man, Charlie's Angels,* and *The Amazing Spider-Man,* all in 1977."

He was also a magician and demonstrated two of his tricks to Lucille off screen. He tore a newspaper into pieces and then, with a wave of his arm, restored it whole again. He also knew how to levitate a young woman on the tips of three swords.

He was also a dedicated Scientologist, frequently extolling its virtues over a period of thirteen years. He later broke from the movement, claiming that it didn't deliver the spiritual gains it had promised.

As Lucille's grandson, Kevin, actor Philip Amelio II was a New Englander born in 1977. He and his younger sister, Lindsey Cook Amelia, were better known for their TV commercials. From the age of four, Philip had promoted commercial products, including becoming the first "pitch person" for Jell-O Pudding Snacks. Later, Lindsey appeared with Morris the Cat promoting 9Lives cat food.

After departing from *Life With Lucy,* Philip enjoyed a three-year run (1988-1991) in the daytime soap, *All My Children*. He also hyped *All,* a laundry detergent, and *Shake 'n' Bake* bread crumbs.

Amelio's life would end tragically at the age of 27 when he developed a bacterial infection of a heart valve.

Las Vegas born Jenny Lewis played Becky, Lucille's granddaughter. She was one of the most talented members of the cast. She was not only an actress, but a singer-songwriter and musician becoming the lead singer and rhythm guitarist for the indie rock band, "Rilo Kiley." Born in 1976, she became a child actress in the 1980s, appearing on such shows as *Bay-*

watch, *The Golden Girls,* and *Murder, She Wrote.*

Critic Jessica Roy later defined her as "a style icon to music-loving young people. For a particular brand of suburban girl who fancied herself cooler than her peers, Jenny was a fire-haired figure of worship. With her endless supply of cool sunglasses, vintage dresses, and hats. She was a beacon of hope for introspective teens, a microgenerational sad-girl touchstone."

Born in Chico, California in 1947, Donovan Scott, cast in the role of Leonard Stoner in *Life With Lucy,* studied at the American Conservatory Theater in San Francisco. He later toured as both an actor and artistic director of a theatrical troupe, After settling into Los Angeles, he made his film debut in Steven Spielberg's *1941.*

Before working with Lucille, he was best known for the 1984 film *Police Academy,* in which he was part of an ensemble cast led by Steve Guttenberg.

***

The premiere episode of *Life With Lucy* was *One Good Grandparent Deserves Another,* telecast on the night of September 20, 1985 on ABC for half an hour.

Curtis MacGibbon (Gordon) returns from a vacation in Hawaii, planning to move in with his son Ted (Larry Anderson). He finds that Lucy Barker has also moved in with Ted and her daughter Margo (Ann Dusenberry).

Not only that, but there are two grandchildren as well, eight-year-old Becky (Jenny Lewis) and six-year-old Kevin (Philp Amelio).

The family occupies a three-story clapboard house in Pasadena. The viewer can expect zany antics and predictable disasters very similar to those within so many other Lucy episodes.

Curtis also learned that Lucy has become a partner in his hardware store. He not only is forced to work with the out-of-control Lucy but has to undergo the stress of living under the same roof with her as well.

The guest star was Ruth Kobart, cast as Mrs. Finlay. In a career that spanned six decades, she was also an opera singer, noted for her big body, big voice, and ugly face.

She had appeared with Clint Eastwood in *Dirty Harry* (1971) and also had a regular role starring with Bob Newhardt on his TV show.

For the most part, big name stars were not booked on *Life With Lucy.* An exception was the September 27 telecast, *Lucy Makes a Hit with John Ritter.* Purse-swinging Ruth Buzzi as Mrs. Wilcox was also

John Ritter's slapstick interaction with **Lucille** in this episode of *Life With Lucy* sometimes appeared to be forced and "trying way too hard.".

hired for comic relief. Ritter played himself.

Lucille had long expressed her admiration for Ritter, the son of cowboy star Tex Ritter. Praising him both as a person and a performer, she called her affection for him "Ritter-itis."

In the plot, Ritter is in Pasadena starring in a play. He visits the hardware store to buy some door handles. Although Lucy means to be helpful, she ends up injuring both of his hands and his feet. She insists he stay at her home so she can look after him during his recovery.

When the leading lady drops out of Ritter's play, guess who volunteers to replace her?

For episode three, *Lucy Among the Two-by-Fours* (October 4), Marc Daniels, who had directed all those *I Love Lucy* sitcoms in the 1950s, returned to helm her once again. Her co-star would be Peter Graves, the brother of actor James Arness, who was cast as Peter Marshall.

Graves was known for his role of Jim Phelps in the hit TV series *Mission: Impossible* from 1967 to 1973. He also made more fans when he co-starred in two feature films, *Airplane!* (1980) and its 1982 sequel, *Airplane II*.

Graves didn't go over too well with Lucille. He asked her if she were Jewish, perhaps assuming she might be since she had a Jewish husband. It turned out he was a devout Christian, and he wanted her to come with him to a Sunday Service where she might be "Born Again."

She assured him that a single instance of being born was enough for her.

Cast as a building contractor, Graves enters the hardware store run by Lucy and Curtis (that is, Gale Gordon). He is seeking some plumbing fixtures. As it turns out, Graves was Lucy's first big crush, and he seems eager "to rekindle the old flame."

On a date, she wears a dress instead of her usual slacks. But, as it turns out, she no longer harbors a romantic feeling for him. Both her husband, Gary Morton, and also Leslie Nielson, had been considered for the Graves role.

For an October 18 telecast, *Lucy Gets Her Wires Crossed*, Peter Baldwin was the director. In this episode (No. 4), Dick Gautier, with a strong supporting cast, played a TV talk show host.

He visits the store run by Lucy and Curtis, who are facing a fall-off in business because of the opening, nearby, of a superstore chain.

Gautier was a comedian, singer, and caricaturist known for his role of "Hymie the Robot" in the hit TV show, *Get Smart*.

Lucy hopes to publicize the hardware store to help its sagging sales. She persuades Gautier to invite Curtis onto his TV show as "Mr. Fix-It." Somehow, she manages to get in on the act, which leads to another misstep when she accidentally ends up gluing herself to Curtis.

Also cast in the show was Kellie Martin as Patty. She was soon to become a familiar face on TV when she played Becca Thatcher in *Life Goes On* (1989-1993) on ABC.

Hoping to beef up the sagging series, director Baldwin Hired Arthur Marx to write episode No. 5, *Lucy as a Sex Symbol*, telecast on October 25.

He was the son of Groucho Marx, and Lucille shared her experiences of working in the 1938 comedy film, *Room Service,* with all the Marx Brothers.

The plot was anemic. Lucy comes across an old saxophone while searching for items for a garage sale. She decides to turn her granddaughter, Becky, into a sax player, but it soon becomes apparent that developing saxophone-playing skills is not a natural fit for Becky.

Coincidentally, Lucille was a hit when she starred in the September 22, 1952 episode of *I Love Lucy* that depicted her playing the saxophone, making it a comic highlight.

Between filming episodes of *Life With Lucy,* she took time out to be a guest star on *The Late Show Starring Joan Rivers,* a 60-minute telecast on Fox that aired on October 30.

Rivers' other guest was First Lady Nancy Reagan.

During Rivers' stint as a substitute host for Johnny Carson on *The Tonight Show,* she had interviewed Lucille, and had a lot of shared references Likewise, Lucille had also met Nancy Reagan before—in her case when she was known as Nancy Davis, then a starlet under contract to MGM in the late 1940s.

Lucille had not been alerted that both the First Lady and Rivers would be formally attired, and she appeared in a purple outfit that looked like it had been purchased at a second-hand clothing store.

Lucille had been one of Rivers' first guests on *The Late Show,* which had premiered on October 9.

JOAN RIVERS

Many consumers found **Joan Rivers** inspirational, a prophet whose bittersweet wisdom transcended her acerbic wit and her gut-busting (sometimes scathing) indictments of other celebrities, especially politicians.

Bouncing Back reviewed her survival from, in her words, "EVERYTHING," in her case, the suicide of her husband, Edgar, her (temporary) estrangement from her only child, Melissa, and the on-again, off-again insecurities associated with roller-coaster career.

Lucille eventually configured Rivers as one of her best and most understanding friends.

MOTHER KNOWS BEST

In one TV format or another, **Joan Rivers** *(left)* managed to interview "movers and shakers" in hip and humorous ways that the public tended to remember.

One of her talk shows included conversations with both Nancy Reagan and Lucille Ball.

River's daughter, **Melissa** *(right),* who was sometimes mentioned as an object of her mother's affection in her comedy acts, is depicted above, too.

After Melissa's divorce was legally concluded, Joan — with her distinctive style and delivery—advised her "to be as sexually free as you like," and "to be much sluttier. You need to put it out there., Enjoy it while you're young, girl. Shorten that skirt, push up those boobs, put on some lifts."

Unlike Lucille, Rivers was an advocate of plastic surgery. She told Lucille, "I've had so many eyelifts, tummy tucks, and other forms of plastic surgery that when I die, I'm gonna donate my body to Tupperware."

Lucille had long admired Rivers for her comedic style, calling her "a troublemaker, trailblazer, and pioneer for women comedians." Both Rivers and Lucille had continuously fought against the legend that women can't be comedians.

The teaming of Lucille and Rivers on *The Late Show* did not produce comedy but struck a sad note that brought Lucille to tears. It started on a friendly note as Rivers told her she hoped she would be on television for another twenty-five years.

Lucille started counting the years on her fingers, asking, "Do you know how old I will be twenty-five years from now?"

Teary-eyed, she expressed her disappointment at the harsh press criticism directed her way for appearing on *Life With Lucy* at her age. "I had no idea I'd be chastised for working at my age. I get lousy notices for coming back at all, which I find strange. I was so amazed at the assault in the press. I can take critique about a show…I'm used to that. But being criticized for coming back on TV—that was all too much."

Rivers would soon confront unexpected disasters of her own. When she challenged the Fox executives who had fired her husband, Edgar Rosenberg, from his job as her show's producer, the networks had also fired her—in her case on May 15, 1987.

Three months later, on August 14, Rosenberg, from within a hotel room in Philadelphia, committed suicide, as has been mentioned before. Rivers blamed Fox for the tragedy, claiming that they had humiliated him.

Later, Rivers credited Nancy Reagan for helping her recover from the firing and the suicide.

Fox continued with *The Lucy Show,* but with Rivers gone, the producers of *The Late Show* backed a rotating list of celebrity hosts.

***

It was back to work for Lucille when she returned to the studio to star in *Lucy Makes Curtis Byte the Dust, episode 6.* Telecast on November 1, it was helmed by veteran director Marc Daniels.

In this plot, Lucy and Curtis purchase a computer to organize the financial records of their hardware store. When she uses the computer to order some non-returnable merchandise, she tries to get the bank to stop a check from being cashed. While doing so, she accidentally informs the bank that Curtis is dead.

One of the guest stars was Dave Madden as Stanley Bigelow. Canada-born, he had become known in the 1970s, when he starred with The Partridge Family, playing the group's manager opposite Shirley Jones. He later had a recurring role as a diner Earl Hicks, in the hit sitcom, *Alice,* that ran from the mid-1970s to the mid-1980s.

Lucille's other co-star was Billy Van Zandt, who was both an actor and playwright. He had written such Off-Broadway plays as *You've Got Hate*

Mail and *Drop Dead!*.

He would later be nominated for an Emmy for a special he wrote called *I Love Lucy: The Very First Show*. Later, he would write a best-selling memoir, *Get in the Car, James (Adventures in the TV Wasteland)*.

Episode 7, *Lucy, Legal Eagle* (November 8), was based on a very anemic script. During a clean-up yard sale, Lucy tries to pass off her grandson's teddy bear as her own because she doesn't want Kevin to be mocked by his friends as a sissy. She sticks it in a bag, which is then purchased by a horrible woman, Hilda Loomis (Dena Dietrich). Lucy offers a $50 reward for the return of the teddy bear, but the Loomis character demands $500. Lucy takes her to small claims court.

Several talented but relatively unknown actors were cast in this episode. Dietrich, a native of Pittsburgh, was seen a lot on television, portraying "Mother Nature" in Chiffon margarine commercials from 1971 to 1979. Mel Brooks also cast her in *The History of the World, Part I* (1981).

Brooklyn-born Don Diamond portrayed "Crazy Cat," the sidekick of Chief Wild Eagle on the popular 1960s TV sitcom, *F-Troop* (1965-1967). Diamond had also starred as "El Toro," the sidekick of Bill Williams cast as Kit Carson in 105 episodes of an early TV series, *The Adventures of Kit Carson* (1951-1955).

ONLY IN AMERICA Can an talented actor's long-standing career be most clearly remembered, generations later, by its associations with campy, over-the-top ads—in this case, *Chiffon* margarine.

Such was the case of **Dena Dietrich**, depicted above as "Mother Nature" in an ad campaign that's remembered by pop cultists many decades after its heyday in the 70s.

Dena, with less spectacular after-effects (and probably lower residuals, too) later appeared in one of the final episodes of the ill-fated *Life with Lucy*—a series reviewed by some critics as "a disaster."

***

Bruce Bilson was brought in to direct the last telecast of *Life With Lucy*, episode 8, *Mother of the Bride,* which aired on November 15.

Audrey Meadows was cast as Lucy's sister, who arrives to oversee a ceremony where Margo and Ted renew their wedding vows. She immediately starts to take over, arousing the ire of Lucy. A highlight of the episode was a "cake fight" between the two sisters.

In 1952, a fledgling actress, Meadows, left a successful Broadway show to join an emerging new TV sitcom headlined by a brash comic Jackie Gleason. The show, *The Honeymooners,* was destined to go down in television history.

Meadows, the sister of Jayne Meadows, appeared as Alice, the deadpan wife, of Ralph Kramden (Gleason). Supporting actors were Art Carney, a sewer worker, married to Joyce Randolph, their upstairs neighbors.

Later, Meadows became the only member of *The Honeymooners* who drew residuals from all those reruns. Her brother, Edward, a lawyer, had inserted a provision in her contract, and it later brought her millions. She hardly needed all that loot because in time, she would wed two multi-millionaires.

The last *Life With Lucy* telecast was also the best. Hoping to save the show, Aaron Spelling talked to Meadows about becoming a regular on the show, somewhat like Vivian Vance (as Ethel Mertz) was in all those *I Love Lucy* episodes. Meadows rejected the offer.

Her sister, Jayne Meadows, later claimed, "I cannot reveal it, but there is a personal problem between my sister and Miss Ball. There is no way that Audrey would work with her on a regular series. No way in hell."

Both Spelling and Gary Morton learned of ABC's cancellation but did not tell Lucy right away. She was filming the *Mother of the Bride* sequence, and they didn't want her to know until the end of the shoot.

Spelling later blamed Lucille for the demise of the series. "She didn't want enough innovation in her Lucy character. First off, she should not have insisted on being called Lucy again. I wanted to name her Myrtle. She simply refused to update the Lucy character. Long ago, it was fresh and original. By 1986, she had gotten very stale with those tired old jokes."

In 2002, *TV Guide* ranked *Life With Lucy* as 26th on its list of the all-time worst TV sitcoms. Some earlier critics had defined it as "Disaster No. One."

***

The premiere episode of *Life With Lucy* was the highest rated among viewers of the entire eight-part series. After the first telecast, ratings plummeted. Most viewers preferred to watch such shows as NBC's *The Facts of Life* or CBS's *Downturn*.

Variety wrote, "*Life With Lucy* is on the Nielsen critical list. Lucille Ball's TV series comeback is heading for an inglorious end."

When that article came out, the series had dropped to No. 75 among viewers. "That puts Ball in the graveyard shift," one viewer claimed.

After watching its first episode, critic Pauline Kael "stuck a knife in my back," in Lucille's opinion.

"Like most older stars who wear too much makeup, Lucille Ball ends up looking like a drag queen," Kael claimed.

Steve Allen, once her friend and supporter, watched two episodes and commented: "Lucille's comedy hasn't aged well. Her gags are from the 1950s and don't work in the 1980s. It's a different world out there."

The reviewer for *Channels* wrote: "That wasn't Lucy up on the screen in *Life With Lucy*, but some elderly imposter. Caked with makeup, she looks mummified. Her voice, deep and hoarse, sounds like a bullfrog in agony. What used to be cute and girlish in a younger woman like Lucy Ricardo turns out to be embarrassing in a senior citizen today."

Another critic said, "One of the key problems of the show seems to be less with Lucy than with her supporting actors. With the exception of Gale

Gordon and Donovan Scott, the young cast she surrounded herself with seems to be overacting, shouting their lines, not offering much support to the aging star in any way."

Lucille would always remember the day she and Morton closed down their offices and walked toward their cars. "People who were normally friendly turned their backs on us and pretended not to notice us. They seemed too embarrassed to face us. It was like we were lepers."

Ann Sothern, her longtime friend, was the first person she called when she got home. "ABC has fired me," she blurted out in a tear-choked voice. "That has never happened to me before. I think they wanted Lucy Ricardo of long ago and got beaten down me, a has-been."

Sothern offered what sympathy she could, but she, too, would face the dilemma of being a has-been, a sparkling star of yesterday now growing old, fat, and outside the mainstream.

The next day, Lucille was told that a tabloid had run her career obit. Once hailed as "The Queen of Television," that newspaper in "Second Coming" headlines proclaimed: "THE QUEEN IS DEAD."

***

Lucille had been so certain of her daughter's talent that she felt she was ready to star in her own show back in 1972 when her daughter was working as a regular on *Here's Lucy*.

A noteworthy episode was aired on February 14 entitled *Kim Finally Cuts You-Know-Who's Apron Strings*. In *Here's Lucy*, Lucie played Lucy's daughter, Kim. She moves out of her mother's home, rents her own apartment, and meets new friends.

Although the episode was viewed as a potential pilot for a new series, there were no takers. Lucie, therefore, resumed playing daughter Kim for seasons 5 and 6. In vivid contrast, Desi Jr. had long ago bolted from the series.

Escaping from the long shadow cast by her famous mother, Lucie Arnaz was finally given her own television show. From April 2 until June 11 in 1985, CBS telecast *The Lucy Arnaz Show*.

Lucie played Dr. Jane Lucas, a psychologist who answers questions from the public on her radio show and also writes an advice column for a newspaper.

Her character was obviously inspired by Ann Landers or Abigail Van Buren who wrote the popular

"Dear Abby" column.

The Arnaz show was directly based on the British TV drama, *Agony*, which aired on London Weekend Television from 1979 to 1981. *[In London, advice columnists were called "Agony Aunts."]*

Coincidentally, in 1981, as *Agony* went off the air in Britain, Desi Jr. made a TV movie entitled *Advice for the Lovelorn,* starring Cloris Leachman. That telefilm was supposed to be a pilot for a series that was never picked up.

Just a year before Lucie's show was aired, PBS presented the latest version of *Miss Loneyhearts* starring Eric Roberts. The film was a latter-day version of another movie that had starred Montgomery Clift. Both stories were based on the famous Nathanael West novel *Miss Lonelyhearts.*

Promotional material for the new Lucie Arnaz show heralded it as "YOU'RE GOING TO LOVE THIS LUCY."

The series was filmed in New York during which time Lucie found out she was pregnant. Therefore, the first six episodes had to be rushed to completion.

[Coincidentally, the same thing had happened to Lucille when she became pregnant with Lucie during the filming of the first pilot for I Love Lucy *in 1951.]*

In Lucie's new series, she not only has to deal with her radio broadcasts and her newspaper advice column, but faces a chauvinistic boss, Jim Gordon (Tony Roberts); her eccentric secretary, Loretta (Karen Jablons-Alexander); her immature co-host Larry Love (Tod Waring), and her interfering sister, Jill (Lee Bryant).

The show also features Jane having to contend with her overly protective mother, who is not seen but calls frequently. Guess who that mother is?

Cast as her boss, Tony Roberts and Lucie were both presenters in 1981 at the Tony Awards aired on CBS. *[Coincidentally, Roberts had appeared on Broadway in They're Playing Our Song, although he joined the cast after Lucie's departure.]*

The pilot for the first episode of *The Lucie Arnaz Show* was called *The Old Boyfriend.* Lucie, as Jane, discovers that her old beau had been a big liar. Ruefully, she decides that "After twelve years, I can put down the torch."

At the end of the show, she advises her listeners, "Happiness is being aware of the fact that you're not going to be happy all the time."

Playing her former boyfriend, Scott, was the Iowa-born actor, John Getz. He had been the standby for Robert Keith in the Broadway production of *They're Playing Our Song,* which had, of course, starred Lucie.

Getz was far better known to Americans when he was the "Shampoo Man" in a Johnson & Johnson Baby Shampoo commercial shot in the late 1970s. His latest appearance on TV has been with Jane Fonda and Lily Tomlin in *Grace and Frankie.*

On her first telecast of *The Lucie Arnaz Show,* the new pilot attracted 20% of viewers, just a sliver over the viewer percentages for *Three's a Crowd* on ABC, but far below *The A-Team* on NBC, which came in with 37% of viewers.

[Three's a Crowd (*also known as* Three's Company, Too) *was produced as a spin-off and continuation of Three's Company. Starring John Ritter, it aired from September 1984 till April 1985.*]

Even so, the executives at CBS chose to cancel The Lucie Arnaz Show for the fall season of 1986.

Lucie told *The Los Angeles Times:* "I wasn't anxious to do a television series. I have no desire to become any more famous than I already am—and I don't mean that egotistically, I've been well known for...well, really ever since I was born, because of whose daughter I was. I've never had a burning ambition to be famous. I grew up with it. I know what it's like."

Lucie had come to the show with impressive credentials: She had been the recipient of The Carbonel Award (1978); the Los Angles Drama Critics Award (1979); the Theatre World Award (1979); and the Sarah Siddons Award (1986).

During the early part of their married life, Lucie and her second husband, Laurence Luckinbill, also a performer, lived in an apartment on Central Park West in Manhattan. They eventually left the cramped quarters and moved to a farm about eighty miles north of the city of Rhinebeck in New York State. Their new home was an Early American farmhouse in the town of Katomah.

In the wake of the death of her father, Desi Arnaz, Lucie, with her husband and three children, decided to move to the upper reaches of Beverly Hills, a short drive from the home of her mother. Perhaps she knew that Lucille's days were numbered, and she wanted to be close at hand.

***

Beginning in 1985, death seemed to hover over Desi Sr., and to a lesser degree, over Lucille herself, who found herself growing weaker every month or so. "Death is like a stage actor on Broadway, waiting in the wings, soon to make his ghoulish entrance into Desi's life and, eventually, I'm sure, my own. I don't know how much longer I can go on."

It was Lucie's stepmother, Edie (aka Mrs. Desi Arnaz), who went first, dying in 1985 after a three-year battle with cancer. Up until that spring, she had led a fairly normal life, experiencing the usual ups and downs in her turbulent 22-year marriage to Desi. In her final weeks, she grew weaker and weaker, and Desi knew her time was near.

Upon Edie's death, Desi went into a long, slow decline, having lost his wife and also his once-flourishing empire. "I never realized how much I needed and depended on Edie until she's gone," he told Lucie. "I think I will soon follow her."

His financial losses had mounted because of his gambling debts and his excessive medical bills. He admitted, "Edie and I have run up staggering medical costs."

He'd been forced to sell off his real estate, having sadly departed from his horse-breeding ranch.

He still kept his beach house at Del Mar but found it an isolated and lonely retreat after Edie's death.

Although his mother, Lolita Arnaz, was still alive, he was forced to put her in a nursing home because, in his present condition, he could no longer look after her.

In the wake of his wife's death, Desi resumed his heavy drinking and even returned to smoking five Cuban cigars a day.

It was reported that Desi Jr., no stranger to booze himself, tried to intervene and keep his father away from the bottle. But it seemed too little, too late. "Dad is too far gone," he was alleged to have said.

When Desi needed to be closer to medical services, Lucille, with Morton's permission, moved her former husband into the cottage behind her main house in Beverly Hills.

The day he moved in, he turned to her and looked nostalgically at the main house. "There once was a day when I lived there. Not only lived there but was the master of the house. Now I'm a guest in the cottage. At least I can see more of my kids and get to know my three grandchildren. Actually, because of my son, the babe magnet, I felt I have more than a trio of grandkids. But who's counting?"

Early in 1986, Desi Sr. phoned Lucille to welcome her to the new year. His voice suddenly choked up. As he confessed: "This morning, my doctor told me I have lung cancer, and it's far advanced. I know this will be my last year occupying my small place on the planet. I want to thank you for all your love and support over the years. I wish I could have been a better husband."

She burst into tears. "Let's forget about what could have been and deal with the reality of getting you all the care the medical profession can provide."

She often functioned as his chauffeur, driving him to and from Scripps Memorial Hospital at La Jolla. Privately, his doctor told Lucille, "He's undergoing radiation and chemotherapy, but it's hopeless. He's too far gone."

Back in Del Mar, living alone, he didn't want to see any old friends and soon no longer took their phone calls. One old friend, Marcella Rabwin, who lived nearby, did come to visit, and he agreed to see her. The two of them talked in his bedroom, and she later reported that she found him living with the regrets of yesterday and thinking of what might have been.

"Finally, I asked him, 'Are you still in love with Lucille?'"

"I've never stopped loving her," he answered.

Putting her husband, Larry Luckinbill, temporarily on hold, Lucie journeyed to Del Mar to aid and assist her father. She was there with him on March 2 when he turned sixty-nine. "I don't think I will ever make it to the big 7-0."

His chemotherapy had caused him to lose his gray hair, and his weight dropped to under one-hundred pounds. "Imagine that...I used to be a bit chubby."

Lucille phoned frequently, and wanted to visit him at Del Mar, but he refused. Finally, she drove down there anyway, against his wishes. He told her, "I want you to remember me as I used to be, a handsome, studly Cuban bandleader."

At first, after Lucille arrived, he would only talk to her through the closed door. But she finally forced her way in and tried to conceal the shock on her face upon viewing his physical decline.

She spent three hours with him, sitting by his bedside, and holding his hand. As she recalled, "This final episode of Lucy and Ricky Ricardo was never filmed. What a sad ending. Even Ethel and Fred Mertz were no longer with us. Gone was the laughter of yesterday. Gone With the Wind. A storm was brewing."

Daughter Lucie sensed that her father was nearing his death, and she phoned her mother, "I think he's going. He hardly utters a word, and he's refused food for three days. I'm not sure if he even understands what's going on anymore. I'm going to put the phone up to his ear and hold it if you want to say some final words to him."

She did just that, telling her father, "There's a redhead on the phone who wants to speak to you."

As Lucille recalled, "Desi hardly said a word to me. I don't think he could. But I told him, 'I love you, Desi, and I always have. I always will.'" Then she put down the phone.

As she learned, Desi died forty-eight hours later in the arms of his daughter.

Death had come to Desi on December 2, 1986.

The morning Desi died, Lucille was starring with Betty White on *Super Password*. Once witty and sharp in playing the game on TV, she now appeared confused and seemed stumped, lacking the mental agility to come up with any good clues.

After the show, she told White "You know, it's the damndest thing… God damn it! I promised myself I would not get upset. But I'm devastated. I bet I'll cry all night, not only for Desi, but for myself. I know I, too, will soon be joining him."

Leaving the studio, she had to face the press, putting up a brave front. "Desi has been ill with cancer for many months. My family and I have been praying for his release from all the pain and suffering he has been forced to endure. My relationship with Ricky Ricardo has remained steadfast over the years, although we have gone on to find love in the arms of others. Gary and Desi respected each other and remained on amiable terms. I'm grateful to God that Desi's suffering is over. His children, Desi Jr. and Lucie, are in mourning over the loss of their father. He loved them very much, and his love was returned. He adored them, and also his grandchildren."

Lucie, too, faced the press. "He was a good father," she said, "but a very lonely man at times. He chose a difficult path to follow in life. My dad was bright, a genius of sorts, and he was also a bundle of emotions, like an open wound. One that never heals. My mother and the rest of the family have been expecting his death for months. He suffered a great deal. Even though expecting his death, it was like a stab in my own heart. That heart of mine is filled with nothing but love for a kind and gentle man, a loving husband and a loving family man."

Desi had left instructions in his will that his body was to be cremated, his ashes tossed to the winds. "I think having an open coffin is ghoulish, something out of a Dracula film. I don't want my friends and family to see what has happened to Ricky Ricardo displayed in a casket. I want only my picture on display, perhaps how I looked in 1955, perhaps a loving picture taken of Lucy and me."

Only a select group of friends and relatives appeared at the actual ceremony at his home parish. St. James Roman Catholic Church at Solana Beach. A few hundred fans, some driving in from Arizona and Nevada, were amassed outside.

Danny Thomas, a longtime friend and business associate, delivered the eulogy: "I will never, never forget Desi Arnaz. That son of Cuba who came to America to forge a new life. I speak of not only what he did for me, but for what he achieved for the entire television industry. We owe him a big debt of gratitude. No one, but no one, has ever come close to the kind of television that he and Miss Ball brought to the emerging industry that changed all of our lives."

In a pew up front, Lucille sat with Gary Morton. She did not wear black but appeared in a light-colored outfit. Every now and then she removed her large sunglasses to wipe away tears.

As she left the church, a little girl, perhaps six years old, emerged from the crowd and handed her a red rose.

The press, including television newscasts, hailed Desi's passing. *The New York Times* called him, "an important figure in the history of television. *I Love Lucy* is being shown twenty-four hours a day, somewhere, in some language."

Newsweek was muted in his obit, recognizing him as an innovative producer and shrewd businessman as head of Desilu. "Yet to all the world, he is still second banana to Lucy Ricardo."

Variety hailed him as "the great architect of the *I Love Lucy* series. He'll have a prominent position in Hollywood heaven."

Growing more feeble by the day, Lolita Arnaz in her nursing home was never told of her son's death. The news was held from her because of the fear of what it might do to her condition.

On occasion, and in a weak voice, she inquired, "Where is my Desiderio? Why doesn't he come to see me anymore? Does he no longer love his *madre?*"

Lolita outlived her son, dying less than three years after the death of Desi Sr. She was ninety-one years old.

***

Long after his death, Desi's role in television was re-evaluated. Critic Douglas McGrath wrote: "Even more than Arnaz's presence behind the screen, his presence on screen is missed. This is the last great secret of the appeal of *I Love Lucy.* Arnaz is a wonderful performer. Undervalued in his time, he was the only one of the four principals never nominated for an Emmy (as an actor—he won as a producer). Yet what he created in Ricky Ricardo was infinitely more advanced and complicated than William Frawley's cheap grump. Arnaz has to play the full range of feelings a man has for his wife: Love, desire, frustration, fury, forgiveness, delight, amusement."

In an article in *The New York Times* appeared this evaluation:

> "There is no question that the best work Desi Arnaz and Lucille Ball ever did was the I Love Lucy *series of the 1950s. After their divorce, Ball became her own producer, and it is no coincidence that none of her subsequent series ever approached the quality of* I Love Lucy*. In fact, under her supervision, each series was worse than the one before. One of the things people mention when they talk about Lucy as a producer was how cheap she was. On that pleasant* The Lucy Show, *the unspeakable* Here's Lucy, *and the pathetic* Life With Lucy, *everything feels stunted, rented, used (including the scripts). Without Arnaz's taste and guidance, these shows did not serve her. They exploited her. The airborne elation an audience felt during* I Love Lucy, *a feeling akin to the joy of watching great silent comedians, was gone. The shows were earthbound and more often than not left their viewers weary, the very sensation* I Love Lucy *so magically erases."*

***

As a host, Lucille's last TV special was *An All-Star Party for Clint Eastwood*, that tall, laconic, squinty-eyed star of "spaghetti westerns" and cop thrillers who morphed his way into super-stardom.

Produced and written by Paul W. Keyes, with whom Lucille had worked before, the 120-minute tribute was telecast by CBS on December 15, 1986. That night, Lucille got a lot of hugs and kisses, even from Cary Grant. Mostly, she was surrounded by loving faces, including Sammy Davis Jr., Merv Griffin, the ever-present Bob Hope, Don Rickles, and one of her oldest friends James Stewart. Roberta Flack and Marsha Mason added some female charm.

Although choreographed as a tribute to Eastwood, the telecast was actually a fund raiser to help put some money into the bank account of Variety Clubs International.

The days after Christmas found Lucille in Washington, D.C. for *The Kennedy Center Honors*, telecast 120 minutes on CBS. Beginning in 1978, the center honored men and women who had made a significant contribution to American Culture through the Performing Arts.

The festivities also included a series of private parties and a ceremony where the honorees were presented to the President, in this case, Ronald Reagan, Lucille's longtime friend.

It was also a sad occasion

since Desi had originally been set to host the event. In the wake of his death, Robert Stack, whom Desi had once cast in the hit TV crime drama, *The Untouchables* (1959-1963), delivered the speech that Desi had written for the occasion.

Lucille, although looking her age, was beautifully groomed, wearing a black and gold designer gown. She listened to a musical tribute from Bea Arthur, Pam Dawber, and Valerie Harper. Backstage, Valerie recalled the days when she was a chorus girl in the Broadway musical, *Wildcat,* that had starred Lucille in 1960.

"The tribute sparked up my sagging spirits," Lucille recalled. "I felt I was still loved and appreciated, even though I had been fired from ABC, my series cancelled. And of course, I was still in mourning over the death of Desi."

Instead of Desi as host, the anchor that night was Walter Cronkite, the most famous news anchor in America.

He was joined by an array of celebrities that featured Glenn Close, Agnes de Mille, José Ferrer, the ballerina Margot Fonteyn, Rosemary Harris, Quincy Jones, Walter Matthau, Liv Ullman, and Peter Ustinov, among others.

Tears came to Lucille's eyes as she was hailed as "a superb clown of infinite range whose side-splitting buffoonery was carved into her bone marrow by her exquisite understanding of the tragic sense of life."

In addition to Lucille, other honorees that night included Ray Charles, Hume Cronyn and his wife, Jessica Tandy, and the violinist and conductor, Yehudi Menuhin.

Fonteyn introduced Lucille to a fellow honoree, London-born Antony Tudor, the fabled choreographer and dancer. Lucille later told Gary Morton, "Tudor was a bit highbrow for me, but later, I learned how important he was. Of course, I knew his last name. I made a stupid joke: 'Are you descended from Henry VIII? If so, how many wives have you had beheaded?'"

"None, my dear girl," he answered. "I have a lover, a life partner, Hugh Laing. He is the greatest thing that ever happened to me. That, and dance, have made my life worth living."

"Prima ballerina assoluta," **Dame Margot Fonteyn**.

Her most famous partner was the Russian-born defector from his native land, Rudolf Nureyev. She danced with him at his debut with the Royal Ballet in London in 1962. As a team, they became an international sensation.

The fabled dancer and choreographer **Antony Tudor** shows how it's done.

Lucille was very provocative with him: "Male ballet dancers in those tight, tight pants show basket. What if a guy doesn't have much basket to show?"

"They stuff it with a sock," he answered.

Tudor died just months after Lucille met him. But his legacy lives on as expressed by Mikhail Baryshnikov. "We do Tudor's ballets because we must. His work is our conscience."

***

After the Kennedy Center honors, Lucille would end the decade by making a few more public appearances, mainly testimonials and tributes, but also award shows.

She knew that time was running out for her, and the Oscar she coveted was now far beyond her reach. But was it?

She didn't expect even an honorary Oscar for her relatively lackluster film career.

One possible script appeared that, in her words, "had Best Actress Oscar written all over it." It was said that producer Richard D. Zanuck briefly considered suggesting her for the co-starring role in *Driving Miss Daisy,* which had already been cast with Morgan Freeman.

This was a comedy drama directed by Alfred Uhry, who had presented it as a play in 1987. It would be released as a film in 1989, the year of Lucille's death.

A publicity photo of **Jessica Tandy** and **Morgan Freeman** in *Driving Miss Daisy.*

Near the end of her life, Lucille felt that her only chance to win an Oscar involved being cast as Miss Daisy in that 1989 film.

"The old Jewish lady was said to possess the kind of stubborness that one hesitates to crack, since underneath there is something fragile," Lucille said. "Yet there is also a fierce intelligence that comes through. That's me, baby!"

Had she been offered, or had she accepted, the role, of Daisy Werthan, Lucille would have been nicknamed "Miss Daisy." She would have played a rich, widowed, 72-year-old retired Jewish schoolteacher who lives alone in Atlanta.

Her 40-year-old Jewish son (Dan Aykroyd) buys her a 1949 Hudson Commodore and hires a black man, "Hoke," (Morgan Freeman) as her chauffeur.

The film deals with racism in the South and anti-Semitism, including the bombing of her synagogue.

As it turned out, no official offer was ever made to Lucille. The producers and directors ultimately decided that Jessica Tandy was the ideal choice. Lucille had met Tandy in Washington when both of them had been honored at the Kennedy Center.

An English actress, she had experienced a peak in her stage career when she had starred opposite Marlon Brando in 1948, cast as Blanche DuBois in Tennessee Williams' *A Streetcar Named Desire.* She became the oldest actress to receive an Academy award for *Driving Miss Daisy* in 1989.

Lucille had been right. That Golden Globe statuette awaited the star of *Miss Daisy*, since it was such a powerful part.

***

One of the most star-studded galas Lucille ever attended was for the telecast of *Happy Birthday, Hollywood,* lasting 180 minutes on ABC on the night of May 18, 1987. Jack Haley Jr. produced the show with "More Stars than there are in Heaven."

Just a fraction of celebrities included not only Lucille, but Milton Berle, Carol Burnett, Sid Caesar, Sammy Davis Jr., Robert Goulet, Lillian Gish, Alice Faye, Richard Gere, Charlton Heston, Dustin Hoffman, Bob Hobe, Tony Martin, Debbie Reynolds, Robert Stack, Lana Turner, Esther Williams, and Loretta Young.

Callow newcomers dismissed Lucille and Bob Hope's ode to *Gigi* (winner of nine Academy Awards in 1958) as corny. Depicted above are **Hermione Gingold** and **Maurice Chevalier**, portraying lovers who meet decades after their passions have faded, in a scene from that film.

But to members of the generation that had loved that (Vincente Minnelli-directed) film, Lucille and Hope's replication of that scene moved some of them to tears.

The lyrics of the song they replicated? *"I Remember It Well."*

Lucille remembered the occasion also for meeting Luise Rainer, born one year before her. The delicate actress was the first performer to bring home back-to-back Oscars, first for *The Great Ziegfeld* (1936) and for *The Good Earth* (1937), in which she played a weary and overworked Chinese peasant woman.

That same month (May 25), Lucille once again was a guest star on yet another salute to Bob Hope. This time it was called *Bob Hope's High-Flying Birthday Extravaganza* telecast for 120 minutes on NBC honoring his 84th birthday.

Hugging and kissing her former co-star, Lucille told Hope "Let's you and I dance the Charleston when we celebrate your 100th birthday."

She appeared well-groomed, carefully styled, and gowned in a mauve creation for the taping at the Pope Air Force Base in North Carolina.

She and Hope performed a duet, "I Remember It Well," that had been so brilliantly sung before by Maurice Chevalier and Hermione Gingold in *Gigi* (1958).

This was a historical occasion for Lucille, as it marked the last time she would perform a comedy skit on TV. She'd played a hillbilly before. This time, she is a gun-toting, backwoods mother trying to maintain the virginity of her daughters (cast with Phyllis Diller, Brooke Shields, and Barbara Mandrell) from the lecherous Hope.

At the age of 84, Hope did not appear to be much of a threat to the virginity of either of these women, especially Shields.

Joining in that night of fun was Dolores, Hope's wife, along with Glen Campbell, Don Johnson, and surprise of surprise, Ronald Reagan, President of the United States and former star of *Bedtime for Bonzo* (1951) in which a chimp stole the picture from him.

Gary Morton and **Lucille**, looking puffy, celebrate the marriage ceremony of dancer/teacher/choreographer **Amy Bargiel** with **Desi Jr.**

Later, Lucille told her husband, "My son's first marriage was all wrong, right from the honeymoon. But on this second time around, I think it's going to work. Amy is a fine girl."

***

The days of Desi Jr., a "babe magnet" with a roving eye, came to an end when he met and married Amy Laura Bargiel on October 8, 1987. A recovering addict, he was introduced to her at a meeting of the New Life Foundation, that organization inspired by the teachings of Vernon Howard, dedicated to spiritual and physical renewal.

In time, Desi Jr. would purchase the Boulder Theatre in Boulder, Nevada, then on the brink of ruin, and restore it. He and his wife turned it into the Boulder City Ballet Company.

Although Desi, Jr., had only a small but symbolic role in *The Mambo Kings*, everyone in the entertainment industry fully understood that his performance had been configured as an homage to his father's (Desi Sr.'s) life and career as "The Conga King."

In the right-hand photo, **Desi Jr.** older and careworn, with few traces of his youthful beauty, appears as an incarnation of his father. He's positioned between **Antonio Banderas** *(left)* and the Italian actor, **Armand Assante**. Each of them portrays high-testosterone Latino musicians of the ilk once personified by Desi Sr.

Amy was a dancer who had taught ballet at the University of Nevada. As executive director of the new ballet company in Boulder, she was affectionately known as "Miss Amy" by her students.

Unlike his first marriage to actress Linda Purl, Desi seemed to have gotten it right the second time around. Amy turned out to be a supportive wife.

"I give and get lots of hugs every day and wouldn't change my profession for anything," she said. "I love children and find great pleasure in providing them this magical world where they can dance and sing and express themselves. Along with pink roses, kittens, and God's abundance, ballerinas are certainly one of the most beautiful gifts our eyes can behold."

In addition to running their ballet theater, Desi and Amy were also animal activists, supporting the rescue of baby elephants that have been made orphans because of the lucrative ivory trade.

***

In the wake of the death of Desi Sr., his son would impersonate him in a 1992 film, *The Mambo Kings,* a French-American musical drama based on the 1989 Pulitzer Prize-winning novel, *The Mambo Kings Play Songs of Love* by Oscar Hijuelos. The actual Mambo Kings were brilliantly portrayed by Armand Assante and Antonio Banderas. Desi appears later in the movie as Desi Sr.

The story begins in the early 1950s, when two brothers, musicians Cesar and Nestor Castillo, flee Havana and settle into New York. After much struggle, they get a job at a night club. There, they are discovered by a Cuban bandleader and TV star. Desi Arnaz Sr. (cast with Desi Jr.). He invites the struggling Castillos to sing and act in an episode of his sitcom, namely, *I Love Lucy.*

Before appearing as his father, Desi Jr. dyed his hair jet black. "I wasn't trying to look exactly like Dad," he said. "I was more into getting his essence and mannerisms."

The first scenes were shot at Re-Mar Studios, the former home of Desilu Productions. A set designer recreated the setting of the Tropicana Night Club in pre-Revolution Havana. Lucille appears on the scene in vintage footage taken from a 1952 episode of *I Love Lucy* called "Cuban Pals."

The Mambo Kings opened to a limited release in February of 1992, grossing just under $7 million. Critical reaction was mostly positive, and the

Some historians define **James ("Jimmy") Stewart** as the personification of the best aspects of America during its mid-20th-century heyday. Here's how he appeared early in his spectacularly successful movie career.

On stage, with Lucille, at a shared TV gala celebrating his long associations with Christmas—including *It's a Wonderful Life*—he reminisced about the highs and lows of their parallel but usually separate years in Hollywood.

movie received Oscar and Golden Globe nominations for its original song, "Beautiful Marie of my Soul."

[After a long battle with cancer, Amy, at the age of 63, died on January 23, 2015, four days after Desi's 62nd birthday. He had supported her and suffered along with her ever since she had been diagnosed with brain cancer in January 2013. Amy was survived by her husband and daughters, Hayley, Nichole, and Julia.]

***

Lucille's days were narrowing to a precious few, as her body grew weaker, yet she continued to appear before TV cameras.

In November of 1987, her longtime friend, James Stewart, asked her to come onto a show he was hosting for Fox called *A Beverly Hills Christmas*. This would mark her first and only religious broadcast *["I'm no female Billy Graham," she said]* and she would actually read a passage from the Bible.

Burt Reynolds was also on the show, and she came up to him to hug and embrace him. "Hello, preacher. Half the women in Hollywood told me how you spread the 'gospel' to them."

Over dinner that night, Stewart talked about being semi-retired. He confessed to having turned down the role of Norman Thayer in the movie, *On Golden Pond* (1981), the role going to his best friend, Henry Fonda. "The picture was far better with Hank and his daughter, Jane. Their father-daughter relationship was always troubled."

"Guess what" he said. "I don't know if you caught it or not, but Bette Davis and I did this HBO office drama, *Right of Way* (1983). Right now, I've got this great gig. I'm doing voiceovers for Campbell's Soups."

Beginning in the 1950s, **Ray ("Brother Ray") Charles** has been credited as a pioneer of "soul music."

He did this, it's said, through a combination of musical styles that include jazz, blues, gospel, rhythm & blues, and country music.

Blind since childhood, probably from undiagnosed glaucoma, he was recognized with Kennedy Center Honors, the National Medal of Arts, and 18 Grammy Awards.

Frank Sinatra called him "the only genius in show business," and Billy Joel said, ""This may sound like sacrilege, but I think Ray Charles was more important than Elvis Presley."

She congratulated him on all the many awards he had received in the 1980s, including the Presidential Medal of Freedom and an honorary Oscar in 1989 presented by Cary Grant, his former co-star in *The Philadelphia Story* (1940) with Katharine Hepburn.

"I've loved my wife Gloria," he said. "But the only person who I have loved consistently over the years, in spite of our many differences, is Hank Fonda. He was my soulmate throughout life. I'll never recover from his death in 1982."

Stewart went into seclusion after his beloved wife, Gloria, died. He passed away on July 2, 1997.

***

At the very end of 1987, Lucille appeared on the CBS telecast of *The Kennedy Center Honors*. This time, she was not an honoree. She was there to host a segment devoted to her longtime friend, Sammy Davis Jr.

Joining her to honor the veteran performer was Ray Charles, whom she'd long admired. She told Gary Morton, "Ray never let being blind keep him from rising to the top in show business."

He had been blinded since he was a kid by glaucoma.

Rolling Stone ranked Charles No. 2 on its list of the 100 greatest singers of all time.

Joining Lucille and Charles in their salute to Davis were the Nicholas Brothers, two dancing brothers who excelled in a highly acrobatic technique known as "Flash Dancing." The African America duo was also the greatest tap-dancing team of their day.

Charming, smooth, musically gifted, and easy to like: **Perry Como.**

Lucille said, "if, in my salad days, I was shopping for a husband, Perry Como and Dean Martin would have been at the top of my list. I found both of them sexy and adorable. Faced with a choice, I would have chosen Perry. Dean couldn't be trusted to keep it zipped up."

Another honoree that night was Perry Como, a singer Lucille had long admired. Hugging and kissing him, she told him, "If a certain Cuban bandleader had not come into my life, I would have nailed you, boy."

Bette Davis, also an honoree, came face to face with Lucille. "Let's bury the hatchet," Lucille said. "I don't know what our so-called feud was ever about."

"Whatever it was, I've forgotten it," Bette answered. "I've reserved my forever-lasting anger for Joan Crawford. My greatest delight was pushing the bitch around in *What Ever Happened to Baby Jane?* and serving her a dead rat for dinner."

Oh, Bette," Lucille said. "You are a trip. There will be only one Bette Davis, and the world can be grateful for that."

Lucille congratulated another winner, Nathan Milstein, a Russia-born virtuoso violinist, hailed as one of the finest of the 20th Century.

A final honoree, Alwin Nikolais, also received warm congratulations from Lucille. One of America's greatest choreographers, he was said to have "redefined" dance, calling it "the art of motion which, left to its own merits, becomes the message as well as the medium."

Perhaps suspecting it would be their final farewell, Lucille and Sammy Davis Jr. hugged and kissed each other, holding onto each other for more than a minute. "It's been a hell of a ride, hasn't it, baby?" he asked.

"You can say that again, Sammy boy," she said. "If I have any regrets, it's not what I did, but what I didn't do."

Davis outlived Lucille by a few months, dying on May 16, 1990.

***

Lucille would make three more appearances with Bob Hope on TV. She came together with him in her capacity as a co-host on *America's Tribute to Bob Hope* (telecast on NBC on March 5, 1988). It was obvious to her that he, too, was cutting back. *Variety* had run a story saying that his long-enduring popularity was entering "the twilight zone." NBC cut the number of his specials to four a year, as he did not seem to be going over to a new generation of TV watchers.

The TV event marked the opening of the Bob Hope Cultural Center in Palm Springs. Hope and his wife Dolores sat in a box with Ronald and Nancy Reagan watching the show.

Lucille, who appeared at the opening of the telecast, was one of the moderators, along with Diahann Carroll, Vic Damone, and John Forsythe.

An array of guest stars was also featured, including names known to her such as Phyllis Diller, Ann-Margret, Alan King, Barbara Mandrell, and her beloved George Burns.

She embraced Donald O'Connor. "I still think you're one of the most talented actors ever to grace the screen. It breaks my heart that I was unable to sell that pilot featuring you. You would have been terrific."

Wil Haygood, a staff writer for *The Washington Post*, summed up **Sammy Davis Jr.** like this:

"The life of Sammy Davis Jr appeared to be the fulfillment of the American Dream. From his rise to top billing on the nightclub circuit to his recording contracts, his featured roles on Broadway to his Hollywood stardom, his fame and fortune in Las Vegas to his Rat Pack heyday, Davis seemed to have it all and have done it all."

"Yet despite his successes, his celebrity friendships, and his untold romances, the entertainer was a rolling storm of contradictions and conflicts. Admired and reviled by both blacks and whites, he was tormented by his raging insecurities, never coming to terms with his own skin."

That's show biz," he said. "You take the heartbreaks with the triumphs—in fact, you're lucky to have any triumphs."

Lucille had dinner that night with Dinah Shore, who was also a guest. She would see Dinah one more time in a subsequent tribute to Hope.

"Like you, I'm doing a lot of tributes, one to Dutch Reagan. A special on Jack Benny is in the works. I'll be returning to TV in a show called *Conversation With Dinah*. I want you on as a guest."

After appearing in her spot on *America's Tribute to Bob Hope*, Lucille, along with Gary Morton, was seen dining with two other guests on that show, Danny Thomas and O.J. Simpson.

***

As a new birthday approached, Bob Hope told NBC executives that he was not certain that he wanted to go on the air and announce to America that he was 85 years old. "I fear I've become an anachronism." But he was convinced to go ahead with a star-studded celebration. *Happy Birthday Bob*, a 180-minute program, was telecast May 16, 1988.

Lucille was called upon to perform "Comedy Is a Serious Business" by James Lipton and Cy Colman. Dressed like Judy Garland used to do, she appeared in a tuxedo jacket with no skirt. She and Diahann Carroll agreed, "The legs are the last to go."

Brooke Shields later was quoted as saying, "I sensed something was the matter with Lucille right from the beginning. Her steps didn't match the music from the orchestra. I felt sorry for this old-time trouper, still trying to hang in there after all these years. Would I one day, in my distant future, be trying to do the same thing?"

> With a sinking feeling, and the knowledge that the world she'd struggled to understand and to thrive in was coming to an end, Lucille noted the deaths of many of her friends, frenemies, rivals, and mentors.
>
> Such was the case of **George Burns** in 1996, as noted on the front page of New York's *Daily News*.

Lucille led an impressive list of celebrities on this star-studded night. She was especially gracious to Dolores, Hope's wife. Lucille greeted Sammy Davis Jr., Angie Dickinson, Phyllis Diller, Michael Landon, John Forsythe, Donald O'Connor, Vic Damone, Tony Randall, Don Rickles, Dinah Shore, James Stewart, Danny Thomas, and Betty White, among others.

Lucille spent the most time talking with Dorothy Lamour, who had starred in all those World War II Road Pictures with Hope and Bing Crosby.

"I may be an old lady," Lamour told Lucille, "but I'm still here. I keep busy…you know, concerts, dinner theater, spots on such TV shows as *Hart to Hart*. I sing the old songs and talk about Bob and Bing. I reflect on how I started out at Paramount making $200 a week, ending up pulling in $450,000 per picture. I feel wonderful, Age is just a state of mind, and I'm grateful that God has taken care of me. I'm also grateful for the sarong that made me famous, although I detest wearing a sarong."

At the age of 81, Lamour died at her home in North Hollywood on September 22, 1996. She was interred at Forest Lawn.

In addition to Hope, two of Lucille's oldest friends were also on the show. All three comedians would survive her.

One of Milton Berle's most popular gigs was in 1992 in the TV sitcom,

The Fresh Prince of Bel-Air, in which he was cast as a womanizing, wise-cracking patient, Max Jakey. He later said, "I was just playing myself."

After doing his telecast with Lucille, Berle appeared on the show of Howard Stern, the syndicated radio "shock jock." All of Stern's questions dealt with the size of Berle's penis, as he was famous in Hollywood for the size of his organ, something Lucille could have attested to back in the late 1930s.

Phil Silvers recalled standing next to Berle at a urinal, telling him, "You'd better feed that thing or it will turn on you!"

In later life, Berle found solace in Christian Science, later announcing, "I'm a Christian Scientist Jew."

In April of 2001, he announced to the press that he had a malignant tumor growing in his colon, but that he was declining surgery. He was dead on March 27, 2002.

A memorial service was held for him at the New York Friars Club, Freddie Roman solemnly announcing, "The penis of our beloved Milton Berle has been buried."

Lucille had long admired the comedic talent of George Burns, telling him, "You'll live forever, but I fear I'm checking out," she told him.

"Forget that!" he told her. "At the age of 110, you'll be dancing the Joan Crawford Charleston on television. I'll be in the front row applauding you."

In July of 1994, Burns suffered a head injury after falling in his bathtub, and he underwent surgery to remove the fluid in his skull. He never fully recovered, and his performing career came to an end.

On March 9, 1996, 49 days after his centenary, Burns died in his Beverly Hills home.

Hope would live to celebrate his 100th birthday on May 29, 2003, becoming one of the small group of centenarians in the entertainment field. Known for his self-deprecating humor, he told the press, "I'm so old they've canceled my blood type."

In 1998, five years before his death, an "incorrect" obituary went out over the wires of the

Her involvement in the "Happy Birthday Bob" celebration was particularly pithy to **Lucille**, who had appeared with him—long before her *Lucy* period—in many vintage movies, and in more TV specials than with any other actor.

The middle photo shows **Bob Hope** as "Happy Hope" on the cover of the May 11, 1962 edition of *Life*.

The bottom photo depicts Lucille with **Hope** and **William Demarest** in *Sorrowful Jones*, released in 1949.

Associated Press. His death was announced from the floor of the U.S. Congress.

Actually, he would live until July 27, 2003, dying of pneumonia at his home in Toluca Lake, just two months after his 100th birthday. Dolores died in 2011, four months after her 102nd birthday.

Happy Birthday, Bob would mark Lucille's final TV variety show appearance. Shortly after filming the tribute, she suffered a minor stroke.

***

Lucille, every day, was growing more alarmed over her health. She suffered from high blood pressure and was subject to angina attacks. That shoulder injury she incurred on a ski slope in Colorado continued to give her sharp pain.

She hired Oona White, the choreographer of *Mame,* her last feature film, to help her work out the kinks in her shoulder, easing her pain. Early in January of 1988, she'd had a cyst removed from her thyroid.

On May 10, following in the wake of her latest appearance on the Bob Hope special, she was rushed to the hospital in an ambulance. She later related what had happened to her friend, Jim Brochu, who had become her regular backgammon partner. He wrote about the incident in a book, *Lucy in the Afternoon: An Intimate Memoir of Lucille Ball,* published by William Morrow in 1990.

He quotes her:

"I woke up about four-thirty in the morning and went to the bathroom. I didn't turn on the lights since I knew my way in the dark. After a minute, I felt this heavy object crash into my lap. I thought a piece of the ceiling had fallen down. It hit me so hard. I reached into my lap to see what it was and almost screamed. I felt my arm there. My own right arm! It had fallen asleep. It was over my head when I got up, and I never felt it or thought anything was wrong until it fell in my lap. I started back to bed but fell down before I got there. Gary picked me up and I was rushed to Cedars-Sinai Medical Center."

At the hospital, she underwent intensive around-the-clock care and was heavily medicated. After four days, she became hysterical and started screaming. She reported that large cockroaches were crawling all over her stomach, terrifying her.

Morton was alerted, and he rushed to the hospital. Once there, she ordered him, "get me out of this god damn hell hole. And now! I can't stand another day here."

In an ambulance, she was hauled back to her home in Beverly Hills, where she was under the constant care of a registered nurse and trained therapist, Trudi Arcudi.

It took several weeks of intense therapy, but her condition began to improve, and she lost that slight facial droop that had followed in the wake of the stroke. Slowly, she regained her speech, although not fully. Day after day, she rehearsed vowel sounds.

Although not fully recovered, she received an invitation she could not refuse. She was invited to join Bob Hope for a presentation at the Academy Awards ceremony that year.

***

The Academy Awards ceremony was presented on NBC on March 19, 1989. She and Bob Hope had been asked to introduce a group of young stars of tomorrow, billed as "Oscar Winners of the Future."

Heavily made up, she was glamourously attired in a black sequined gown designed by Ret Turner. It contained a slit that went all the way up her left thigh.

Before going on, and noting how nervous she was, Hope tried to reassure her. "Kid, you may be seventy-eight years old, but you have the look and glamour of a woman half your age. You still look radiant after all these years, and I know you'll knock 'em dead."

Frank Liberman, the publicist for Hope, also offered his assurance. She had asked him if her eyes looked baggy. "When the bright lights go on you, two old war horses like you and Bob will each look thirty years younger. Those wrinkles will disappear. Just vanish. Your shoulders will go from stooped to straight. You'll also be a foot taller."

On the arm of Hope, she walked out onto the stage. Immediately, these two veteran comedians received one of the longest and loudest standing ovations in the history of the Academy.

The occasion would mark her last appearance on television. After she hugged and kissed Hope goodbye, she would never see her longtime co-star again.

As *Variety* reported the next day, "Millions of viewers around the world were treated to 162 years of longevity with the appearance of Lucille Ball and Bob Hope last night."

***

After the Oscar ceremony, Lucille fell into a deep depression. On April 17, she called for Gary Morton, claiming that she was experiencing "excruciating chest pains." He quickly packed a suitcase for her and then drove her to Cedars-Sinai Medical Center, even though she told him, "I loathe the joint."

After examinations from three doctors, the best in the clinic, she was rushed to an operating room. There, she spent seven hours enduring open-heart surgery for a ruptured aorta.

News of her being in the hospital spread across the country, and flowers and get-well cards arrived by the hour.

After time in intensive care, she was moved to a private room. Morton slept on a cot near her bed, keeping a 24-hour vigil.

Urgent calls swamped the switchboard. One observer noted that her floor of Cedars-Sinai resembled a combination botanical garden and a U.S. Post Office.

Her son and daughter rushed to her side, offering what comfort they could but no doubt fearing the worst.

In the early morning hours of April 26, 1989, Lucille woke Morton from his sleep on a cot nearby. She raised herself off the pillow, claiming, "I'm in pain." Those were the last words she ever spoke before descending into unconsciousness.

He immediately summoned her doctors. Although they worked frantically to save her, they knew from the beginning that their cause was hopeless. She was experiencing the throes of death. Her aorta had ruptured again.

It was at 5:47 that morning when her doctor pronounced her dead.

Someone on the hospital staff immediately alerted the Associated Press. The wire service carried the news as Americans were waking up. New Yorkers and other people in the East were the first to hear the news, as TV and radio stations interrupted their regular broadcasting. One Chicago paper ran the headline—LUCILLE BALL DEAD. LUCY RICARDO LIVES."

EPILOGUE

On the night of Lucille's death, hosts Mary Hart and John Tech went on the air for another episode of *Entertainment Tonight,* telecast for 30 minutes on April 26, 1989. The syndicated gossip and entertainment round-up program became the longest-running entertainment magazine show of all time (1982-2011). It had its widest audience that night.

Lucille's longtime home studio also presented a special that night simply entitled *CBS News Special: Lucy.* Dan Rather was the host, and he was joined by other TV reporters, Charles Osgood and Mike Wallace. They interviewed such guests as Dick Van Dyck, Ronald Reagan, Dinah Shore, and even Jerry Lewis. Lewis was the wrong guest to have been invited, but he kept his wisecracks about Lucille to himself, venting them later. He had never liked her, but out of respect, he concealed his animosity on that night of mourning.

William S. Paley, the former chief honcho of CBS, was eighty-eight when he, too, appeared on the show. Putting aside their past differences, he claimed, "Lucille Ball was in a class by herself. She will always be the First Lady of CBS."

When the next issue of *Time* magazine came out, it compared Lucille to other stars. "She was as deft and daring as Harold Lloyd. As rubber faced as Bert Lahr. As touching as Chaplin, More 'ladylike' than Milton Berle."

Newsweek claimed, "She was the most popular woman in the history of television."

Former President Ronald Reagan called her "an American institution." Her long-time friend, Sammy Davis Jr., named her as "one of the world's greatest clowns."

President George H.W. Bush said, "Lucille Ball possessed the gift of laughter. She also embodied an even greater treasure—the gift of love. She appealed to the gentler impulses of the human spirit."

The New York Times claimed that "Lucille Ball helped inaugurate the age of television just as Charlie Chaplin did with silent pictures."

A rival comedian, Carol Burnett, was nonetheless a friend. Hearing of Lucille's demise, she said, "It was like a death in the family."

In a bit of fanciful speculation, a devoted fan told a reporter for *The Miami Herald,* "Today, Lucille Ball joined Desi Arnaz in heaven. They are going to be remarried by God himself. Ethel and Fred Mertz are going to end their long-running feud, and also will be renewing their marriage vows. These couples will be living forever in our hearts."

Gary Morton made a surprise statement. "I guess Lucille is happy tonight. She's in heaven with Desi."

The notorious underground filmmaker John Waters (*Hairspray* and *Polyester*) remembered watching *I Love Lucy* when he was only eight years old. "I thought she was a drag queen. You know, dyed red hair (so I was told), fake eyelashes, and all that lipstick."

In private, Jerry Lewis gave his spectacularly tasteless review: "I don't like female comics. Never did. Ball had no innate sense of humor. She read from cue cards written by others. Frankly, I think women are good for only two things: To provide a hole for a man to get off in, and that same hole to be used for birthin' babies."

Morton revealed that Lucille had been horrified at the public spectacle of the Marilyn Monroe funeral in 1962. She wanted her memorial to be attended by only three people—Morton himself, and her son and daughter. It was conducted without a clergyman at an undisclosed location. Her cremated remains were interred at Forest Lawn in a family plot she'd purchased.

In 2002, her ashes were removed and shipped to her hometown of Jamestown, New York, for burial there.

The cremated remains of her brother, Fred Ball, were also interred next to hers upon his death.

The details of her estate were never revealed but estimated at a low of $20 million and skyrocketing to $350 million. Trust funds had already been arranged for Lucie and Desi Jr. It is assumed that the estate was divided among Lucie, Desi Jr., and Morton. He ended up getting the home in Beverly Hills.

Word of Lucille's death eventually reached Eva Gabor. She and her sister, Zsa Zsa, liked to marry millionaires. She phoned Morton and asked him out on a date, which led to a night of seduction. They dated for a few weeks before she broke it off. "He's never in bed with me. Always on some damn golf course."

In 1996, Morton married golf pro Susie McAllister.

Lucille's second husband, the former "Borscht Belt" stand-up comedian, Gary Morton, became a studio executive and producer only because of his famous marriage. He would live to the age of 74, dying of lung cancer in Palm Springs.

***

The highest honor ever bestowed on Lucille came after her death. She was among five Americans awarded the Medal of Freedom on July 6, 1989, during the administration of George H.W. Bush. She was cited as "The First Lady of Television and one of America's greatest comediennes."

"Her face on the TV screen was seen by more viewers more times than the face of any human being who ever lived," the citation stated.

Another woman honored at the time was Maine Senator Margaret Chase Smith. She was the first woman to serve in both houses of the U.S. Congress.

Also cited was Jimmy Doolittle, the aviator pioneer famous for his daring bombing raid on Tokyo early in America's declaration of war against Japan.

Charles Douglas Dillon was recognized for shaping American foreign policy during his tenure as Ambassador to France (1953-1957) and for his innovative term as the 57th Secretary of the Treasury (1961-1965).

George F. Kennan was acknowledged as an advocate of containment against Soviet expansion during the Cold War.

***

Writing in *The New York Times*, Joyce Millman said:

"Watching I Love Lucy *today, you realize how complex Lucy Ricardo really was, And this complexity is what makes the show so enduringly hilarious, so relevant. Let's face it: Lucy Ricardo is a lot more fun to watch than, say, saintly Donna Reed. Lucy never tidied up her character flaws. She was envious, stubborn, undisciplined, imperfect. Lucy wanted it all, large and small: Family, fame, a part in Ricky's latest movie, admittance to an exclusive ladies' club, a Paris frock, a movie star's autograph. Nearly every plan Lucy understood was rooted in the desire to be somebody, to express herself, to create a life of her own. Lucy Ricardo was no dumbbell. Her schemes were creative, impeccably logical, and courageous."*

But why did we love Lucy? A photo sometimes expresses it better than words. Here's **Lucille Ball** with **Vivian Vance**, in an early episode of her first TV series.

Lucille Ball
First Lady of Comedy, an American Icon
1911-1989
She Made Us Laugh. She Helped Us Hope.

LONG AGO AND FAR AWAY, IN THE SNOWY FORESTS OF
WESTERN NEW YORK STATE,
LUCILLE BALL BEGAN HER ICONIC JOURNEY.

HERE'S HOW THEY REMEMBER HER TODAY:

For years, the statue of Lucille Ball on the left, the work of Dave Poulin, was displayed at the **Lucille Ball Memorial Park in Celeron, New York**, near her childhood home. Inspired by her "Vitameatavegamin" skit, it did not look like Lucille and was often referred to as "Scary Lucy." (*left photo*)

Fans demanded a better representation, and they got it on August 6, 2016 when the more likable and more recognizable bronze sculpture (*right photo*) by Carolyn D. Palmer was unveiled. It occurred on what would have been the 105th birthday of Lucille Ball, gone but hardly forgotten.

None of this was lost on residents of Palm Springs, California's desert retreat for rich celebrities and their fans. With the understanding that the resort considers itself "Lucille's real home," it erected a "sitting on a bench" statue of Lucille (*inset photo*) in 1995 on one of the town's busiest pedestrian thoroughfares, the corner of Tahquitz Canyon Way and Palm Canyon Drive.

According to one fan, after posing beside it for a selfie, "She was such a lively, lovely woman, and now she just sits there, day in, day out. Lucy deserves better. Perhaps it's time for it to be spruced up."

Authors' Bios

DARWIN PORTER

As a precocious nine-year-old, **Darwin Porter** began meeting entertainers through his mother, Hazel, a charismatic Southern girl whose husband had died in World War II. Migrating from the Depression-ravaged valleys of western North Carolina to Miami Beach during its most ebullient heyday, Hazel became a personal assistant to the vaudeville comedienne **Sophie Tucker**, the kind-hearted "Last of the Red Hot Mamas."

Loosely supervised by his mother, Darwin was regularly dazzled by the likes of **Judy Garland, Dinah Shore, Frank Sinatra, Ronald Reagan** (at the time near the end of his Hollywood gig), and **Marilyn Monroe**. Each of them made it a point, whenever they were in Miami (either on or off the record), to visit and pay their respects to "Miss Sophie."

At the University of Miami, Darwin edited the school newspaper, raising its revenues, through advertising and public events, to unheard-of new levels. He met and interviewed **Eleanor Roosevelt** and later invited her, as part of a sponsored event he crafted, to spend a day ("Eleanor Roosevelt Day") at the university, and to his delight, she accepted. Years later, in Manhattan, during her work as a human rights activist, he escorted her, at her request, to many public functions.

On another occasion, he invited **Lucille Ball and Desi Arnaz**, then at the pinnacle of their fame and popularity, to the University. On campus, after the photographers and fans departed, Lucille launched a bitter attack on her husband, accusing him of having had sex the previous night with two showgirls. Because of that and other upsets that unfolded that day, Darwin learned early in his life that Lucille Ball and Desi Arnaz were definitely not Ricky and Lucy Ricardo.

After his graduation, Darwin, in a graceful transition from his work as editor of the University's newspaper and his sponsorship by **Wilson Hicks** (Photo Editor and then Executive Editor of Life magazine) became a Bureau Chief of The Miami Herald (the youngest in that publication's history) assigned to its branch in Key West. At the time the island outpost was an avant-garde literary mecca and—thanks to the Cuban missile crisis—an flash point of the Cold War.

Key West had been the site of Harry S Truman's "Winter White House" and Truman returned a few months before his death for a final visit. He invited young Darwin for "early morning walks" where he used the young emissary of The Miami Herald to "set the record straight."

Through Truman, Darwin was introduced and later joined the staff of **Senator George Smathers** of Florida. His best friend was a young senator, **John F. Kennedy**. Through "Gorgeous George," as Smathers was known in the Senate, Darwin got to meet Jack and Jacqueline in Palm Beach. He later wrote two books about them—The Kennedys, All the Gossip Unfit to Print, and one of his all-time bestsellers, Jacqueline Kennedy Onassis—A Life Beyond Her Wildest Dreams.

Buttressed by his status as The Miami Herald's Key West Bureau Chief, Dar-

win met, interviewed, and often befriended **Tennessee Williams. Ernest Hemingway, Tallulah Bankhead, Gore Vidal, Truman Capote, Carson McCullers,** *and a gaggle of other internationally famous writers and entertainers:* **Cary Grant, Rock Hudson, Marlon Brando, Montgomery Clift, Susan Hayward, Warren Beatty, Christopher Isherwood, Anne Bancroft, Angela Lansbury, and William Inge.**

Eventually transferred to Manhattan, Darwin worked for a decade in television advertising with the producer and arts-industry socialite **Stanley Mills Haggart.** *In addition to some speculative ventures associated with Marilyn Monroe, they also jointly produced TV commercials that included testimonials from* **Joan Crawford** *(then feverishly promoting Pepsi-Cola);* **Ronald Reagan** *(General Electric); and* **Debbie Reynolds** *(Singer sewing machines). Other personalities they promoted, each delivering televised sales pitches, included* **Louis Armstrong, Lena Horne, Rosalind Russell, William Holden***, and* **Arlene Dahl,** *each of them hawking a commercial product.*

Beginning in the early 1960s, Darwin joined forces with the then-fledgling **Arthur Frommer** *organization, playing a key role in researching and writing more than 50 titles and defining the style and values that later emerged as the world's leading travel guidebooks,* **The Frommer Guides.** *Darwin's particular journalistic expertise on Europe, New England, California, and the Caribbean eventually propelled him into authorship of (depending on the era and whatever crises were brewing at the time), between 70 and 80% of their titles. Even during the research of his travel guides, he continued to interview show-biz celebrities, discussing their triumphs, feuds, and frustrations. At this point in their lives, many were retired and reclusive. Darwin either pursued them (sometimes though local tourist offices) or encountered them randomly as part of his extensive travels.* **Ava Gardner, Lana Turner, Hedy Lamarr, Ingrid Bergman, Ethel Merman, Andy Warhol, Elizabeth Taylor, Marlene Dietrich, Bette Davis***,* **Judy Garland,** *and* **Paul Newman** *were particularly insightful.*

Porter's biographies—at this writing, they number sixty-two— have won thirty first prize or "runner-up to first prize" awards at literary festivals in cities or states which include New England, New York, Los Angeles, Hollywood, San Francisco, Florida, California, and Paris.

Darwin, also a magazine columnist, can be heard at regular intervals as a podcast commentator, reviewing the ironies of celebrities, tabloid culture, politics, and scandal.

A resident of New York City, where he spent years within the social orbit of the Queen of Off-Broadway (the eccentric and very temperamental philanthropist, **Lucille Lortel),** *Darwin is currently at work on a biography of the dysfunctionally fascinating father/daughter team of* **Henry Fonda** *and his rebellious daughter,* **Jane.**

DANFORTH PRINCE

A graduate of Hamilton College and a native of Easton and Bethlehem, Pennsylvania, he's president and founder (in 1983) of the Porter and Prince Corporation, the entity that produced the original texts and updates for dozens of key titles of **THE FROMMER GUIDES**—travel "bibles" for millions of readers during the travel industry's go-go years in the 80s, 90s, and early millennium.

He also founded, in 1996, the Georgia Literary Association, precursor to what morphed, in 2004, into **Blood Moon Productions**, the corporate force behind dozens of political and Hollywood biographies. Its vaguely apocalyptic name was inspired by one of Darwin Porter's popular early novels, **Blood Moon**, a thriller about the false gods of power, wealth, and physical beauty. In 2011, Prince was named "Publisher of the Year" by a consortium of literary critics and marketers spearheaded by the J.M. Northern Media Group.

Prince has electronically documented his stewardship of Blood Moon in at least 50 videotaped documentaries, book trailers, public speeches, and TV or radio interviews. Most of these are available on **YouTube.com** and **Facebook** (keyword: "Danforth Prince"); on **Twitter** (#BloodyandLunar); or by clicking on **BloodMoonProductions.com**.

Hearkening back to his days as a travel writer, Prince is also an innkeeper, maintaining and managing a historic bed & breakfast, **Magnolia House (www.MagnoliaHouseSaintGeorge.com)**. Affiliated with AirBnb, and increasingly sought out by filmmakers as an evocative locale for moviemaking, it lies in St. George, at the northern tip of Staten Island, the "sometimes forgotten" Outer Borough of New York City. A landmarked building with a "formidable" historic and literary pedigree, it lies in a neighborhood closely linked to Henry James, Theodore Dreiser, the Vanderbilts, and key moments in America's colonial history.

Set in a terraced garden with views over New York Harbor and nearby Manhattan, it's been visited by show-biz stars who have included **Tennessee Williams, Gloria Swanson, Joan Blondell, Edward Albee, Jolie Gabor** (mother of Zsa Zsa, Eva, and Magda), soap opera queen **Ruth Warrick**, the Viennese chanteuse **Greta Keller,** and many of the luminaries of Broadway. It lies within a twelve-minute walk from the ferries regularly chugging their way across the harbor to Wall Street and Lower Manhattan.

Publicized as "a reasonably priced celebrity-centric bed & breakfast with links to the book trades," and the beneficiary of rave ("superhost") reviews (including "New York's most fascinating B&B") from hundreds of previous guests, **Magnolia House** *is loaded with furniture and memorabilia collected from around the world during his decades as a travel journalist for the Frommer Guides.* **Since the onset of the Covid Crisis, social distancing and regular decontamination regimens have been rigorously enforced.** *For photographs, testimonials from previous guests, and more information, click on*

www.AirBnb/H/Magnolia-House

Magnolia House is a proud, architecturally protected landmark within the St. George, Staten Island Historical District.

It's depicted here in a photo snapped by New York City's Department of Finance as part of its 1940 Tax Census.

Some visitors liken Magnolia House to a *grande dame* with a centuries-old knack for nourishing high-functioning eccentrics. Many have lived or been entertained here since New York's State Senator Howard Bayne, a transplanted Southerner, moved in with his wife, the daughter of the Surgeon General of the Confederate States of America, in the aftermath of that bloodiest of wars on North American soil, the War Between the American States.

Since then, dozens of celebrities have whispered their secrets and rehearsed their ambitions within its walls. They've included movie vamps from the silent screen, midnight cowboys, dancers from the dance, *Butterflies in Heat,* a heavyweight boxing champ, writers from every hue, faded film goddesses, playwrights who crafted blockbusters for both Marilyn (Monroe) and Elizabeth (Taylor), *ultra-avant-garde* diarists, every known variety of *prima donna* and *diva,* including some from the world of opera, and a world-class Olympic athlete.

They've also included authors Darwin Porter and Danforth Prince, who spent decades here renovating it and within its walls, producing a stream of FROMMER TRAVEL GUIDES and award-winning celebrity biographies.

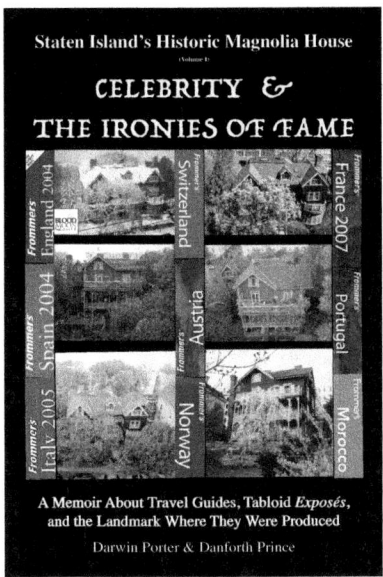
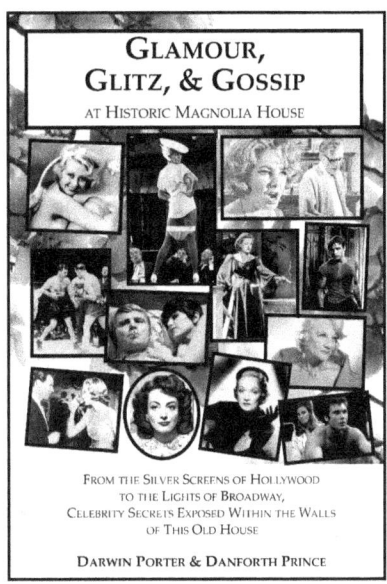

HOW TO BUILD A MAGNOLIA-SCENTED MONUMENT

As depicted above, **Volumes One and Two** of Blood Moon's Magnolia House Series were conceived as affectionate testimonials to a great American monument, **MAGNOLIA HOUSE,** a nurturing and very tolerant historic home in NYC with a raft of stories to tell—some of them about how it adapted to America's radically changing tastes, times, circumstances, and values.

VOLUME ONE (ISBN 978-1-936003-65-5) focuses on its construction by a prominent lawyer during the booming (Northern) economy before the Civil War; its Gilded-Age purchase by the widow of the Surgeon General of the Confederate States of America; and later, its role as a branch office for dozens of travel titles during the heyday of THE FROMMER GUIDES, with detailed insights into the celebrity secrets their reporters (privately, until now) unveiled.

VOLUME TWO (ISBN 978-1-936003-73-0) is an *haute* celebrity romp through the half-century of Broadway, Hollywood, and publishing scandals swirling around Magnolia House's visitors and their frenemies…a "Reporters' Notebook" with everything that arts industry publicists didn't want fans and critics to know about at the time.

Each of these books is a celebration of the fast-disappearing PRE-COVID AMERICAN CENTURY,
And both are available now through internet purveyors worldwide.

BLOOD MOON PRODUCTIONS
Award-Winning Entertainment about
America's Legends, Icons, & Celebrities

In reference to Magnolia House's status as an AirBnb, your host, handler, concierge, and problem-solver, **Danforth Prince**, says, "Come with your friends for the night and stay for breakfast.

Even with social distancing, Covid cautiousness, and a lot more 'scrub-a-dub-dubbing,' it's about healing, recuperation, razzmatazz, show-biz, Classic Hollywood, sightseeing, and conversation in the greatest city in the world.

*Stay with Us! Learn more about "Celebrity-Centric Sleepovers" at Blood Moon's **Magnolia House**, a historic and moderately priced "Airbnb" in New York City.*

 www.AirBnB/H/Magnolia-House

Judy Garland & Liza Minnelli
Too Many Damn Rainbows

Judy and Liza were the greatest, most colorful, and most tragic mother-daughter saga in show biz history. Darwin Porter and Danforth Prince have compiled a compelling "post-modern" spin.

Their memorable stories unfold through eyewitness accounts of the typhoons that engulfed them. There were depressions "as deep as the Mariana Trench," suicide attempts, and obsessive identifications on deep psychological levels with roles that include Judy's Vicky Lester in *A Star is Born* (1954) and Liza's Sally Bowles in *Cabaret* (1972).

Lesser known are the jealous actress-to-actress rivalries.

As Judy faded into the 1960s, Liza roaringly emerged as a star in her own right. She survived the whirlwinds of her mother's drug addiction with a yen for choosing all the wrong men in patterns that weirdly evoked those of Judy herself.

For millions of fans, Judy will forever remain the cheerful adolescent (Dorothy) skipping along a yellow brick road toward the other side of the rainbow. Liza followed her down that hallucinogenic path, searching for the childhood, the security, and the love that eluded her.

Judy Garland, an icon whose memory is permanently etched into the American psyche, continues to thrive as a cult goddess. Revered by thousands of die-hard fans, she's the most poignant example of both the manic and depressive (some say "schizophrenic") sides of the Hollywood myth.

Deep in her 70s, Liza is still with us, too, nursing memories of her former acclaim and her first visit as a little girl to her parents at MGM, the "Dream Factory," during the Golden Age of Hollywood.

Judy Garland & Liza Minnelli: Too Many Damn Rainbows
Darwin Porter & Danforth Prince
Softcover, 6" x 9", with hundreds of photos.   ISBN 978-1-936003-69-3
Available Everywhere Now

The Seductive Sapphic Exploits of
Mercedes de Acosta
Hollywood's Greatest Lover

IF YOU ASSUMED THAT THE GREATEST LOVERS ARE MEN, some of the most famous "cult goddesses" of the early- and mid-20th-Century might emphatically disagree.

At Magnolia House, in the final years of her life, the notorious, once-fabled Spanish beauty, **MERCEDES DE ACOSTA** (1892-1968) was a frequent visitor. To Darwin Porter, she confessed and recited fabulously indiscreet stories about her romantic same-sex exploits among the theatrical and cinematic elite of New York, London, Paris, and Hollywood.

It reveals "Sapphic Standards" from the heyday of Silent Film and the early Talkies that no other book—even her own (*Here Lies the Heart*, published in 1960)— ever dared to make public.

Mercedes de Acosta's love affairs were with women, each a figurehead in art, the theater, and the filmmaking and literary scenes. They included Greta Garbo, Marlene Dietrich, Nazimova, Gertrude Stein, Alice B. Toklas, Eva Le Gallienne, Tallulah Bankhead, Jeanne Eagels, Katharine Cornell, Eleanora Duse, Isadora Duncan, and both of Valentino's wives. This is probably the best portrait of *avant-garde* Broadway and early 20th-century filmmaking ever published.

The Seductive Sapphic Exploits of
MERCEDES DE ACOSTA
Hollywood's Greatest Lover

Darwin Porter and Danforth Prince
ISBN 978-1-936003-75-4.
A pithy, photo-packed softcover with 474 pages, available now from online purveyors everywhere, including Ingram's Lightning Source and Amazon.com

LOVE TRIANGLE:
Ronald Reagan, Jane Wyman, & Nancy Davis

THIS BOOK EXPOSES THE SHOW-BIZ SCANDALS THAT THE REAGANS DESPERATELY WANTED TO FORGET.

Unique in the history of publishing, this triple biography focuses on the Hollywood indiscretions of former U.S. president Ronald Reagan and his two wives. A proud and Presidential addition to Blood Moon's Babylon series, it digs deep into what these three young and attractive movie stars were doing decades before two of them took over the Free World.

As reviewed by Diane Donovan, Senior Reviewer at *California Bookwatch and The Midwest Book Review:*

"This is lurid Hollywood *exposé* writing at its best. It outlines the truths surrounding one of the most provocative industry scandals in the world."

"*Love Triangle* is a steamy, eye-opening story that blows the lid off the Reagan illusion. Black and white photos liberally pepper an account of the careers of all three and the lasting shock of their stormy relationships in a delightful pursuit especially recommended for any who relish Hollywood gossip."

In the year of its publication (2015) *LOVE TRIANGLE* was designated by the Hollywood Book Festival as Runner-Up to Best Biography of the Year.

LOVE TRIANGLE
Ronald Reagan, Jane Wyman, & Nancy Davis

Darwin Porter & Danforth Prince
Softcover, 6" x 9", with hundreds of photos.   ISBN 978-1-936003-41-9

THIS BOOK ILLUSTRATES WHY GENTLEMEN PREFER BLONDES, AND WHY MARILYN MONROE WAS TOO DANGEROUS TO BE ALLOWED TO GO ON LIVING

Less than an hour after the discovery of Marilyn Monroe's corpse in Brentwood, a flood of theories, tainted evidence, and conflicting testimonies began pouring out into the public landscape.

Filled with rage, hysteria, and depression, "and fed up with Jack's lies, Bobby's lies," Marilyn sought revenge and mass vindication. Her revelations at an imminent press conference could have toppled political dynasties and destroyed criminal empires. Marilyn had to be stopped…

Into this steamy cauldron of deceit, Marilyn herself emerges as a most unreliable witness during the weeks leading up to her murder. Her own deceptions, vanities, and self-delusion poured toxic accelerants on an already raging fire.

> **"This is the best book about Marilyn Monroe ever published."**
> —**David Hartnell**, Recipient, in 2011, of New Zealand's Order of Merit (MNZM) for services to the entertainment industry, as defined by Her Majesty, Queen Elizabeth II.

Winner of literary awards from the New York, Hollywood, and San Francisco Book Festivals

"Darwin Porter is fearless, honest and a great read. He minces no words. If the truth makes you wince and honesty offends your sensibility, stay away. It's been said that he deals in muck because he can't libel the dead. Well, it's about time someone started telling the truth about the dead and being honest about just what happened to get us in the mess in which we're in. If libel is lying, then Porter is so completely innocent as to deserve an award. In all of his works he speaks only to the truth, and although he is a hard teacher and task master, he's one we ignore at our peril. To quote Gore Vidal, power is not a toy we give to someone for being good. If we all don't begin to investigate where power and money really are in the here and now, we deserve what we get. Yes, Porter names names. The reader will come away from the book knowing just who killed Monroe. Porter rather brilliantly points to a number of motives, but leaves it to the reader to surmise exactly what happened at the rainbow's end, just why Marilyn was killed. And, of course, why we should be careful of getting exactly what we want. It's a very long tumble from the top."

—**ALAN PETRUCELLI**, Examiner.com, May 13, 2012

MARILYN: DON'T EVEN DREAM ABOUT TOMORROW
SEX, LIES, MURDER, AND THE GREAT COVER-UP, BY DARWIN PORTER
ISBN 978-1-936003-79-2

A Revised Edition of Darwin Porter's Investigative Classic from 2012
MARILYN AT RAINBOW'S END

CARRIE FISHER & DEBBIE REYNOLDS
PRINCESS LEIA & UNSINKABLE TAMMY IN HELL

This is history's first comprehensive, unauthorized overview of Debbie Reynolds ("hard as nails and with more balls than any five guys I've ever known") and her talented, often traumatized daughter, Carrie Fisher ("one of the smartest, hippest chicks in Hollywood"). Evolving for decades under the unrelenting glare of public scrutiny, each became a world-class symbol of the social and cinematic tastes that prevailed during their heydays as celebrity icons in Hollywood.

It's a scandalous saga of the ferociously loyal relationship of the *"boop-boop-a-doop"* girl with her intergalactic *STAR WARS* daughter, and their iron-willed, "true grit" battles to out-race changing tastes in Hollywood.

Loaded with revelations about "who was doing what to whom" during the final gasps of the film industry's "Golden Age," it's an All-American story about the price of glamour, career-related pain, family anguish, romantic betrayals, lingering guilt, and the volcanic shifts that affected a scrappy, mother-daughter team—and everyone else who ever loved the movies.

CARRIE FISHER & DEBBIE REYNOLDS
Princess Leia & Unsinkable Tammy in Hell

ANOTHER OUTRAGEOUS TITLE IN BLOOD MOON'S BABYLON SERIES
DARWIN PORTER & DANFORTH PRINCE

"Feeling misunderstood by the younger (female) members of your gene pool? This is the Hollywood exposé every grandmother should give to her granddaughter, a roadmap like Debbie Reynolds might have offered to Billie Lourd."
—Marnie O'Toole

"Hold onto your hats: the "bad boys" of Blood Moon Productions are back. This time, they have an exhaustively researched and highly readable account of the greatest mother-daughter act in the history of show business: Debbie Reynolds and Carrie (Princess Leia) Fisher. If celebrity gossip and inside dirt is your secret desire, check it out. This is a fabulous book that we heartily recommend. It will not disappoint. We rate it worthy of four stars."
—MAJ Glenn MacDonald, U.S. Army Reserve (Retired), © MilitaryCorruption.com

"How is a 1950s-era movie star, (TAMMY) supposed to cope with her postmodern, substance-abusing daughter (PRINCESS LEIA), the rebellious, high-octane byproduct of rock 'n roll, Free Love, and postwar Hollywood's most scandal-soaked marriage? Read about it here, in Blood Moon's unauthorized double exposé about how Hollywood's toughest (and savviest) mother-daughter team maneuvered their way through shifting definitions of fame, reconciliation, and fortune."
—Donna McSorley

Winner of the coveted "Best Biography" Award from the 2018
New York Book Festival

CARRIE FISHER & DEBBIE REYNOLDS,
UNSINKABLE TAMMY & PRINCESS LEIA IN HELL
Darwin Porter & Danforth Prince

630 pages Softcover with photos. Now online and in bookstores everywhere
ISBN 978-1-936003-57-0

This is What Happens When A Demented Billionaire Hits Hollywood

HOWARD HUGHES

HELL'S ANGEL
BY DARWIN PORTER

From his reckless pursuit of love as a rich teenager to his final days as a demented fossil, Howard Hughes tasted the best and worst of the century he occupied. Along the way, he changed the worlds of aviation and entertainment forever.

This biography reveals inside details about his destructive and usually scandalous associations with other Hollywood players.

"The Aviator flew both ways. Porter's biography presents new allegations about Hughes' shady dealings with some of the biggest names of the 20th century"
—New York Daily News

"Darwin Porter's access to film industry insiders and other Hughes confidants supplied him with the resources he needed to create a portrait of Hughes that both corroborates what other Hughes biographies have divulged, and go them one better."
—Foreword Magazine

"Thanks to this bio of Howard Hughes, we'll never be able to look at the old pinups in quite the same way again."
—The Times (London)

Winner of a respected literary award from the Los Angeles Book Festival, this book gives an insider's perspective about what money can buy
—and what it can't.

814 pages, with photos. **Available everywhere now, online and in bookstores.**

ISBN 978-1-936003-13-6

LANA TURNER

The Sweater Girl: Hollywood's OTHER Most Notorious Blonde

Beautiful and Bad, Her Full Story Has Never Been Told. UNTIL NOW!

Lana Turner was the most scandalous, most copied, and most gossiped-about actress in Hollywood. When her abusive Mafia lover was murdered in her house, every newspaper in the Free World described the murky dramas with something approaching hysteria.

Blood Moon's salacious but empathetic new biography exposes the public and private dramas of the girl who changed the American definition of what it REALLY means to be a blonde.

Here's how *California Bookwatch* and *The Midwest Book Review* described this book:

"*Lana Turner: Hearts and Diamonds Take All* belongs on the shelves of any collection about the evolution of Hollywood. It's a weighty survey packed with new information about her life."

"It offers many new revelations about the movie industry in the aftermath of World War II. Lana's introduction of a new brand of covert sexuality, her scandalous romances, her extreme promiscuity, her search for love, her notorious flings - even her involvement in murder - are all probed in a revealing account of glamour and movie industry relationships that bring Turner and her times to life."

"This is a 'must have' pick for any collection strong in Hollywood history, gossip, scandals, the real stories behind them, and Lana Turner's tumultuous career, in particular."

Lana Turner, Hearts & Diamonds Take All
Winner of the coveted "Best Biography" Award from the San Francisco Book Festival

By Darwin Porter and Danforth Prince

Softcover, 622 pages, with photos. ISBN 978-1-936003-53-2
Available everywhere, online and in bookstores.

SCARLETT O'HARA
DESPERATELY IN LOVE WITH HEATHCLIFF, TOGETHER ON THE ROAD TO HELL

This is the definitive and most revelatory portrait ever published of the most talented and tormented actor and actress of the 20th century.

Damn You, Scarlett O'Hara
The Private Lives of **Vivien Leigh** and **Laurence Olivier**

Here, for the first time, is a biography that raises the curtain on the secret lives of **Lord Laurence Olivier**, often cited as the finest actor in the history of England, and **Vivien Leigh**, who immortalized herself with her Oscar-winning portrayals of Scarlett O'Hara in *Gone With the Wind*, and as Blanche DuBois in Tennessee Williams' *A Streetcar Named Desire*.

Dashing and "impossibly handsome," Laurence Olivier was pursued by the most dazzling luminaries, male and female, of the movie and theater worlds.

Lord Olivier's beautiful and brilliant but emotionally disturbed wife (Viv to her lovers) led a tumultuous, off-the-record life, too. Her paramours ranged from A-list celebrities to men she selected randomly off the street. But none of the brilliant roles depicted by Lord and Lady Olivier, on stage or on screen, ever matched the power and drama of personal dramas which wavered between Wagnerian opera and Greek tragedy. Darwin Porter is the principal author of this seminal work.

"The folks over at TMZ would have had a field day tracking Laurence Olivier and Vivien Leigh with flip cameras in hand. Damn You, Scarlett O'Hara can be a dazzling read, the prose unmannered and instantly digestible. The authors' ability to pile scandal atop scandal, seduction after seduction, can be impossible to resist."

—THE WASHINGTON TIMES

DAMN YOU, SCARLETT O'HARA
THE PRIVATE LIFES OF LAURENCE OLIVIER AND VIVIEN LEIGH

Darwin Porter and Roy Moseley

Winner of four distinguished literary awards, this is the best biography of Vivien Leigh and Laurence Olivier ever published, with hundreds of insights into the London Theatre; the role of the Oliviers in the politics of World War II; and the passion, fury, and frustration of their lives together as actors in London's West End, on Broadway, and in Hollywood.

ISBN 978-1-936003-15-0   Hardcover, 708 pages, with about a hundred photos.

DONALD TRUMP
IS THE MAN WHO WOULD BE KING

This is the most famous book about our incendiary ex-President you've probably never heard of.

Winner of three respected literary awards, and released three months before the Presidential elections of 2016, it's an entertainingly packaged, artfully salacious bombshell, a scathingly historic overview of America during its 2016 election cycle, a portrait unlike anything ever published on CANDIDATE DONALD and the climate in which he thrived and massacred his political rivals.

Its volcanic, much-suppressed release during the heat and venom of the 2016 Presidential campaign was heralded by *The Midwestern Book Review, California Book Watch, The Seattle Gay News*, the staunchly right-wing WILS-AM radio, and also by the editors at the most popular Seniors' magazine in Florida, *Boomer Times*, which designated it as their September 2016 choice for BOOK OF THE MONTH.

TRUMPOCALYPSE: *"Donald Trump: The Man Who Would Be King* is recommended reading for all sides, no matter what political stance is being adopted: Republican, Democrat, or other.

"One of its driving forces is its ability to synthesize an unbelievable amount of information into a format and presentation which blends lively irony with outrageous observations, entertaining even as it presents eye-opening information in a format accessible to all.

"Politics dovetail with American obsessions and fascinations with trends, figureheads, drama, and sizzling news stories, but blend well with the observations of sociologists, psychologists, politicians, and others in a wide range of fields who lend their expertise and insights to create a much broader review of the Trump phenomena than a more casual book could provide.

"The result is a 'must read' for any American interested in issues of race, freedom, equality, and justice—and for any non-American who wonders just what is going on behind the scenes in this country's latest election debacle."

Diane Donovan, *California Bookwatch* and *The Midwest Book Review*

DONALD TRUMP, THE MAN WHO WOULD BE KING
WINNER OF "BEST BIOGRAPHY" AWARDS FROM BOOK FESTIVALS IN
NEW YORK, CALIFORNIA, AND FLORIDA
by Darwin Porter and Danforth Prince
Softcover, with 822 pages and hundreds of photos. ISBN 978-1-936003-51-8.

Available now, everywhere

LINDA LOVELACE
INSIDE LINDA LOVELACE'S DEEP THROAT
Degradation, Porno Chic, and the Rise of Feminism

This is the most comprehensive biography ever written of an adult entertainment star, her tormented relationship with Hollywood's underbelly, and how she changed forever the world's perceptions of censorship, sexual behavior patterns, and pornography.

Darwin Porter, author of more than fifty critically acclaimed celebrity exposés of behind-the-scenes intrigue in the entertainment industry, was deeply involved in the Linda Lovelace saga as it unfolded in the 70s, interviewing many of the players, and raising money for the legal defense of *Deep Throat's* co-star, Harry Reems.

Emphasizing her role as an unlikely celebrity interacting with other celebrities, he brings inside information and a never-before-published revelation to almost every page.

"This book drew me in..How could it not?" Coco Papy, Bookslut.

This Was The Beach Book Festival's
Grand Prize Winner for
"Best Summer Reading of 2013"

Runner-Up to "Best Biography of 2013" The Los Angeles Book Festival

Another ironic and insightful commentary about major and sometimes violently controversial conflicts of the American Century, from Blood Moon Productions.

Inside Linda Lovelace's Deep Throat, by Darwin Porter
Softcover, 640 pages, 6"x9" with photos.
ISBN 978-1-936003-33-4

HOW THE FBI INVESTIGATED HOLLYWOOD
Winner, in 2012, of literary awards from the Los Angeles and the Hollywood Book Festivals

Darwin Porter's saga of power and corruption has a revelation on every page—cross dressing, sexual indiscretions, hustlers for sale, alliances with the Mafia, and criminal activity by the nation's chief law enforcer.

It's all here, with chilling details about the abuse of power on the dark side of the American saga. Mostly it's about the decades-long love story between two of America's most powerful men—lovers who could tell presidents "how to skip rope." (Hoover's words.)

*****

"EVERYONE'S" dredging up J. Edgar Hoover. Leonardo DiCaprio just immortalized him, and now comes Darwin Porter's paperback, *J. Edgar Hoover & Clyde Tolson: Investigating the Sexual Secrets of America's Most Famous Men and Women.*

It shovels Hoover's darkest secrets dragged kicking and screaming from the closet. It's filth on every VIP who's safely dead and some who are still above ground."

— **Cindy Adams,** *The New York Post*

"This book is important, because it destroys what's left of Hoover's reputation. Did you know he had intel on the bombing of Pearl Harbor, but he sat on it, making him more or less responsible for thousands of deaths? Or that he had almost nothing to do with the arrests or killings of any of the 1930s gangsters that he took credit for catching?

"A lot of people are angry with its author, Darwin Porter. They say that his outing of celebrities is just cheap gossip about dead people who can't defend themselves. I suppose it's because Porter is destroying carefully constructed myths that are comforting to most people. As gay men, we benefit the most from Porter's work, because we know that except for AIDS, the closet was the most terrible thing about the 20th century. If the closet never existed, neither would Hoover. The fact that he got away with such duplicity under eight presidents makes you think that every one of them was a complete fool for tolerating it."

— Paul Bellini, *FAB Magazine* (Toronto)

J. EDGAR HOOVER AND CLYDE TOLSON
Investigating the Sexual Secrets of America's Most Famous Men and Women
Darwin Porter
Softcover, 564 pages, with photos   ISBN 978-1-936003-25-9.   Also available for E-Readers

PINK TRIANGLE

The Feuds and Private Lives of

TENNESSEE WILLIAMS, GORE VIDAL, TRUMAN CAPOTE,

& Famous Members of their Entourages

This book, the only one of its kind, reveals the backlot intrigues associated with the literary and script-writing enfants terribles of America's entertainment community during the mid-20th century.

It exposes their bitchfests, their slugfests, and their relationships with the *glitterati*—Marilyn Monroe, Brando, the Oliviers, the Paleys, U.S. Presidents, a gaggle of other movie stars, millionaires, and international *débauchés*.

This is for anyone who's interested in the formerly concealed scandals of Hollywood and Broadway, and the values and pretentions of both the literary community and the entertainment industry.

"*A banquet... If PINK TRIANGLE had not been written for us, we would have had to research and type it all up for ourselves...Pink Triangle is nearly seven hundred pages of the most entertaining histrionics ever sliced, spiced, heated, and serviced up to the reading public. Everything that Blood Moon has done before pales in comparison.*"

"*Given the fact that the subjects of the book themselves were nearly delusional on the subject of themselves (to say nothing of each other) it is hard to find fault. Add to this the intertwined jungle that was the relationship among Williams, Capote, and Vidal, of the times they vied for things they loved most—especially attention—and the times they enthralled each other and the world, [Pink Triangle is] the perfect antidote to the Polar Vortex.*"
—**Vinton McCabe in the NY JOURNAL OF BOOKS**

"*Full disclosure: I have been a friend and follower of Blood Moon Productions' tomes for years, and always marveled at the amount of information in their books—it's staggering. The index alone to Pink Triangle runs to 21 pages—and the scale of names in it runs like a* Who's Who *of American social, cultural and political life through much of the 20th century.*"
—**Perry Brass in THE HUFFINGTON POST**

"*We Brits are not spared the Porter/Prince silken lash either. Pink Triangle's research is, quite frankly, breathtaking. It will fascinate you for many weeks to come. Once you have made the initial titillating dip, the day will seem dull without it.*"
—**Jeffery Tayor in THE SUNDAY EXPRESS (UK)**

PINK TRIANGLE—*The Feuds and Private Lives of Tennessee Williams, Gore Vidal, Truman Capote, and Famous Members of their Entourages*

Darwin Porter & Danforth Prince
Softcover, 700 pages, with photos   ISBN 978-1-936003-37-2   Also Available for E-Readers

THOSE GLAMOROUS GABORS
Bombshells from Budapest

Zsa Zsa, Eva, and Magda Gabor transferred their glittery dreams and gold-digging ambitions from the twilight of the Austro-Hungarian Empire to Hollywood. There, more effectively than any army, these Bombshells from Budapest broke hearts, amassed fortunes, lovers and A-list husbands, and amused millions of *voyeurs* through the medium of television, movies, and the social registers.

In this astonishing "triple-play" biography, designated "Best Biography of the Year" by the Hollywood Book Festival, Blood Moon lifts the "mink-and-diamond" curtain on this amazing trio of blood-related sisters, whose complicated intrigues have never, until now, been fully explored.

"You will never be Ga-bored...this book gives new meaning to the term compelling. Be warned, Those Glamorous Gabors is both an epic and a pip. Not since Gone With the Wind *have so many characters on the printed page been forced to run for their lives for one reason or another. And Scarlett making a dress out of the curtains is nothing compared to what a Gabor will do when she needs to scrap together an outfit for a movie premiere or late-night outing.*

"For those not up to speed, Jolie Tilleman came from a family of jewelers and therefore came by her love for the shiny stones honestly, perhaps genetically. She married Vilmos Gabor somewhere around World War 1 (exact dates, especially birth dates, are always somewhat vague in order to establish plausible deniability later on) and they were soon blessed with three daughters: Magda, the oldest, whose hair, sadly, was naturally brown, although it would turn quite red in America; Zsa Zsa (born 'Sari') a natural blond who at a very young age exhibited the desire for fame with none of the talents usually associated with achievement, excepting beauty and a natural wit; and Eva, the youngest and blondest of the girls, who after seeing Grace Moore perform at the National Theater, decided that she wanted to be an actress and that she would one day move to Hollywood to become a star.

"Given that the Gabor family at that time lived in Budapest, Hungary, at the period of time between the World Wars, that Hollywood dream seemed a distant one indeed. The story—the riches to rags to riches to rags to riches again myth of survival against all odds as the four women, because of their Jewish heritage, flee Europe with only the minks on their backs and what jewels they could smuggle along with them in their decolletage, only to have to battle afresh for their places in the vicious Hollywood pecking order—gives new meaning to the term 'compelling.' The reader, as if he were witnessing a particularly gore-drenched traffic accident, is incapable of looking away."

—**The New York Review of Books**

Those Glamorous Gabors, Bombshells from Budapest
by Darwin Porter & Danforth Prince
Softcover, 730 pages, with hundreds of photos   ISBN 978-1-936003-35-8

ROCK HUDSON EROTIC FIRE

IN THE DYING DAYS OF HOLLYWOOD'S GOLDEN AGE, ROCK HUDSON WAS THE MOST CELEBRATED PHALLIC SYMBOL AND LUST OBJECT IN AMERICA.

THIS BOOK DESCRIBES HIS RISE AND FALL, AND THE INDUSTRY THAT CREATED HIM.

Rock Hudson charmed every casting director in Hollywood (and movie-goers throughout America) as the mega-star they most wanted to share PILLOW TALK with. This book describes his rise and fall, and how he handled himself as a closeted but promiscuous bisexual during an age when EVERYBODY tried to throw him onto a casting couch.

Based on dozens of face-to-face interviews with the actor's friends, co-conspirators, and enemies, and researched over a period of a half century, this biography reveals the shame, agonies, and irony of Rock Hudson's complete, never-before-told story.

In 2017, the year of its release, it was designated as winner ("BEST BIOGRAPHY") at two of the Golden State's most prestigious literary competitions, the Northern California and the Southern California Book Festivals.

Darwin Porter & Danforth Prince
Another Outrageous Title in Blood Moon's Babylon Series

It was also favorably reviewed by the *Midwestern Book Review, California Book Watch, KNEWS RADIO, the New York Journal of Books,* and the editors at the most popular Seniors' magazine in Florida, *BOOMER TIMES.*

ROCK HUDSON EROTIC FIRE
By Darwin Porter & Danforth Prince
Softcover, 624 pages, with dozens of photos, 6" x 9"
ISBN 978-1-936003-55-6

Available everywhere now, online and in bookstores.

HOLLYWOOD BABYLON

IT'S BACK! (VOLUME ONE) AND
STRIKES AGAIN! (VOLUME TWO)

Profoundly outrageous, here are Blood Moon's double-header spins on exhibitionism, sexuality, and sin as filtered through a century of Hollywood indiscretion

Winner of the Los Angeles Book Festival's Best Nonfiction Title of 2010, and the New England Book Festival's Best Anthology for 2010.

"If you love smutty celebrity dirt as much as I do, then have I got some books for you!"
—The Hollywood Offender

"These books will set the graves of Hollywood's cemeteries spinning."
—London's Daily Express

"Monumentally exhaustive...The ultimate guilty pleasure"
—Shelf Awareness

Hollywood Babylon It's Back!
& Hollywood Babylon Strikes Again!

Darwin Porter and Danforth Prince
Hardcover, each 380 outrageous pages, each with hundreds of photos

[Whereas Volume One is temporarily sold out, and available only as an e-book, Volume Two, also available as an e-book, still has hard copies in stock]

ISBN 978-1-9748118-8-8 and ISBN 978-1-936003-12-9

CONFUSED ABOUT HOW TO INTERPRET THEIR RAUCOUS PAST? THIS UNCENSORED TALE ABOUT A LOVE AFFAIR THAT CHANGED THE COURSE OF POLITICS AND THE PLANET IS OF COMPELLING INTEREST TO ANYONE INVOLVED IN THE POLITICAL SLUGFESTS AND INCENDIARY WARS OF THE CLINTONS.

BILL & HILLARY
SO THIS IS THAT THING CALLED LOVE

"This is both a biographical coverage of the Clintons and a political *exposé*; a detailed, weighty exploration that traces the couple's social and political evolution, from how each entered the political arena to their White House years under Bill Clinton's presidency.

"Containing gossip, scandal, and biographical sketches, it delves deeply into the news and politics of its times, presenting enough historical background to fully explore the underlying controversies affecting the Clinton family and their choices.

"Sidebars of information and black and white photos liberally peppered throughout the account offer visual reinforcement to the exploration, lending it the feel and tone of both a gossip column and political piece - something that probes not just Clinton interactions but the D.C. political milieu as a whole.

"The result may appear weighty, sporting over five hundred pages, but is an absorbing, top recommendation for readers of both biographical and political pieces who will thoroughly enjoy this spirited, lively, and thought-provoking analysis."

—THE MIDWEST BOOK REVIEW

***

Shortly after its release in December of 2015, this book received a literary award (Runner-up to Best Biography of the Year) from the New England Book Festival. As stated by a spokesperson for the Awards, "The New England Book Festival is an annual competition honoring excellence in books, with particular focus on projects that deserve closer attention from the academic community. Congratulations to Blood Moon and its authors, especially Darwin Porter, for his highly entertaining analysis of Clinton's double-barreled presidential regime, and the sometimes hysterical over-reaction of their enemies."

Available Everywhere now, in Bookstores and Online
BILL & HILLARY—SO THIS IS THAT THING CALLED LOVE
Softcover, with photos. ISBN 978-1-936003-47-1 by Darwin Porter and Danforth Prince

BURT REYNOLDS
PUT THE PEDAL TO THE METAL

How a Nude Centerfold Sex Symbol Seduced Hollywood

In the 1970s and '80s, Burt Reynolds represented a new breed of movie star: Charming and relentlessly macho, he was a good old Southern boy who made hearts throb and audiences laugh. He was Burt Reynolds, a football hero and a guy you might have shared some jokes with in a redneck bar. After an impressive but tormented career, rivers of negative publicity, a self-admitted history of bad choices, and a spectacular fall from Hollywood grace, he died in Jupiter, Florida, at the age of 82 in September of 2018.

For five years, both in terms of earnings and popularity, he was the number one box office star in the world. *Smokey and the Bandit* (1977) became the biggest-grossing car-chase film of all time. As he put it, perhaps as a means of bolstering his image, "I like nothing better than making love to some of the most beautiful women in the world." Perhaps he was referring to his romantic and sexual involvements with dozens of celebrities from New Hollywood. More unusual dalliances occurred with Marilyn Monroe, whom he once picked up on his way to the Actors Studio in New York City. Love with another VIP came in the form of that "Sweetheart of the G.I.s," Dinah Shore, sparking chatter. "I appreciate older women," he once said in a moment of self-revelation. According to Sally Field, "Burt still lives in my heart." But then she expressed relief that, because of his recent death, he never read what she'd said about him in her memoir.

Men liked him too: He played poker with Frank Sinatra; shared boozy nights with John Wayne; intercepted a "pass" from closeted Spencer Tracy; talked "penis size" with Mark Wahlberg; went "wench-hunting" with Johnny Carson; and threatened to kill Marlon Brando, to whom his appearance was often compared. He also hung out with Bette Davis. ("I always had a thing for her.")

His least happy (some said "most poisonous") marriage—to Loni Anderson—was rife with dramas played out more in the tabloids than in the boudoir. According to Reynolds, "She's vain, she's a rotten mother, she sleeps around, and she spent all my money."

This biography—the first comprehensive overview of the "redneck icon" ever published—reveals the joys and sorrows of a movie star who thrived in, but who was then almost buried by the pressures and insecurities of the New Hollywood. A tribute to "truck stop" America, it's about the accelerated life of a courageous spirit who "Put His Pedal to the Metal" with humor, high jinx, and pizzazz. He predicted his own death: "Soon, I'll be racing a hotrod in Valhalla in my cowboy hat and a pair of aviators." On his tombstone, he wanted it writ: "He was not the best actor in the world, but he was the best Burt Reynolds in the world."

BURT REYNOLDS
PUT THE PEDAL TO THE METAL
Darwin Porter & Danforth Prince; ISBN 978-1-936003-63-1; 450 pages with photos.
Available Everywhere Now

PETER O'TOOLE

HELLRAISER, SEXUAL OUTLAW, IRISH REBEL

At the time of its publication early in 2015, this book was widely publicized in the *Daily Mail,* the *New York Daily News,* the *New York Post,* the *Midwest Book Review, The Express (London), The Globe,* the *National Enquirer,* and in equivalent publications worldwide

One of the world's most admired (and brilliant) actors, Peter O'Toole wined and wenched his way through a labyrinth of sexual and interpersonal betrayals, sometimes with disastrous results. Away from the stage and screen, where such films as *Becket* and *Lawrence of Arabia,* made film history, his life was filled with drunken, debauched nights and edgy sexual experimentations, most of which were never openly examined in the press. A hellraiser, he shared wild times with his "best blokes" Richard Burton and Richard Harris. Peter Finch, also his close friend, once invited him to join him in sharing the pleasures of his mistress, Vivien Leigh.

"My father, a bookie, moved us to the Mick community of Leeds," O'Toole once told a reporter. "We were very poor, but I was born an Irishman, which accounts for my gift of gab, my unruly behavior, my passionate devotion to women and the bottle, and my loathing of any authority figure."

Author Robert Sellers described O'Toole's boyhood neighborhood. "Three of his playmates went on to be hanged for murder; one strangled a girl in a lovers' quarrel; one killed a man during a robbery; another cut up a warden in South Africa with a pair of shears. It was a heavy bunch."

Peter O'Toole's hell-raising life story has never been told, until now. Hot and uncensored, from a writing team which, even prior to O'Toole's death in 2013, had been collecting under-the-radar info about him for years, this book has everything you ever wanted to know about how THE LION navigated his way through the boudoirs of the Entertainment Industry IN WINTER, Spring, Summer, and a dissipated Autumn as well.

Blood Moon has ripped away the imperial robe, scepter, and crown usually associated with this quixotic problem child of the British Midlands. Provocatively uncensored, this illusion-shattering overview of Peter O'Toole's hellraising (or at least very naughty) and demented life is unique in the history of publishing.

PETER O'TOOLE: HELLRAISER, SEXUAL OUTLAW, IRISH REBEL
Darwin Porter & Danforth Prince   Softcover, with photos.   ISBN 978-1-936003-45-7

HUMPHREY BOGART
The Making of a Legend

Darwin Porter

A "cradle-to-grave" hardcover about the rise to fame of an obscure, unlikely, and frequently unemployed Broadway actor

With startling information about Bogart, the movies, &
Golden Age Hollywood

Whereas Humphrey Bogart is always at the top of any list of the Entertainment Industry's most famous actors, very little is known about how he clawed his way from Broadway to Hollywood during Prohibition and the Jazz Age.

This pioneering biography begins with Bogart's origins as the child of wealthy (morphine-addicted) parents in New York City, then examines the love affairs, scandals, failures, and breakthroughs that launched him as an American icon.

It includes details about behind-the-scenes dramas associated with three mysterious marriages, and films such as *The Petrified Forest, The Maltese Falcon, High Sierra,* and *Casablanca*. Read all about the debut and formative years of the actor who influenced many generations of filmgoers, laying Bogie's life bare in a style you've come to expect from Darwin Porter. Exposed with all their juicy details is what Bogie never told his fourth wife, Lauren Bacall, herself a screen legend.

Drawn from original interviews with friends and foes who knew a lot about what lay beneath his trenchcoat, this *exposé* covers Bogart's remarkable life as it helped define moviemaking, Hollywood's portrayal of macho, and America's evolving concept of Entertainment itself.

This revelatory book is based on dusty unpublished memoirs, letters, diaries, and often personal interviews from the women—and the men—who adored him.

There are also shocking allegations from colleagues, former friends, and jilted lovers who wanted the screen icon to burn in hell.

All this and more, much more, in Darwin Porter's exposé of Bogie's startling secret life.

542 pages, with hundreds of photos   ISBN 978-1-936003-14-3

PAUL NEWMAN

The Man Behind the Baby Blues
His Secret Life Exposed

Drawn from firsthand interviews with insiders who knew Paul Newman intimately, and compiled over a period of nearly a half-century, this is the world's most honest and most revelatory biography about Hollywood's pre-eminent male sex symbol.

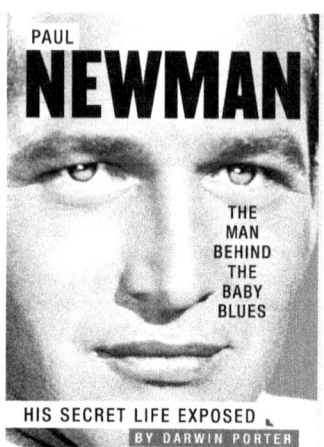

This is a respectful but candid cornucopia of once-concealed information about the sexual and emotional adventures of an affable, impossibly good-looking workaday actor, a former sailor from Shaker Heights, Ohio, who parlayed his ambisexual charm and extraordinary good looks into one of the most successful careers in Hollywood.

Whereas the situations it exposes were widely known within Hollywood's inner circles, they've never before been revealed to the general public.

But now, the full story has been published—the giddy heights and agonizing crashes of a great American star, with revelations and insights never before published in any other biography.

"Paul Newman had just as many on-location affairs as the rest of us, and he was just as bisexual as I was. But whereas I was always getting caught with my pants down, he managed to do it in the dark without a *paparazzo* in sight. He might have bedded Marilyn Monroe or Elizabeth Taylor the night before, but he always managed to show up for breakfast with Joanne Woodward, with those baby blues, looking as innocent as a Botticelli angel. He never fooled me. It takes an alleycat to know another one. Did I ever tell you what really happened between Newman and me? If that doesn't grab you, what about what went on between James Dean and Newman? Let me tell you about this co-called model husband if you want to look behind those famous peepers."

—Marlon Brando

Paul Newman, The Man Behind the Baby Blues,
His Secret Life Exposed, by Darwin Porter
Recipient of an Honorable Mention from the New England Book Festival
Hardcover, 520 pages, with dozens of photos.
ISBN 978-0-9786465-1-6   Available everywhere, online and in bookstores.

JAMES DEAN
Tomorrow Never Comes

HONORING THE 60TH ANNIVERSARY OF HIS VIOLENT AND EARLY DEATH

America's most enduring and legendary symbol of young, enraged rebellion, James Dean continues into the 21st Century to capture the imagination of the world.

After one of his many flirtations with Death, which caught up with him when he was a celebrity-soaked 24-year-old, he said, "If a man can live after he dies, then maybe he's a great man." Today, bars from Nigeria to Patagonia are named in honor of this international, spectacularly self-destructive movie star icon.

Migrating from the dusty backroads of Indiana to center stage in the most formidable boudoirs of Hollywood, his saga is electrifying.

A strikingly handsome heart-throb, Dean is a study in contrasts: Tough but tender, brutal but remarkably sensitive; he was a reckless hellraiser badass who could revert to a little boy in bed.

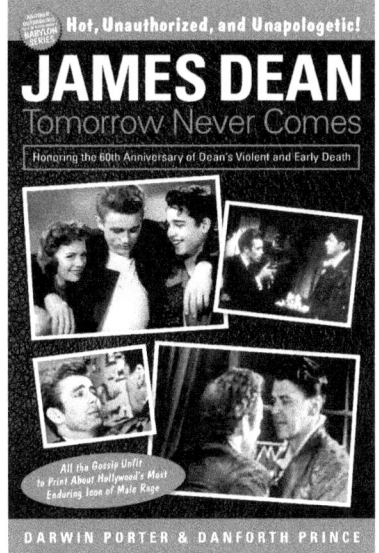

A rampant bisexual, he claimed that he didn't want to go through life "with one hand tied behind my back." He demonstrated that during bedroom trysts with Marilyn Monroe, Rock Hudson, Elizabeth Taylor, Paul Newman, Natalie Wood, Shelley Winters, Marlon Brando, Steve McQueen, Ursula Andress, Montgomery Clift, Pier Angeli, Tennessee Williams, Susan Strasberg, Tallulah Bankhead, and FBI director J. Edgar Hoover.

Woolworth heiress Barbara Hutton, one of the richest and most dissipated women of her era, wanted to make him her toy boy.

Tomorrow Never Comes is the most penetrating look at James Dean to have emerged from the wreckage of his Porsche Spyder in 1955.

Before setting out on his last ride, he said, "I feel life too intensely to bear living it."

Tomorrow Never Comes presents a damaged but beautiful soul.

JAMES DEAN
TOMORROW NEVER COMES
Darwin Porter & Danforth Prince
Softcover, with photos. ISBN 978-1-936003-49-5

From Blood Moon:
The Comprehensive, Unauthorized Exposé Every Playboy and Every Playmate Will Want to Read

Hugh Hefner, the most iconic Playboy in human history, was a visionary, an empire-builder, and a pajama-clad pipe-smoker with a pre-coital grin.

In 1953, he published his first edition of *Playboy* with money borrowed from his puritanical, Nebraska-born mother. Marilyn Monroe appeared on the cover, with her nude calendar inside.

Rebelling against his strict upbringing, he lost his virginity at the age of 22.

His magazine, punctuated with nudes and studded with articles by major literary figures, reached its zenith at eight million readers. As a "tasteful pornographer," Hef became a cultural warrior, fighting government censorship all the way to the U.S. Supreme Court. As the years and his notoriety progressed, he became an advocate of abortion, LGBT equality, and the legalization of marijuana. Eventually, he engaged in "pubic wars" with Bob Guccione, the flamboyant founder of *Penthouse*, which cut into Hef's sales.

Although lauded by millions of avid readers, he was denounced as "the father of sex addiction," "a huckster," "a lecherous low-brow feeder of our vices," "a misogynist," and, near the end of his life, "a symbol of priapic senility."

During his heyday, some of the biggest male stars in Hollywood, including Warren Beatty, Sammy Davis, Jr., Mick Jagger, and Jack Nicholson, came to frolic behind Hef's guarded walls, stripping nude in the hot tub grotto before sampling the rotating beds upstairs. Even a future U.S. president came to call. "Donald Trump had an appreciation of Bunny tail," Hef said.

Hefner's last Viagra-fueled marriage was to a beautiful blonde, Crystal Harris, 60 years his junior. "There's nothing wrong in a man marrying a girl who could be his great-granddaughter," he was famously quoted as saying.

This ground-breaking biography, the latest in Blood Moon's string of outrageously unvarnished myth-busters, was the first published since Hefner's death at the age of 91 in 2017. It's a provocative saga, rich in tantalizing detail. Not recommended for the sanctimonious, and loaded with ironic, little-known details about the trendsetter's epic challenges, it 's available everywhere now.

PLAYBOY'S HUGH HEFNER
EMPIRE OF SKIN
by Darwin Porter and Danforth Prince
978-1-936003-59-4

BLOOD MOON'S RESPECTFUL FAREWELL TO A GREAT AMERICAN MOVIE STAR

KIRK DOUGLAS
MORE IS NEVER ENOUGH
How a young horndog, oozing masculinity, set out to conquer Hollywood and to bed its leading ladies.

Of the many male stars of Golden Age Hollywood, Kirk Douglas became the final survivor, the last icon of a fabled, optimistic era that the world will never see again. When he celebrated his birthday in 2016, a headline read: *LEGENDARY HOLLYWOOD HORN-DOG TURNS 100.*

He was both a charismatic actor and a man of uncommon force and vigor. His restless and volcanic spirit is reflected both in his films and through his many sexual conquests.

Douglas was the son of Russian-Jewish immigrants, his father a collector and seller of rags. After service in the Navy during World War II, he moved to Hollywood, oozing masculinity and charm. He became the personification of the American dream, moving from obscurity and (literally) rags to riches and major-league fame.

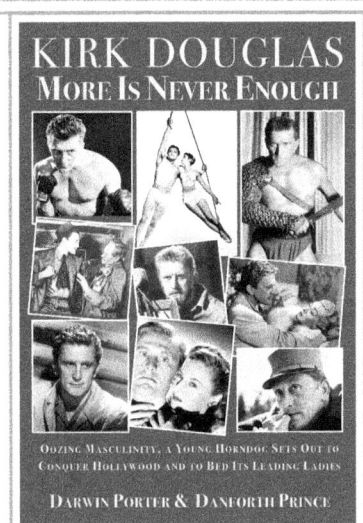

The *Who's Who* cast of characters roaring through his life included not only a daunting list of Hollywood goddesses, but the town's most colossal male talents and egos, too. They included his kindred hellraiser and best buddy Burt Lancaster, John Wayne, Henry Fonda, Billy Wilder, Laurence Olivier, Rock Hudson, and a future U.S. President, Ronald Reagan, when his winning the highest office in the land was virtually unthinkable.

Over the decades, Douglas immortalized himself in film after film, delivering, like a Trojan, one memorable performance after another. He was at home in *film noir*, as a western gunslinger, as an adventurer (in both ancient and modern sagas), as a juggler, as Tennessee Williams' "gentleman caller," as a Greek super-hero from Homer's *Odyssey*, and as roguish sailor in the Jules Verne yarn, exploring the mysteries of the ocean's depths.

His performances reflected both his personal pain and the brutalization of the characters he played. In *Champion* (1949), he was beaten to a fatal bloody pulp. As the sleazy, heartless reporter in *Ace in the Hole* (1951), he was stabbed with a knife in his gut. As Van Gogh in *Lust for Life* (1956), he writhed in emotional agony and unrequited love before slicing off his ear with a razor. His World War I movie, *Paths of Glory* (1957) grows more profound over the years. He lost an eye in *The Vikings* (1958), and, as the Thracian slave leading a revolt against Roman legions in *Spartacus* (1960), he was crucified.

All of this is brought out, with photos, in this remarkable testimonial to the last hero of Hollywood's cinematic and swashbuckling Golden Age, an inspiring testimonial to the values and core beliefs of an America that's Gone With the Wind, yet lovingly remembered as a time when it, in many ways, was truly great.

KIRK DOUGLAS *MORE IS NEVER ENOUGH*
Darwin Porter & Danforth Prince; ISBN 978-1-936003-61-7; 550 pages with photos.
Available everywhere now

ONE OF THE 20TH CENTURY'S MOST FASCINATING WOMAN was sired by one of its most widely heralded movie stars. As a precocious but love-starved child raised amid the bizarre abnormalities of Hollywood, **Jane Fonda** admitted, "I sometimes did naughty things to attract my father's attention."

Two of Hollywood's leading biographers turn klieg lights on two emotionally intertwined Oscar winners, the lanky and boyish American hero, **Henry Fonda, and his beautiful daughter Jane,** a political activist and superstar beloved by millions despite her formerly poisonous reputation as "Hanoi Jane."

This book, unlike any other previously published, reflects the private agonies of a father and daughter engulfed by the divisions of their respective generations and the ironies of The American Experience.

JANE AND HENRY FONDA
To Each His (or Her) Own

Coming soon from Ingram and from Amazon.com, worldwide
ISBN 978-1-936003-77-8
Softcover, 450 pages, with hundreds of photos.